The Politics of American Government

Brief Edition

The Politics of American Government

Brief Edition

Stephen J. Wayne
Georgetown University

G. Calvin Mackenzie
Colby College

David M. O'Brien
University of Virginia

Richard L. Cole
University of Texas at Arlington

St. Martin's Press
New York

Sponsoring editor	Beth A. Gillett
Associate editor	James Headley
Assistant editor	Jayme Heffler
Development editor	John Elliott
Manager, Publishing services	Emily Berleth
Senior editor, Publishing services	Douglas Bell
Project management	York Production Services, Inc.
Senior production supervisor	Dennis Para
Marketing manager	John Britch
Photo research	Rose Corbett Gordon
Text design	Dorothy Bungert/EriBen Graphics
Cover design	Lucy Krikorian
Cover photo	Westlight © W. Cody

Library of Congress Catalog Card Number: 97-80010

Manufactured in the United States of America.

3 2 1 0 9 8
f e d c b a

For information, write:

St. Martin's Press, Inc.
175 Fifth Avenue
New York, NY 10010

ISBN: 0-312-17786-0

Acknowledgments and copyrights can be found at the back of the book on page R-10, which constitutes an extension of the copyright page.

Dedication

These pages bear the fruits of our country's proud political tradition. Enjoy them. Improve them. Live them. And give them to your children.

To

Jonathan C. Cole
Mary Ashley Cole
Andrew C. Mackenzie
Peter W. Mackenzie
Rebecca M. Knight
Benjamin M. O'Brien
Sara A. O'Brien
Talia M. O'Brien
Jared B. Wayne
Jeremy B. Wayne

Brief Contents

Features *xv*
Preface *xvii*
About the Authors *xxiii*
Chapter 1 The American Political Environment xxvi

Part I Constitutional Politics

Chapter 2 The Contitutional Basis of American Politics 24
Chapter 3 Federalism in Theory and Practice 46

Part II The Politics of Liberty and Equality

Chapter 4 Civil Rights and Liberties 70
Chapter 5 Issues of Freedom and Equality 90

Part III The Politics of Participation

Chapter 6 Political Socialization, Participation, and Public Opinion 114
Chapter 7 Interest Groups and Political Parties 148
Chapter 8 Campaigns and Elections 186
Chapter 9 Politics and the News Media 220

Part IV American Political Institutions

Chapter 10 Congress 246
Chapter 11 The Presidency 276
Chapter 12 The Executive Bureaucracy 308
Chapter 13 The Judiciary 332

Part V Politics and Public Policy

Chapter 14 The Policy-Making Process 358

Appendixes

A The Declararation of Independence *A-1*

B The Constitution of the United States of America *B-1*

C From *The Federalist,* Nos. 10 and 51 *C-1*

D Presidential Elections *D-1*

Glossary *G-1*

References *R-1*

Index *I-1*

Contents

Features xv

Preface xvii

About the Authors xxiii

Chapter 1 **The American Political Environment** **xxvi**

One Basic Concept: Politics 3

Two Other Concepts: Government and Public Policy 5

Politics and Power: A Critical Relationship 5

Personal freedom and social welfare 6 Concentrated and distributed power 7 Majority rule and minority rights 7 Government and authority 9

The American Political Culture 10

The "American ethos" 11 Subcultures and diversity 14 Consensus, conflict, and apathy in American democracy 17

Part I **Constitutional Politics**

Chapter 2 **The Constitutional Basis of American Politics** **24**

The Founders' Constitution 27

The revolutionary background 27 The Articles of Confederation 28 The Constitutional Convention 28 Ratification 31

Enduring Ideas and Essential Tensions 32

Popular sovereignty 32 Limited government 33 Unalienable rights 33 Separation of powers 34 Federalism 36 Judicial review 37

The Living Constitution 39

Day-to-day operation of government 39 Formal amendment 40 Judicial review 41

Chapter 3 **Federalism in Theory and Practice** **46**

Federalism as a Political Issue 48

The Changing Nature of American Federalism 48

National supremacy versus states' rights, 1787–1865 49 Redefining state and national roles, 1865–1933 51

Expansion of the federal government, 1933–1968 51
From grants-in-aid to mandates and regulations, 1968–1994 53 Devolution federalism, 1994–? 54

Federal–State–Local Relations: Power and Politics 55

National regulation of states and localities 55
Conditions of aid 57 Grants-in-aid: a typology 57
Distribution criteria 58 The regional controversy over grant distribution 59 State and local influences on national policy making 60

Part II The Politics of Liberty and Equality

Chapter 4 Civil Rights and Liberties 70

Rights, Liberties, and Constitutional Politics 72

The Nationalization of the Bill of Rights 74

Civil Rights and Criminal Justice 76

Due process of law 76 Freedom from unreasonable searches and seizures 78 Government interrogations and the right to counsel 79 The right to a fair trial 81
The prohibition against cruel and unusual punishment 82

Rights and Liberties versus Economic Interests 83

Chapter 5 Issues of Freedom and Equality 90

Freedom of Religion 92

Separation of church and state 94 Freedom of religious exercise 96

Freedom of Speech and Press 96

Protected speech 97 Unprotected speech 98
Symbolic speech, speech-plus-conduct, and freedom of association 100

The Quest for Equality 101

The extension of voting rights 101 Redistricting and equal representation 103 Ending racial discrimination 104 Nonracial discrimination 105
Affirmative action and reverse discrimination 106

Part III The Politics of Participation

Chapter 6 Political Socialization, Participation, and Public Opinion 114

Political Socialization 117

Changes over the life cycle 117 Agents of political socialization 119

Political Participation 121

Ways of participating 121 Who participates? 124

Political participation and public policy 125

Public Opinion 126

Discovering public opinion 126 Characteristics of public knowledge: lack of information 128 Characteristics of public opinion: ambivalence and diversity 129 Political ideologies 130 Democratic beliefs 135

Public Opinion and Governance 140

Chapter 7 Interest Groups and Political Parties 148

Political Interest Groups and Public Policy 151

Electoral Activity 154

Spending by PACs 155 PACs: pro and con 157

Lobbying 158

Types of lobbying 159 Targets of lobbying 160 Changes in lobbying and lobbyists 163 Regulation of lobbying 164 Consequences of lobbying 164

The American Party System 166

Major parties 166 Minor parties 167

A Brief History of the Two-Party System 169

Party Organization 171

The national level 171 The state and local levels 172

Parties and Elections 173

Parties, Policy, and Government 175

Determining the party's positions 175 Converting positions into public policy 176 Influencing Congress 177 Influencing the executive and judiciary 177

Chapter 8 Campaigns and Elections 186

Elections and Democracy 189

Suffrage: Who can vote? 189 Meaningful choice: How are elections structured? 190 Political equality: Do all citizens have an equal voice? 191

The American Voter 193

Turnout 194 Voting behavior 196

The Election Campaign 198

The presidential nomination process 199 Nonpresidential nominations 204 Nonpresidential elections 205 Midterm elections 207

Analyzing the Results 207

The presidential election 208 Midterm elections 210

Elections and Governance 212

Chapter 9 Politics and the News Media 220

News Media in a Democratic Society 223

History of the news media 223 Recent developments 228

News Media and Politics 230

The news slant 230 Manipulation of the news 232 Political advertising 234 The impact of the media on electoral politics 234

News Media and Government 235

Coverage of the president 236 Coverage of Congress 237 Coverage of the judiciary 239

The Impact of the News Media on Public Policy 239

Part IV American Political Institutions

Chapter 10 Congress 246

The Institution of Congress 248

The members of Congress and their work environment 248 Staff and support services 249

The Organization of Congress 250

Congressional parties 251 The committee system 253

The Functions of Congress 257

Legislation 257 Representation 262 Administrative oversight 267

Congressional Reform and Its Impact 268

Chapter 11 The Presidency 276

The Authority of the Presidency 279

Exercising Leadership 280

Bargaining 281 Going public 281

Institutional and Personnel Resources 283

The cabinet 283 The Executive Office of the President 284 The president's spouse 289 The vice presidency 290

The Personal Dimension 293

Physical health 293 Character 295 Managerial style 296 Belief system 297

The Politics of Presidential Policy Making 297

Setting the agenda 297 Influencing the legislature 298 Building public support 300 Implementing priorities in the executive branch 302 Presidential leadership 302

Chapter 12 The Executive Bureaucracy 308

The Organization of the Federal Bureaucracy 310

Types of organizational structures 311 Staffing the bureaucracy 314

Functions of the Executive Bureaucracy 317

Implementation 317 Policy making 320 Determinants of bureaucratic influence 324

Problems of Accountability 326

Legal controls 326 Legislative controls 327 The adequacy of controls 327

Chapter 13 The Judiciary 332

Judicial Federalism 335

Federal courts 336 State courts 336

The Power of Judicial Review 336

The political question doctrine 338 Judicial review and political influence 338 Activism versus self-restraint 338

How Judges Are Chosen 340

Appointment of federal judges 341 Appointment of Supreme Court justices 342

The Supreme Court 344

The Court's caseload 344 Deciding what to decide 344 Oral argument 348 Discussing cases and voting in conference 348 Writing opinions 348 Opinion days 349 Supreme Court decision making as a political process 350

The Politics of Judicial Policy Making 350

Part V Politics and Public Policy

Chapter 14 The Policy-Making Process 358

Types of Policy 361

Stages in the Policy-Making Process 362

Problem recognition 362 Policy formulation and adoption—subgovernments and issue networks 364 Policy implementation 366 Policy evaluation 366 Policy reconsideration or termination 367

Politics and the Policy Process 368

Incrementalism 368 Major policy shifts 368 Mixed results 369

Appendixes

A The Declaration of Independence *A-1*

B The Constitution of the United States of America *B-1*

C From *The Federalist*, Nos. 10 and 51 *C-1*

D Presidential Elections *D-1*

Glossary *G-1*

References *R-1*

Index *I-1*

Features

Practicing Democracy

Finding Supreme Court Decisions 93
Getting Involved in Partisan Activities 174
How to Register to Vote 194
Using the Freedom of Information Act and the Privacy Act 224
Contacting Your Representatives in Washington 263
Keeping Up with the President 292
Using the *Federal Register* 320
Following an Issue through Congress 370

Where on the Web?

State Governments 61
Public Opinion Data 134
Interest Groups and Political Parties 152
Congress 266
The Presidency 294
The Federal Bureaucracy 318
Supreme Court Decisions and Other Legal Materials 351

Case Studies

Immigration: The Natives Get Restless 17
The Watergate Crisis and Constitutional Politics 42
Federalism and Same-Sex Marriage 63
The Battle over Abortion 84
Affirmative Action versus Reverse Discrimination 109
Generation X: Individualistic and Involved 141
Buying Influence: Is Public Policy for Sale? 179
The Campaign Finance Debacle 213

'Indecency' on the Internet 240
Mandatory Term Limits 271
The Clinton Health-Care Fiasco 303
Government Regulates Too Much! Or Does It? 328
The Battle over Bork 353
Making Welfare Work 371

Other Features

The Bill of Rights 32
Federalism North and South of the Border 50
The *Miranda* Warnings 80
Lobbying on the Internet to Save Student Loans 159
The 18-Year-Old Vote 191
How to Find Information about Federal Elections 201
Congressional Leadership 254
Requirements for Gaining Standing 338

Preface

Changes and continuity have characterized the American political landscape in the 1990s. Forty years of Democratic dominance of Congress ended as did 12 years of Republican control of the White House, but the struggle between Congress and the presidency persists. The new congressional Republican majority has proposed an agenda to reverse the trend toward big government programs at the national level. Although President Clinton has resisted some of the Republican cutbacks in popular social and economic programs, particularly in education, the environment, and health care, he has also conceded that "the era of big government is over." The 1997 agreement to balance the federal budget by the year 2002 with both spending and tax cuts is one more example of the more conservative economic philosophy that is dominating American politics today.

For its part, the public is content, cynical, and apathetic. The contentment stems from peace and prosperity: The end of the Cold War has removed the major threat to the nation's military security, a nuclear-armed, communist adversary in the form of the Soviet Union. The resurgent economy, with low inflation, low unemployment, large profits, huge increases in stock prices, and an expansion of trade, has contributed to the sense of well-being at home. Public officials of both parties have benefited from these conditions.

Underlying the serene surface, however, is a deepening cynicism about politicians and government. Allegations of campaign finance excesses and possible illegalities, misuse of government perquisites by public officials of both parties, the perception that government still does not operate efficiently, economically, and in a people-friendly manner—all have contributed to the public's sense that the political system is not working properly, that the politicians are basically self-interested, and that wealthy individuals and groups exercise disproportionate influence on the political process and policy outcomes. Voting turnout has decreased despite a new law that makes it much easier for people to register and vote and despite the huge increase in campaign expenditures in recent elections.

But certain things in American political life also remain the same. Most newsworthy political activity still focuses on conflict, conflict within and between the executive branch and Congress, conflict within and between the major parties, conflict among politicians vying for position and power. This is a book about that conflict. It is about *politics,* pure and simple.

NEW BRIEF EDITION

In this new brief edition of ***The Politics of American Government,*** we have tried to capture the nature of the struggle that characterizes the American political scene. In doing so, we have worked carefully to maintain our *critical but not cynical* perspective. Our objective remains the same: to demonstrate to students that politics matters *to them,* that they can affect it, and that the country will be better off if they become more involved. To this end we have retained many of the features of the larger book that provide opportunities for students to learn how to participate in the political process, such as the *Practicing Democracy* and *Where on the Web?* boxes. We have also retained and updated the chapter-opening vignettes, designed to spark student interest and connect chapter concepts with real-life politics. Finally, we have created a case study at the end of each chapter that gives students a vivid illustration of the chapter topic and provides a forum for discussion. Questions at the end of these case studies challenge students to think further about the issues and provide ample opportunity for classroom debate.

INSTRUCTIONAL PACKAGE

As authors, publishers, and instructors, we continue to seek to create and assemble the most diverse range of materials to support the teaching of American government. Each component of ***The Politics of American Government*** is designed to make teaching more effective and to heighten students' interest in American government and, particularly, their American government course.

Instructor's Manual and Test Item File The Instructor's Manual portion of this combined ancillary includes, for each chapter, an outline and overview, learning objectives, key terms and concepts, recommended assignments, and discussions. The Test Item File offers over 1,400 questions that are also available on disk.

Lecture Outlines and Lectures The outlines list topics that follow the major headings of each chapter of the textbook; they also suggest a range of supplementary topics and issues that relate to, but do not repeat, material in the text. These outlines and lectures are available on-line to allow you to access, customize, and print at will.

Documents These primary sources include Supreme Court cases, major laws, political speeches, presidential decisions, even excerpts from *The Federalist Papers* which are now available on-line at St. Martin's easily accessible web site.

The Politics of American Government *Interactive Web Page* When you log on to this page, you will find a bulletin board where instructors can exchange ideas, activities, and syllabi with the authors and other instructors. The page is updated by the authors to offer suggestions for incorporating current debates into your classroom. An Internet activities and exercise section offers a series of Internet activities that give your students practice in finding electronic information. *The St. Martin's Political Science Links* page gives professors and students over 1,000 annotated linked references to topics in every chapter. The Web Page can be found at **http://www.smpcollege.com/smp_govt/**.

Untangling the Web: A Beginner's Guide to Politics on the World Wide Web This guide offers hands-on advice for learning how to get onto the Internet and access information.

The St. Martin's Student Survey of Political Attitudes This survey is designed for use in American government classes. When the survey is given at the beginning of the course and sent to St. Martin's Press for tabulation, the results will be returned to the professor for use during the semester. The results allow students to explore the relationship between their political opinions and those of students across the country.

The St. Martin's Resource Library in Political Science This resource comprises a series of brief, supplementary books on a range of topics to complement your teachings and customize your focus. Upon adoption of ***The Politics of American Government,*** an instructor can select one of these texts to receive free of charge with the main text.The series includes:

- *Ralph Nader's Practicing Democracy, 1997: A Guide to Student Action*
- *Big Ideas: An Introduction to Ideologies in American Politics,* by Mark Tiller of Houston Community College.
- *The Real Thing: Contemporary Documents in American Government,* by Fengyan Shi of Georgetown University.

The Politics of American Government *Presentation CD-ROM* This easy-to-use CD-ROM allows professors to enhance their lectures with graphics from the text.

"In Action: Students Making It Happen in Government" This 25-minute video follows students as they work on the Republican and Democratic campaigns for the 1996 elections.

St. Martin's Video Resource Library This is an additional series of 25-minute videos for use in class. Each video is accompanied by a guide that includes a summary of the video, test and discussion questions, and a list of supplemental classroom activities. Topics covered include "Women in Politics,""Interest Groups in America,""Presidential Leadership,""The Selection and Confirmation of Supreme Court Justices," and "The Politics of Midterm Elections: The Case of the 104th Congress."

For information about these ancillaries or about special packages and discounts for those who want to use ***The Politics of American Government*** with other books published by St. Martin's Press, please contact your local representative or call or write St. Martin's Press, College Desk, 345 Park Avenue South, New York, NY 10010 (phone 1-800-446-8923).

ACKNOWLEDGMENTS

We wish to acknowledge and thank some of the many people who contributed to this book. Bert Lummus conceived of the text, initially contracted for it, and encouraged us with good humor, patience, support, and many meals. Don Reisman orchestrated the first edition at St. Martin's with skill and imagination; Beth Gillett presided over this edition, making numerous suggestions on how to improve and enliven the book. John Elliott and Joanne Tinsley, developmental editors, greatly improved the manuscript's style, organization, and presentation. Thanks also to others at St. Martin's who helped us with this edition: photo researcher Rose Corbett Gordon, designer Patricia McFadden, senior production supervisor Dennis Para, senior editor Doug Bell, assistant editor Jayme Heffler, associate editor James Headley, and marketing manager John Britch, as well as Dolores Wolfe at York Production Services.

The authors owe a considerable debt to our research assistants, particularly Rachel Goldberg, who helped us with this brief edition.

We cannot close without saying how much we have appreciated the sacrifices and support we have received from our families as we worked on this book. Our children, especially, have patiently endured our writing and rewriting with only an occasional quip "haven't you finished *that* book yet?" We have dedicated this book to them, not only because of their patience but also because they and their peers, who will read this book, embody the hopes and hold the keys to the future of our political system.

Finally, we wish to thank our many colleagues in the political science profession who have answered questionnaires, reviewed chapters, found mistakes, and conveyed extremely useful suggestions to us—all of which have helped us improve this book:

Phillip J. Ardoin, Louisiana State University; David G. Adler, Idaho State University; Claude W. Barnes, North Carolina Agricultural and Technical State University; William T. Bianco, Duke University; Stephen A. Borrelli, University of Alabama; Sheryl Breen, University of Minnesota; John Burke, University of Vermont; William E. Carroll, Sam Houston State University; Roger H. Davidson, University of Maryland at College Park; Laura Ebke, University of Nebraska, at Lincoln; David E. England, Arkansas State University; Brian L. Fife, Ball State University; Janet E. Frantz, University of Southwest Louisiana; John Geer, Vanderbilt University; Micheal Giles, Emory University; Nirmal Goswami, Texas A & M University–Kingsville; David R. Harding, Arkansas State University; Kenneth Hartman, Longview Community College; Michael W. Hirlinger, Oklahoma State University; Herbert Hirsch, Virginia Commonwealth University; Michael J. Horan, University of Wyoming; Leon H. Hurwitz, Cleveland State University; Butch Kamena, Western Washington University; Matthew R. Kerbel, Villanova University; James P. Lester, Colorado State University; Thomas Lobe, Union College; Brad Lockerbie, University of Georgia; Burdett A. Loomis, University of Kansas; Bonnie G. Mani, East Carolina University; Cecilia G. Manrique, University of Wisconsin–La Crosse; Janet M. Martin, Bowdoin College; Valerie Martinez-Ebers, University of North Texas; James L. McDowell, Indiana State

University; Lauri McNown, University of Colorado at Boulder; Donald Melton, Arapahoe Community College; Michael Moore, University of Texas, Arlington; J. Keith Nicholls, University of South Alabama; Arthur Paulson, Southern Connecticut State University; Jeff Pickering, Kansas State University; George Pippin, Jones County Junior College; Edward E. Platt, Indiana University of Pennsylvania; David Reed, SUNY Cortland; Ronald G. Shaiko, The American University; Steven S. Smith, University of Minnesota; John W. Soule, San Diego State University; Bartholomew Sparrow, University of Texas at Austin; C. Michael Swinford, Kennesaw State College; Andrew J. Taylor, North Carolina State University; Roy Thoman, West Texas State University; Roberto J. Vichot, Florida International University; David J. Webber, University of Missouri; Herbert F. Weisberg, The Ohio State University; and Gary D. Wekkin, University of Central Arkansas.

Stephen J. Wayne
G. Calvin Mackenzie
David M. O'Brien
Richard L. Cole

About the Authors

Stephen J. Wayne (Ph.D., Columbia University) is a professor and the head of the American government section at Georgetown University. Besides being a veteran instructor of American government, he has been a Washington insider specializing in presidential politics for over twenty-five years. He has authored numerous articles and published several books about the presidency, including *The Road to the White House, The Legislative Presidency,* and *Presidential Leadership* (with George C. Edwards III). Invited frequently to testify before Congress and to lecture to senior federal executives, distinguished international visitors, and college students in the United States and abroad, Wayne also has shaped public opinion about the presidency and electoral politics as a commentator for radio, television, and newspapers.

G. Calvin Mackenzie (Ph.D., Harvard University) is the Distinguished Presidential Professor of American Government at Colby College. With expertise in presidential appointments, Congress, and public policy, Mackenzie is among the foremost American scholars and commentators on the staffing of national administrations. He is a former congressional staff member and has worked in or advised executive-branch agencies, including the departments of Defense and the Treasury. *The Politics of Presidential Appointments* and *The Irony of Reform* are among his many books; he also has contributed to a wide range of academic and popular journals and is interviewed often on television and radio.

David M. O'Brien (Ph.D., University of California, Santa Barbara) is the Leone Reaves and George W Spicer Professor in the Department of Government and Foreign Affairs at the University of Virginia. A former Judicial Fellow at the Supreme Court and Fulbright Scholar in Great Britain and Japan, O'Brien is one of the most prominent political scientists studying the Supreme Court. His several books about the judiciary include *Storm Center: The Supreme Court in American Politics*, which in 1987 received the American Bar Association's Silver Gavel Award. His most recent publication is *To Dream of Dreams: Religious Freedom in Postwar Japan.*

Richard L. Cole (Ph.D., Purdue University) is dean of the School of Urban and Public Affairs at the University of Texas, Arlington, where he is also a professor specializing in political science methodology, urban politics, and public policy. He is a former president of the Southwest Political Science Association and former president of the North Texas chapter of the American Society for Public Administration. In addition to dozens of monographs, journal articles, and book reviews, Cole's publications include *Texas Politics and Public Policy* and *An Introduction to Political Inquiry*. His latest book is *Introduction to Political Science and Policy Research*, also with St. Martin's Press.

1

The American Political Environment

PREVIEW

- Three concepts: *politics, government,* and *public policy*
- Politics and power: personal freedom and social welfare; concentrated and distributed power; majority rule and minority rights; government and authority
- The American political culture: the "American ethos"; subcultures and diversity; consensus, conflict, and apathy

It began as a bitter, no-holds-barred battle, pitting political parties, governing institutions, and strong and ambitious people against one another. It ended in compromise with both sides claiming victory. It illustrates the politics of American government. Ostensibly, the battle of the budget was about money: could a balanced federal budget be achieved after decades of deficit spending? The Republicans believed that it could and should; their candidates for the House of Representatives campaigned on this proposition in 1994 and won a majority of seats for the first time in forty years. The Democrats were more wary. Where would spending cuts be made? Who would be affected? Would the public approve reductions in popular programs?

Within the first 100 days of the 104th Congress, the House of Representatives enacted a proposal for a constitutional amendment requiring a balanced budget; but when it fell one vote short of the required two-thirds in the Senate, the Republicans turned to ordinary legislation that needed only a majority. They proposed a budget that would eliminate the deficit in seven years. President Clinton's support was crucial to obtain this objective, since the Republicans did not have the two-thirds majority in both houses required to override a presidential veto. Although Clinton had said that he favored a balanced budget, he had not submitted one in his first three years in office, nor did he agree with the Republicans on their timetable for such a budget or their methods for achieving it.

Preventing a presidential veto was only part of the problem. Garnering public support for specific cuts in government programs, particularly popular programs, was another. Although most Americans agreed with the goal of a balanced budget, they did not agree on how to achieve it.

The Republicans' task was also complicated by the promise contained in their *Contract with America* to reduce taxes as well as spending. The only way to meet these dual objectives was to shrink expenditures on so-called entitlements, ongoing programs that account for more than half of federal spending and that automatically give benefits to all individuals who meet certain qualifications. With both the Republicans and Clinton unwilling to risk the political dangers of cutting back the largest entitlement program, Social Security, the main targets for cuts included Medicare, which provides health-care coverage for those age 65 and older; Medicaid, a health-care program for the poor; and various welfare programs such as food stamps and Aid to Families with Dependent Children.

Ever since Medicare began in 1965, it enjoyed broad and strong public support. Realizing this, the Democrats linked Republican proposals to save billions by changing Medicare to the GOP proposal to cut income taxes for those earning up to $200,000 a year—a proposal that would cost the government approximately what it would save from the proposed changes in Medicare. The implication was hardly subtle: the elderly were being asked to sacrifice to benefit the wealthy.

Interest groups entered the fray. The American Association of Retired Persons, with a membership of 33 million, announced its opposition to the Medicare premium increases and benefit cuts. The American Medical Association objected to any plan that might benefit group health organizations at the expense of private physicians; naturally, the Health Insurance Association of America and the Group Health Association of America took the opposite stand. Meanwhile, groups especially concerned about budget deficit reduction, such as the Concord Coalition, or about lower taxes, such as the National Taxpayers Union, weighed in with their own public statements and lobbying efforts.

With the political debate heating up, the Republicans needed a strategy to force the president's hand, and they turned to the "power of the purse" to do so. The Constitution states that no money can be drawn from the treasury unless it is appropriated by Congress. That is why Congress must enact annual appropriations bills to fund federal departments and agencies; without them or a resolution to continue spending at a certain level, the government cannot operate. Twice during the winter of 1995, much of the government had to shut down because appropriations bills acceptable to the president had not been enacted. The first shutdown lasted six days; the second, three weeks. By early January 1996, unable to visit national parks and museums, obtain passports, or get federally guaranteed mortgages, the public was becoming weary of and angry about the stalemate; and by a two-to-one margin, they blamed the Republicans. Fearing that the electorate would take its anger out in the 1996 election, the Republicans gave in and passed appropriation bills that were acceptable to the president. The crisis was over, but the issue remained.

The partisan battle continued into the 1996 presidential campaign, with Democratic, Republican, and Reform presidential candidates offering different budgetary solutions. The budget remained a contentious issue as the reelected Republican Congress and Democratic president took office in January 1997. But the public mood had clearly mellowed, and the problem seemed less severe as government deficits declined substantially. As a consequence, bipartisan oratory began to replace partisan haggling.

In February 1997, President Clinton submitted his plan to balance the budget by the year 2002. Leery of the president's proposal but sensitive to the cost of opposing him in the current political environment, congressional Republicans muted their criticism and did not even provide an alternative budget of their own, leaving the president's to serve as the basis for negotiations. These negotiations began in earnest in the spring. They were initiated by the White House, and they occurred behind closed doors. Although the parties were not that far apart on the overall revenue and expenditure figures, they were far apart on the politics of what to cut, how much, and who should pay. Each side needed ingredients in the budget to which they could point to claim victory: the president needed to protect his priorities in education, the environment, and health care; and the Republicans needed to achieve additional spending and tax cuts. Neither side could afford to alienate a major population group such as senior citizens or veterans by substantially reducing the benefits of popular entitlement programs.

Just when the negotiations seemed to be faltering because the parties could not find enough money to achieve everyone's objectives, the Congressional Budget Office (CBO) found a pot of gold at the end of the rainbow. Revising its five-year revenue estimates upward because of the vigorous economy, the CBO projected that the government would receive $230 billion more in income from 1997 to 2002 than had been anticipated by the president's Office of Management and Budget. This amount was sufficient to give the negotiators what they needed to sell the agreement to their partisans, members of Congress, and their constituents. Only the ideologues, the most liberal Democrats and conservative Republicans, were unhappy and opposed the deal.

The politics of reason had replaced the politics of principle. Agreement overcame intransigence because the parties to the agreement found it in their political self-interest to compromise, and because the money was found to seal the deal.

The battle of the budget demonstrates the political character of the American electoral and governing systems: the volatility of public opinion, and the responsiveness of most elected officials to that opinion, but also the resistance of the constitutional framework to major policy changes. It indicates how the public can alter the political climate; how voting decisions can affect the politics of governing, which in turn influences public policy making. In this way the battle of the budget reveals the *life cycle of American politics:* how politics affects government, how government tries to resolve contentious political issues, and how that resolution or lack of it generates new political pressures and policy solutions.

That is why we have titled our book *The Politics of American Government.* We believe that government can be best understood when it is viewed through the lens of politics. If **politics** consists of struggles by individuals and groups in pursuit of their own interests and goals, then practically everything government does, every action it takes, is the result of political activity of one kind or another. *Politics* thus provides the framework for understanding how *government* works and what it does.

ONE BASIC CONCEPT: POLITICS

Today the word *politics,* like *politician,* is often used disparagingly. Political candidates who accuse their opponents of "playing politics" imply that they are doing things primarily to enhance themselves in the eyes of those whose

Although in the 1990s many Americans have become highly cynical about politics, many others continue to get involved. The Rock the Vote campaign aimed to register voters between the ages of 18 and 25 at rock concerts across the country.

support they need. In the 1996 presidential campaign, the stands Robert Dole and Bill Clinton took in favor of lowering taxes after they had supported sizable tax increases in 1993 made them look like "typical politicians."

Originally, however, *politics* had a positive meaning. The modern term derives from the Greek word *polis*, roughly translated as "city-state." In ancient Greece, the polis, an independent city and the land that surrounded it, formed the basic unit of political organization. Early Greek philosophers such as Plato and Aristotle believed that loyalty to a polis was part and parcel of being human; in fact, Aristotle referred to the citizens of a city-state as "political animals." In these small communities, "government" meant face-to-face discussions of community issues among all citizens.

In the ancient world, politics was the process by which the community determined how its will would be implemented. Politics involves that same process today. Contemporary society has become much more diverse and complex, of course, and so has politics. But it is still the means through which who gets what, when, and how is determined, and is still fundamental to the operation of government. In a world where values and beliefs conflict, where resources are limited and desires and ambitions seem virtually limitless, the quest for political gain is inevitable.

Although politics sometimes leads to excesses and abuses, in itself it is neither bad nor dangerous. Insofar as it facilitates the expression of disagreement and the building of consensus, politics is critical to the health of a democratic society. Without it, there would be no mechanism other than force to resolve disagreements.

Politics is an end as well as a means. It is an *end* because it is an activity that has value in and of itself. It links citizens to their government and guides that government as it goes about its principal tasks. It is a *means* to other ends because it gives people the opportunity and the tools to advance their own interests by influencing who gets into office and what actions those officeholders take while they are there.

TWO OTHER CONCEPTS: GOVERNMENT AND PUBLIC POLICY

The term **government** refers to the *formal institutions* within which decisions about public policy are made and to the *processes and procedures* of decision making. For example, the California State Assembly, the Federal Trade Commission, and the local motor vehicles bureau and school board are all governing institutions. So is your school's student council. They and other governing institutions exercise their authority by means of various processes and procedures that permit policies to be made and carried out and disputes to be judged and settled. The ratification of treaties by the United States Senate, the vetoing of legislation by the president, the inspection of meat-processing plants by the Department of Agriculture, and the conduct of criminal trials all exemplify the exercise of formal government power.

Public policy is what governments decide. Codified in the form of laws, of executive agreements, orders, and actions, and of Supreme Court decisions, public policy consists of established rules, procedures, and practices that are determined by and protected by the authority of government.

The federal government and some state governments impose and collect taxes on personal incomes. They also spend money on public services such as education, police, and health-related programs. The personal income tax and public services, therefore, are public policy. The federal government does not ban the ownership of handguns or the drinking of liquor by those over a certain age. The freedom to own handguns or consume alcoholic beverages, therefore, is public policy in the United States. Some states and many cities ban the possession of handguns and some counties are "dry," however, which demonstrates that public policy may differ at different levels of government.

Policies are not necessarily the same as laws, and how laws are implemented has a lot to do with what public policies really are. If the law says that the speed limit is 55 miles per hour on a particular highway but the state police never stop any drivers unless their speed exceeds 65 miles per hour, then public policy is really 65 miles per hour because no penalty is imposed as long as drivers stay under that speed. Those who implement a policy—the state police, in this instance—often have considerable discretion in defining what that policy really is.

POLITICS AND POWER: A CRITICAL RELATIONSHIP

For political activity to succeed, it must be accompanied by the exercise of power. **Power**, in this sense, is the ability to get someone to do something that he or she might not otherwise do. Power may be wielded through persuasive skills, rewards, legal authority, threats, or even force.

Power is exerted by and within all institutions of government. Presidents exercise power when they persuade reluctant legislators to support their policy positions, as President Clinton did in 1993 when he persuaded a majority of the members of Congress to support his deficit reduction proposal despite their many misgivings. Congress exercises power when it exerts its constitutional authority over government spending, as the Republican majority did in 1995 and 1996 when it got President Clinton to accept reductions in domestic spending that were larger than he wanted. At the state and local levels, power is exercised by governors when they commute a death sentence or allow it to be carried out, as well as by police officers when they make an arrest or even merely cruise the streets in patrol cars. Those outside the government also attempt to get their way by promising support or threatening opposition to legislators before they vote on particular issues.

Does the public exercise power when those in government act in accordance with its opinion? Probably, because in a democracy public officials need to be sensitive to public opinion. Failure to do so could result in their defeat in a subsequent election or, less commonly, their recall by the voters or impeachment by Congress.

Power is a normal, everyday component of politics. There can be no politics without power.

Personal Freedom and Social Welfare

The exercise of power often affects individuals and the community in very different ways. One person's liberty, after all, may be another's constraint. For example, many Americans cherish the right to possess and use firearms. Yet we all know that firearms are dangerous and that their use can cause harm. Legislators have struggled with the dilemma of how to design public policy that satisfies both those who want to own guns and use them legally and those who believe that the very availability of guns contributes significantly to violence in our society and thus restricts their freedom in less obvious ways (by discouraging them from walking around their neighborhoods in fear for their safety).

To take another example, free speech is a basic individual right without which a democracy could not exist. But speech also can be harmful. Words themselves are not as lethal as bullets, but they can cause psychological injury or lead directly to violence. Should speech, then, be as restricted as the possession of firearms? Should it be limited at all, and if so, under what conditions? Should a society be able to outlaw obscene language on the telephone, indecent pictures on the Internet, or public appeals to break the law?

These questions pit the rights of individuals to say and do what they like, and to protest policies and laws that they believe to be unjust, against the obligation of society to protect the health and well-being of its members, which includes maintaining laws that the majority in the community supports. How can the freedom of an individual be protected while the rights of others are preserved? Should people be allowed to protest abortion by blocking entrances to clinics? Should they be allowed to defend animal rights by destroying medical laboratories, sabotaging hunters' traps, or spraying paint on fur coats? Should those who preach hatred and advocate violence be allowed to do so on the public airwaves such as on radio talk shows? Would your answer be the same if they did so at a much publicized rally at which violent reactions were likely to occur?

Drawing the line between personal liberty and the needs of the community is a difficult task, but one that government must perform. In accomplishing this function, government makes policy judgments that are shaped and conditioned by the political climate in which they occur. In short, *politics influences government, which in turn influences politics*. In both cases, the exercise of power drives the process.

Concentrated and Distributed Power

How power is distributed within the government affects not only which public policies are made but also who makes them and who benefits most from them. When power is concentrated in the hands of a few individuals or groups, decision making is more efficient and government can act more quickly and decisively. But those with the power are likely to make decisions that advance their own goals and interests, often at the expense of others.

When power is widely distributed, there is less opportunity for a few people or groups to dominate decision making and determine policy outcomes. But arriving at a consensus, much less agreeing on the details of public policy, is a much harder undertaking. This is the problem usually faced by the United States Congress and other American legislative bodies when they try to draft public policy into law. Both the membership of Congress and the distribution of power within Congress are designed to reflect the diversity of American society; but this diversity makes it difficult, and sometimes impossible, for the party in control of Congress to agree among itself on legislation. In more homogeneous countries such as the United Kingdom and Germany, the legislative majority tends to be more cohesive.

How to overcome the lack of concentrated power evident in large, broad-based parties is the challenge legislatures encounter in the United States. One technique is for the winners of an election to claim a public mandate and use that claim to help them achieve a consensus, as Newt Gingrich, the newly elected Republican Speaker of the House of Representatives, did in 1995.

Another technique is to use a crisis as an action-forcing and coalition-building mechanism. During periods of national peril, support for public officials tends to be greater, opposition is muted, and partisanship often suspended. But reason must also give way to emotion, and the rights of individuals, particularly those in the minority may be jeopardized by government responses to the needs and fears of the majority. After the bombing of the federal office building in Oklahoma City on April 19, 1995, the Senate quickly enacted antiterrorist legislation proposed by President Clinton. The bill gave broad investigative powers to the FBI and other law enforcement agencies, powers that some claimed infringe on individual rights protected by the First Amendment to the Constitution. Partly because of this concern, the House did not rush to support this legislation; it enacted a modified bill almost a year later.

Obviously, then, there are tradeoffs between concentrated and distributed power, tradeoffs that can have a profound effect on politics and policy making. Generally speaking, the more concentrated the power, the better able the government to function. On the other hand, the more distributed the power, the better able are minorities to protect their rights and interests, even against a determined majority.

Majority Rule and Minority Rights

The tension between minorities and majorities, especially when it involves the exercise of personal freedom and the establishment of community standards that restrict that freedom, is one of the principal ongoing problems in the American political system. It is inherent in any democracy, although different societies try to resolve this tension in different ways. What is a democracy, and why does it inevitably produce this clash between the majority and various minorities?

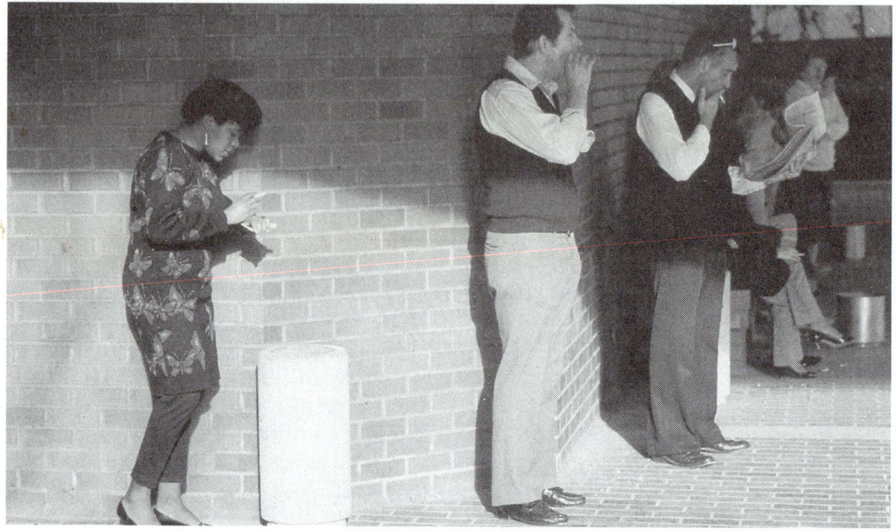

The interests of the community often conflict with the freedom of individuals. Ordinances that prohibit smoking in offices, for example, constrain the freedom of smokers.

A **democracy** is a form of government in which citizens have a right to control their own destiny. Democracy works on the principle of popular consent. The term itself comes from the Greek word *demos*, meaning "people," and *kratos*, meaning "authority." In a democracy the people have the final authority; they have the right to make or at least influence decisions that affect their everyday lives.

Thus in a democracy every citizen should have an equal opportunity to influence public policy through equal representation in government. Rule by the people, or "popular rule," is accomplished by having a majority of citizens or their representatives decide the policies that affect the whole society. If the wishes of the majority are *not* reflected in such decisions, the system itself is not democratic, even though public officials may have been selected in a democratic manner.

Majority rule is vital for a democracy, but it has its dangers. Those in the majority can—and sometimes do—disregard the needs of those in the minority, threaten their interests, and deny them their basic rights. Consider the issue of smoking in public places, for example. When government bans that activity, the ability of smokers to satisfy their needs and desires is adversely affected, yet the health of the majority is enhanced. Is that an acceptable tradeoff? Most people believe it is, or antismoking laws would not have been enacted and would not remain public policy today.

However, the majority cannot always have its way. The principle of majority rule sometimes must be modified in practice. As limits are placed on individual behavior, so too must they be placed on group behavior, *even if the group constitutes a majority.*

The United States Constitution was designed to do just that—to create a government that people of all opinions could influence but that no single group, including the majority, could easily control. James Madison, one of the architects of the Constitution, argued that this was a major strength of the new system. But it has also been perceived by some as a weakness. The very difficulty that people have in manipulating the system to their own advantage makes that system resistant to change. This resistance is a source of constant frustration to those who want quick, efficient, and popular solutions to problems.

Government and Authority

When a government makes public policy, it does so on the basis of its **authority**, that is, its lawful power. In a democratic society that authority is derived, directly or indirectly, from the people. In most cases, people do not make policy decisions themselves; but by voting, they have a voice in selecting those who do. Voters choose policy makers to represent them, and then they may try to influence the decisions their representatives make. Thus we frequently hear the terms *representative democracy* or *representative government* used to describe the American political system and distinguish it from *direct democracy*, in which every citizen has an opportunity to participate in making policy decisions (such as in town meetings).

The authority of the government is embodied in *law*. The Constitution is the supreme law of the United States, but it is not the only law. Treaties, statutes, executive orders, and judicial opinions are also part of the body of rules that must be observed by all members of society, including those in government.

Like decisions themselves, the rules by which decisions are made benefit some people and hurt others. Thus they can impinge both on the principle of majority rule and on the rights of individuals and groups in the minority. For example, the power of the Supreme Court to determine the constitutionality of both local and national law restricts the ability of those in the majority to determine public policy, because no legislature can take any action that violates the Constitution. In 1995, for instance, the Supreme Court's decision in *U.S. Term Limits v. Thornton* overturned the laws of twenty-two states that had imposed limits on the number of terms members of Congress from those states could serve.

The divisions of authority mandated by the Constitution contribute to the politics of the governing process. By separating the institutions of government and assigning each one a primary sphere of authority, then imposing elaborate internal checks and balances on the exercise of that authority, the Constitution builds competition into the system. The president cannot appoint officials to the executive departments and agencies without Senate approval. Congress cannot appropriate money unless the president approves; however, Congress can override presidential disapproval of its legislation by a two-thirds vote in each house. The Supreme Court cannot enforce its own rulings; only the president has that power. Congress cannot determine the constitutionality of its own legislation; the Supreme Court has assumed that prerogative. The federal system, too, with its divisions of authority between the national government and the states, often plays off competing interests, needs, and policy goals against each other. In short, politics—the competition among conflicting interests—is built into the design and operation of the system.

Over the years, the dispersion of authority among the branches and levels of government has given well-organized and well-funded groups more opportunities to exert influence on public officials than those with fewer resources at their disposal have had. This influence is often used to prevent policies that adversely affect the interests of powerful groups from becoming law. For years, for example, the American Medical Association effectively prevented Congress from enacting legislation creating a government-run health-care system for the general population. Similarly, domestic automobile manufacturers delayed and subsequently weakened the automobile emissions standards that environmentalists sought to impose on them. But powerful groups do not always get their way. The tobacco industry has not been able to prevent the passage of laws that restrict smoking in public places, and the gambling industry has not yet been able to overcome local opposition in several states to legalized casinos.

The dispersion of authority also leads to the dilution of policy decisions. To make policies acceptable to as many people as possible and to gain sufficient support to get them enacted, policy makers find that they must add, alter, or remove items that particular groups desire or oppose. This practice builds consensus, but it often weakens a policy's scope or impact and may even change its character.

In normal times, politics usually produces only small, incremental changes in public policy. In determining what those changes will be, the advantage clearly goes to those with the resources to influence who is selected to hold political power and what decisions they make in office. Those with greater resources are also likely to be benefiting from government policy already, and thus they are reluctant to support changes that might undercut their advantage. For this reason, government officials tend more often to tinker with the distribution of resources rather than to redistribute them on a larger scale.

Occasionally, however, a crisis of national proportion propels the public to demand more sweeping changes. In the Great Depression of the 1930s, for example, President Franklin Roosevelt proposed and Congress promptly enacted legislation to provide federal aid to small farmers, unemployed laborers, and older Americans, all of whom had been hit especially hard by the economic downturn. Though modest by the standards of later social welfare programs, these measures were unprecedented in the United States and seemed almost revolutionary at the time—especially to Roosevelt's Republican critics. In the early 1980s, reacting to a public perception of a weakened United States (a perception fueled by the holding of American diplomats as hostages in Iran and the invasion of Afghanistan by the Soviet Union), President Ronald Reagan got Congress to agree to a large increase in defense spending to bolster the country's national security and image as a superpower. During 1995–1996, the Republican-controlled Congress responded to public displeasure with the size, cost, and implementation of the national government's welfare programs by devolving financial and administrative responsibility for one of these programs, Aid to Families with Dependent Children, to the states.

THE AMERICAN POLITICAL CULTURE

Even during the worst crises, however, most Americans would not allow their leaders to do certain things, such as assume dictatorial powers in violation of the Constitution and laws of the land. Underlying the political system of any nation are the dominant values, beliefs, and attitudes held by citizens about their governance, their nation's unique history, and their rights and responsibilities in society. Together these values, beliefs, and attitudes constitute the unique **political culture** of a people. That culture largely determines the structure and rules of a political system and the bounds of acceptable behavior within it.

The political culture of the United States has been unusually hospitable to a republican form of government, one that is based on popular consent, as opposed to one in which a central authority imposes its will on the people. That culture also favors democratic rules of participation in which citizens can influence who gets elected, what decisions they make, and when and how they make them. Indeed, over time, principles of both republicanism and democracy have become enshrined in America's public institutions. Whether they be a student council, local school board, state legislature, or even the presidency, these institutions are expected to be sensitive to public opinion and responsive to public needs and interests.

However, American political life is not guided by a single, cohesive theory like monarchism or communism. Even the American Revolution lacked the kind of guiding idea that inspired other national revolutions. Most of the American revolutionaries seemed to mean it when they said that they simply wanted protection of their rights as Englishmen, even as that desire led them to the conclusion that they could no longer endure British rule. It was not the charm of a new or more appealing philosophy that lured them away from their British loyalties; it was a practical need to run their own affairs in a way they thought would best suit their interests.

Throughout subsequent American history, practical needs, not theoretical concerns, have given rise to the major political issues that the country has had to address: how to broaden political participation; how to meet the challenges of industrialization and immigration; how to adjust to new realities wrought by technological sophistication, including nuclear weapons. In recent years public officials have been debating how and at which level of government to address the problems of the poor, not whether those problems are a legitimate concern of government. It is politics, not philosophy, that shapes the issue and conditions the solution.

The "American Ethos"

Although the American political culture is a composite of pragmatic attitudes, values, and traditions, two beliefs lie at its core: (1) the commitment to democracy, a political system that stresses personal liberty and political equality, and (2) the commitment to capitalism, an economic system based on individual initiative and private property. These ideas are the basis of the **American ethos**.

Democracy In democratic America, many people believe that a primary responsibility of government is to protect individual liberty. This belief, articulated in the Declaration of Independence, was reaffirmed in the Bill of Rights, the first ten amendments to the Constitution, which guarantee freedom of speech, freedom of religion, and other basic forms of liberty.

To preserve liberty, Americans believe that political processes must be open and responsive to the needs and opinions of individual citizens. But people must have more than mere *access* to government. They must also be *equal* in its eyes. In general, the American ethos enshrines equality in two different forms: political equality and equality of opportunity.

In application, *political equality* means that every citizen's vote counts the same, that all citizens have the same rights and obligations, that they are all subject to the same laws and entitled to the same treatment. Americans have consistently supported this kind of equality.

They have differed, however, over how to achieve *equality of opportunity.* Although Americans widely endorse the principle, they disagree over its applications. Should government take steps to improve opportunities for those who start out or become "less equal," even if they do so by reason of their own shortcomings? Americans disagree, often violently, on their answers to this question (see Figure 1-1 and Table 1-1).

Why the disagreements? Intrinsic tensions between equality and liberty are to blame, as they have been for much of the conflict in American political history. The contemporary debate over affirmative action is a good example. Some people believe that achievement of genuine equality of opportunity requires policies designed to make up for previous practices of discrimination. They feel that extraordinary measures are necessary to offset previously limited opportunities for disadvantaged groups. Employers, for example may be forced by affirmative action guidelines to undertake vigorous recruitment programs for female or minority-group job applicants. Failure to do so would leave them open to loss of government contracts or benefits or to lawsuits by those who claim discrimination.

But is such "increased equality" true "equality"? Critics argue that most if not all affirmative action policies put members of historically advantaged groups—generally whites, males, and members of the middle and upper classes—at a competitive disadvantage, depriving them of a fair shake when they compete with members of the groups targeted by affirmative action programs for jobs, college admissions, loans, and scholarships. Further, it is argued that

FIGURE 1-1

Changes in Public Attitudes toward Government Efforts to Improve Equality of Opportunity

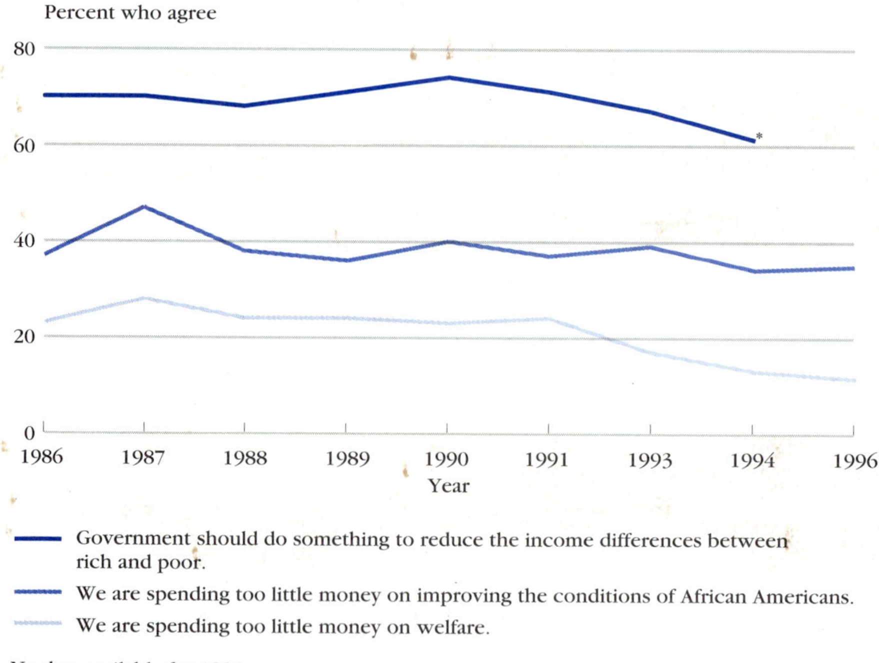

No data available for 1992.

* Not available for 1996.

SOURCE: General Social Surveys, University of Chicago, National Opinion Research Center.

TABLE 1-1 ***Changes in Public Attitudes toward Political Equality and the Role of Government***

Statements about Equality	Those who agree (percent) 1984	1996
1. Our society should do whatever is necessary to make sure that everyone has an equal opportunity to succeed.	90	82
2. We have gone too far in pushing equal rights in this country.	45	54
3. One of the big problems in this country is that we don't give everyone an equal chance.	49	48
4. It is not really that big a problem if some people have more of a chance in life than others.	36	37
5. The country would be better off if we worried less about how equal people are.	53	53
6. If people were treated more equally in this country, we would have many fewer problems.	64	61

Statements about the Role of Government	Those who agree (percent) 1984	1996
1. There should be a government insurance plan that would cover all medical and hospital expenses.	38	39
2. The government should see to it that every person has a job and a good standard of living.	34	26
3. The government should make every possible effort to improve the social and economic positions of African Americans.	32	19
4. The government should provide fewer services, even in areas such as health and education, in order to reduce spending.	34	37

SOURCE: Based on data from the 1984 and 1996 American National Election Studies, conducted by the University of Michigan, Center for Political Studies, Ann Arbor, Michigan Data provided by the Inter-University Consortium for Political and Social Research, Ann Arbor, Michigan.

these programs curtail individual liberties because they limit the freedom of employers or others, such as college administrations and banks, to choose whomever they wish. The political debate on this issue, waged with great intensity and emotion in the 1990s between liberals and conservatives, Democrats and Republicans, and minority and majority racial groups, has forced policy makers at the national and state levels to modify and curtail many affirmative action programs.

Affirmative action is not the only kind of policy that helps some at the expense of others and exacerbates the natural tensions between liberty and equality. In fact, it is difficult to think of any policy decision that does not benefit some people and hurt others.

Capitalism Americans believe not only in political liberty but also in economic liberty. The American economy operates as a **free-enterprise system**. The "free" in "free enterprise" means that individuals are encouraged to pursue their own financial interests, creating products and services that they can sell for a profit.

The American free-enterprise system is an example of **capitalism**, a system of economic organization that is based on private ownership and private control of the means of production and distribution. Its roots lie in a commitment to individualism, which helps explain the lack of interest that collectivist theories like communism and socialism have usually inspired in the United States.[1] Americans have never believed that government, or any designated planning agency, could generate as much productivity or as high a standard of living as a free market in which economic freedom encourages individual initiative and stimulates the creativity that leads to success. Freedom thus fuels the engine of economic progress. This belief in the social benefit of individual initiative is another component of the American ethos.

Subcultures and Diversity

Although certain common values and beliefs shape culture, there is still considerable diversity within that culture. Many subcultures coexist, such as the Cajuns of Louisiana, the Amish of Pennsylvania, the Cubanos of Miami, the Mexicans of San Antonio, the Hasidic Jews of New York. These and many other groups have distinctive traditions, perceptions, and values.

Although the presence of diverse ethnic, racial, and religious groups has often been celebrated as a strength of American society, it has also given rise to much of the tension within it. One of the more controversial issues in recent years has been the proposal to establish English as the official language of the United States, a measure already adopted by several states. Proponents argue that a common tongue has helped to unify our diverse society into a single nation, in contrast to other countries in which ethnic and tribal groups who continue to speak different languages and dialects have often come into serious conflict with one another. Opponents, however, contend that the proposal is unnecessary and undesirable: unnecessary because speaking English is essential to advancement in the United States, and undesirable because it may impede learning if it prohibits or discourages bilingual education.

Racial and ethnic groups For many years the United States was often described as a huge melting pot, a place where Old World cultures were gradually dissolved and blended into the culture of a newer American nation. Today, however, the melting-pot image does not capture America as accurately or stir Americans as powerfully as it once did. Recent immigrants and the descendants of earlier ones have become increasingly conscious of and interested in preserving or rediscovering their ancestral heritages, as have African Americans and indigenous peoples. In general, recent immigrants and racial minorities have felt less of a desire to blend in and adopt the values and mores of the dominant group, whites of European descent.

With this heightened pride in historical roots has come a proliferation of organizations to promote, preserve, and in some cases exalt various ethnic identities. Many of these groups, such as the American Jewish Congress, the Arab American Institute, National Council of La Raza, and the Japanese American Foundation, have gotten involved in the political process. In general, their concerns focus on aid to and trade with the members' homelands, foreign policy toward these countries, immigration from them, and certain domestic issues of particular groups, such as bilingual education for the children of Spanish-speaking parents.

The increasing self-awareness of racial and ethnic groups has generated conflict among them, as well as between them and groups that are part of or closer to the majority culture. Much of the conflict stems from inequality in wealth and income, education and employment opportunities, and political influence. In the past three decades, much political debate has focused on what, if anything, government should do about this inequality. The debate over tax and spending cuts is a good example. Some contend that they would benefit society as a whole by returning money and political control to individuals and the state governments; others see the spending cuts, particularly those that would affect health and welfare, as hurting the most vulnerable: minorities, the poor, the young, and the old. They also believe the tax cuts disproportionately benefit the rich.

In addition to the politics of economic inequality, issues of social justice also generate considerable political controversy. Congress has debated civil rights legislation, Native-American treaty rights, and the eligibility of legal and illegal aliens for government aid. The Supreme Court has considered cases involving school desegregation, financial inequalities in public education, affirmative action, and legislative districts designed to ensure minority representation. Presidents have been pressured to appoint members of minority groups to public office; to develop and promote programs that prohibit discrimination on the basis of race, gender, and sexual orientation in both the public and private sectors; and to encourage minority businesses.

Interest group activity has fueled the politics of inequality. The Urban League, the Congress of Racial Equality (CORE), the Southern Christian Leadership Conference (SCLC), and many other predominantly African-American groups have championed the cause of the poor within the political arena, as has the "rainbow coalition," a grassroots organization that supported Jesse Jackson's candidacy for the Democratic presidential nomination in 1984 and 1988. More recently, Louis Farrakhan and the organization he heads, the Nation of Islam, have also gotten involved in political activity, sponsoring a "Million Man March" on Washington in 1995 and a day of atonement in 1997.

Hispanic-American groups such as the National Council of La Raza and the Mexican American Legal Defense and Education Fund have also become more politically active, particularly in states with large Hispanic populations, such as Florida, Texas, and California. Asian Americans are well organized in California and other Pacific Coast states. These and other, smaller ethnic groups have commanded recognition within the political parties and Congress, and special presidential aides now provide liaison to them on a regular basis.

In sum, the increased self-awareness and unhappiness of racial and ethnic groups about their economic and social conditions has prompted them to organize and enter the political arena. They are not alone.

The women's movement American women, too, have experienced inequality in various forms; and in the last few decades the women's movement has profoundly changed politics and public policy. During the first half of this

The ethnic and religious diversity of American society presents challenges for government in trying to devise public policy. Highway safety on the New York State Thruway was jeopardized because so many Hasidic Jews stopped to pray along the roadside and flagged down others. Finally, officials created a special "Mincha area" for the afternoon prayer.

century, men took a more active part in politics than did women. Men voted more regularly, and they determined the issues that went on the public policy agenda. American women were not universally guaranteed the right to vote until 1920. Even after they obtained suffrage, their political attitudes and voting behavior did not differ significantly from men's for many years—a fact that some attributed to the stratification of social roles, which encouraged women to be more concerned about family issues and men more concerned about national and world affairs. As a result, married women—and a larger percentage of women were married then—tended to follow their husbands' lead on political matters.

Times have changed. In the late 1960s and 1970s, women surged into the work force and entered the political arena. In both areas they found many traditional patterns and procedures not to their liking, and they became intensely concerned with issues that affected them directly: abortion and other women's health concerns, maternity leave and child-care policies, equal pay and equal job opportunities, legal rights within marriage, and the equity of divorce laws. At the same time, the proportion of women who were divorced or separated or who had never been married increased sharply.

Consistent with the growing awareness of their economic needs, women began to develop distinctive political attitudes. As a group, women became more sympathetic than men to a larger government role within the economic and social spheres and less supportive of a foreign policy based on military force. In response to the differing positions taken by the political parties on these issues, a gender gap emerged, with women more likely to vote for Democratic candidates and men more likely than women to support Republicans. This gap, which reached 17 percentage points in the 1996 presidential election, has reinforced the policy positions and ideological differences between the parties, making the Republicans more conservative and the Democrats more liberal.

In addition, women began to form their own interest groups, such as the National Organization for Women (NOW) and the Women's Political Caucus; through them, they began to join causes and support women's issues more successfully than in the past. More women also began to seek and win elective office, at both the state and the national levels. These developments have introduced a new gender-based dimension into American politics.

Consensus, Conflict, and Apathy in American Democracy

Both consensus and conflict grow from the soil of the American culture, and both help to shape American politics and government. The consensus, which emerges from shared fundamental beliefs and values, embraces the need for government, the rules of the political process, and the general nature of public policy. The conflict, which springs from the diversity of the population and from the different needs, interests, and goals that flow from that pluralism, usually swirls around the content of specific policies and generates much of the activity within the political and governing arenas.

Consensus provides a broad base of support for the government and whatever policies the government produces. The wide diversity of interests, on the other hand, produces political battles over specific issues. Most of this activity occurs among those groups, whether large or small, that are directly interested in or affected by a particular issue. The general public is likely to get involved only when the policy goes into effect or its cost must be paid. Most of the time, only a small portion of the population knows or cares much about public policies, and an even smaller portion gets involved and tries to influence the content of those policies.

The strength of the American system is that it permits those who are interested to participate in politics and affect policy outcomes. It also gives the general citizenry regular opportunities to get involved. Thus periodic elections, a free critical press, and abundant opportunities for citizens to petition and protest keep public officials responsive to society, even though many people choose not to involve themselves in day-to-day political activities. The weakness of the system is that because many people do not get involved, even by voting, they do not have a significant impact on government and public policy. Their lack of involvement reinforces the unequal distribution of wealth and benefits within the society. The system is oriented toward the maintenance of the status quo; it makes it easier to keep government and policy as they are than to change them.

CASE STUDY

Immigration: The Natives Get Restless

Immigration. For most of American history, this has been a word that inspired warm feelings and rich memories. "A nation of immigrants," Americans were called. "Give me your tired, your poor, / Your huddled masses yearning to breathe free," American schoolchildren recited from Emma Lazarus's poem about the Statue of Liberty. Americans looked with pride on their immigrant heroes, retold stories of the struggle and determination of their own ancestors to make a better life in a new country, and regarded their country as a beacon of hope, opportunity, and democracy for people from all over the world.

But today immigration often strikes a different chord in the American psyche and evokes less sentimental images. To some, it has come to mean illegal entry and increased taxes to pay for government "handouts" to those who come here for such bounty; to others, it brings to mind criminal gangs and a lowering of educational standards in public schools. Still others see cheap immigrant labor as putting Americans out of work. In the 1990s, many Americans have wanted to put the brakes on immigration, and they found responsive politicians to lead the effort.

Why now? The answer lies in a very powerful demographic reality: the United States population has never been more diverse than it is today, and one reason is a recent acceleration in immigration. Net immigration (the number of people arriving minus the number leaving) has been steadily rising since World War II. But the rush of new immigrants in the 1980s accounted for more than 30 percent of all population growth, the largest proportion since the first decade of the twentieth century.

Equally important in stimulating a political backlash has been the concentration of these new immigrants in a few areas where their swelling numbers have made them a significant economic and cultural presence. Among foreign-born citizens and legal aliens counted in the 1990 consensus, 25 percent were from Mexico and Central America and another 25 percent from Asia. These populations are highly concentrated in a few states and within certain parts of those states: Hispanics, for example, now outnumber all other ethnic and racial groups combined in dozens of counties in New Mexico, Texas, Arizona, Colorado, and California.

More than any other state, California has been dramatically affected by recent immigration patterns. According to the 1990 census, 10 percent of California's population is Asian and 25 percent Hispanic; the portion that is non-Hispanic white has dropped to 57 percent from 76 percent in 1980. Believing that immigrants, many of them illegal, were costing the state millions of dollars in education, health care, and other public services, a group of citizens initiated a ballot referendum in 1994 that would deny these benefits to illegal aliens. Californians voted overwhelmingly in favor of this referendum, Proposition 187. In doing so, they sent a loud and clear message across the country's political landscape.

Meanwhile, the Arizona legislature enacted a law making English the state's official language and requiring state officials to conduct all business in English. When a bilingual employee challenged the law, however, a federal court ruled that the English-only provision could not be enforced by the state. In 1994, Congress imposed proficiency in English and a knowledge of civics as qualifications for citizenship, exempting only the mentally disabled from this requirement.

Two years later, these qualifications became even more important when the Republican-controlled 104th Congress enacted a welfare reform bill that made noncitizens ineligible for most benefits, such as food stamps, Medicaid, and Supplemental Security payments. The legislation was notable in that it imposed these cutbacks not only on illegal but also on legal immigrants, who critics say often abuse immigration laws by using loopholes to bring in large extended families to the United States. (Supplemental Security payments for legal aliens were later restored by the 1997 budget agreement.) The 104th Congress also tried to curb the flow of immigration by attaching to an omnibus spending bill provisions that would have prevented noncitizens from receiving a host of other federal benefits, including Social Security. When opposition developed to denying benefits to legal aliens (as well as to raising the income level for those who sponsor them when they come to the United States), the bill was amended to apply only to illegal aliens, who have been entering the country at the rate of approximately 300,000 per year.

The omnibus spending bill also contained money to hire more border guards and more Immigration and Naturalization Service investigative agents and to build a 3-tiered, 14-mile fence along the California–Mexico border. Congress considered even harsher measures against illegal aliens, such as imposing tough sanctions against employers who hire them, creating a national verification program to screen them out from welfare rolls, and even allowing states to deny public education to their children. But these proposals were eventually stricken from the bill in order to gain sufficient support for its passage and for presidential approval.

Curbing legal immigration remains a controversial issue, one that continues to divide the country. Should quotas, the number of people allowed into the United States from each foreign country, be reduced? If so, how much, and on the basis of what criteria? Should we continue to prevent those with communicable diseases or those who would require extensive health care, such as people with AIDS, from entering the country? Should exceptions to these rules be made for those who can demonstrate that they have suffered from political persecution? Should economic persecution or other conditions also qualify? What about practices that most Americans find abhorrent, such as female circumcision—should women from societies who practice this ritual qualify as well?

Proponents of curbs argue that too many people are coming to the United States, at too great economic and social costs to American society. However, a coalition of immigrant and employer groups argues that the United States has greatly benefited over the years from the contribution of immigrants, who have enriched its culture with their diversity; have provided a vital source of labor, taking hard, unpleasant, and low-paying jobs that citizens have not wanted; and have produced cheap goods and services from which all Americans have profited.

A report published in 1997 by the National Academy of Science supports this view. The Academy's report estimates that immigrants add about $10 billion a year to the United States economic output, thereby benefiting most people in the society, who consume the products of this labor. The only group that may not benefit are unskilled or lower-skilled workers, whose job opportunities and wages may be adversely affected by immigrant competition

To get more information about this issue or to become involved in the debate, contact one of the following groups:

Supporting efforts to curtail legal immigration:

Federation for American Immigration Reform
1666 Connecticut Ave., N.W., Suite 400
Washington, DC 20009
1-800-395-0890
e-mail: fair@fairus.org; http://www.fairus.org

Opposing most efforts to curtail legal immigration:

The National Network for Immigrant and Refugee Rights
310 8th Street, Suite 307
Oakland, CA 94607
(510) 465-1984
(510) 465-7548 (fax)
e-mail: nnirr@igc.apc.org

Discussion Questions

1. What are the principal issues about legal and illegal immigration that continue to divide Americans? Which of them do you believe to be the most serious?
2. Who are the principal protagonists on these issues, and what would they like to see happen?
3. What should be the criteria for legal immigration and for citizenship? And what should we do about illegal immigration?
4. Should noncitizens be eligible for government social benefits? Should they pay taxes?

SUMMARY

In a culture where disagreement and self-interest are the norm, where individual liberty and the common good may be mutually exclusive, and where rewards are limited whereas desires are virtually insatiable, the quest for political gain is never-ending. If *politics* is the ongoing struggle among people to influence the values, beliefs, and policy of the society, then *government* is the institutional mechanism for determining the rules of that contest and, within those rules, who wins and who loses. Government determines who gets what and when by formulating policy decisions that distribute resources, allocate funds, and make and enforce rules.

When government makes decisions, it exercises *authority*. In a democracy, it must do so in a way that reflects the desires of the majority but does not violate the rights of the minority. This is a difficult task. The Constitution provides general guidelines, but each generation must decide for itself how to interpret those guidelines, that is, where to draw the line between the majority's interests, desires, and rights, and the minority's rights.

How government makes decisions may be controversial as well. The rules by which any political system operates are not neutral: they benefit some at the expense of others. Those who understand the rules are best able to benefit from them. And those who understand the rules and can most effectively manipulate them to their advantage have tended to be the best-organized, best-funded, and best-led groups. This is why the political system in the United States seems to advantage the advantaged. This is also why the government tends to maintain the status quo, and why policy changes are more often incremental than innovative.

That Americans accept the political system and the rules by which it functions, even though they do not always agree with or benefit from the policy it establishes, is testimony to the consensus underlying the basic values and beliefs of American culture. Most Americans believe that *democracy* is the best type of government and *capitalism* is the best type of economic system. Both are predicated on the concept of individual liberty—the idea that people should be free to pursue their own interests as long as that pursuit does not impinge on the general welfare of the society. When it does, law may impose restraints. Americans also believe in political equality, the idea that all citizens have equal rights and responsibilities under law. These shared beliefs in individual liberty and political equality provide the foundation on which the political system rests, and the political system in turn provides the mechanisms for the debate and resolution of disagreements.

Society in the United States consists of many different ethnic, racial, and religious groups. This diversity has contributed to the strength and vitality of American society and its political system. But it has also led to continuous struggles over *public policy*, struggles that pit individuals and groups against one another as they pursue their own interests, values, and beliefs. These battles are the essence of contemporary politics, the fuel that fires the engines of government and keeps them running.

KEY TERMS

- politics
- government
- public policy
- power
- democracy
- authority
- political culture
- American ethos
- free-enterprise system
- capitalism

RESOURCES

READINGS

Dahl, Robert A. *A Preface to Democratic Theory*. Chicago: University of Chicago Press, 1963. An extended discussion of the concept of democracy.

Dionne, E. J. *Why Americans Hate Politics*. New York: Simon and Schuster, 1992. A leading journalist's account of why so many Americans have been turned off by politics and politicians and what can be done about the situation.

Ellis, Richard J. *American Political Cultures*. New York: Oxford University Press, 1993. This book postulates the thesis that there are a variety of political cultures in America and that the debate over policy is really a conflict among these cultures.

Greider, William. *Who Will Tell the People: The Betrayal of American Democracy*. New York: Simon and Schuster, 1993. A thoughtful critique of what is wrong with our democratic system and how it can be fixed.

Lasswell, Harold. *Politics: Who Gets What, When, How*. New York: Meridian Books, 1958. A classic study of the politics of influence by a scholar who helped shape the discipline of political science.

Lipset, Seymour Martin. *The First New Nation: The United States in Historical and Comparative Perspective.* New York: Norton, 1979. An inquiry into the economic, historical, and sociological factors that shaped the American character.

Tocqueville, Alexis de. *Democracy in America.* Edited by J. P. Mayer. New York: Harper and Row, 1988. A classic study of American democracy as seen through the eyes of a French traveler in the United States in the 1830s.

ORGANIZATIONS

Common Cause, 1250 Connecticut Ave., NW, Suite 600, Washington, DC 20036; phone (202) 833-1200, fax (202) 659-3716, Internet http://www.commoncause.org A citizens' lobby, interested in the operation of government and its responsiveness to the people.

Congress Watch, 215 Pennsylvania Avenue, S.E., Washington, DC 20003; phone (202) 546-4996, fax (202) 547-7392, Internet http://www.citizen.org/public_citizen/congress/cwhome.html A part of activist Ralph Nader's organization, this group examines Congress and the behavior of its members.

Public Citizen, 1600 20th Street, N.W., Washington, DC 20009; phone (202) 588-1000, fax (202) 588-7799, Internet http://www.citizen.org/ Another group in Ralph Nader's organization, it promotes democratic practices and tries to coordinate citizen action campaigns.

2

The Constitutional Basis of American Politics

PREVIEW

- The Founders' Constitution: the revolutionary background; the Articles of Confederation; the Constitutional Convention; ratification
- Enduring ideas and essential tensions: popular sovereignty; limited government; unalienable rights; separation of powers; federalism; judicial review
- The living Constitution: day-to-day operations of government; formal amendment; judicial review

Have you ever registered to vote? If not, did you know that you will be offered a chance to do so the next time you go to renew your driver's license? The story of how the federal government came to use state motor vehicle offices to register voters—and how state governments unsuccessfully challenged its authority to do so—reveals many facets of the complex relationship between politics and government within the American constitutional system.

Determining who may vote has generated recurring political controversy throughout American history. During the Constitutional Convention, the framers struggled with the issue, agreeing on the need for a representative government but disagreeing over who would choose the representatives. In the end, they gave the states the right and obligation to conduct elections for federal officials, with such exceptions and regulations as Congress might determine.

The framers' decision not to decide on the voting question did not end the controversy, however. In fact, it ensured that it would be extended to later generations. Over the years, Congress has instituted constitutional amendments to extend suffrage to all citizens eighteen years of age and older, including racial minorities and women, and has enacted laws limiting the states' discretion in conducting elections for federal officials. The most recent example of this limitation is the so-called motor-voter law, officially known as the National Voter Registration Act of 1993. The law requires states to permit registration by mail or in a variety of state offices, including departments of motor vehicles, social services, vocational training, and military recruitment. Moreover, it prohibits states from purging from their registration lists those who have not voted in the past.

Enacted by a Democratic Congress, the motor-voter law aimed to increase the proportion of citizens who actually vote. That proportion had been declining for three decades, leaving voter turnout in the United States lower than in many other democratic countries. But the Democrats had a political motive as well. People who are older, better educated, and of higher income levels are more likely to vote than those at the lower end of the age, education, and income scales. Because the Republicans have tended to receive a larger proportion of their vote than have the Democrats from people in the upper education and income brackets, the Democrats hoped and the Republicans feared that the impact of the law would be to increase the potential Democratic vote. That is one reason why an earlier version of legislation, passed by Congress during the Bush administration, was vetoed by the president. Reenacted during the first year of the Clinton presidency, it was signed into law with considerable fanfare and took effect in 1995, one year before the president was to run for reelection.

After the bill became law, however, a number of states challenged its constitutionality and refused to comply with its requirements. These states—California, Illinois, Kansas, Michigan, Pennsylvania, South Carolina, and Virginia—had one thing in common: they all had Republican governors. The results of the 1994 congressional elections, in which the Republicans gained control of both houses of Congress, reinforced the resolve of these governors and Republican legislators in these states to oppose the law. In response to the states' opposition, the United States Justice Department countersued in an attempt to force compliance.

The states could not argue in a court of law that registering more people was bad because the new voters were more likely to register and vote Democratic (a charge that in fact was not borne out by the response to the law in its first year). Instead, their claim had to be couched in constitutional terms. The Tenth Amendment states, "The powers not delegated to the United States by the Constitution, nor prohibited by it to the States, are reserved to the States respectively, or to the people." California's Governor Pete Wilson thus charged that "'Motor Voter' is the Clinton Administration's latest assault on states' sovereign rights to run their own agencies and to determine the jobs of their own employees." Likewise, Virginia's Governor George F. Allen claimed that the law was "an unfunded mandate" from the federal government that required state employees, in the departments of motor vehicles and social services, to perform work other than that for which they were hired. The governors also claimed that the law would open the door to voter fraud and cost their states "excessive amounts of money."

The federal courts that ruled on the constitutionality of the law unanimously disagreed, however. In rejecting the Republican governors' arguments, the courts cited Article I, Section 4, of the Constitution, which states, "The Time, Places and Manner of holding Elections for Senators and Representatives, shall be prescribed in each State by the Legislature thereof; but the Congress may at any time by Law make or alter such Regulations," except as to the places of choosing senators. Under this provision, Congress had the power to pass the motor-voter law because the Constitution gives it, not the states, the power to alter state voter regulations governing congressional elections. Moreover, the courts noted that although Article I, Section 2, of the Constitution gives the states the power to set the qualifications of voters for senators and representatives, the motor-voter law did not intrude on that power since it did not alter the qualifications themselves. In the words of the Court of Appeals for the Ninth Circuit, "Congress may conscript state agencies to carry out voter registration for the election of representatives and senators." In January 1996, the Supreme Court decided not to review California's appeal of this ruling, thus settling definitively the question of the law's constitutionality.

The controversy over the motor-voter law illustrates how the Constitution can be both a prescription for political struggle and a framework for resolving political conflict. Politics involves contests over competing interests and powers. The dispute over the motor-voter law was a partisan disagreement between Republicans and Democrats. But when the dispute was taken to the courts, it became a conflict over federalism and the powers of the national government versus the states. The Constitution also provides that the Supreme Court and the lower federal courts may review and decide such cases and controversies. Through constitutional amendments and legislation like the motor-voter law, American government has become more and more democratic. The Constitution thus is as much a framework for government as a blueprint for a dynamic political process in which individuals and interest groups compete for influence and power.

Politics in America differs from politics in other countries because of the nature of the Constitution. The United States Constitution, the oldest written constitution in the world, is unique because it combines the idea of the rule of law with the idea that government is based on the consent of the governed. This chapter examines the basic principles and structure of the Constitution. We discuss the historical context in which this document was drafted and ratified, the original Constitution of 1787, and how the Constitution has changed over the years, as well as the ways in which constitutional change may occur.

THE FOUNDERS' CONSTITUTION

The founders' Constitution, as the historian Max Farrand observed, was a "bundle of compromises."[1] It was forged by a group of pragmatic statesmen who had to overlook, if not reconcile, their conflicting views about the politics of government. How did the Constitution come about?

The Revolutionary Background

In 1774, twelve of the original thirteen British colonies sent delegates to the First Continental Congress. This gathering had no official status; rather, it was convened to pass resolutions denouncing the British Parliament and Crown. The colonies had unsuccessfully demanded their own representatives in Parliament, arguing that only by this means could they defend their economic interests. When Britain imposed taxes on goods imported into the colonies, the demand for political representation intensified and the slogan "No taxation without representation" became a popular rallying cry. In addition, the colonists opposed the use of judges appointed by King George III to enforce laws they deemed unconstitutional.

In response to growing opposition to the Crown, the First Continental Congress recommended economic sanctions against Britain and boycotts of its goods. It also declared some acts of Parliament unconstitutional and urged colonists to arm themselves and form their own militias. In April 1775, fighting broke out between colonial and British troops, and in May a Second Continental Congress passed a resolution putting the colonies in a state of defense. Hostilities spread, and pressure grew for complete separation from Britain.

In the spring of 1776, a committee of the Continental Congress began work on a resolution proclaiming the colonies free and independent. Committee members decided that Thomas Jefferson would draft the resolution—the Declaration of Independence. Drawing on the Enlightenment philosophy of rationality and a science of human affairs that included the idea of individuals having unalienable rights to "life, liberty and the pursuit of happiness," Jefferson compiled a long list of despotic "abuses and usurpations" of power by King George. On July 1, 1776, the Continental Congress began debating Jefferson's draft and making changes in the wording. Three days later, on July 4, it approved the Declaration of Independence.

Later in 1776, the Continental Congress also considered a proposed set of "Articles of Confederation and Perpetual Union." The **Articles of Confederation**, the United States' first constitution, was approved in 1777 but was not ratified by all thirteen of the former colonies until 1781.

The Articles of Confederation

The Articles of Confederation provided for a unicameral, or one-house, legislature known as the Continental Congress, composed of delegates from the states. But this Congress had no effective power to regulate commerce or collect taxes; and tariffs, weights and measures, and currency varied from state to state. There was no separate executive or national judiciary; neither was there a national army. Instead, each of the original thirteen colonies was an independent and sovereign state that could conduct its own foreign policy without reference to the policies of other states.

This lack of a national political authority presented grave problems. For example, when several states refused to repay debts they had incurred during the Revolutionary War, the Continental Congress had no power to compel them to do so. In fact, it had no enforcement powers in any area. It could only ask each state to comply with and enforce its laws and policies voluntarily.

Also of growing concern were the economic problems facing the country and the tensions between creditors and debtors. In the aftermath of the Revolutionary War, imports and exports declined sharply, wages fell by as much as 20 percent, and money was in short supply. In 1786 and 1787, tensions came to a head in economically depressed western Massachusetts when the state legislature refused to respond to petitions from debt-ridden farmers demanding the issuance of paper money and legislation to stop banks from foreclosing on their homes and farms. The angry farmers, led by Daniel Shays, formerly a captain in the Revolutionary army, rebelled against the state government and eventually marched on the federal arsenal at Springfield. It took the Massachusetts militia a year to put down Shays's rebellion.

Shays's Rebellion dramatically underscored the weakness of the national government under the Articles of Confederation. It also coincided with the states' selection of delegates to the Constitutional Convention, which opened in Philadelphia in May 1787. And it was fresh in the minds of convention delegates, who planned to revise the Articles of Confederation but ended up drafting an entirely new constitution, one that greatly strengthened the powers of the national government.[2]

The Constitutional Convention

Despite their diverse interests and conflicting views of government, delegates to the Constitutional Convention agreed that the Articles of Confederation were defective. The Continental Congress lacked three important powers: to regulate commerce, to raise funds to support a national army, and to compel compliance by the states. Within five days after the convention convened, on May 25, 1787, delegates had decided that "a *national* Government ought to be established consisting of a supreme legislative, executive and judiciary."[3]

Although they agreed that government must rest on the consent of the governed, the delegates shared a distrust of direct democracy. They feared a tyranny of the majority as much as they feared a tyranny of a minority—the concentration of power in too few hands. From the outset, therefore, the convention was inclined toward creating a **republic**, or representative form of government. Such a government would have considerable power to make and enforce laws but would derive its authority directly or indirectly from the citizens through popular elections. The objective, in the words of James Madison, a delegate from Virginia, was a "mixed" form of government, one that combined democratic and representative elements so as to minimize the possibility of tyranny by either the majority or a minority.[4]

The Great Compromise Although in agreement on the broad outlines of the new republic, the delegates were sharply divided over the precise form it should take. Conflicts between large states and small states over their representation in Congress and between states in the North and those in the South over taxation and representation proved to be the major problems.

During the first few weeks, debate focused on the **Virginia Plan**, which was drafted by James Madison and presented by Edmund Randolph, the governor of Virginia. It called for a strong central government with a *bicameral legislature*—a legislature with two houses. Members of the lower house would be elected by voters in the states, and members of the upper house would be chosen by those in the lower house from nominees submitted by the state legislatures. Representation of states in the national legislature would be based on wealth and population; thus the large states—Virginia, Massachusetts, and Pennsylvania—would

James Madison, the primary force behind the creation of the Constitution, later played a key role in the dispute that established the power of the Supreme Court to interpret the document.

dominate. In addition, the Virginia Plan called for an executive chosen by the legislature, for a judiciary with considerable power, and for a council of revision (comprising members of the executive and the judiciary) with the power to veto legislation.

Delegates from small states opposed this plan and supported the **New Jersey Plan**, proposed by William Paterson of New Jersey. It called for a *unicameral legislature* with considerable regulatory and taxing power, in which all states would be represented equally. Executive powers would be exercised by a group that would not have the power to veto legislation.

By the end of June, the convention had reached an impasse, and a committee known as the Committee of Eleven was given the task of hammering out a compromise. On July 5, it presented the solution that became known as the **Great Compromise**: a bicameral legislature in which representation in the lower house (the House of Representatives) would be based on population, and representation in the upper house (the Senate) would be equal for every state. House members were to be chosen by popular election, whereas senators were to be chosen by the state legislatures.

The three-fifths compromise Slavery was another divisive issue. Delegates from southern states wanted slaves to be counted as part of a state's population, which would increase the South's representation in the House of Representatives (because most slaves lived in the South). Delegates from northern states insisted on the principle of equal representation of all citizens, which discounted slaves because they were not considered citizens. The delegates finally agreed to the **three-fifths compromise**, which stated that "three-fifths of all other Persons [that is, slaves]" would be counted for purposes of

The Signing of the Constitution, *commissioned to celebrate the Constitution's bicentennial in 1987, was based on authenticated portraits of those who attended the Constitutional Convention and on architectural records of the time.*

representation but that the same standard would apply for any taxes assessed on the basis of a state's population. As a concession to the southern states, the larger issue of slavery and trading in slaves was put off for two decades by Article I, Section 9, which prohibited Congress from outlawing the slave trade before 1808.

After negotiating the three-fifths compromise, the convention spent more than a month debating issues involving the powers of Congress and those of the president. But the major conflicts over state representation and the structure of government had been resolved. On September 17, 1787, thirty-nine of the remaining delegates signed the document; only three refused to do so.[5]

Ratification

Although the delegates had approved the Constitution, they still had to secure its ratification by the states. To outmaneuver the opposition, they recommended (in Article VII) a novel method of ratification. Amendments to the Articles of Confederation were supposed to be ratified by *all* state legislatures, but instead of submitting the Constitution to the legislatures, the Constitutional Convention recommended that the Congress of the Confederation send the document to the states for ratification by special conventions of the people. Article VII provided that the Constitution would be ratified if at least *nine* of the thirteen states gave their approval. Congress and the thirteen states agreed to this plan.

Ratification by special state conventions was politically significant because, in James Madison's words, it meant that the Constitution was not a mere treaty "among the Governments and Independent States" but the expression of "the supreme authority of the people themselves."[6] Requiring only nine states for ratification was also a defensive strategy, because it was far from certain that all thirteen states would give their approval. The erosion of the states' power and the repudiation of their sovereignty did not escape the attention of those who were opposed to the new Constitution. Known as the Anti-Federalists, they saw the document as concentrating too much power in a national government and retaining too little authority for the states, both individually and collectively. In the words of Patrick Henry of Virginia, "what right had they [the delegates] to say, *We, the People?* . . . Who authorized them to speak the language of, *We, the People*, instead of *We, the States?* States are the characteristics, and the soul of the confederation. If the States are not the agents of this compact, it must be one great consolidated National Government of the people of all the States."[7] But Henry lost, not only in Virginia but in all the other states.

Delaware ratified the Constitution on December 7, 1787. Within weeks, Pennsylvania, New Jersey, Georgia, and Connecticut gave their approval. Massachusetts followed in February 1788, but with a close vote of 187 to 168. In the spring of 1788, Maryland and South Carolina gave their overwhelming endorsements. Then, in June, close votes in New Hampshire and Virginia secured the nine states needed for ratification. But the battle was not over. New York's ratification convention was bitterly divided, and New York's approval was crucial for the success of the union because this large commercial state separated New England from the states in the South. Opponents feared that the national government was being granted too much power and that representatives from small states might conspire in Congress against New York's commercial interests. It was largely owing to the leadership of Alexander Hamilton that

New York finally voted in favor of ratification.[8] (North Carolina did not ratify until November 1789, and Rhode Island held out until May 1790.)

In New York and several other states—notably Massachusetts and Virginia—the price of ratification was agreement that the First Congress would adopt a bill of rights that specifically guaranteed individuals' civil rights and liberties. In 1789, the First Congress adopted twelve amendments to the Constitution and promptly submitted them to the states. Ten of the amendments, known as the **Bill of Rights**, were ratified by the states on December 15, 1791. The protections contained in the Bill of Rights are listed in the box.

THE BILL OF RIGHTS

First Amendment Freedom of religion, speech, the press, and assembly.

Second Amendment The right to bear arms.

Third Amendment Protection against the quartering of soldiers in one's home.

Fourth Amendment The right to be secure against unreasonable searches and seizures.

Fifth Amendment The right to "due process of law," protection against double jeopardy, and the privilege against self-incrimination.

Sixth Amendment The right to counsel for one's defense and to a speedy and public trial by an impartial jury.

Seventh Amendment The right to a jury trial in civil law cases.

Eighth Amendment Prohibition of excessive bail and fines and of "cruel and unusual punishment."

Ninth Amendment The retention by the people of rights that are not enumerated in the Constitution.

Tenth Amendment The retention by the states or by the people of powers not delegated to the national government.

With the ratification of the Constitution and the Bill of Rights, the framework for a dynamic political process was in place. It remained for succeeding generations to work out the details of government.

ENDURING IDEAS AND ESSENTIAL TENSIONS

In just 4,300 words, the Constitution provides a blueprint for self-government. The Constitution provides for both continuity and change because of the interplay of certain enduring ideas: the principles of popular sovereignty, limited government, and individual unalienable natural rights. These ideas led the founders to establish a system of checks and balances by distributing power among the branches of the national government, dividing power between the national and state governments, and creating the basis for judicial review.

Popular Sovereignty

As the Declaration of Independence stated, the Revolutionary War was fought because of a "long train of abuses" by the British Crown. The colonists charged that King George III, among other things, taxed them but denied them representation and made judges dependent on his will.

In rejecting the British monarchical model of government, in which sovereignty rested with the Crown, the colonists proposed the revolutionary idea of **popular sovereignty**, the idea that government is based on the consent of the people and is accountable to the people for its actions.[9] Although the framers of the Constitution were not inclined to support direct popular involvement in government, they did subscribe to the principle that government authority is based on the consent of the governed. This principle is expressed in the opening lines of the Preamble to the Constitution: "We, the People of the United States, . . . do ordain and establish this Constitution for the United States of America."

Limited Government

The idea of **limited government** follows from the notion of popular sovereignty. Fearful that the only alternative to constitutionally limited government was political tyranny, the founders sought to ensure that the authority of government—its ability to make and enforce laws that limit individual freedom—would be restricted to **express powers**, that is, powers specified and delegated to the national government by the Constitution.[10] These express powers are listed in the first three articles of the document: Article I details the legislative powers of Congress, Article II describes the executive powers of the president, and Article III indicates the powers of the federal judiciary.

In addition to express powers, the Constitution confers on Congress certain **implied powers**, that is, powers that might be inferred from those that are expressly delegated. The basis for implied powers is the "necessary and proper" clause (Article I, Section 8), which gives Congress the power "to make all laws which shall be necessary and proper for carrying into execution the foregoing powers, and all other powers vested by this Constitution in the government of the United States." Because this clause gives Congress such wide-ranging authority, it is often referred to as the "elastic clause." Yet, how far Congress may go in exercising its implied powers has often been a matter of controversy.

In addition to express and implied powers, in the conduct of foreign affairs the national government has **inherent powers**, that is, powers that are not specifically enumerated in the Constitution. The states may make no claims in this area. But political contests between Congress and the president occasionally arise over claims of inherent powers, particularly in times of international crisis. These disputes force presidents to defend their actions in terms of the Constitution and to be accountable to Congress and the American people.

Unalienable Rights

One of the founders' main objectives in constraining the powers of government was to ensure the **unalienable rights** of individuals. According to the social theory of the English philosopher John Locke, people are born with certain rights granted to them in advance by "nature." Among these, as the Declaration of Independence proclaims, are "Life, Liberty and the Pursuit of Happiness." Because these rights precede the creation of government, they are not granted by government and therefore cannot be taken away by government. Instead, so this theory goes, it is the duty of government to protect its citizens against any encroachment on those rights.[11]

By limiting government power to that which is specifically granted in the Constitution, the founders hoped to safeguard individuals' unalienable rights. That was one of the arguments used by Madison, Hamilton, and other defenders of the Constitution to win its ratification by the states. In *The Federalist, No. 84,* one of a series of newspaper essays defending the new Constitution, Hamilton wrote: "The Constitution itself, in every rational sense, and to every useful purpose, is a bill of rights." By this he meant that a government with limited and delegated powers would not expand to usurp individuals' rights, and thus those rights would be secure.

Those who opposed the Constitution were unpersuaded, however. Fearful that the national government's power would be too great and would expand at the expense of the states and the people, they urged the adoption of a separate bill of rights, which was ratified in December 1791.

Separation of Powers

Because the founders were wary of the concentration of government power, they distributed power among the three branches of the national government (see Figure 2-1). This **separation of powers** was designed to create a delicate structure in which the legislative, executive, and judicial branches would check and balance each other in various ways. "Ambition must be made to counteract ambition," Madison argued in *The Federalist, No. 51.*

The principle of separation of powers is embodied in the Constitution's grant of legislative power to Congress, executive and other powers to the president, and judicial power to the Supreme Court and other federal courts. This system stands in contrast to unitary systems such as that of Britain, in which the majority party in Parliament (the legislative branch) appoints the prime minister and cabinet (the executive branch). Nevertheless, the powers given to the three branches are not entirely or completely separate; the branches are actually separate institutions that share political power. For instance, Congress passes legislation

FIGURE 2-1

Separation of Powers among the Branches of Government

President:
- Commander-in-chief of the military
- Makes treaties with other countries
- Appoints ambassadors, federal judges, Supreme Court justices, other federal officials
- Administers U.S. laws
- Acts as head of state

Congress:
- Passes federal laws
- Raises taxes
- Regulates foreign and interstate commerce
- Declares war
- Raises and funds the military
- May borrow money by issuing bonds for sale

Supreme Court:
- Reviews lower federal court rulings and appeals from state courts that involve federal law or constitutional issues
- Hears cases involving foreign ambassadors as first and final court
- Rules on disputes between states

SOURCE: Adapted from *Scholastic Update,* vol. 119, no. 1 (September 8, 1986).

FIGURE 2-2

Checks and Balances among the Branches of Government

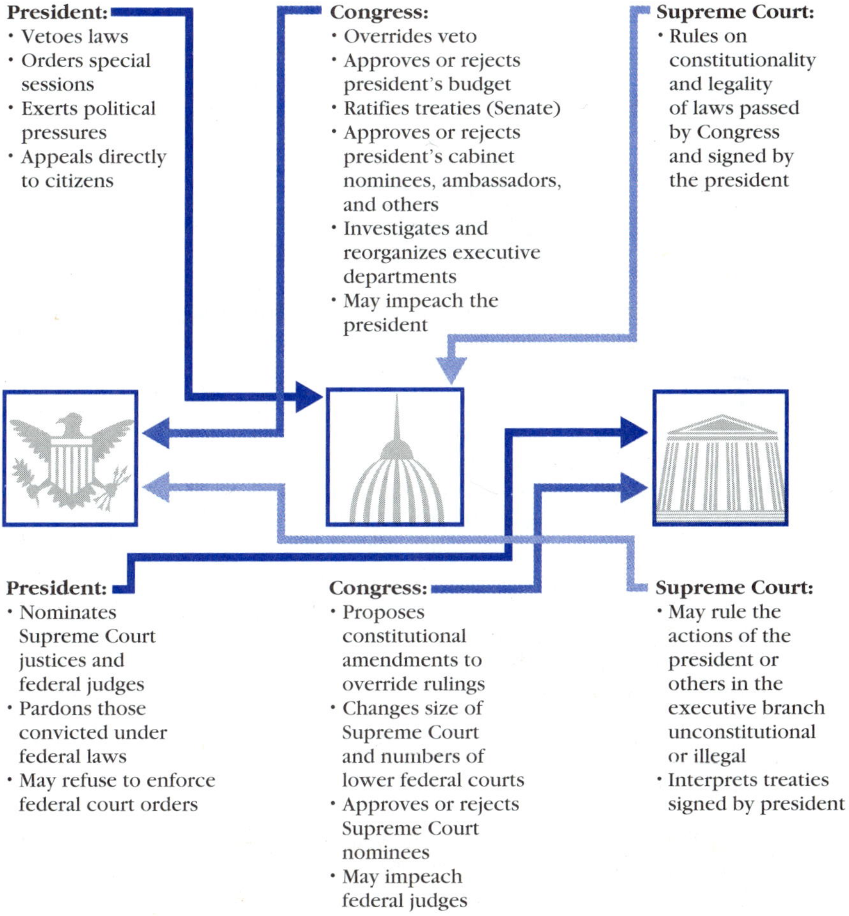

President:
- Vetoes laws
- Orders special sessions
- Exerts political pressures
- Appeals directly to citizens

Congress:
- Overrides veto
- Approves or rejects president's budget
- Ratifies treaties (Senate)
- Approves or rejects president's cabinet nominees, ambassadors, and others
- Investigates and reorganizes executive departments
- May impeach the president

Supreme Court:
- Rules on constitutionality and legality of laws passed by Congress and signed by the president

President:
- Nominates Supreme Court justices and federal judges
- Pardons those convicted under federal laws
- May refuse to enforce federal court orders

Congress:
- Proposes constitutional amendments to override rulings
- Changes size of Supreme Court and numbers of lower federal courts
- Approves or rejects Supreme Court nominees
- May impeach federal judges

Supreme Court:
- May rule the actions of the president or others in the executive branch unconstitutional or illegal
- Interprets treaties signed by president

SOURCE: Adapted from *Scholastic Update,* vol. 119, no. 1 (September 8, 1986).

that the president must approve or veto; a two-thirds vote by both the House of Representatives and the Senate may override a presidential veto. The president makes treaties with foreign governments and appoints members of the federal judiciary, but presidential treaty making and judicial appointments are subject to ratification or confirmation by the Senate.

Congress, the president, and the judiciary share various other powers as well, so that they check and balance each other both directly and indirectly (see Figure 2-2). This division and sharing of powers makes political change difficult and slow. In the words of Justice Louis D. Brandeis,

> The doctrine of separation of powers was adopted by the Convention of 1787, not to promote efficiency but to preclude the exercise of arbitrary

> power. The purpose was not to avoid friction, but, by means of the inevitable friction incident to the distribution of the governmental powers among three departments, to save the people from having one institution dominate the government.[12]

The effects of power sharing by separate institutions are evident in the operation of constitutional checks and balances through the years. The president has vetoed congressional acts more than 2,400 times, and Congress has overridden about 100 of those vetoes. The Supreme Court has ruled more than 180 congressional acts or parts of acts unconstitutional. The Senate has refused to confirm 29 nominees to the Supreme Court (out of 143 nominations) and has rejected at least 9 cabinet nominations as well as many subcabinet appointees. Congress has impeached 14 federal judges and convicted 7. Congress has passed, and the states have ratified, 5 amendments to the Constitution overturning decisions of the Supreme Court. In short, separation of powers is often a prescription for political struggle.

On the other hand, power sharing also encourages cooperation and compromise. For example, Congress and the president must work together to enact legislation and appropriate funds for the operation of government, and the Supreme Court sometimes depends on the other two branches to enforce its rulings. In fact, when the Court handed down its landmark rulings mandating school desegregation, in *Brown v. Board of Education* (1954 and 1955), both presidential action and congressional action were required to overcome opposition in the South.

Federalism

By dividing power not only among the branches of the national government but also between the national and state governments, the Constitution created a system known as **federalism**.[13] The framers of the Constitution had no real alternative to establishing a federal system. They could not abolish the thirteen original states or deny them most of their governing powers, but they *could* establish a national government with its own independent powers and leave intact the powers of the states that were not exclusively delegated to the national government. Thus each state retained its own executive branch, legislature, and judicial system. Individuals were to be subject to both state and national laws. This division has made the politics of government decentralized, as well as flexible and responsive to the heterogeneous population of the United States.

The Constitution reserves to the states all powers that are not granted to the national government and not expressly denied to the states; in addition, states may exercise other powers that are not given exclusively to the national government. These powers, exercised by both the national government and the states, include the power to tax, to regulate commerce, and to make and enforce criminal laws. The distribution of power between the national government and the states is shown in Table 2-1.

Because the national and state governments share certain powers, conflicts may arise between them. The Constitution requires that federal law prevail in such conflicts. Rarely, however, do state laws directly contradict federal law. More frequent—and more troubling—are cases involving the concurrent powers of the national and state governments, such as the powers to tax and regulate commerce. Conflicts between the national and state governments are ultimately decided by the Supreme Court. For instance, when state and federal laws governing highway safety or telecommunications come into conflict, the Court must

TABLE 2-1 ***Distribution of Power between the National Government and the States***

POWERS RESERVED TO THE NATIONAL GOVERNMENT	POWERS RESERVED TO THE STATES	POWERS EXERCISED BY BOTH
Coining money and currency Conducting foreign relations Making treaties Regulating foreign and interstate commerce Providing an army and navy Declaring war Establishing post offices Protecting patents and copyrights Regulating weights and measures Admitting new states Making laws necessary and proper to carrying out specifically delegated powers	Establishing local governments Regulating trade within the state Conducting elections Ratifying amendments to the Constitution Exercising powers not granted to the national government or denied to the states	Taxing Borrowing money Establishing courts Chartering banks Spending for the general welfare

decide whether Congress has preempted state regulation or whether the existence of a variety of different state laws interferes with the need for national and uniform regulations.

Judicial Review

Article III, Section I, of the Constitution states, "The judicial power of the United States shall be vested in one Supreme Court, and in such inferior courts as the Congress may from time to time ordain and establish." Nowhere does the Constitution give the federal courts the power to strike down any congressional or state legislation or any other government action because it violates a provision of the Constitution. Yet the courts have assumed this power of **judicial review**, a power that makes them the final arbitrator of major political conflicts and places them in the role of guardian of the Constitution.[14]

The power of judicial review was a distinctive American contribution to the practice of government and remains so today. For example, there is no such power in Britain, which does not have a written constitution. In other European democracies, only in the last fifty years have special courts been created to decide constitutional questions.

Despite the absence of a specific constitutional provision, the Supreme Court's power to interpret the Constitution is a logical implication of the Constitution. After all, the Constitution is the supreme law of the land, and judges take an oath to uphold it—that was the argument made by Chief Justice

John Marshall in *Marbury v. Madison* (1803). The case of *Marbury v. Madison* grew out of one of the great episodes of early American politics. Shortly after the ratification of the Constitution, two rival political parties emerged with widely different views of the Constitution and government power. The Federalists supported a strong national government in which the federal courts would have the power to interpret the Constitution. Their opponents, the Anti-Federalists and later the Jeffersonian Republicans, favored the states and state courts.

The struggle came to a head with the election of Thomas Jefferson as president in 1800. In that election, the Jeffersonian Republicans defeated the Federalists, who had held office since the creation of the republic. Fearful of what the Jeffersonian Republicans might do once they assumed office in March 1801, President John Adams and the Federalist-dominated Congress created a number of new judgeships in January and appointed Federalists to fill them all. Appointed as chief justice was Adams's secretary of state, John Marshall. Marshall, continuing to work as secretary of state, delivered commissions for the new judgeships in the final days of Adams's term but failed to deliver them all before Adams's term expired.

The Federalists' attempt to "pack" the courts with Federalist judges infuriated the Jeffersonian Republicans, and President Jefferson instructed his secretary of state, James Madison, not to deliver the rest of the commissions. William Marbury, one of the newly appointed judges whose commission was not delivered, decided to sue to force Madison to give it to him. In his suit he sought a *writ of mandamus*, a court order directing a government official (Madison) to perform a certain act (hand over the commission). Marbury argued that Section 13 of the Judiciary Act of 1789 authorized the Supreme Court to issue such writs. He saw this strategy not only as a way of getting his commission but also as a means by which the Court could take a stand against Jeffersonians.

The Supreme Court faced a major dilemma. On the one hand, if it ordered Madison to deliver Marbury's commission, President Jefferson would likely refuse to let Madison comply. The Court would then be revealed as powerless, perhaps permanently. On the other hand, if it refused to issue the writ, it could appear to be confirming the Jeffersonian argument that the courts had no power to intrude on the executive branch.

Chief Justice Marshall handed down the Court's decision on February 24, 1803. Marbury had a right to his commission, Marshall observed. But, he went on to say, the Court had no power to issue the writ of mandamus; the Judiciary Act's authorization of the Court to issue such a writ was unconstitutional because it expanded the Court's original jurisdiction beyond that provided in the Constitution. According to Marshall, Article III of the Constitution granted the Court original jurisdiction *only* in cases involving ambassadors, foreign ministers, and states. William Marbury, however, was none of these. Thus the Court declared Section 13 of the Judiciary Act unconstitutional and simultaneously established the Court's power to declare acts of Congress unconstitutional. Marshall's brilliant opinion not only asserted the power of judicial review, but defused the political controversy surrounding the case. Because the Court's decision went against Marbury on the immediate point at issue, it gave President Jefferson no opportunity to retaliate. The Jeffersonians fervently disagreed with the reasoning behind the decision, but there was little they could do about it.

During the first half of the nineteenth century, the Court struck down a number of state laws, thereby reaffirming the power of the national government over the states. But it was not until 1857, in *Dred Scott v. Sanford,* that the Court declared another act of Congress unconstitutional. In that case, the Court struck down the Missouri Compromise, which had prohibited slavery in the nation's territories. The decision badly damaged the Court's reputation and helped to precipitate the Civil War. However, it confirmed the precedent and practice of judicial review established in *Marbury v. Madison* and reaffirmed the Supreme Court's position as a coequal branch of government having considerable influence on the politics of government and the direction of public policy.

THE LIVING CONSTITUTION

The Constitution is a flexible document. Indeed, the major conflicts of American politics—between the national government and the states, and between majority rule and individual and minority rights—are fueled by conflicting interpretations of the meaning of the Constitution. During the past two hundred years, constitutional change has been in the direction of making the Constitution a more democratic document than it was in 1787 and expanding its protection of the civil liberties and rights of individuals. Change has occurred through applications of the Constitution to the day-to-day operation of government, through formal amendments, and by means of judicial review.

Day-to-Day Operation of Government

The Constitution sets out only a broad framework for the governing process. Within that framework, politics determines the day-to-day workings of government and the outcome of public policies. Through elections and interest group activities, the people influence the direction of government and the formulation of public policies, which in turn influence future elections and interest groups as they compete for influence over what the government does.

As the nation's population has increased from barely 4 million in 1787 to more than 250 million today, government institutions have changed profoundly. The size of Congress, for instance, has expanded from the 22 senators and 54 representatives elected in 1789 to the 100 senators and 435 representatives (assisted by a staff of more than 25,000) serving today. The power vested in the president now resides in a large executive branch with more than 3 million employees. The federal judiciary has likewise grown, from 19 to more than 1,000 judges, plus more than 15,000 supporting personnel—law clerks, magistrates, and secretaries, among others. In addition, new kinds of government agencies, corporations, and regulatory agencies have powers that cut across and combine the authority of Congress, the executive branch, and the judiciary.

Advances in science and technology—in nuclear energy, telecommunications, biomedicine, and other areas—have created new political conflicts and required numerous adjustments in the workings of government. For example, in the age of sailing ships, when the ocean protected the United States against hostile nations, there was ample time for Congress to establish war policy. Now, the existence of nuclear weapons and missiles calls for rapid decision making and action. The result has been a shift of power from Congress to the president in the area of foreign affairs—in effect, a modification of the Constitution.

Social forces, rising expectations, and decreasing resources have resulted in other modifications. For example, interest groups and broad political coalitions forged in the 1960s to promote equal civil rights and liberties succeeded in pressuring the government to enact new laws and to amend the Constitution. As a result, the Constitution became more democratic than it was originally. By the late 1980s and 1990s, however, there was a reaction against the growth of federal bureaucracy and regulation that these changes had produced, and appeals for reducing the size of government became more popular.

Formal Amendment

Although tens of thousands of proposed amendments have been introduced in Congress, the Constitution has been amended only twenty-seven times in two hundred years. These figures give some indication of how difficult the amendment process (spelled out in Article V) was designed to be. Two-thirds of the members of Congress (or a national constitutional convention called for by two-thirds of the states) must pass an amendment, and then three-fourths of the states must ratify it. To date, only Congress has initiated amendments. The idea of a national constitutional convention worries many political observers, who fear that such a gathering might seek to revise the Constitution as much as the Constitutional Convention in 1787 "revised" the Articles of Confederation. Among recent proposals that have failed to win approval were the Equal Rights Amendment, which would have outlawed discrimination on the basis of gender, and a proposal to grant home rule (self-government) and Senate representation to residents of the District of Columbia.

As noted earlier, the first ten amendments—the Bill of Rights—were ratified just four years after the adoption of the Constitution. They were necessary to quell fears about the coercive power of the national government and to secure the rights of individuals. Five later amendments overturned rulings by the Supreme Court—a remarkably small number, given the thousands of decisions handed down by the Court. The Eleventh Amendment (1798) granted the states sovereign immunity from suits by citizens of other states. The Thirteenth (1865) and Fourteenth (1868) Amendments (known as the Civil War Amendments) abolished slavery and made African Americans citizens of the United States. The Sixteenth Amendment (1913) gave Congress the power to enact a federal income tax, and the Twenty-sixth Amendment (1971) extended the right to vote in all federal and state elections to citizens who are age 18 and older.

The majority of the remaining amendments to the Constitution have made government processes more democratic. The Seventeenth Amendment (1913) provided for the popular election of senators. Voting rights were extended to African Americans by the Fifteenth Amendment (1870), to women by the Nineteenth Amendment (1920), to residents of the District of Columbia by the Twenty-Third Amendment (1961), and to indigents (through the ban on poll taxes) by the Twenty-Fourth Amendment (1964). Together with the Supreme Court's rulings promoting the principle of *one person, one vote* (that is, all electoral districts within the same state must be approximately equal in population), these amendments have made the Constitution a more democratic document and the political process more open, accessible, and responsive to the people.

Judicial Review

Through judicial review, the Court gives authoritative meaning to the Constitution in light of new claims and changing conditions. And it does so by bringing new claims, such as a right to privacy, within the language, structure, and spirit of the Constitution.

Through its interpretation of the Constitution, therefore, the Court legitimates and occasionally initiates constitutional change. In the nineteenth century, for example, it expanded the power of Congress to regulate a broad range of social and economic activity. Moreover, it has sanctioned presidents' claims of inherent power in foreign affairs and of *executive privilege*—the power to withhold some White House communications in the interest of national security. In this century, the Court has enforced the Bill of Rights against the states. Previously, it had interpreted those amendments as applying only to the national government.

Given the enormous power wielded by the Court in interpreting and applying the Constitution, *how* it should interpret that document remains highly controversial. The controversy has embroiled both liberals and conservatives at different times. In the late nineteenth and early twentieth centuries, liberals attacked the Court for becoming a "superlegislature" because it overturned progressive economic legislation. On the other hand, in the last few decades conservatives have cried "judicial imperialism" when criticizing the Court's decisions in the areas of civil liberties and civil rights.

Even the justices themselves disagree on how to interpret the Constitution. Some argue for what is known as **strict construction**, that is, interpretation that is confined to a literal reading of the constitutional text, supplemented by historical precedent and whatever can be learned about the historical context of specific provisions. Others urge a **broad reading** of the text, structure, and spirit of the Constitution, an approach that may require judges to formulate a broad principle that is applicable to different cases in light of changing circumstances. The debate over how to interpret the Constitution is almost as old as the document itself and is likely to continue as long as the American system of constitutional politics survives. As Justice Felix Frankfurter wisely observed, "Constitutional law is not at all a science, but applied politics."[15]

Constitutional interpretation evolves with the Court and the country, and constitutional law is best viewed as a constantly evolving dialogue between the Supreme Court and the American people. By deciding particular cases, the Court infuses constitutional meaning into the resolution of the surrounding political controversies that those cases represent. Yet the Court by itself cannot lay political controversies to rest. In *Marbury v. Madison*, for example, Chief Justice Marshall resolved the dispute at hand but by no means laid to rest the larger controversy over judicial review and the Court's power to strike down congressional legislation.

The Court's power turns on the cooperation of other political institutions and, in the end, on the public's acceptance of its rulings. In the words of Chief Justice Edward White, the Court's power to interpret the Constitution "rests solely on the approval of a free people."[16] In sum, the major confrontations that the Court attempts to resolve—such as controversies over school desegregation, school prayer, and abortion—are determined as much by the possibility of developing consensus in a pluralistic society as by what the Court says about the meaning of the Constitution.

CASE STUDY

The Watergate Crisis and Constitutional Politics

On the night of June 17, 1972, five men broke into the headquarters of the Democratic National Committee, housed in the Watergate complex in Washington, D.C. Their purpose was to plant bugging devices so that they could monitor the Democratic party's campaign plans for the fall presidential election. The "plumbers," as they were called, were caught by some off-duty police officers. The next day it was learned that one of them, E. Howard Hunt, a former agent for the Central Intelligence Agency, worked for President Richard M. Nixon's reelection committee. The stage was set for what would become over the next two years one of the most monumental constitutional crises in American history.

Nixon and his associates managed to cover up their involvement in the break-in, and the president easily won reelection in November. But reporters and congressional committees continued to search for links between the break-in and the White House. Judge John Sirica, who presided over the trial of the five burglars, pressed for a full disclosure of White House involvement. These investigations led to further cover-ups.

In the spring of 1973, the Senate Select Committee on Presidential Activities of 1972, chaired by Senator Sam Ervin of North Carolina, began its investigation. The proceedings were carried on national television. Nixon's former counsel, John Dean, became the star witness, revealing much of the president's involvement in the cover-up. Another aide disclosed that Nixon had installed devices to tape conversations in the Oval Office. The possibility that the tapes contained evidence of Nixon's involvement in the cover-up escalated the crisis.

The Senate Select Committee and a special prosecutor appointed to investigate illegal activities of the White House, Archibald Cox, immediately sought a small number of the tapes. Nixon refused to relinquish them, claiming an executive privilege to withhold information that might damage national security interests. The special prosecutor then subpoenaed Nixon's attorneys to turn over the tapes. When Nixon again refused, Judge Sirica ordered the release of the tapes. But Nixon still did not comply. Cox appealed to the United States Court of Appeals for the District of Columbia, which urged that an attempt be made to reach a compromise. When that failed, the court ruled that Nixon had to hand over the tapes.

After the court of appeals ruling, Nixon announced his own compromise. On October 19, 1973, he offered to provide summaries of relevant conversations. When Cox declared the deal unacceptable, Nixon ordered him dismissed, unleashing a wave of public anger. Within four days, Nixon was forced to tell Sirica that nine tapes would be forthcoming.

The public outcry against Nixon did not subside, nor did the release of the nine tapes end the controversy. It was soon discovered that an eighteen-minute segment of the first conversation between Nixon and his chief of staff after the break-in had been erased. That and other revelations prodded the House of Representatives to establish a committee to investigate the possibility of impeachment of the president. Three months later, in February 1974, the House directed its Judiciary Committee to begin hearings on impeachment. Nixon continued to refuse to give additional tapes to the Judiciary Committee and to Leon Jaworski, who had replaced Cox as special prosecutor.

After a federal grand jury investigating Watergate indicted top White House aides and secretly named Nixon as an unindicted coconspirator, the House Judiciary Committee subpoenaed the release of all documents and tapes related to the Watergate break-in. Nixon remained adamant about his right to decide what to release. This confrontation between the special prosecutor and the president set the stage for the case of *United States v. Nixon*.

The Supreme Court heard oral arguments for the case on July 8, 1974. The fundamental issue, the special prosecutor contended, was "Who is to be the arbiter of what the Constitution says?" Nixon's claim of executive privilege in withholding the tapes, the prosecutor insisted, was an attempt to place the president above the law. In contrast, Nixon's attorney, James St. Clair, asserted that the case should be dismissed because there was a "fusion" between the criminal prosecution of Nixon's aides and the impeachment proceedings against the president. He argued that this fusion violated the principle of separation of powers and that the president should decide what would be made available to the House Judiciary Committee. The dispute, he insisted, was essentially a political one, one that the Supreme Court should avoid.

The Court disagreed. Just sixteen days after hearing oral arguments, it unanimously rejected Nixon's claim of an absolute and unreviewable executive privilege. Writing for the Court, Chief Justice Warren E. Burger, whom Nixon had appointed just a few years earlier, ruled that the president's claim of executive privilege was inconsistent with "the fundamental demands of due process of law in the fair administration of justice."

The new tapes that the ruling forced the president to release contained even stronger evidence of his guilt, and within a week the House Judiciary Committee had voted three articles of impeachment against him. On August 9, facing almost certain impeachment by the full House and conviction by the Senate, Nixon became the first president to resign his office.

Discussion Questions

1. What was the major political issue in *United States v. Nixon?*
2. Who were the principal protagonists, and what did they want?
3. How was the issue resolved?
4. Who won, who lost, and what impact has this case had on American politics?

SUMMARY

The Constitution is a political document. In laying out a blueprint for government, it provides a basis for political struggles. Based on the ideas of popular sovereignty and limited government as the means for securing individuals' unalienable rights, the Constitution provides for a separation of powers among the three branches of the national government, for a federal system dividing power between the national government and the states, and for judicial review. These divisions of power give rise to ongoing conflicts that animate the politics of American government.

The First Continental Congress met in 1774 to pass resolutions denouncing the English Parliament and Crown. In 1776, the Second Continental Congress drafted a resolution—the Declaration of Independence—that proclaimed the American colonies to be free and independent states. In 1777, it approved the *Articles of Confederation*, the nation's first constitution. Under the Articles, Congress lacked the power to regulate commerce, collect taxes, or enforce its legislation.

In 1787, delegates from the states met in Philadelphia to revise the Articles of Confederation but quickly decided to establish a national government with legislative, executive, and judiciary branches. The new government would be a *republic*; it would have the power to make and enforce laws but would derive its authority from the citizens through popular elections.

The Constitutional Convention recommended that the new constitution be sent to the states for ratification by special conventions. The Constitution would be ratified if nine of the thirteen states gave their approval. In some states—especially New York, Virginia, and Massachusetts—the Constitution met with opposition from those who were concerned that it gave the national government too much power. Their approval was finally obtained when it was agreed that the First Congress would adopt a group of amendments that guaranteed the civil rights and liberties of individuals. These first ten amendments constitute the *Bill of Rights*.

Central to the Constitution is the idea of *popular sovereignty*, which holds that government is based on the consent of the people and is accountable to the people for its actions. From this notion follows the idea of *limited government*, the restriction of government authority to *express powers*, which are powers specified and delegated to the national government by the Constitution. The national government also has certain *implied powers*, which can be inferred from its express powers, as well as *inherent powers* in the area of foreign affairs.

One of the main reasons for limiting the powers of government is to safeguard the *unalienable rights* of individuals. These natural rights were ensured not only through the passage of the Bill of Rights but also through the distribution of power among the three branches of the national government. The *separation of powers* creates a delicate structure in which the three branches check and balance each other in various ways. In reality, the powers of the government are not truly separate but are shared. The Constitution also distributes power between the national and state governments, in a system known as *federalism*.

Although the Constitution does not give the judiciary the power of *judicial review*—the power to strike down any legislation or other government action that violates constitutional provisions—the federal courts have assumed this power because the Constitution is the supreme law of the land and judges take an oath to uphold it.

During the last two hundred years, constitutional change has occurred in three ways: through applications of the Constitution to the day-to-day operation of government, through formal amendments, and through judicial review. Changes in government institutions, scientific and technological advances, and social forces have brought about modifications of the constitutional structure of government. In addition, the Constitution has been amended twenty-seven times, and the Supreme Court has occasionally initiated change through its interpretation of the Constitution.

KEY TERMS

Articles of Confederation
republic
Virginia Plan
New Jersey Plan
Great Compromise
three-fifths compromise
Bill of Rights
popular sovereignty
limited government
express powers
implied powers
inherent powers
unalienable rights
separation of powers
federalism
judicial review
strict construction
broad reading

RESOURCES

READINGS

Farrand, Max. *The Framing of the Constitution.* New Haven, Conn.: Yale University Press, 1913 (paperback ed., 1962). A classic introduction to the creation of the Constitution by the editor of the definitive collection of papers and proceedings of the Constitutional Convention.

Kammen, Michael. *A Machine That Would Go of Itself: The Constitution in American Culture.* New York: St. Martin's Press, 1994. Shows how the Constitution has survived amid the myriad changes that have taken place in the country over the past two hundred years.

Wood, Gordon S. *The Creation of the American Republic, 1776–1787.* New York: Norton, 1993. A widely acclaimed and pathbreaking study of the intellectual trends and political conflicts that led to the creation of the Constitution.

PRIMARY SOURCES

Farrand, Max, ed. *The Records of the Federal Convention of 1787.* 4 vols. New Haven, Conn.: Yale University Press, 1913 (paperback ed., 1986). The definitive collection of the debates at the Constitutional Convention. In 1987, a fifth volume based on additional documents was added to the set.

Hamilton, Alexander, John Jay, and James Madison. *The Federalist Papers.* This collection of eighty-five essays, written to help win support of the Constitution by the New York ratifying convention, contains some of the most illuminating arguments about the nature of the Constitution. It has gone through many editions and many editors; the edition by Clinton Rossiter contains a fine introduction (New American Library, 1961).

Kurland, Philip, and Ralph Lerner. *The Founders' Constitution.* 5 vols. Chicago: University of Chicago Press, 1987. An easy-to-use guide to what the framers said about each part of the Constitution. It contains most of their statements, arranged according to each provision in the Constitution.

3

Federalism in Theory and Practice

PREVIEW

- Federalism as a political issue
- The changing nature of American federalism
- Federal–state–local relations: national regulation of states and localities; grants-in-aid, conditions, politics, distribution criteria, and regional controversies; state and local influence on national policy making
- Federalism in action: the minimum age for alcohol consumption; control and management of water resources

On March 10, 1992, Alfonso Lopez Jr., a senior at Edison High School in San Antonio, Texas, was caught carrying a .38 caliber handgun, along with five bullets, to school. He was arrested and charged under Texas law with possession of a firearm. The following day, the state charges were dismissed after federal law enforcement agents charged Lopez with violating the 1990 Gun-Free School Zones Act, a federal law banning possession of guns in or near schools. Lopez was convicted in United States district court and sentenced to six months in prison.

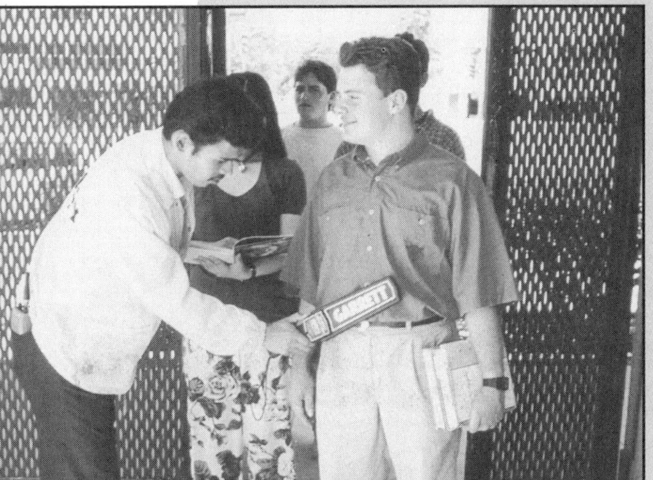

Lopez and his attorney appealed, claiming the federal law to be "unconstitutional as it is beyond the power of Congress to legislate control over our public schools" [131 L Ed 2d, 632, 1995]. In a stunning 5-to-4 decision announced in April 1995, the United States Supreme Court agreed, striking down the Gun-Free School Zones Act.

The decision in *United States v. Lopez,* which directly pitted the constitutional authority of the states against that of the national government, was remarkable because it was the first time in sixty years that the Court had *limited* the reach of national authority under the clause of the Constitution that gives Congress the power to regulate interstate commerce. In its defense, the federal government argued that gun violence represents a drain on national commerce because guns affect learning and learning affects the nation's economic strength. But in this case the Court ruled that Congress had gone too far and that the possession of guns at or near schools was not sufficiently related to interstate commerce to justify federal involvement.

Control of guns in and around public schools, the Court reasoned, was an area legitimate for *state*, but not federal, regulation. Writing for the majority of the Court, Chief Justice William H. Rehnquist stated, "If we were to accept the [federal] Government's arguments, we are hard pressed to posit any activity by an individual that Congress is without power to regulate." In dissent, Justice John Paul Stevens stated, "The welfare of our future . . . is vitally dependent on the character of the education of our children. [Therefore] Congress has ample power to prohibit the possession of firearms in or near schools."

The *United States v. Lopez* case illustrates some fundamental principles of politics and decision making in the American federal system. In nonfederal countries such as Great Britain, political debate ordinarily is limited to whether government *should* get involved in some activity. In the United States, the debate is about not only *whether* government should be involved but *which level* of government should be responsible for a particular activity.

FEDERALISM AS A POLITICAL ISSUE

Throughout the nation's history, the debate over what the Founding Fathers actually intended when they created a federal form of government has been fueled by the ambiguous language of the Constitution. They provided no clear definition of the precise relationships between the various levels of government. But the debate continues for other reasons as well. For one thing, national legislators are elected from local districts and are responsible to local constituents. In addition, many Americans view government activities at the state and local levels more favorably than those at the national level. For those reasons, even more than a constitutional vagueness, federalism is likely to remain an intensely political issue.

Debates over the "true" meaning of federalism have been at the heart of some of the most important political battles in United States history, including those over slavery, the regulation of business and industry, the civil rights movement, and environmental protection. The legalistic and scholarly terms in which debates over the proper roles of different levels of government are couched often disguise other, more political concerns. When interest groups, political parties, and individuals advocate more or less control by Washington or by the states, they frequently do so to achieve specific policy goals. People who believe that state and local governments are likely to support their views on an issue—be it welfare, gun control, abortion, or prayer in public schools—will argue that the Constitution "clearly" reserves authority for such decisions to the states and communities. People who believe the national government is likely to be supportive of their views will make the opposite argument. The Constitution, they say, "obviously" delegates responsibility in these areas to the national government.

In this chapter, we examine the political aspects of federalism. We trace the evolution of the American federal experience and look at power and influence in the federal system, focusing especially on the ways in which the national government and the states and localities attempt to regulate and influence each other's behavior.

THE CHANGING NATURE OF AMERICAN FEDERALISM

Since the nation's founding, advocates for the national, state, and local governments have sparred over the meaning of federalism and over the proper division of power and responsibility in the American political system. In the 1860s, these debates erupted in the Civil War. In the 1950s and 1960s, the civil rights movement raised the question of whether states had the right to maintain a system of racial segregation in defiance of the federal government. In the 1990s, welfare, health care, abortion, and the environment continue to raise questions about the balance of national, state, and local responsibility.

Not surprisingly, the founders did not foresee all the issues of federalism that would confront subsequent generations. As such, the concept of federalism has been evolving since 1787, and it will go on evolving as the nation faces new issues and continues to debate how best to deal with old ones. In short, federalism is, as some people say, "unfinished business."

National Supremacy versus States' Rights, 1787–1865

During the period from the ratification of the Constitution to the end of the Civil War, the constitutional debate continued over the proper role of governments in the American system. Those seeking more power and responsibility for the national government vied for power with those seeking to protect and enhance the rights of the individual states.

Those who maintained a *nation-centered* view—the Federalists—believed that the Constitution emanated from and was applicable to the American people as a whole, that it was not simply a pact among the states. From the Federalist perspective, the national government had a legitimate interest in protecting and promoting the health, safety, and welfare of the people themselves; its interests and obligations did not end with its dealings with state governments. As Chief Justice John Marshall stated in 1819 in the case of *McCollough v. Maryland,* the national government "is the government of all; its powers are delegated by all, it represents all, and acts for all."[1]

In contrast, those who held a *state-centered* view—the Anti-Federalists—believed that the Constitution was a compact among the states and that the states themselves were the legitimate center of power and authority in the federal system. This position was eloquently advanced in 1798 in the Virginia and Kentucky Resolutions, drawn up by James Madison and Thomas Jefferson, which implied that the national government did not have *all* government power, that its powers were limited by the language of the Constitution, that some rights were reserved for the states, and the states could protect their rights.[2]

This position was taken to its extreme in the 1820s and 1830s by many advocates of states' rights, especially by Senator John C. Calhoun of South Carolina, whose **doctrine of nullification** argued that *sovereignty*—ultimate government power—could not be divided among levels of government but instead resided with the states. The Constitution, Calhoun thought, was an agreement made by sovereign states that had established a central government to perform certain tasks for them. Viewing the central government as an agent of the states, he argued that whenever a state found an act of Congress to be in violation of the Constitution, that state could declare the congressional act null and void within its own borders.

By the 1840s, slavery had become the dominant issue dividing advocates of the nation-centered and the state-centered notions of federalism. As always, both groups pointed to the Constitution for support. Opponents of slavery cited the due process clause of the Fifth Amendment, which states that "No person . . . shall be . . . deprived of life, liberty, or property, without due process of law." They further argued that since Congress had full sovereignty over the territories by virtue of its treaty and war powers, Congress could limit or abolish slavery in the territories as it wished.

Federalism North and South of the Border

Among the countries that have opted for a federal form of government are our closest neighbors to the north and south, Canada and Mexico. Although all federal governments share some characteristics, there are many dissimilarities as well. The governments of Canada and Mexico illustrate this diversity.

The Canadian federal union was created in 1867 and today consists of ten provinces and two territories. Working just after the American Civil War and reflecting on what they saw as defects in the American Constitution that had helped to bring about the conflict, the framers of the Canadian government wanted to make sure that supreme power would not reside at the provincial level. By its act of creation, the Canadian parliament was given explicit control over defense, trade, transportation, and foreign affairs. If only constitutional provisions are considered, Canada appears to be a more centralized federal system than the United States. But because of the country's vast extent, its strong support of local cultural and linguistic heritages (including the legal right of French Canadians to retain their language), and the tendency of the provinces to have developed around a few key metropolitan centers, provincial governments actually exercise considerable power and authority. In fact, the degree of influence exercised by the Canadian provincial governments exceeds that of state and provincial governments in many other federal nations.

Furthermore, the Canadian combination of federalism with a parliamentary form of government has meant that cabinets and cabinet officials, as well as civil service professionals, play a significant role in both levels of government. This characteristic has led some to apply the term *executive federalism* to the Canadian system.

The Mexican constitutional convention of 1917 created a federal system of government that today consists of thirty-one states and the federal district of Mexico City. From the outset, the Mexican system was designed to produce a strong central government, and the persistent strength of the ruling party, Partido Revolutionario Institucional (PRI), has contributed to Mexico's centralizing tendencies. Mexico's president operates with relatively few restraints. Not only are both houses of the federal legislature typically dominated by representatives of the PRI, but those elected to public office at all levels are usually appointed as candidates by higher-ups in the party apparatus.

The Mexican system is sometimes labeled one of "political centralism," meaning that each level of government exercises more political authority than the one below it. The federal government controls most public revenues, so that state and local governments depend heavily on it for resources. While creating inequalities in the distribution of public investments and access to services, the resulting system of centralized control has contributed to Mexico's long-term political stability.

SOURCES: Wayne A. Cornelius and Ann L. Craig, *Politics in Mexico: An Introduction and Overview* (Glenview, Ill: Scott, Foresman, 1988); R. MacGregor Dawson and W. F. Dawson, *Democratic Government in Canada,* 4th ed. (Toronto: University of Toronto Press, 1989); and Ronald L. Watts, "Canadian Federalism in the 1990s," *Publius: The Journal of Federalism* (Summer 1991), 169–190.

Proponents of slavery argued that since the national government was merely an agent of the states, it could not administer the territories against the interest of any of the states. Therefore, they said, slaveholders had a constitutional right to bring slaves into any territory without legal hindrance. They also relied on the Fifth Amendment, arguing that since slaves were property, legislation abolishing slavery would be a destruction of property without compensation and therefore a violation of the amendment's due process protections.

Redefining State and National Roles, 1865–1933

The Civil War permanently altered federal–state relations. Nullification theory was discredited by the outcome of the strife, and the Union was preserved.

Between 1865 and 1933, a new relationship known as **dual federalism** emerged, which recognized separate and distinct spheres of authority for the national and state governments. The staunchest advocates of dual federalism viewed the distribution of power between the levels of government as fixed and unchangeable. The states were judged to be on an equal plane with the national government, and the Tenth Amendment was cited as the Constitutional evidence of an area of authority reserved for the states.[3]

During this period, the United States was rapidly industrializing, and the public began looking to government at all levels for greater social and economic regulation. However, because state attempts to curb business excesses and monopolies proved largely ineffective, it fell to Congress to regulate economic practices and the social effects of big railroads and other industrial giants. Much of the debate over proper federal–state relations centered on the interpretation of the interstate commerce clause of the Constitution (Article I, Section 8) and on the proper role of Congress in regulating the nation's commerce.

Attempting to distinguish between *inter*state commerce, which Congress could regulate, and *intra*state commerce which was under the authority of the states, the Supreme Court invalidated a number of regulatory actions by Congress on the grounds that they usurped state authority. In 1895, for example, the Court significantly weakened the effects of the Sherman Anti-Trust Act of 1890 (a federal act attempting to prevent monopolies) by declaring that monopolistic manufacturing activities were not within the scope of national regulatory influence because manufacturing activities were not within the scope of national regulatory influence because manufacturing is not commerce.[4] During the 1890s, the Court also severely curtailed the powers of the Interstate Commerce Commission, which had been created in 1887 to regulate commerce, particularly the railroads.

Expansion of the Federal Government, 1933–1968

The Court's affirmation of dual federalism lasted until the 1930s. At that time the Great Depression ushered in **cooperative federalism**, which stressed a partnership and a sharing of functions, responsibilities, and programs between the states and the national government. Since the late 1930s, the courts have generally interpreted the Constitution so as to extend the national government's control and regulation of business and commerce. Actions by Congress and the courts greatly enlarged the role of the national government in such areas as education, housing, transportation, civil rights, environmental protection, and social services.

The period from 1933 to 1968 was marked by the increased use of **grants-in-aid**, that is, programs through which the national government shares its

During the War on Poverty of the 1960s federal grants to states and localities for social welfare programs rose dramatically. The Head Start program still provides food, medical care, and early education to prepare disadvantaged children for school.

fiscal resources with state and local governments. By 1930, fifteen grant programs were allocating about $120 million to the states annually. Between 1930 and 1960, the number of grants-in-aid programs increased dramatically. During the period sometimes called the "First New Deal"—about 1933 to 1935—new grant programs were enacted for the distribution of surplus farm products to the needy and for free school lunches, emergency highway expenditures, emergency relief work, general relief, administration of unemployment insurance, and assistance in meeting local government costs. During the "Second New Deal"—about 1935 to 1939—additional grant programs were created for child welfare, mothers' and children's health, services for crippled children, old-age assistance, aid to dependent children, aid to the blind, and general health services.

By 1960, some 132 grant programs existed, allocating almost $7 billion annually. Most of the grants made available during this period went to state governments; a few went directly to cities. Because most of the grants were for specific purposes or programs defined by Congress, the regulatory role of the national government (in the form of rules that had to be followed and conditions that had to be met in order for grants to be awarded) increased significantly. So did national reliance on the grants-in-aid system for achieving a range of objectives, especially in social welfare, housing, and transportation.[5]

During the 1960s, the number of federal grants available to state and local governments exploded. In 1965 and 1966 alone, Congress enacted 130 new grant programs. By 1968, almost $19 billion was allocated through the grant programs, many of which provided money directly to cities, bypassing the state governments.

From Grants-in-Aid to Mandates and Regulations, 1968–1994

When the Republicans gained control of the White House in 1968, a new chapter in the history of federalism was written. Calling his approach the **new federalism**, President Richard M. Nixon deemphasized the use of grants for specific purposes and focused instead on large grants to local governments in general policy areas. In theory, such grants, known as block grants, gave the recipient governments greater discretion in the expenditure of funds, and they also removed from the national government a degree of control over how the funds were spent.

Following his election in 1980, President Reagan announced a program known as New Federalism, but his approach differed from Nixon's. The Reagan administration deemphasized grants-in-aid as a tool for national policy making. But a higher proportion of grants went to state governments than to local governments, and states had greater authority over the funds. This policy continued during the Bush administration, contributing to what some observers believed to be a revitalization of state governments. However, it also left local governments with considerably less revenue to deal with the myriad problems facing America's cities. Bill Clinton, during his presidency, proposed a few modest assistance programs for distressed cities and neighborhoods, but his focus on deficit reduction precluded any major new spending on grants-in-aid.

Throughout this period, whether grants were expanding or shrinking, the federal government—through various mechanisms discussed later in this chapter—greatly increased its *monitoring and regulation* of state and local activities. From 1970 to 1990, for example, it issued more than two hundred "preemptive statutes" that displaced or replaced state and local laws. This was twice as many such statutes as had been passed in the *entire history* of the United States until then.

Throughout this period, too, the Supreme Court adopted an increasingly nationalistic perspective on issues of federalism. In an important case in 1976, *National League of Cities v. Usery*, the Court held that some areas of state activity—in this instance, the setting of minimum wages for municipal employees—are exempt from national-level encroachment. The Tenth Amendment, the Court had ruled, provides absolute protection for at least some areas of state (and municipal) government functions.

Soon, however, the Court began issuing decisions that served to erode severely the principle of state sovereignty established in the case.[6] In *Garcia v. San Antonio Metropolitan Transit Authority* (1985), the Court ruled that local governments must adhere to minimum-wage standards set by Congress.[7] In this 5-to-4 decision, the Court ruled that except in rare situations the Constitution *does not* limit the national government's power to interfere in state affairs.[8]

To some, these and other related court decisions seemed virtually to have eliminated any vestige of protected state or local sovereignty. As Justice Sandra Day O'Connor lamented in her dissenting opinion in the *Garcia* case, "The States as States retain no status apart from that which Congress chooses to let them retain." Together, the cases seemed to imply that officials of the national government would be the sole judges of the limits of national power and that, in fact, there would be almost no arena of state activity beyond the regulatory authority of the national government.

Devolution Federalism, 1994–?

Many believe that the stunning Republican party victories in the 1994 elections—in which Republicans won control of both houses of Congress as well as thirty governorships—ushered in a new era of intergovernmental relations. Called by some **devolution federalism**, this era would be marked by a return to state and local governments of many responsibilities that in recent decades had been assumed by the federal government.

The 1995 *Lopez* decision, in which the Supreme Court curtailed expansion of national power in regulating firearm possession, has already been discussed. Another significant court case was decided in 1997. In that case (*Printz v. United States*) the Court further restricted national powers by ruling that Congress has required states to help administer federal programs. Here, the Court struck down a provision of a 1993 gun-control bill in which Congress had required local law enforcement officials to perform background checks on prospective handgun buyers.

But the center of action for the new emphasis on devolution has been the U.S. Congress. Republicans in 1994 ran on a platform they called the Contract with America, much of which dealt with federal–state relations. Among other provisions, the contract promised a reduction of unfunded mandates—federal requirements imposed on state and local governments without any federal funding to cover the costs of implementation. The contract also promised reductions in grants-in-aid and a greater emphasis on block grants.

After winning majorities in the House and Senate, Republicans were quick to introduce many of their ideas into proposed legislation. Among the first significant pieces of legislation passed by the new Congress—in March 1995—was one limiting congressional use of unfunded mandates; it requires Congress to study the costs of a mandate before imposing it and to find ways to pay those costs—or to vote specifically to waive the funding requirement in that case. A few months later, Congress repealed the national 55-mile-an-hour speed limit it had established twenty-one years earlier, saying states should be permitted to decide speed limits.

By far the strongest indication of the shift to devolution federalism, however, was congressional action in 1996 that converted the Aid to Families with Dependent Children program, a central component of the nation's welfare policy, to block grants—an action that virtually ceded control of national welfare policy to the states. Although similar proposals to convert the Medicaid program, along with various employment and job-training programs, to block grants were not enacted, the abolition of AFDC alone represented a significant change of direction in federal responsibilities.

Proponents of greater state and local responsibility argue that governments closest to the people will be able to make better decisions for their citizens. Opponents fear, however, that these governments will not be able to adequately carry out this responsibility. It is too early to tell which of these forecasts will be correct. It is too early to tell even if these recent developments really do mark a fundamental shift in American federal–state relations or if they are only temporary aberrations in long-term trends. But they certainly do show that the principle of federalism, created more than two hundred years ago by the founders of the Constitution, remains a central feature of American politics today. Federalism continues to adapt in response to changing situations and public attitudes.

FEDERAL–STATE–LOCAL RELATIONS: POWER AND POLITICS

The federal system of the United States poses particular challenges for the national government, as it attempts to influence and regulate local governments, and for local governments, as they in turn attempt to affect activities at the national level. The national government, in its attempts to regulate states and localities, may issue direct orders and may preempt state and local activities. Further, through grants-in-aid and the *conditions* attached to these grants, the national government may encourage certain state and local activities and discourage others.

National Regulation of States and Localities

Direct orders Occasionally, the national government issues direct orders that local governments must comply with or else face civil or criminal penalties. For example, the Americans with Disabilities Act of 1990 requires local governments to see to it that all fixed-rate public transportation systems be made accessible to the disabled, that all new buses and transit facilities be equipped with wheelchair lifts, and that transit services be provided to people who cannot use public transit facilities. In 1991, the Environmental Protection Agency issued a ruling requiring all municipal landfills to meet certain conditions designed to prevent contamination of soil and underground water supplies—at a cost to local governments of about $330 million per year—thereby establishing the first comprehensive federal standards for city dumps.

Preemption Early in the nation's history, Congress assumed the authority to *preempt*, or remove from state activity, policy areas having broad national implications. In 1984, for example, Congress preempted the power of local governments to regulate cable television rates. In such situations, national-level authority expands to occupy a field previously administered by state and local governments.

A process known as **partial preemption** occurs when the national government establishes minimum standards in certain areas and authorizes state and local governments to exercise primary responsibility for the function *as long as* they maintain standards at least as high as those set by the national government. States may impose stricter standards, but if a state or locality fails to enforce the base-level standard set by Congress, the national government assumes responsibility for doing so. Partial preemption occurred, for example, when Congress passed the Water Quality Act of 1965. The law gave states one year in which to set acceptable standards of quality for interstate waters within their boundaries. After that year passed, the secretary of health, education, and welfare (and, more recently, the head of the Environmental Protection Agency) was authorized to enforce federal standards in any state that failed to do so.

Since the ratification of the Constitution, more than 350 preemption statutes have been passed by Congress. However, only a handful were passed prior to 1900, and more than half have been adopted in the past two decades. This concentration reflects the growing complexity of contemporary policy issues and the real need for uniform national standards in many areas. But the increased use of preemptive legislation reflects political considerations as well. In the 1960s, liberals relied on preemptive legislation as a key weapon in implementing policies in the areas of civil rights, fair housing, age discrimination, and voting rights.

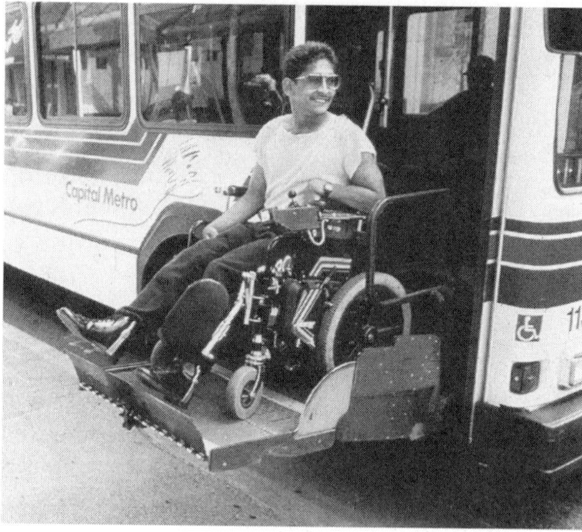

For state and local governments, federal policies rarely provide a free ride (in any sense of the term). The threat of losing federal highway funds pushed states to adopt mandatory motorcycle helmet laws by 1994, but the following year the new Republican Congress repealed the requirement. Under the Americans with Disabilities Act of 1990, localities must spend millions of dollars to buy and maintain buses with wheelchair lifts.

In the 1980s and early 1990s, on the other hand, business and industry groups (especially in banking, communications, and transportation) repeatedly sought federal preemption as protection from more aggressive state regulations. For example, the Bus Regulatory Reform Act, signed by President Reagan in 1982, nullified the authority of states to engage in economic regulation of the busing industry. Today, virtually all authority to engage in economic regulation of airline, bus, and trucking activities has been removed from the states.

Grants-in-aid The use of grants-in-aid is an even more common, and in many instances more effective, way for the national government to see that its objectives are carried out at the state and local levels. Today, more than $225 billion is allocated annually through grants-in-aid, which have enabled the national government to motivate state and local governments to pursue objectives that otherwise might have been politically difficult or impossible. Grants-in-aid have been used to fund projects in mass transportation, urban renewal, housing, drug rehabilitation, crime reduction, health care, low-income home energy assistance, pollution control, nuclear-waste disposal, solid-waste disposal, highway beautification, and aid to homeless youth, as well as in many other areas.

Conditions of Aid

The many conditions that recipients must satisfy to receive federal grants can influence state and local policies. These conditions are of two types: crosscutting requirements and crossover sanctions.

Crosscutting requirements, which are attached to almost all federal grants, pertain to nondiscrimination, environmental protection, planning and coordination, labor standards, and public access to government information and decision making. As an example, the 1964 Civil Rights Act guarantees nondiscrimination in all federally assisted programs. Today, there are approximately sixty such requirements.

Crossover sanctions impose national sanctions or penalties in one area to influence state or local policy in another area. The Intermodal Surface Transportation Act of 1991, for example, contained over a dozen crossover sanctions, including one requiring states to adopt mandatory motorcycle helmet and seat belt laws by 1994. (The motorcycle helmet provisions of this act were repealed in 1995.) States that failed to adopt these laws had to spend up to 3 percent of the federal funds they received for highway projects on highway safety activities. In 1996, when Congress renewed the Ryan White Act—a measure funneling millions of dollars to state and local governments to help with the care of people with AIDS—it included a provision to cut off funds to states that do not wish to establish mandatory procedures to test newborns for the virus that causes the disease. In 1997, the House passed a bill offering $1.5 billion to states to fight juvenile crime on condition that states change their laws to require that young people accused of violent crimes be tried as adults in state courts.

Such requirements almost always reflect worthy objectives. Nevertheless, local officials frequently claim that the requirements fail to take local conditions into account, are unnecessary and duplicative, and are too costly. By the mid 1990s, it was estimated that the cost of compliance with federal mandates amounted to more than $6 billion annually for cities and almost $5 billion annually for counties.[9]

Figure 3-1 shows the growth of the major forms of federal regulation of state and local governments between 1931 and 1990.

Grants-in-Aid: A Typology

There are two types of grants: categorical grants and block grants. **Categorical grants** are made for specific purposes defined by Congress, such as library construction, child welfare, adoption assistance, and bridge and road construction. Categorical grants can be used only for the purposes stated in the legislation that creates and funds the program, and state and local decision makers thus have little discretion in how the grant money is spent. As of 1995, there were 618 categorical grants, the largest number of categorical grant programs in history.

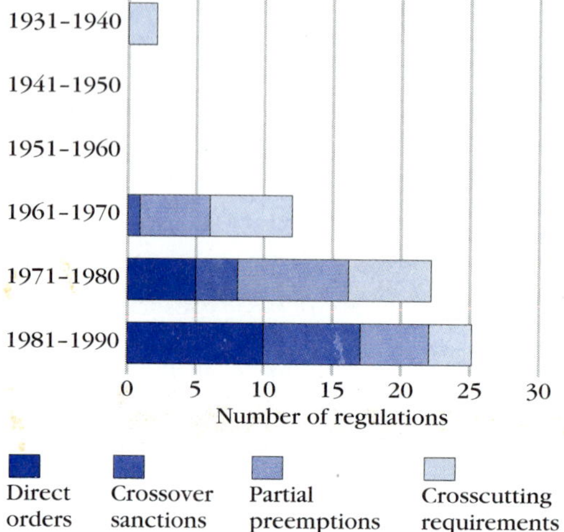

FIGURE 3-1

Major Forms of National Regulation of State and Local Governments, 1931–1990

SOURCE: Adapted from Timothy J. Conlan, "And the Beat Goes On: Intergovernmental Mandates and Preemption in an Era of Deregulation," *Publius: The Journal of Federalism* 21 (Summer 1991): 51. Reprinted by permission.

Block grants allow appropriated funds to be used in broad policy areas such as job training, health, and public housing. Congress establishes the areas in which the funds are to be used, and state and local officials determine how the money is actually spent. Today, there are sixteen block grants in the areas of education, health and human services, housing, criminal justice, job training, and transportation. President Clinton in his 1996 budget proposal called for combining 271 categorical grant programs into a few block grants. However, the only additional block grant approved in 1996 was the one that replaced the AFDC program.

In general, block grants are popular among conservatives and advocates of states' rights, in part because they believe most local electorates and local officials will not want to use them for liberal social programs, especially those designed to sharply redistribute resources from upper- to lower-income populations. Block grants also tend to be popular among state and local officials because they allow them greater discretion in spending the funds.

Categorical grants are more appealing to liberals, particularly those who believe the national government should be actively involved in addressing highly pressing social and urban problems. Congress, too, generally prefers categorical grants because they allow greater congressional influence in determining and monitoring how the money is spent.

Distribution Criteria

Grants may be categorized as formula grants or as project grants, depending on the criteria used for distribution of the money. **Formula grants** follow a formula that is applied proportionally to all eligible recipients. For example, a grant program to aid education might allocate money to all school districts, with the amount for each district determined by the number of pupils in the district whose families' incomes are below a certain level. By simply calculating the number of pupils who will fall into this category, all school districts across the country will immediately know how much they are entitled to receive.

The political controversies surrounding formula grants concern the elements to be included in the formula and the weighting of those elements. For example, a bitter fight broke out in 1988 when Congress considered changing the formula for distributing money through the Alcohol, Drug Abuse, and Mental Health (ADAMH) block grant. The original formula included a factor that benefited states receiving funds under the older categorical grants that had been eliminated when the ADAMH block grant was approved. Critics argued that this element of the formula gave too much of the ADAMH money to northern states and too little to the southern and western states.

Project grants are ones for which potential recipients must apply directly to the agency responsible for administering the grant. That agency reviews the proposals and determines which ones are to be funded and at what level. Because there is not enough money to fund every potential project, competition for the funds may be keen.

Federal agencies and departments maintain greater control and authority over project grants than over formula grants. Project grants, which proliferated in the 1960s, have been used for policy areas that might not receive sufficient attention from state and local decision makers in the absence of national funding—areas such as education for disabled youth, programs for the aging, AIDS research, drug rehabilitation, and bilingual education. Like formula grants, however, project grants are often a focus of much political controversy. Those whose applications are not approved may attribute their failure to obtain funds to federal bureaucrats who make poor decisions or are out of touch with local problems. They argue that project grants place too much control at the national level, ignore the specialized needs of local areas, and give an advantage to jurisdictions that are large and wealthy enough to hire staffs with the skills required for drafting federal grant proposals.

The Regional Controversy over Grant Distribution

As the controversy over the ADAMH formula suggests, conflicts sometimes arise over the regional distribution of grants-in-aid funds. Some states and regions receive considerably higher per-person allocations than do others. Table 3-1 shows the per-person distribution of federal grants-in-aid to the top and bottom five states as of 1994.

State and local officials in the Frostbelt (the Midwest and Northeast) often express the opinion that their social and economic problems, such as decaying cities and aging industrial infrastructures, justify higher proportions of federal grant assistance. On the other side, officials in the Sunbelt (the South and Southwest) argue that rapid population growth in their sections of the country brings unique problems calling for increased federal aid. The dispute has led to clashes between coalitions of legislators, mayors, and governors over distribution formulas, a rivalry that has been described as a "regional war."[10]

In 1995, for example, when Congress was debating welfare reform, representatives from the Frostbelt states generally wanted each state's share of the proposed welfare block grant to be based on what it had previously received from the federal government in categorical grants for welfare programs. Representatives from the Sunbelt states, though, argued that funding should favor those regions with high population growth rates.

Competition for federal funds has been growing as the proportion of dollars

TABLE 3-1 Per-Person Federal Aid Received by Selected States in Fiscal Year 1994

TOP FIVE RECIPIENTS	PER-PERSON GRANTS TO STATE AND LOCAL GOVERNMENTS
Wyoming	$1,456
Alaska	1,444
New York	1,058
Rhode Island	1,012
North Dakota	953
BOTTOM FIVE RECIPIENTS	**PER-PERSON GRANTS TO STATE AND LOCAL GOVERNMENTS**
Virginia	462
Florida	471
Texas	530
Nevada	535
Kansas	564

SOURCE: *Advisory Commission on Intergovernmental Relations,* Significant Features of Fiscal Federalism, 1994 Edition. vol. 2 (Washington, D.C.: ACIR, 1994), 186.

distributed by the federal government through grants-in-aid programs has been declining. So regional clashes over federal aid are likely to continue and to increase in intensity.

State and Local Influences on National Policy Making

Officials of state and local governments, and local constituencies in general, use certain tools of their own in an attempt to influence national policy making, including the allocation and distribution of grants. All national legislators are elected from states or local districts and ultimately are responsible to voters at the local level. Thus members of Congress are sure to give some attention to the concerns of their constituents. Furthermore, state and local governments can go to court to challenge the actions of the national government and thus may, at least temporarily, halt or delay national initiatives. Sometimes just the threat of court action will influence an agency or department to modify policy. Two additional tools that local officials may use to influence national policies are grantsmanship and the intergovernmental lobby.

Grantsmanship The efforts of local officials to maximize the amount of federal grants they receive and to have grant rules interpreted so as to achieve the best funding distribution for their areas are termed **grantsmanship**. Cities and states that are most capable of exploiting the various options and opportunities provided by the grant program are able to garner far more than their "fair" share of federal grants.

Grantsmanship is frequently criticized by those who believe that federal grants should go to local areas because of demonstrated problems or needs, not because of officials' skills in obtaining grants. Moreover, officials at the national level seek to prevent what they consider the "manipulation" of grant programs.

WHERE ON THE WEB?

STATE GOVERNMENTS

Are you interested in finding information about a particular department or agency of your state government, or in identifying the departments and agencies involved with a specific policy issue? Are you looking for a job with a particular state government? Do you need a list of the hundreds of documents and manuals published by state governments, sorted by subject area—a perfect resource for a research paper?

In the past few years, the amount of information available online about state governments has mushroomed. Virtually every state has at least one website where basic facts and figures and general policy may be accessed; many states have more than one. For example, the site http://www.ca.gov/ provides basic information about California and links to more than two dozen other websites maintained by California state agencies, such as the education department, the energy commission, and the fish and game department.

To find the website for your state, try asking your instructor or calling your state legislator for the address.

The intergovernmental lobby One of the most effective strategies used by state and local governments in recent years has been to organize the **intergovernmental lobby**. Following the explosion of grants-in-aid in the 1960s, representatives of state and local governments began organizing themselves into lobby groups to press for more federal aid for states and communities, to see that grants are designed to meet state and local needs, and to keep abreast of new rules and regulations affecting grants. Unlike other Washington lobbies, the intergovernmental lobby is funded almost exclusively with public money—state and local funds and even federal grants.

The most important organizations in the intergovernmental lobby are listed in Table 3-2. But these national organizations are just a few of the dozens of groups that represent state and local interests.

In addition, many states and cities, believing that these national organizations cannot adequately represent their particular interests, have opened their own offices in Washington. By the mid 1990s, about thirty states, one hundred cities, and a dozen counties maintained offices there. California had the largest presence in Washington of all the states: separate offices represented the state, twenty-three cities, and seven counties. Sometimes all this lobbying activity can lead to awkward situations and even conflicting efforts. The state of New York, for example, has separate lobbyists serving the interests of the governor, the state assembly, and the state senate. In the debate over President Reagan's block grant proposals, lobbyists for the Democratic-controlled New York state assembly opposed the block grants, and lobbyists for the Republican-controlled state senate supported them.

The 1960s and 1970s were in many ways a golden age for the intergovernmental lobby. Federal aid to states and cities grew steadily during that time, reaching $91.5 billion by 1980—just over 25 percent of total state and local fiscal

TABLE 3-2 The Intergovernmental Lobby

Organization	Employees	Budget (approx.)	Major issues
National Conference of State Legislatures 40,000 legislators and staff	140	$14 million	1. Unfunded federal mandates 2. Medicaid 3. Welfare reform
National League of Cities 20,000 cities	85	$11 million	1. Unfunded federal mandates 2. Public safety 3. Tax reform
U.S. Conference of Mayors 1,000 cities with populations over 30,000	57	$10 million	1. Unfunded federal mandates 2. Toxic waste 3. Sports franchise relocations
National Association of Counties 2,000 counties	75	$10 million	1. Community development 2. Transportation 3. Welfare reform, job training
National Governors' Association 55 state and territorial governors	89	$14 million	1. Medicaid 2. Welfare reform 3. Safe drinking water
National Association of Towns and Townships 13,000 local governments in areas with populations of 25,000 or less	4	$700,000	1. Rural transportation 2. Indian issues 3. Environment

SOURCE: Authors' interviews with officials of each organization, 1996.

outlays. The passage of the general revenue sharing program in 1972 was perhaps the crowning achievement of these organizations. By contrast, the Reagan-Bush years were a time of declining political influence for the intergovernmental lobby. It was not able to prevent the elimination of the general revenue sharing program and the urban development action grants, and it could not overcome a slowdown in federal funds for housing, transportation, and many social programs.

With the election in 1992 of former Arkansas governor Bill Clinton to the presidency, the intergovernmental lobby hoped for more productive relationships with the federal government. Yet Clinton's early focus on cutting the budget deficit made it clear that expansive new programs to assist state and local governments would not be priorities of his presidency. As discussed earlier, however, along with the Republican Congress elected in 1994, the intergovernmental lobby did succeed in 1995 in passing the

Unfunded Mandates Reform Act, making it more difficult for Congress to impose costly mandates and certain conditions of grants-in-aid on state and local governments.

CASE STUDY

Federalism and Same-Sex Marriage

Representative Barney Frank (D, Mass.): "We are talking here about a desperate search for a political issue. . . . Nobody has come to me and said, "Gee, Congressman, I've been married for seven years and now my marriage is threatened because two women have fallen in love a couple of blocks away."

Representative Henry J. Hyde (R, Ill.): "There is a moral issue. . . . People don't think that the traditional marriage ought to be demeaned, or trivialized, by same-sex unions."[1]

This emotional exchange between an openly gay member of Congress and one of the leading congressional conservatives on moral issues took place on the floor of the House of Representatives on May 30, 1996. It was part of the debate over a bill called the Defense of Marriage Act, which was intended to register the opposition of the federal government to marriages between persons of the same sex. Although many people see same-sex marriage as an issue of justice or of sexual morality, its sudden appearance in the political arena in the 1990s prompted a lively debate in the field of federalism as well.

The immediate issue grew out of a court case in Hawaii, where in 1990, the State Department of Health had denied marriage licenses to three homosexual couples in Honolulu. The couples then sued the state, contending that its law prohibiting same-sex marriage was unconstitutional. The trial judge upheld the state law, and the plaintiffs appealed to the state supreme court. In 1993, the court held that the state's denial of marriage licenses to same-sex couples is a form of sexual discrimination under Hawaii's constitution. The court did authorize another trial to determine whether the discrimination was permissible because it was supported by a "compelling state interest." Because the state was thought unlikely to be able to demonstrate such an interest, however, the likelihood arose that Hawaii would become the first state to legalize same-sex marriage.

After the Hawaii Supreme Court's decision, many conservative state legislators nationwide introduced bills to block legal recognition of same-sex marriages. These legislative skirmishes escalated into a national battle with the introduction of the Defense of Marriage Act in Congress in 1996. (At that time, eight states had passed such measures; similar legislation had been defeated, withdrawn, or vetoed in fifteen states and was pending in eight others. Introduced by Senator Don Nickles of Oklahoma and Representative Bob Barr of Georgia (both Republicans), the Defense of Marriage Act passed both houses of Congress by wide margins and was signed into law by President Clinton in September 1996. The act defines marriage as the union of one man and one woman. It authorizes states to refuse to recognize single-sex marriages performed elsewhere; and it withholds from married gay and lesbian couples recognition for federal tax, welfare, pension, health, immigration, and survivor benefits that are available to married heterosexual couples.

Opponents charged that the act, as well as the state laws of the same nature,[2] violates the United States Constitution, specifically, "the full faith and credit" clause. This clause, Section 1 of Article IV, states: Full Faith and Credit shall be given in each State to the public Acts, Records, and judicial Proceedings of every other State. And the Congress may by general Laws prescribe the Manner in which such Acts, Records and Proceedings shall be proved, and the Effect, thereof." In legal terms, this language means that each state must accept as valid the public acts, statutes, and records of every other state and must enforce the civil judgments of the courts of other states.

In general, the full faith and credit clause has been interpreted to require states to recognize as valid marriages that are valid under the laws of another state. Some opponents of same-sex marriage thus feared that if same-sex marriage was legalized in Hawaii, gay and lesbian couples from all over the nation might travel to Hawaii to get married and return to their home states, which would then have to recognize the marriages as legally valid. (In fact, a Hawaiian judge did rule in late 1996 that the state lacked a compelling interest in banning same-sex marriages, but the prospects for legalization ultimately depended on a final ruling by the state supreme court and a 1998 referendum on a proposed state constitutional amendment banning such marriages.)

There is, however, one recognized exception to the general rule requiring states to honor and recognize legal actions of other states. The courts have ruled that the paramount interests of an individual state—as reflected in its traditions, laws, customs, notions of justice, and moral attitudes—may on occasion outweigh the full faith and credit mandate. A valid marriage in one state may not have to be accepted in another state if such recognition would run counter to the clearly expressed public policy of the state. Bigamous or polygamous marriages, for example, are explicitly prohibited by law in most states.

Moreover, supporters of the Defense of Marriage Act maintain that the second sentence of the full faith and credit clause gives Congress the explicit authority to pass legislation to restrict the applicability of one state's laws to another state. Many constitutional scholars are critical of that interpretation, however. For example, Cass Sustein, a law professor at the University of Chicago, told the Senate Judiciary Committee on July 11, 1996: "A good deal of the entire federal system could be undone. Under the proponents' interpretation, Congress could simply say that any law Congress dislikes is of no effect in other states."[3]

Whatever its outcome, the same-sex marriage controversy raises interesting questions about the obligations states have to each other in our federal system. Federalism is more than just a way of describing the relationship between the national government and the states. It describes the relationships between and among the states as well. Obviously, cooperation among the states is essential if the nation is to survive intact. The Framers recognized this by including in the Constitution, primarily in Article IV, specific provisions that deal with the obligations and responsibilities states have to one another. These prevent states from discriminating against citizens of other states and guarantee freedom of movement from one state to another, as well as ensuring that states recognize as valid the laws and public acts of other states.

To get more information about this issue or to become involved in the debate, contact one of the following groups:

Supporting legalization of same-sex marriage:

Human Rights Campaign
1101 14th Street NW, Suite 200
Washington, D.C. 20005
ph: (202) 628-4160
fax: (202) 347-5323
e-mail: hrc@hrcusa.org

Opposing legalization of same-sex marriage:

Family Research Council
700 13th Street, Suite 500
Washington, D.C. 20005
ph: (202) 393-2100
fax: (202) 393-2134
e-mail: frc@sojourn.com

Discussion Questions

1. In what ways can federalism be viewed as a "political issue?" How has it been used to advance political agendas of various groups over the history of the country? What issues today are being debated largely from a "federal" perspective?

2. Identify some indicators of the recent "devolution" of American federalism, and discuss what you believe to be some of the likely consequences of such devolution (e.g., who do you believe will win and who will lose from such change)?

3. What are some of the most important ways in which the national government attempts to influence policy at the state and local level, and what are some of the most important ways by which state and local governments try to affect decision making at the national level? Which of these tactics (or others) do you believe will continue to be most effective? Why?

[1] *New York Times,* May 31, 1996, p. A18.

[2] By mid-April 1997, eighteen states had enacted such laws.

[3] "GOP Bill Restricting Gay Unions Clears . . . But Does Not Yield Political Dividends," *Congressional Quarterly Weekly Report,* September 14, 1996, pp. 2598–2599.

SOURCE: William N. Eskridge, Jr., *The Case for Same-Sex Marriage: From Sexual Liberty to Civilized Commitment* (New York, The Free Press, 1996).

SUMMARY

Throughout the nation's history, there have been conflicts over the meaning of federalism and the proper division of power and responsibility among federal, state, and local governments. During the period following ratification of the Constitution, those who favored more power and responsibility for the national government were opposed by those who sought to protect and enhance the rights of individual states.

The conflict over national supremacy versus states' rights intensified along with opposition to slavery, finally culminating in the Civil War. After the war, a new relationship known as *dual federalism* emerged. It recognized separate and distinct spheres of authority for the national and state governments.

The Great Depression of the 1930s ushered in a period of *cooperative federalism,* which stressed a partnership and a sharing of functions, responsibilities, and programs between the states and the national government. This era was marked by increased use of *grants-in-aid,* programs through which the national government shared its fiscal resources with state and local governments.

For much of the past half-century, Supreme Court rulings have been interpreted by many as eliminating—or at least significantly reducing—state and local sovereignty. But within recent years, some Court decisions seem to have restored a measure of state and local independence. Moreover, the Republicans who won control of Congress in the 1994 elections mounted a strong effort to return to the state and local governments many responsibilities that had been assumed by the federal government in recent decades, such as welfare, job training, and Medicaid. These shifts suggested a trend toward a new era in intergovernmental relations, which some have called *devolution federalism*.

In its attempts to regulate state and localities, the national government may issue direct orders, preempt state and local activities, or use grants-in-aid to encourage certain activities and discourage others. Occasionally, the national government issues direct orders, such as antidiscrimination and environmental regulations, that local governments must comply with or else face civil or criminal penalties. Preemption removes a certain policy area, such as regulation of copyrights or cable television rates, from state authority.

A more common approach to regulation is the use of grants-in-aid. Grants have been used to fund projects and efforts in a wide variety of areas, ranging from mass transportation to nutrition programs for the elderly. National influence over state and local policies is accomplished through the conditions and requirements that recipients must satisfy in order to receive the aid.

Some states and regions receive considerably higher per-person allocations of grant monies than do others. As a result, controversies and conflicts sometimes arise over the regional distribution of grant funds. In particular, officials in Frostbelt states and in Sunbelt states often clash over the formulas for distribution of federal funds.

State and local governments naturally attempt to influence the adoption and distribution of federal grants. The term *grantsmanship* refers to efforts by local officials to maximize federal grants received and to influence the interpretation of grant rules in ways that are favorable to their locality. State and local governments have also organized an *intergovernmental lobby* to press for more federal aid, see that grants are designed to meet their needs, and keep abreast of new rules and regulations.

KEY TERMS

doctrine of nullification
dual federalism
cooperative federalism
grants-in-aid
new federalism
devolution federalism
partial preemption
crosscutting requirements
crossover sanctions
categorical grants
block grants
formula grants
project grants
grantsmanship
intergovernmental lobby

RESOURCES

READINGS

Conlan, Timothy. *New Federalism: Intergovernmental Reform from Nixon to Reagan*. Washington, D.C.: Brookings Institution, 1988. A thorough account of events in American federal relations focusing especially on the presidencies of Richard Nixon and Ronald Reagan. The author presents an interesting analysis of the "politics" of intergovernmental relations during those years.

Hamilton, Christopher, and Donald T. Wells. *Federalism, Power, and Political Economy*. Englewood Cliffs, N.J.: Prentice-Hall, 1990. A contemporary overview of federalism, suggesting that conflicts between the states and the national government are central to politics and economics in America.

Kincaid, John, ed. *American Federalism: The Third Century*. Annals of the American Academy of Political and Social Science. Newbury Park, Calif.: Sage, 1990. A collection of essays by scholars examining various aspects of federalism in the 1990s, including fiscal roles, finance, regulation, and court decisions.

Nice, David C., and Patricia Fredericksen. *Federalism: The Politics of Intergovernmental Relations*. 2d ed. Chicago: Nelson-Hall, 1995. A good textbook on federalism, with a useful look at various models of federal systems as well as a discussion of interstate relations.

Peterson, Paul E. *The Price of Federalism*. Washington, D.C.: Brookings Institution, 1995. An excellent examination of contemporary political debates in the federalism arena, with special focus on the policy consequences of devolution.

Peterson, Paul E., Barry G. Rabe, and Kenneth K. Wong. *When Federalism Works*. Washington, D.C.: Brookings Institution, 1987. An examination of the operation of nine federal programs in education, health, and housing. The study attempts to assess why some federally sponsored programs work well and others do not.

Riker, William H. *The Development of American Federalism*. Boston: Kluwer Academic Publishers, 1987. A collection of essays addressing various aspects of federal relations. The book presents an especially interesting look at institutions such as Congress, the presidency, and the military in a federal context.

Swartz, Thomas R., and John E. Peck. *The Changing Face of Fiscal Federalism.* Armonk, N.Y.: M. E. Sharpe, 1990. A collection of essays examining federalism from a fiscal perspective, focusing primarily on the Carter, Reagan, and Bush presidencies. The book looks especially at the "winners" and "losers" in the changing system of federal finance.

Walter, David B. *The Rebirth of Federalism.* Chatham, N.J.: Chatham House Publishers, 1995. An excellent brief overview of the most important aspects of American federalism. The book presents an especially insightful look at the various stages of development of the American federal system.

ORGANIZATIONS

Advisory Commission on Intergovernmental Relations, 800 K Street, N.W., Washington, DC 20575; phone (202) 653-5540; fax (202) 653-5429; e-mail ir002529@interramp.com. A government commission that publishes useful studies and reports on various aspects of American federalism. Especially useful is its annual report, *Significant Features of Fiscal Federalism,* which presents detailed fiscal information on numerous intergovernmental programs and issues.

American Society for Public Administration, 1120 G Street, N.W., Washington, DC 20005-2885; phone (202) 393-7878; fax (202) 638-4952; e-mail dcaspa@ix.netcom.com. A scholarly organization focusing on many aspects of American federalism. Especially useful is its journal *Public Administration Review,* which contains articles dealing with the funding, administration, implementation, and evaluation of intergovernmental programs.

Center for the Study of Federalism, 1616 Walnut Street, Temple University, Philadelphia, PA 19103; phone (215) 204-1480; fax (215) 204-7784; e-mail v2026r@vm.temple.edu. An interdisciplinary educational and research institute located at Temple University. Its publication, *Publius: The Journal of Federalism,* is an excellent source of scholarly research dealing with federal issues.

4

Civil Rights and Liberties

PREVIEW

- Rights, liberties, and constitutional politics
- The nationalization of the Bill of Rights
- Civil rights and criminal justice: due process of law; freedom from unreasonable searches and seizures; government interrogations and the right to counsel; the right to a fair trial; the prohibition against cruel and unusual punishment
- Rights and liberties versus economic interests

In the late 1980s, school officials in Vernonia, a small logging community in Oregon, noticed a sharp increase in drug use and disciplinary problems among their students. Student athletes, in the officials' view, not only were among the users but were actually the leaders of the drug culture. As a result, in 1989, the school board approved a policy under which athletes had to sign a form consenting to drug testing and obtain the written consent of their parents as well. At the beginning of the season of each sport, every athlete playing that sport was tested for drugs. Then, throughout the season, 10 percent of the athletes were randomly selected to be tested each week.

When the parents of James Acton, a 12-year-old seventh grader, sued the Vernonia School District over the constitutionality of the drug-testing policy, a federal district court rejected their claim that it violated the Fourth Amendment's guarantee against "unreasonable searches and seizures." But a federal court of appeals reversed that ruling, and school officials appealed to the Supreme Court. Lawsuits challenging similar drug-testing programs adopted by other schools and colleges throughout the country had resulted in conflicting rulings in the state and federal courts. It was therefore important for the Supreme Court to resolve the controversy.

Not only students but also public employees have increasingly been required to submit to random drug testing since the 1980s. Whereas proponents of testing insist that it is a necessary part of the country's "war on drugs" and important to ensuring the health and safety of students, employees, and the general public, opponents counter that it violates individuals' right of privacy as well as the guarantee against "unreasonable searches and seizures." Typically, they point out, a search requires a showing of "probable cause," or at least a "reasonable suspicion," that a person is engaged in illegal activities. Random drug testing, however, requires no such showing.

Political controversies such as the one over drug testing of students eventually find their way to the Supreme Court. The Court decides only important cases, and most have a political dimension. They involve people or institutions that are in conflict with one another or with the government. When that conflict enters the judicial arena, it concerns rules of law and how those rules are interpreted. The law may be the Constitution, statutes, or prior rulings known as precedents. In any case, it is for the courts to resolve the legal issue. Their judgments often have widespread implications, affecting not only the individuals in a specific case but the society as a whole. In this sense, courts interact with and affect the political environment.

Prior to ruling on drug testing in public schools, the Supreme Court had approved a drug-testing program for federal employees, in *National Treasury Employees Union v. Von Raab* (1989), as well as mandatory drug tests for railroad workers involved in serious accidents, in *Skinner v. Railway Labor Executives' Association* (1989). Both of those cases had sharply divided the justices. And by a 6-to-3 vote in *Vernonia School District 47J v. Acton,* the Court reversed the appeals court's decision and upheld the school district's policy.

In his written opinion explaining the reasoning of the Court's majority, Justice Antonin Scalia cited as precedents those earlier decisions upholding the drug testing of public employees. In addition, he emphasized that students are subject to the supervision of teachers and have fewer constitutional protections than adults. Since every student athlete was tested for drugs, he reasoned, school officials were not being arbitrary in choosing whom to test, and students' expectations of privacy were less because all athletes were tested.

By contrast, in a dissenting opinion on behalf of herself and two others, Justices John Paul Stevens and David H. Souter, Justice Sandra Day O'Connor wrote that the Court's majority wrongly minimized students' privacy interests and the constitutional requirement for probable cause for government searches. In her words, "The population of our Nation's public schools, grades 7 through 12, numbers around 18 million. By the reasoning of today's decision, the millions of these students who participate in interscholastic sports, an overwhelming majority of whom have given school officials no reason whatsoever to suspect they use drugs at school, are open to an intrusive bodily search."

The controversy over drug testing in public schools illustrates how civil rights and liberties are linked to larger political struggles. Interest groups on both sides of the controversy were mobilized and divided over the competing values at stake. Even the justices disagreed with each other when deciding *Vernonia School District.* The Court is a political institution, and its rulings respond to and may invite political conflicts. Civil rights and liberties ultimately depend not only on the Court's rulings but also on the achievement of political consensus in the country.

RIGHTS, LIBERTIES, AND CONSTITUTIONAL POLITICS

One of the great ongoing struggles in American politics involves the protection of civil rights and civil liberties. **Civil rights** are rights, such as the right to vote, that government may not categorically deny or infringe on because of an individual's race, gender, ethnicity, or various other characteristics. **Civil liberties** are freedoms that government must respect, such as the freedom to think, express oneself, and act in a manner that conforms to one's beliefs and values.

The government has not always respected every individual's civil rights and liberties. For example, women, African Americans, and other minority groups have been discriminated against, and for much of American history so-called subversive political ideas and speech have been punished. As a result, American politics has been animated by political struggles aimed at guaranteeing equal civil rights and liberties for all people.

Political struggles over civil rights and liberties stem from the competing demands for majority rule and for individual or minority rights. We have seen already how difficult it is to have a government based on majority rule that also respects the rights of individuals and minorities. Conflicts between the majority and minority often arise over issues such as free speech, school prayer, the rights of those accused of crimes, abortion, and the rights of homosexuals. Resolving those disagreements is crucial to the stability and vitality of the political system.

Conflicts over civil rights and liberties can be traced to the development of guarantees for individual rights in England. The Magna Carta (1215), the Petition of Right (1628), and the English Bill of Rights (1689) recognized the equality of individuals before the law and placed certain limitations on government power. Together with the philosophical tradition of unalienable natural rights, those basic charters inspired America's founders when they drafted the Declaration of Independence, the Constitution, and the Bill of Rights. The core idea of these documents is that all people enjoy certain rights and liberties that are essential to their personal freedom and well-being and to their equality before the law.

The Constitution itself was viewed by some as a bill of rights. Alexander Hamilton argued that individuals' rights and liberties would remain secure because the powers of the national government were limited to those expressly granted to it in the Constitution. In addition, he said, the states would continue to safeguard civil rights and liberties because the states were closer to the people and directly accountable to them. But the Anti-Federalists, who feared that the national government would not only usurp the powers of the states but also deny individuals their rights and liberties, were not persuaded. To ensure that their concerns were satisfied, they made the addition of the first ten amendments to the Constitution—that is, the **Bill of Rights**—more or less a condition for its ratification in Massachusetts, Virginia, and New York. Their fears were probably well founded, since the 1787 Constitution contained only five provisions that directly protected civil liberties. In any case, however, all the states ratified the Bill of Rights in 1791.

James Madison, the principal drafter of the Bill of Rights, had also sought to include protection for individuals' "rights of conscience" and limitations on the powers of the states to deny civil rights and liberties, but Congress rejected those proposals. Initially, then, the guarantees of the Bill of Rights were viewed as limitations only on the federal government, not on the states. Congress assumed that the states would ensure individuals' civil rights and liberties under their own constitutions, but these varied widely in their safeguards. As a result, the Supreme Court finally *nationalized* the Bill of Rights, making its guarantees applicable to the states as well as to the federal government by construing them to be included in the Fourteenth Amendment's guarantee of due process of law. The nationalization of the Bill of Rights has involved the Court in political controversy, because it expanded the judiciary's supervision over state legislation and made the Court a powerful arbitrator in the struggle for civil rights and liberties.

We now turn to the functions of the Supreme Court as an arbitrator of civil rights and liberties. How has it sought to balance civil rights against societal interests? In particular, how has it interpreted the constitutional guarantees of the rights of the accused? And what about other rights, such as the right of privacy, that are not explicitly mentioned in the Constitution? (In the next chapter, we take up issues of political freedom—the freedoms of speech, press, and religion—along with the quest for equality and the elimination of racial and nonracial discrimination.)

THE NATIONALIZATION OF THE BILL OF RIGHTS

The guarantees in the Bill of Rights are stated in broad terms. The First Amendment is the only one that specifically singles out the national government in its provisions, which prohibit Congress from passing laws establishing religion and from denying the free exercise of religion and the freedoms of speech, press, and assembly. Nevertheless, the view that the first ten amendments limited the powers *only of the national government* prevailed until the twentieth century.

But with the adoption of the Fourteenth Amendment in 1868, there was a new basis for applying the Bill of Rights to the states.[1] Like the Fifth Amendment, the Fourteenth contains a due process clause, but that clause specifically limits the power of the states: "No State shall make or enforce any law which shall abridge the privileges or immunities of citizens of the United States; nor shall any State deprive any person of life, liberty, or property, without due process of law; nor deny to any person within its jurisdiction the equal protection of the laws."

Immediately after the adoption of the Fourteenth Amendment, lawyers tried to convince the Supreme Court that the Fourteenth Amendment "incorporated" or "absorbed" the guarantees of the Bill of Rights and applied them to the states. Yet with one exception, the Court refused to go along with that argument in the nineteenth century. The exception came in 1897, when the Court held that the concept of eminent domain, which is contained in the Fifth Amendment's guarantee that private property shall not be taken "without just compensation," also applies to the states.

In a revolutionary decision in 1925, however, the Court ruled in *Gitlow v. New York* that a major provision of the First Amendment (the guarantee of the freedoms of speech and press) applies to the states. Justice Edward T. Stanford simply announced that "for present purposes we may and do assume that freedom of speech and press, which are protected by the First Amendment from abridgment by Congress, are among the fundamental personal rights and 'liberties' protected by the due process clause of the Fourteenth Amendment from impairment by the States."[2] In the 1930s and

TABLE 4-1 ***The Nationalization of the Guarantees of the Bill of Rights***

YEAR	GUARANTEE AND AMENDMENT	CASE
1897	Eminent domain (V)	*C, B & Q Railroad v. Chicago*
1925	Freedom of speech (I)	*Gitlow v. New York*
1931	Freedom of press (I)	*Near v. Minnesota*
1932	Right to counsel in *capital* cases (VI)	*Powell v. Alabama*
1934	Free exercise of religion (I)	*Hamilton v. Regents of the Univ. of California*
1937	Assembly and petition (I)	*DeJonge v. Oregon*
1947	Establishment of church and state (I)	*Everson v. Board of Ed. of Ewing Township*
1948	Public trial (VI)	*In re Oliver*
1949	Unreasonable searches and seizures (IV)	*Wolf v. Colorado*
1961	Exclusionary rule (IV)	*Mapp v. Ohio*
1962	Cruel and unusual punishment (VIII)	*Robinson v. California*
1963	Right to counsel in criminal cases (VI)	*Gideon v. Wainwright*
1964	Compulsory self-incrimination (V)	*Malloy v. Hogan*
1965	Confrontation of witnesses (VI)	*Pointer v. Texas*
1965	Right of privacy[a]	*Griswold v. Connecticut*
1966	Trial by impartial jury (VI)	*Parker v. Gladden*
1967	Right to a speedy trial (VI)	*Klopfer v. N. Carolina*
1968	Jury trial in nonpetty criminal cases (VI)	*Duncan v. Louisiana*
1969	Double jeopardy (V)	*Benton v. Maryland*
1972	Right to counsel in all cases involving a jail term (VI)	*Argersinger v. Hamilton*

[a]The right of privacy is not enumerated in the Bill of Rights, but the Supreme Court found it in the "penumbras" or "shadows" of the provisions of the First, Third, Fourth, and Fifth amendments.

1940s, the Court applied the remaining First Amendment guarantees—those dealing with religion and the right of assembly—to the states on a case-by-case basis. But the Court remained reluctant to apply to the states the rest of the Bill of Rights, particularly the rights of the accused contained in the Fourth through Eighth Amendments.

During the 1960s, however, when the Court was headed by Chief Justice Earl Warren, a liberal, it selectively incorporated the other principal guarantees of the Bill of Rights into the Fourteenth Amendment's due process clause and made them applicable to the states (see Table 4-1).[3] In addition, in 1965 it found a "right of privacy" (which is not specifically mentioned in the Constitution) and applied it to the states under the Fourteenth Amendment. By the 1970s, all the major provisions of the Bill of Rights had been held to apply to the states. The only ones that do not apply are the right to bear arms (Second Amendment); the provision against the quartering of troops in private homes (Third); the provision for grand jury indictments (Fifth); the right of a jury trial in civil cases (Seventh); and the provision that the other enumerated rights "shall not be construed to deny or disparage others retained by the people" (Ninth).

CIVIL RIGHTS AND CRIMINAL JUSTICE

Americans enjoy a great number of civil rights and liberties that limit the coercive powers of government. Some are a result of both the Supreme Court's interpretation of the Constitution and congressional legislation designed to ensure equal access to justice and equality before the law. Others are contained in state constitutions and bills of rights. Many, such as due process of law and freedom from unreasonable searches and seizures, are rooted in principles that originated in the English common law—judge-made law in England—and are embodied in the guarantees of the Bill of Rights. The following discussion examines the provisions of the Bill of Rights that limit the powers of state and federal governments in criminal procedures and law enforcement. The major stages in the criminal-justice process are presented in Figure 4-1.

Due Process of Law

Under the due process clauses of the Fifth and Fourteenth Amendments, no person shall be deprived of "life, liberty, or property, without due process of law." But what is **due process**? What "process" is "due"?

Those are vexing questions, for the concept of due process is broad and elusive. It can be traced to the English Petition of Right and then even further back to

FIGURE 4-1

The Criminal-Justice Process

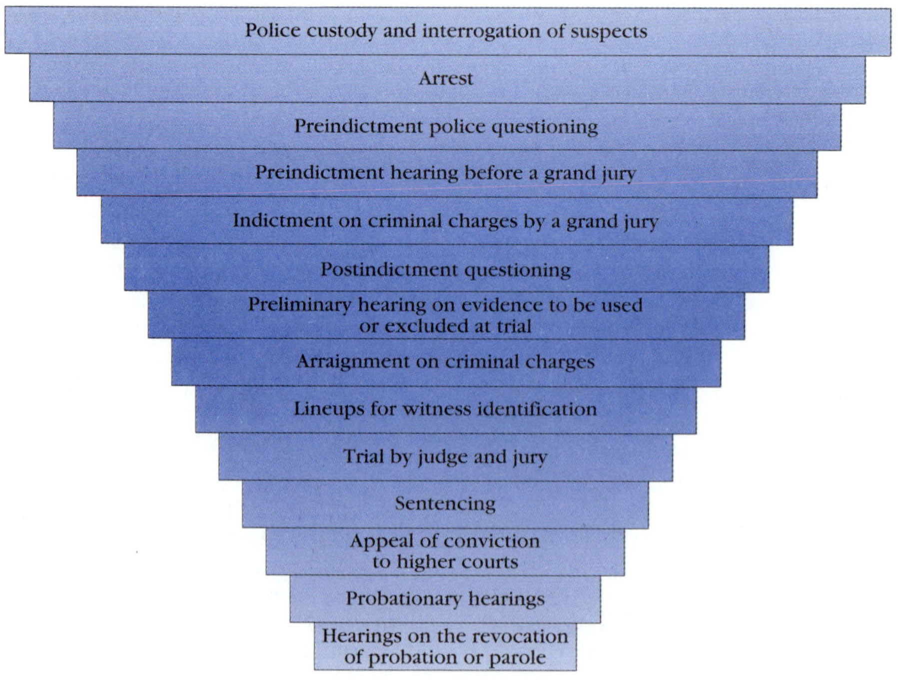

the Magna Carta, where it originally meant simply "the law of the land." Due process, as Justice Felix Frankfurter once explained, "is compounded of history, reason, the past course of decisions, and stout confidence in the strength of the democratic faith which we profess. Due process is not a mechanical instrument. It is not a yardstick. It is a delicate process of adjustment inescapably involving the exercise of judgment by those whom the Constitution entrusted with the unfolding of the process.[4]

As Frankfurter's statement suggests, many complex elements enter into due process. To understand this issue more clearly, it is helpful to think of due process as being divided into two basic kinds: procedural and substantive.

Procedural due process is concerned with *how* the law is carried out—whether through police, judges, legislatures, or administrative agencies. Although procedural due process often pertains to the specific rights and procedural guarantees mentioned in the Bill of Rights, the Supreme Court has also sought to enforce a more general standard of fairness in criminal procedures and law enforcement. In *Rochin v. California* (1952), for example, the Court reversed the conviction of Antonio Richard Rochin for selling and possessing narcotics. Police with no arrest or search warrant had broken into Rochin's home and found him in bed, where he immediately swallowed two morphine capsules that were on a table next to the bed. The police attempted to make him cough up the evidence, repeatedly kicking him and trying to make him gag. Finally they took him to a hospital and ordered a doctor to pump his stomach. At Rochin's trial, the prosecution introduced the regurgitated morphine as evidence. In an opinion for the Supreme Court overturning Rochin's conviction, Justice Frankfurter observed that the conduct of the police "shocks the conscience. . . . Due process of law [means that] convictions cannot be brought about by methods that offend 'a sense of justice.'"[5]

The Court has further held that some laws are unconstitutional because they are overly broad or *void for vagueness*. For instance, laws that made it a crime to treat the American flag "contemptuously" have been struck down because they do not make clear exactly what is permitted and what is prohibited and thus give arbitrary and unfair discretion to prosecutors, judges, and others who carry out such laws.

Substantive due process is concerned with the subject matter of a law, regulation, or executive order; it places limitations on *what* government may do. The Court looks at the substance of the law itself, why it was enacted, and whether it is "unreasonable," "irrational," or "arbitrary" in light of the concept of due process and other constitutional guarantees. Because the Court may overturn laws, substantive due process is highly controversial. For example, between 1897 and 1937, the Court was dominated by conservatives who opposed most social welfare legislation and used substantive due process to strike down many laws that regulated the economy, such as those that controlled the prices of goods and the wages and hours of workers. The Court based its actions on a "liberty of contract," which, though not specifically mentioned in the Constitution, it found to be implicit in the concept of due process. In 1937, President Franklin Roosevelt—whose early New Deal economic legislation had fallen victim to the Court's invalidations—threatened to increase the number of justices from nine to fifteen in order to secure a majority willing to uphold his programs. At that point, the Court stopped using substantive due process on matters of economic regulation, and it has not done so since.

More recently, however, the Court has employed substantive due process to overturn laws infringing on noneconomic civil liberties. Notably, in the 1965 case of *Griswold v. Connecticut,*[6] the Court invoked the right of privacy under the Fourteenth Amendment's due process clause to overturn a law prohibiting the use of contraceptives. In its highly controversial 1973 ruling in *Roe v. Wade,* the Court went even further by striking down most laws forbidding abortion. It did so on the basis of the right of privacy and a balancing of the interests of women against the interests of the state. Since *Roe,* however, a more conservative Supreme Court has been reluctant to rely on substantive due process to protect or extend benefits to individuals.

Freedom from Unreasonable Searches and Seizures

Like many other rights, the freedom from "unreasonable searches and seizures" provided for in the Fourth Amendment is rooted in the history of the English common law and the American colonial experience. During the colonial period, royalist judges issued *writs of assistance* or *general warrants,* which allowed British authorities to search and ransack homes. The purpose of the Fourth Amendment was to prevent such intrusions—to forbid police from conducting "arbitrary," "unreasonable," and "general" searches and seizures.

The key to this protection is the requirement that a magistrate issue a warrant before a search or an arrest can be made. To obtain a warrant, the police must swear under oath that they have "probable cause" for its issuance, and the warrant must describe the specific places that will be searched and persons or things to be seized. The police are barred from conducting more wide-ranging searches.

Exceptions to the warrant requirement may be allowed when the arrest is made in a public place, when the police are in "hot pursuit" of a suspect, or when someone's life is in danger. Even when the police arrest or "seize" a person in a public place, they must still have *probable cause* to believe, or a *reasonable suspicion,* that the person had committed or was about to commit a crime. In *California v. Hodari D.* (1991), however, the Rehnquist Court held that police may chase a person even without probable cause or reasonable suspicion.[7] Hodari D., a teenager standing with others on a streetcorner at night, ran away at the sight of an undercover police car. The police then chased him and recovered a piece of crack cocaine that he had thrown away, and the crack was used as evidence at trial against him. Even though the police had not had a basis for questioning or detaining Hodari D. before he threw away the crack, the Court held that, for the purposes of the Fourth Amendment, he had not been "seized." When the police arrest a person, moreover, they may search him or her as well as whatever area and items are in "plain view."

The provisions of the Fourth Amendment apply not only to people's houses but also to their apartments, their offices, and (under some circumstances) their cars and other personal effects, such as clothing and luggage. In general, the Court has held that the amendment "protects people, not places" and applies in cases which the Court deems someone to have a "reasonable expectation of privacy."

Other threats to personal privacy posed by new technologies and changing law enforcement techniques have been addressed by the Court as well. When initially confronted by the issue of whether wiretapping constituted an "unreasonable search and seizure" in the 1928 case of *Olmstead v. United States,* a bare majority of the Court said no.[8] But forty years later, in *Katz v. United States* (1967), the Court reversed itself. It held that police must obtain a search warrant before conducting wiretaps—even wiretaps placed in public telephone booths—because the amendment safeguards individuals' "reasonable" and "legitimate expectations of privacy."[9] Subsequently, in the Crime Control and Safe Streets Act of 1968, Congress established federal guidelines for the use of electronic surveillance by law enforcement officials.

Government Interrogations and the Right to Counsel

Individuals enjoy a number of rights under the Fifth and Sixth Amendments, which bar the government from coercing confessions and forcing the disclosure of incriminating evidence. One of these, known as the privilege against **self-incrimination**, is a fundamental principle of an **adversary** (or **accusatory**) **system** of justice. In such a system, people are not required to prove their innocence and may not be forced to testify against themselves; in the American adversary system, the government has the burden of proving guilt and may not compel a defendant to testify at all. In contrast, under the **inquisitorial system** used in France and other European countries, the accused person is presumed guilty, interrogated by magistrates and required to answer their questions, and denied many of the other rights afforded under an adversary system.

Although the Fifth Amendment protection against self-incrimination literally applies only during criminal trials, it has been extended to protect individuals who are summoned to appear before other government institutions and agencies. It may be invoked in the proceedings of grand juries, congressional and state investigatory committees, and some administrative agencies. Individuals cannot lose their government employment because they claim the privilege before a disciplinary board. But individuals may invoke the privilege only when their disclosures would in fact prove incriminating, not merely embarrassing.

The Supreme Court has also sanctioned the practice of **plea bargaining**, in which an accused person, in order to obtain probation or a reduced sentence, pleads guilty to a lesser offense than the one with which he or she was originally charged. In exchange for a lighter sentence, defendants who plea-bargain must surrender their constitutional rights against self-incrimination, as well as their right to a speedy and public jury trial and to confront witnesses against them. Plea bargaining is advantageous for the government as well as for the accused because it eliminates the time and cost of going to trial. Approximately 90 percent of all guilty pleas in American courts result from plea bargains that are struck between the accused and the prosecution.

The most controversial extension of the protection against self-incrimination is the Supreme Court's use of it to limit police interrogations of criminal suspects. In the 1960s, the Court handed down several landmark rulings on this matter. In *Escobedo v. Illinois* (1964), it held that whenever a person becomes the primary suspect in a criminal investigation, he or she has the right to request the assistance of counsel.[10] A year earlier, in *Gideon v. Wainwright* (1963), it had ruled that any individual accused of a criminal offense but too poor to hire a lawyer has the right to a court-appointed attorney.[11] Both cases acknowledged that without the assistance of counsel, individuals may not fully understand their rights and may be intimidated by police and by the judicial process itself.

Subsequently, in *Miranda v. Arizona* (1966), Chief Justice Earl Warren sought to establish objective standards for determining whether confessions were coerced.[12] Ernesto Miranda, a 23-year-old indigent with a ninth-grade education, had been arrested and charged with kidnapping and raping an 18-year-old girl on the outskirts of Phoenix, Arizona. At the police station, the rape victim identified Miranda in a police lineup; two officers then took him into a separate room for interrogation. At first denying his guilt, Miranda eventually confessed and wrote out and signed a brief statement admitting and describing the crime. After his trial and conviction, Miranda's attorneys appealed, contending that the use of a confession obtained during police interrogations, in the absence of an attorney, violated Miranda's Fifth Amendment right to remain silent. The Court agreed, holding that confessions cannot be introduced at trial unless the police had initially informed the suspect of his or her constitutional rights. This procedural safeguard is known as the ***Miranda* warnings**.

Escobedo, Gideon, Miranda, and other rulings were crucial to ensuring individuals' Sixth Amendment right to counsel and to achieving equality before the law for rich and poor citizens alike. Subsequent decisions held that the right to counsel applies to virtually every stage of the criminal-justice process—from initial police interrogations and preliminary hearings, through trials and sentencing, to the first appeals of convictions and sentences. Only when individuals do not face the possibility of imprisonment has the Court held that they have no right to a court-appointed attorney.

The *Miranda* Warnings

1. You have the right to remain silent and refuse to answer questions. Do you understand?
2. Anything you do say may be used against you in a court of law. Do you understand?
3. You have the right to consult an attorney before speaking to the police and to have an attorney present during any questioning now or in the future. Do you understand?
4. If you do not have an attorney available, you have the right to remain silent until you have had an opportunity to consult with one. Do you understand?
5. If you cannot afford an attorney, you have the right to have one appointed for you. Do you understand?
6. Now that I have advised you of your rights, are you willing to answer questions without an attorney present?

A California state criminal court jury found O. J. Simpson not guilty of the murders of his ex-wife and a friend, but a federal civil court jury later found him responsible for their deaths and awarded a huge financial settlement to the victims' families. Acquitted criminal defendants may not be tried again in the same court for the same crime, but they may be subject to prosecution or lawsuits in both state and federal systems.

The Right to a Fair Trial

When a criminal case goes to trial, a number of other safeguards come into play to ensure that the accused gets a fair trial. In addition to being guaranteed the assistance of counsel, accused individuals are guaranteed the *right to be informed of the nature and cause of the accusation* against them. It is the responsibility of the prosecutor—the attorney representing the government and the public—to bring the charges. Usually this is done through an indictment by a grand jury. A **grand jury** comprises twelve or more citizens who, first, hear the government's charges against a suspect on the basis of a preliminary presentation of the evidence and, then, may approve an **indictment**, a written statement of the charges or offenses for which the accused will stand trial. Not all states require grand jury indictments, however. About half permit the prosecution to present a **bill of information**, a document specifying the charges and evidence against an accused, to a judge at a preliminary hearing. The accused's attorney may then seek to exclude particular evidence from being used at the defendant's trial.

During the trial, the defendant has the *right to confront witnesses.* After the prosecution introduces witnesses and questioning designed to prove the defendant's guilt, the defendant (or the defense attorney) may question these witnesses to try to persuade the judge and jury that their testimony is unreliable. In addition, the defense may call its own witnesses to challenge the prosecution's case or establish the defendant's innocence; the prosecution in turn may question these witnesses. This confrontation—or "fight"—between advocates is the essence of an adversary system of justice.

The Sixth Amendment requires the federal government to give a person accused of a crime *a speedy and public trial before an impartial jury,* and the Seventh Amendment guarantees the right to a jury trial in civil cases involving controversies concerning amounts that exceed $20. These provisions for jury trials are based on the English common law principle that a trial by a jury of one's peers is the surest way to safeguard against arbitrary and vindictive prosecutions. They may temper the enforcement of unpopular and outdated laws, and they serve as a hedge against a corrupt or overzealous prosecutor and a biased or eccentric judge.

Moreover, criminal suspects may not be subject to **double jeopardy**—that is, after an acquittal they may not be retried for the same offense in the same court, whether state or federal. However, they may be tried in both state and federal courts for an offense that violates both state and federal laws.

The Prohibition against Cruel and Unusual Punishment

After trial and conviction, the accused is sentenced. In federal and most state courts, the laws provide for a range of terms of imprisonment for particular offenses, and judges and juries have some discretion in sentencing within that range. The federal government and some states, however, have systems of **determinate sentencing** by which a mandatory length of imprisonment is specified for each offense.

The only limitation on sentencing and punishment provided in the Constitution is the Eighth Amendment, which forbids the levying of "excessive fines" and the inflicting of "cruel and unusual punishment." According to the Supreme Court, the ban on cruel and unusual punishment limits sentencing in two ways. First, it prohibits barbaric forms of punishment, such as torture and unnecessary infliction of pain. Second, it forbids punishment that is grossly disproportionate to the crime committed.

In the past few decades, a major controversy has centered on whether the death penalty is a cruel and unusual punishment and hence unconstitutional. Justice William J. Brennan Jr. maintained that it is, arguing that whenever the state takes a life, it violates the fundamental principle of respect for human dignity embedded in the Constitution. Chief Justice Rehnquist countered that capital punishment was permissible when the Constitution was drafted and that state legislatures, not the courts, should decide whether the death penalty should be imposed.

In an important ruling in *Furman v. Georgia* (1972), a bitterly divided Court held that the death penalty is not cruel and unusual punishment but that there must be precise standards for imposing it in order to minimize the potential for injustice and ensure the equal protection of the law.[13] Without standards for guiding a jury's discretion in imposing death sentences, the Court said, some individuals convicted on the basis of similar facts and offenses could be executed, whereas others might not. *Furman* essentially invalidated most of the capital punishment laws in effect at that time. Within the next decade, however, thirty-six states redrafted their laws and reintroduced the death penalty.

When reviewing challenges to these new laws, the Court ruled that capital punishment may be imposed only in cases involving murder and not in those involving rape or other crimes unrelated to murder.[14] It also overturned laws requiring mandatory death sentences for certain crimes, including the killing of police officers. States are required to specify the circumstances (such as the age or role of the accused and the circumstances of a murder) that allow a judge and jury to sentence the accused to death rather than to life imprisonment. Moreover, juries must be allowed to consider all mitigating factors when deciding whether to impose the death penalty.

RIGHTS AND LIBERTIES VERSUS ECONOMIC INTERESTS

The Supreme Court assumed the role of "guardian of civil rights and liberties" after 1937. Before then, it was preoccupied with protecting economic and property interests. With the gradual nationalization of the Bill of Rights, the Court began devoting more attention to cases involving civil rights and liberties and the equal protection of the law, abandoning its role as a champion of economic interests. As a result, a **judicial double standard** evolved. Since 1937 the Court has upheld, under the Fourteenth Amendment's due process clause, virtually all legislation regulating economic interests. But it has given greater scrutiny to, and has often invalidated, legislation that impinges on individuals' civil rights and liberties.

In addition to enforcing the guarantees of the Bill of Rights, the Court has struck down numerous laws that infringe on rights and liberties not specifically mentioned in the Constitution. The Court's application of the *right of privacy* in overturning laws forbidding abortions remains perhaps the most controversial of these actions. But the right of privacy actually embraces a broader concept, "the right to be left alone."

Accordingly, the Court has sought to ensure various other constitutionally protected privacy interests, such as the right of *associational privacy*—that is, the right to form and join groups and organizations of one's own choosing.[15] The Court has also defended privacy interests in a person's home, papers, property, and effects as protected by the Fourth Amendment's guarantee against "unreasonable searches and seizures," as well as privacy interests under the Fifth Amendment's privilege against self-incrimination. It has not, however, extended the right of privacy to cover all matters of personal autonomy. In *Bowers v. Hardwick* (1986), for instance, it rejected the claims of a homosexual that laws prohibiting sodomy between consenting adults violate the constitutional right to privacy.[16]

The Court's exercise of its supervisory powers over civil rights and liberties is likely to remain controversial. Its post-1937 double standard of protecting civil rights while not scrutinizing laws that infringe on economic interests has been widely criticized. Still, the Bill of Rights contains explicit language that guarantees a variety of civil rights and liberties; only the Fifth Amendment mentions economic interests, in providing that a person may not be deprived of "life, liberty, or property" without the due process of law and that private property may not be taken "for public use without just compensation."

The Court's enforcement of the guarantees enumerated in the Bill of Rights is, in James Madison's words, "an auxiliary precaution" against the tyranny of the majority. Because the Court has the task of enforcing the guarantees of the Bill of Rights, it often thwarts the will of the majority and becomes the center of political controversy. Yet the Court accomplishes little unless its rulings have the support of other branches of government and, ultimately, command a national consensus. In Chief Justice Edward White's words, "The Court's power rests solely on the approval of a free people."[17]

CASE STUDY

The Battle over Abortion

When the Supreme Court handed down its watershed ruling on abortion, in *Roe v. Wade* (1973), the issue of abortion was elevated to the national political agenda. After the *Roe* decision, states could no longer outlaw all abortions or impose criminal penalties on doctors who perform medically safe abortions. The Court declared that during the first trimester (about three months) of a pregnancy, women have the right to decide whether to continue or terminate it. States may regulate abortions during the second trimester, but only to safeguard the health of women and the unborn. In the third trimester, the Court decided, states' interests in preserving the life of the unborn become compelling, and they may limit, even ban, abortions except when necessary to save a woman's life.

Until the midnineteenth century, most states had permitted abortions before the quickening, or first movement, of the fetus, and an abortion at a later stage of pregnancy was usually considered only a minor offense. After the Civil War, however, states gradually began to toughen their laws. By 1910, every state except Kentucky had made abortion a felony. After the sexual revolution of the 1960s, however, women's groups began pressuring states to liberalize their abortion laws. Prior to *Roe,* fourteen states had liberalized their laws to permit abortions when the woman's health was in danger, when fetal abnormality was likely, and when the woman was a victim of rape or incest. Four states had also repealed all criminal penalties for abortions done in early pregnancy. Thus, the legal status of abortion had returned to about where it was a century earlier.

Roe sparked a heated controversy and led to the formation of numerous new antiabortion groups, including the National Right to Life Committee—the largest and most influential antiabortion organization in the country. *Roe* also left numerous questions unanswered and afforded ample opportunities for noncompliance. Although most states adapted new laws to conform to *Roe,* many also sought to limit the availability of abortion by such means as withholding Medicaid funds for abortion and denying the use of public hospitals for the performance of abortion. Likewise, Congress passed several laws restricting the availability of abortion

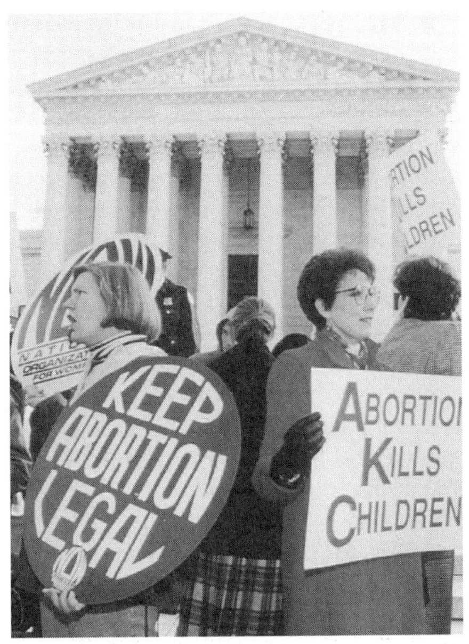

Friends and foes of legalized abortion often take their fight literally to the steps of the Supreme Court. Ever since 1973, when the Court ruled that most laws prohibiting abortion violated constitutional guarantees of substantive due process, opponents have tried through demonstrations, legislation, and other means to overturn the decision or at least narrow its scope.

and barring the use of federal funds for programs in which abortion is included as a method of family planning.

By the 1980s, the Court's ruling on abortion was an issue in presidential politics as well. Republican platforms endorsed by Ronald Reagan and George Bush supported a constitutional amendment "to restore protection of the right to life for unborn children." Moreover, the Reagan and Bush administrations appointed only judges opposed to abortion to the federal judiciary, including the Supreme Court. They also encouraged and joined in litigation that might undercut and ultimately lead to the reversal of *Roe.*

Interest groups on both sides of the controversy held rallies for their supporters, lobbied Congress and state legislatures, and participated in litigation challenging the enactment of more restrictive abortion laws. Some antiabortion groups, like Operation Rescue, picketed and demonstrated at abortion clinics. Even more extreme opponents bombed clinics and shot doctors and others involved in abortion. But most in the antiabortion movement remained peaceful and lawful in competing for influence with abortion rights groups.

As the Supreme Court's composition changed in the 1980s and early 1990s, speculation mounted that *Roe* might be overturned. Despite six Reagan and Bush appointments, however, a bare majority of the justices upheld the "essence of *Roe*" in *Planned Parenthood of Southeastern Pennsylvania v. Casey* (1992). In a surprising majority opinion, Justices Sandra Day O'Connor, Anthony Kennedy, and David Souter were joined in part by Justices Harry Blackmun and John Stevens. In their dissent, Chief Justice William Rehnquist and Justices Clarence Thomas, Antonin Scalia, and Byron White argued that *Roe* should be completely overturned.

Although not overruling *Roe,* the majority in *Casey* did uphold most of Pennsylvania's restrictions on access to abortions. Women must be informed by doctors about fetal development, give their consent (minors must obtain parental consent), and wait at least twenty-four hours after giving their consent before obtaining an abortion. The majority also imposed certain reporting and public disclosure requirements on doctors who perform abortions. However, it struck down as an "undue burden" a requirement that married women notify their husbands of their desire to obtain an abortion because that requirement potentially exposed women to violence and economic hardship. In sum, a bare majority reaffirmed *Roe* while rejecting much of the analysis on which it was based. States may not completely ban abortions, but the Court signaled that it would uphold restrictions that do not "unduly burden" women seeking abortions.

With the 1992 election of Democratic president Bill Clinton and his appointment to the Court of Justices Ruth Bader Ginsburg and Stephen Breyer, it became even more unlikely that *Roe* would be overruled. Still, interest groups for and against abortion remain active and the controversy is not likely to vanish from American politics, at least in the foreseeable future.

To get more information about this issue, or to become involved in the debate, contact one of the following groups:

National Abortion Rights Action
League Foundation
1101 14th Street, N.W.
Washington, D.C. 20005
(202) 973-3000

National Right to Life Committee
419 7th Street, N.W.
Washington, D.C. 20004
(202) 626-8800
http://www.nrlc.org/nrlc

Discussion Questions

1. What is the major political issue in this case?
2. Who are the principal protagonists, and what do they want?
3. How was the issue resolved?
4. Who won and who lost, and what impact has this case had on American politics?

SUMMARY

Civil rights and liberties are guaranteed in the Bill of Rights and other legislation. Yet they often become matters of intense political debate and conflict. When the

Supreme Court hands down controversial rulings on civil rights and liberties, it invites larger political struggles between competing interest groups. Ultimately, civil rights and liberties depend not only on the Court's rulings but also on the achievement of political consensus.

Civil rights are rights, such as the right to vote, that government may not categorically deny or infringe on because of an individual's race, gender, ethnicity, or various other characteristics. *Civil liberties* are freedoms that government must respect, such as the freedom to think, communicate, and behave in a manner that conforms to one's beliefs and values. Political struggles over civil rights and liberties stem from the competing demands for majority rule and for individual or minority rights.

During the struggle over ratification of the Constitution, the Federalists argued that it would protect individuals' rights and liberties because the powers of the national government were limited to the powers expressly granted to it. The Anti-Federalists believed that this protection was not sufficient. Their concerns resulted in the passage of the *Bill of Rights*, the first ten amendments to the Constitution. Initially, the guarantees contained in the Bill of Rights were viewed as limitations only on the federal government, not on the states. But because the state constitutions varied widely in their protection of individual rights and liberties, the Supreme Court eventually nationalized the Bill of Rights—that is, made its guarantees applicable to the states as well as to the federal government. The due process clause of the Fourteenth Amendment specifically limited the power of the states. Until the middle decades of the twentieth century, however, the Supreme Court did not use this clause to apply the guarantees of the Bill of Rights to the states. By the 1970s, all the major provisions of the Bill of Rights had been held to apply to the states.

Under the due process clause of the Fifth and Fourteenth Amendments, no person shall be deprived of "life, liberty, or property, without due process of law." There are two kinds of *due process*. *Procedural due process* is concerned with how law is carried out. *Substantive due process* is concerned with the subject matter of a law, regulation, or executive order.

Individuals enjoy a number of rights under the Fifth and Sixth Amendments, which bar the government from coercing confessions and forcing the disclosure of incriminating evidence *(self-incrimination)*. The most controversial aspect of the protection against self-incrimination is its use to limit police interrogations of criminal suspects. In 1966, the Supreme Court ruled that confessions cannot be introduced as evidence at trial unless the suspect had originally been informed of his or her constitutional rights by the police. This procedural safeguard is known as the *Miranda warnings*. Related Court rulings require that suspects be allowed to request the assistance of counsel and that criminal suspects who cannot afford counsel be assisted by court-appointed attorneys.

Since 1937, a *judicial double standard* has evolved by which the Supreme Court has upheld virtually all legislation regulating economic interests but has invalidated much legislation impinging on individuals' civil rights and liberties. In addition to enforcing the guarantees of the Bill of Rights, the Court has struck down laws that infringe on rights and liberties not specifically mentioned in the Constitution, such as the right of privacy.

KEY TERMS

civil rights
civil liberties
Bill of Rights
due process
procedural due process
substantive due process
self-incrimination
adversary (accusatory) system
inquisitorial system
plea bargaining
Miranda warnings
grand jury
indictment
bill of information
double jeopardy
determinate sentencing
judicial double standard

RESOURCES

READINGS

Abraham, Henry J., and Barbara Perry. *Freedom and the Court.* 5th ed. New York: Oxford University Press, 1994. A highly readable and enjoyable survey of the Supreme Court's rulings in the areas of civil liberties and civil rights.

Berns, Walter. *The Death Penalty: Cruel and Unusual Punishment.* New York: Basic Books, 1979. A provocative argument for the imposition of capital punishment, based on society's moral outrage at heinous crimes.

Black, Charles L. Jr. *Capital Punishment: The Inevitability of Caprice and Mistake.* New York: Norton, 1974 (rev. ed., 1982). A classic and provocative condemnation of the death penalty, based on the inevitability of injustice in its imposition.

Cortner, Richard C. *The Supreme Court and the Second Bill of Rights: The Fourteenth Amendment and the Nationalization of Civil Liberties.* Madison: University of Wisconsin Press, 1981. A detailed discussion of the cases in which the Supreme Court has applied the guarantees of the Bill of Rights to the states.

Craig, Barbara, and David M. O'Brien. *Abortion and American Politics.* Chatham, N.J.: Chatham House, 1993. A case study of the controversy over abortion and how it has played out in the courts, the states, Congress, the executive branch, public opinion polls, and the activities of pro-life and pro-choice interest groups.

Schwartz, Herman, ed. *The Burger Court Years.* New York: Viking, 1987. A fascinating collection of essays assessing the Burger Court years and their legacy for civil rights and liberties in a number of important areas.

ORGANIZATION

United States Civil Rights Commission, 1121 Vermont Avenue, N.W., Washington DC 20425; (202) 376-8312. A government agency authorized by Congress to study and recommend changes in laws bearing on civil rights and liberties.

5

Issues of Freedom and Equality

PREVIEW

- Freedom of religion: separation of church and state; freedom of religious exercise
- Freedom of speech and press: protected, unprotected, and symbolic speech; speech-plus-conduct; freedom of association
- The quest for equality: the extension of voting rights; redistricting and equal representation; ending racial discrimination; nonracial discrimination; affirmative action and reverse discrimination

Outside the 1984 Republican National Convention in Dallas, Gregory "Joey" Johnson and other members of the Revolutionary Communist Youth Brigade held a rally in protest of the Reagan administration's policies toward Latin America and its support of the contras in Nicaragua. After a march through the streets, Johnson set fire to an American flag while the crowd chanted, "America, the red, white, and blue, we spit on you." Police officers moved in and arrested Johnson.

During Johnson's trial, his attorney argued that like the Vietnam War protesters of the 1960s and 1970s, Johnson had burned the flag as a form of political expression, a form protected by the First Amendment guarantee of freedom of speech. Nevertheless, Johnson was convicted of violating a Texas law forbidding abuse and destruction of the American flag. He appealed to the Texas Court of Criminal Appeals, which reversed his conviction on First Amendment grounds. The ruling was then appealed to the Supreme Court by the state's attorney general in *Texas v. Johnson* (1989).

For protest as well as patriotism, the American flag provides one of the most potent political symbols in the United States. The Supreme Court has often been involved in controversies over the flag. One of the issues that has come before the Court is the authority of government to require participation in symbolic acts honoring the flag; another is the legitimacy of punishing those who abuse the flag as a way of expressing their political views. In 1943, for example, the Court struck down a law requiring children in public schools to salute the flag at the beginning of each schoolday. In this case, the Court upheld the claim of a Jehovah's Witness that the law denied his First Amendment rights by forcing his children to worship a graven image in violation of their religious beliefs. Subsequently, the Court overturned the conviction of a protester who had burned the flag, of an individual who had worn a small flag on the seat of his pants, and of a student who had hung a flag upside down with a peace symbol attached to it from the window of his dormitory room.

Despite the more conservative composition of the Court in the late 1980s, it again upheld the First Amendment protection of political expression in *Texas v. Johnson*. The Court struck down the Texas law as well as laws in forty-seven other states that made it a crime to desecrate the American flag. In the opinion announcing the majority's decision, Justice William J. Brennan wrote, "if there is a bedrock principle underlying the First Amendment, it is that the Government may not prohibit the expression of an idea simply because society finds the idea itself offensive or disagreeable."[1]

President George Bush immediately denounced the Court's ruling. "Flag burning is wrong—dead wrong," exclaimed Bush, continuing to sound a theme of his 1988 campaign.[2] In the aftermath of the Court's ruling, numerous congressional leaders in both parties joined the president in calling for a constitutional amendment to reverse the Court's judgment. Instead, Congress passed the Federal Flag Protection Act of 1989, which authorized the prosecution of individuals who desecrate the American flag. That law was immediately challenged, and was overturned by the Court in *United States v. Eichman* (1990).[3] Following the ruling, another attempt to overturn the Court's ruling by means of a constitutional amendment failed. The House of Representatives voted 254 to 177 in favor of the amendment—34 votes short of the required two-thirds needed to propose a constitutional amendment. The proposed amendment also fell 9 votes short of a two-thirds majority in the Senate.

Flag desecration quickens the pulse of American politics. Most Americans agree that it is wrong, and few actually burn the flag. But the ruling in *Texas v. Johnson* illustrates the difficult role the Supreme Court plays in safeguarding the rights of minorities and those who express unpopular views. It also illustrates the controversy and opposition the Court is likely to generate when it takes a position that supports those who speak or behave in a manner that the majority finds objectionable. Finally, it demonstrates that the Court cannot avoid political issues as it fulfills its government role as an interpreter of the Constitution.

Among the political freedoms that are essential to free government are those that James Madison called "the equal rights of conscience"—the freedom of religion and the freedoms of speech and press. Under the First Amendment, individuals are equally free to worship or not worship according to their own conscience and to express their opinions as they please. But these basic freedoms are not (and cannot be) absolute. Individual and societal interests often collide—for example, in disputes over prayer in public schools and the advocacy of unpopular ideas like revolution.

We focus in this chapter on the fundamental freedoms of religion and expression, as well as on the quest for greater equality. How has the Supreme Court defined the boundaries of those freedoms in response to major political controversies and shifts in public opinion? And what has been the Court's special role in applying the Fourteenth Amendment to eliminate racial and nonracial discrimination and to achieve equal voting rights and greater access to the political process for all people?

FREEDOM OF RELIGION

Many of the people who settled in the American colonies were escaping from religious persecution and state churches in England and on the European continent. Although some colonists professed support for religious freedom, the colonies

PRACTICING DEMOCRACY

Finding Supreme Court Decisions

Cases pending before the Supreme Court are analyzed in *Preview of United States Supreme Court Cases,* published regularly during each Court term by the Public Education Division of the American Bar Association. Each discussion summarizes the issues, facts, background, significance, arguments (for and against), and amicus briefs (for and against) for each case. *Preview* is an excellent source for clearly written descriptions of the cases awaiting decision; it can be found in law and research libraries.

Once a case has been decided, the justices issue their opinion. The final draft is given to the reporter of decisions—the Court official responsible for overseeing the publication of opinions. The reporter adds a headnote at the beginning summarizing the decision and adds a list at the end of how each justice voted. When a decision is announced, 275 copies (called "bench opinions") are made. They are distributed to the news media and other interested parties. One copy is immediately sent to the Government Printing Office, which prints several thousand copies (called "slip opinions") for immediate distribution, primarily to federal and state courts and agencies and to the public. Finally, the decision, along with any corrections from the slip-opinion version, is incorporated by the Government Printing Office into the formal record of Supreme Court decisions, *United States Reports.*

When a Supreme Court decision is referred to, or cited, in a formal text, a specific format is followed. Court citations always begin with the names of the parties to the case, starting with the appellant (the person or party bringing the case), followed by *v.* (meaning "versus," or "against"), followed by the name of the appellee (the person or party responding)—all usually underscored or italicized. Next comes the volume number of *United States Reports* in which the decision appears, followed by the page number on which the decision begins. Next, if a specific quotation from the decision is being cited, the word *at* and the page number of the quote appear. In parentheses following the page number is the year in which the decision was made. For example, the case *McCulloch v. Maryland,* 17 U.S. 316 at 317 (1819), is found in volume 17 of *United States Reports* starting on page 316, with the particular quote cited appearing on page 317; the decision was made in 1819.

Information about Supreme Court decisions can also be found in commercial publications such as *Supreme Court Reporter, United States Law Week,* and *United States Supreme Court Reports, Lawyer's Edition.* In addition, computerized legal databases such as LEXIS contain Supreme Court decisions. Sources like these are found in all law libraries and in many research libraries.

as a whole were far from tolerant of religious diversity. Most provided financial support to an established religion and required holders of public office to adhere to it. Catholics, Jews, and atheists, as well as Protestants belonging to nonestablished sects, were excluded from office and sometimes persecuted.

In the original Constitution, Article VI indicated that the founders deemed freedom of religion a fundamental political freedom. Article VI provides that "no religious test shall ever be required as a qualification to any office or public trust under the United States." With the adoption of the Bill of Rights, the First Amendment provided a broader and more explicit statement: "Congress shall make no law respecting an establishment of religion, or prohibiting the free exercise thereof." Note that the amendment provides a dual protection for religious freedom. First, the **establishment clause** expressly forbids the creation of a national religion; it separates church and state. Second, the **free exercise clause** guarantees that individuals may worship as they please.

These two provisions raise more vexing questions than they settle about the scope of religious freedom. Does the Amendment forbid the establishment of a national church but allow the states to sponsor particular religions? Does any state aid to religious schools constitute an establishment of religion, or do only certain forms of aid do so? Religious *beliefs* are protected, but how far may states go in prohibiting certain religious *practices,* such as the use of poisonous snakes in religious services? And what should be done when the provisions for separation of church and state and for free exercise of religion conflict?

Separation of Church and State

According to James Madison and Thomas Jefferson, the establishment clause embodies "a high wall of separation" between church and state. This was the view taken by the Supreme Court in *Everson v. Board of Education of Ewing Township* (1947), in which it ruled that the principle of separation applies to the states no less than to the national government. In this case, the Court held that a state must be *"neutral* in its relations with groups of religious believers and non-believers" but that religious organizations may benefit from government programs that have a clearly secular purpose. The Court approved New Jersey's providing free bus rides to schoolchildren regardless of whether they were attending public schools or private religious schools.

In 1995 the Supreme Court ruled that the Ku Klux Klan had to be allowed to erect a cross on the lawn of the statehouse in Columbus, Ohio, for four days during the Christmas season. But the story did not end there, as anti-Klan protesters knocked the cross over into the mud.

Critics of the wall-of-separation theory argue, however, that the Court has gone too far in its emphasis on strict neutrality, which they contend has actually led to state hostility toward religion. In their view, the government is forbidden not from aiding religion but only from showing *favoritism* toward any particular religion.[4] The controversy over religious establishment came to a head in 1948 in a case involving a "released-time" program for religious education, in which children in public schools could attend one-hour classes of Protestant, Catholic, or Jewish instruction during school hours and in the school building. The Court held that this program violated the wall-of-separation doctrine that organized religion in the public schools establishes religion over nonreligion. But in a second "released-time" case a few years later, the Court allowed children to have the option of attending classes in religious instruction held *off* the school grounds.

Despite the Court's decisions, and its distinction between religious activities held in public schools or away from them, many schools chose to interpret the ruling narrowly by arguing that it applies only to formal instruction in a religion. This argument was used to defend a practice that had become customary in many schools: requiring children to begin the schoolday with a prayer. In time, however, this practice was also challenged, in the landmark cases of *Engel v. Vitale* (1962) and *Abington School District v. Schempp* (1963).[5] In *Engel,* at issue was the New York State Board of Regents' recommendation for the daily recital in the public schools of a brief nonsectarian prayer: "Almighty God, we acknowledge our dependence upon Thee, and we beg Thy blessings upon us, our parents, our teachers, and our country." *Schempp* involved a challenge to the required recital of the Lord's Prayer in schools in Pennsylvania and Maryland. In both cases, the Court found that the "high wall of separation" had been breached by these religious activities.

In recent years, the Court has moved somewhat away from enforcement of a high wall of separation and has adopted instead an "accommodationist" or "preferentialist" approach to church–state relations. Chief Justices Warren Burger and William Rehnquist, among others, have championed this interpretation of the First Amendment, which holds that government may aid or extend benefits to religion as long as it does not prefer one religion over another. In advancing this view, the Court has evolved a three-part test. If a law or program is to avoid violating the establishment clause, (1) it must have a *secular legislative purpose,* (2) its *primary effect* must neither advance nor inhibit religion, and (3) it must *avoid excessive government entanglement with religion.*

Under the accommodationist approach, the Court must draw some very fine lines in determining what the establishment clause forbids and permits. In *Witters v. Washington Department of Services for the Blind* (1986), for example, it approved a state's giving higher-education grants to blind students even though one recipient, Larry Witters, chose to study at a Christian college. According to Justice Thurgood Marshall, the state's grant program did not violate the establishment clause because it had a secular purpose, and denying a grant to Witters would violate his right of free exercise under the First Amendment. Likewise, in *Rosenberger v. Rector and Visitors of the University of Virginia* (1995), the Court held that the university could not deny funds used for extracurricular student activities to a Christian student group that published a newspaper. Funding for the newspaper did not violate the establishment clause, Justice Anthony Kennedy held, and the university's denial of funding infringed on the Christian students' First Amendment rights of free speech and religious exercise.[6]

Freedom of Religious Exercise

The free exercise clause embodies the principle of government neutrality with respect to the religious convictions held by individuals and to the ways in which they act on those convictions. Religious *beliefs* may never be prescribed or coerced by the state; for example, people may not be required as a condition of government employment to take an oath that they believe in God. But in some circumstances, the government may regulate and even ban *actions* or *practices* that grow out of those beliefs, as well as require actions that offend beliefs.

Basing its decisions on the distinction between beliefs and practices, the Supreme Court has sought to ensure religious freedom by enforcing a **secular regulation rule**. This rule requires that all laws must have a reasonable secular purpose and that they must not discriminate on the basis of religion. But the rule also means that people may not claim exemption from reasonable government regulations on religious grounds because that would amount to religious favoritism and would violate the establishment rule. In *Reynolds v. United States* (1879), for instance, laws forbidding polygamy were upheld over the objections of Mormons, even though at the time the practice was part of Mormon religious beliefs.[7] Subsequently the Court ruled that states may require schoolchildren to have smallpox vaccinations, denying claims for exemption by Christian Scientists. The Court has also upheld laws restricting the sale of pamphlets and books in public buildings, dismissing objections by the Hare Krishna that such sales are part of their religious rituals.

In these cases, the Court has argued that the state, because of its obligation to protect the health and well-being of all citizens, may limit practices that might adversely affect society. The Court has avoided trying to define religion, however. The First Amendment does not protect only traditional or orthodox religions; rather, it guarantees the right of each person to define his or her own religious beliefs. And that is the greatest guarantee of religious freedom.

FREEDOM OF SPEECH AND PRESS

The freedom of speech and press is often called the "preferred freedom" because it is integral to the politics of a constitutional democracy. Campaigns, elections, and government accountability to the people would have little value without free and uncensored exchanges of opinion. In Justice William J. Brennan's words, the First Amendment registers "a profound national commitment to the principle that debate on public issues should be uninhibited, robust, and wide-open, and that it may well include vehement, caustic, and sometimes unpleasantly sharp attacks on government and public officials."[8]

In fact, however, the broad protection accorded freedom of speech and press today is a product of Supreme Court rulings in only the past forty years. The prevailing view of the First Amendment throughout the nineteenth century was that it incorporated freedoms inherited under English common law. In this view the Amendment required only that there be *no prior restraint* on publications—in other words, censorship *before* publication was prohibited. Although that remains an important guarantee, there was no protection against *subsequent punishment;* books could be banned and newspapers closed. Moreover, under English law, individuals could be prosecuted for **seditious libel**—that is, for defaming or criticizing the government or its officials.

James Madison, the author of the First Amendment, insisted that it embodied greater protection than the mere requirement of no prior restraint. But not until after World War I did the Supreme Court begin to articulate the constitutional principles and rules that ensure freedom of speech and press today.

Protected Speech

The First Amendment guarantee of free speech and press is not self-interpreting. The Court must give it meaning by developing tests or standards that define the scope of protected speech and press. The **clear and present danger test**, perhaps the Court's best-known test in this area, was formulated by Justice Oliver Wendell Holmes in *Schenck v. United States* (1919). In that case, the Court upheld the conviction of Charles T. Schenck under the Espionage Act of 1917 for urging resistance to the draft and distributing antidraft leaflets during World War I. Schenck's antidraft advocacy at a time of war constituted, in the Court's view, "a clear and present danger" to the country. In Justice Oliver Wendell Holmes's familiar words:

> The character of every act depends upon the circumstances in which it was done. . . . The most stringent protection of free speech would not protect a man in falsely shouting fire in a theater and causing a panic. . . . The question in every case is whether the words used are used in such circumstances and are of such a nature as to create a clear and present danger that they will bring about the substantive evils that Congress has a right to prevent. It is a question of proximity and degree.[9]

Despite the Court's ruling against Schenck, the clear and present danger test was formulated as a broad measure to protect individuals against prosecution for unpopular ideas. Majorities may be tempted to suppress minority views, but "the theory of our Constitution," Holmes contended, is that government has no power to say what is true or false. Each individual has the right to express his or her own beliefs. Subsequent cases have strengthened this decision. Today, speech that has **social redeeming value**, because it addresses matters of public concern, is fully protected. The government may neither exercise prior restraint on nor subsequently punish individuals for speech or publications that touch on political, scientific, literary, or artistic matters. Even speech that might threaten national security is protected. In 1971, at the height of the Vietnam War, the Court rejected the Nixon administration's attempt to prevent the *New York Times* and the *Washington Post* from publishing excerpts from the *Pentagon Papers,* a forty-seven volume documentary history of America's involvement in the war that had been classified as top secret. In this watershed ruling, the Court maintained that the government "carries a heavy burden" of justifying its attempts at censorship.[10]

Determining what speech has social redeeming value, however, is often politically controversial. The interests of communities in discouraging certain types of speech conflict with those of individuals who claim that the First Amendment protects their right of self-expression. In the late 1980s and the 1990s, for example, more than thirty states, as well as numerous localities, colleges, and universities, enacted "hate-crime" and "hate-speech" laws. St. Paul, Minnesota, made it a crime to place on public or private property a burning cross, swastika, or other symbol likely to arouse "anger, alarm, or resentment in others on the basis of race, color, creed, religion, or gender." But the constitutionality of that ordinance was challenged by Robert A. Vicktora, who along with several other white youths burned a cross after midnight on the lawn of the only African-American family in his neighborhood. In *R.A.V. v. City of St. Paul, Minnesota* (1992), the Supreme Court ruled that the ordinance violated the First Amendment because it punished certain kinds of speech on the basis of their content. Writing for the Court, Justice Antonin Scalia observed that "the First Amendment does not permit St. Paul to impose special prohibitions on those speakers who express views on disfavored subjects."[11]

In *Wisconsin v. Mitchell* (1993), however, the Court upheld laws that give defendants longer prison terms if they commit crimes that are determined to have been motivated by racial, religious, or gender bias. In that case, an African American who said "go get that white boy" and then assaulted the individual received a four-year instead of a two-year prison sentence under Wisconsin's prison-enhancement statute for so-called hate crimes.[12]

Unprotected Speech

The broad protection afforded the freedoms of speech and press is not absolute. Historically, there have been four categories of unprotected speech: obscenity, libel and slander, fighting words, and commercial speech. Yet defining standards for each category has proven extraordinarily vexing.

Obscenity For centuries, **obscenity** has been subject to government censorship, but defining what is obscene has been a persistent problem. Prior to *Roth v. United States* (1957), federal courts permitted state and local governments to ban even major literary works under an English common law rule set forth in 1868. Known as the *Hicklin* rule, it permitted the banning of books on the basis of isolated passages that might tend to "deprave and corrupt those whose minds are open to such immoral influences." This was a very broad standard and, as Justice Felix Frankfurter put it, would eliminate virtually all literature "except that only fit for children."

In the *Roth* decision, the Court held that obscenity is "not within the area of constitutionally protected speech," but it also rejected the *Hicklin* rule for determining what is obscene. Justice Brennan, in his opinion for the Court in *Roth*, announced a new test: "whether to the average person, applying contemporary community standards, the dominant theme of the material taken as a whole appeals to prurient interests."[13] Basically, the *Roth* test meant that only hard-core pornography was outside the scope of First Amendment protection. But the justices remained unable to agree on how to define obscenity. That problem led Justice Potter Stewart to confess that although he could not define it, "I know it when I see it."

The *Roth* ruling ignited considerable political controversy because it appeared to open the floodgates for purveyors of pornographic materials. Presidential commissions studied the problem, and state and local law enforcement agencies sought tougher standards. Under pressure to overturn *Roth,* the more conservative Court of the 1970s redefined the basis for determining whether material is obscene. In *Miller v. California* (1973), the Court stipulated three tests for judging allegedly obscene material: (1) whether the average person, applying local community standards, would find that a work, taken as a whole, appeals to a prurient interest; (2) whether the work depicts in a patently offensive way sexual conduct specifically defined as "obscene" in law; and (3) whether the work, taken as a whole, lacks "serious literary, artistic, political, or scientific value."[14]

Although many law enforcement agencies thought the *Miller* decision gave them broader power to prosecute purveyors of obscenity, the Court subsequently reaffirmed that only hard-core pornography lies outside the First Amendment's protection. The use or public display of "four-letter words" may not be banned.[15] However, students in public schools may be disciplined for the use of indecent as well as obscene language.[16] Furthermore, states may forbid the sale of pornographic materials to minors (those under the age of 18), completely ban pornography depicting minors,[17] and prohibit sexually explicit live entertainment and films in bars.[18] In *Reno v. American Civil Liberties Union* (1997), however, the Court struck down the Communications Decency Act of 1996 and held that the Internet is a unique medium that receives full protection under the First Amendment.

Libel and slander In legal terms, **libel** is false statement of fact about a person or defamation of his or her character by print or by visual portrayal on television. **Slander** is such a statement or defamation by speech. Both damage an individual's reputation by holding the person up to contempt, ridicule, and scorn, and both may be subject to civil lawsuits.

The landmark ruling in *New York Times Co. v. Sullivan* (1964) established the standards for determining when public officials and public figures may recover damages in cases of libel and slander. Such individuals must prove "actual malice"; they must show that statements about them were made with knowledge of their falsity or with reckless disregard of their truth or falsity. This standard makes it exceedingly difficult for public figures to win libel awards. By contrast, private individuals, those who neither hold public office nor have wide reputations and have not been thrust into the limelight, may recover damages on a lesser standard. They simply must show that the statements were false and that the publisher was negligent in its reporting.

The Court's standards make it relatively easy for private individuals to bring libel suits to trial, and when juries rule in their favor, they tend to make large awards. But in about two-thirds of the cases the awards are later reduced or overturned by appellate courts. Some critics contend that the Supreme Court has made it too difficult for public officials and public figures to win libel cases. Publishers, on the other hand, claim that the law of libel has a chilling effect on freedom of the press. They frequently face high court costs in defending their publications, and reporters and editors may be challenged to justify their editorial decisions.

Fighting words So-called **fighting words** have been held to be unprotected speech because they are likely to incite violence or lead to a breach of the peace and public order. In recent years, however, the Court has reversed every conviction for controversial or "fighting" words. So it is uncertain that any prosecution under this category of unprotected speech would be upheld.

Commercial speech Advertising or **commercial speech** was for many years deemed to be outside the scope of First Amendment protection, ostensibly because it does not bear on political matters. In addition, governments have important interests in regulating some kinds of advertising. The Court still upholds regulations aimed at ensuring truth in advertising, but it also recognizes that in some cases the public's interests in obtaining information may justify extending First Amendment protection to commercial speech. Accordingly, it has overturned state and local laws forbidding the advertising of the price of prescription drugs, routine legal services, the availability of abortion services, and some other kinds of professional services. In addition, the Court has ruled that corporations' advertisements, newsletters, and mailings are protected under the First Amendment.[19]

Symbolic Speech, Speech-plus-Conduct, and Freedom of Association

Besides extending First Amendment protection to virtually all forms of *pure speech,* the Supreme Court has ruled that certain other kinds of expression are protected by the First Amendment because they involve the communication of ideas. These include symbolic speech, speech-plus-conduct, and the freedom of association.

Conduct that involves the communication of political ideas, often as a protest, is known as **symbolic speech**. The Court has held, for example, that wearing a black armband in school,[20] displaying a red flag,[21] and turning the American flag into a peace symbol in order to protest the Vietnam War[22] are protected forms of expression under the First Amendment.

Speech-plus-conduct also involves the communication of ideas, but the ideas are conveyed through marching, picketing, and holding sit-ins on sidewalks and streets and in other public areas. Protection for these kinds of expression is rooted not only in the First Amendment's guarantee of free speech but also in its provision for freedom of association and "the right of the people peaceably to assemble, and to petition the government for a redress of grievances."

In public places such as streets and parks, individuals have the right to engage in political activities subject only to *reasonable time, place,* and *manner* restrictions. Thus cities may limit the hours that parks may be used or the times that sound trucks may travel the city streets. In 1989, for example, the Court upheld a New York City ordinance requiring the use of the city's sound system and city engineer for all concerts held in Central Park. Time, place, and manner restrictions must apply equally and not discriminate against particular kinds of political expression.

The protection accorded to the **freedom of association** is broader than that accorded to the freedom to organize rallies and peaceful protests. It also includes the right to join political parties and religious, economic, and other kinds of organizations. As a result, the disclosure of an organization's membership list cannot be compelled by election officials[23] or by legislative investigating committees.[24] Nor may individuals be dismissed from employment because of their political associations[25] or be required to disclose their associations in order to gain admission to the bar.[26]

However, the Court has ruled that the freedom of association may be limited in certain ways when there are overriding societal interests in doing so. For example, it has upheld the Hatch Act of 1940, which forbids federal employees from actively campaigning in elections and assuming leadership positions in political parties.[27] Such federal and state laws have been found to be a reasonable way of ensuring a neutral civil service.

By protecting the rights of individuals and minorities to express their political views through marches, pickets, and other kinds of demonstrations, the Court has challenged the views of the majority and invited more political controversy. Yet in defending the right to express unpopular views, it ensures the freedom of public discussion and debate that is essential to democratic self-governance and a free society.

THE QUEST FOR EQUALITY

The concept of equality and equal freedoms for all citizens is mentioned in neither the Constitution nor the Bill of Rights. Nevertheless, it is the bedrock of a political system based on the consent of the governed. The Declaration of Independence was emphatic about equality of political freedoms: "We hold these truths to be self-evident: That all men are created equal; that they are endowed by their Creator with certain unalienable Rights." But not until 1868, with the ratification of the Fourteenth Amendment, did the Constitution expressly provide that no person shall be deprived of "the equal protection of the laws." Achieving that equality in practice has proven to be extraordinarily difficult. There remains no greater struggle in American politics than the struggle to guarantee all citizens their basic civil rights without discrimination due to their race, religion, national origin, or sex. That struggle reflects the impact of social movements and the increasing diversity of American society on the politics of government.

The Extension of Voting Rights

The narrow victory of General Ulysses S. Grant in the 1868 presidential election convinced the Republican party that to maintain its control of Congress it needed the votes of African Americans. So it proposed the Fifteenth Amendment (ratified

In 1960 a group of African American college students staged a sit-down protest after they were refused service at a lunch counter reserved for white customers at a Woolworth's store in Greensboro, North Carolina. These three stayed seated throughout the day. Over the next few years civil rights activists often used such protests, and the litigation they sparked, to desegregate public accommodations like restaurants and buses.

in 1870), which forbade the abridgment of any citizen's right to vote "on account of race, color, or previous condition of servitude."

Although the amendment did not mention discrimination on the basis of gender, some women hoped that they might win **suffrage**, or the right to vote, in federal elections by claiming that this right was guaranteed by the Fourteenth Amendment's clause forbidding the abridgment of any citizen's "privileges and immunities." Susan B. Anthony gave this as her defense when she was prosecuted for casting a ballot in a federal election in 1872, but the argument was rejected by a federal court. In 1875, the Supreme Court dashed the hopes of a woman who sought to vote in a Missouri election when it held that "the Constitution of the United States does not confer the right of suffrage upon anyone."[28] By 1913, only nine states allowed women to vote.

Political pressure in support of women's suffrage mounted during World War I as large numbers of women entered the work force and contributed to the war effort. In 1918, President Woodrow Wilson endorsed women's suffrage, and during the next year Congress submitted to the states a constitutional amendment granting women the right to vote. The Nineteenth Amendment was ratified in 1920.

Although African Americans were guaranteed the right to vote by the Fourteenth and Fifteenth Amendments and many were elected to office in the South during Reconstruction, white-dominated state governments and party organizations soon erected barriers such as poll taxes and literacy tests. Poll taxes required a payment in order to vote and thereby discouraged the poor from voting. Likewise, literacy tests were used in the South to discourage African Americans from voting by requiring them to first answer questions—often obscure questions—about American law and politics. By the turn of the century, African Americans were effectively disenfranchised.

In 1937, the Supreme Court ruled that poll taxes did not violate the Fourteenth and Fifteenth Amendments, a decision that sparked a campaign to get the states and Congress to abolish poll taxes. The campaign had considerable success in the states; by 1960, only Alabama, Arkansas, Mississippi, Texas, and Virginia retained poll taxes. Congress finally banned poll taxes in federal elections with the Twenty-Fourth Amendment, ratified in 1964, and two years later the Court decided that the Fourteenth Amendment's equal protection clause forbids poll taxes in the state elections.

Among the goals of the civil rights movement of the 1950s and 1960s was the elimination of all barriers to voting rights for African Americans. Rev. Martin Luther King Jr. launched voter registration drives in the South, where there was widespread and often violent resistance. Congress passed civil rights acts in 1957 and 1960, but they proved ineffective in ending the discriminatory practices that discouraged African Americans from voting. Not until the Voting Rights Act of 1965 was suffrage for African Americans effectively guaranteed.

The Voting Rights Act bans the use of literacy tests or tests for educational achievement and understanding, as well as requirements that voters prove "good moral character" or present certificates verifying their qualifications, in any state or locality where less than 50 percent of the citizens of voting age were registered on November 1, 1964, or voted in an election that November. Moreover, it authorizes the U.S. Civil Service Commission to appoint federal examiners to register voters where the attorney general deems it necessary for the enforcement of the Fifteenth Amendment.

Because it limits the powers of the states to determine the qualifications for voting, the Voting Rights Act has remained controversial. However, the Supreme Court affirmed its constitutionality in 1966, and the act has been extended several times since then. It was last extended by Congress in 1982 and is not scheduled to lapse until 2007.

Redistricting and Equal Representation

Besides striking down poll taxes and other barriers to exercising voting rights, the Supreme Court has become involved in issues of **redistricting**, that is, redrawing the boundaries of legislative districts. Traditionally, the courts avoided districting issues on the grounds that they involve "political questions," which must be resolved by legislative bodies. However, in a landmark decision (*Baker v. Carr,* 1962)[29] the Court ruled that such controversies contain issues of fairness and justice that open them to judicial review as well.

The issues of fairness and justice to which the Court referred pertain to the relationship between population and representation. In a democracy all voters must be equal; one person's vote cannot count for more than another's. Yet representation is decidedly unequal when members of the House of Representatives or members of state legislatures represent districts with different numbers of residents, a condition that was prevalent in many states after the Civil War. In most cases, rural districts enjoyed representation equal to or even greater than urban areas, even though their populations were smaller. For example, the Court's ruling in *Baker v. Carr* involved a challenge to the districting of Tennessee's state legislature. Despite growing urbanization and population changes over a sixty-year period, Tennessee had not changed the boundaries of its legislative districts since 1901. As a result, the population ratio between urban and rural districts in the state was more than 19 to 1.

In *Baker v. Carr,* the Court's majority opinion was limited to the jurisdictional question: was districting an issue that courts could decide? The Court's answer was yes. In two subsequent cases in the 1960s, the Court ruled on the merits of this issue, applying the principle of **one person, one vote** to congressional districts and to state legislative districts. This principle requires that the weight of a vote cast in each election district (and usually the total population in each district) must be roughly equal. In the 1970s and 1980s, the Court extended the rule to virtually all local elections as well.

The Court's rulings meant that district lines for congressional, state, and local elections must be redrawn every ten years, after the national census, to ensure equal representation. This redistricting requirement has made the American electoral process at all levels more open, accessible, and democratic. It has also made redistricting a partisan issue that reemerges every ten years.

When congressional district lines were redrawn following the 1990 census, racial and ethnic issues also came to the fore. Citing a provision of the 1982 Voting Rights Act and several Supreme Court decisions, the Justice Departments of both the Bush and the Clinton administrations pressed state legislatures to create more so-called minority–majority voting districts, in which a majority of the voters were African Americans or Hispanics. As a result, the number of minorities elected to the House of Representatives more than doubled. Because African Americans and Hispanics tend to vote heavily Democratic, however, their heavy concentration in certain districts made other, "whiter" districts more likely to elect Republicans and thus provided an overall Republican advantage. White Democrats in some southern states challenged the constitutionality of such "racial gerrymandering," and in *Miller v. Johnson* (1995) a bare majority of the Court agreed that racial gerrymandering violates the Fourteenth Amendment's equal protection clause and ruled that race may not be the sole or primary factor in congressional redistricting.[30]

Ending Racial Discrimination

Despite the Fourteenth and Fifteenth Amendments (as well as the Thirteenth, which prohibited slavery), new barriers to racial equality emerged in the late nineteenth century in the form of so-called **Jim Crow laws**, which separated the races in public transportation and accommodations and discriminated against African Americans in other ways. Moreover, segregation persisted in housing, education, and employment and was permitted by the Supreme Court. In 1883, the Court struck down as unconstitutional the Civil Rights Act of 1875, which had forbidden discrimination in public accommodations such as hotels, theaters, and railroad carriages. According to the Court, Congress had exceeded its power under the Fourteenth Amendment by prohibiting *private* individuals from discriminating; the amendment, in the Court's view, forbade only *state* discrimination.

Subsequently, in the case of *Plessy v. Ferguson* (1896), the Court affirmed the **separate but equal doctrine** by upholding Louisiana's law requiring separate but equal facilities for the races in railroad cars.[31] Although it struck down laws specifically denying or limiting the right of nonwhites to acquire property, it upheld until 1948 the enforcement of **restrictive covenants**, that is, contracts in which property owners agree not to sell or lease their property to members of certain racial or religious groups.

Beginning in the 1930s, individuals and organizations such as the National Association for the Advancement of Colored People (NAACP) began filing lawsuits to force the end of racial segregation in housing, education, and employment. Like the other branches of government, the Court was slow to respond to these demands. Not until 1954 did it step firmly into the racial discrimination controversy with its landmark decision in *Brown v. Board of Education of Topeka* (1954).[32] In that case, the Court finally rejected the separate but equal doctrine, holding that racially segregated public schools violated the equal protection clause of the Fourteenth Amendment.

Even in *Brown,* the Court was reluctant to press too hard too quickly for desegregation; the justices knew how much political controversy their ruling would stir. It was another year before the Court handed down its remedial decree stating that school boards must proceed with "all deliberate speed to desegregate public schools at the earliest practical date."[33] The decree of "all deliberate speed" was a compromise between requiring precise deadlines for school desegregation and simply allowing states and localities to comply with *Brown*'s mandate at their own discretion.

In fact, the *Brown* decision and its enforcement decree did meet with massive resistance, in the form of widespread evasion, occasional violence, and even a year-long shutdown of an entire school system. The vagueness of the phrase "with all deliberate speed" actually served to justify noncompliance; progress toward achieving integrated schools was deliberately slow and uneven.

By the late 1960s, the Supreme Court also made it clear that it would no longer abide delays in complying with *Brown*'s mandate. In proclaiming that "continued operation of racially segregated schools under the standard of 'all deliberate speed' was no longer permissible," the Court stated that school districts had to "terminate immediately dual school systems based on race and operate only unitary school systems."[34]

During the 1970s, 1980s, and early 1990s, the issue of bringing an end to segregated schools was replaced by the issue of achieving integrated schools. This was a particularly troublesome question in the North and West, where schools were segregated as a result of housing patterns **(de facto segregation)**, not because of laws and official policies **(de jure segregation)**. One device for overcoming de facto segregation is busing children to schools they would not ordinarily attend. Although busing can be a means of achieving integrated schools, it violates the tradition of neighborhood schools, creates lengthy travel for some students, and sometimes increases racial tensions within schools. The Court's position on busing is clear: it has upheld the power of federal judges to order busing *within* school districts but not *between* them as a remedy for segregated schools. Given the racial composition of many school districts, this position has not enabled proponents of integrated public schools to achieve their goal. However, it may have contributed to the movement of white families from the cities to suburban neighborhoods to escape busing.

More than forty years after the landmark ruling in *Brown v. Board of Education*, approximately five hundred school desegregation cases remain in the lower federal courts around the country. Most involve the issue of whether school systems have eliminated vestiges of past discrimination. The decisions being made by the Court in the 1990s recognize both the importance of equal opportunities in education and the limitations of what courts and local school boards can do in areas that remain or are becoming racially segregated due to housing patterns and population changes.

Nonracial Discrimination

All legislation and government policy, by its very nature, discriminates because it confers burdens or benefits on some groups and not on others. For example, most states require that individuals be at least 16 years old and pass a driving test before they can operate a motor vehicle. From the standpoint of civil rights, the question is whether laws and regulations are reasonable and do not unfairly discriminate against particular groups.

When considering challenges to law and policy under the Fourteenth Amendment's equal protection clause, therefore, the Supreme Court must decide whether the discrimination is invidious and unconstitutional. During the mid 1950s and the 1960s, the Court evolved a two-tier approach to applying the equal protection clause. When reviewing challenges to legislation that deals solely with economic matters, it uses a **minimal scrutiny test**, meaning that it simply looks to see whether the legislation in question has a rational basis. Using this test, the Court has not struck down any federal or state economic legislation under the equal protection clause since 1937.

When legislation is based on a "suspect classification" or denies individuals their "fundamental rights," the Court uses a **strict scrutiny test** for determining its constitutionality. The strict scrutiny test puts the burden of proof on the state, which must demonstrate a "compelling interest" to justify the law or policy in question. Suspect classifications include race, nationality, and alien status. Because those characteristics are immutable—individuals cannot choose or

Five-year cadet Kim Messer (center) joins the ranks at The Citadel, a state military college in Charleston, South Carolina, in 1996. The school began admitting women after the Supreme Court ruled that the all-male admissions policy of its Virginia counterpart, the Virginia Military Institute, violated the Constitution.

change their race or nationality—laws that impose burdens or deny benefits on the basis of them invariably fail to pass the Court's strict scrutiny test.

In the past two decades, the Court has confronted an increasingly broad range of claims of nonracial discrimination, including claims of discrimination based on gender, age, and wealth. In response to these new challenges, the Court has created a third, intermediate test—the **strict rationality test**, also known as the **exacting scrutiny test**. It has done so primarily because a majority of the justices have refused to consider gender a "suspect classification" under the Fourteenth Amendment, even though it is an immutable characteristic.

Under the strict rationality test, legislation must in a reasonable way further some legitimate government policy. Such a standard is necessarily more subjective or flexible than strict scrutiny. For example, gender-based discrimination has been approved by the Court in cases challenging an all-male military draft,[35] the enforcement of statutory rape laws against males but not females,[36] the sale of 3.2 percent beer to males (but not females) under the age of 21,[37] the assignment of female guards in prisons,[38] and the denial of health benefits to women who miss work because of pregnancy leaves.[39] On the other hand, the Court has struck down laws discriminating against women in cases involving the denial of benefits for dependents of female (but not male) military personnel,[40] and the denial of seniority status to women who take pregnancy leaves from work.[41] Moreover, in 1986, the Court unanimously agreed that female employees could sue employers for sexual harassment under the Civil Rights Act.[42]

Affirmative Action and Reverse Discrimination

Affirmative action in education and employment has been especially controversial. Designed to help women and members of minority groups advance in areas in which they have historically been discriminated against (see Figure 5-1), **affirmative action** originated with Lyndon Johnson's Democratic administration in 1964–1965. Affirmative action programs give special consideration to women and minorities in, for example, admission to college and promotion in

Percentage of people living in poverty

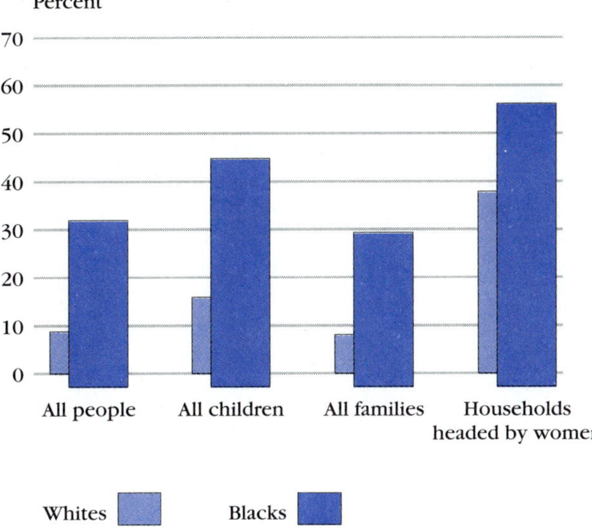

Black workers' earnings

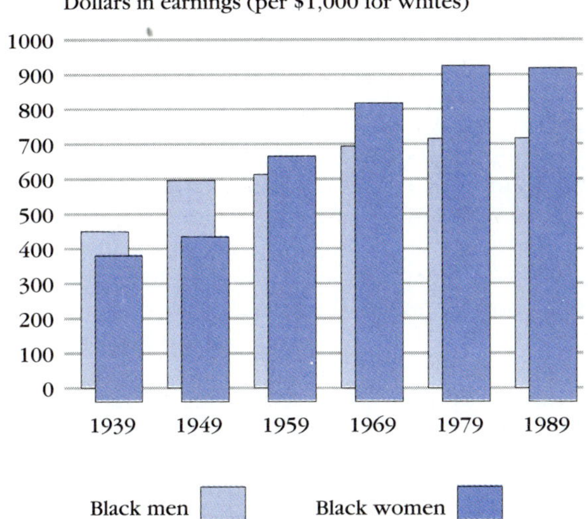

FIGURE 5-1
Racial and Gender Differences in Economic Status

SOURCE: Andrew Hacker, *Two Nations: Black and White, Separate, Hostile, Unequal* (New York: Scribner's, 1992), 100, 101, 105.

the workplace. Consequently, these programs have been attacked for practicing **reverse discrimination**—that is, for penalizing whites and males in violation of their rights under the Fourteenth Amendment's equal protection clause. Critics argue that what affirmative action does is move beyond the principle of **equality of opportunity** in education and employment in an effort to ensure **equality of result**.

When confronted with challenges to affirmative action programs, the Supreme Court initially was as sharply divided as the rest of the country. One of the most important cases was *Regents of the University of California v. Bakke* (1978).[43] Alan Bakke, a white who had been denied admission to the medical school at the University of California at Davis, contended that his application had been rejected because the school set aside 16 out of 100 admissions for African Americans, Chicanos, Asians, and Native Americans—groups that had previously been underrepresented in the student body. He claimed that this policy violated his rights under the Civil Rights Act and the Fourteenth Amendment, because some of the minority students admitted under the school's affirmative action program had grade-point averages and test scores lower than his.

The Court agreed in part with Bakke. The majority opinion stated that *quota systems* (programs that set aside a precise number of openings for minorities) like the one at the University of California are unconstitutional. At the same time, however, the Court upheld the constitutionality of affirmative action programs that consider race as one among many factors in student admissions.

Affirmative action programs in employment have proven even more divisive. In 1979, the Court ruled that employers and labor unions may agree to adopt private affirmative action programs despite the objections of white members of the union. In the following year, it upheld Congress's power to set aside 10 percent of federal funds for public works projects to be used to pay for supplies and services provided by minority-owned businesses. The Court's decisions offered little clear guidance for policy makers, however, since in every case the justices split 5 to 4 or 6 to 3, with those in the majority often disagreeing on why they should uphold or strike down particular programs. Still, in three out of four rulings during the 1980s, the Court upheld the constitutionality of affirmative action programs, basing its decisions on its exacting scrutiny test. Programs aimed at promoting African Americans and other minorities and women over white employees with more seniority have proven particularly troublesome. The Court was unable to establish a principle for judging the constitutionality of such programs. From 1984 to 1987, it upheld some programs and struck down others.

By 1989, however, changes in the composition of the Court resulted in a conservative majority inclined to oppose most affirmative action programs. In *City of Richmond v. J. A. Croson* (1989), the Court struck down a program in Richmond, Virginia, that required nonminority building contractors to subcontract 30 percent of all city-awarded projects to minority-owned businesses.[44] This set-aside quota was as much a way to help black construction companies penetrate the local building industry as it was a remedy for past discrimination. Half of Richmond's population was black, but minority-owned firms had won less than 0.6 percent of the $25 million awarded in city contracts in the preceding five years.

In announcing the Court's ruling, Justice Sandra Day O'Connor noted that Richmond's affirmative action program was not narrowly targeted to the city's

African Americans, because minority-owned businesses from all over the country were eligible to bid on projects. The ruling held that state and local governments may no longer adopt affirmative action programs unless they are designed specifically as remedies for past discrimination in denying opportunities for African Americans and other minorities.

J. A. Croson was a major break with prior rulings because the Court abandoned its use of the exacting scrutiny test for upholding affirmative action programs and signaled that henceforth the tougher strict scrutiny test would be employed. Under this standard, states and localities must have a "compelling interest" in adopting any program that discriminates on the basis of race, regardless of whether that discrimination is for the purpose of conferring benefits, rather than burdens, on racial minorities and women. This and other decisions have thrown into question the constitutionality of hundreds of federal, state, and local affirmative action programs and have forced governments to redraft their laws in anticipation of further challenges.

As the controversy over affirmative action programs shows, political struggles over civil rights and liberties usually involve more than a conflict between an individual and the state. They often reflect deeper divisions in society and competing interests in how to balance liberty and equality that must be reconciled over time.

CASE STUDY

Affirmative Action versus Reverse Discrimination

During the 1996 election campaign, leading Republican politicians declared their opposition to affirmative action programs, which give preference to women or minorities in college admissions or in hiring and promotions in business. They portrayed all such programs as "reverse discrimination," contending that they necessarily and unfairly elevate women and minorities above more-qualified white males. Although this stance did not seem to help Republican presidential candidate Bob Dole, in the late 1990s, affirmative action remains a divisive "wedge issue" in American politics. This is so even though the Supreme Court has outlawed quotas in affirmative action programs. Any such program is extremely difficult to defend in court unless it is a narrowly tailored remedy for past discrimination.

Historically, affirmative action programs were developed with the support of both Democratic and Republican presidents. Following the enactment of the Civil Rights Act of 1964, which prohibits discrimination in employment and education, Democratic president Lyndon B. Johnson signed a 1965 executive order requiring federal contractors to "take affirmative action to ensure that applicants are employed, and that employees are treated during employment, without regard to race, color, religion, sex, or national origin." In 1966, a federal court ordered the first race-conscious hiring program, to recruit African Americans into a New Orleans union that had for decades excluded minorities. Under Republican president Richard M. Nixon, then, the Department of Labor adopted the so-called Philadelphia plan requiring federal contractors to set goals and timetables to end underrepresentation of women and minorities in their work force.

These early programs were expanded by Republican president Gerald R. Ford and Democratic president Jimmy Carter. More than 160 federal programs, involving tens of billions of dollars in government contracts, ultimately affected a quarter of all United States businesses. Similar programs were also enacted in all fifty states and by thousands of local governments. In the 1970s, the University of California led other colleges in adopting an affirmative action admissions program.

Political opposition to affirmative action programs also began in the 1970s, however, and grew throughout the 1980s and early 1990s. During the administrations of Republican presidents Ronald Reagan and George Bush, the Department of Justice opposed affirmative action and rather successfully urged lower courts and the Supreme Court to limit those programs in cases like *City of Richmond v. J. A. Croson.* In 1995, California's Republican governor Pete Wilson spearheaded a bitterly fought campaign that ended the University of California's historic program. As a result, the enrollment of African Americans at the university is projected to drop as much as 50 percent, and Hispanic enrollment more than 10 percent.

In the face of Republican attempts to capitalize on the issue in the 1996 presidential election, President Bill Clinton undertook a review of all federal affirmative action programs. After a five-month study, he announced a "mend it, don't end it" policy and issued an executive order directing all departments to review their programs in light of four tests. "Any program must be eliminated or reformed," according to his executive order, if it: creates a quota, creates preferences for unqualified individuals, creates reverse discrimination, or continues after its equal opportunity purposes have been achieved. In addition, Clinton's Department of Justice issued guidelines for agencies to reexamine affirmative action programs in light of the Supreme Court's 1995 ruling in *Adarand Constructors, Inc. v. Pena,* requiring such programs to be narrowly tailored to remedy past discrimination.

The controversy is not likely to go away in the near future. Supporters of affirmative action argue that past discrimination against women and minorities persists and that there remains a need for diversity in education and employment. They point to studies showing that in the early 1990s no more than 3 percent of the employment discrimination cases brought in federal courts were for reverse discrimination; the vast majority were for discrimination against women and minorities. African Americans remain more than twice as likely as whites to be unemployed, and those with jobs earn, on average, more than 20 percent less than whites. And in spite of affirmative action programs in construction unions, for instance, the percentage of minorities there has declined over the last decade. For these reasons, even some Republican governors and prominent black Republicans have said that they favor continuing affirmative action programs.

The issue is complex and further complicated by how pollsters pose questions about affirmative action. An overwhelming majority of the public opposes giving "preferences to unqualified individuals." At the same time, a majority favors programs that "fight discrimination," "promote equal opportunity," and "treat everyone fairly." A smaller percentage supports giving "special treatment" to women and minorities, but quotas are overwhelmingly opposed. In short, as Alexis de Tocqueville observed in the nineteenth century, Americans remain very individualistic: they both want individuals to be treated fairly and respect individual merit.

Discussion Questions

1. What is the major political issue in this case?
2. Who are the principal protagonists, and what do they want?
3. How has the issue been addressed?
4. Who won and who lost, and what impact has this case had for American politics?
5. What directions might the debate over this issue take in the future? Why?

SUMMARY

Individual freedom and the quest for equality often collide and become the focus of political struggles and competing political movements, which in turn put pressure on government. The Supreme Court plays an important role in responding to political controversies over issues of freedom and equality. In drawing lines that define those freedoms, the Court has historically sought to ensure that those freedoms are enjoyed equally by all citizens.

The First Amendment provides a dual protection for religious freedom. The *establishment clause* forbids the creation of a national religion, and the *free exercise clause* guarantees that individuals may worship as they please.

The First Amendment also guarantees freedom of speech and press. Before 1925, however, the First Amendment was viewed as requiring only that there be no prior restraint on publications; individuals had no protection against subsequent punishment for what they said or wrote. But, the Supreme Court held that speech that touches on political matters or has *social redeeming value* because it addresses matters of public concern is fully protected.

Historically, there have been four categories of unprotected speech: obscenity, libel and slander, fighting words, and commercial speech. In recent years, however, the Court has struck down many of the cases based on the latter two categories.

With the ratification of the Fourteenth Amendment in 1868, the Constitution expressly provided that no person shall be deprived of "the equal protection of the laws." However, it has been extremely difficult to achieve that equality in practice. When considering issues of discrimination, the Court uses a *minimal scrutiny test* to review legislation dealing with economic matters, but it uses a *strict scrutiny test* to review matters involving individuals' fundamental rights. When considering claims of nonracial discrimination, it uses a *strict rationality,* or *exacting scrutiny, test*. Under this test, legislation that discriminates on the basis of gender, age, or wealth is unconstitutional unless it furthers some legitimate government policy in a reasonable way.

Affirmative action is a policy designed to help women and minority groups advance in areas in which they have historically been discriminated against. The goal of affirmative action programs is to move beyond *equality of opportunity* to *equality of result*. Critics claim that such programs are a form of *reverse discrimination*. During the 1980s, the Supreme Court tended to uphold the constitutionality of affirmative action programs. In the early 1990s, however, it handed down several decisions that made it harder for women and minorities to prove discrimination in the work place and easier for white males to attack affirmative action programs in the courts.

KEY TERMS

establishment clause
free exercise clause
secular regulation rule
seditious libel
clear and present danger test
social redeeming value
obscenity
libel
slander
fighting words
commercial speech
symbolic speech
speech-plus-conduct
freedom of association
suffrage
redistricting
one person, one vote
Jim Crow laws
separate but equal doctrine
restrictive covenants
de facto segregation
de jure segregation
minimal scrutiny test
strict scrutiny test
strict rationality (exacting scrutiny) test
affirmative action
reverse discrimination
equality of opportunity
equality of result

RESOURCES

READINGS

Edsall, Thomas, and Mary Edsall. *Chain Reaction: The Impact of Race, Rights, and Taxes on American Politics*. New York: Norton, 1992. A provocative study of how the civil rights era has affected American politics in the 1990s.

Graham, Hugh Davis. *The Civil Rights Era: Origins and Development of National Policy, 1960–1972*. New York: Oxford University Press, 1992. A fine historical analysis of the civil rights movement and its impact on American politics.

Levy, Leonard W. *Emergence of the Free Press*. New York: Oxford University Press, 1985. A rich account of freedom of speech and press during the founding period.

O'Brien, David M. *Constitutional Law and Politics: Civil Rights and Civil Liberties*. 3d ed. New York: Norton, 1997. A comprehensive collection of the Supreme Court's most important rulings on civil rights and liberties. Also contains introductory essays on the history and politics of the Court's interpretive decisions regarding the Bill of Rights and the Fourteenth Amendment.

ORGANIZATION

U.S. Civil Rights Commission, 1121 Vermont Avenue, N.W., Washington DC 20425; (202) 376-8312. A government agency authorized by Congress to study and recommend changes in laws bearing on civil rights and liberties.

6

Political Socialization, Participation, and Public Opinion

PREVIEW

- Political socialization: changes over the life cycle; agents of political socialization
- Political participation: ways of participating; who participates; political participation and public policy
- Public opinion: discovering public opinion; characteristics of public knowledge and opinion; political ideologies; democratic beliefs; public opinion and governance

Bill Clinton's first brush with national politics came in July 1963, when he was an Arkansas delegate to Boys Nation, the annual civics celebration for high school juniors sponsored by the American Legion. The high point of the week was a trip to the White House, where President John F. Kennedy would briefly address the delegates. David Maraniss, a reporter and Clinton biographer, describes that day:

> It got quiet inside the Boys Nation buses as they pulled through the White House gate from the South. . . . Bill Clinton was at the front of the first bus. He wanted a prime spot in the Rose Garden. . . . [After some brief remarks, Kennedy moved to the audience.] . . . As the president walked toward them, the boys surged forward. Clinton was the first to shake his hand. The sixteen-year-old from Hot Springs lost his breath, his face contorted in what he would later call "my arthritis of the face." The Boys Nation photographer was nearby, snapping away.
>
> The next morning, their last in Washington, they returned from a day at the FBI and the Capitol to find a bulletin board . . . cluttered with photographs taken during the week by a Legion photographer. Each picture was numbered so that the boys could order copies. They mobbed the board, writing down their selections. Along with an overwhelming feeling that in Washington he had seen the career he longed for, Bill Clinton brought home a captured moment bonding his joyous present with his imagined future.

A year later, when Clinton went back to Washington to begin college at Georgetown University, he began immediately to run for freshman class president. Maraniss describes that campaign:

> Clinton had lost two elections in a row—to Jack Hanks, Jr., of Texas for the Nationalist party vice-presidential nomination at Boys Nation, and to Carolyn Yeldell for senior class secretary at Hot Springs High. In both cases he had run for offices below his aspirations and therefore had done so halfheartedly. Now he would run as hard as he could. Within a few days of settling in Room 225 he had been off and running for president of the freshman class. [Tom] Campbell helped him distribute leaflets and [Thomas] Caplan advised him on speeches, but Clinton ran his own show.

His candidacy was nonideological, and he developed a platform of dry moderation. He called for better communications through a campus government newsletter and referendum powers for the student body. "I believe this is a possible platform," he assured potential voters. "The feasibility of every plank has been carefully examined."

In surveying the political landscape, Clinton learned that student politicians from Long Island tended to dominate. Another Long Island power play was taking shape, [but] Campbell could help Clinton cut into [the] Long Island vote. . . . Clinton saw great potential support among the women at the language institute, especially after he talked one of them out of running against him. He mimeographed his platform and signed copies by hand while eating breakfast. And then he set out to meet every voter on the East Campus.

On Halloween Eve, Clinton was elected president of the freshman class. He took office with a phalanx of Long Islanders, who were somewhat surprised to find him in their midst. "Bill Clinton[,] who looks and sounds like an amiable farm boy, is the latest to ascend to that position of status supremacy known as freshman class president," the next issue of *The Courier* proclaimed.[1]

Bill Clinton's political career was under way. It was to be a frantic one: president of his freshman and sophomore classes at Georgetown, Rhodes scholar, Yale Law School, Arkansas attorney general at 30, and governor at 32, the youngest in the country. Defeated for reelection, Clinton regained the governorship two years later, was reelected four more times, and achieved national prominence as leader of the National Governors' Association and head of the Democratic Leadership Conference. Even after his reelection as president in 1996, he still seemed driven to keep campaigning.

Clinton explains his nonstop political career as a kind of reaction to the death of his biological father before Bill was born:

> For a long time I thought I would have to live for both of us in some ways. . . . I think that's one reason I was in such a hurry when I was younger. I used to be criticized by people who said, "Well, he's too ambitious," but to me, because I grew up sort of subconsciously on his timetable, I never knew how much time I would have. . . . It gave me an urgent sense to do everything I could in life as quickly as I could.[2]

Americans learn about and participate in politics in different ways and for different reasons. Our interest in politics is inspired by our family, our friends, and our life experiences; if and when that interest has been established, we must learn how to function politically.

For most of us, these experiences do not include shaking hands with a president, much less becoming one. For some people, in fact, political interest never develops even to the point of voting. For others, it leads to active kinds of involvement like signing a petition, donating to a candidate, joining a political interest group, or participating in a protest demonstration. And for those like Clinton, it reaches a level that makes them want to actually become part of government.

This chapter explores the processes by which Americans become—or do not become—political. It considers how we orient ourselves to the American political culture and political system and then examines how we participate—or why we do not participate—in politics and government. The chapter concludes with an examination of the role of public opinion in politics, a factor that has had a growing impact as polling and communication become ever faster and more sophisticated.

POLITICAL SOCIALIZATION

Political socialization is the ongoing process by which individuals acquire the information, beliefs, attitudes, and values that help them comprehend the workings of a political system and orient themselves within it. Through political socialization, people learn to be **citizens**, or members of a political society.

Studying political participation helps in comprehending broad patterns of behavior within a political system. Just as a chemist would find it essential to identify the characteristics of molecules before explaining chemical elements, so it is important to explore the characteristics of American citizens before trying to describe and explain the politics of American government. Later chapters look at group and mass political behavior; here the focus is on individuals and the way they become citizens.

Changes over the Life Cycle

No one is sure exactly how early political socialization begins, but by the second grade many children already possess some knowledge and ideas about the political system in which they live. At this age, most of them are aware of the existence of a government and are able to identify two important authority figures: the president of the United States and the police officer. They may also be familiar with political symbols such as the flag, the national anthem, and George Washington. Most American children, for example, learn to recite the Pledge of Allegiance before they have any idea what its words mean.

In the preadolescent period, the majority of American children develop positive feelings about their nation's government and its leaders. Most see the police officer as a helper and protector, and the president as a good and wise person who is interested primarily in the welfare of the nation. In fact, many children in this age group compare the president to their father and place the president near the top of their list of favorite people.

The positive character of most children's early perceptions of the American political system is important because it facilitates the bonding between citizen and government that is essential to the government's legitimacy, the citizens' belief in its right to rule. If citizens do not believe that a government is legitimate, they are unlikely to participate faithfully in its processes or support its decisions. In the United States, there is widespread acceptance of the legitimacy of the government. Most children become patriotic before they have acquired enough information to explain the loyalty they feel. Although these strongly positive feelings tend to be modified as children grow older, they play an important role in the maintenance and stability of the American political system by securing the support of most of its citizens early in their lives.

As children move into adolescence, their perceptions of the political world become more sophisticated. They begin to recognize that there is more to government than presidents and police officers; they become aware of Congress, courts, cabinet members, and the distinctions among various levels of government. As children begin to recognize that individuals may take sides in disagreements among candidates, political parties, and interest groups on controversial

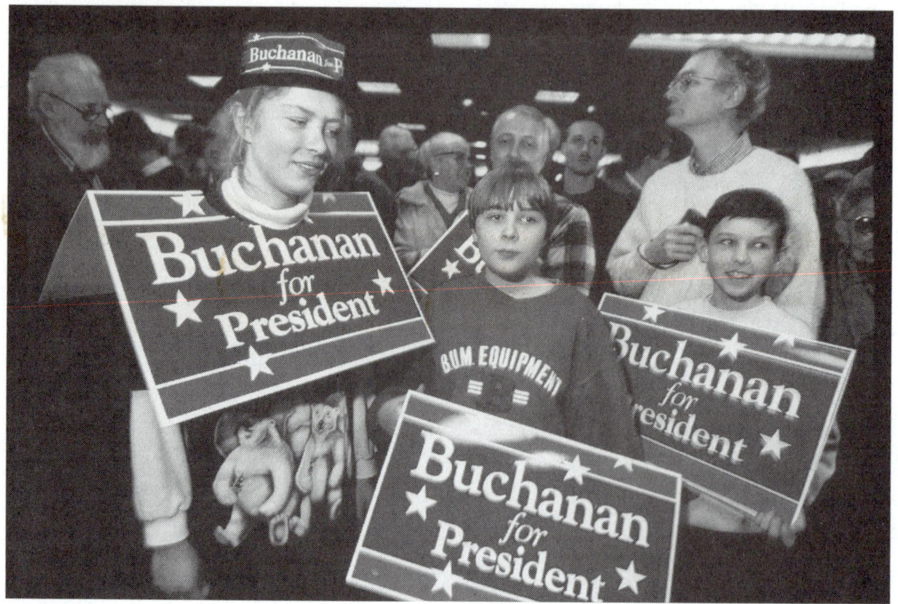

Political attitudes take root early, and even schoolchildren often identify with a particular party. But they have little understanding of ideological differences until adolescence. After that, their political attitudes and patterns of participation may last a lifetime.

issues, they are confronted by the need to choose a side, to position themselves within the political universe. This is a critical stage in the process of political socialization because it shapes the lifelong attitudes of many Americans.

Party affiliation One of the most important of these choices is that of an affiliation with a political party. In the United States, citizens do not join a party in the way that they join a club or a church. They make no formal profession of membership, they receive no membership card, and they are not required to pay dues. What they tend to do instead is simply to identify with a particular political party (or, in many cases, to identify themselves as independents). Because the political party identification that begins for many children in elementary school structures their orientation to politics throughout their lifetimes, party identification is an important concept in American political analysis.

In the early elementary grades, many children have a notion of the existence of Republicans and Democrats and can identify themselves with one party or the other. By the twelfth grade, according to another study, almost two-thirds of a national sample had a clear party preference. More recently, however, increasingly large numbers of children are identifying themselves as independents or adopting no partisan preference.[3]

As you might expect, most early partisan attachments are based on very little knowledge. Awareness of substantive differences between the parties rarely comes before the last years of elementary school, and even then less than 10 percent of children can make distinctions based on issues or ideology.[4] Not until high school do most people acquire an understanding of the substantive differences between political parties.[5]

Along with the increase in knowledge about politics and partisanship that occurs in the adolescent years comes a modification of the positive attitudes held in earlier years. Teenagers' political views become more realistic, and teens begin to perceive political figures in less heroic terms as they begin to understand the complexities and controversies of politics. It is also during the teenage years that most people begin to perceive government as a constraint on personal behavior by means of local curfews, minimum ages for driving and drinking, and school attendance requirements.

Major political events Major events, especially those occurring during the formative years, may have a lifelong impact on the generation that experiences them. For example, the generation of southern whites who came of age during and immediately after the Civil War, when the Republican party controlled the presidency and Congress, mostly learned to view Republicans as the villains of that war and as "carpetbaggers" who rode roughshod over the South during Reconstruction. Their allegiance to the Democratic party was tightly forged as a result. Similarly, the generation of Americans who reached adulthood during the Great Depression of the 1930s tended to blame the Depression on President Herbert Hoover and other Republicans who were in office when it started, and to attach their loyalties to the Democrats. In both cases, party loyalties remained in place long after the passing of the events that created them. The Depression generation, for instance, remained a core component of the Democratic party for many decades after helping to elect Franklin Roosevelt to the presidency and a Democratic Congress in 1932.

People who have come of age politically since the 1960s have been affected less by any single major event than by the general movement away from strong political party orientations that has been characteristic of this period. The effects of the Vietnam War, the Watergate and Iran-contra affair, and other political scandals and failures have combined to create a trend toward alienation—or at least disconnection—from politics. At the same time, the organization of political campaigns has shifted away from the political parties. Even though some young people have found themselves attracted to charismatic political figures (such as Ronald Reagan in the 1980s and Bill Clinton in the 1990s), that attraction has not appeared to translate into deep and abiding loyalty to a particular political party.

Agents of Political Socialization

How do young Americans acquire their information and attitudes about politics? Two theories have been proposed.[6] According to one theory, individuals are taught most of what they come to know and feel about politics by **agents of political socialization**, that is, people and institutions with an active interest in influencing their beliefs. The other theory suggests that individuals themselves have considerable autonomy in acquiring the political information they find useful and the political attitudes they find comfortable. Actually, the two theories are not necessarily at odds. In American society, as in every other society, certain agents do attempt to socialize young people to accept and adapt to the prevailing political culture. But American society also gives young people ample opportunities to shape their own political socialization through

Most children first come into contact with the political world through patriotic rituals in school, like the Pledge of Allegiance to the flag and observance of national holidays.

independent acquisition and evaluation of political information. The principal agents of political socialization include the family, school, religious organizations, peer groups, and organized groups such as professional associations and labor unions.

Another potential socializing agent is the mass media, particularly television—after all, Americans watch television a lot, averaging almost fifty hours per week per household.[7] However, the evidence that the media play a significant role as political socializing agents is mixed. Recent studies have indicated that television is an important source of news and political knowledge for young people and for immigrants, helping those new to the political system to get their bearings and orient themselves in partisan or ideological debates. Subsequently, however, people tend to sustain and enlarge their political interests by turning to newspapers and other print media. In this regard, television can be seen as important in helping to socialize politically, people who are not yet ready to use print media for this purpose.[8] In any event, little evidence suggests that any medium people use to obtain political information has much independent effect on their political attitudes. In other words, most people's opinions are not altered significantly by their exposure to the mass media.

But even if the mass media do not seem to shape partisan or ideological preferences to any significant extent, they may affect political socialization in another, perhaps more profound way. Some recent studies have suggested that the cumulative effect of television watching may be to increase disaffection and cynicism among Americans. The lengthening of election campaigns combined with extensive television coverage often leads to boredom rather than to heightened interest, and intensive scrutiny of political scandals and the private lives of public officials inevitably makes American leaders seem less heroic than they often appeared in the days before television.[9] Such findings are especially noteworthy because in the political socialization of younger Americans, increasing reliance on television now often substitutes for the role that parental communications once played.

POLITICAL PARTICIPATION

Political participation is a critical ingredient in a successful democracy. To use the language of Abraham Lincoln, government cannot be "for the people" if it is not also "of the people and by the people." Specifically, the public must participate in policy making enough to ensure that public policy accurately reflects both the intensity and the direction of popular concerns. But participating in politics and government is not easy. It takes time and energy; it requires knowledge of political and government processes; and it requires that people feel that their political activity will make a difference.

Some people participate; others do not. Some people participate extensively, others only minimally. Why? Part of the answer comes from variations in the socialization patterns discussed earlier. Part also results from differences in opportunities or incentives to participate, from external factors that have a direct effect on people's lives. Three important aspects of political participation are (1) the ways in which Americans most commonly participate in political life, (2) the characteristics of those who participate and those who do not, and (3) the impact of participation on public policy.

Ways of Participating

Political participation encompasses a variety of activities. Some, such as running for political office, are very demanding. Others, such as voting, require only minimal amounts of time and knowledge. Between these extremes is a wide range of other activities.

Campaign activity Short of getting elected to office oneself, securing the election of people who share one's views is probably the most direct way to get those views embedded in public policy. Participating in a political campaign is not difficult if a person has the desire to do so. Campaign activity may consume a lot of time, but the amount of time invested is usually up to the volunteer. Some people support candidates with their money as well as, or instead of, their time. Increasingly, in fact, financial contributions to candidates are coming to replace volunteered time as a meaningful form of political participation.[10] The fact that so many Americans have never participated in campaign activities (see Table 6-1) suggests that even this level of interest is not very common. Indeed, much current research suggests that levels of political interest in elections and government are in decline in the United States, especially among the young.[11] Because of their mobility and willingness to do the menial work of politics, young people normally constitute the core of campaigns, but in recent decades disaffection with conventional politics has kept many young people away.

Voting Voting is widely regarded as the simplest form of political activity. Not surprisingly, therefore, it is also the form that is engaged in most frequently; in fact, it is the only political activity in which many Americans participate regularly. Nevertheless, as Table 6-1 indicates, more than one-fourth of the American people do not even identify themselves as regular voters.

TABLE 6-1 ***Americans Participating in Various Political Activities, 1976–1996 (in percent)***

TYPE OF ACTIVITY	1976	1980	1984	1988	1992	1996
Voted*	72	71	74	70	75	77
Worked for party or candidate	4	4	4	3	3	3
Attended rallies or meetings	6	8	8	7	8	6
Tried to persude others how to vote	37	36	32	29	38	29
Wore campaign button; displayed bumper sticker	8	7	9	9	11	10
Contributed money to campaign	16	8	13	9	6	6

*These are self-identified voters. This figure generally exceeds the percentage of eligible adults who participate in any single national election. The actual percentage of eligible adults who voted in the 1996 presidential election was 49.

SOURCE: Data for 1976 and 1980 are adapted from David B. Hill and Norman R. Luttbeg, *Trends in American Electoral Behavior* (Itasca, Ill.: Peacock, 1983), 99. Data for 1984–1996 are adapted from the National Election Studies.

Why do people not vote? Some say that they lack time, interest, or motivation. Historically, registration requirements in many states have also been an impediment. Although much is made of the relatively low percentage of eligible Americans who vote (in comparison with rates in other democracies), there are a number of other ways to affect the political process—and even nonvoters may engage in them.[12]

Cooperative activity In politics, there is strength in numbers. The greater the number of people who support a particular course of action, the greater is the likelihood that such a course will be pursued by public officials.

An emphasis on cooperative forms of participation is evident at both the local and the national levels of American politics. In most communities, policy decisions are frequently influenced by the efforts of organized groups of citizens: the PTA working for increases in school budgets, the chamber of commerce trying to hold down the tax rate in order to attract new business investment, the city employees' union supporting candidates for local office who will vote for increases in salaries or benefits. Similarly, at the national level, most significant interests in American public life are now organized as groups with their own lobbyists in Washington. There are thousands of such organizations, reflecting interests as diverse as those of autoworkers, milk producers, the mentally retarded, summer camp operators, and importers of exotic animals. Interest groups are a commanding presence in contemporary American politics, and we look at their role more closely in the next chapter.

Having a high level of information is not a requirement. In fact, for many people the combination of high interest and low information is what motivates them to join a group and participate in its activities.

Unconventional participation Not all efforts at political participation follow conventional channels. Some circumvent them and in this sense, may be termed **unconventional participation**. These include such activities as protest demonstrations, sit-ins, rent strikes, riots, and other forms of violence, including bombings, kidnappings, and assassinations.

Unconventional activities most often occur when individuals or groups of citizens do not know how to follow conventional participation channels or do not believe that they can influence public policy by going through those channels. In many cases, they are frustrated or believe themselves powerless to compete effectively in conventional politics. A good example is student activism against the Vietnam War in the 1960s. Under the laws in effect at the time, most students could not vote. They did not have the money or the organizational skills necessary to establish effective national interest groups, nor did their individual contacts with government officials seem to produce much change in the conduct of the war. Consequently, many students chose to express their opposition to the war outside the routine channels of political participation: in street demonstrations, mass marches, sit-ins, and other kinds of organized protest.

Social scientists have little reliable data on the number of people who participate in unconventional political activities, but most analysts believe that it is not very large, perhaps 1 or 2 percent of the population. Among certain groups, however, the percentage may be substantially higher. Moreover, because of their intensity and, in the age of television, their visibility, unconventional forms of participation may affect public policy more than one would anticipate from the proportions of people typically involved in them. During the civil rights movement of the 1950s and 1960s, only a small percentage of the American people—even of African Americans—participated personally in public protest activities, but those who did captured national attention and became important symbols of the issues involved.

Lacking power to influence policy through normal political channels, college students who opposed the Vietnam War were forced to use unconventional strategies, some with tragic outcomes. On May 4, 1970, Ohio National Guardsmen fired tear gas into a crowd of antiwar protesters at Kent State University. In the confusion that followed, the Guardsmen panicked and fired live bullets at the students, killing four.

Nonparticipation A sizable number of Americans do not participate in political activities at all. They do not vote regularly; they engage in no direct contacts with public officials; they are not members of any group involved in political action; and they do not participate in unconventional forms of political activity. They are politically inactive.

Among these inactive citizens are several different types of people: those who are elderly and infirm, mentally incompetent, or incarcerated in prisons or other confining institutions; those who live lives of poverty and desperation and lack the skills, confidence, or energy necessary to take part in political life; and those who believe that political life is inherently corrupt or unfair and inequitable. Still others are inactive because they are basically satisfied with their own lives and with the state of national affairs and see no reason to invest any time or effort in political activities directed at change.

Whatever their reasons, approximately one-fifth of American adults are politically inactive. What does it say about democracy in the United States if one-fifth of its citizens take no active part in choosing their leaders or in shaping the public policies that affect their lives? Although many believe that so much nonparticipation threatens the vitality of the democratic process, others contend that as long as participation is possible and encouraged, the system meets democratic criteria. A democracy could become unstable and unworkable if everyone participated extensively at all levels and on most issues. Thus some level of nonparticipation may be necessary for stability and efficiency in public life.

Who Participates?

Answers to the question of who participates must be given with caution. Participation patterns are complex, and no simple formulation can adequately describe or accurately predict the participation level of all individuals. Nevertheless, some patterns do exist, and examining these may shed light on the role of political participation in shaping American politics and public policy. Keep in mind, however, that these are broad patterns to which there are numerous exceptions.

The impact of socioeconomic status One of the most consistent findings of studies of American political participation is that participation correlates closely with an individual's **socioeconomic status** (SES), or social and economic standing relative to other citizens. The higher one's SES, the greater is the likelihood that one will participate actively in politics. Most citizens who are active participants are well educated and well-off, and among the inactives and those whose only activity is voting are a disproportionate number with low levels of education and income.

The relationship among interest, participation, and SES is not very surprising. Because of their greater knowledge of politics, higher-SES individuals are more likely to follow political issues on television and in the press. Their higher levels of income may indicate that they have a substantial financial interest in many public policy decisions (taxes and investment regulations, for example). Most important, studies of political participation suggest that people of high socioeconomic status tend to have a stronger belief that they can bring about the change they desire.

Other demographic correlates No other demographic characteristic matches the impact of socioeconomic status on participation, but several others appear to affect participation levels. Age is one. In general, young adults—particularly those under age 30—and people over age 65 are less likely to be active partici-

FIGURE 6-1

The Effect of Age on Political Participation, 1996

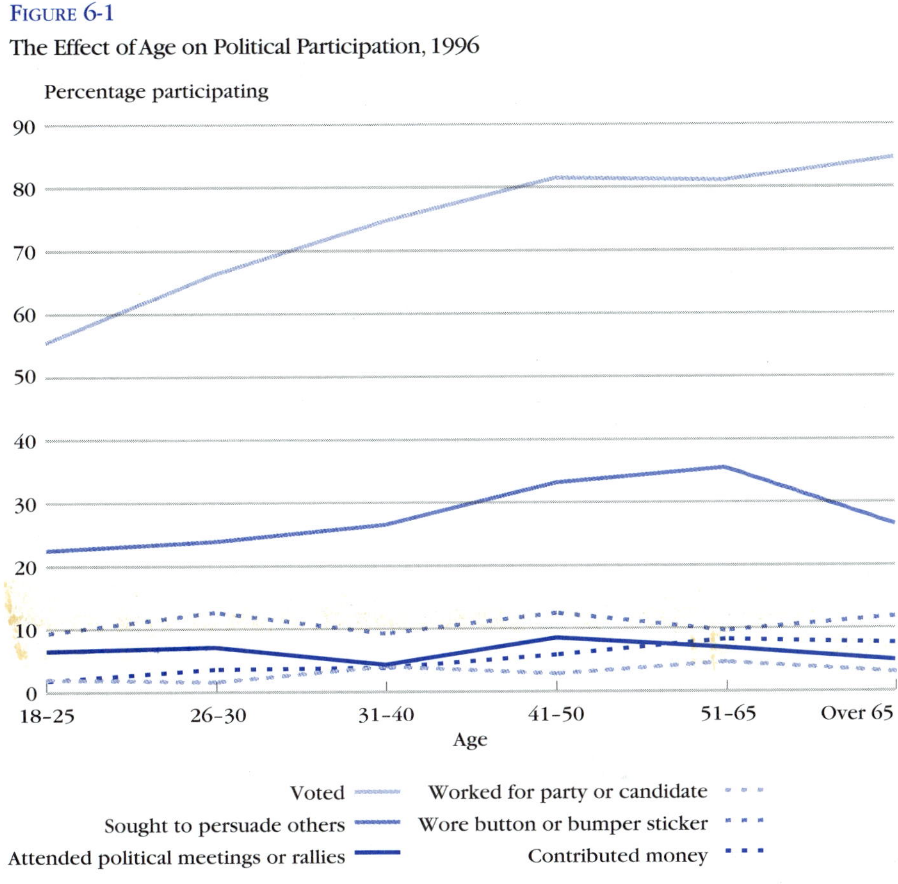

SOURCE: American National Election Study, 1996. Data are based on poll responses and may overstate actual participation, particularly for voting.

pants than are those in between. As Figure 6-1 indicates, participation levels tend to increase as one gets older, level off in middle age, and then drop as one moves into the traditional retirement years.

Race, gender, and religion are also factors in participation. African Americans, for example, are less likely than whites to be politically active, in part because they are overrepresented in the lower socioeconomic status groups. Women are less likely to be active than men, although the gap between the sexes has been narrowing in recent years and has disappeared in voting participation.[13] And people who participate significantly in religious activities are more likely to be politically active than people who don't attend religious services regularly.

Political Participation and Public Policy

Two important pieces of information emerge from this material on political participation: (1) the American people vary greatly in the extent to which they participate in political life, and (2) socioeconomic status is the major cause of that variation. What are the implications of these findings?

If participants and nonparticipants were scattered randomly throughout the population, the actual level of participation might not make much difference in terms of public policy. But participation patterns are not random, and the political views of those who do participate are often quite different from the political views of those who do not.[14] To the extent that policy decisions are a response to what public officials hear from the public, that response is skewed toward the views of those who are most likely to make themselves heard: the active participants. Thus the haves tend to speak with a louder, steadier, and more influential voice than the have-nots, and they can perpetuate their advantage.

The policies of government result from the processes of politics. When some people participate and others do not, both process and policy are affected. The question of who participates and who does not directly and deeply affects the politics of American government: what it does; how it does it; who benefits and who does not.

PUBLIC OPINION

Direct participation is not the only way to affect politics, government, and public policy. Just having an opinion and letting it be known can have an impact. **Public opinion** consists of people's *opinions,* or judgments, on current issues; *attitudes,* or broad orientations toward policy areas; and *values,* or basic ideals and beliefs. In a government based on the consent of the governed, what the people know, believe, and want influences government, particularly in an age of rapid communications.

Discovering Public Opinion

How do policy makers discover what people think about an issue? They observe their behavior, monitor their communications, and ask them questions. However, some individuals in every group are more demonstrative and outspoken than others, perhaps because their opinions are more intense or because their personalities create a need for them to express themselves. Since it is important to determine the opinions of a range of people, not just those who are vocal, most policy makers survey the population as a whole. The most efficient way to do this is through **public opinion polls**.

Polls can indicate the **direction**, the **stability**, and even the **intensity** of public opinion. Direction refers to the proportion of the population that holds a particular view. Evaluations of that direction over time indicate how stable that opinion is. Intensity refers to the depth of feelings on particular issues. Each of these characteristics is an important component of public opinion.

Polls can also reveal the **salience** of issues, which ones arouse the most public attention and interest. These are the issues that are most likely to have an impact on politics and government. Conversely, issues that concern only a small portion of the population are not apt to become the focus of political attention and public policy.

Candidates for office and incumbent officials use polls to discern which groups of people are most likely to support certain policies, be concerned about certain issues, and vote for particular candidates. During an election campaign, polls provide feedback to candidates about voters' perceptions, their political

Because of David Duke's past as a Nazi sympathizer and Grand Dragon of the Ku Klux Klan, many Louisianans were embarrassed to tell pollsters the truth—that they planned to vote for him for governor. People's tendency to say what they think they should causes particular problems in polls based on personal interviews.

attitudes, and their reactions to the symbols, issues, and images that the candidates are using. Indeed, this information is now available so quickly that candidates are able to assess the damage caused by an opponent's charges almost immediately and respond to them quickly. The failure to do so can be fatal, as Democratic presidential candidate Michael Dukakis found out in 1988 when he did not respond to Republican George Bush's charge that he was soft on crime, weak on defense, and out of step with basic American values. In 1992 and again in 1996, effective polling enabled Democratic candidate Bill Clinton to anticipate and reply to charges against him within twenty-four hours.

Polls cannot predict what opinions people will hold in the future, however, and that is why those taken several days before an election may not accurately forecast the results if a large number of voters make up or change their minds after the polls are completed. Voter preferences for Harry Truman in 1948 and Ronald Reagan in 1980 crystallized during the week before the election, confounding pollsters who had sampled opinion earlier. There are other limitations as well. Some polls—those that rely on personal interviews, for example—may encourage responses that are considered socially acceptable or desirable and suppress those that are not. A good illustration of this tendency occurred during the nonpartisan primary in Louisiana in 1991, when the number of people who voted for David Duke, a former Grand Dragon of the Ku Klux Klan and supporter of Nazi ideology, was much higher than the number who had told interviewers they would do so in surveys taken before the election.

In addition, error can also be introduced by the way survey results are interpreted. In early preelection polls, the candidates who tend to do best are those who are best known, not necessarily those who ultimately prove to be the most electable. Senator Gary Hart led all other Democratic presidential candidates in the December 1987 preelection poll in Iowa, even though he had only recently reentered the race after withdrawing in May following allegations of adultery. In the caucus election one month later, he finished in fifth place. The

Hart example suggests that the interpretation of polls, and the prognoses that often follow from them, must be made with great care.

Characteristics of Public Knowledge: Lack of Information

Survey after survey conducted in the past thirty years has shown that the public is poorly informed about government officials and political issues. Not only do Americans know little about specific issues, but most people would be hard-pressed to name their representatives in Congress and their state legislature, much less recall the representatives' performance in office unless they have been involved in a scandal or abused their position. For example, a national poll conducted in 1995 by the *Washington Post,* Kaiser Family Foundation, and Harvard University found that only 60 percent of those surveyed could name the current vice president of the United States, 53 percent the Speaker of the House, and 34 percent the Senate majority leader. Only one in four knew the length of a senator's term in office.[15] Some of the other results of the poll are shown in Figure 6-2.

Knowledge about entertainers in the movies and television tends to be greater than knowledge about most public officials, even the high-ranking ones. The same poll found that only 6 percent of respondents knew the name of the chief justice. Even Justice Clarence Thomas, who was confirmed in a very controversial hearing shown on national television (a hearing that included explicit charges against him of sexual harassment), was known by only 30 percent. Another national poll in 1995 found that only 17 percent of respondents could name three of the nine justices on the Supreme Court, but 59 percent could name the Three Stooges.[16]

Not only higher levels of education but also higher income is associated with greater political information. The relationship between income and information can be attributed in part to the demands of a professional or business life, which require that one be aware of what is going on in the political arena. The relationship may also be due to efforts to protect one's income or profession from those who might threaten it. In addition, education and income tend to be associated with each other. Better-educated people generally make more money, and those who make more money tend to be the better educated.

Q: Do you happen to know the names of the U.S. senators from your state, or not? What are their names?

Q: Do you happen to know the name of the person who serves in the U.S. House of Representatives from your congressional district, or not?

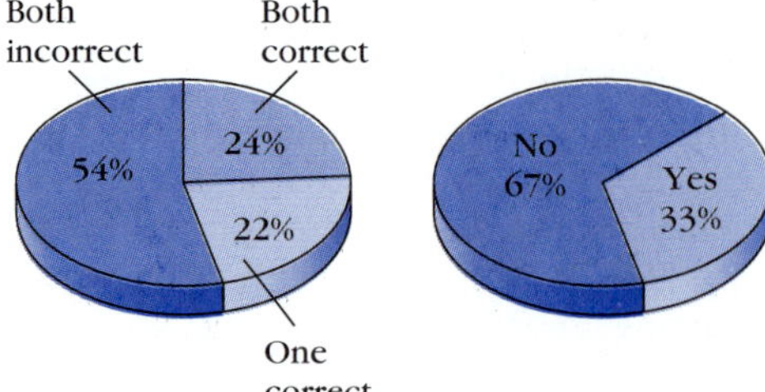

FIGURE 6-2
How Much Do Americans Know About Their Elected Officials?

SOURCE: *Washington Post*/Kaiser Family Foundation/Harvard University national survey, conducted Nov. 28–Dec. 4, 1995, of 1,514 randomly selected adults as reported in the *Washington Post,* January 29, 1996, A6.

Age is also strongly associated with a person's level of information on political issues. As people get older, as they develop greater stakes in their community and profession, they become more aware of the effects of political decisions on their lives and well-being. As the number of government policies affecting senior citizens increases, older people have an incentive to remain informed and involved.

Generational differences may also be a factor. The Pew Research Center for The People & The Press analyzed historic polling data in 1990 and found that "Americans under 30 represented a generation that knew less, cared less, and read newspapers less than previous generations of young people." The Center's subsequent studies have confirmed this conclusion. They have found that only one out of five people between 18 and 29 pays close attention to the news.[17]

What implications does the low level of information have for the politics of government? For one thing, it gives government leaders more initial discretion in making policy decisions. With less direction from the public, they have more flexibility to fashion a solution. This is particularly evident in foreign affairs and in complex economic and technological issues such as telecommunications policy, nuclear energy, and biomedical research. In contrast, where the public is better informed, public officials have much less leeway.

Even in the absence of discernible public concern, government officials rarely have a blank check. Certain proposals cannot be enacted because they lie outside the values and beliefs of most people. For example, few considered a national health system run by the government, often referred to as "socialized medicine," to be a viable solution to recent health-care problems in the United States, even though it has been utilized in other Western democracies such as Canada, Sweden, and Great Britain.

Another consequence of limited public knowledge is that it tends to encourage short-term solutions. Not understanding the full complexity of issues, the public expects and demands results here and now. These demands are readily converted into political pressure on government officials for quick fixes rather than longer-term solutions.

A third implication of the low level of public information is that it seems to increase the power of interest groups and their leaders. When many people are uninformed and uninterested, opinion leaders—particularly those who represent large and powerful groups—exercise more clout. A poorly informed public is easier to manipulate.

Characteristics of Public Opinion: Ambivalence and Diversity

The consistency with which beliefs and opinions are held varies. People are often ambivalent about issues—they seem to talk out of both sides of their mouths. For instance, surveys of public opinion indicate that Americans want to protect and preserve their interests around the world but shy away from involving United States forces in that effort; they want to help those who cannot help themselves but are opposed to welfare programs in which individuals automatically receive funds, food, or other benefits without earning them; they believe in the sanctity of human life as well as the right of individual choice. This ambivalence stems in part from clashing values. Americans cherish numerous values such as liberty, equality, and opportunity. Unless they are able to order these values in terms of their relative importance, however, conflicts are likely to develop and persist.

One way to resolve such conflicts is to adopt a **belief system**, a set of related ideas that helps people understand and cope with the world around them and that also provides guidelines for behavior. Examples of a belief system include a religion (such as Christianity, Islam, or Judaism) or an ideology (such as communism or capitalism). Frequently, however, people do not accept all the tenets of a belief system; and they may adhere to religious, political, and economic belief systems that are not logically congruent, that do not easily mesh with one another. That is a major reason why public opinion often lacks consistency.

Education is a key variable in determining the consistency of someone's beliefs. People with more education tend to be more consistent in the political positions they take and the political beliefs they hold and express. Not only does education increase their awareness of issues, but it gives them the skills to think logically and spot inconsistencies in their beliefs.

In addition to low levels of information and ambivalent attitudes, public opinion in the United States is characterized by diversity. That diversity reflects the heterogeneity of the population—its various subcultures, races, and levels of education and income. Table 6-2 (pages 132–133) illustrates these differences in opinion on a number of contemporary issues. The table indicates the percentage of people who agree with each statement. Notice that education and income often vary directly with each other, and that significant differences exist between those in the youngest and oldest age groups on several issues. It is also interesting that opinion differences between the races tend to be greater than those between the genders.

The ambivalence and contradictions in people's attitudes and opinions can be very frustrating for policy makers who look to public opinion for guidance. What should public officials do, for example, when people demand deficit reduction and lower taxes, but no reduction in levels of spending for specific programs? This is precisely what the American people said they wanted in the 1990s.[18]

Political Ideologies

As noted earlier, many people seek to orient themselves to the political world by adopting a system of beliefs called an ideology. A **political ideology** is a set of interrelated attitudes that shape judgments about and reactions to political issues. Ideologies provide a general stance toward the political system, a perceptual lens through which to view and evaluate events.

In the United States, the two dominant political ideologies are **liberalism** and **conservatism**. Liberals are those who believe that government can and should be used as a powerful force in achieving greater social and political equality and greater economic opportunity for all. They support government intervention to protect civil rights and promote equal opportunity for minorities who have not been afforded the same privileges and opportunities as the majority. In contrast, they oppose government actions that threaten to deprive people of their basic personal and political freedoms, particularly the freedom to deviate from social norms. Liberals' desire for greater social equality and personal freedom extends to foreign policy as well, where they tend to favor policies of accommodation, reject the threat of force as an instrument of diplomacy, and support programs designed to help the economically and politically deprived.

Conservatives fear government involvement *more* in the economic sphere, particularly where such involvement places restrictions on the free-enterprise system, and *less* in the social realm, particularly in matters of law and order where individual behavior is constrained. They have usually voiced opposition to increased taxation, especially as a device to redistribute wealth. As proponents of private enterprise, conservatives prefer to keep capital in the hands of individuals and nongovernment groups, to be spent and invested as they see fit. Compared with liberals, conservatives seem to be more satisfied with the status quo, more willing to accept economic and social inequalities as natural consequences of the human condition, and more resistant to large-scale social change.

Although conservatives accept the notion of individual liberties, they also see the need for an ordered and stable society in which property is protected and entrepreneurship encouraged. They contend that government has a major responsibility for providing that protection as well as protection against external threats to the national interests and security of the United States. Since World War II, conservatives have generally supported a foreign policy based on military strength.

Do people actually think along these ideological lines? Do they use liberalism and conservatism as a basis for formulating opinions and making decisions? The evidence suggests that they do. It also suggests that the more information people have, the more likely they are to maintain views on policy issues that are consistent with their ideological orientation.

Although that orientation does not dictate positions on issues for most people, it is a useful device for self-identification and for explaining and even rationalizing policy positions and candidate preferences. But whether ideology is the principal reason for forming an opinion, taking a position, or arriving at a political judgment remains difficult to say. Nonetheless, ideological awareness has grown. In recent presidential elections, there has been a strong association between ideological self-identification and voting patterns, although there is little evidence that ideology itself causes people to vote as they do.[19]

Who are the liberals and conservatives in the American electorate? According to statistics assembled by political scientists between 1982 and 1996 (see Table 6-3, page 136) men are more conservative than women, whites are more conservative than nonwhites, and older Americans are more conservative than younger Americans.

The ideological orientation of the American electorate has had an impact on partisan politics. Conservatives tend to ally themselves with the Republican party and liberals with the Democratic party. Ideology also affects policy making in that problems that are defined in ideological terms tend to be more difficult to resolve. Ideologues are not good compromisers. Although the ideological orientation of the American polity has shifted in a conservative direction during the 1980s and 1990s, the people continue to display considerable latitude in the application of their political views to the issues of the day. That is why American politics is characterized more by pragmatism than by rigid adherence to ideological beliefs.

Changes in public attitudes on some major economic and social issues have been influenced by shifting patterns in ideological identification. Since the mid 1970s, the public has shown less support for large-scale government programs than it did during the previous two decades.[20] Cynicism toward the

TABLE 6-2 ***Diversity of Public Opinion, 1996 (percentage agreeing)***

ISSUES*	GENDER		RACE		AGE			
	MALE	FEMALE	WHITE	NONWHITE	18–29	30–49	50–64	65+
1. Women and men should have equal roles.	77.3	77.0	77.0	77.7	84.4	81.9	76.0	61.7
2. The death penalty should be abolished.	17.1	24.9	17.8	43.1	25.7	19.4	23.4	20.3
3. Government should see to it that people have good jobs and an acceptable standard of living.	21.3	30.0	22.7	46.2	35.7	25.9	21.7	23.4
4. Government should improve the social and economic conditions of African Americans.	16.5	20.3	15.8	35.3	22.6	18.1	19.9	14.9
5. Government should provide fewer services to reduce government spending.	44.0	31.7	40.5	16.8	33.5	38.2	36.8	38.7
6. Welfare benefits should be limited to two years.	78.1	77.8	79.9	66.2	81.2	78.4	76.4	76.3
7. Prayers should not be allowed in public schools.	13.0	11.5	12.8	8.3	14.1	13.2	11.3	9.6
8. Immigration should be decreased.	56.1	58.7	58.6	51.0	52.5	55.0	59.7	64.2

ISSUES*	EDUCATION				INCOME (IN THOUSANDS OF DOLLARS)			
	DROP-OUT	HIGH SCHOOL	SOME COLLEGE	COLLEGE GRAD.	UNDER 15	15–24	25–49	50+
1. Women and men should have equal roles.	64.3	73.5	81.2	83.0	68.1	78.9	78.1	83.9
2. The death penalty should be abolished.	27.7	16.0	22.7	22.7	28.3	23.5	22.1	15.0
3. Government should see to it that people have good jobs and an acceptable standard of living.	36.7	28.2	22.8	22.6	37.5	31.2	24.6	18.2
4. Government should improve the social and economic conditions of African Americans.	22.3	13.6	17.2	23.7	23.1	24.6	15.1	16.7
5. Government should provide fewer services to reduce government spending.	30.2	30.7	37.8	45.9	23.8	26.7	41.2	47.3
6. Welfare benefits should be limited to two years.	77.1	75.1	80.7	78.9	68.8	78.3	81.4	81.2
7. Prayers should not be allowed in public schools.	7.9	8.4	10.8	19.7	9.9	12.3	11.1	14.8
8. Immigration should be decreased.	63.9	64.7	60.3	44.0	61.4	55.7	61.0	51.9

TABLE 6-2 *Diversity of Public Opinion, 1996 (percentage agreeing) (continued)*

*The questions put for each issue were these:

1. Recently there has been a lot of talk about women's rights. Some people feel that women should have an equal role with men in running business, industry, and government. . . . Others feel that a women's place is in the home. . . . Where would you place yourself on this scale (1 . . . 7), or haven't you thought much about this? ("Percentage agreeing" is the total of scaled responses 1-3.)
2. Do you favor or oppose the death penalty for persons convicted of murder?
3. Some people feel the government in Washington should see to it that every person has a job and a good standard of living. Others think the government should just let each person get ahead on his or her own. Where would you place yourself on this scale (1 . . . 7), or haven't you thought much about it? ("Percentage agreeing" is total of scaled responses 1-3.)
4. Some people feel that the government in Washington should make every effort to improve the social and economic position of African Americans. Others feel that the government should not make any special effort to help African Americans because they should help themselves. Where would you place yourself on this scale (1 . . . 7), or haven't you thought much about this? ("Percentage agreeing" is total of responses 1-3.)
5. Some people think the government should provide fewer services, even in areas such as health and education, in order to reduce spending. Other people feel it is important for the government to provide many more services even if it means an increase in spending. Where would you place yourself on this scale (1 . . . 7), or haven't you thought much about it? (Percentages are totals of responses 1-3.)
6. Another proposal is to put a two-year limit on how long someone can receive welfare benefits. Do you favor or oppose this two-year limit?
7. Which of the following views comes closest to your opinion on the issue of school prayer?
   By law, prayers should not be allowed in public schools.
   The law should allow public schools to schedule time when children can pray silently if they want to.
   The law should allow public schools to schedule time when children, as a group, can say a general prayer not tied to a particular faith.
   By law, public schools should schedule a time when all children would say a chosen Christian prayer.
8. Do you think the number of immigrants from foreign countries who are permitted to come to the United States to live should be increased a little, increased a lot, decreased a little, decreased a lot, or left the same as it is?

SOURCE: The American National Election Studies, conducted by the University of Michigan, Center for Political Studies, Ann Arbor, Michigan. Data provided by the Inter-University Consortium for Political and Social Research, located at the University of Michigan, Center for Political Studies, Ann Arbor, Michigan.

WHERE ON THE WEB?

Public Opinion Data

What is the public's opinion on contemporary issues, and how can you find it out? The findings of national public opinion polls started to appear on the Internet in 1996. Among them are data provided by the Gallup Poll, the Wirthlin Group, the *New York Times,* and CBS News. In addition to these national surveys, almost every website of a major news organization contains the findings of its latest polls.

If you want to research trends in American public opinion over time, the best places to locate these data are the archives at several universities. The Documents Center at the University of Michigan has the best collection of academic public opinion surveys, and the Roper Center at the University of Connecticut has a collection of survey data from all the major polling organizations, television networks, and major newspapers and magazines. However, much of the data at the university websites is available only to subscribers, those who pay a fee for access. Check with your instructor to see whether your school has subscriber privileges at one of these library data sites.

You can acquire much of this information by accessing the political science links at the St. Martin's Press website (http://www.smpcollege.com). If you wish to go directly to some sites, here are some useful addresses:

Current Public Opinion Pollsters

Gallup Organization
http://www.gallup.com/

Louis Harris
http://www.techsetter.com/harris

The Wirthlin Group
http://user.aol.com/wirthlin.htm

Selected News Media Sites with Polling Data

AllPolitics (CNN and *Time* magazine)
http://AllPolitics.com/

national government has increased. Government-run agencies such as the United States Postal Service, the Internal Revenue Service, the Bureau of Alcohol, Tobacco, and Firearms, the Federal Bureau of Investigation, the Central Intelligence Agency, and the Immigration and Naturalization Service have been the targets of much criticism, and there continue to be endless complaints about government regulations and paperwork. Within the social sphere, Americans—particularly young Americans—have become more tolerant of certain kinds of behavior, such as single motherhood and homosexuality, than they were in the past. But they are also more supportive of harsh penalties for criminal behavior, such as the death penalty for those who commit heinous crimes.

New York Times
http://www.nytimes.com/

Washington Post
http://www.washingtonpost.com/

Public Opinion Data Libraries and Data Archives

Electronic Data Services (Columbia University)
http://www.columbia.edu/acis/eds/

Inter-University Consortium for Political and Social Research (University of Mighigan)
http://www.icpsr.umich.edu/

National Election Studies (University of Michigan—Center for Political Studies)
http://www.umich.edu/~NES/

Princeton Survey Research Center
http://www.princeton.edu/~abelson/

Roper Center for Public Opinion Research (University of Connecticut)
http://www.lib.uconn.edu/RoperCenter/

Social Sciences Data Center (University of Virginia Library)
http://www.lib.virginia.edu/socsci/

Social Sciences Data Collection (University of California at San Diego)
http://ssdc.ucsd.edu/

Statistical Resources on the Web—Political Science (University of Michigan)
http://www.lib.umich.edu/libhome/Documents.center/stpolisc.html

Yahoo
http://www.yahoo.com/

Democratic Beliefs

In addition to their varying levels of political knowledge and differing ideological perspectives, Americans hold a range of attitudes toward government, society, and the interaction between the two. These attitudes condition the kinds of issues public officials must consider and the range of options they can follow in dealing with them. In particular, attitudes have an impact in four areas that are critical to the operation of a democracy: the role of government, trust in public officials, political efficacy, support for democratic processes, and tolerance of others.

The role of government What do the American people see as the proper role of government? In the economic realm, support for government

TABLE 6-3 ***Political Ideologies: Who Has Them? (percentage agreeing)***

	Liberal			Moderate			Conservative		
	1982	1992	1996	1982	1992	1996	1982	1992	1996
Sex									
Male	30	26	21	37	29	27	33	45	52
Female	29	30	30	42	34	33	29	37	37
Age									
18–29	31	32	36	43	35	32	26	33	31
30–49	35	32	29	36	26	29	29	43	43
50–64	23	21	20	44	33	27	33	46	53
65 and up	24	19	15	38	40	35	38	41	50
Race									
White	42	27	25	35	31	30	23	43	46
Nonwhite	25	36	32	42	37	35	34	28	33
Party									
Democrat	35	44	47	40	32	32	25	24	22
Republican	17	8	5	37	27	18	46	66	77
Independent	31	28	22	49	35	40	20	38	39

Source: The American National Election Studies, conducted by the University of Michigan, Center for Political Studies, Ann Arbor, Michigan. Data provided by the Inter-University Consortium for Political and Social Research, located at the University of Michigan, Center for Political Studies, Ann Arbor, Michigan.

intervention to promote employment, control inflation, and foster growth has remained fairly consistent since the Great Depression. However, there has been disagreement over how much the government should be involved in the economy, and how much it should regulate economic activity. This disagreement is often couched in partisan and ideological terms, with Democrats and liberals supporting a larger government role than Republicans and conservatives.

In the realm of social issues, attitudes do not fit neatly into partisan categories, although they do divide along ideological lines. Liberals in general, and racial and ethnic minorities in particular, favor a more vigorous government role—promoting racial integration, voting rights, and equal opportunity programs—than do conservatives and whites. On issues where moral judgments come into play—pornography, homosexual behavior, abortion—there also tends to be a liberal-conservative cleavage, with conservatives inclining more than liberals toward the imposition of community standards by government intervention.

Trust in public officials The question of what the government should do in certain policy areas becomes meaningless unless citizens can trust public officials to mean what they say, say what they mean, and do what they promise. Without trust, no government can operate successfully; without trust, the motives of public officials will always be suspect and their actions subject to misunderstanding and misinterpretation. The Watergate scandal was one of a series of events, including the Vietnam War, that resulted in a steady decline of trust in the United States government by its citizens during the 1960s and 1970s. As the economy improved in the early 1980s, trust in government

FIGURE 6-3

Trust in Government, 1968–1996

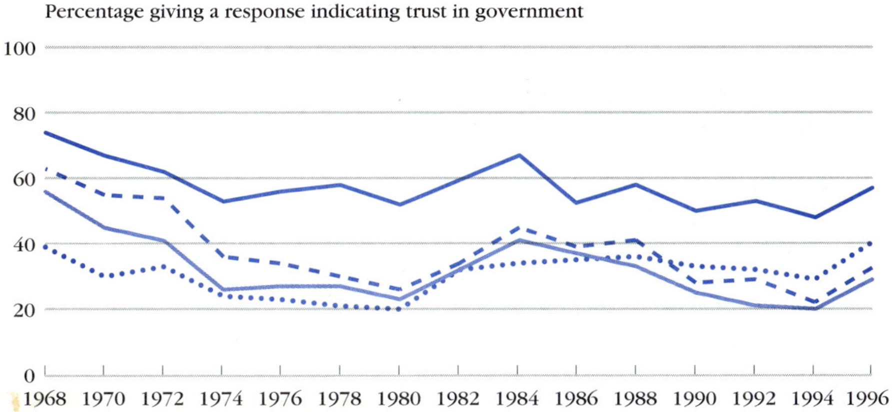

Percentage giving a response indicating trust in government

100 80 60 40 20 0

1968 1970 1972 1974 1976 1978 1980 1982 1984 1986 1988 1990 1992 1994 1996

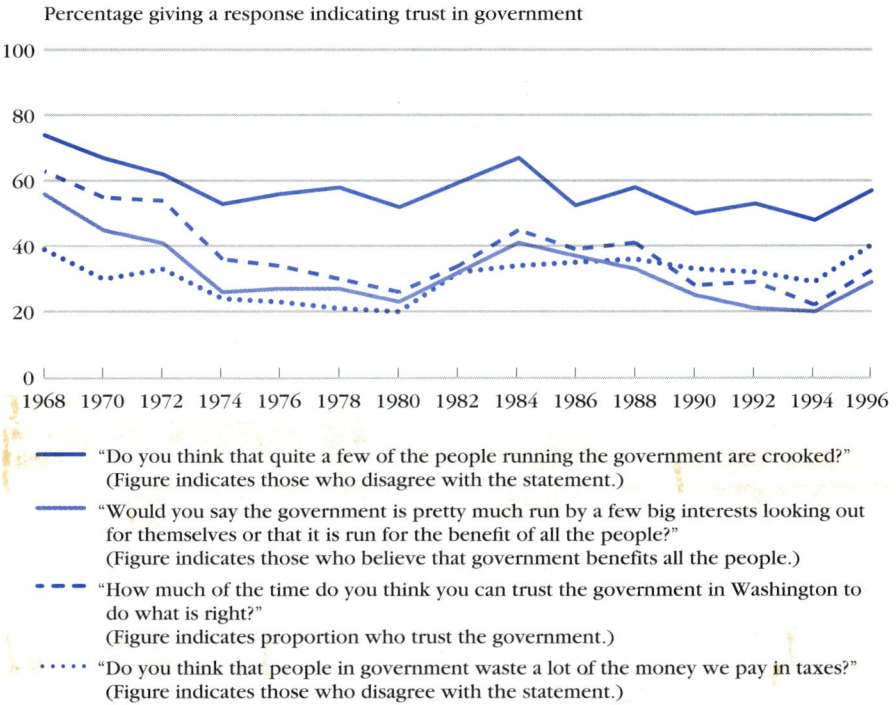

"Do you think that quite a few of the people running the government are crooked?" (Figure indicates those who disagree with the statement.)

"Would you say the government is pretty much run by a few big interests looking out for themselves or that it is run for the benefit of all the people?" (Figure indicates those who believe that government benefits all the people.)

"How much of the time do you think you can trust the government in Washington to do what is right?" (Figure indicates proportion who trust the government.)

"Do you think that people in government waste a lot of the money we pay in taxes?" (Figure indicates those who disagree with the statement.)

SOURCE: Analysis based on data from the American National Election Studies, conducted by the University of Michigan, Center for Political Studies, Ann Arbor, Michigan. Data provided by the Inter-University Consortium for Political and Social Research, located at the University of Michigan, Center for Political Studies, Ann Arbor, Michigan.

increased; but as Figure 6-3 shows, it leveled off by the middle of the decade. During the early 1990s (with the exception of brief periods such as those following the Persian Gulf War and the Oklahoma City bombing), it was on the decline once again until the economic prosperity improved people's evaluation of how the government was doing. Nonetheless, the misuse of campaign funds for which Speaker Newt Gingrich was reprimanded by the House in 1996 and President Clinton and Vice President Gore's use of the White House to raise campaign funds are recent examples of behavior that continues to fuel public mistrust.

People tend to be less willing to give government officials leeway in developing policy if they have little trust in the ability of those officials to find acceptable solutions. A decline in trust also shortens the length of time the public is willing to wait for results. It increases cynicism and discourages the participation in the political process that is so important in a democracy.

Levels of trust are not uniform throughout the population. Young people traditionally exhibit more trust in government than their elders do.

In the aftermath of the 1995 bombing of the federal office building in Oklahoma City, media attention to the strident anti-government stance of paramilitary groups like the Michigan Militia generated a public backlash against them.

Although political trust among young people declined during the late 1960s and early 1970s, by the mid 1970s young people were again the most trusting of any age group, and they have remained so since that time. Political trust is also generally greater among people with higher education; however, African-American college graduates have been less trusting than African Americans who do not have a college education. Trust also varies among racial groups, largely in response to their ability to identify with the policies of a particular president.

People are not only less trusting of government; they are also less trusting of each other. In 1964, approximately half of Americans believed that others could be trusted most of the time. By the mid 1990s, that percentage had dropped to 35.[21]

Political efficacy For civic responsibility to be taken seriously, citizens must believe that they can make a difference, that they can bring about a desired political outcome. This belief, known as **political efficacy**, has declined in recent years. Evidence of lower political efficacy can be seen in the decreasing levels of voter turnout since the 1960s, when a little over 60 percent of the eligible population voted. During the 1970s and 1980s, that percentage declined to the point where barely more than half the electorate voted in the 1988 presidential election. Although turnout did increase to 55 percent in 1992, it was only in the range of 36 percent in the 1994 midterm elections and 49 percent in 1996, the lowest level in a presidential election since 1924. A sizable proportion of American voters still apparently believes that their vote does not really matter.

As a group, both African Americans and Hispanics have a lower sense of efficacy than whites do. Their lower levels of education explain some of the difference, because studies conducted regularly since the 1950s have consistently found that education is correlated with higher levels of political efficacy. Yet the increase in education levels in the general public has not resulted in an overall increase in political efficacy, nor has it led to an increase in the portion of the population that votes. Among the factors that contribute to lower efficacy today are the weakening of party loyalties, cynicism caused by the news media's attention to conflicts of interest and unethical behavior on the part of public officials, and the size and complexity of modern government and the average citizen's difficulties in dealing with it.

Trust and efficacy are related. People who trust government tend to feel that they can affect its decisions, whereas those who lack trust often feel helpless and become alienated and angry.[22] In the 1990s, much of this anger has been directed against the federal government and those who run it. The votes against the presidential incumbent in 1992 and against the Democrats (the party controlling Congress) in 1994 reflected much unhappiness with the way those in power were behaving and governing. More extreme manifestations of this anger have included the growth of private militia groups around the country and terrorist acts such as the 1995 bombing of the federal office building in Oklahoma City.

For a democratic system to exist and thrive, the people must value the principles and processes on which it is based. If people perceive the rules as unfair, they are likely to be content with electoral or policy decisions made in accordance with those rules, and they may choose not to abide by those decisions.

Support for democratic processes and tolerance of others Fortunately, most Americans value the norms that underlie their political system.[23] Although they have been increasingly critical of their government, they strongly oppose taking violent actions against it, as can be seen in the reaction to the Oklahoma City bombing. In fact, public support for the principles of majority rule and minority rights remains high.

Surveys conducted during the last two decades have also found greater tolerance for diverse groups and nontraditional behaviors, including changes in gender roles. In theory at least, people seem more willing today than they were in the past to tolerate homosexual behavior, accept women in what were traditionally considered male jobs, and vote for minority candidates for office. In practice, however, certain beliefs and affiliations (atheism, racism, communism, and Nazism, for example), certain forms of speech (obscenity, blasphemy, and speech that is perceived as sexual harassment), and certain kinds of behavior (desecration of patriotic symbols, lesbian motherhood, and interracial marriage) are not as readily tolerated.

How to prevent people from being intolerant of others is an extremely difficult problem. Attempts to protect minority rights by prohibiting discrimination have themselves become controversial. In the late 1980s, some colleges and universities created codes of conduct that punished those whose speech and actions denigrated or offended others, particularly women and certain minority groups. Proponents of these codes contend that some words constitute or can lead to behavior that violates people's rights, behavior that society has a right to prevent. However, critics contend that the codes establish what kinds of language and behavior are **politically correct** and limit individual rights protected by the First Amendment. Several codes have subsequently not met the test of constitutionality, and others have been modified or rescinded by the schools that issued them.

Tolerance is a learned behavior. It is influenced by family, school, community, and the many associations people have in the course of their daily lives. Once again, level of education seems to be the most important factor. The more education a person has, the more likely it is that he or she will be tolerant of those who are different.

PUBLIC OPINION AND GOVERNANCE

Regardless of what different groups of Americans believe about issues that are vital to democratic government, the general public does not dictate policy. It cannot. Relatively few people have the time, interest, or motivation to contact government representatives directly. Moreover, specific policy issues have minimal influence on the voting behavior of most Americans.

What is the role of public opinion in the determination of policy? It helps establish the salience of issues and, to some extent, identifies acceptable and unacceptable policy alternatives. For example, consider the drug problem. Policy options range from educational campaigns in schools, to methadone treatment centers for addicts, to criminal prosecution for those who sell illegal drugs. To date, however, the legalization of "hard" drugs, even marijuana, has not been seen as a viable option because it conflicts with the public's strongly held view that these drugs are dangerous and their use should be discouraged.

A high level of public interest and concern indicates that an issue is important and, usually, that something must be done about it. If there is a dominant mood or opinion, public officials tend to follow it. Scholars who have studied opinion change and policy outcomes have found a correlation between the two;[24] they have also found that opinion change *precedes* rather than *follows* policy change, a pattern that one would expect in a democracy.[25]

For most issues, however, there is not a single dominant opinion but a variety of opinions. These opinions are developed, publicized, and communicated by the opinion makers, who have the skills, contacts, and motivation to try to convert them into policy decisions. Specific courses of action are more likely to be influenced by the interchange between opinion makers and government officials than by the general public. However, the values and beliefs of the people are still important because they set the parameters within which policy debate occurs and policy decisions are made.

Government officials have been extremely sensitive to public opinion, so much so that they have been accused of pandering to it and also of manipulating it to their advantage. Such accusations, however, do not take account of the fine line between leading and following. A good leader gets out in front, but not too far. Although Americans may fault their political leaders for failing to heed public opinion or to lead it, government officials still must make many of their decisions without knowing exactly how the public will react.

Moreover, effective policy may demand that decision makers do what they think is right and what will benefit the country the most in the long run, regardless of the public mood and the short-run consequences of a decision. But there is a danger here, too. American history is filled with examples of policies that failed or had to be curtailed because of lack of public support. Prohibition is one outstanding example; the Vietnam War and President Clinton's proposals to reform the health-care system are others.

Finally, what is the impact of public opinion on the politics of American government? The public's values and beliefs constitute the intellectual foundation on which the political system rests; the public's opinions frame the policy debate and influence the government's decisions. Those decisions, in turn, are continuously subject to public evaluation and reevaluation. Public opinion therefore is a critical component of democratic politics.

CASE STUDY

GENERATION X: INDIVIDUALISTIC AND INVOLVED

How many times have you heard or read that the so-called Generation X—those born between 1961 and 1981, who may well include you—is less politically aware and involved than previous generations of Americans? In one sense, this is true. Compared with their parents, members of Generation X are less informed; they vote less regularly; they have weaker partisan attachments; and they join fewer national political organizations. But this sketch may be too broadly drawn. Research into the interests and activities of Generation Xers paints a more complex picture—one that suggests they may conceive of "politics" in an entirely different manner from the way their elders see it.

The Pew Research Center for The People & The Press, as well as other polling organizations, has conducted surveys throughout the 1990s to determine levels of interest and involvement of various age groups. Pew researchers reported that in 1995 only 20 percent of the people they surveyed between the ages of 18 and 20 paid close attention to major news stories, as compared with 23 percent of those between the ages of 30 and 49 and 29 percent of those above the age of 50. The report continued: "The generation gap was especially large for news stories that dealt with politics and policy (both domestic and international) and the economy. It all but disappeared for stories that dealt with social issues, celebrity scandals, and sports."[1] These findings led the Pew analysts to conclude: "Americans under 30 represented a generation that knew less, cared less, and read newspapers less than previous generations of young people."[2]

Similar trends are evident in partisan affiliation and voting turnout. Generation Xers have not developed strong allegiances toward political parties. Although they do tend to identify themselves as Republicans or Democrats rather than independents, they switch their identification more readily than do their elders. Moreover, they turn out to vote less than does any other age group in the electorate.

It is important to note that partisan identification in general has been weakening over the last several decades and that voting turnout (with the exception of the 1992 election) has also been declining among all population groups. Thus, the profile of Generation X is not all that different from that of the preceding Baby Boomer generation when the "Boomers" were between 18 and 30 years of age. On the other hand, Generation Xers are also less involved in other types of partisan political activity than Boomers and older Americans were at their age. They join fewer traditional political organizations and are less likely to participate in electoral campaigns or other types of political activism, particularly at the national level.

Why does this generation seem so turned off to politics? If you are part of it, you may be able to answer this question on the basis of your own feelings and experiences. But scholars who have studied this subject suggest that the answer may have to do with the formative experiences Generation Xers have had—or perhaps not had—growing up and the ways in which they have acquired their information and beliefs about politics.

Generation X has come of age in a conservative era, one characterized more by endings than beginnings. The cold war ended, and with it the principal threat to United States military security. The civil rights and women's rights movements have aged, and with that aging has come increasing public skepticism toward claims that government should be actively promoting equal rights and greater opportunities for all. An era of big government and large-scale social and economic programs has given way to a reduction in the size of the national government, a devolution of some of its social and economic responsibilities to the states, and tighter constraints on government spending. Broadly speaking, then, public perceptions of the role of government, of what it can and cannot do, should and should not do, have narrowed.

Moreover, the nuclear family structure has been weakened by divorce; and parental nurturing has been affected by the dual careers of fathers and mothers, producing what some refer to as a "latch key" generation. These changes could not help affecting the values, beliefs, and activities of Generation X much as the Great Depression, World War II, and the onset of the Cold War affected their grandparents' generation and as the Vietnam War, the Watergate scandal, and the civil rights, feminist, and other social movements identified with the 1960s (and the reactions to them) influenced their parents' generation. For example, the shift toward a smaller role for government may have made Generation Xers see politics as simply less important and less relevant to their lives than their elders do. And the changes in family life may have left many young people with the attitude that they are on their own and have little connection with a larger community or society, including such cooperative endeavors as politics and government.

The so-called communications revolution, which began in the midtwentieth century and accelerated in the 1980s and 1990s, has also had a profound impact on the availability, form, and dissemination of knowledge about politics and government. For Generation X, television has replaced newspapers as the principal source of information. It has weakened the impact of family and community as socializing agents, particularly as the principal purveyors of partisan beliefs and political learning. And as noted earlier in this chapter, it may have helped produce boredom and cynicism about politics among Americans in general, and especially the younger people.

But being turned off to traditional partisan politics does not necessarily mean that Generation X does not care or is not involved. In fact, an increase in voluntary activities by Americans at the community level in recent years has been particularly strong among the young. Whether because of the service component that many secondary schools, colleges, and religious groups emphasize or even require today, or of the activities in which environmentalists, preservationists, crime fighters and others concerned with quality of life are engaged, or even of organizations created to foster and promote ethnic, racial, and other forms of diversity (sexual orientation, for example), volunteerism has increased. And Presidents Bush and Clinton have both sought to increase it still further.

The volunteerism of Generation X and the values that underlie it may not accord with traditional political attitudes and activities in a democracy, but they do suggest that on a highly personal level Generation Xers care about and are very much involved in their communities. Perhaps we need to broaden our definition of what is political.

Discussion Questions

1. What criteria should be used to measure political activity?
2. On the basis of these criteria, how involved are you and your friends in politics?
3. What have been the primary influences on the development of your political attitudes and involvement—or lack of involvement—in politics?
4. What are your beliefs about civic responsibility in a democracy? Do you think political parties and frequent elections are essential for a democracy? Are there other vital needs?

1. Pew Research Center for The People & The Press, "Times Mirror News Interest Index: 1989–1995," p. 7.
2. Ibid.

SUMMARY

Political socialization is an ongoing process through which people learn to be *citizens,* or members of a political society. It continues throughout the life cycle. During the preadolescent period, the majority of American children develop positive feelings about their government and its leaders. These feelings play an important role in the maintenance and stability of the political system. Adolescents begin to recognize that individuals may take sides in disagreements among candidates, political parties, and interest groups. They are confronted by the need to make choices, of which the most important is the choice of a party affiliation.

Agents of political socialization are groups and individuals from whom citizens acquire political information and learn political attitudes and values. The family is the dominant agent of political socialization in the early years. With the increase in single-parent families, however, the family is becoming a less potent source of political attitudes.

Although much of a child's time is spent in school, schools play a limited role in political socialization. When peer groups actively engage in political discussions or activities, they are likely to be very influential in shaping the political orientations of their members. The mass media, in contrast, provide political information but do not have a significant effect on political attitudes.

People vary greatly in the extent to which they participate in politics and in the types of activities in which they engage. Because levels of political interest have been declining in the United States, campaign activity is a relatively rare form of political participation. The most frequent form is voting, the only political activity in which many Americans participate regularly. Many people do not even vote; however, saying that they lack time, interest, or motivation or that registration requirements create an impediment. Although some citizens directly contact a political figure or public agency for the purpose of altering public policy, most people are more likely to engage in cooperative activity toward this end, and organized groups are active at all levels of government.

Unconventional participation includes activities such as protest demonstrations and riots. Although they attract only a small proportion of citizens, these forms of participation may have a significant effect on public policy because of their intensity and visibility.

About one-fifth of American adults does not participate in political activities at all. Participation correlates closely with an individual's *socioeconomic status* (SES), or relative social and economic standing. The higher one's SES, the greater is the likelihood that one will participate actively in politics.

Participation is not the only way to affect politics. The identification and expression of public opinion is another. Although public opinion influences the issues the government tackles and when and how it tackles them, it does not usually dictate specific solutions. Rather, public opinion sets the parameters within which policy debate occurs and contentious issues are resolved by those with the knowledge, power, and responsibility to do so.

The most efficient way to discover what the public thinks is by conducting a *public opinion poll,* which can provide useful information on the direction, stability, and intensity of public opinion so long as the poll is an accurate and valid indicator of the opinion it purports to measure.

Over the years, surveys have found that most Americans are poorly informed about politics and government. Those who have the most information tend also to be better educated and have higher incomes. A poorly informed public gives government leaders more flexibility in making policy decisions, but it also encourages short-term solutions that have an immediate impact and increases the influence of interest groups.

Because Americans are ambivalent about many issues, they often adopt a *belief system,* a set of simplified ideas that helps them understand and cope with the world. A *political ideology* is a belief system that shapes responses to policy issues and positions. The two dominant political ideologies in the United States are *liberalism* and *conservatism.*

Although most Americans agree that government should promote employment, control inflation, and foster growth, they disagree over how extensive such involvement should be. Indeed, attitudes toward the overall role of government vary widely, as do levels of trust in public officials and levels of belief in *political efficacy,* the idea that political participation can make a difference. In general, however, the American public supports the concepts of democracy and the principles of majority rule and minority rights. It opposes violating the law and disobeying the government despite a trend of declining confidence in and increasing cynicism about government and the performance and behavior of those who work in it. In terms of applying the principles of tolerance, there is less agreement.

Public opinion does not dictate policy, but it does establish the salience of issues and set limits on acceptable policy alternatives. A high level of public interest indicates that an issue is important and requires action. But in most cases, no single opinion dominates. When many different opinions exist, policy is more apt to be produced by negotiations between opinion makers and government officials than by the general public.

KEY TERMS

political socialization
citizen
agents of political socialization
unconventional participation
socioeconomic status
public opinion
public opinion polls
direction
stability
intensity
salience
belief system
political ideology
liberalism
conservatism
political efficacy
politically correct

RESOURCES

READINGS

Abramson, Paul R. *Political Attitudes in America: Formation and Change.* San Francisco: Freeman, 1983. A comprehensive examination of what Americans believe and the factors that shape and alter those beliefs.

Conway, M. Margaret. *Political Participation in the United States.* 2d ed. Washington, D.C.: Congressional Quarterly, 1991. A recent survey of scholarship on many elements of political participation.

Craig, Stephen C. *The Malevolent Leaders: Popular Discontent in America.* Boulder, Colo.: Westview, 1993. A study of the trends in and causes of public distrust in government.

Erikson, Robert S., Norman R. Luttbeg, and Kent L. Tedin. *American Public Opinion: Its Origins, Content, and Impact.* 4th ed. New York: Macmillan, 1991. An excellent summary of the literature on political opinion by three political scientists.

Greenstein, Fred I. *Children and Politics.* New Haven, Conn.: Yale University Press, 1965. An original and imaginative exploration of the ways in which children come to know and relate to the political world.

Herbst, Susan. *Numbered Voices: How Opinion Polling Has Shaped American Politics.* Chicago: University of Chicago Press, 1993. A historical account of how polling data have come to play an important role in American politics.

McClosky, Herbert, and Alida Brill. *Dimensions of Tolerance: What Americans Believe About Civil Liberties.* New York: Russell Sage, 1983. A study of political beliefs that argues that tolerance is a learned behavior reinforced by group associations.

Sapiro, Virginia. *The Political Integration of Women.* Urbana: University of Illinois Press, 1984. A thorough analysis of the development of women's political consciousness in the 1980s.

Smith, Robert C., and Richard Seltzer. *Race, Class, and Culture: A Study in Afro-American Mass Opinion.* Albany: State University of New York Press, 1992. Examines racial attitudes and opinions within the African-American community and contrasts those attitudes and opinions with those of the white majority in the United States.

Stimson, James A. *Public Opinion in America: Moods, Cycles, and Swings.* Boulder, Colo.: Westview, 1991. Presents a theory of how public moods change and the impact of those changes on politics and elections.

Verba, Sidney, Kay Lehman Schlozman, and Henry Brady. *Voice and Equality: Civic Voluntarism in American Politics*. Cambridge, Mass.: Harvard University Press, 1995. A study of 15,000 Americans and the reasons for variance in their political participation patterns.

Verba, Sidney, and Norman H. Nie. *Participation in America: Political Democracy and Social Equality*. Chicago: University of Chicago Press, 1972. A landmark study of impressive scope, analyzing participation patterns in the United States.

Zaller, John. *The Origins and Nature of Mass Opinion*. New York: Cambridge University Press, 1992. Another major study of opinion formation.

ORGANIZATIONS

Committee for the Study of the American Electorate, 421 New Jersey Avenue, S.E., Washington, DC 20003; phone (202) 546-3221; fax (202) 546-3571. A nonpartisan research group that studies issues involving low and declining voter turnout.

The Gallup Poll, 53 Bank Street, Princeton, NJ 08540; phone (609) 924-9600; fax (609) 924-2584; Internet http://www.Gallup.com/

Inter-University Consortium for Political and Social Research, Institute for Social Research, University of Michigan, Ann Arbor, MI 48106; phone (313) 764-5494; fax (313) 764-8041; e-mail netmail@um.cc.umich.edu; Internet http://www.icpsr.umich.edu/

League of Women Voters of the United States, 1730 M Street, N.W., Washington, DC 20036; phone (202) 429-1965; fax (202) 429-0854; Internet http://www.electriciti.com/~/wvus/ A nonpartisan organization that works to increase participation in government.

Partnership for Democracy, 2335 18th Street, N.W., Washington, DC 20009; (202) 483-0030. A foundation that provides technical and financial assistance to grassroots citizen and community organizations concerned with public policy issues.

Roper Center for Public Opinion Research, User Services Department, P.O. Box 440, Storrs, CT 06268; phone (203) 486-4440; fax (203) 486-6308; Internet http://www.lib.uconn.edu/RoperCenter/

7

Interest Groups and Political Parties

PREVIEW

- Political interest groups and public policy
- Electoral activity: spending by PACs; PACs: pro and con
- Lobbying: types; targets; changes in lobbying and lobbyists; regulation; consequences
- The American party system: major and minor parties
- A brief history of the two-party system
- Party organization at the national, state, and local levels
- Parties and elections
- Parties, policy, and government: determining party positions and converting positions into public policy; influencing Congress, executive, and judiciary

Americans care about the environment, but they also care about the economy. In the last three decades, these concerns and the interests that support them have continually clashed with one another. On one side are the environmental groups, such as the Sierra Club, the National Wildlife Federation, the Environmental Defense Fund, and the Natural Resources Defense Council; their allies from state and local governments; concerned members of the scientific community; and a generally sympathetic Democratic party. On the other side are various economic groups: trade associations such as the American Manufacturers Association, the National Lumber Association, and the U.S. Chamber of Commerce; energy producers and consumers; the workers who are employed in these industries; and a Republican party leery of too much federal regulation.

In their battles over legislation to establish environmental standards and regulations to implement them, each side has developed a strategy for achieving its policy objectives. Each has worked with its own allies on Capitol Hill and in the executive branch. Each has tried to mobilize public support. And each has been involved in electoral politics. This ongoing struggle illustrates the way in which interest groups and political parties can affect the governmental system and public policy.

During the 1970s, the environmentalists had the upper hand. Not only did they gain legislation to reduce pollution into the air, water, and soil, to protect endangered species, and to conserve and manage the nation's natural resources, they also saw the creation of the federal Environmental Protection Agency (EPA), charged with issuing regulations, monitoring activities, and prosecuting violators. In 1980, Congress even created a Superfund to help pay the costs of cleaning up sites contaminated with toxic wastes.

With the election of Republican President Ronald Reagan later that year, however, the fortunes of the environmental proponents began to change. The Reagan administration, more sympathetic to economic concerns and wanting to decrease the federal government's regulatory activities, ordered the EPA to reduce its aggressive enforcement of environmental standards. Moreover, Congress, particularly the Republican-controlled Senate from 1981 to 1987, resisted new and more far-reaching environmental legislation.

In 1986, environmental and economic groups began a major battle over clean air legislation, in which the economic forces were initially successful. With the backing of the Reagan administration, they prevailed on their congressional allies to block the bill in committee. But the battle resumed in subsequent Congresses. By the end of the decade, growing public concern over the environment and Democratic control of both houses of Congress generated sufficient political pressure to make the adoption of some legislation likely. Consequently, Republican President George Bush proposed a bill to tighten controls on utilities that burned soft coal and to institute new, tougher auto emissions standards. Praised at first by environmentalists and criticized by energy producers and users, his proposals became the basis for a compromise in 1990, known as amendments to the Clean Air Act.

In politics, however, defeat is rarely final if the issue and the protagonists remain. This time it was the business community that took the lead, urging the president to avoid stringent rules for implementing the new law. Facing enormous pressure from organized groups that had supported his administration, as well as a tough reelection campaign, Bush gave in, leaving it to the new, Democratic Clinton administration to issue the regulations.

But the pendulum has kept swinging. In 1993, President Clinton was forced to seek a compromise between loggers and environmentalists in the Northwest over the threat posed to the spotted owl, an endangered species, by continued logging in the forests it inhabited. After their victory in the 1994 elections, congressional Republicans tried to limit the EPA's regulatory clout by substantially restricting its authority to enforce parts of the Clean Air Act and the Clean Water Act. But divisions within the party combined with Democratic opposition not only prevented the restrictions from being enacted but also forced the Republicans to restore funding they had initially proposed be cut from the agency's budget and to enact a law that requires state and local governments to inform people about health-threatening substances in their drinking water. The Clinton administration then issued even more stringent regulations in the summer of 1997, thereby forcing business opponents back to the Republican Congress to try to soften their "economic" impact. And the fight continues.

The clash over environmental issues illustrates the pervasiveness of interest group and party politics in practically all aspects of contemporary policy making, both foreign and domestic, and in all arenas of government from the legislative to the executive to the judicial. Whether the concern be clean air and water, wetlands, endangered species, private property rights, grazing and mining fees, pesticides, farm conservation, fishing, nuclear and chemical waste disposal, interstate garbage dumping, international trade, or the costs of toxic-waste cleanup, diverse groups and political parties cooperate with or contend against one another to influence government and affect public policy.

The ebb and flow of interest group activity, of conflict between and within political parties, and of shifting coalitions between groups on the one hand and parties on the other is another aspect of the politics of American government.

This activity occurs within a political system that encourages people to organize to pursue their objectives and protects them when they do so, but also limits their activities by laws that establish the bounds of acceptable behavior. Who wins and who loses these political battles, and how much do they gain or lose, is determined by several factors: the size and clout of the groups, the political environment in which they must operate, and the partisan composition of government. Those best able to mobilize large coalitions, to shape and activate public opinion, and to gain access to and influence over those in power are apt to be most successful. The openness of the process to outside interests and to partisan debate is consistent with democracy; the advantages certain groups and the major parties have and the benefits they receive may not be. Therein lies the dilemma of interest-group and party politics for a democratic society.

Political parties have existed since the 1790s. Interest groups have been around even longer, but they have become more numerous, more focused, and better organized in the last three decades. As these groups have gained influence over the policy process, political parties have lost some of their traditional power. This dynamic between parties and interest groups has energized the American political system and affected its representational character as well as public policy. This chapter will examine how interest groups and parties have affected the politics of American government.

POLITICAL INTEREST GROUPS AND PUBLIC POLICY

To achieve their objectives, groups have to become involved in the political and governing processes. Those that do are referred to as **political interest groups**. They have three primary characteristics: (1) shared interests and goals, (2) an organizational structure, and (3) a desire to influence public policy.

All groups are not equally influential. Their power varies according to a number of factors: their size, the composition of their membership, their unity and sense of purpose, their leadership, and the resources at their disposal. Their goals are also a factor, because goals that are grandiose or lie outside the mainstream of public norms, values, or beliefs (the termination of Medicare or Social Security, for example, or the public financing of all federal elections) are not likely to be achieved. Among interest groups, then, some begin with a considerable advantage.

Consider the factor of size. Groups with a large membership such as the American Association of Retired Persons (AARP), with more than 33 million members, or the American Automobile Association (AAA), with about 31 million, exercise influence by virtue of their numbers. However, larger groups are more likely to be plagued by internal divisiveness, and issues that are salient to some of their members are less important to others. As a result, dissension may dissipate the group's impact or even discourage it from taking a position.

Large labor unions like the AFL-CIO, business federations like the U.S. Chamber of Commerce, and groups like the National Organization for Women are others that fall into this category. Although their leaders are interested in numerous public issues, their members are united on only a few of them. Business groups and labor groups each unify (usually in opposition to each other) on bread-and-butter issues such as the minimum wage, health benefits, job security, and working conditions; but their members divide on social issues such as affirmative action. For women's groups, the issues that are most likely

WHERE ON THE WEB?

Interest Groups and Political Parties

Do you want to join a group that protects the welfare of animals, the environment, or the right to own a gun? Or maybe you'd like to find out more about what Libertarians believe. Interest groups and political parties are great avenues to becoming involved in local or national civic life. The Internet provides a useful way to find out about them as well as to get up-to-the-minute information on their activities.

You can access many interest groups by using the **political science links** on the St. Martin's Press homepage for this book **(http://www.smpcollege.com)**. Once you have accessed the links, go to "American Government" and from there to "Public Policy and Interest Groups." From the list provided, look up the type of group and then the specific organization. There is also a selection of indexes for accessing groups interested in public policy.

If you wish to cast an even wider net, you can do so through one of the World Wide Web servers such as **Yahoo** (http://www.yahoo.com/government/politics/interestgroups) which is a particularly useful, well-organized search that includes "gopher" and "ftp" sites as well as websites on its menu. In Yahoo, look first under the general category of "Interest Groups." Under the title "Government/Politics/Interest Groups/Public Interest Groups," you will find many political organizations as well as a long list of other groups.

When a group does not fit the category of interest group on the Internet, try looking under specific subjects. For example, the Christian Coalition is listed under the entry "Society and Culture/Religion/Organizations/Christianity," even though the sites (like the coalition itself) seems heavily involved in political activism.

It is much easier to find political parties on the Internet. The major parties, their state affiliates, and their Senate and congressional policy and fund-raising committees all have sites. To access them, simply contact the major parties at their Internet addresses:

Democratic National Committee http://www.democrats.org

Republican National Committee http://www.rnc.org

and continue to the state, local, or congressional party links that you desire.

Most minor parties also have Internet addresses. Here are some of them:

Communist party http://www.hartford-hwp.com/cp-usa

Libertarian party http://www.lp.org

Reform party http://reformparty.org

Socialist party http://www.socialist.org

U.S. Taxpayers party http://www.USTaxpayers.org

If you can't find the site you want here, check the political party link on the St. Martin's Press homepage.

to produce a consensus include equal employment opportunity and equal pay, reproductive rights, and child care; for senior citizens they include health and retirement benefits.[1] Smaller organizations, such as the Milk and Ice Cream Association, the National Association of Home Builders, and the National Bankers Association, have a narrower membership base and fewer policy interests, but there is greater consensus among members about which of these issues are salient. Unity brings strength to the smaller interest groups.

A related factor is emotional intensity. To some extent, depth of feeling can compensate for lack of numbers. For years the National Rifle Association's membership was less than 2.5 million, yet it was able to derail federal gun control legislation.[2] Success has also been experienced by organizations with even smaller memberships, such as the American Civil Liberties Union, in protecting First Amendment rights.

Financial resources are also very important, not only for staffing an organization and keeping the members informed but also for lobbying and supporting candidates for office. The better the financial resources a group has, the more likely its communications facilities will be state of the art.

For organizations with staffs in Washington, an important source of influence is contact with people "in the right place" in government. Washington is full of former members of Congress and former executive branch officials, including senior White House aides, who represent organized interests in the private sector—a practice referred to as **revolving door politics**. Former top-level Department of Defense officials, both military and civilian, may be found working for major government contractors or even for foreign governments. Conversely, federal

Success need not depend on numbers for groups whose followers care enough about their cause. For the 2.5 million members of the National Rifle Association, "stick to your guns" is both the style and the goal. Here Marion P. Hammer, the first woman president in the NRA's 125-year history, sounds the call to arms at the group's national convention in 1996.

regulatory agencies are often composed of people who have worked in the industries they are charged with regulating. It is the personal contacts within the relevant government agencies that enhance an interest group's ability to influence those agencies.

ELECTORAL ACTIVITY

How do political interest groups influence the politics of American government? A group that is interested in influencing public policy has three electoral options. It can support specific candidates either in an election or when the president proposes a nomination to the Senate. In some states, it can also introduce a recall petition to remove elected officials. A recall election occurred in California in 1995 when Los Angeles County voters removed a representative to the state legislature who had been elected as a Republican but switched to independent, thereby denying the Republicans a majority in the lower chamber. The third option, permitted by some states but not the national government, is to petition to get policy initiatives directly on the ballot, usually by obtaining the signatures of 10 percent of the voters in the most recent statewide election. Citizens groups that favor term limits for legislators and groups supporting and opposing homosexuals' rights have actively used the initiative petition route to achieve their policy objectives.

Political interest groups have become extremely active in political campaigns. Before the 1970s, groups channeled most of their campaign activity through the Democratic and Republican party organizations, which exercised more control over nominations and general election campaigns than they do now. Indeed, federal legislation prevented corporations and labor unions from making direct contributions to political campaigns, so they had to work within the parties to exert influence. Today, the nomination process is less subject to the dictates of party leaders and more a product of activities initiated by candidates and regulated by government. Laws that limit private contributions, subsidize presidential elections, and require candidates to report revenue and expenditures govern the financial environment in which federal elections occur.

The law does not allow business organizations, labor unions, or other interest groups to make direct contributions to candidates for national office. But it does allow them to form groups among their employees, stockholders, or members. Known as **political action committees** (PACs), these groups (see Figure 7-1 for types of PACs and their number) solicit voluntary contributions and use the money to influence political campaigns and policy outcomes. PACs can contribute up to $5,000 to individual candidates (except for the major parties' presidential and vice presidential nominees), spend an unlimited amount of money independently in support of or in opposition to candidates, and educate, mobilize, and register voters on behalf of candidates. And there are even ways to circumvent the contribution limits. In one such technique, called **bundling**, a PAC solicits donations for a group of candidates but requests that the checks be made out directly to specific candidates, not to the PAC. It then bundles together the checks for each candidate and sends them to the candidates. This technique was pioneered by Emily's List, a PAC that solicits contributions for women candidates.

FIGURE 7-1
The Growth of PACs, 1980–1997

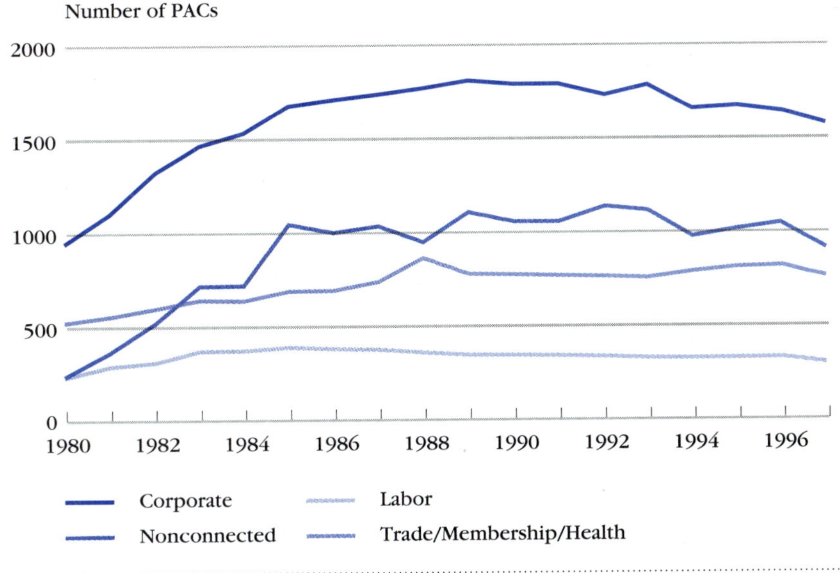

SOURCE: Federal Election Commission, *Record*, July 25, 1997.

In addition to contributing to federal candidates, PACs can contribute to state and local candidates and political parties in an effort to turn out a large vote. They can also communicate directly with their members and sympathizers. The opportunity to affect who wins and who loses provides a powerful incentive for PACs to organize and participate in the electoral process, and they have done so in a big way.

Spending by PACs

Where does PAC money go? That question is fairly easy to answer because PACs are required to report their receipts and expenditures to the Federal Election Commission, a government agency. At the national level, most of the money goes to incumbents, primarily because they have the power to make decisions on public policy that affect the interests of contributing PACs and their constituents.

PACs did not always give primarily to incumbents. When they were first created, in the 1970s, they gave money to candidates who were most sympathetic to their interests and needs; business PACs gave mostly to Republican candidates and labor PACs to Democrats, the party that controlled Congress at that time. During the 1980s, however, Democratic congressional leaders applied pressure on business leaders to allocate more of their PAC contributions to Democratic incumbents, who controlled the House of Representatives. They warned these PACs that if they wanted to maintain their access and get a fair deal, they should support those who have the power to hear them out and make decisions. The business PACs complied; they became the House Democrats' largest financial backers, giving them even more money than their labor counterparts did in the 1980s and early 1990s.

FIGURE 7-2
The Million Dollar Club: PAC Contributions to All Federal Candidates, Including Money to the Political Parties to Get Out the Vote

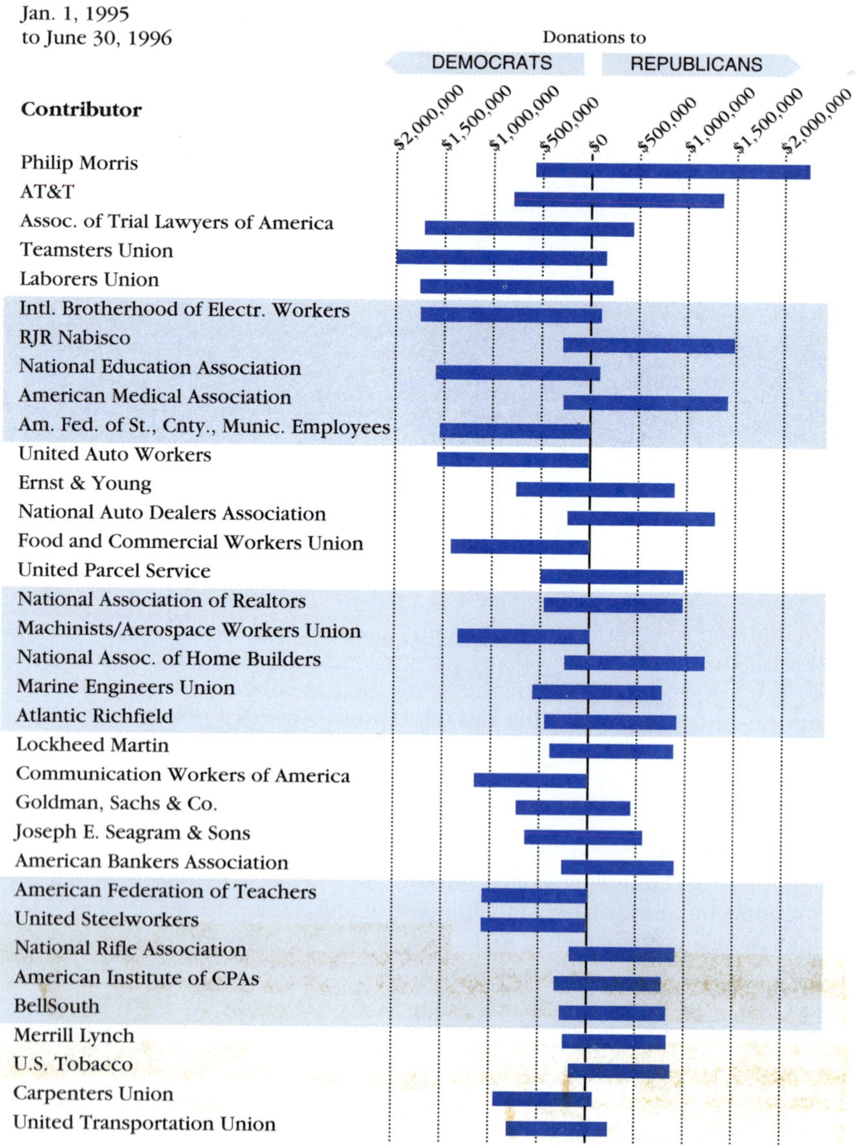

SOURCE: Center for Responsive Politics, as published in "The 50 Largest Political Contributors," *New York Times*, December 26, 1996, D9.

Then came the Republicans' surprising victory in the 1994 midterm elections. The GOP reaped the financial benefits of this victory, as business and trade association PACs reverted to their natural ideological and issue leanings and gave more of their contributions to Republican members of Congress, and they have maintained it since then (see Figure 7-2). During the 1995–1996 election cycle,

PACs contributed $217.8 million to federal candidates, an increase of $28.5 million over the same period during the previous cycle. Incumbents received $146.4 million, challengers $31.6 million, and candidates for open seats $39.8 million. Of the total contributed, Republican candidates received $118.2 million and Democrats $98.9 million.[3]

PACs play a more important role in congressional politics than they do in presidential politics. Within Congress, PAC money is more critical for members of the House of Representatives than for members of the Senate and, as noted previously, more important for incumbents than for challengers. At the presidential level, PAC contributions account for a very small percentage of the total contributions candidates receive in their quest for their party's nomination. In 1992, they accounted for less than 1 percent. In 1996, they were approximately 1.1 percent of total revenues (including matching funds); Dole received the most, amounting to about 2.7 percent of his total revenues.

Although PAC contributions are permitted during the nomination process, they are not allowed to be given directly to candidates in presidential elections. However, the grassroots activities and voluntary efforts of PACs can be a vital supplement to a campaign. In 1996, for example, organized labor waged a $35 million "nonpartisan" voter education campaign that was aimed at turning out a sizable pro-labor vote and defeating incumbents, primarily Republicans, who were considered antilabor. The campaign was only partially successful.

PACs: Pro and Con

The increasing involvement of PACs in the electoral process has generated considerable criticism and led to proposals for reform. Critics contend that PACs exercise undue influence on public officials. Since PACs have contributed disproportionately to incumbents, it is natural to infer that they are seeking to obtain the sympathetic ear of those who are already in power. Not only does PAC money gravitate toward incumbents, but it goes disproportionately to party leaders and the chairs of committees and subcommittees because PACs believe that these individuals have the most power to help or hurt the interest group. These patterns raise the suspicion that the more money a candidate receives from a particular PAC, the more difficult it will be for that person to make independent decisions about the PAC's issues once in office.

This distribution of funds would not elicit so much objection were all segments of society equally represented by PACs, but they are not. Corporate and trade association PACs are more numerous and raise and spend more money than their chief adversaries, the labor PACs. And all three groups raise and spend much more than consumer groups. Similarly, nonconnected and ideologically conservative PACs have been more active and more successful fund-raisers than have their liberal opponents.

Another controversial aspect of PACs is their effect on political parties. Most political scientists believe that PACs hurt parties. In addition to siphoning funds away from them, PACs encourage policy-oriented candidates who may not have a history of party involvement or allegiance, and they promote their own relatively narrow agendas. These activities detract from the ability of the parties to take consistent positions on a broad range of issues, to attract candidates who support those positions and are willing to toe the party line, and to hold candidates responsible for how they perform once they gain office.

In contrast, proponents of PACs note that PACs help finance elections, thereby reducing the burden on taxpayers and the general public; they increase knowledge of the issues among their members and the public at large; and they encourage people to vote and to participate in the electoral process in other ways. These activities contribute to the functioning of a democratic society. Moreover, by supporting candidates who are sympathetic to their points of view and are in a position to help them achieve their policy objectives, PACs link the public with its representatives—another important objective of democracy. Finally, proponents point out that group association and election activity are protected by the First Amendment to the Constitution.

Nonetheless, there have been frequent proposals to reform the system and limit the influence of PACs. Recent proposals have included imposing spending limits on congressional candidates, lowering or eliminating the amount of money PACs are allowed to contribute to campaigns, and even providing public funding as is done in presidential elections.

LOBBYING

Once an election is over, what can a group do to ensure that its point of view is forcefully presented when issues of concern arise on Capitol Hill or in a state legislature? It can **lobby**, a term that describes the behavior of people who accost their elected representatives in the lobbies of legislatures and other government buildings and try to persuade them how to vote on an issue. Unfortunately, the word also suggests some of the seamy sides of representation, and it is often associated in the public's mind with illegal and unethical behavior in politics.

Lobbyists do indeed congregate in and around legislative lobbies, but they do much more than that. Their principal function is to provide public officials with information to influence their opinions and positions. Although lobbyists can use a variety of positive and negative inducements in this effort, they must

Lobbyists are a common sight lined up outside the door of the House Ways and Means Committee room as they wait to buttonhole legislators and plead in their clients' interest. This corridor is known as Gucci Gulch because of the expensive Italian loafers that lobbyists favor.

be careful not to exceed the bounds of what officials consider proper conduct or to make permanent enemies. Moreover, because lobbyists typically deal with the same officials again and again, they take care to see that the information they provide is correct. Most lobbyists believe that their ability to persuade is directly related to their credibility; they fear that if they mislead, either purposely or accidentally, their information and arguments will always be viewed skeptically by those they are trying to influence.

Types of Lobbying

Lobbying can take many forms: a memo or statement to a public official indicating a group's position, a trip by influential constituents to Washington to plead an organization's case, or a public relations campaign in which millions of people participate and millions of dollars are spent. In general, however, lobbying techniques may be divided into direct and indirect types. In direct lobbying, group representatives themselves contact public officials; in indirect lobbying, they encourage others to do so. Whether direct or indirect, lobbying activity has the same goal: to influence the decisions of public officials and thereby affect public policy in a manner that accords with the group's interests.

Lobbyists attempt to influence the policy process directly by testifying at public hearings and by providing detailed policy statements, briefings, and supporting material to public officials and their staffs. Sometimes they even draft proposed bills or regulations for use by a committee considering legislation or an agency attempting to implement it. Even when lobbyists do not testify or prepare position papers, they make a point of attending hearings when proposals in which they are interested are being considered.[4]

These same groups have been active in indirect lobbying as well, writing speeches for their sympathizers to deliver and instituting grassroots campaigns to build support for their side within the general public—particularly among

Lobbying on the Internet to Save Student Loans

In 1995, considerable consternation arose within the academic community about proposals to cut appropriations for student loans. Around the country, students demonstrated to protest the proposed cuts. They even formed groups, such as the Coalition to Save Student Aid, which went into action after the House of Representatives approved legislation that would have reduced the amount of money available for loans by $18.7 billion.

Using the Internet, the Coalition issued a legislative alert and devoted two homepages to information about the issue and what students could do about it. The group also sent e-mail to student leaders and student newspapers around the country, urging opponents of the legislation to flood Senate offices with e-mail and come to Washington to stage a public protest. Recent graduates were also mobilized for the effort. The lobbying paid off. The Senate modified the House proposal, and in the end the loan program was only modestly reduced.

people who feel strongly about the issue and are likely to communicate their feelings to those in government. Computer technology makes it possible to target precisely large groups and quickly generate letters to them to raise money, solicit memberships, and mobilize support for a particular policy.

Grassroots campaigns have been in vogue for some time, but now interest groups have begun to engineer these campaigns for their own purposes. This practice is known as **astroturfing**, a name that conveys the artificiality or deceptiveness of the public response that such a campaign creates. Astroturfing is frequently generated by advocacy advertising, such as that engaged in by the health insurance industry to defeat the Clinton administration's health-care reform proposal in 1994.

Industry groups that direct, fund, and profit from an astroturfing campaign often try to hide their involvement so as to create the impression that the movement is public-spirited, not privately motivated. Thus when the American Tort Reform Association mounted a highly successful campaign to reform liability laws on the state and federal level—making it more difficult and less profitable for individuals to sue builders, manufacturers, or service providers—they publicized the community groups such as the little leagues and school boards that supported their coalition, not the large manufacturers, insurance companies, and retail chains that provided the money and would be the primary beneficiaries of the legislation.

A related tack is to point to a common enemy to generate public support. When President Clinton vetoed product liability legislation that Congress had enacted in 1996, critics immediately charged that he was beholden to trial lawyers who had contributed heavily to his campaign and who opposed the limits on monetary awards.

Targets of Lobbying

Most Americans tend to equate lobbying with efforts to influence the legislative process. However, any experienced lobbyist knows that this process is only one part of the government, and that it is not always the most important or most pertinent part for a particular group or a particular issue. At the national level, the president has an active role in the legislative process and the executive agencies have a great deal of discretion in the administration of the laws. Moreover, the courts have the power to interpret and, in some cases, invalidate laws passed by Congress. At the state level, similar patterns of interaction and spheres of influence are evident. What determines the best place for a group to lobby, and what kinds of activities are most successful in different branches or levels of government?

Legislatures Legislators are relatively easy to lobby. They are open and accessible; as elected representatives, they have to be sensitive to outside pressures, particularly when those pressures come from their constituencies. Lobbyists can also provide things that legislators need and want as they carry out their legislative responsibilities: information about how legislation will affect their constituents, political support for the legislation, and financial backing in the next election. For these reasons, lobbyists are generally welcome or at least tolerated in the halls of legislatures and in lawmakers' offices.

How successful lobbyists are in getting what they want from legislators is another matter. The main challenge facing those who hope to influence legislative bodies is the relatively large size of most legislatures and consequently the large number of members who must be contacted and persuaded. It takes time, which costs money. A second problem, particularly at the national level, stems from the degree of activity and number of groups interested in any particular issue. Legislators must deal with a variety of issues and be receptive to a range of special pleaders, and thus lobbyists are rarely alone in presenting their position or unified in the advice they give. Normally, they meet with opposition from other lobbyists. Moreover, legislators frequently behave as if they do not owe lobbyists anything. They may use the professional and personal services provided by lobbyists (such as legislative research, political support, financial contributions, electoral endorsement, and grassroots activity) without promising anything in return.

The proliferation of lobbying has resulted in coalition building among diverse political interest groups. The formation of alliances in support of and in opposition to clean-air and clean-water laws (described at the beginning of this chapter) illustrates the alliance making that regularly occurs among groups with similar interests and objectives. To cite another example, even before President Clinton proposed his health-care reform package to the nation, health-care groups began to form alliances in support of or opposition to his plan.

The executive branch Chief executives—the president and the state governors—and their administrative agencies have also become a major focus of lobbying activities. As in the legislature, lobbying in the executive branch is viewed as legitimate and is usually not discouraged. Indeed, lobbyists and executive branch officials tend to have mutual needs and interests. Whereas interest groups desire access, visibility, and support for their objectives, chief executives and their administrations require political allies within the public arena. Particularly at the national level, where political parties are weak, interest groups can be mobilized to build support for the president's programs.

In addition to trying to influence policy making in the executive branch, interest groups try to shape the content and application of rules governing policy implementation. Indeed, most executive agencies are required to publish proposed regulations and hold public hearings on them to solicit input from the interested public. Moreover, lobbyists specializing in executive branch activities frequently have served in the very departments and agencies they seek to influence. They know how the game is played, who the principal players are, and which arguments and information are apt to be most persuasive.

Groups may also try to influence the selection of political appointments. For example, the Christian Coalition, the Family Research Council, various pro-life groups, and other conservative organizations that opposed Clinton's nomination of Dr. Henry Foster to be surgeon general testified against the nomination in the Senate hearings and mounted considerable public opposition. In contrast, business groups were delighted with the appointment of Chicago businessman William Daley as secretary of commerce at the beginning of Clinton's second term.

Presidents are not defenseless against groups. In fact, they have tried to mobilize them to support their key policy initiatives.[5] President Clinton succeeded in encouraging multinational corporations to lobby for the free trade agreements his administration advanced in its first term, but he was much less successful in building support for health-care reform among business and consumer groups. Since 1978, a public liaison office has operated in the White House to maintain ties and coordinate lobbying activities with a variety of community and interest groups. Some of these activities, however, particularly those involving White House invitations to potential contributors to the Democratic party and the Clinton reelection campaign, raised concerns that the administration had violated the law by using government facilities and computer lists of executives for partisan political purposes.

The judiciary The judicial arena is also a focus of group activity, since political interest groups that have little or no hope of achieving their ends through the legislative and executive processes often turn to the courts for help. How do groups lobby the judicial branch? One way is through the selection of judges. Although the judicial selection process, particularly at the federal level, is often portrayed as nonpolitical, partisan considerations are almost always involved in the nomination and confirmation processes. The vast majority of federal judicial nominees are of the same partisan affiliation as the president. Although most are confirmed by the Senate without much challenge, occasionally a nominee provokes considerable controversy and lobbying of senators by interest groups. This was the case when federal judges Robert Bork (1987) and Clarence Thomas (1991) were nominated to fill vacancies on the Supreme Court; Bork was rejected, and Thomas was barely confirmed. (The conflict over the Bork nomination is described in the case study at the end of Chapter 13.)

Another way to influence the judiciary is through litigation. For those who wish to prevent a hostile majority from depriving them of what they consider their basic rights, the courts are a last resort. Business groups, for instance, have regularly appealed to the courts to invalidate government attempts to regulate their operations. In the early part of this century, they successfully challenged

Was this room for rent? In the Clinton White House the historic Lincoln Bedroom, whose Victorian furnishings include the massive bed where Abraham Lincoln supposedly slept, provided a night's stay for a number of "friends," many of whom also happened to be prominent political contributors to the Democratic party. Although the president said such invitations were entirely appropriate, Republicans charged that he was "renting the room" to the highest bidders.

state and national laws that limited the hours employees could work and established the minimum wage they could be paid. Today, business groups continue to contest restrictions on how they do business, including regulations on health, safety, and environmental concerns and even personnel practices such as hiring, firing, and promoting.

The area of civil rights also provides many illustrations. The landmark school desegregation case of *Brown v. Board of Education* (1954) was brought in the absence of legislation because a law making segregation illegal was unlikely to be enacted by Congress or southern state legislatures in the 1950s. Similarly, groups have gone to court to require state-supported military colleges such as the Citadel and Virginia Military Institute to admit women.

In addition to instituting legal challenges, an interest group may file an **amicus curiae** ("friend of the court") **brief**. This is a legal argument that a group makes to influence a decision on a pending case. For example, more than one hundred different groups filed briefs with the Supreme Court in connection with *Regents of the University of California v. Bakke* (1978), a case dealing with the issue of whether states or the federal government could require affirmative action programs to make up for past discrimination. "Friends of the court" in this case included such diverse organizations as the American Federation of Teachers, the American Indian Bar Association, the American Jewish Congress, the NAACP Legal and Education Fund, the United Farm Workers, and the United Mine Workers. Eleven years later, the Court received seventy-eight amicus briefs in the case of *Webster v. Reproductive Health Services;* of these, forty-six favored the Missouri abortion law that was at issue in the case, and thirty-two opposed it. Similarly, more than one hundred organizations and groups filed amicus briefs in the case of *Planned Parenthood of Southeastern Pennsylvania v. Casey,* which was decided by the Supreme Court in 1992. These briefs debated issues ranging from when life begins, to the legislative history of abortion in America, to the constitutionality of the *Roe v. Wade* decision.

Efforts to influence the justices by means of legal arguments have been supplemented by more visible demonstrations of public support. Public protests, along with organized letter-writing and advertising campaigns, obviously serve the interest groups' needs for visibility and public education (and, indirectly, for their own fund-raising). But whether these activities have much impact on Supreme Court decisions is questionable.

Changes in Lobbying and Lobbyists

As American society grows more pluralistic, many new groups are seeking to influence government. Lobbying activities have increased manyfold, not only in Washington, D.C., but in most state capitals as well. Foreign interests have also found new ways to be represented.

Large lobbying expenditures by governments, political groups, and private companies from other countries, combined with foreign contributions to United States' political parties and their electoral campaigns, raise serious questions about how much non-Americans should be permitted to influence public policy in the United States. In response to these concerns, President Clinton requested all major appointees in his administration to promise that they would *never* represent foreign interests after they left government. He also supported legislation to make it illegal for people who were not United States citizens to contribute to political parties and candidates for office.

Legal changes have already affected lobbying. Sunshine laws mandating that congressional committee meetings and executive agency deliberations be open to the public have forced lobbyists and decision makers to operate in the public spotlight much of the time.[6] New ethics and finance laws have imposed more stringent requirements on public officials who interact with lobbyists, and the news media also report more on improprieties.

Regulation of Lobbying

Some activities by lobbyists and those they lobby, such as the "buying" of support through campaign contributions and personal gifts, are obviously illegal.[7] In other cases, behavior may be legal but inconsistent with the principles of a democratic political system, in which the influence of the wealthy should be no greater than that of the poor. One such practice includes selling tickets to party or candidate fund-raisers in which participants are prominent public officials. The Clinton administration got into trouble when it was revealed that it hosted 103 coffees in 1995–1996 in which prominent individuals were invited to the White House to chat with the president and later solicited for partisan political contributions. The president was also criticized for inviting donors to spend a night at the White House or ride with him on Air Force I.

Over the years, there have been numerous attempts to control lobbying activities, but in recent years, Congress has really tightened the registration and reporting requirements for lobbyists. In 1995, it enacted legislation that broadened the definition of lobbying to include not only direct contact with government officials but also the preparation of information to influence those officials. Those who spend at least 20 percent of their time lobbying members of Congress, their staffs, and executive branch officials are required to register and report the identity of their clients, the issues on which they were involved, and the amount of money they were paid for their services. In addition, the law precludes members of Congress, their staffs, and presidential appointees from earning outside income, although income derived from educational activities such as teaching or writing is excluded as long as these activities are not performed during government time. Presidential appointees may not accept gifts or even a free meal. However, "finger food" at a reception attended by twenty-five people or more is all right. The law goes so far as to prohibit the director and deputy director of the office that represents the United States in trade negotiations with other countries from *ever* representing foreign interests after they leave public service. Other legislation has been directed at establishing guidelines for ethical behavior by current and former public officials.

There still is considerable controversy not only about the effectiveness of these laws but even about their desirability. Is it necessary to encourage ethical conduct in and after public office? Proponents argue that it is; they note that the careers of public officials often begin and end in the private sector, creating a need for rules that prevent private gain at public expense. Others, however, fear that the requirements for financial disclosure, the limits placed on private employment after government service, and the restriction of foreign representation may keep some of the best-qualified people out of government.

Consequences of Lobbying

When resources are limited, it is almost inevitable that some people will benefit more than others. In 1960, E. E. Schattschneider suggested that the beneficiaries of the struggle among political interest groups are the people in higher socioeconomic brackets—those with the most money, the best organizations, and the greatest influence.[8] Today, almost four decades later, there are many more organized interests, but the system still favors the "haves" in the sense that it is resistant to large-scale policy change. Moreover, corporations, educational institutions, and local governments still outnumber public interest and consumer groups and have a larger and more pronounced presence in Washington. They have more resources to hire high-powered lawyers, lobbyists, and public relations firms, which they believe give them greater ability to influence policy makers' decisions.

How effective are political interest groups in actually affecting policy outcomes? The answer depends on how much competition there is among groups within a particular policy sphere and on who will benefit from and who will pay for a new policy. In general, if there is little competition, an interest group seeking change will be more likely to get what it wants than if there is much competition among groups with comparable resources. A good example of a noncompetitive situation is "pork-barrel" legislation (such as medical research grants or public works projects), in which the benefits are concentrated but the costs are widely dispersed. In such a situation, those who stand to gain a lot from creation of the programs or a lot to lose from their elimination have much more incentive to organize and try to influence policy than do those who will pay or save a relatively small amount as a result of the change.

But if there is competition between groups (such as over pollution standards between environmental and energy groups, or over highway speed limits between motorists and truckers on one hand and the insurance industry on the other), there may be a standoff until the competitors can make a deal (as in the case of clean air) or until one side wins (as in the case of removing the national speed limit of 55 miles per hour on interstate highways). In general, the American system puts the burden on those who wish to change policy, not those who wish to maintain it.

Change *is* possible, but it is usually incremental; and it is often the product of strong political leadership, most often but not exclusively emanating from the White House. In the 1960s, Presidents Kennedy and Johnson refocused public policy with their New Frontier and Great Society programs designed to provide direct and indirect aid to those in the lower socioeconomic groups. In the 1980s, President Reagan sought to reverse these policies, reducing the federal government's role in social and economic policy. He did so despite pressure from interest groups that had benefited from these programs and had organized to protect their benefits. In the 1990s, President Clinton proposed streamlining the federal government and reforming the nation's health-care and welfare systems although powerful forces prevented him from achieving many of his legislative objectives. In turn, congressional Republicans offered their own comprehensive plans to balance the budget and devolve many federal government responsibilities onto the states, but they too were forced to modify or abandon some of their proposals in the face of strong pressure from constituents and opposition from the president.

In short, organized interests try to influence what government does, but their influence may be offset or deflected by other interests, the public mood, or skilled political leadership. Thus political interest groups do not usually dictate policy, but they certainly influence it, especially in a government system designed to respond to public pressures.

So, of course, do political parties. They, too, influence the people in government and the timing and content of their policy decisions. When doing so, they, too, are sensitive to public pressures. But they tend to have larger and more diverse constituencies than do interest groups and thus are more interested in issues, although perhaps with less intensity than a group directly affected by a particular policy. And parties also tend to be more candidate oriented than interest groups; in fact, elections are often their principal reason for existing.

THE AMERICAN PARTY SYSTEM

A **political party** is an organization whose goal is to win elective office in order to influence what the government does and how it does it. It comprises three interacting groups of **partisans**: rank-and-file supporters; professionals, who run the organization and manage its operations; and candidates and public officials.

Parties have been adversely affected by the growth and proliferation of interest groups, although they have contributed to that growth and proliferation as well. The loyalties of rank-and-file partisan supporters have weakened; party leaders exercise less control over the nomination of candidates for office and the running of their campaigns; and the mass media, not the political parties, now provide the principal link between candidates and the voters.

Nevertheless, parties still play important roles in the electoral and governing processes. In elections, they raise money, recruit candidates, articulate policy, and mobilize voters. If they are successful, they help organize the legislature, influencing its structure and the voting of its elected representatives. They also affect the executive branch, primarily through the appointments that the chief executive makes and the policies that the executive pursues. Finally, at the national level and also in some states, parties shape the composition of the judiciary and thereby indirectly affect some of its judgments.

Major Parties

Although the major parties have evolved in composition, organization, and power, they continue to be characterized by three principal features: diversity, decentralization, and pragmatism. In contrast, political parties in multiparty systems such as those of France, Israel, Italy, and Russia tend to be more exclusive in composition, narrowly focused on policy issues, and ideological in orientation.

What explains the character of the major parties in America? Part of the explanation has to do with the federal system of government. The Constitution vests substantial powers and responsibilities in the states, including the conduct of elections for all federal and state officials. In fact, except for the election of the president and vice president, all elections in the United States are for state or local officials or for state representatives to Congress. The party system reflects this decentralized federal structure. Candidates are recruited at the state or local level and are responsive primarily to their own constituencies. At the national level, the major parties consist of representatives of the fifty state parties; at the state level, they consist of local representatives. This parochialism affects the policy positions that parties take and the decisions that their elected officials make.

The decentralized and inclusive nature of the major parties is reinforced by another characteristic of the American electoral system. Most officials are chosen in a district in which only one candidate is elected (known as a **single-member district**); there is no prize for coming in second. As a result, each candidate must try to obtain a majority (more than half the votes) or a plurality (more votes than any other candidate) within the district, and candidates of smaller parties have little chance of winning. Members of the British House of Commons are also chosen in single-member districts. However, in Britain the national party leaders designate the candidates, whereas in the United States they are chosen mainly by party supporters in state and local primaries and caucuses. Hence the parties must be receptive to a variety of candidates from different districts.

Since the United States encompasses a large geographic area with a highly diverse population, its major parties must be broad based and adopt positions that are acceptable to as much of the electorate as possible. Hence the parties' policy positions tend to be in the mainstream of public attitudes and opinions, and when they are not, that itself becomes an issue as it was for Republican Barry Goldwater in 1964 and Democrat George McGovern in 1972. Their ideological orientations—Goldwater was very conservative and McGovern very liberal—resulted in high rates of defection by party supporters, who voted for the candidate of the other party.

Minor Parties

In contrast, minor parties have been more concerned with promoting a particular ideology, issue, or candidate.

Ideological parties have had the greatest staying power but the least political impact. (In multiparty systems, they often have a greater impact because their support is needed to form a majority in the legislature; examples include the religious parties in Israel and the Free Democratic party in Germany.) Ideological parties in the United States, such as the Socialists, the Communists, and the Libertarians, have advocated a new way of thinking about the relationship between government and society, a set of ideas that differ significantly from those of the major parties. Because their beliefs lie outside those of mainstream America, however, their followings have been loyal but not large.

Issue parties have had more political success. Created out of dissatisfaction with one or both of the major parties when they ignored an important issue or took an unpopular stand, these parties have sought to get the major parties to change their ways. They have done so largely by attracting support for their own candidates, thereby reducing the electoral coalitions of the major parties. Although issue parties have not usually managed to get their candidates elected, they have drawn attention to their interests, reduced the vote going to the major parties, and forced one or the other to take the actions or support the positions that prompted their protest in the first place. An example is the Populist party, which supported farmers, miners, and small ranchers who favored the unlimited coinage of silver and government regulation of commerce when both major parties rejected these positions at the end of the nineteenth century. After the Democrats adopted a "free-silver" policy, however, the Populists lost their reason for existing and gradually dissolved as a political force.

Although issue parties have continued to emerge from time to time, in recent decades they have become heavily candidate oriented, dominated by individuals who have used them as vehicles for promoting themselves and their own policy agenda. A good example is the party created from the organization that H. Ross Perot established for his presidential campaign of 1992. It was Perot's decision to create the Reform party, which, not surprisingly, adopted many of his policy positions such as reducing the budget deficit and reforming the campaign finance system. Other **candidate** parties include those that supported George Wallace in 1968 and 1972 and John Anderson in 1980.

Minor-party candidates, however, are disadvantaged by the two-party system. They face legal obstacles to getting on the ballot and have difficulty raising sufficient funds to run a viable campaign.

At the presidential level, minor parties are hurt by the mechanics of the Electoral College, which benefit candidates who can win a statewide popular vote. Even if a third-party candidate could win enough electoral votes to prevent either major-party candidate from getting a majority, the next step in the process, in which the House of Representatives must determine the winner, also favors major-party candidates because almost all the representatives are aligned with one of the major parties. These election rules also create a powerful psychological disincentive to voting for minor-party candidates, since in all likelihood, such a vote will be "wasted"; it will not directly determine the winner. In addition, minor-party candidates do not automatically receive government funding unless the party received at least 5 percent of the vote in the previous election. They are still subject to the limits on individual and group contributions during the campaign, however. The only way to skirt these limits is for candidates to use their own money, as Perot did in the 1992 general election (and as Steve Forbes did in the 1996 Republican nomination campaign). In 1996, however, Perot accepted $29 million in government funds and supplemented it by soliciting private contributions. He could spend only $50,000 of his own money on his campaign. Since the Reform party received 8.5 percent of the vote in 1996, it will again be eligible for federal funding in 2000.

Ross Perot (right) with former Colorado governor Richard Lamm at the 1996 convention of the Reform party, where the two competed for the party's presidential nomination. Perot, who had founded and funded the party as a vehicle for his own presidential candidacy, used his control of its machinery to easily brush off Lamm's challenge.

A BRIEF HISTORY OF THE TWO-PARTY SYSTEM

American political parties have changed significantly over the years. Their evolution has been influenced not only by the federal character of the political system in the United States but also by major events such as the Civil War, the recession of the early to mid 1890s, and the Great Depression of the 1930s.

Parties are not mentioned in the Constitution. They began to take shape during the administration of George Washington. The first parties, the *Federalists* and the *Democratic-Republicans* (or Republicans), had little popular support. By the 1820s, the Federalists had faded from the scene and the Republicans had split into feuding factions, one of which formed the coalition that succeeded in electing Andrew Jackson president in 1828.[9] Jackson's followers became known as the *Democrats* and were opposed by a new party known as the *Whigs*.

In 1854, the party known today as the *Republicans* was organized. When the Democrats split over the slavery issue in 1860 and the Whig party collapsed, Republican candidate Abraham Lincoln was elected president. Originally composed of small-business owners, laborers, and farmers, the Republican party increasingly became influenced by big business. At the turn of the century, economic conflict between rural and urban interests ended with the Republicans becoming dominant in national politics for the next three decades, until the election of Franklin Roosevelt in 1932.

During the Great Depression of the 1930s, the electorate divided along economic class lines, with less prosperous voters more likely to be Democratic and more prosperous voters more likely to be Republican. The Democrats expanded their support among white southerners and racial and religious minorities. Since the end of the 1960s, the Democratic New Deal coalition has frayed but not completely disintegrated. Beginning in the 1960s, white southerners, disillusioned with the advocacy of school desegregation, civil rights legislation, and other social programs by Presidents John F. Kennedy and Lyndon Johnson and the Democratic Congress, started voting Republican, first at the presidential level and later at the congressional levels as well. Even moderate southern Democrats such as Jimmy Carter and Bill Clinton were unable to win a majority of the white vote in the South, although with the help of African Americans, Carter did win a majority of the total southern vote in 1976. Clinton did not, however, in either of his elections.

The Democrats have also suffered declining support from several other key groups of the New Deal coalition. Organized labor, for example, remains Democratic, but the decreasing proportion of blue-collar workers (especially union members) in the population has made labor a smaller and hence less important component of the electorate. Catholic identification with the Democratic party has also weakened, although Catholic backing of Clinton increased from 1992 to 1996.

On the other hand, the Democrats have continued to benefit from the support they receive from minority groups, notably African Americans and Hispanics. With the exception of those of Cuban descent, who tend to be Republican, African Americans and Hispanics overwhelmingly think of themselves as Democrats and vote for Democratic candidates at all levels of government. Relatively low socioeconomic status has worked to reinforce the Democratic inclinations of many of these minority voters, but it has also lowered their turnout at the polls. Demographic differences in the parties are revealed in Table 7-1.

Since 1980, discernible differences have developed in the partisan identities and voting patterns of men and women: women are more likely than men to

TABLE 7-1 ***Demography of Democrats and Republican in the mid 1990s (percentages)***

	Republican	Democrat	Independent
National	30	31	39
Sex			
Male	31	26	43
Female	28	37	35
Age			
18–29 years	29	26	45
30–49 years	30	29	41
50–64 years	30	33	37
65 and older	29	42	29
Region			
East	27	31	42
Midwest	29	29	42
South	31	34	35
West	31	30	39
Race			
White	34	26	36
Nonwhite	11	52	33
Black	6	62	28
Education			
College graduate	35	28	37
Some college	31	29	40
High school graduate	29	32	39
Less than high school grad.	22	38	40
Family Income			
$75,000 and over	42	24	34
$50,000-$74,999	37	27	36
$30,000-$49,999	32	29	39
$20,000-$29,999	27	33	40
Under $20,000	22	38	40

SOURCE: "Republicans: A Demographic and Attitudinal Profile," *The Pew Research Center For The People & The Press,* August 7, 1996, 7-9.

identify with the Democratic party, and men are more likely than women to prefer the Republican party. In presidential voting, this "gender gap" reached its maximum in 1996, when men voted for Dole over Clinton by 44 to 43 percent, whereas women backed Clinton by 54 to 38 percent. The gender gap has tended to be larger among whites than among nonwhites, larger among better educated and wealthier voters than among less advantaged groups, and larger among unmarried people than among married ones.

Another important shift in the partisan electoral coalitions has been the movement of new voters, particularly youth. After being more Democratic than their elders for several decades, younger voters (those age 18 to 29) began to change their political allegiances, ideological orientations, and voting patterns in the 1980s. They became more conservative than the general public on a host of economic and social issues and more Republican in their voting behavior, supporting Ronald Reagan in 1980 and 1984 and

George Bush in 1988. During this decade, a majority of the younger voters entering the electorate also identified with the Republican party. However, the 18- to 29-year-old voters returned to the Democratic fold in 1992 and have remained there. In 1996, this age category provided Clinton and Democratic congressional candidates with stronger support than did any other age group.

As for the Republicans, in the last three decades they have gained adherents, probably more from new voters than from a wholesale shift of existing ones. As an electoral coalition, Republicans have become more white, more male, and more suburban. While gaining support in the South and Southwest, they have lost support in the Northeast. While they have maintained the traditional loyalties of white Protestants, they have gained support from Protestant fundamentalists who backed Democratic candidates through 1976. The core constituency of the contemporary Republican party thus consists of members of racial and religious majorities and higher socioeconomic groups.

What conclusions can be drawn about the parties today? The old electoral coalitions have changed and, in the case of the Democrats, weakened to the point where they have lost their partisan advantage. Indeed, by the end of the 1980s, the major parties were at or near parity, with an increasing portion of the electorate identifying themselves as independent.

It is clear that a partisan **dealignment**—a weakening of the attachments that people feel toward political parties—has been occurring over the last thirty years. This dealignment has led more people to think of themselves as independents and vote more for the candidate and less for that candidate's partisan affiliation. It is not nearly as clear, however, whether a *realignment* has occurred or is occurring.

A **realignment**—a shifting in the partisan attitude of the electorate—normally occurs over a series of elections and is characterized by changes in the allegiances of some existing voters from the majority party to the minority party and by the development of preferences for the new emerging majority party among many new voters. With the exception of white southerners, who have switched their partisan allegiances from Democratic to Republican, wholesale shifts from one electoral coalition to another have not occurred. Nor have overwhelming proportions of young voters aligned themselves with one party.

Shifts in partisan attitudes *have* produced a more volatile electorate, however, one on which neither party can depend as confidently as before. These shifts have also contributed to the decline in the party's influence over its candidates, the electorate, and elected officials.

PARTY ORGANIZATION

In the decentralized organization of the major political parties, power is dispersed. Separate structures at the national, state, and local levels operate largely independently of one another. Each exercises autonomy over its nominations and campaigns as well as over the election of its own officials.

The National Level

At the national level, parties have traditionally been weak. For most of their existence, they operated more like confederations of state parties than as independent entities. Today, they are more centralized and have developed extensive and independent fund-raising apparatuses. The Democrats also impose national rules on their state parties in the presidential election; the Republicans do not.

The chair of the national committee serves as the party's chief public spokesperson and liaison to state party leaders. The chair also oversees the party's administrative operation, although sometimes day-to-day responsibilities are performed by an executive director if the chair holds another position, usually that of an elected official.

Generally speaking, the national parties direct the bulk of their energies to presidential campaigns. They raise and dispense funds, identify and target voters, survey and communicate with the public, develop policy positions, and generate partisan appeals. They also provide assistance directly to candidates as well as to state and local party organizations.

The Republicans have led the Democrats in those activities. During the 1970s, they aggressively expanded their fund-raising and technical services while the Democrats, saddled with a divided party and a sizable debt from their 1968 presidential campaign, were unable to do so. In the 1980s the Democrats began to emulate the Republicans in providing some of these benefits for their candidates, but they still lag in fund-raising and campaign support even with their control of the White House and its aggressive fund-raising activities.

In addition, the major parties have established elaborate in-house media facilities that can be used by their candidates and elected officials. The Republicans produce a regular one-hour television program that is transmitted via satellite to stations around the country, and both parties have engaged in generic television and radio advertising to promote their policy positions. They have also devoted considerable resources to surveying public opinion on a regular basis.

Another development that has strengthened the national Democratic party has been changes in that party's rules for the selection of delegates to nominate its presidential and vice presidential candidates. Beginning in the 1970s and continuing into the 1990s, a series of party commissions have reformed the delegate selection process and, with the approval of the national committee, have tried to impose these reforms on the state parties. The new rules deal with the issues of who can participate in party primaries and caucuses, when these contests can be held, how the delegates to the Democratic national convention are apportioned among states and other units, and for whom they can vote.

Although the Democrats' nationalization of party rules and the centralization of fund-raising and campaign services by both parties have significantly increased the influence that national party organizations have on their state and local affiliates, the national organizations do not control the selection of the party's nominees, the platforms on which they run, or the conduct of their campaigns.[10] Nor do they control nominations or campaigns at the state or local levels.

The State and Local Levels

Some of the developments that have changed national party organizations have also affected their state and local counterparts. The organizational structure of many of them has been strengthened, and their operations have been institutionalized. Most state parties now have a permanent staff. Their fund-raising capabilities have been substantially improved, their operating budgets have increased, and their ability to train and assist candidates in the general election has been enhanced.[11] In general, state Republican parties have done a better job of organizing and raising money than have their Democratic counterparts.[12]

State and local party structures are decentralized. In most states, there is a party committee comprising representatives from different geographic subdivisions, usually counties. State party committees vary in size, composition, and function. Local party organizations also tend to be loosely structured. Most of their leaders and workers are volunteers; there may be no paid staff. Most of their activities, like those of the state parties, are organized around election campaigns: arranging fund-raising events, contributing money to candidates, and publicizing themselves and their candidates through media advertising, press releases, telephone campaigns, and the distribution of campaign literature. The local organization also maintains lists of registered voters and organizes get-out-the-vote campaigns.

State and local campaign activity has increased in recent years. Some of the increase seems to be the result of greater competition between the parties. For years, local party organizations in the South were less active than those in the Northeast, the Midwest, or the Pacific Coast, because they had less competition. But Republican gains in the South over the last three decades have forced Democratic party organizations there to take their membership-building and campaign activities more seriously.

PARTIES AND ELECTIONS

Parties are election oriented: their principal function is to get their candidates into office. To do this, they need to influence the electoral process. Today, the parties exercise less influence over the conduct of elections—the nomination of

After the 1996 elections, both major political parties chose a new national committee chair from Colorado: Roy Romer, the state's governor (right), for the Democrats and Jim Nicholson, a land developer and building contractor (left), for the Republicans. The chair serves as the party's chief public spokesperson and liaison to elected officials.

PRACTICING DEMOCRACY

Getting Involved in Partisan Activities

The easiest way to get involved in a political party is to join the chapter of the Young Democrats or Young Republicans at your school. At some schools, there may also be affiliates of other parties, such as the Libertarians, the Green party (in California), and the Socialist Workers. If there is no party chapter at your school, it is relatively easy to organize one.

Both major national parties have a youth division with a staff to coordinate activities within the party's college and university chapters around the country. The national parties also have speaker's bureaus, run campaign seminars, and organize volunteers for campaigns and elections.

But joining a party's college chapter is not the only way to get involved. Most state and local parties need a lot of help during campaigns, mostly with fund-raising, grassroots organizing, and get-out-the-vote activities. (You can find party headquarters through the local phone directory.) Because candidate organizations do much the same thing, parties compete with them for volunteers. The advantage of working with a party at the local or state level is that you come in contact with a variety of campaign workers and candidates. The disadvantage is that the campaign is not likely to garner as much public attention as national campaigns.

During nonelection periods, the parties have less need of help, but there are still jobs associated with party meetings, ongoing fund-raising, and membership solicitation.

There are opportunities at the national level as well, but you usually have to be in Washington to take advantage of them. The Republican and Democratic National Committees always have need of volunteers. You can contact the Republican committee on the Internet at http://www.rnc.org and the Democratic committee at http://www.democrats.org. Here are some of the telephone numbers (all in area code 202) you can call for specific offices at the national party headquarters.

	Republican	Democrat
Main Number	863-8500	863-8000
Chairman	863-8700	863-8121
Treasurer	863-8720	863-7150
Counsel	863-8638	863-7110
Communications	863-8614	863-8148
Press Secretary	863-8550	863-8148
Political/Campaign/ Executive Director	863-8600	863-8047
Research Director	863-8666	479-5130
Finance Director	863-8720	863-7125
Membership/Marketing	863-8630	863-7121
Fax	863-8774	863-8174

candidates, the structure of the campaign, and the vote itself—than they did three or four decades ago. One of the reasons for their declining influence has been the growth of primary elections that give the rank and file a greater voice in the selection of party candidates and, conversely, reduce the ability of the party's leaders to control this aspect of the nomination process.

Primaries have improved participation and affected representation. They have also encouraged a different type of candidate, one who can appeal to partisans and not simply to the party's leadership. In this way, primaries have encouraged factions built on personal followings. They have also made it more difficult for parties themselves to maintain consistent policy positions, because the parties can no longer control who is nominated or what appeals those nominees make.

Another reason for declining party influence has been the changes in the conduct of contemporary campaigns. The increased use of television and other electronic media has reduced the traditional role of parties as the principal link between candidates and voters. Since candidates need to raise much of their own campaign money, particularly during the nomination process, and discern public opinion throughout the campaign, they have increasingly turned to a new group of professionals who have rivaled and in many instances replaced party pros as campaign strategists and technical advisers. Professional campaign consultants and interest group leaders not only compete for influence in the campaign; they continue to vie for the candidate's ear after the election is over. In this way, they challenge party leaders and their organizations.

PARTIES, POLICY, AND GOVERNMENT

Despite its emphasis on elections, the party's ultimate objective is to influence the formulation of public policy in accordance with the interests and needs of its supporters. These interests and needs are articulated by the party in its quadrennial platform, by its candidates during the campaign, and by its leaders and elected officials during nonelection periods.

Determining the Party's Positions

A **party platform** is a formal statement of beliefs, opinions, and policy stands tied together by a set of underlying principles based on the party's ideological orientation. It is drafted by a platform committee composed of delegates to the party's national convention and then approved (occasionally with modifications) by the convention itself. Over the years, the platforms of the two major parties have differed significantly.[13]

The sharpest distinctions between Democrats and Republicans have been evident in relation to the economy, welfare, and social and cultural issues where the Democrats have favored greater government involvement on economic issues and the Republicans supported government-imposed community standards on social issues such as abortion, prayer in school, and homosexuality. Foreign affairs did not produce many clear-cut or consistent differences between the two parties until the 1990s, when partisan divisions have become evident in the debates over the role and participation of the United States in peacekeeping operations led by international and regional organizations such as the United Nations and NATO, and the expansion of NATO to include countries in eastern Europe.

Differences between party platforms are important because elected officials do attempt to redeem the promises they and their parties make. One study of party platforms and campaign promises made during presidential election campaigns between 1960 and 1984 found that presidents "submitted legislation or signed executive orders that are broadly consistent with about two-thirds of their campaign pledges." Of this legislation, a substantial percentage was enacted into law, ranging from a high of 89 percent of that proposed during the Johnson administration to a low of 61 percent of that proposed during the Nixon years.[14]

More recently, Newt Gingrich, the leading architect of the Republicans' 1994 Contract with America, pledged to vote on the proposals within that contract during the first 100 days of the new Congress if his party won control of the House of Representatives. It did; and as Speaker, Gingrich made it a point to redeem this pledge in less than 100 days. The Republican-controlled Senate, marching to the tune of different drummers, did not act with as much dispatch, however.

Converting Positions into Public Policy

The successful conversion of a partisan agenda into legislative enactments and executive actions is an important measure of **responsible party government**, that is, holding the party accountable for its platform and the promises made by its candidates for national office.[15]

Officials who abandon their party's positions may jeopardize the benefits they receive from their party's leaders—such as legislative committee assignments and presidential support. However, this is often not a very serious risk to run, as indicated by what happened to Phil Gramm when he was a Democratic representative from Texas. As a member of the House budget committee, Gramm supported the budget proposals of the Reagan administration in 1981 to reduce domestic spending and allegedly conveyed the content of confidential Democratic discussions to the Republicans. The Democratic leadership punished him by denying him a seat on the budget committee in the next Congress. Gramm responded by switching parties and winning reelection as a Republican, an example that was not lost on subsequent party leaders. In 1995, when Senator Mark Hatfield of Oregon broke ranks to oppose a major Republican proposal (a constitutional amendment to require a balanced federal budget), a party caucus that considered his actions did nothing.

A party organization has limited leverage over public officials, regardless of their partisan affiliation. The heterogeneous nature of the major parties and their decentralized structures result in policy positions that are not equally attractive and salient to all candidates and officeholders. Moreover, platforms become dated over time. Although legislators of both parties maintain committees and caucuses to define partisan policy positions, during nonelection years the parties have had difficulty articulating and promoting stands on issues. An exception was the Republicans' Contract with America, which served as a basis for the 104th Congress's legislative agenda.

Finally, in the United States system of separate branches of government sharing powers, there may not be one controlling party. Control of the legislative and executive branches by opposite parties has been the rule, not the exception, since 1968, a period during which the public has made significant demands on government. In such a situation, credit or blame for inaction is difficult to assess. Thus, party is but one influence among many on public policy.

Influencing Congress

Parties shape the structure and operation of Congress, as they do those of most legislatures. The vote on legislative leadership occurs along party lines: the Speaker of the House and the Senate majority leader are chosen on straight party votes. In addition, the majority party controls committees, recruits most of the staff, and influences rule making, personnel, and policy matters.

Although the effect of partisanship on substantive matters varies with the issue, it tends to be greater than any other factor in affecting the outcome of voting in Congress at the final stage of deliberation.[16] For example, from 1954 through 1986 a majority of Republicans opposed a majority of Democrats on an average of 43.2 percent of the roll-call votes in the House and 42.9 percent of those in the Senate.[17] Since that time, the parties have become even more unified, with partisan majorities opposing each other even more of the time.

A continuing difficulty for the parties, however, is that there are few sanctions they can impose on members who refuse to support the party's position. Unlike their counterparts in the United Kingdom, for example, where members of Parliament who do not support their party may be denied the opportunity to run for reelection, party leaders in the United States cannot control or in some cases effectively influence the nomination, campaign, and election of those who wear their party label, although they may exercise leverage over the financial resources candidates can receive. Hence the ability of the leadership to affect legislative decision making rests primarily on persuasion. In situations where constituency, executive, or other strong pressures push against the party's position, however, persuasion may be difficult.

Influencing the Executive and Judiciary

Traditionally, chief executives perform a number of functions that may be subject to party influences. They set the agenda for public debate, choosing which initiatives they wish to emphasize. They nominate certain people to high-level executive positions and, in the federal government, to judicial positions as well. They even exercise some discretion over the performance of government services. In each of these activities, they are affected by partisan considerations, but they also influence those considerations.

Even if a president, governor, or mayor does not hold a formal position within a party, he or she is considered to be the party's leader at the national, state, or local level. As such, a chief executive can make policy decisions and personnel choices (including the choice of national committee chair) and also have an impact on a party's financial and electoral support. Some choose not to do so, however.

American presidents often cause divisions within their own party by taking a stand that is unpopular with some of their own partisans, as George Bush did when he supported a tax increase in 1990 and Bill Clinton did when he supported free trade agreements in 1993–1994, welfare reform in 1996, and fast track authority in 1997. These divisions reduce presidents' political capital and may weaken them in subsequent elections. Indeed, the costs of dividing a party or even neglecting it can be significant even for presidents, who ran as outsiders and did not depend on members of Congress to get elected, because they do need congressional support to govern effectively.

Legislators are likely to support a chief executive of their own party because they and the chief executive share similar goals and objectives, and their political fates are also usually bound together. The electoral fates of the legislature and executive are not as closely linked as they once were, however. Presidential "coattails," to which candidates of the president's party may cling during presidential elections, have gotten shorter.[18] And presidents have even less influence over the election of fellow partisans during nonpresidential elections and practically no influence over nominations other than their own at any time. In 1986, a popular president, Ronald Reagan, campaigned actively for the reelection of eight Republican senators. Although he helped them raise money and may have increased the size of their vote, six of them lost. Reagan's experience indicates the very limited ability of contemporary presidents to share their popularity with candidates of their own party.

Chief executives have some rewards that they can bestow on partisan supporters, rewards such as patronage appointments, campaign resources, and media exposure. On the other hand, an unpopular president or governor hurts the party and can affect the success of legislators running on the same ticket in the next election. In 1994, for example, many conservative and some moderate Democrats "jumped ship," distancing themselves from President Clinton and the liberal policies that were associated with his administration. They were more willing to associate themselves with the president when his job approval ratings increased.

Partisanship is an important consideration in the appointment of federal judges and some state judges, and partisan divisions are evident even in states where judges are selected on the basis of merit alone.[19] However, the influence of party on judicial decision making is more difficult to discern. Although studies have found that Republican and Democratic judges differ on certain types of issues, these studies have not been able to determine whether the differences are a result of partisanship or differing values, ideology, and judicial philosophy.[20]

Moreover, the mores of judicial decision making require judges to make their decisions on the basis of law, not politics, although personal and partisan factors may intrude on these decisions. The sentence given to a person convicted of a heinous crime could affect a state judge's reelection; the determination of whether a redistricting plan accords with federal guidelines could affect a party's chances in the next election. Nonetheless, partisan considerations do not affect the judiciary in the same way they affect the legislative or executive branches.

The political party is thus an instrument for governance although it does not control government. What it does is link institutions on the basis of common ideas and overlapping interests and promote cooperation through a system of rewards and occasional sanctions. Parties help produce an agenda and contribute to consensus building within institutions and among the general public. In theory, this linkage between politics and government also contributes to public accountability, although weak party discipline and separate institutions that may be controlled by different parties make that accountability harder to achieve in practice. Nevertheless, the performance of a party's public officials affects the election prospects of others who run on the same party label.

The crucial relationship between party and government puts a premium on building and maintaining party unity. Only by converting public choices into coherent partisan positions can the parties minimize internal struggles and thereby maximize their chances of winning. Party unity also facilitates governance. It promotes accountability by making it easier for the public to allocate responsibility for the government's decisions and actions. That is why political parties are an important component of a democratic system and why partisan politics are essential to its operation.

CASE STUDY

Buying Influence: Is Public Policy for Sale?

PACs and lobbyists spend millions of dollars yearly in their attempts to influence public policy. PACs contribute to electoral campaigns and to party treasuries; they also mount their own organized efforts for and against candidates, parties, and the policy positions they take. Lobbyists may also provide public officials with amenities such as food and trips; they buy tickets to fund-raising dinners and galas as well as host elaborate affairs at party conventions. But what do they get for their money? And are their activities undercutting the democratic process?

From the perspective of the news media, they get plenty, and their activities unlevel the playing field. The press senses that something potentially or actually undesirable, unethical, or illegal may be going on. The public obviously shares some of this concern, displaying a continuing suspicion that political contributions affect public policy. When a 1997 *Washington Post* poll asked the question "How much are you bothered by political contributions from companies that do business with the government or are regulated by Congress or a government agency?" 59 percent of the respondents said, "A lot." When the same respondents were asked how often they thought members of Congress decide what to do based on what their political contributors want, rather than what they really believe, 69 percent said half the time or more.

Are these press suspicions and public beliefs justified? Can money buy votes or at least "rent" them on occasions? Do coffees and dinners with the president and vice president, sleepovers at the White House, and meetings between big contributors on one hand and members of Congress and top executive officials on the other influence the content of public policy? Here is one case in which political contributions and lobbying activities seemed to do so.

As the 1996 election year approached, congressional Democrats, anxious to please their low-income political supporters, introduced legislation to raise the minimum wage. Many Republicans initially opposed the increase, arguing that it would raise the costs of doing business, fuel inflation, cause employers to create fewer jobs, and even lay off current employees. However, they also felt pressure from constituents who could not make ends meet on the existing minimum wage of $4.25 per hour (amounting to $170 per forty-hour week, or $8,500 per year), as well as from public sympathy for these so-called working poor.

Not wanting to reinforce their image as the party of the rich, one that was unsympathetic to the plight of the less fortunate, the Republicans looked for political cover that would allow them to vote for the legislation while helping their supporters within the business community. They turned initially to the 600,000-member National Federation of Independent Businesses to aid them in this effort. House Speaker Newt Gingrich put the party's plight to the NFIB representatives this way: "We need to be able to say that while we're doing something that kills jobs, we're doing other things to create jobs. So you guys need to tell us items on your agenda that fit that bill. Just give us the list."

Gingrich was not disappointed. The NFIB had worked closely with the Republican leadership throughout the 104th Congress, and during the 1995–1996 election cycle, its PACs had contributed $1.2 million to 300 mostly Republican House and Senate candidates. More than $500,000 of that money had gone to members of the House Ways and Means Committee, the committee charged with writing tax legislation. Members of Ways and Means, like their counterparts on the Senate Finance Committee, traditionally benefit from their committee membership by receiving more campaign contributions than do most other members of Congress. In the last election, corporate and trade PACs gave them more than $36 million in the form of direct contributions and indirect expenditures on their behalf.

Organized labor was also in the ring, contributing to and campaigning for congressional candidates who supported its position policy issues. In 1996, labor launched a $35 million effort directed toward seventy-five congressional districts that had sizable labor constituencies but, in many cases, Republican representatives. Thirty-one of these Republicans had opposed an increase in the minimum wage.

Although the lobbying on this legislation was fierce, much of it was conducted behind closed doors. The NFIB proposed a list of tax incentives designed to make the minimum wage increase more palatable to its members. Included were adjustments in pension laws that provided businesses with more flexibility and greater tax breaks, including increases in their depreciation allowances. Placed on the House bill by Ways and Means Chairman Bill Archer, these proposals attracted little media attention or public debate, even though their estimated cost to the treasury over a ten-year period was more than $10 billion. Other tax credits exceeding $1 billion were appended to the legislation in the House to help carry-out food chains such as Dominos, Pizza Hut, and Grandfather's Pizza.

When the bill reached the Senate Finance Committee, more business incentives were added. The National Association of Convenience Stores, whose PACs had also made sizable contributions to members of both the House and the Senate tax-writing committees, was given a seemingly innocuous benefit, a reduction from thirty-nine to fifteen years in the period of time over which these stores could depreciate the cost of their gasoline pumps. The Senate committee also extended the tax credit for companies that had set up manufacturing plants in Puerto Rico, which included corporate giants such as Johnson & Johnson, Bristol-Myers Squibb, General Electric, Hewlett-Packard, Coca-Cola, and Pepsi. Created in the 1970s to spur investment and job opportunities on the island, which had been hurt by a severe economic downturn, by the 1990s, the credit had come under attack from a group of fiscal conservatives and business critics as "corporate welfare." But pharmaceutical, electronic, and soft-drink manufacturers are well represented in Washington by large and powerful law, lobbying, and public relations firms as well as by their own corporate officials. These informed and influential insiders convinced Senate committee members to keep the credit on the books for an additional ten years, at a cost of $18 billion in lost revenues.

The joint House–Senate conference committee that considered the legislation ultimately reported out a bill that looked more like a Christmas tree with expensive ornaments and presents for all than a simple 90-cent increase in the minimum wage over two years. Congress passed the bill in August 1996, and Clinton signed it with much fanfare on the South Lawn of the White House, hailing the legislation as a great victory for the working class in America. The Democratic president devoted less than a minute of his laudatory remarks to the business tax breaks.

Each side got what it wanted. Labor got its increase in the minimum wage; business got its tax breaks; the political parties got hurrahs from their constituents as the November election approached. Congress got credit for responding to the problem and passing legislation. Moreover, the Democrats got credit for initiating it, the president for signing it, and the Republicans for not opposing it. Only the taxpayers suffered, in this case to the tune of about $30 billion. Now do you see why it has been so difficult for politicians to balance the federal budget?

Discussion Questions

1. How much do PACs and interest groups influence party positions and public policy outcomes?
2. Is this influence beneficial or harmful, and to whom: to the parties, to the interest groups, to society, to the democratic process?
3. Should and could a more concerned public counter the effects of group activity and party collusion in the electoral and governing processes?
4. Should the law be changed to limit political contributions to parties and candidates, and to restrict their expenditures and campaign activities by interest groups?

SOURCE: Eric Pianin, "How Business Found Benefits in Wage Bill," *Washington Post,* February 11, 1997, A1+.

SUMMARY

Political interest groups can strengthen the democratic process by educating people about their civic responsibilities, increasing public awareness, providing an outlet for public expression, and encouraging participation in the electoral and governing processes. However, they can also produce consequences that are not nearly as beneficial. For groups, the danger is that some will dominate decision making, shaping public policy in their interest. For parties today, the danger may be just the opposite—the decentralization of power within the parties, the presence of competing policy agendas, and the inability to hold their elected officials accountable for their positions, votes, and activities.

Although political interest groups have existed throughout the nation's history, they have undergone their greatest development since the middle of the twentieth century. The rapid increase in the number of interest groups after 1950, spurred by the growth of government programs and regulatory activity and by the political movements of the 1960s and 1970s, has contributed to the increase in group activity, thereby weakening the parties and providing groups with greater incentives and opportunities to influence who is nominated, what positions candidates take, who wins the election, and what policy decisions they make in office.

Lobbyists' targets include not only legislatures but also the executive branch and the judiciary. Interest groups lobby executive officials and agencies to gain access, visibility, and support for their interests. In exchange, they offer their members' political support for the administration, its personnel, and its policies.

In recent years, the amount of lobbying activity in Washington, D.C., and in state capitals has increased dramatically. Foreign companies and governments regularly hire American firms to represent them. Sunshine laws force lobbyists to operate more in public view, and new ethics and finance laws and regulations have imposed stringent requirements on public officials who interact with lobbyists or become lobbyists after they leave office.

The influence of parties has declined. The partisan loyalties of voters have become less intense, whereas the proportion of voters considering themselves independent has increased; primary elections have reduced the influence of party leaders on the nomination process; and the mass media have become the primary link between candidates and voters. These trends have factionalized the parties and contributed to the fluidity of the electorate.

The composition of the parties has changed as well. The Democrats have lost their majority status. The defection of southern whites to the Republican party, the weakening of support for Democrats among the general population, and the reduction of the blue-collar labor vote as a proportion of the electorate have placed the parties at rough parity today. The Democrats receive disproportionate support from racial, religious, and ethnic minorities, whereas Republicans benefit from the increasing number of white-collar workers as well as from the backing they receive from Christian fundamentalist groups. In recent years, a gender gap in partisan identification and voting behavior has also appeared, with women more Democratic and men more Republican.

Despite their decline, the major political parties remain important entities within the political system. Primarily oriented toward elections, they raise money, target voters, communicate with the public, get out the vote, and provide other assistance to their candidates. After the election, they continue to try to shape policy outcomes. They do so by organizing legislatures, developing positions, and mobilizing support for these positions among their elected officials. Their chief executives, be they president or governor, also make policy and personnel decisions and attempt to use partisan affiliation as a vehicle for building support for their initiatives and nominations. Partisanship is also a major factor in the appointment of the federal judiciary and some state judiciaries, but it has a less direct impact on judicial judgments.

KEY TERMS

political interest groups
revolving door politics
political action committee (PAC)
bundling
lobby
astroturfing
amicus curiae brief
political party
partisan
single-member district
ideological party
issue party
candidate
dealignment
realignment
party platform
responsible party government

RESOURCES

READINGS

Abramson, Paul R., John H. Aldrich, Phil Paolino, and David W. Rohde. "Third-Party and Independent Candidates: Wallace, Anderson, and Perot." *Political Science Quarterly* 110 (Fall 1995), 349–367. A recent article that explains why it is so difficult for third-party and independent candidates to win presidential elections.

Beck, Paul Allen, and Frank J. Sorauf. *Party Politics in America*. 8th ed. New York: HarperCollins, 1996. A recent revision of a highly regarded text on political parties.

Cotter, Cornelius P., James L. Gibson, John F. Bibby, and Robert Huckshorn. *Party Organizations in American Politics*. Pittsburgh: University of Pittsburgh Press, 1989. A comprehensive study of party organizations in the states.

Key, V. O., Jr. *Southern Politics*. Knoxville: University of Tennessee Press, 1984. The classic study of southern politics from the end of the Civil War until the middle of the twentieth century.

Lowi, Theodore. *The End of Liberalism: Ideology, Policy, and the Crisis of Public Authority*. 2d ed. New York: Norton, 1979. A classic analysis and criticism of interest group politics in America.

Pomper, Gerald M. *Passions and Interests: Political Party Concepts of American Democracy*. Lawrence: University Press of Kansas, 1992. A study that focuses on the role of American political parties in theory and practice in the democratic process.

Rothenberg, Lawrence S. *Linking Citizens to Government: Interest Group Politics at Common Cause*. New York: Cambridge University Press, 1992. A comprehensive case study of the public interest group Common Cause: its composition, organization, decision-making processes, and impact on public policy.

Schlozman, Kay L., and John T. Tierney. *Organized Interests and American Democracy*. New York: HarperCollins, 1990. A comprehensive text about interest groups and their impact on the American system, based in part on interviews with 175 Washington representatives of major organizations.

Walker, Jack L. Jr. *Mobilizing Interest Groups in America: Patrons, Professions, and Social Movements.* Ann Arbor: University of Michigan Press, 1991. Pointing out that all interest groups in the United States are not equally represented, the author discusses the disparity as well as the forces behind the expansion of interest groups at the national level.

Watenberg, Martin P. *The Decline of American Parties, 1952–1992.* Cambridge, Mass.: Harvard University Press, 1994.

ORGANIZATIONS AND AGENCIES

Common Cause, 1250 Connecticut Ave, N.W., Washington, DC 20036: phone (202) 833-1200: fax (202) 659-3716; Internet http://www.commoncause.org A self-described citizens' lobby, concerned with issues of governance such as campaign finance, lobbying practices, federal government salaries, and the availability of government information.

Democratic Congressional Campaign Committee and Democratic Senatorial Campaign Committee, 430 S. Capitol Street, S.E., Washington, DC 20003; DCCC phone (202) 863-1500, fax (202) 485-3512; Internet http://www.dccc.org; DSCC phone (202) 224-2447, fax (202) 485-3120 These committees raise and distribute funds for Democrats who seek election or reelection to the House of Representatives and the Senate, respectively.

Democratic National Committee, 430 S. Capitol Street, S.E., Washington, DC 20003; phone (202) 863-8000, fax (202) 863-8174; Internet http://www.democrats.org This committee, supported by a large staff, makes and implements policy and personnel decisions for the Democratic party.

Federal Election Commission, 999 E Street, N.W., Washington, DC 20463; phone (202) 219-3440; (800) 424-9530 (information division); flashfax (202) 501-3413; Internet http://www.fec.gov Collects, analyzes, and sends out information on election laws, contributions, and other campaign activities; releases annual reports as well as election summaries.

National Republican Congressional Committee, 320 1st Street, S.E., Washington, DC 20003; phone (202) 479-7000, fax (202) 863-0693; Internet http://www.nrcc.org National Republican Senatorial Committee, 425 2nd Street, N.E., Washington DC 20002; phone (202) 675-6000, fax (202) 675-6058; Internet http://www.nrsc.org These committees raise and distribute funds for Republicans who seek election or reelection to the House of Representatives and the Senate, respectively.

Office of Public Liaison, The White House, 1600 Pennsylvania Avenue, N.W., Washington, DC 20500; phone (202) 456-2930; fax (202) 456-6218; no direct e-mail. Handles the president's relations with organized political interest groups, including servicing their needs, keeping track of their positions, and trying to mobilize them behind key presidential initiatives.

Republican National Committee, 310 1st Street, S.E., Washington, DC 20003; phone (202) 863-8500, fax (202) 863-8774; Internet http://www.rnc.org This committee, supported by a large staff, makes and implements policy and personnel decisions for the Republican party.

Senate Democratic Policy Committee, S-118 Capitol Building, Washington, DC 20510; phone (202) 224-5551; Internet http://www.senate.gov./~dpc This committee establishes policy for the Democratic party in the Senate.

Senate Republican Policy Committee, 347 Russell Office Building, Washington, DC 20510; phone (202) 224-2946, fax (202) 224-1235; Internet http://www.senate.gov./~rpc This committee establishes policy for the Republican party in the Senate.

8

Campaigns and Elections

PREVIEW

- Elections and democracy: suffrage, meaningful choice, and political equality
- The American voter: turnout and voting behavior
- The election campaign: presidential and nonpresidential elections
- Analyzing the results: presidential and midterm elections
- Elections and governance

On March 6, 1991, President George Bush delivered an address to Congress in which he declared that the United States and its allies had been victorious in the Persian Gulf War. The first public opinion poll following Bush's speech revealed that almost 90 percent of the American people approved of the job he was doing as president. But less than two years later, in November 1992, Bush was defeated in his quest for reelection, receiving just 38 percent of the vote.

On January 21, 1993, Bill Clinton was sworn in as president. The first Democrat to be elected since 1976, he was also the first president since Jimmy Carter whose party controlled both houses of Congress. In his inaugural address, Clinton promised to end the legislative gridlock that had gripped the Bush years. He also proposed new Democratic policies for old problems: "to end welfare as we know it," to reform lobbying and campaign finance, to promote investment, to reduce crime, to improve education, to clean the environment, and to end discrimination on the basis of sexual orientation. And that was not all. His three principal legislative priorities were to stimulate the economy, reduce the federal budget deficit, and reform health care.

Two years later, only a few of those proposals had become public policy. Some had been defeated in Congress, others were modified by Congress. Of the president's major priorities, his stimulus plan was killed by a filibuster in the Senate, his deficit reduction plan was passed narrowly after being completely overhauled, and his health-care proposal died in the legislature. With his party divided, his White House staff an embarrassment, his wife a polarizing figure, and his administration marred by allegations of illegal and unethical behavior, the president's performance in office was disapproved of by almost as many as had approved of it during his first two years in office.

Congress was also in bad repute. The Democratic leadership's inability to transform the legislature into an effective policy-making institution and to prevent its members from engaging in self-interested and self-aggrandizing behavior led to increasing public dissatisfaction and anger with the government in general and with Clinton and the Democratic Congress in particular. The voters responded the first chance they had: in November 1994, they elected the first Republican Congress since 1954. In their Contract with America, the Republicans promised to do things differently; but within one year the level of public dissatisfaction rose again, and this time the Republicans were the principal target.

How could a governor from a small state with no experience in Washington and little national exposure, such as Bill Clinton, a candidate with considerable personal vulnerabilities, defeat an incumbent president who had successfully prosecuted one war and presided over the end of another, the Cold War? How could little-known Republican challengers, campaigning in local areas with a national program, do so well against an entrenched Democratic party that had been in power for forty years? How could these very same Republicans so quickly become the objects of public unhappiness? And then how could public opinion change again so quickly that in 1996 both President Clinton and the Republican congressional majority were reelected? The answers lie in the rules under which nominations and elections are conducted, in the advantages the system gives to incumbents, and in the turbulent contemporary political environment.

During the nomination period, the rules and procedures prescribed by the political parties favor those candidates with the best organization and the most money. In 1992, these were George Bush and Bill Clinton and the congressional incumbents of both parties. In 1994 and 1996, the insiders again had the advantage. Clinton was not challenged for the Democratic nomination, and Robert Dole, Senate majority leader, started off as the odds-on favorite for the Republican nomination and easily won it. Only one congressional incumbent was not renominated.

In the general election, the system also usually favors the incumbents—candidates who are well known, have had contact with voters, and have done favors for them. This was the case in 1992 and 1996 for most members of Congress, but it was not for the Democrats in 1994.

The political environment is another key factor in determining an election's outcome. In the early 1990s, the public mood shifted from euphoria over victory in the Persian Gulf War to pessimism over the economy, social conditions, and the country's future direction, then to anger over alleged abuses by public officials in Congress and the executive branch and frustration over government's inability to address pressing national issues. These attitudes proved fatal to President Bush in 1992 and to Democrats in 1994. But in 1996, the public was more contented. People perceived the economy to be stronger; they saw themselves as better off than they were four years earlier; and more saw their country moving in the right direction. Under these circumstances, incumbents of both parties benefited.

The elections of the 1990s are prime examples of a dynamic political process at work, of candidates who defied initial odds and an electorate that reconsidered its early impressions and reevaluated its performance judgments, of effective versus ineffective campaigns, and of the powerful impact of perceptions of economic and social conditions on voting behavior. These are some of the key features of American electoral politics. The elections also demonstrate the principal way in which voters hold those in government accountable for their decisions and actions and, by their voting behavior, change the direction of government and its public policy.

This chapter discusses these and other political aspects of the electoral process. It first looks at the relationship between elections and democracy and then focuses on the American voter, on who votes and why. Finally, it examines the stages of the electoral process, election returns, and the implications of elections for government and public policy.

ELECTIONS AND DEMOCRACY

Elections are a mechanism for making important political choices. They frame policy debate, select public officials, and influence the decisions of those officials. Such functions are essential for a democratic government because they establish and reaffirm popular control.

If elections are to link the people to their representatives, they must meet three criteria: universal suffrage, meaningful choice, and political equality. **Universal suffrage** means that all citizens who are responsible for their own actions are permitted to vote in order to protect and promote their own interests.[1] **Meaningful choice** implies that there is some opportunity to select among different options. **Political equality** requires that the votes of all who choose to participate should be equal and that the majority rule, that the candidates with the most votes win.

Each of these democratic criteria seems logical, straightforward, and noncontroversial; yet each has generated considerable conflict. In the United States, much of the conflict has turned on the issue of suffrage—the question of who may vote. Another problematic issue is how to structure elections so as to ensure meaningful choice. A third controversy in recent years concerns the application of the principle of equality. Should individual candidates have the right to spend their own money and utilize their own resources during a campaign, or does this violate a basic democratic assumption that no person or group should exercise greater influence in an election simply on the basis of wealth?

Suffrage: Who Can Vote?

The framers of the Constitution struggled with the suffrage issue, but in the end they evaded it. They made the states responsible for deciding who would be eligible to vote, retaining for Congress the power to legislate on these matters if it desired.

Initially, most states required property ownership as a condition of voting. Since property was owned primarily by white men, this requirement effectively disenfranchised women and racial minorities. Some states imposed an additional requirement: belief in a Christian God. By the middle of the 1830s, however, property ownership and religious beliefs had been dropped as qualifications for voting in most states. Gender and racial barriers remained, and it took the enactment of constitutional amendments and voting rights legislation to remove them. (The debate over lowering the voting age to 18 is described in the box on page 191.)

Restrictions on suffrage, which prevented the United States from achieving the goal of political equality, benefited those in power, generally the more well-to-do members of society. They made challenges to those in power more difficult, especially at the state and local levels. As suffrage was gradually extended,

The extension of suffrage to women met with considerable resistance, and women who demanded it were often depicted as mannish or even lewd. In this Currier and Ives print, The Age of Brass *(1869), women wear men's hat's, smoke cigars, expose their legs, and look downright nasty. The one man on the scene holds a baby, a sign of frightful role reversal to come if women should get the same rights as men.*

however, these consequences were also gradually reversed. As women and minority groups increased their representation in government, policies that benefited these newest members of the electorate were enacted and implemented. The party system became more competitive at all levels of government, and within the parties there were more opportunities for the rank and file to be heard and to influence the selection of nominees.

Meaningful Choice: How Are Elections Structured?

In the early days of the republic, the states had extensive authority to determine the conduct of federal elections. Subsequently, constitutional amendments and congressional statutes limited that discretion—particularly the right to set qualifications for voting and, more recently, the procedures for voter registration. Nevertheless, state laws that control ballot access, electoral challenges, and even the time, place, and manner of voting continue to have an important impact on the electoral process in both primary and general elections.

In two landmark decisions, *Cousins v. Wigoda* (1975) and *Democratic Party of the U.S. v. La Follette* (1981), the Supreme Court held that the parties may determine their own rules for selection of delegates to their national conventions and may refuse to seat delegates who are not chosen in accordance with those rules. Despite these rulings, however, increased popular participation in the nomination process has weakened the ability of party leaders and organizations to select candidates for office. As a result, the responsiveness of many elected officials to the constituencies that elected them has increased, but in a way that fragments rather than concentrates political power. This may produce a more representative political system, but it also produces a more divided government.

The 18-Year-Old Vote

Americans take it for granted today that any citizen who is 18 years of age or older should have the right to vote. But thirty years ago, that was not the case. States used to set their own minimum age for voting, and most required that their citizens be 21 years of age or over.

There was not much support to establish a national minimum voting age of 18 until the development of massive opposition to the Vietnam War in the late 1960s, when "conscription without representation" became an issue. If men were old enough to be drafted into the armed services and sent to fight in Vietnam, putting their lives on the line in the process, it was argued, then they were old enough to choose public officials responsible for this policy. The increasing educational levels among younger people and the desirability of expanding the electorate in a democracy were other reasons offered for lowering the voting age.

Nonetheless, considerable opposition remained. Proponents of states' rights, particularly those in the South, contended that the establishment of national voting qualifications denied the states their constitutional right to set the voting age. Others believed that younger Americans were not sufficiently mature, responsible, or informed to vote. Some even felt that allowing 18-year-olds to vote could adversely affect public policy by, for example, creating pressure to lower the drinking age (which also varied from state to state) or encouraging candidates to make unrealistic promises as a means of gaining votes in certain elections, such as those for school boards.

The good news is that the Twenty-Sixth Amendment—which established 18 as the age at which states must permit their citizens to vote—went into effect on July 1, 1971. The bad news is that relatively few 18- to 21-year-olds actually do vote. In fact, this group has had the lowest percentage of voter registration and turnout of any age cohort within the population.

Political Equality: Do All Citizens Have an Equal Voice?

The criterion of making sure that all citizens have an equal voice in the electoral process has generated a decades-long debate over campaign finance, and specifically over whether the American tradition of unrestricted private funding of political campaigns undercuts the basic principles of a democratic electoral process. Before the mid 1970s, campaigns were financed entirely by individual contributions. Both parties depended on a small number of wealthy donors for much of their funding. After campaign expenditures increased, primarily as a result of rising media costs (for television advertising, in particular), Congress enacted legislation in the 1970s to limit campaign spending and provide government support for presidential nomination and election campaigns. The Federal Election Campaign Act required public disclosure of all contributions and expenditures above a certain amount and created the Federal Election Commission to monitor activities and oversee compliance. Parts of this legislation were highly controversial. In particular, some saw the limits on contributions as a restraint on freedom of speech. In *Buckley v. Valeo* (1976) the Supreme Court took the middle ground. Arguing that personal expenditures can be a form of expression but that campaign finance can be regulated, the Court upheld the right of Congress to restrict the amount that individuals and groups could contribute to candidates in any federal election, but not the amount they could spend *independently* on behalf of those candidates.

Even after the Court's decision, however, partisan debate over the law continued. Republicans were generally opposed to it for practical as well as philosophical reasons. Not only did they believe that limits on individual contributions denied their party its traditional financial advantage, but some of them also objected to the very idea of government subsidies, arguing that the government should not support semipublic political organizations. Democrats, in contrast, contended that such support for parties and their nominees was a legitimate function of government and that equalizing the amount of money candidates had available to them would produce a more democratic result. This debate has continued throughout the 1990s.

Although the campaign finance legislation did correct some problems it was designed to address, it has also had several unintended consequences. Most federal funds and some private contributions go directly to the candidates, not to the party. As a result, candidates are forced to create and use their own campaign organizations rather than relying on the party's. Thus the legislation has contributed to factionalism within the parties and has reduced the parties' influence over the campaigns of their own candidates.

In 1979, Congress reacted to the parties' plight, as well as to a decline in voter turnout, by amending the law to permit parties to raise and spend unlimited funds on efforts to encourage people to register and to vote. These so-called **soft-money** expenditures, which have created a huge loophole in the limits on contributions and expenditures, have been substantial in recent years. In 1996, the soft-money expenditures reported to the Federal Election Commission were $149.7 million for the Republicans and $121.8 million for the Democrats, a staggering increase over 1992.

Not only have soft-money contributions increased, but the ways in which they have been solicited, who has solicited them, and who has contributed have also become controversial issues.

After winning renomination in Chicago in 1996, President Clinton and Vice President Gore campaign in Illinois. Campaign finance legislation has had the unintended effect of forcing candidates to create their own campaign organizations. In this way, they have become increasingly independent of party control.

TABLE 8-1 *Suffrage and Turnout*

Year	Total Adult Population (Including Aliens)[a]	Total Presidential Vote	Percentage of Adult Pop. Voting
1824	3,964,000	363,017	9.0
1840	7,381,000	2,412,698	33.0
1860	14,676,000	4,692,710	32.0
1880	25,012,000	9,219,467	37.0
1900	40,753,000	13,974,188	35.0
1920	60,581,000	26,768,613	44.0
1932	75,768,000	39,732,000	52.4
1940	84,728,000	49,900,000	58.9
1952	99,929,000	61,551,000	61.6
1960	109,672,000	68,838,000	62.8
1964	114,090,000	70,645,000	61.9
1968	120,285,000	73,212,000	60.9
1972	140,777,000	77,719,000	55.5
1976	152,308,000	81,556,000	53.5
1980	164,595,000	86,515,000	52.6
1984	174,447,000	92,653,000	53.1
1988	182,600,000	91,602,291	50.2
1992	187,033,000	104,552,736	55.9
1996	196,511,000	96,277,223	49.1

[a]Restrictions based on sex, age, race, religion, and property ownership prevented a significant portion of the adult population from voting in the nineteenth and early twentieth centuries. Of those who were eligible, however, the percentage casting ballots was often quite high, particularly during the last half of the nineteenth century.

Source: Population figures for 1824 to 1920 are based on estimates and early census figures that appear in Neal R. Pierce, *The People's President* (New Haven, Conn: Yale University Press, 1979). Copyright © 1979. Reprinted with the permission of the publisher. Population figures from 1932 to 1984 are from the U.S. Department of Commerce, Bureau of the Census Statistical Abstract of the United States (Washington, D.C., 1987), 250. Figures for 1988 to 1996 were compiled from official election returns published by the Federal Election Commission.

THE AMERICAN VOTER

Who *can* vote and who *does* vote are two different questions. The expansion of suffrage has made the American political system more democratic—at least in theory. In practice, however, there has always been a gap between eligible voters and actual voters, a gap that has traditionally been widest for newly enfranchised voters. Table 8-1 indicates the magnitude of this gap.

What explains the gap between those who can vote and those who actually cast ballots? Part of the answer may have to do with the time required for people to develop the interest, knowledge, and incentive to vote. Women, for example, received the right to vote in 1920 but voted at a lower rate than men until 1986. Similarly, African Americans in the southern states effectively gained the ability to vote in the mid 1960s, but their rate of participation still lags behind that of whites.

PRACTICING DEMOCRACY

How to Register to Vote

Since 1995, the federal motor-voter law has required states to permit people to register to vote by mail or when applying for a driver's license. The Federal Election Commission has designed a single national registration form, which is reproduced here. In addition to motor vehicle offices, those offices that dispense welfare, aid people with disabilities, or supervise elections also have registration forms as do most military recruitment offices.

If you have any problems obtaining a voter registration form, contact the Federal Election Commission at (800) 424-9530; the staff should be able to tell you where and how to obtain the mail-in form and where to send it when you have completed it.

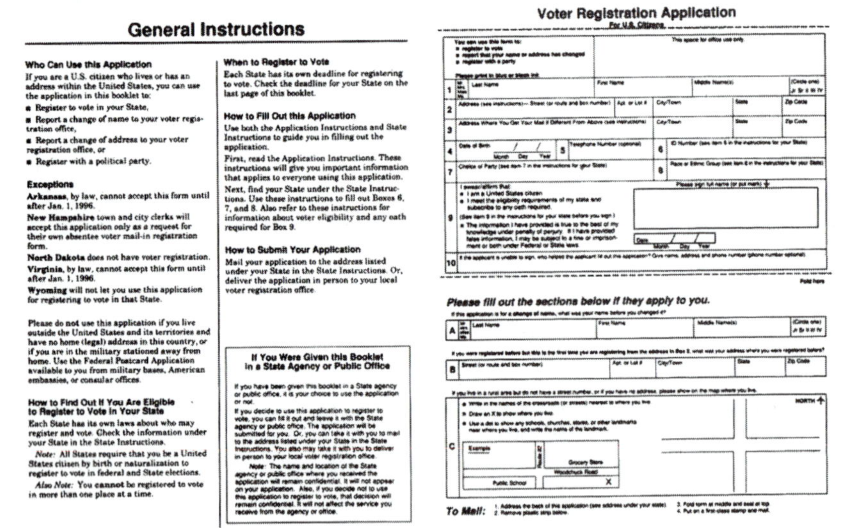

General Instructions

Who Can Use this Application

If you are a U.S. citizen who lives or has an address within the United States, you can use the application in this booklet to:

- Register to vote in your State,
- Report a change of name to your voter registration office,
- Report a change of address to your voter registration office, or
- Register with a political party.

Exceptions

Arkansas, by law, cannot accept this form until after Jan. 1, 1996.

New Hampshire town and city clerks will accept this application only as a request for their own absentee voter mail-in registration form.

North Dakota does not have voter registration.

Virginia, by law, cannot accept this form until after Jan. 1, 1996.

Wyoming will not let you use this application for registering to vote in that State.

Please do **not** use this application if you live outside the United States and its territories and have no home (legal) address in this country, or if you are in the military stationed away from home. Use the Federal Postcard Application available to you from military bases, American embassies, or consular offices.

How to Find Out If You Are Eligible to Register to Vote in Your State

Each State has its own laws about who may register and vote. Check the information under your State in the State Instructions.

Note: All States require that you be a United States citizen by birth or naturalization to register to vote in federal and State elections.

Also Note: You **cannot** be registered to vote in more than one place at a time.

When to Register to Vote

Each State has its own deadline for registering to vote. Check the deadline for your State on the last page of this booklet.

How to Fill Out this Application

Use both the Application Instructions and State Instructions to guide you in filling out the application.

First, read the Application Instructions. These instructions will give you important information that applies to everyone using this application.

Next, find your State under the State Instructions. Use these instructions to fill out Boxes 6, 7, and 8. Also refer to these instructions for information about voter eligibility and any oath required for Box 9.

How to Submit Your Application

Mail your application to the address listed under your State in the State Instructions. Or, deliver the application in person to your local voter registration office.

If You Were Given this Booklet in a State Agency or Public Office

If you have been given this booklet in a State agency or public office, it is your choice to use the application or not.

If you decide to use this application to register to vote, you can fill it out and leave it with the State agency or public office. The application will be submitted for you. Or, you can take it with you to mail to the address listed under your State in the State Instructions. You also may take it with you to deliver in person to your local voter registration office.

Note: The name and location of the State agency or public office where you received the application will remain confidential. It will not appear on your application. Also, if you decide not to use this application to register to vote, that decision will remain confidential. It will not affect the service you receive from the agency or office.

Voter Registration Application

For U.S. Citizens

Please fill out the sections below if they apply to you.

To Mail:

Turnout

The motivations for voting are complex. They have to do with interest in the campaign, concern about the outcome, feelings of civic responsibility, and a sense of political efficacy. Generally speaking, people who identify with a political party are more strongly motivated to vote than those who do not. They tend to have more interest in the campaign, more knowledge about the candidates and issues, and more concern about the outcome of the election.[2]

Demographic characteristics also contribute to political involvement. Of these, as noted in Chapter 6, the most important is education: the more educated a person is, the more likely that person will vote. Education enhances one's ability to understand the issues, to follow the campaign, and to discern the difference between the candidates' positions. More education also usually leads to higher income, which in turn may increase a person's perceived stake in the outcome of elections.[3]

FIGURE 8-1
Age and Voting, 1996

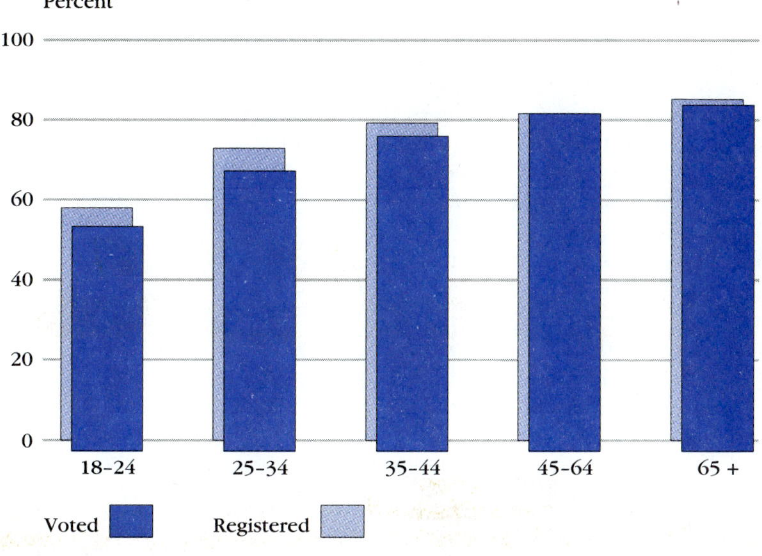

SOURCE: Data from the *American National Election Studies,* conducted by the University of Michigan, Center for Political Studies, Ann Arbor, Michigan. Data provided by the Inter-University Consortium for Political and Social Research, located at the University of Michigan, Center for Political Studies, Ann Arbor, Michigan.

Given the effects of education and income on voting, it is a little surprising that since 1960, electoral turnout has mostly decreased even though education and income levels for the population have increased. To understand why this has occurred, it is necessary to look at other factors that affect the vote.

One of these factors is age. Studies have shown that the younger groups of eligible voters, those under the age of 30, vote less regularly than people in the middle age groups (see Figure 8-1). Older people—those over age 75—also are less likely to vote. Among the young, greater mobility, weaker partisanship, and a less developed sense of community contribute to lower rates of participation, whereas poor health and decreased interest are the major reasons for lower turnout by senior citizens. Democratic trends that have resulted in larger proportions of younger and older voters have undoubtedly helped to reduce voting turnout since 1960, but these trends do not fully explain the decline because all age groups have experienced lower turnout.

Another contributing factor has been the public's increasingly negative feelings about poor performance of those in government, feelings that have led to greater apathy, more cynicism, and lower efficacy. This discussion of voter motivation may suggest why turnout declined from 1960 to 1990 and again in 1994 and 1996, but it does not explain why turnout increased in 1992. Factors unique to the 1992 election appear to be more directly responsible for the 5 percent increase in turnout from the previous presidential election. People seemed to be more aware of the issues and more concerned about them in 1992 than they were in 1984, 1988, and 1996. That concern undoubtedly aroused by the recession, generated a higher-than-normal vote, as did H. Ross Perot's independent candidacy.[4] Finally, there was the campaign itself, especially the candidates' use of television talk shows to reach and motivate a portion of the electorate usually less affected by traditional campaign events.

Who votes is as important a question to a democracy as *who is eligible to vote*. The answer not only indicates the extent to which the ideal of equal participation and influence is being achieved but also reveals levels of satisfaction and dissatisfaction among the population. It forecasts how representative the government is likely to be and which segments of the society are likely to benefit the most.

Turnout has partisan implications as well. The Republican party, composed of a larger proportion of well-educated, higher-income, white-collar workers, usually gets a greater percentage of its adherents to vote than does the Democratic party. However, in 1992 and 1996, turnout among those who identified themselves as Republicans was only marginally higher than among Democrats. But in 1994, it was substantially higher, contributing to the GOP's victory in the congressional elections that year.

Would the results of recent presidential elections have been different if everyone voted? Political scientist Ruy A. Teixeira contends that they would not be. He argues that nonvoters typically have much weaker partisan ties than do voters and therefore would be more likely to be influenced by general perceptions of the candidates than by partisan inclinations. He speculates that their vote would probably reflect the vote of the electorate as a whole, and he supports his argument with the surveys of nonvoters that have been taken after presidential elections.[5]

Voting Behavior

Although *who* votes obviously influences the outcome of the election, so do the political attitudes and social groupings of the electorate. Voters do not come to an election with a completely open mind; they come with preexisting beliefs and attitudes. Of these, the most important is partisan identification. A majority of the electorate still identifies with a political party, a commitment that is relatively stable and has both direct and indirect influences on voting.

People develop political attitudes early in life and generally maintain and strengthen them as they get older. Although partisan attitudes can change, they are less likely to vary than positions on issues and perceptions of candidates. Moreover, when people do drop their partisanship identity, they are more likely to think of themselves as independents than as supporters of another party, and they are still more likely to vote for candidates of their former party than for those of other parties. Actually, not only do two-thirds of those who claim to be independent lean toward one party or the other, but these *independent leaners* often vote in a more partisan fashion than do people who continue to claim a weak partisan allegiance.[6] Thus partisan predispositions directly affect the vote of those who feel strongly about their party and its candidates, and they indirectly affect the vote of those who feel less strongly but still tend to view their party's nominees more favorarably than they view the opposition's.

Party identification is important because it provides a framework for analysis; it offers cues for evaluating the candidates and their stands. In general, the less that is known about the candidates, particularly those who are running for state or local office, the greater is the influence of party, because it becomes the primary factor that people consider in deciding how to vote. In contrast, at the presidential level more information is usually available to voters, such as the experience, character, leadership potential, and issue positions of the candidates.

Today, about two-thirds of American voters consider themselves either Democrats or Republicans, compared with the three-fourths who identified with one of the two major parties in 1952. Not only does a smaller proportion of the electorate identify with the major parties, but the strength of their partisan attitude has also weakened. The result has been more **split-ticket voting**—that is, voting for candidates of different parties on the same ballot—and more emphasis on candidates' personal characteristics and less on their party affiliation. The weakening of partisan allegiances also tends to make deciding whom to vote for harder for many people. As a consequence, they tend to make their voting decisions later in the campaign. According to data from the huge exit poll conducted by the Voter News Service in 1996, 69 percent of the voters made their decisions at least one month before the election.

Group orientations can also influence voting. Most people see themselves as members of groups. To the extent that groups believe their interests are best served by particular parties, candidates, or issues, they will tell their members how to vote in a given election.

Group associations generate pressures that find expression in the political process. These pressures may reinforce partisan inclinations, or they may undermine them by creating cross-pressures that give mixed signals to voters. In the 1980s, for example, the partisan identities of white blue-collar workers oriented them toward the Democrats and that party's stand on economic issues. Yet their dissatisfaction with the Democratic party's positions on welfare, law and order, and defense and national security issues, combined with their unhappiness with the presidency of Jimmy Carter, led many to support Ronald Reagan in 1980 and 1984. They did, however, return to the Democratic fold in 1992 and stayed Democratic in 1996.

Another group of people whose association produces voting cohesion are white born-again Christians. From the New Deal era of the 1930s until 1978, this group supported Democratic candidates. In 1976, Jimmy Carter, himself a born-again Christian, received a majority of the vote of this group. In 1980, however, born-again Christians deserted the Democratic party over social issues: they opposed the Democrats' liberal positions on abortion, homosexuality, and the feminist movement and sided with the Republicans' emphasis on traditional family values and community standards. And they have remained Republican. In 1992, George Bush received the support of 61 percent of this group, his largest and most cohesive voting bloc; in 1994, born-again Christians voted 3 to 1 for Republican candidates.[7] In 1996 they also voted Republican, with 65 percent of them supporting Robert Dole.

The candidates themselves and the issues of the day also affect how people vote. Voters' perception of candidates have become more important in recent years, largely because of the greater use of television, which tends to emphasize personality and leadership at the expense of substantive policy issues. The specific issues that affect voting behavior vary with the election, the constituency, and the candidates. Whether issues—be they jobs, crime, education, environment, health, or national security—are salient depends on four factors: (1) how much attention they receive from the media, (2) how directly they affect voters, (3) how much the candidates differ on them, and (4) voters' awareness of candidates' differences.[8] Thus important public concerns, particularly those that relate to fundamental values and needs (individual well-being, personal safety, economic prosperity), may not be campaign issues unless the public perceives that the candidates and their parties approach them in different ways. The more direct the perceived impact of the issue, the more likely it is to have a discernible electoral impact.

How do people weigh various factors in arriving at their decisions, and what questions do they try to answer? Political scientists have proposed two models of voting: retrospective and prospective. **Retrospective voting** is based on an assessment of the past performance of the parties and their elected officials in the light of the promises they made, political events that have occurred, and the conditions that currently exist.[9] In this model, voters base their judgment on their accumulated political experience, asking themselves, "Am I better off now than I was when the other party and its leaders were in power?" In contrast, **prospective voting** anticipates the actions of candidates once they assume office. Voters compare their own values, beliefs, and opinions with those of the candidates and parties; then they base their judgment on their sense of which party and which candidates are likely to benefit them the most after the election.

The retrospective and prospective models are theoretical formulations of the thought processes that people go through when they decide how to vote. In practice, voters undoubtedly do both; they look backward and forward to arrive at their electoral judgments. They evaluate the candidates and their parties and how well they have done largely on the basis of how good or bad conditions seem to be. If the economy is strong, society appears harmonious, the nation feels secure, and government seems to be functioning normally, people assume that their leaders—particularly the president—must be doing a good job. If conditions are not favorable, they tend to blame those in power, especially the president. This judgment—how conditions are and who is responsible for them—is part of the voting decision, but not the only part. Voters must also anticipate which of the candidates and parties, given the record of the past, is likely to do better in the future. Thus both retrospective and prospective analyses help people arrive at the rationales they use for their voting decisions.

THE ELECTION CAMPAIGN

Every candidate's objective is to win, to convince voters that he or she is the most qualified and will do the best job. The campaign is the mechanism used to achieve this objective. Frequently, candidates must conduct two campaigns: one to gain their party's nomination, and another to compete in the general election. Because they are conducted at different times under different rules, appeal to different electorates, and often emphasize different issues, positions, and leadership traits, these campaigns are quite different.

Of the two, the nomination campaign has changed the most during the twentieth century. Formerly an internal matter decided by party leaders, the quest for nomination today occurs within the public arena, usually in primary races among self-declared aspirants for office. Candidates are selected on the basis of their appeal to primary voters. If successful, they must run again in the general

In 1968, with Democrats bitterly divided over the Vietnam War, thousands of anti-war protesters clashed with police outside the party's convention hall in Chicago. The ugly televised spectacle alienated many voters and helped to doom the chances of Democratic presidential nominee Hubert Humphrey. In 1996, unified behind the reelection of President Clinton, the Democrats returned to Chicago for the first time since 1968—this time demonstrations were few and peaceful.

election, refocusing their campaign and broadening and moderating their message for the entire electorate. In doing so, they may have to soften their partisan rhetoric, reposition themselves toward the center of the political spectrum, and stress those issues and personal traits that will attract the votes of independents, supporters of the other party, and partisans of their own party who did not vote for them in the primaries.

The quest for office is also conditioned by the rules that govern the election, the environment in which the election occurs, and the electorate to which the candidates must appeal. Of these, the economic and social environment is the most variable factor, changing from election to election. The rules are more predictable, but they too have changed, particularly those that pertain to the presidential nomination process. The electorate is stable but not static, as we note in Chapter 7.

The Presidential Nomination Process

In theory, national nominating conventions still designate the major parties' nominees for president and vice president and formulate the platforms on which they will run. In practice, party activists have the greatest influence on those judgments. The movement toward increased popular control of the nomination process came during the 1970s, when the Democratic party revised its rules for delegate selection to its nominating convention in order to encourage greater public participation and more equitable representation of rank-and-file voters.

These changes made primary elections the preferred mode of selection. Today, approximately three-fourths of the delegates, pledged to particular candidates at both the Democratic and the Republican national conventions, come from states that hold some form of primary. All the remaining Republican pledged delegates and some of the remaining Democratic ones come from states that utilize a multistage party **caucus** system of selection. In addition to the pledged delegates, the Democrats choose a number of unpledged delegates from among the party's elected and appointed leaders; in 1996, these **superdelegates**, as they are called, constituted about 18 percent of the total number of delegates who attended the Democratic convention.

Another major objective of the Democratic rule changes was to more accurately reflect popular preferences in the selection of delegates. That is why the Democrats adopted the principal of **proportional voting**, in which delegates are rewarded to each candidate in a primary or caucus in proportion to the number of popular votes the candidate receives. To be eligible for delegates, however, a candidate must receive a minimum percentage of the total vote, or *threshold,* usually 15 percent.

The Republicans have not imposed similar national rules. Nevertheless, state Republican parties operate under rules that have increased rank-and-file participation and have broadened representation at their conventions. The chief difference is that the Republicans permit states to have **winner-take-all voting** and the Democrats do not.

In such a system, the candidate or delegates (if they run separately) with the most votes win and the losers get nothing. Such a system benefits front-running candidates and puts them in that position to wrap up the nomination earlier than Democratic candidates usually can.

The changes in the way the parties select their delegates have resulted in greater public involvement in the nomination process. Although a larger portion of the electorate now participate in the primaries, these participants are not equally distributed among all segments of society. Generally speaking, better-educated, higher-income, older party members participate more frequently than do younger people with less education and lower incomes. Racial minorities in particular have tended to be poorly represented among those who vote in primary elections.

Representation at the nominating convention has also improved for various groups within the parties. The percentages of delegates who are women or minorities have increased significantly since 1968. But even though conventions are demographically more representative of the American electorate, they are not necessarily ideologically more representative. Studies of recent convention goers have found Republican delegates to be more conservative and Democratic delegates more liberal than their party's rank-and-file members and much more conservative or liberal than the electorate as a whole.[10] The stronger ideological position of the delegates may explain why recent party platforms have contained unequivocal stands on controversial issues such as abortion, taxes, capital punishment, and the balanced budget and Equal Rights amendments,[11] positions that many of the party's rank and file—and even the presidential nominees—may not accept.

The changes in rules have affected party leaders as well, by reducing the leaders' ability to choose delegates and influence delegates' behavior at the convention. The greater openness of the nominating process and increased

How to Find Information about Federal Elections

The Federal Election Commission (FEC) is a good source for a variety of information about campaigns and elections for federal offices, including regulations, forms, schedules, and any legal actions the commission initiates or advisory opinions it offers. Because its mission is to provide information about these activities to the general public, the commission offers a large number of services for little or no charge. The monthly newsletter *Record,* which lists press releases and other published FEC reports, should be available in your college library. If it is not, you may obtain a free subscription by calling the FEC's public records office at (800) 424-9530. Copies of the documents listed can be obtained at little or no charge by calling or by writing the FEC at 999 E St. N.W., Washington, DC 20463.

If you are in a hurry, the documents can be faxed to you at government expense. All you have to do is call (202) 501-3413 using a touch-tone phone. (The system operates twenty-four hours a day.) You will be asked for the identification numbers of the documents you want, your fax number, and your telephone number. The documents will then be quickly faxed to you, usually within hours.

You can also obtain these documents on the Internet. The FEC also has a homepage **(http://www.fec.gov),** which has several menu options. For example, a *Citizens Guide to Contributions and the Law* contains highlights from various FEC publications and a guide to using the FEC's public records office and its online Direct Access program, as well as summaries, charts, and graphs of presidential and congressional financial campaign information that are updated monthly. News releases and media advisories are also available at this website. You can even obtain information on how to register to vote in your state and a national registration voting form.

If you have any questions about the kind of information the FEC has available, and you do not want to use the Internet, you can call the FEC's public information office at (800) 424-9350.

participation by the rank and file have encouraged people who had not been party regulars in the past to become involved. They have also forced candidates and the delegates who support them to depend less on the party apparatus and more on their own organizing skills.

On balance, the rules for delegate selection have led to an increase in the number of candidates and to the creation of separate candidate organizations. Even incumbents may face opposition, as did Gerald Ford in 1976, Jimmy Carter in 1980, and George Bush in 1992.

Preconvention strategy and tactics Campaigns usually start well before the first caucuses and primaries are held, because candidates need to do well in these early tests of their appeal to voters. By early summer of 1995, more than a year before the 1996 Republican convention, ten candidates had officially thrown their hats into the ring for the Republican nomination. The first contests have assumed great importance because of the attention they attract from the news media and the momentum they can generate.

Another reason for beginning so far ahead of the nomination is that it takes time to raise the money needed for a serious campaign. Millions of dollars are necessary to build an organization, pay its expenses, move around the country, and project an appeal. Financial pressures have forced candidates to devote much of their time to fund-raising, especially since individual donors cannot contribute more than $1,000 and groups more than $5,000 to their campaigns.

The increasing use of mass media, particularly television, by aspirants for their party's nomination has also upped the financial ante. In addition to media, the expenses of building a campaign organization and conducting public opinion polls have increased the financial burden on candidates in recent elections. Assessing public opinion is important because in building an electoral coalition, a candidate has to tailor messages to specific groups within the party, as the Republican aspirants did in 1996.

National nominating conventions After the delegates have been selected, the national nominating conventions are held. The conventions decide on the party's rules, choose its presidential and vice presidential nominees, and adopt the party platform. Despite the conventions' political rhetoric, today they actually decide little that has not been preordained by the delegate selection process. Nevertheless, they do serve several important purposes. They reward the party faithful—activists who were involved in the delegate selection process, those who have toiled for the party, and elected officials, party leaders, and other prominent individuals who desire public recognition and political support. They unify groups that have been divided by the nomination process, stimulating them to pull together during the election campaign. Finally, they constitute a massive public appeal by the parties on behalf of their candidates in the general election.

During the convention, enhancing the party's public image and improving its chances in the election may be difficult because the interests of the party and those of the news media are often in conflict. Both seek to entertain as well as inform. But whereas the party is trying to present a unified front by

It was women and children first at the Republican and Democratic national conventions in 1996, as both parties aimed to showcase their concern for American families. The Republicans featured New York congresswoman Susan Molinari, whose keynote speech made much mention of her two-month-old-baby; in addition, Elizabeth Dole (pictured here), wife of presidential nominee Robert Dole, charmed delegates with a talk-show-style-walk on the convention floor.

scripting the convention proceedings to make them appear interesting and favorable to the party's image—in effect, to conduct a huge pep rally—the media are looking for news, not theater. In 1992, the conservative coup d'état at the Republican convention was the big news, in contrast to the near-unanimity at the Democratic one. In 1996, there was little "hard news" at either major-party convention. As a consequence, the amount of network news coverage declined, as did the number of viewers.

Conventions are one of many stimuli that voters receive during the election campaign. They occur at the midpoint of the process—at the end of the nomination period and the beginning of the general election campaign, months before the final vote. Although they generate more concentrated coverage than any other event to that point, frequently consuming more television time than the rest of the campaign, their impact on the vote is difficult to measure. Political scientists have suggested three major effects of conventions on voters. They heighten interest, thereby potentially increasing turnout. They arouse latent attitudes, thereby raising awareness of the partisan issues. They color perceptions, thereby affecting the electorate's judgments about the candidates, the parties, and their positions.[12] Studies have also found that people who watch the conventions tend to make their voting decisions early in the campaign. About one in five says that she or he does so at the time of the nominating conventions.[13]

General election: strategies and tactics Whereas the nomination process has undergone many changes in recent decades, the federal election process has not. The presidential election still occurs within the context of the **Electoral College** system.

When the framers of the Constitution fashioned the system for choosing the president and vice president, they rejected the idea of a direct popular vote, preferring instead an indirect method in which a group of **electors** would choose the president. Their plan was to have states choose electors in any manner they desired. The electors, equal in number to the total number of senators and representatives from a state, would meet as a group and exercise their own judgment in selecting the president and vice president. It was expected that they would select the most qualified candidates, not necessarily the most popular ones.

Today electors are no longer chosen directly by state legislators; they are chosen by the electorate of each state. When that electorate votes for president, it actually selects electors who are pledged to a particular presidential candidate. Moreover, the electors who are chosen no longer make an independent judgment but instead cast their votes for the candidate of their party.

In all but two states, Maine and Nebraska, the candidate who wins the most popular votes receives *all* the state's electoral votes.[14] This winner-take-all method of voting in the Electoral College is known as the **general ticket system**. A majority of the votes in the Electoral College, 270 out of 538, is needed to win. The candidate can win a majority in the Electoral College and thus be elected president without winning a majority or even a plurality of the total popular vote. This situation has occurred twice: in 1876 and 1888.

If no candidate wins a majority in the Electoral College, the House of Representatives selects the president; voting takes place by state, with each state's delegation having one vote. It is thus possible for the candidate with the most votes in the Electoral College to lose the presidency in the House. That is what happened in 1824 to Andrew Jackson who led with popular and electoral votes in a four-way race but did not have a majority of electoral votes.

If no vice presidential candidate receives a majority in the Electoral College, the Constitution puts the responsibility for choosing a vice president on the Senate. In fact, the Senate has chosen a vice president in this manner only once. In 1837, because of a personal scandal, Richard Johnson, Martin Van Buren's running mate, fell one vote short of a majority in the Electoral College. The Senate elected him anyway.

The structure and operation of the Electoral College give the largest states disproportionate influence in presidential elections because they have the most electoral votes and cast those votes as a bloc. By giving an advantage to the large states, the Electoral College benefits groups that are concentrated in those states and tend to vote cohesively: these include such groups as Jews, Hispanics, and African Americans living in urban areas. The Electoral College also favors the very smallest states, those with four electoral votes or less; these states gain more influence than they would from a direct popular vote.

Presidential candidates take the Electoral College into account when planning their strategy for the general election. Their primary objective must always be to win a majority of the college, not necessarily a majority of the popular vote. To do this, they need to concentrate much of their resources in the large industrial states with the most electoral votes, because failure to win a majority of these states makes it extremely difficult to put together a winning coalition. In building their electoral coalitions, candidates begin with states where they are strong, try to add states in which they have some support, and compete in most of the large states regardless of the odds.

In addition to the Electoral College, the incumbency factor is usually important in the presidential election. Of the fifteen presidents who sought reelection in the twentieth century, ten won. Franklin D. Roosevelt was reelected three times. However, between 1976 and 1992, three out of four incumbents who ran for reelection lost. They suffered from increasingly negative media coverage of the presidency, an increasingly hostile public mood toward government, the weakening of party allegiances and divisions within the parties' electoral coalitions, and the persistence of adverse economic and social conditions. These factors were muted in 1984 and 1996 by the perception of growing prosperity and the absence of a threat to the national security. Being an incumbent is an advantage in good times.

Incumbency is a two-edged sword, however, which can both strengthen and weaken a president's claim to leadership. Incumbency usually helps presidents demonstrate those traits deemed essential for the office: experience, knowledge, direction, decisiveness, and forcefulness. But it also highlights character weaknesses, such as inconsistency, indecisiveness, or inability to stand up to opposition or to demonstrate empathy. Presidents can use their position to gain media attention, promote policies, affect events, and dispense favors. But they also are subject to more critical media scrutiny than other politicians, get blamed for conditions and events they cannot foresee or control, and are often accused of having political motivations for whatever they do.

Nonpresidential Nominations

Some of the changes that have affected presidential selection have affected the election campaigns for other offices as well. The nomination process, especially, has changed. There are now more contested nominations within the parties, and more people are likely to vote in them, particularly when they occur in presidential election years. Fund-raising has become a necessity for most candidates; the mass media have become the principal communication link for reaching large numbers of voters.

The strategy and tactics for nomination campaigns are similar for national, state, and local offices. The principal differences in these contests involve the cost of the campaigns, the use of media, and the ability to employ sophisticated campaign techniques, including public opinion polling. Most money tends to be spent in races for governor and United States senator. These statewide nomination campaigns are also likely to depend more on visual media, primarily television, to convey a message. Because of the cost of buying television time, candidates for other state and local offices have to rely more on radio and print journalism and try to generate more coverage on local news. Similarly, public opinion surveys, a staple for presidential, senatorial, and gubernatorial candidates, are too expensive for most other candidates, who must depend more on their own impressions, instincts, and skills.

Nonpresidential Elections

All elections except for the presidential election are conducted by the states according to state law. This law establishes the districts in which elections are held and the rules and procedures by which they are conducted and the winners determined. Of these factors, the process and product of districting can be especially controversial.

The legal environment: reapportionment and redistricting The Constitution requires that seats in the House of Representatives be redistributed among the states every ten years on the basis on the national census. The stakes are high in this redistribution, known as **reapportionment**, since it may affect not only the number of congressional representatives a state has but also the amount of federal aid it receives. Which states gain and lose representation as a consequence of reapportionment may also affect the partisan balance or control of Congress.

Whether or not the number of congressional seats allocated to a state changes, after each census the state legislature may have to redraw the boundaries of the state's congressional and other legislative districts to reflect geographic shifts in population within the state. This process is known as **redistricting**. The party in control of the legislature naturally uses its power to draw the districts in such a way as to maximize its political advantage.[15] This practice is often referred to as **gerrymandering**, a term coined in 1812 or 1813 to describe the shape of particular legislative district in Massachusetts during the governorship of Elbridge Gerry. The district, which looked a little like a salamander and was dubbed a "Gerry-Mander," is shown in Figure 8-2.

From the 1930s through the 1980s, the principal beneficiaries of gerrymandering were the Democrats, who used it to preserve their dominance of both state legislatures and the House of Representatives. Beginning in the 1990s, however, federal judges began to play an active role in resolving redistricting disputes. At that time a majority of the federal judiciary had been appointed by Presidents Reagan and Bush, so the judges' decisions tended to be more favorable to redistricting plans designed by Republican-controlled legislatures than to Democratic-sponsored ones.[16]

FIGURE 8-2
The First Gerrymandered Congressional District

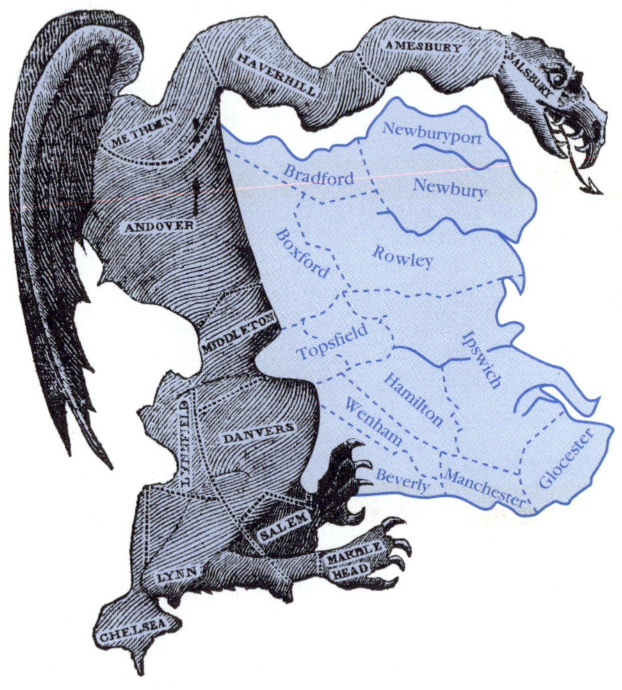

SOURCE: Library of Congress.

The institutional environment: the incumbency advantage? Partisan gains from redistricting are reinforced in large part by incumbency. Incumbency provides recognition, which in turn generates support. Barring a high level of public dissatisfaction, the electorate is more likely to vote for candidates that it knows than for those it does not, and challengers are usually not nearly so well known.

Incumbents can also use the perquisites of their office to help themselves get reelected. The availability of staff, travel funds, and free mailings gives incumbents a head start and at the same time discourages qualified people from challenging them.[17] In addition, they have a fund-raising advantage: potential contributors see incumbents as better able to help them because of their established position in government. The ability of incumbents to raise money, combined with the high costs of running (particularly for statewide office), also discourages would-be challengers.

During the 1980s, more than 90 percent of incumbents in the House of Representatives were renominated and reelected, compared with less than 80 percent of those in the Senate. In the early 1990s, when public frustration with government and the self-interested behavior of those in office reduced the power of incumbency, the reelection rate for House incumbents declined. But even with the shift in partisan control of Congress in 1994, the incumbency reelection rate was still relatively high, and it remained so in 1996. The incumbents who tend to be most vulnerable are freshmen who won their seats by narrow margins. Of the seventy Republicans who were first elected in 1994, thirteen were defeated in 1996.

In addition to its effect on individual candidates, the incumbency advantage works to perpetuate the ruling group within all levels and branches of government, be that group defined in partisan, demographic, or ideological terms. This advantage is one of the reasons that women, who constitute a majority of the population and vote at the same rates as men or even higher rates, have not achieved elective office in anywhere near the proportion that men have.

Midterm Elections

Midterm elections, the congressional elections held in the even-numbered years between presidential elections, tend to work to the disadvantage of the party that controls the White House. Since the Civil War the president's party has lost seats in the House of Representatives in every midterm election except 1934, the election that occurred in the midst of the Great Depression. In some years, these losses have been significant: 1946, 1958, 1966, 1974, and 1994. In only two of them, however (1946 and 1994), has control of Congress actually changed from one party to the other, in both cases going from a Democratic to a Republican majority.

Why does the president's party lose at midterm? Some analysts believe that it has to do with the previous presidential election, in which the victorious candidate sweeps into office fellow party members who come from marginal congressional districts, that is, districts that can be won by either party. In the midterm elections, without the president running, there are no "coattails" to help members of the president's party. Besides, some voters who supported the winning candidates for president and Congress will have become alienated by the decisions they made in office.

Moreover, with the president's coattails being no threat, the outparty can usually attract stronger candidates and raise more money than it can when the president is running for reelection. The Republicans accomplished this feat in 1994 with aggressive recruiting of their congressional candidates.

ANALYZING THE RESULTS

When the campaigns are over and the voters have made their decisions, political pundits, media analysts, party officials, and the winning and losing candidates dissect and evaluate the election. This analysis is important for several reasons. It helps the winners define and claim their electoral mandate—what the people want them to do. It helps the losers know why they lost and, equally important, what they might do to win the next time around. For other observers, it helps clarify the meaning of the election, obviously an important concern for a government based on popular consent.

Most interpretations of elections have focused on the presidency. The midterm election of 1994 is an exception. The magnitude of the Republicans' victory at the national and state levels generated more than the usual amount of interest and led many to view the results in national rather than local terms.

To understand who voted for whom and why, researchers conduct surveys in which voters are asked to identify the principal reasons for their choices and how they feel about the candidates and issues. The two most frequently cited surveys of this sort are the large exit polls conducted for the major news networks, newspapers, and wire services on election day (see Table 8-2) and a smaller but more comprehensive pre- and postelection survey conducted by the National Election Center at the University of Michigan for scholars across the country. Interpretations of these data often produce mixed messages, but they do suggest the dominant issues, images, and partisan allegiances that seem to have shaped the retrospective and prospective judgments of the electorate.

The Presidential Election

The 1992 election was a retrospective vote in which an unhappy electorate turned George Bush out of office because they were disgruntled about his leadership, his economic policies, and a myriad of other domestic problems. Although people had serious reservations about Bill Clinton's character and lack of national experience, they still saw him as more likely to effect change, particularly with respect to the economy. And the economy was the most important issue for a majority of voters. Thus Clinton won despite his personal vulnerabilities.

The mood of the country also provided the climate that permitted the independent candidacy of H. Ross Perot to get off the ground. Tapping the anger and frustration of the voters, Perot promised to do something about the problems of the deficit, the faltering economy, and a deadlocked and out-of-touch government. His straight talk and unconventional campaign, targeted to those who were "sick and tired" of the way things were going—those who had lost confidence in the major parties and their candidates—won him almost as many votes among independents as Clinton and Bush got (see Table 8-2). However, Perot failed to persuade enough Republicans and Democrats to support his candidacy. His failure to do so attests to the difficulty that independent candidates face with the American electorate and in the Electoral College. Perot won no states and received no electoral votes even though he received 19 million popular votes.

By 1996, the economy was stronger, crime had decreased, and the nation remained at peace—all conditions that favor incumbents. Voters responded accordingly, reelecting the Democratic president and the Republican congressional majority. Clinton won more popular and electoral votes than in 1992, although the regional composition of his vote remained essentially the same (see Figure 8-3). Despite misgivings about some aspects of the president's character—notably his honesty, his ideological leanings, and his willingness to stand up for his beliefs—voters saw him as more caring, more in touch with the times, and more visionary than his Republican opponent, Robert Dole. In comparison to 1992, the population groups that shifted most strongly toward the president were women, who responded to his pledges to preserve federal social welfare programs and to strengthen government support for families, and voters under age 30. Dole, in his fourth campaign for national office, and Perot, in his second, also suffered from no longer being new faces to which voters could look for a fresh alternative to the incumbent. As the candidate of the newly organized Reform Party, Perot drew less than half the number of votes he had in 1992.

In short, the 1996 election was a referendum on the Clinton presidency, and Clinton won. Not only did the electorate evaluate his first term favorably, but they saw the president as more capable than either of his major oppo-

FIGURE 8-3
The Electoral College Vote, 1992 and 1996

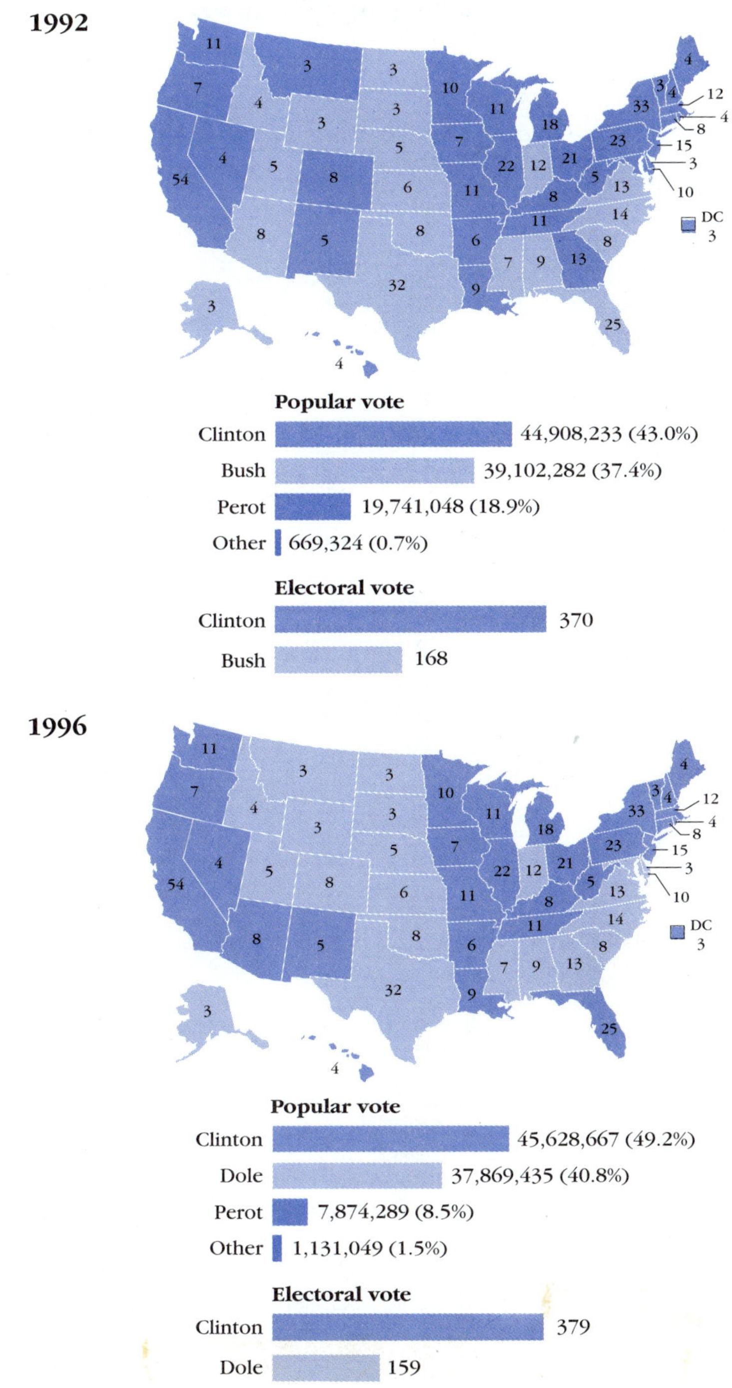

SOURCE: Data for 1992 and 1996 from the Federal Election Commission.

TABLE 8-2 ***Portrait of the Electorate, 1992 and 1996 (percentages)***

		1992			1996		
	1996 TOTAL	CLINTON	BUSH	PEROT	CLINTON	DOLE	PEROT
Total Vote:		43	38	19	49	41	8
Men	48	41	38	21	43	44	10
Women	52	46	37	17	54	38	7
Whites	83	39	41	20	43	46	9
Blacks	10	82	11	7	84	12	4
Hispanics	5	62	25	14	72	21	6
Asians	1	29	55	16	43	48	8
Married	66	40	40	20	44	46	9
Unmarried	34	49	33	18	57	31	9
18–29 years old	17	44	34	22	53	34	10
30–44 years old	33	42	38	20	48	41	9
45–59 years old	26	41	40	19	48	41	9
60 and older	24	50	38	12	48	44	7
Not high school grad.	6	55	28	17	59	28	11
High school graduate	24	43	36	20	51	35	13
Some college education	27	42	37	21	48	40	10
College grad. or more	43	44	39	18	47	44	7
College graduate	26	40	41	19	44	46	8
Postgraduate edu.	17	49	36	15	52	40	5
White Protestant	46	33	46	21	36	53	10
Catholic	29	44	36	20	53	37	9
Jewish	3	78	12	10	78	16	3
White born-again Christian	17	23	61	15	26	65	8
Union household	23	55	24	21	59	30	9
Family's financial situation compared with four years earlier							
Better today	33	24	62	14	66	26	6
Same today	45	41	41	18	46	45	8
Worse today	20	61	14	25	27	57	13

nents of understanding and handling the challenges of the late 1990s and, in his words, "building a bridge to the twenty-first century."

Midterm Elections

Most midterm elections do not lend themselves to a single interpretation, although the results of those elections—that is, the composition of the new Congress—affect public policy for the country as a whole. Even though the news media read into the election certain national trends and issues, the dominant concerns for most voters most of the time are local personalities, parties, and constituency-related issues.

TABLE 8-2 ***Portrait of the Electorate, 1992 and 1996 (percentages) (continued)***

		1992			1996		
	1996 Total	Clinton	Bush	Perot	Clinton	Dole	Perot
Family Income							
under $15,000	11	59	23	18	59	28	11
$15,000–$29,999	23	45	35	20	53	36	9
$30,000–$49,999	27	41	38	21	48	40	10
$50,000 and over	39	39	44	17	44	48	7
$75,000 and over	18	36	48	16	41	51	7
$100,000 and over	9	—	—	—	38	54	6
From the East	23	47	35	18	55	34	9
From the Midwest	26	42	37	21	48	41	10
From the South	30	42	43	16	46	46	7
From the West	20	44	34	22	48	40	8
Republicans	35	10	73	17	13	80	6
Independents	26	38	32	30	43	35	17
Democrats	39	77	10	13	84	10	5
Liberals	20	68	14	18	78	11	7
Moderates	47	48	31	21	57	33	9
Conservatives	33	18	65	17	20	71	8
Employed	64	42	38	20	48	40	9
Full-time student	—	50	35	15	—	—	—
Unemployed	36	56	24	20	49	42	8
Homemaker	—	36	45	19	—	—	—
Retired	—	51	36	13	—	—	—
First-time voters	9	48	30	22	54	34	11

Notes: Data for 1992 collected by Voter Research and Surveys and based on questionnaires completed by 15,490 voters leaving 300 polling places around the nation on Election Day. Data for 1996 collected by Voter News Service and based on questionnaires completed by 16,627 voters. Those who gave no answer are not shown. Dashes indicate that a question was not asked or a category was not provided in a particular year. "Born-again Christian" was labeled "born-again Christian/fundamentalist" in 1992. In 1996, "Employed" includes only those employed full time; all others are listed as unemployed.

Source: *New York Times,* November 28, 1993, B9, and November 10, 1996, 28.

The midterm elections of 1946 and 1994 were different. In 1946, the voters reacted against sixteen years of Democratic control, against a Democratic president, Harry Truman, who was not perceived to be of the same stature as his much revered predecessor, Franklin Roosevelt, and against various scandals that had marred the Truman presidency.

In 1994, the voters protested against Democratic leadership. They reacted against a Democratic president who had not lived up to expectations, to a Democratic Congress that seemed unable or unwilling to follow his lead, and to a Democratic philosophy of government that seemed out of tune with the public's antigovernment, anti-Washington mood.

Republican presidential candidate Robert Dole campaigns at the 1996 Veterans of Foreign Wars convention. But voters seemed satisfied with President Clinton's performance and rewarded him with another term.

ELECTIONS AND GOVERNANCE

Elections influence what government does, particularly in the year following the election. That is why understanding the meaning of the election is so important. Contrary to popular belief, campaign promises and party platforms do get translated into public policy. Media scrutiny, frequent elections, and the desire to be reelected provide incentives for redeeming campaign promises and staying responsive to the electorate.

On the other hand, elections are rarely clear mandates, even though public officials may claim them. A poll taken before the 1994 elections found that even of those respondents who planned to vote Republican, only about 25 percent knew anything about their Republicans' Contract with America. Moreover, Republican senators did not as a group declare their allegiance to the Contract as their House counterparts had done.

A mixed judgment is not unusual. People vote for the same candidate for different reasons, and they vote for different candidates for the same reason. They also vote for many different officials. As a consequence, the results of the election may yield seemingly contradictory messages. Differing national, state, and local constituencies also tend to produce outcomes that mirror the political system's decentralization and diversity more than a dominant public mood. Perhaps this is why divided partisan control at the national level has been the rule, not the exception, since 1968. Separate institutions and divided control of them has made governing more difficult precisely because the Republicans and Democrats have different and often competing priorities and policy agendas.

Finally, the length of the electoral process and the promises made by candidates to obtain and retain office have increased public expectations of government performance and, at the same time, made these expectations harder to meet. Today's successful candidates usually owe less to their party leaders and organizations than to themselves, their campaign organizations, and their constituencies. Once in office and over time, they tend to behave independently, guided more by the people who elected them than by their party's official position on current issues. At the national level, especially, this has produced more elected public officials who wish to lead and fewer who are willing to follow them.

CASE STUDY

THE CAMPAIGN FINANCE DEBACLE

Money is said to be "the mother's milk of politics," and the love of money to be "the root of all evil." These two aphorisms seemed particularly appropriate during and after the 1996 elections. In this period, the Speaker of the House, Newt Gingrich, was reprimanded by his colleagues for violating House rules by misleading a congressional committee looking into his fund-raising activities on behalf of the Republican party. President Clinton and Vice President Al Gore became the targets of allegations that they had misused their offices to raise money for their presidential election campaign. The head of the House committee investigating these charges, Dan Burton (R, Ind.), was himself accused of "shaking down" a Democratic lobbyist for campaign contributions. The National Committee, faced with revelations that it had accepted millions of dollars in contributions from foreign donors, many of whom were not permitted to contribute under United States law, returned millions to those whose legal status could not be verified. The party was left heavily in debt.

Why has the solicitation of campaign funds suddenly become such an issue? The short answer to this question is that the costs of conducting electoral campaigns have skyrocketed in recent years. In addition, the law regulating these activities contains gigantic loopholes that have encouraged candidates to go on a fund-raising rampage. As a consequence of these trends, the campaign finance system has broken down. And the Federal Election Campaign Act no longer serves the purposes for which it was intended—to promote democratic elections and facilitate the politics of Ameican government.

In the 1995–1996 election cycle, the major parties broke fund-raising records. Together, at state and national levels, they raised $881 million, a 73 percent increase over the previous election period. The Federal Election Campaign Act, enacted during the mid 1970s, did not envision revenues and expenditures of this magnitude. In fact, one of the goals of the original legislation was to relieve the presidential candidates of much of the burden of fund-raising so that they could concentrate on getting their message across to the voters. Yet in this election cycle, President Clinton hosted 103 "koffee klatsches" in the White House to encourage and reward contributors to the Democratic party. White House spokespeople defended the president's actions by pointing out that Clinton's Republican predecessors had also engaged in these and similar activities. In response, Republicans pointed to the discrepancies in scale between those of the Clinton White House and past Republican administrations.

The law was intended to limit individual and group contributions to candidates and political parties. Yet, ever since 1979, when an amendment was added to permit unlimited donations for voluntary "nonpartisan" efforts to get out the vote, candidates and their parties have used this loophole to solicit huge contributions of so-called soft money. In the 1995–1996 election cycle alone, the Republicans raised around $141 million in soft money and the Democrats about $122 million, almost three times as much as these parties raised four years earlier. Nearly four hundred corporations, labor unions, and individuals gave more than $100,000 each in soft money to the major parties during this period. Seven of these groups gave more than $1 million.

To make matters more complicated, the legislation enacted in the mid 1970s did not anticipate that the Supreme Court would void any congressionally imposed limits on independent campaign expenditures by individuals and groups. But in *Buckley v. Valeo,* the Court held that independent expenditures were protected by the free speech provision of the First Amendment to the United States Constitution, thereby opening the door to the wealthy to try to influence the political process with large expenditures of funds, even for their own election. As a candidate for the Republican nomination in 1996, Steve Forbes alone spent more than $37 million in his unsuccessful quest. In the previous presidential election, Ross Perot spent more than $64 million of his own money on his campaign.

As a consequence of these developments, the Pandora's box of financing campaigns has been opened wide. In the 1996 election, an estimated total of $1.5 billion dollars was spent on federal and state races. Raising funds of this magnitude requires considerable coordination, time, and effort; and some of these efforts got the winning candidates and their parties into big trouble.

Take Speaker Gingrich, for example. Beginning in 1986, as chair of a political action committee known as GOPAC, he was instrumental in soliciting large sums of money to be used to recruit and train Republican candidates for federal and state office. As part of this effort, Gingrich, a former college history professor, taught a course entitled "Renewing American Civilization," which was beamed by satellite to colleges around the country. The course naturally reflected Gingrich's conservative ideological perspective and his political views and objectives, and funding for it came from a tax-exempt foundation set up as an adjunct of GOPAC. By law, however, tax-exempt foundations are not permitted to engage in partisan political activities.

Charged with violating the law by not properly differentiating his political activities from the educational efforts of the foundation, Gingrich added to his problems by providing misleading information to the House Ethics Committee that was investigating the controversy. When a special counsel appointed by the House revealed this misinformation, the Speaker was forced to admit his indiscretion and was subsequently reprimanded by the House and fined $300,000.

Even before the Gingrich matter had come to a vote, the fund-raising activities of the Democratic National Committee and the White House had become the focus of attention and criticism. The news media reported that the party, in apparent violation of the Federal Election Campaign Act, had accepted millions of dollars from foreign residents, noncitizens, and some American affiliates of foreign companies. Moreover, many of the donors had received special treatment such as entry to White House events and audiences with the president, vice president, and cabinet members, opportunities ordinary citizens do not have. Not only had the party not checked into the eligibility of the donors, but the White House had not run the usual background checks on many of these visitors. Warnings from the FBI and others in the administration that certain foreign countries, companies, and individuals were attempting to gain influence through their campaign contributions went unheard or unheeded.

The president actively encouraged these activities. He approved the solicitation of funds from foreign-related sources and the use of the White House events, such as coffee hours and "sleep overs," for donors. In all, 938 "friends of Bill," as the administration described them, slept in the White House during the president's first term, leaving observers to ponder whether they were "friends of Bill" because they contributed or contributed because they were friends of Bill.

The vice president was also an active participant in the Democrats' fund-raising efforts, making numerous telephone calls from his White House office to solicit money for the 1996 campaign. Although he did so on a phone line paid for by the Democratic National Committee, with individual calls billed to a credit card from Gore's campaign organization, federal law prohibits political solicitation in or from government buildings.

As the news media revealed the scope of these activities, Congress began to investigate the alleged illegalities, irregularities, and unethical practices that had come to light. Meanwhile, Representative Burton, who chaired the Government Reform and Oversight Committee, charged with conducting this investigation for the House, found himself the subject of the "shakedown" allegations, which he vehemently denied.

These financial activities and allegations raise serious questions, many of which relate to the high cost of campaigning. Are such expenditures necessary, and if so, who should pay for them? Should it be the taxpayers, through public financing of elections, the mass media, through laws requiring them to provide free-advertising for candidates, or those who choose to contribute, as is now the case? Should limits be placed on the size of all campaign contributions and expenditures (including soft money)? If so, wouldn't such limits violate the First Amendment? If not, doesn't the current system advantage the wealthy and undercut the democratic electoral process? Finally, to what extent should federal office holders be permitted to use their offices, their staffs, and their perquisites—travel allowances to go to their districts, franking privileges for mail, media access and public relations, and especially their ability to gain legislation that benefits the folks back home—to solicit money?

Discussion Questions

1. How serious are these issues, and what if anything do you think should be done about them?
2. Who would have to find solutions, and why has it been so difficult for these individuals to do so?
3. Can and should these items be legislated? Should the Constitution be amended?
4. Ideally, how should Americans finance their electoral system?

SUMMARY

Electoral politics are the foundation upon which a democratic political system rests. They frame policy debate, determine legislative and top executive officials, and influence the decisions these officials make as well as the initial agenda they pursue. In this way, electoral politics shape the who, when, and what of American government.

Yet in the early years of the nation, suffrage was extremely limited. It took three amendments to the Constitution to remove racial and gender barriers to voting and extend *suffrage* to all citizens 18 years of age and older. The expansion of suffrage increased the number of eligible voters, but not the percentage of those who actually vote. Turnout has generally declined since 1960. Among the factors that have contributed to lower turnout are weakening party identification, mobility among younger voters, and the growing number of elderly people with poor health and less interest in politics. Government scandals have also increased the apathy and cynicism of the electorate as a whole.

In recent years, one of the critical issues concerning the democratic character of elections has been money. Congress has sought to regulate contributions and expenditures through the enactment of campaign finance legislation. That legislation has placed limits on campaign spending, provided government support for presidential nomination and election contributions and expenditures over a certain amount. But these laws have loopholes through which millions of dollars have been funneled to the two major parties, causing public concern and prompting proposals to restrict such fund-raising.

Despite the excesses of the parties, they are still important because they provide voters a framework for analysis and offer cues for assessing the candidates and their stands. Group associations, the candidates, and the issues also affect how people vote.

Candidates and parties contrive their campaigns to affect the electorate's judgment. There are usually two campaigns: one is to gain a party's nomination and, if that is successful, the other is to win the general election. Of the two, the quest for the nomination has changed the most during the twentieth century, particularly at the presidential level.

Most presidential campaigns usually start well before the *caucuses* and *primaries* are held. One reason for this is that it takes time to raise the money needed for a serious campaign. Millions of dollars are needed to build an organization, pay for television time, conduct public opinion polls, and develop voter appeals.

The national nominating convention formally decides the party's rules, chooses its presidential and vice presidential nominees, and approves its election platform. Usually, however, the nominees have been preordained by the delegate selection process. An important function of the convention is to unify groups that have been divided by the nomination process and launch the general election campaign with a broad national appeal.

The president is actually chosen by a group of *electors*, meeting as the *Electoral College*. The voters in each state select a group of electors equal in number to the state's senators and representatives; these usually vote as a bloc for the presidential and vice presidential candidates who have won the popular vote in the state. Candidates take the Electoral College into account when divising their campaign strategy.

Some of the changes that have affected the presidential election process have affected nonpresidential selection as well. Primaries have become the route to nomination at most levels of government. These primaries have led to more competition within the parties and have left them more factionalized. To win the nomination, candidates must build their own strategy, and mount a campaign that appeals to those partisans who are most likely to participate.

Who wins does matter in terms of what government does, particularly in the year following the election. Most elections are referendums on the officials and the policies of those in power. The electorate evaluates how the government has worked and credits or blames those in office.

Elections are important because they provide an agenda of priorities as well as a potential coalition of supporters. It is up to those in power to convert that agenda into a series of proposals and mobilize a coalition to support them. They usually claim an election mandate to do so.

KEY TERMS

- universal suffrage
- meaningful choice
- political equality
- soft money
- split-ticket voting
- retrospective voting
- prospective voting
- caucus
- superdelegate
- proportional voting
- winner-take-all voting
- Electoral College
- elector
- general ticket system
- reapportionment
- redistricting
- gerrymandering

RESOURCES

READINGS

Abramson, Paul R., John H. Aldrich, and David W. Rohde. *Change and Continuity in the 1992 Elections*. Washington, D.C.: Congressional Quarterly, 1993, and volumes for previous elections. A thorough analysis of the vote in presidential elections.

Campbell, Angus, Philip E. Converse, Warren E. Miller, and Donald E. Stokes. *The American Voter*. Chicago: University of Chicago Press, 1980. A classic study that postulates a theory of voting behavior that is still applicable. Not easy reading, but worth the effort.

Jacobson, Gary C. *The Politics of Congressional Elections*. 3d ed. New York: HarperCollins, 1991. A thorough analysis of the impact of party, incumbency, money, and other factors on the outcome of congressional elections.

Pomper, Gerald M. et al. *The Election of 1996*. Chatham, N.J.: Chatham House, 1997. Prominent political scientists evaluate the 1996 election.

Rosenstone, Steven J., and John M. Hansen. *Mobilization, Participation, and Democracy in America*. New York: Macmillan, 1993. A comprehensive study of political participation. The authors suggest that economic interests may be less important motivating factors than moral values and ideological perspectives.

Sabato, Larry, ed. *Toward the Millennium: The Elections of 1996*. Boston: Allyn & Bacon, 1997. A book of essays on the 1996 presidential election.

Sorauf, Frank J. *Inside Campaign Finance: Myths and Realities*. New Haven, Conn.: Yale University Press, 1992. A good source of information about campaign finance.

Wattenberg, Martin P. *The Rise of Candidate-Centered Politics*. Cambridge, Mass.: Harvard University Press, 1991. An examination of presidential elections during the 1980s and their increasing candidate orientation.

Wayne, Stephen J. *The Road to the White House, 1996*. New York: St. Martin's Press, 1996, postelection edition, 1997. A nuts-and-bolts description of the arduous quest for the nomination and the general election.

ORGANIZATIONS

House Oversight Committee, 1309 Longworth Office Building, Washington, DC 20515; phone (202) 225-8281, fax (202) 225-9957; Internet http://www.house.gov/cho/ Holds hearings on legislation dealing with the electoral process and publishes transcripts of them; oversees the Federal Election Commission.

Federal Election Commission, 999 E Street, N.W., Washington, DC 20463; phone (800) 424-9530, fax (202) 219-3880; Internet http://www.fec.gov Issues a monthly newsletter, press releases, and various other reports in addition to its public computer file on campaign expenditures for all national campaigns.

Inter-University Consortium for Politicial and Social Research, University of Michigan, Ann Arbor, MI 48104; phone (313) 763-5010, fax (313) 764-8041; Internet http://www.icpsr.umich.edu/ Has conducted national surveys during presidential and congressional elections since 1952 and disseminates data to scholars for analyses of voting behavior.

League of Women Voters, 1730 M Street, N.W. Suite 1000, Washington, DC 20036; phone (202) 429-1965, fax (202) 429-0854; Internet http://www.lwv.org/ Provides information to voters on election rules and procedures at the national, state, and local levels; also provides information on candidates' positions.

Senate Committee on Rules and Administration, 305 Russell Office Building, Washington, DC 20510; phone (202) 224-6352, fax (202) 224-3036; Internet http://www.senate.gov/committee/rules.html Holds hearings on legislation dealing with the electoral process and publishes transcripts of them; oversees the Federal Election Commission.

9

Politics and the News Media

PREVIEW

- News media in a democratic society
- History and modern communications technology
- News media and politics: the news slant; manipulation of the news; political advertising; the impact of the media on electoral politics
- News media and government: coverage of the president, Congress, and the judiciary
- The impact of the news media on public policy

The first bomb went off in Chicago in 1978. A security guard was hurt, but no one was killed. The second exploded a year later at nearby Northwestern University, injuring a graduate student. The third explosion occurred on an airline flight originating in Chicago. Constructed in a similar manner, the bombs seemed to suggest that a serial bomber was at work.

When the fourth went off in Chicago in 1980, injuring the president of United Airlines, the FBI dubbed its investigation of the case UNABOM after the apparent targets, universities and airlines.

The bombings continued but spread beyond the Chicago area to Vanderbilt University and the University of California at Berkeley. The first fatality occurred in 1985, when a person was killed outside a computer store in Sacramento, California, to which a bomb was mailed. No one claimed responsibility for any of these blasts, and the FBI had few solid leads.

In 1993, after explosions occurred again at UC Berkeley and at Yale University, injuring two faculty members, the *New York Times* received a letter from an alleged anarchist group, the Freedom Club, claiming that it had set off the bombs. More letters, threats, and bombs followed—all widely publicized by the news media. By this point, the FBI had put together a profile of the culprit, who appeared to be a well-educated man, perhaps with a graduate degree in engineering or mathematics, who had a grudge against modern industrial society and those who contributed to it.

In 1995, after a threat to bomb a plane at Los Angeles International Airport was made, the *New York Times* and the *Washington Post* each received a fifty-six-page manifesto entitled "Industrial Society and Its Future." Along with this document, the author sent a letter promising to end the bombings if the newspapers published his essay. The promise placed the newspapers and law enforcement officials in a dilemma. Publication of the document could be viewed as a victory for the "Unabomber" and might encourage others to engage in similar illegal activities or threats to public security in order to gain a podium for their views. On the other hand, the bombings, which had killed three people, injured many others, and caused widespread public anxiety, might cease. After considerable debate and with no apparent break in the case, the newspapers decided to produce a joint publication that was printed and distributed by the *Post* in September 1995. The Unabomber had achieved his principal objective, the dissemination of views criticizing modern technology, and had done so with the help of the news media. Were they now accomplices in the crimes?

But the communication intended to warn of technology's evils soon became technology's captive. Long after copies of the manifesto had disappeared from newsstands, it continued to circulate on the Internet, kept alive by a Unabomber cult that regularly exchanged information about their mysterious, inventive "hero." It was on the Net that David Kaczynski read portions of the Unabomber's views, which he concluded bore a remarkable resemblance to his brother's thoughts and writings. After much soul-searching, Kaczynski alerted federal authorities to the similarities. Theodore Kaczynski was arrested on April 3, 1996, at his primitive cabin in the mountains of Montana and charged with the bombings. A search of the cabin found three typewriters that officials believe he had used to write his letters to the newspapers, addresses for the mail bombs, and the manifesto itself.

Thus the media, responsible in large part for the publicity the Unabomber received for his actions, threats, and beliefs, were also responsible for warning society about his terrorism and for providing the information that may have ultimately resulted in his capture. Obviously, the dissemination of information is a critical function of the press in a democratic society. However, by reporting an event, the media can become part of it, influencing the very story they cover. That happened with the Unabomber, and it wasn't the first time—nor will it be the last.

The Unabomber case also illustrates the delicate relationship between the news media and government in the United States. In fact, it was somewhat unusual in that two major newspapers cooperated with a government agency to try to work out a course of action that would best serve the public interest. More commonly, the American media consider that they best serve this interest by taking an adversarial, critical stance toward the people and institutions of politics and government. Especially in recent decades, this role has often had a significant impact.

The exposure of the White House connection to the Watergate burglary during the Nixon administration, the reporting of atrocities during the Vietnam War, the nightly television news program on the captivity of American diplomats held hostage in Iran, the revelation of arms sales to Iran, and later, the diversion of funds to rebels fighting the Marxist government in Nicaragua—all helped focus public attention on major problems, forced government officials to react to those problems, and set off a series of decisions and actions that ultimately affected government, public policy, and the political environment.

The news media affect the politics of American government in a variety of ways: they focus attention on salient issues; create a time frame in which those issues are addressed; influence the content, tone, and parameters of public debate; and convey and evaluate the decisions and actions of those in power. Thus they play two critical roles for democratic government: they constitute principal vessels through which information is transmitted, and they influence that very information and how people may react to it by the manner in which they report it. In this sense, the news media continually affect the reality they purport to describe and assess. That is why they are often referred to as the fourth branch of government. This chapter examines the news media and their impact on American politics.

NEWS MEDIA IN A DEMOCRATIC SOCIETY

Newspapers, radio, and television are essential for a democracy. They are a vital link between the people and their public officials. They provide information and analysis about policy issues; they also sensitize those in government to public opinion, enabling policy makers to respond to the needs and desires of the population. Moreover, the news media play an important role in reporting and evaluating the decisions of government, a role that is critical for holding those in power accountable for their decisions and actions.

To perform those functions adequately, the news media need to operate freely, with as few restrictions as possible on their collection and dissemination of information. They need to be a "marketplace of ideas," a forum in which the truth will emerge. In a government based on the consent of the governed, such a forum is essential not only for discerning truth but for evaluating the performance of public officials.

The First Amendment guarantees the press the right to investigate and report about people and events, but the Supreme Court has also ruled that it must be balanced by the rights of others to privacy, truthfulness, and fairness and by the need of the country to protect its national security. It is up to the judiciary to determine the boundaries between freedom of the press and individual and societal rights.

Limits placed on print journalism are less extensive than those on the electronic media. Because broadcasters use the public airwaves, they are required to operate in the public interest and have been subject to rules designed to ensure *fairness* in the discussion of important issues, *equal time* for candidates to present their views to the electorate, and the *right of rebuttal* for those attacked on the air. The result of these rules, however, has been to discourage the electronic media from becoming a forum for debate because of the requirement to provide free and equal time for opposing points of view.

Free time costs money, and the American media are predominantly private and profit oriented. Being profit oriented forces them to entertain as they inform in order to capture and hold the attention of as large an audience as possible. Thus they emphasize competition, conflict, and human interest and deemphasize detailed discussion of policy issues.

History of the News Media

The history of the news media in the United States illustrates the tension between the democratic goals of informing the public and the economic interests of maintaining as large an audience as possible. Mass journalism developed during the nineteenth century, spurred by the invention of the telegraph and later by sensational *yellow journalism*. During the twentieth century, as radio and then television became the most important medium for reporting fast-breaking news stories and foreign news, the number of daily newspapers and the proportion of the public getting their news from them began to decline.

PRACTICING DEMOCRACY

Using the Freedom of Information Act and the Privacy Act

Did you ever wonder about what government officials considered when they made important decisions or whether certain groups were given greater access than others or more information on policy that affected them? What about the various investigations in which the government has engaged under the guise of promoting national security or maintaining law and order? Has this information been used to create a file on you or someone you know, or a group that you are considering joining? Now you can find out.

Journalists, students of government, even ordinary citizens can use the Freedom of Information Act and the Privacy Act to obtain copies of government reports, memorandums, and files. The Freedom of Information Act (FOIA), enacted in 1966, requires agencies and departments of the executive branch of the United States government to provide the fullest possible disclosure of information to the public. The Privacy Act of 1974, a companion to FOIA, provides safeguards against invasions of individuals' privacy through the misuse of records by federal agencies. The Privacy Act allows most individuals to gain access to federal agencies' records about themselves and to seek to change any incorrect or incomplete information.

Both laws make federal agencies accountable for information disclosure policies and practices. Although neither law grants an absolute right to examine government documents, both laws establish the right to request records and to receive a response to the request. If a record cannot be released, the requester is entitled to be told the reason for the denial and has the right to appeal the denial and, if necessary, challenge it in court.

Radio In addition to being faster than newspapers in reporting the news, radio had the advantage of being better able to convey the excitement and color of a scene. Politicians soon became aware of the power of radio to transmit ideas. Franklin Roosevelt was the first president to use it effectively to appeal directly to the people and mobilize support for his political agenda. Roosevelt's "fireside chats" fostered a personal relationship between the president and the public, and his technique became the model for his successors in the White House.

Although radio lost its national audience to television in the 1950s, it did not fade away. Instead, stations began broadcasting specialized programming aimed at smaller, local, homogeneous audiences. Today, there are more radio stations operating than in radio's supposed "glory days" in the 1940s.[1] One factor that has kept radio flourishing has been the increasing amount of time Americans spend in their cars; unlike reading or watching television, listening to the radio is not difficult or dangerous to do while driving.

The 1990s have seen the expansion of talk radio, where listeners are encouraged to telephone the host with questions and comments. Many of the people who host such shows have strong ideological convictions that they share, usually with like-minded listeners. Rush Limbaugh, G. Gordon Liddy, Michael Reagan,

Often the most difficult part of obtaining information under the provisions of the FOIA and the Privacy Act is determining which agency has the records. There is no central government records office that handles all FOIA requests, nor is there a central index of federal government records about individuals. To find the correct agency, you must consult a government directory such as the *United States Government Manual* or a commercially produced directory such as *Information USA.* Both are found in virtually every college library. The next step is to write a simple letter to the agency's head or to its FOIA or Privacy Act officer. The letter should contain three important elements. First, state that the request is being made under the FOIA or Privacy Act (or both). Second, identify as clearly as possible the records that are being sought. Finally, include the name, address, and signature of the requester. There is no need to explain the reason for the request. Anyone can write a request letter; there is no need for a lawyer to be involved.

Federal agencies are required to respond to FOIA requests within ten working days, with actual disclosure of the requested information to follow promptly thereafter. Agencies may charge fees for processing some requests, particularly if the requester is going to use the information for commercial purposes. The fees are often reduced or waived for small requests made by individuals seeking information for personal or scholarly use.

The disclosure requirements of the FOIA do not apply to elected officials of the federal government, including the president, vice president, senators, and representatives; to the federal judiciary; or to state or local governments (all states and some localities, however, have passed laws similar to the FOIA). Moreover, under the FOIA an agency may withhold some types of information, such as that which is classified for national security or needs to be kept confidential for the conduct of an agency's business.

In his famous fireside chats on radio, President Franklin Roosevelt reached millions of listeners and built support for his policies. A president's role as "communicator-in-chief" has become critical, as more and more citizens get their information from electronic media rather than the printed press.

FIGURE 9-1

Households with Radios, Televisions, Cable Television, and VCRs, 1940–1995

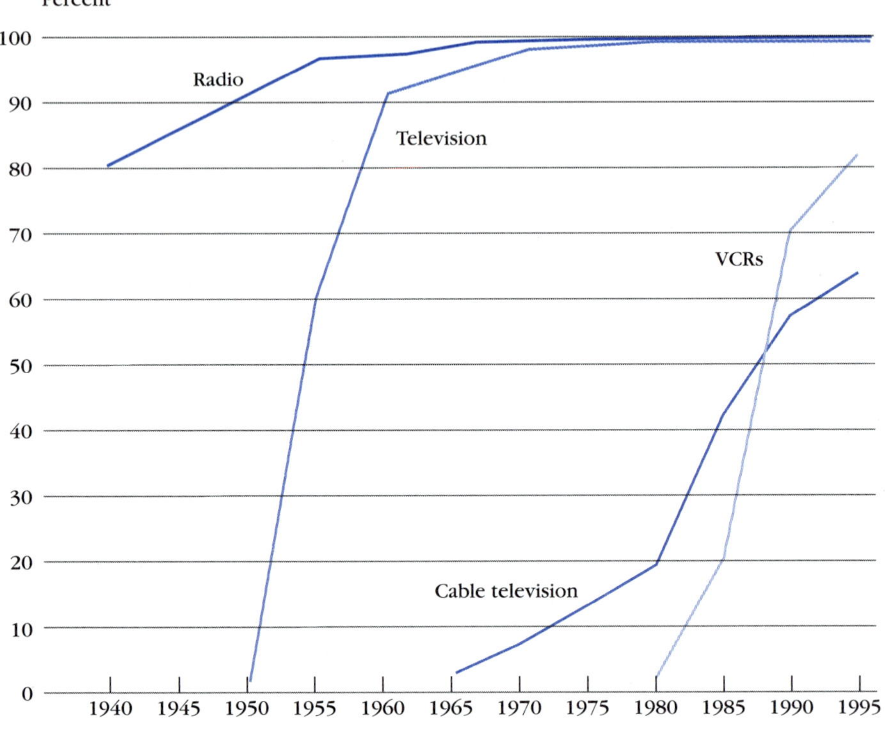

SOURCE: Samuel Kernell, *Going Public,* 3rd ed. (Washington, D.C.: Congressional Quarterly, 1997), 126.

and Oliver North have reached large audiences with their anti-Washington, antiliberal, anti-Clinton rhetoric.

Television After World War II, television quickly transformed the American public into a large viewing audience. In 1950, only 9 percent of the households in the United States had televisions; ten years later, that percentage had grown to 87; by 1980, it had reached over 98 percent. Today, almost 80 percent of American households have at least *two* television sets. Moreover, the average length of time that a television set is turned on each day has risen from approximately four hours in 1950 to about seven hours today, with the average person watching more than nine hundred hours per year. Figures 9-1 and 9-2 document the extent to which radio and television serve as primary sources of communication.

When television started to dominate the American media, three networks—ABC, CBS, and NBC—began to dominate television. During this formative stage, most of the commercial stations in the United States were affiliated with one of these three networks, which provided them with the bulk of their entertainment programming and national news.

Over the next two decades, television's power to shape political images was demonstrated repeatedly. In 1954, it contributed greatly to the downfall of Senator Joseph McCarthy (R, Wis.), who had made a name for himself by charging that communists had infiltrated the government, particularly the State Depart-

FIGURE 9-2

Media Use by Consumers, 1988–1999

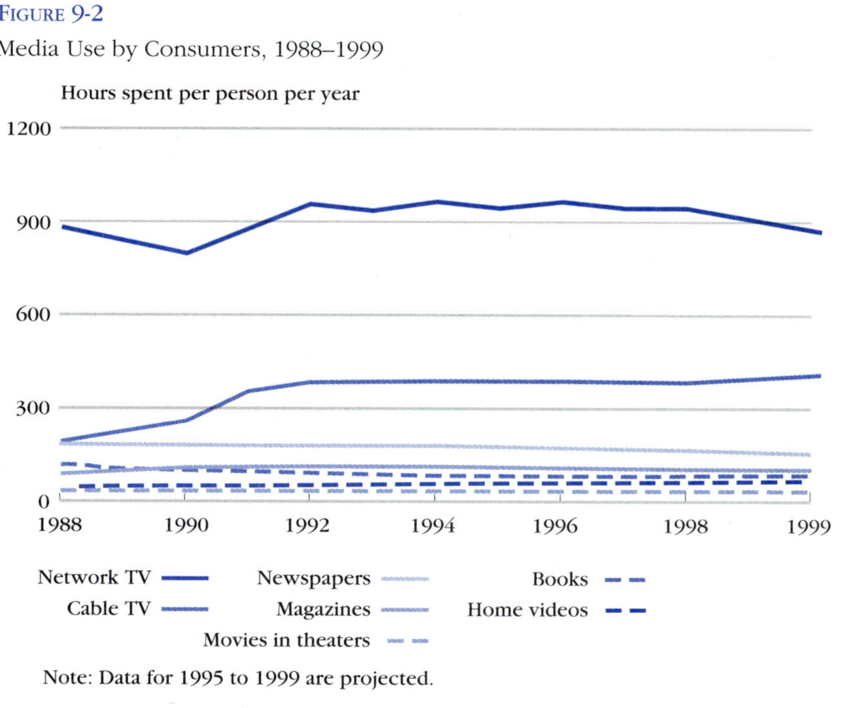

SOURCE: U.S. Bureau of the Census, *Statistical Abstract of the United States,* 1996, 116th ed. (Washington, D.C., 1996), 562.

ment, and the military. During eight weeks of televised hearings by McCarthy's committee into possible communist influence in the Army, the public was able to view and evaluate (negatively, as events proved) the senator's unsubstantiated charges and browbeating of witnesses and others who denied his allegations.

Another example of the power of television came during the four debates held in 1960 between the two major presidential candidates, Senator John F. Kennedy and Vice President Richard M. Nixon, especially the first debate that was seen by more than half the electorate. In that confrontation, the vice president appeared pallid; the color of his suit blended into the background; he seemed to need a shave; and he shifted nervously in his seat with his eyes darting back and forth. He did not look nearly as good as he sounded. In contrast, Kennedy appeared fresh; his clothes made him stand out; and his facial expressions and gestures came across well on television. Those who heard the debate on radio judged Nixon the winner; those who saw it on television were more impressed by Kennedy. The television exposure that both candidates received during the debates contributed to Kennedy's narrow victory.

Television coverage of the civil rights movement, particularly the 1963 protest staged in Birmingham, Alabama, by Dr. Martin Luther King Jr., and the reaction to it by the white police (with attack dogs, water cannons, and cattle prods), created unforgettable images for viewers. For much of the public, television provided the evidence that justified the struggle for civil rights. Coverage of the Vietnam War, the first "living-room war," provides another vivid illustration of the power of television news on public opinion. Nightly pictures of the pain and suffering of the victims of the war, including American military casualties,

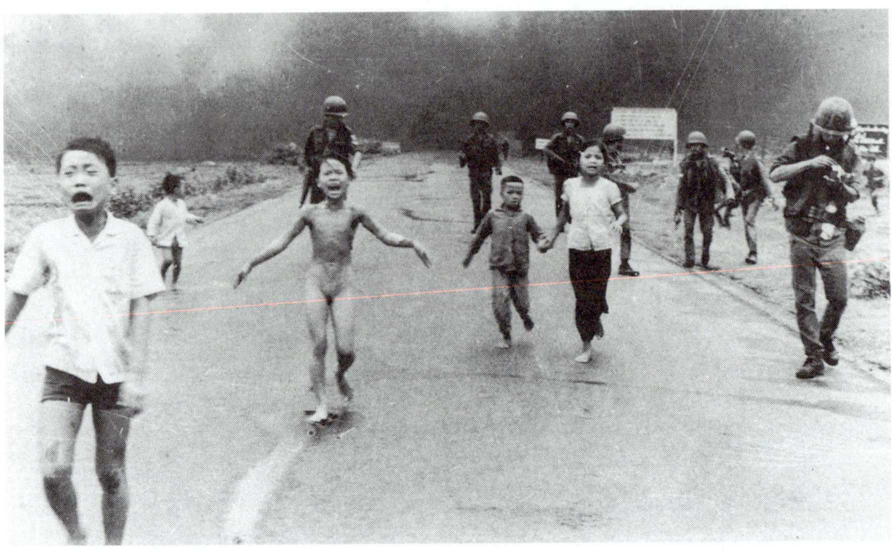

Media coverage of the Vietnam War—especially the nightly televised images of death, destruction, and suffering—helped turn public opinion against American military involvement in Vietnam. In this 1972 photograph, one of the most famous of any war, children flee in panic from an air strike in which napalm bombs were dropped.

and persistent, critical evaluations of the progress of the war by correspondents in the field of operations had a powerful cumulative effect on the public's conscience and helped turn national sentiment against the war.

The decade of the 1960s also saw the increasing importance of television network news and the growth of a large Washington press corps. In 1948, NBC and CBS began airing fifteen-minute evening newscasts. By 1963, the national news was extended to a half-hour. Since that year, Americans have cited television as their principal and most believable source of news.[2]

Television affected the print media as well. Since television reports events at or close to the time they happen, newspapers and magazines had to supplement their coverage and commentary in order to provide an additional dimension and thereby maintain a product that people would want to buy. Moreover, they had to find news by investigating activities that on the surface might not have appeared newsworthy. *The Washington Post*'s reporting of the Watergate scandals during 1972 and 1973 is a good example of the power and profitability of investigative journalism.

Recent Developments

A major change for the public in the 1980s and 1990s has been the growth and accessibility of cable television. Although cable television began to operate in the early 1950s, largely to improve television reception in areas that had difficulty getting a clear picture, it took several decades for the country to become wired for it and for companies to offer a wide selection of programming on it. By the middle of the 1980s, cable was available in most metropolitan areas and, increasingly, in rural areas as well. By the mid 1990s, more than 59 million households were subscribing to a basic cable service, approximately 62.4 percent of the total households with televisions.[3]

The development of cable has more closely paralleled that of contemporary radio than that of television. Instead of appealing to the broadest possible audience, cable stations engage in what political scientist Austin Ranney describes as "narrowcasting," that is, offering specialized programming designed for specialized audiences.[4] For those interested in politics and government, the all-news and public affairs stations like Cable News Network (CNN) and the Cable Satellite Public Affairs Network (C-SPAN) provide a seemingly endless amount of coverage.

Other recent developments in the electronic media include the improvement of satellite technology, which is particularly important for extending broad coverage to rural areas. In addition, low-powered stations that provide specialized programming to local audiences have expanded.[5]

Not only has the diversity of programs increased, but so has the capacity of viewers to shift quickly from one channel to another by using remote controls. These devises have had a profound effect on news coverage. To prevent their audiences from getting bored and switching to other channels, the networks have speeded up the action, shortened the statements they air by candidates and public officials, and emphasized argumentation and conflict in these individual's on-the-air remarks. Moreover, interactive radio and television shows, in which live audiences as well as listeners and viewers comment and question on-the-air personalities, have now become standard fare.

The communications revolution continues to advance at a rapid rate. The Clinton administration has begun the development of a communications "superhighway," a voice, video, and data network that can transmit information in a matter of seconds across the country, enabling users to access hundreds of stations and data banks.

Like television in the 1950s, computers have become a mass medium in the 1990s. According to a survey conducted by the Nielsen Media Research in 1997, 50.6 million people in the United States and Canada were using the Internet and 37.4 million, the World Wide Web and those numbers are growing exponentially.[6] In 1993, the Clinton administration became the first to open itself to communication via the Internet, and the White House began to interact with the public through an electronic mail (e-mail) system. Today, at a website called *Welcome to the White House: An Interactive Citizens' Handbook,* one can access text, pictures, and audio and video files from the White House by simply clicking a computer mouse at the appropriate icons or the highlighted key words. The *Handbook,* which is linked directly to the websites of all cabinet-level departments and the other federal executive agencies, offers the public direct, rapid, and easy-to-use access to an enormous amount of government information.

While the White House was taking the lead in getting into "cyberspace," Capitol Hill was moving in the same direction. The websites of both House and Senate are linked directly to the interface of the Library of Congress, which offers information on daily congressional activities, the full text of bills introduced in Congress since 1973, and information on the library's huge collection, among other things. The number of individual legislators who have ventured onto the Internet has grown very rapidly as well. Today, most senators and representatives can be contacted by e-mail and have their own homepages on the Web.

The judicial branch has lagged behind the other two branches in this area, though the Administrative Office of U.S. Courts has developed a website called *U.S. Federal Judiciary* and the Federal Judicial Center has also established a website.

Since the White House went on line, public access to government information has been improved substantially. The major federal Internet sites are listed in the appropriate chapters of this text. Almost all of them are linked directly, thereby facilitating "surfing" from one site to another.

As the information explosion changes the ways in which people obtain political and other information, the type and amount of information they receive, the ways in which they contact their government, and the time frame in which public officials respond, politics and government are bound to be affected. The next two sections examine some of that impact by describing contemporary news media coverage of elections and government and exploring how that coverage affects the events that are reported.

NEWS MEDIA AND POLITICS

News media coverage of politics and government is not neutral. No coverage can be. What do the news media choose to emphasize, and to whom are their stories directed? How do candidates for political office react, and how do they try to shape the news to their advantage? Finally, what impact does all this have on voters?

The News Slant

The key to news media coverage of political events (as well as other kinds of events) is their **newsworthiness**. This complex concept includes timeliness, importance, conflict, drama, and surprise. To be considered news, an event must have the potential to capture the attention of the public: readers, listeners, and viewers. From the news media's perspective, their job is to emphasize events that have this potential.

What is reported as news is also influenced by factors such as access and convenience. With limited resources, the media have to decide what to cover

Ongoing C-SPAN coverage of the House of Representatives shows members addressing their constituents in speeches that may have little if any legislative impact: the camera does not pan the floor of the House and thus does not reveal members' absences or inattention.

and how much time to devote to it. Along with newsworthiness, the cost of coverage and the amount of time and trouble it will take figure in that decision.

How does the slant of the news color coverage of an event? Consider an electoral campaign. Above all else, in the view of the media, election news must be exciting. Thus campaigns are reported as if they were sporting contests, with correspondents stressing the competitive, gaming aspect. According to the polls, which of the candidates is winning and losing, who is doing better than expected, and who is doing worse? Not only is the game of politics emphasized, but it is stressed at the expense of substantive policy issues—particularly at the beginning of the electoral process, when "horse race" stories tend to dominate the coverage (see Figure 9-3). Once a front-runner emerges, builds a lead, and thus makes the race less interesting, the focus shifts to questions about the candidates' character and to conflicts between candidates, their advisers and staff, and even the news media in the campaign.

Stories about the private lives and personalities of the candidates and their staffs have also become a fixture of campaign coverage. In fact, the issue of personality has received more attention in recent years than have issues of policy. The principal reason is that people find personality more interesting than complex, often abstract policy considerations. Another reason may have to do with the medium of television itself. The average length of a story on the evening news is forty-five to ninety seconds, too short a time to provide in-depth analysis and barely long enough to let candidates discuss the issues.[7] In fact, policy issues accounted for less than one-third of all the campaign stories on the evening news programs broadcast by the three major networks in 1992 and only 37 percent in 1996.[8]

FIGURE 9-3

Focus of Coverage of Primaries on the Evening News, January–March 1992 and 1996

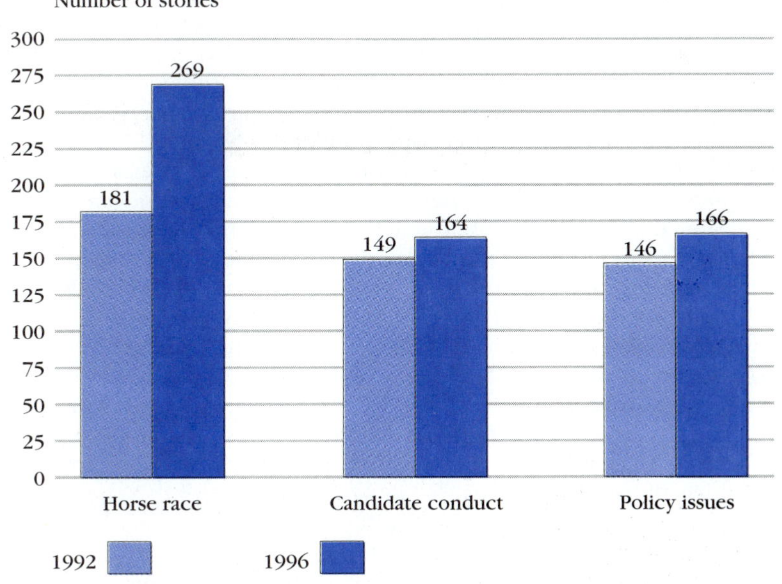

Note: A story may include more than one topic.

SOURCE: "The Bad News Campaign," *Media Monitor,* March–April 1996: 3.

In addition to the presumption about what is newsworthy in a campaign and how it should be presented, there is a larger framework into which that news is made to fit. According to political scientist Thomas E. Patterson, a dominant "story line" emerges in the media, and much of the campaign is explained in terms of it. In 1992, it was Pat Buchanan's surprising showing in the primaries against President Bush that was news, not Bush's easy wins against his Republican rival; in 1996, it was Buchanan's and Steve Forbes's early victories, not Robert Dole's organizational and reputational advantages.

In short, the press fits the news of the campaign into the accepted story rather than create new stories from the changing events of the campaign. Naturally, the story line that the news media present affects the electorate's perception of what is happening.

Not only is the news fit into a story line, but it is increasingly bad news. In an analysis of the evening news on the three major television networks during the 1992 presidential campaign, S. Robert Lichter and his associates found that 69 percent of the evaluations of President Bush were negative, as were 63 percent of the comments about Governor Clinton and 54 percent of those about Ross Perot after he got back into the race.[9] Similarly, during the 1996 primaries, the four leading Republican candidates—Dole, Buchanan, Alexander, and Forbes—all received more negative than positive press. In fact, their speeches, their ads, and their interviews were less critical of their opponents than the media were of the candidates in general.[10] Dole's negative press continued into the general election campaign. Two out of three 1996 campaign stories on Dole were negative, compared with one out of two for Clinton.[11]

What is the reason for all the negativism? Does it represent an ideological or political bias, as Dole charged in the 1996 general election campaign? Although academic experts disagree on whether the news has an ideological bias, they do agree that it has a professional bias that contributes to negative coverage. That bias or orientation is dictated by the definition of what is news. A new face winning or an old face losing is news; an old one winning or a new one losing is not. Similarly, the first time a politician states a position, it may be news; the second time, it is not. Since candidates or public officials cannot provide new positions or new ideas every time they address a group—in fact, candidates normally give the same speech many times over—the correspondents who cover these events look for other things to report. Verbal slips, inconsistent statements, and other mistakes get more attention than would the news that a speech is well delivered or warmly received. Similarly, how the public reacts to what candidates say and do has become almost as newsworthy as the statement, event, or action itself.

Another aspect of contemporary news coverage that adversely affects a candidate's ability to appeal to voters is the increasing mediating role that correspondents play. News programs devote less time to the candidate's own words and more to the correspondents and others for their reaction. In 1968, the average length of a **sound bite** from candidates on the evening television news was 42.3 seconds. In 1992, it was only 8.4 seconds and in 1996, only 8.2 seconds. Under these circumstances, it is not surprising that politicians attempt to manipulate the news of their campaigns.

Manipulation of the News

People in the news, especially politicians, try to affect the coverage they receive. They do this by scheduling and staging events, by releasing information and granting access to reporters, and by preparing speeches and responses. To

To reach larger, less politically involved audiences, presidential candidates have begun appearing on television entertainment shows. Here in 1992, Bill Clinton plays his saxophone for Arsenio Hall. This appearance, like one on MTV, contrasted the younger, "swinging" Clinton with his more aloof, stuffy Republican opponents—a contrast that helped Clinton capture the youth vote in 1992 and 1996.

accommodate television's need for good visual images, newsmakers often pose in dramatic settings to create the image they wish to convey. Reagan's appearance on the shores of Normandy on the fortieth anniversary of the Allied invasion of Europe during World War II, Bush's Thanksgiving dinner with the troops on the Arabian desert during the 1990 buildup of United States forces for the Persian Gulf War, and Clinton's attendance at a memorial service in Oklahoma City following the 1995 bombing of the federal office building there are three illustrations of how recent presidents have used their position to advantage. Those who lack a presidential podium have to use their imagination and creativity to generate a favorable and memorable image.

One of the major changes in the relationship between politicians and the news media in the 1990s has been the use of the "soft news," or talk/entertainment format by candidates and (to a lesser extent) public officials to present their views in their own words. Pioneered by Ross Perot on television and Jerry Brown on radio, this new format provides a user-friendly atmosphere in which to engage the public. In variations of the format such as town meetings and call-in shows, candidates and public officials can demonstrate their responsiveness, sincerity, and empathy by interacting with the audience. Clinton has been particularly effective in such settings.

The talk/entertainment format has several other advantages for politicians, particularly candidates. For one thing, it distances them from the aggressive "gotcha" style of journalism in which national news correspondents frequently engage. They are treated better, more like celebrities than politicians. Their host tends to be more cordial and less adversarial than the national correspondents. And those being questioned can give longer answers that are broadcast in their entirety rather than in one or two sound bites. In fact, the programs themselves are often newsworthy, generating an even larger impact when excerpts from them are rebroadcast or summarized on the news. The larger audience, higher comfort level, and greater ability to project desired images and present seemingly spontaneous but often carefully crafted answers have made this format appealing for politicians who wish to supplement and, where possible, circumvent the national press coverage to reach the general public.

Political Advertising

Paid advertising can also be used to convey political messages. Associated primarily with election campaigns, it has been used as well to generate public support on a wide range of political issues. One of the most effective advertising campaigns in recent years was launched in 1994 by the Health Insurance Industry of America against President Clinton's health-care reform plan. The ads featured an average American couple named Harry and Louise, who voiced their fears that the Clinton plan would not allow them to choose their own doctors, would cost them more money, and would involve them in more government paperwork and red tape. Another very effective series of policy ads, aired in 1995 by the Democratic National Committee, in turn warned against the Republican plan to cut funding from the Medicare program.

The objectives of advertising are to gain recognition, to create images, and to educate people about the merits or liabilities of particular policies or candidates. Bill Clinton skillfully used advertising during his presidential campaigns to project an image of a New Democrat, a moderate, who could deal effectively with economic problems. He also used it to counter and preempt Republican criticism of himself and his administration.

Image making can be negative as well as positive. With the increasing emphasis placed on personal factors in politics, **negative advertising** has grown in importance in recent years, particularly during election campaigns. Researchers have estimated that at least half the advertising in the last three presidential campaigns was negative.[13] As a consequence, voters are becoming more leery of negative ads. Part of their skepticism has stemmed from the controversy generated by some of them, such as the one about Willie Horton that was aired during the 1988 presidential campaign. The ad featured a mug shot of Horton, an African-American prisoner who had raped a white woman while on a weekend furlough from a Massachusetts jail. Aimed at those who were fearful of crime, of African Americans, and of liberals and their "do-good" social policies, it was directed against Democratic candidate Michael Dukakis, the governor of Massachusetts. The commercial, sponsored by a political action committee supporting Bush, was supplemented by other PAC ads featuring relatives of the victims of Horton's crimes. The Bush campaign also produced ads of its own to reinforce the crime issue.

The cumulative impact of these negative ads left the impression that Dukakis released hardened criminals who then recommitted their heinous crimes against other innocent victims. By the end of the campaign, 25 percent of the electorate knew who Willie Horton was, what he did, and who had furloughed him; 49 percent thought Dukakis was soft on crime.[14]

The Impact of the Media on Electoral Politics

With all the effort and energy put into news coverage and the candidates' use of the media, one would think that the news media have a significant impact on the outcome of elections. Yet that impact is difficult to measure.

Research has found that the media (including hard news, soft news, and advertising) affect voters' awareness and impressions of candidates more than they influence their political attitudes or cause them to change their opinions on major issues. The media do, however, elevate the importance of certain issues through the attention they devote to them. In this way, the media are able to influence the criteria that voters use to evaluate candidates and decide for whom to vote.

The news media are usually more influential at the beginning of the electoral process, when people have relatively little knowledge about the candidates and their positions, than at the end. Especially in presidential elections, the disproportionate coverage given to the candidates in the first primaries and caucuses can be crucial to their success in winning the nomination.

News media coverage affects voter turnout. By emphasizing certain issues and personal characteristics, the press sets the campaign agenda and frames discussion. By evaluating the candidates and their campaigns, by reporting public sentiment, and by forecasting the likely outcome, they may influence that outcome. Thus they become participant observers.

The news media have also affected the political parties by becoming today the principal vehicle through which campaigns are communicated. Voters no longer need to turn to the parties for information about candidates. Conversely, candidates gain independence from party organizations by mounting direct media-based appeals.

Not only may the media influence which candidates are elected; they also influence what those candidates do after being elected. Clinton's adherence to his economic stimulus program at the beginning of his presidency in spite of economic recovery, and Gingrich's promise to vote on all the proposals contained in the Republicans' Contract with America within the first 100 days of the 104th Congress, indicate how much the publicity given to campaign promises shapes the policy agenda after an election. Bush's reversal on his "Read my lips, no new taxes" pledge and his subsequent election defeat reveal the costs of breaking a major promise to the American voters.

NEWS MEDIA AND GOVERNMENT

Coverage of public officials and policies does not end with the election. Often the news is an important factor in shaping debates over the issues and the evaluation of political leaders.

Certain journalistic conventions shape the reporting and presentation of national news. The focus on government activities centers on people rather than on institutions or policy, partly because most issues and operations of government are so complex that they are difficult to explain in a news story. Little background or contextual information is provided, particularly by the electronic media. Instead, the personal dimensions of the story are emphasized. For example, the personalities and actions of those who were involved in the Iran-contra affair were more interesting to the American public than were details about the confusing arms sales and ways in which funds were diverted; similarly, it was the Clintons' role in Whitewater and the president's and vice president's in campaign finance matters that captivated public attention, not the complex financial transactions and the legalities of the issues.

In addition, news coverage often stresses the style and strategy employed by government officials to pass or defeat a particular piece of legislation, rather than the effect the policy might have on the country. This is a variation of the "horse race" journalism that commonly appears in election coverage. Policy issues are presented as two-sided arguments. Congressional votes are portrayed as either wins or losses for the president or congressional leadership; conflicts within agencies or committees are seen as pluses or minuses for one individual or group against another. In the mid 1990s, the news media variously described the debate and division over how to balance the budget in seven years as a tug of war between the administration and Congress; between Clinton, Dole, and Gingrich; between Democrats and Republicans; and between liberals and conservatives.

In their watchdog role, the news media tend to emphasize failures rather than successes, what does not work rather than what does. Bad news is almost always reported; good news may not be.

Coverage of the President

In their coverage of the national government, the news media focus on the presidency. The reason the presidency receives so much attention is that the president is seen as the principal initiator and prime mover of the political system, the head of the government and head of state, a chieftain with multiple roles, all deserving attention. Moreover, the presidency provides a "handle" for evaluating the many facets of government. The president personifies the government, at least in the view of the news media.

The news media's focus on the president naturally produces incentives for an administration to try to shape the coverage it receives. Presidents want to place their administration in a favorable light and build support for their policies. They have a variety of instruments to do so.

The release of news may be timed to make the administration look good. If good news is released, it is likely to be the only information made available by the administration at that time. If bad news must be released, other announcements may also be made in an attempt to obscure it; and if possible, it is made public over the weekend, when less attention will be paid to it. The general rule is that good news is announced by the president and bad news by others, often the White House press secretary or a cabinet official.

The White House can also take more direct steps to affect what the media report. Reporters tend to rely on the pictures and stories made available to them by White House sources. Among the services provided to the White House press corps that may help shape the news are briefings, interviews, off-the-record background sessions, photo opportunities, travel arrangements, and handouts and other press releases. The Clinton administration held as many as three press briefings a day not only to present the president's perspective but to give reporters stories, keeping them busy and thereby limiting their time to pursue other leads.

In addition to the comprehensive coverage of presidential activities, the president can usually obtain airtime for major speeches and press conferences in times of crisis or, occasionally, when making a major policy announcement. If the news media perceive that partisan politics is a primary motivation for such a request, however, they are less apt to provide that free time.

Despite the many ways in which the White House can curry favor with reporters, stage events, control access to information, and direct public attention, presidential news is often unfavorable. In an analysis of evening news cov-

FIGURE 9-4
President Clinton's Evaluations on Television and by the Public, 1993–1995

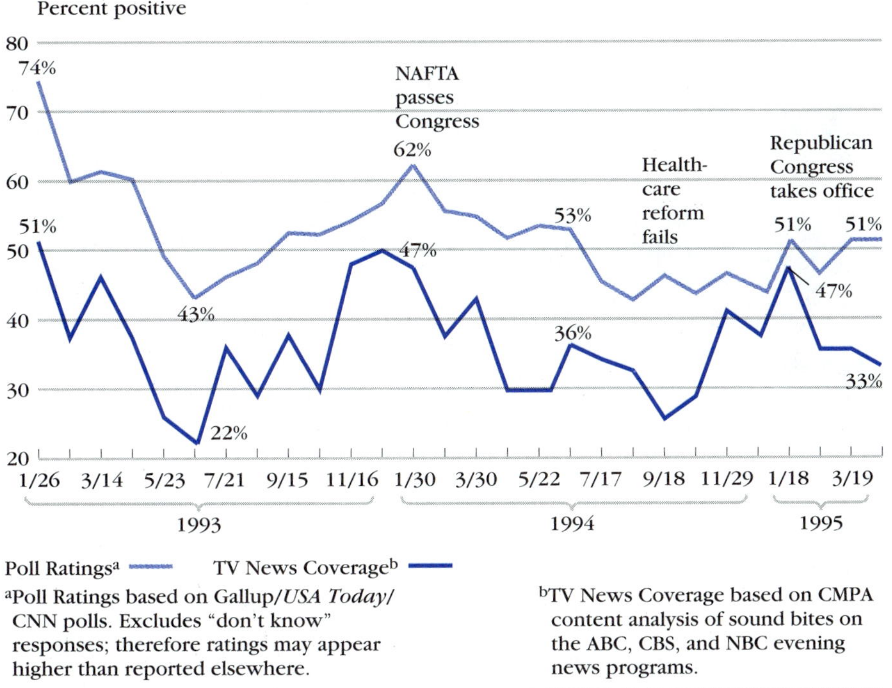

[a]Poll Ratings based on Gallup/*USA Today*/CNN polls. Excludes "don't know" responses; therefore ratings may appear higher than reported elsewhere.

[b]TV News Coverage based on CMPA content analysis of sound bites on the ABC, CBS, and NBC evening news programs.

SOURCE: "The Invisible Man, TV News Coverage of President Bill Clinton, 1993-1995," *Media Monitor,* May-June 1995: 5. Reprinted by permission.

erage of the first twenty-eight months of the Clinton administration, Lichter and his associates found that the president was the object of 3,500 negative comments. His ratio of bad news to good news was 5 to 3 (63 percent bad compared with 37 percent good).[15] Figure 9-4 traces both Clinton's television news coverage and his public-opinion approval ratings during this period.

Coverage of Congress

Congress is less newsworthy than the president most of the time. The commercial television networks and CNN occasionally offer live coverage of events such as major speeches, committee hearings, and floor debates. In recent years, these have included the Senate hearings on campaign finance in 1997, the confirmation of Clarence Thomas as a Supreme Court justice in 1991 and of Dr. Henry Foster as surgeon general in 1995, and the floor debate in the Senate over the authorization of military force against Iraq in 1991. Other famous congressional hearings that have received live coverage include the investigations of the Iran-contra affair during the Reagan administration and of Watergate and related scandals during the Nixon administration, as well as Senator Joseph McCarthy's hunt for communists in the government during the Eisenhower administration.

Most of the coverage on the major broadcast networks is not live, however. Rather, they report snippets of what Congress does or does not do and how

In recent administrations, presidential press conferences have become more formal, made-for-television productions. Here President Clinton meets the press in the East Room of the White House.

representatives and senators behave. The major live coverage is on C-SPAN, which records the official proceedings on the House and Senate floors and, along with CNN, covers selected committee hearings.

With 535 members of Congress, most eager for public attention, there is no shortage of people willing to be interviewed. The open environment encourages the news media to assign a host of reporters and correspondents to the Capitol Hill "beat." However, the major media give little emphasis to the substance of policy and its consequences for society. When substantive policy is discussed, it is frequently presented in a simplified form and as a divisive political issue in which the difficulties members have in reaching agreement and the obstacles to the president's legislative leadership are stressed. Because the internal policy-making processes of Congress are complex, slow-moving, undramatic, and often unpredictable, the media describe Congress as constantly involved in struggles against itself or against the president.

In addition to being harsh on Congress as an institution, the media are tough on its members—when they get any coverage at all. The personal foibles and questionable behaviors of members of Congress—their abuse of banking and postal privileges, periodic charges of sexual escapades and harassment, and investigations into the fraudulent use of public funds—all command attention. The public service, policy positions, and legislative work of most members do not. Only the policy positions of the leaders of the House and Senate and their role on controversial issues receive coverage in the national media, and much of it is not flattering.

How the news media report on Congress and what they report affect the behavior of representatives and senators in several fundamental ways. Members of Congress consciously position themselves to be newsmakers, granting interviews to reporters, attending and participating in committee hearings that the news media are likely to cover, using their staffs to issue press releases about their positions and legislative initiatives, and keeping the press (particularly the local media in their home states and districts) informed about their activities. Most of them take advantage of radio and television studios in Congress to record programs for the folks back home. This media-oriented behavior has led one student of Congress to conclude that "making news has become a crucial component of making laws."[16]

In contrast to the mostly negative coverage by the national media, the local news media present a different picture. They report less on Congress as a whole and more on local representatives, particularly when they are back home in their districts. Local coverage tends to be of the "soft," human interest variety—a speech to the chamber of commerce, a tour of the state fair, a ceremony at a high school graduation, a ribbon cutting at a senior center financed by federal funds that the member helped obtain. Most of this coverage conveys a favorable image of the member, in sharp contrast to the generally harsh evaluation of Congress as an institution.

Coverage of the Judiciary

The third branch of government, the judiciary, is often a stranger to the national media, except during major trials or controversial hearings such as the confirmation hearings for Clarence Thomas. The Supreme Court receives only a small fraction of the attention received by the president and Congress, and only a few news organizations assign reporters to it on a full-time basis.

There are several reasons for the dearth of coverage of the judiciary. The Supreme Court does not welcome attention: justices rarely give interviews or discuss the decision-making process in which they are involved. In addition to the problem of access, many judicial decisions are complex. To understand them, one must give them careful consideration, often applying specialized legal knowledge. Only a few major newspapers, networks, and magazines can afford to hire journalists who have this knowledge. Therefore, the initial reports of Supreme Court decisions are often brief descriptions of the majority and minority opinions, the justices who voted on each side, and the implications of the decision. This information is frequently presented in the context of whose interests were benefited or hurt by the judgment. Reporters who cover the lower federal courts tend not to be lawyers or students of the law. Their focus is often on sensational cases rather than on far-reaching legal issues and trends.

At the state level, coverage of the judiciary is more common because many judges are elected rather than appointed. And some state courts now permit radio and television coverage of trials, some of which appear on the cable court channel. Moreover, highly publicized events involving alleged criminal activity, such as the O. J. Simpson murder trial and the beating of Rodney King by several Los Angeles policemen, gain coverage by virtue of the actions or the people involved.[17]

THE IMPACT OF THE NEWS MEDIA ON PUBLIC POLICY

News media coverage of institutions of government naturally has an impact on the public's evaluation of those institutions. Public approval tends to follow media coverage, not the other way around. At the beginning of the 104th Congress, coverage was favorable and the public more approving than during the same period of the previous Congress. However, as the news media increased the amount of congressional news, emphasizing internal divisions between the

Republicans in the House and the Senate and their failure to reach agreement on a broad range of policy issues (including the principal priorities in the Contract with America), the evaluation of Congress declined sharply. A similar explanation can be made for the judicial system, whose favorable evaluation declined from 43 percent in January 1994 to 35 percent two years later. The drop was caused in part by the unfavorable reaction to the length, legal maneuverings, and verdict of the O. J. Simpson murder trial, which was watched by millions of Americans.[18]

In addition to affecting the public's assessment of how government is working, news coverage affects the content of policy as well as the behavior of public officials. It does so in three ways: it shapes priorities; it shortens time frames; and it limits options.

The news media help set the agenda for government. For example, in 1979–1980, through their extensive daily coverage of the Iranian hostage crisis, when diplomats at the American embassy in Tehran were taken hostage by paramilitary guards loyal to the Iranian government, the news media kept the problem before the public and thereby heightened the demand for a satisfactory solution. The coverage also raised expectations for a quick solution, effectively shortening the response time available to the Carter administration. The daily television coverage began by noting the number of days the hostages had been in captivity and thus reminded the public not only of the problem but also of the administration's inability to deal with it.[19]

How the press covers an event or policy issue and how the public reacts to that coverage may also limit the options available to public officials. At the beginning of the Clinton administration, for example, administration officials "floated" various ideas for reducing the federal budget deficit. One involved a delay in the cost-of-living adjustment for Social Security. Negative public reaction to this report doomed the proposal and even led the president to deny that his administration was seriously considering it.

Although the publicizing of proposed decisions and actions may generate a hostile response, it may also produce public support. In either situation, the news media perform a necessary role in a democratic society, linking the public to their government.

CASE STUDY

'Indecency' on the Internet

The virtual explosion in use of the Internet in recent years, and particularly its accessibility to children, have raised concerns about the availability of sexually explicit images and texts from private home pages and commercial online services. In 1996, Congress reacted to these concerns by tacking on a provision to the omnibus telecommunications bill that was enacted in that year. This part of the legislation, known as the Communications Decency Act, banned the dissemination of "indecent" and "patently offensive" material to minors on the Internet and established penalties of prison terms and large fines for violators.

Civil libertarians, medical educators, and companies offering online and computer services immediately objected. They argued that the enforcement of the law would have a chilling effect on Internet communications, placing the government in the position of censor with public officials determining what is or is not allowed. For example, would a medical journal that depicted parts of the human anatomy or discussed the transmission of AIDS through sexual relations be subject to prosecution under the law? What about a Robert Mapplethorpe photograph that shows an aroused man, or men engaged in sexual activity with one another? Would scenes from a play that depicts nudity and simulates sexual acts be permitted? Critics also contended that under the law text permitted in print or images permitted in a movie could be banned on the Internet, thereby creating a dual standard for different means of communication.

In raising these questions, opponents of the legislation, which included the American Civil Liberties Union, the U.S. Chamber of Commerce, and the Association of National Advertisers, contended that it would impede communication on the Internet as well as involve the government in what should be a parental activity. Since most website providers cannot readily determine the age of those accessing their sites, the opponents noted, they would have to cleanse sites of any material that could be considered indecent or face the possibility of criminal prosecution. Theoretically, parents who allowed their children to use the Internet could also have been prosecuted if the children viewed material that fell under the purview of the legislation. Similarly, minors who corresponded with others in "chat rooms" could have been subject to prosecution if they talked explicitly about sex. The opponents also contended that technology now exists (in the form of computer software) to screen out sexually explicit material on the Internet, another reason for the government not to get involved.

Another issue raised by critics of the law involved material originating from sources outside the United States. About 30 percent of all Internet addresses are currently in other countries and that proportion will undoubtedly grow in the years ahead. Would the Communications Decency Act apply to foreign individuals and groups; and if so, how would it be enforced?

Proponents of the legislation, of course, saw things differently. They noted that obscene material is not protected by the First Amendment to the Constitution. Movies are currently rated on the basis of the violence, sex, and language they contain; those under a certain age may not be admitted to certain films and may attend others only with an adult. Moreover, Congress has established restrictions on television broadcasting that provide for "family programming" during certain hours and require warnings prior to the airing of shows containing dialogue or images that some might find offensive. The proponents also pointed to provisions in the new telecommunications law requiring that broadcasters rate the content of their programming for sex and violence and that new televisions sold in the United States contain a device known as a "V chip," that allows parents to prevent certain programs from being viewed on their own televisions. Besides, they argued, doesn't Congress have a right to protect children whose parents are not able or willing to do so, and a duty to make public policy that reflects community standards and the wishes of the majority?

The clash between individual rights and community standards is an ongoing one, and the arena of free speech is one in which it often occurs. In the case of the Communications Decency Act, the courts acted quickly, clearly, and decisively. A three-judge federal panel in Philadelphia ruled unanimously that key elements of the law that pertained to indecent material were unconstitutional. The court reasoned that the law was too sweeping; that there were other ways, short of government censorship, in which parents could control objectionable material on the Internet; and, finally that information on the Internet had to be afforded at least as much protection under the First Amendment as printed matter. (Calling attention to the new communications technology, the court distributed its decision on a compact disk and published it on its own bulletin board on the Internet.) A federal court in New York issued a similar ruling, and both courts issued injunctions preventing the government from enforcing the law.

The Justice Department immediately appealed these decisions to the Supreme Court, which heard oral arguments in March 1997 and issued its decision in June of that year. In *Reno v. American Civil Liberties Union,* the Supreme Court sided with the appellate courts, invalidating the law. Arguing that the First Amendment's freedom of speech protection applied to online communications as it did to the print media, the Court held the language of the Communications Decency Act, specifically its reference to "indecent and patently offensive" material, was overly vague and its prohibition on the dissemination of such material "an unnecessarily broad suppression of speech addressed to adults." Although the Court acknowledged that the government had a legitimate interest in protecting minors from harmful material, it said such protection could not be achieved in a manner that restricted the communication of nonobscene material among adults.

Discussion Questions

1. Do you think the Supreme Court made the right decision?
2. If government has a right to protect children from harmful material on the Internet, then how can it do so?
3. Is there other material, such as personal information on individuals—credit ratings, family history, buying habits, etc.—whose dissemination on the Internet could or should be restricted by government?
4. What about gambling? Can the government regulate it on the Internet? Can it tax revenues generated from the Internet?

SUMMARY

The news media form a critical link between the public and their government. This link functions as a conduit through which communications flow and by which those communications affect elections, government, and public policy. The politics of American government is shaped by the type of information the media convey, the manner in which they convey it, and the impact that it has on public opinion and public participation in the political process on one hand and on the government's decisions, actions, and public policy on the other. Whatever that impact, it embroils the news media in these politics as the fourth branch of government.

Few would deny that a free press is essential for a democratic society. Although the First Amendment to the Constitution protects freedom of the press, that freedom is not absolute. It must be balanced by individual rights to privacy, social obligations to truthfulness, and the country's national security needs.

The history of the news media in the United states is marked by professional change, economic competition, and technological advancements. Newspapers were the principal source of news for most people until the 1940s, when they were replaced first by radio and then by television. Today, advances in communications technology have supplemented radio and television as communication satellites, fiber optics, and new online technologies have opened up additional channels for communicating quickly. For television, the major change has been the growth of cable and satellite networks. The Cable News Network can report news as it happens almost anywhere in the world, and public service cable channels provide in-depth coverage of some of the official proceedings of government as well as discussion of public issues. Furthermore, the use of the Internet as an interactive link between the people, politicians, and government officials is fast developing as a major vehicle by which information is conveyed and public opinion expressed.

The mass media have had a major impact on politics and government. With coverage slanted toward material that has *newsworthiness,* and material placed within the context of a dominant story line, they frequently utilize the game format to describe campaigning and government. Issues are portrayed as arguments between two sides, congressional votes as victories or defeats for the president or the Congress, the Democrats or the Republicans. The news media also tend to emphasize issues and events that create criticism of candidates for office and officials in office, justifying this emphasis in terms of their watchdog role.

National coverage of the campaign focuses on the major party candidates, particularly those for the presidency; coverage of the government usually focuses on the president and the administration's policy agenda. Although Congress usually gets less coverage, the 1994 election of the first Republican Congress in forty years made the new Congress more newsworthy than its predecessor. As a consequence, it received more coverage but not necessarily more favorable coverage. In general, the national press are often harsh critics. Local news media, however, report more favorably on their own representatives, especially when they are back in their home districts. In contrast to the critical scrutiny of Congress and the president, the judiciary receives little media coverage except during controversial hearings or major trials.

The news media affect politics and government through the issues they choose to cover and the information they choose to disclose. Those choices affect the issues of the campaign, the public's perception of the candidates, and their evaluation of their suitability for office. They also affect the government's agenda and priorities, shorten time frames for policy decisions, and limit the options of government officials. They shape public and government evaluations, analysis, and recommendations. The news media's increasingly critical evaluations of politics and government have contributed to lower public esteem for the political system and how it works.

KEY TERMS

newsworthiness
sound bite
negative advertising

RESOURCES

READINGS

Abramson, Jeffrey B., F. Christopher Arterton, and Gary R. Orren. *The Electronic Commonwealth: The Impact of New Media Technologies on Democratic Politics*. New York: Basic Books, 1990. An insightful analysis of how contemporary changes in the media have affected and may continue to affect democratic politics.

Adatto, Kiku. *Picture Perfect: The Art and Artifice of Public Image Making*. New York: Basic Books, 1994. A well-researched book discussing how and why news media coverage of presidential elections has become increasingly superficial.

Ansolabehere, Stephen, and Shanto Iyengar. *Going Negative: How Political Advertisements Shrink and Polarize the Electorate*. New York: Free Press, 1995. Based on a research project in which the authors conducted experiments to measure the influence of negative advertising on voting behavior, this book shows how such ads depress turnout and lower trust in government.

Fallows, James M. *Breaking the News: How the Media Undermine American Democracy*. New York: Pantheon, 1996. A very critical study of the news media and their impact on politics and government.

Graber, Doris A. *Mass Media and American Politics*. 5th ed. Washington, D.C.: Congressional Quarterly, 1996. A comprehensive discussion of media and government, from ownership patterns to press freedom to characteristics of coverage and its effects.

Patterson, Thomas E. *Out of Order*. New York: Knopf, 1993. A creative, hard-hitting analysis of the news media's coverage of presidential elections, focusing on 1992. The author suggests reforms for the presidential selection process.

Spitzer, Robert J., ed. *Media and Public Policy*. Westport, Conn.: Praeger, 1993. Based on papers delivered at recent conferences, the book presents contributions from fifteen scholars that address the link between the news media and public policy.

West, Darrel M. *Air Wars: Television Advertising in Election Campaigns, 1952–1996*. 2nd ed. Washington, D.C.: Congressional Quarterly, 1997. A study by a political scientist about the influence of television and radio commercials on American voters.

ORGANIZATIONS

Accuracy in Media, 4455 Connecticut Ave., N.W., Washington, DC 20008; phone (202) 364-4401, fax (202) 364-4098; Internet http://www.aim.org An organization with a conservative orientation that researches what it sees as examples of liberal bias in the media.

Center for Media and Public Affairs, 2100 L Street, N.W., Suite 303, Washington, DC 20037; phone (202) 223-2942, fax (202) 872-4014; Internet http://www.cmpa.com./ An organization that conducts scientific studies of how television news treats contemporary social and political issues.

Corporation for Public Broadcasting, 901 E Street, N.W., Washington, DC 20004; phone (202) 879-9600, fax (202) 783-1019; Internet http://www.cpb.org/ A government corporation that funds public broadcasting.

Federal Communications Commission, 1919 M Street, N.W., Washington, DC 20554; phone (202) 418-0126, fax (202) 418-2840; Internet http://www.fcc.gov/ The government agency that regulates the use of the airwaves in the United States.

Freedom Forum, 1101 Wilson Blvd., Arlington, VA 22209; phone (703) 528-0800, fax (703) 284–2836; Internet http://www.freedomforum.org/ A non-partisan foundation that supports media studies, First Amendment debates, and issues pertaining to public affairs and the media.

The Pew Research Center for the People & the Press, 1875 Eye Street, N.W., Suite 1110, Washington, DC 20006; phone (202) 293-3126, fax (202) 293-2569; Internet http://www.people-press.org/ Does national surveys on public opinion, especially about the news media and current issues.

10

Congress

PREVIEW

- The institution of Congress: members, work environment, staff, and support services
- The organization of Congress: congressional parties and the committee system
- The functions of Congress: legislation, representation, and administrative oversight
- Congressional reform and its impact

The faxes came spinning out of National Rifle Association headquarters as soon as the vote was over.

On March 22, the U.S. House of Representatives voted to *repeal* the 1994 Clinton gun and magazine ban! On a bi-partisan 239 to 173 vote, lawmakers put the interests of law-abiding gun owners ahead of the political posturing of Bill Clinton and his anti-gun allies in the House.

It looked like a great victory. And in a sense it was, at least in the ways of contemporary Washington politics. Sometimes merely looking victorious is good enough.

But no public policy was changed when the House voted in 1996 to repeal the ban Congress had placed in 1994 on the sale of assault weapons. Nor did anyone in Washington expect a change. Bob Dole, the Senate majority leader and soon to be his party's nominee for president, had no intention even of bringing the repeal to a vote in the Senate, where he knew it could not survive a filibuster. And President Clinton had promised to veto the repeal if it ever came to his desk. The House vote was about politics, not policy; about an election just past and an election just ahead, about the role that interest groups have come to play in congressional behavior, and about a new political age in which symbolism is often as important as substance.

In 1994, Republicans had regained control of the House of Representatives for the first time in forty years. Many Republican candidates had received significant financial support from the National Rifle Association (NRA). Of the thirty-four Democratic incumbents defeated that year, twenty-nine had voted for the ban.

To ensure the protection of its new supporters, the NRA had already begun to aid the reelection campaigns of many of the Republicans first elected in 1994. Of the $229,993 the NRA's Political Victory Fund contributed to freshmen during 1995, almost 96 percent had gone to Republicans.

But such support rarely comes without strings, or at least strong expectations. Republican leaders had promised the NRA that there would be a vote to repeal the assault weapons ban. Even when it seemed impossible to win such a vote, the leadership felt compelled to fulfill its promise.

Democratic representative Charles Schumer of New York, the House sponsor of the ban, described the event in these terms: "Newt Gingrich bent his knee and is kissing the ring of the NRA."

When the time came, sixty-six of the seventy-four Republican freshmen voted to repeal the ban on assault weapons. They hadn't changed the law, but they had begun the position-taking—and the fund-raising—for reelection in 1996.[1]

As the attention to the assault weapons ban clearly demonstrates, politics is the most persistent and most important element in the legislative process. Members of Congress struggle constantly to build political coalitions for or against particular bills. They fight to change the institution's procedures and organization to gain leverage over legislative decisions. They do constant battle with other political institutions, especially the president and the bureaucracy, to assert their institutional prerogatives and to influence the shape of public policy. And as in the case of the assault weapons ban, they sometimes must go through major legislative maneuvers largely for political reasons.

This chapter examines the central role of Congress in the American government. What sort of institution is Congress? Who are its members? What are its organization and principal functions? What is the role of political parties and legislative committees in organizing and accomplishing its work? Each of these topics reveals something about how politics determines what Congress does.

THE INSTITUTION OF CONGRESS

The United States Congress is a **bicameral legislature**—that is, it comprises two legislative bodies. The larger is the House of Representatives, which has 435 voting members plus 5 other delegates who represent the District of Columbia and the United States territories and possessions. Each member of the House represents a congressional district with a population of about 600,000. The districts are distributed among the states according to population, with each state having at least one and California having the largest number (fifty-two). All House members serve terms of two years.

The smaller legislative chamber is the Senate. It has one hundred members, two from each state. Senators serve six-year terms, but the terms are staggered so that every two years approximately one-third of the seats in the Senate are up for election.

Elections to Congress occur in November in even-numbered years. The new Congress convenes in the following January. Each Congress lasts two years and is numbered; thus the First Congress convened in 1789, and the 105th convened in 1997. The first year of a Congress is called the first session, and the second year is called the second session. The first session of the 104th Congress met in 1995, and the second session in 1996.

The Members of Congress and Their Work Environment

The Constitution establishes minimum requirements for service in Congress. To serve in the House, one must have reached the age of 25, have been a United States citizen for seven years, and be a resident of the state (but not

A special election in Chicago in 1995 sent Jesse Jackson Jr. (center) to Congress. Here after reenacting his taking of the oath of office, he shares a joke with his wife, Sandi; his father (right); and House Speaker Newt Gingrich (left). Despite gains in recent years, most racial and ethnic minorities are still underrepresented in Congress relative to their proportion in the population.

necessarily the district) from which one is elected. Senators must also be residents of the states from which they are elected, and they must be at least 30 years old and have been United States citizens for nine years at the time they begin their service.[2]

In recent decades, service in Congress has become difficult and demanding. Hundreds of thousands of people view the member as their personal representative in the federal government. When they have problems such as a lost Social Security check or when they need help in getting a small-business loan or a passport, they expect their representative to assist them.

Members are also legislators. Each year they must vote on hundreds of issues, many of which are too complex to be grasped in the short time available before the vote. Each member also serves on several congressional committees and subcommittees, where members are expected to involve themselves deeply in the development of new legislation.

In addition, most members of Congress are candidates for reelection. The election campaign requires frequent meetings with the leaders of various interest groups in the home state or district, regular travel to meet with constituents, and contact with political action committees and other funding sources to ensure the availability of campaign funds.

Staff and Support Services

To help them deal with their workloads, senators and representatives are surrounded by thousands of congressional employees whose principal responsibility is to provide various kinds of support. One form of support is provided by personal staffs. Each member has the authority to hire staff employees to work for him or her alone. In recent years, House members have typically had about twenty people on their personal staffs. Senators have larger staffs; those from the largest states employ as many as sixty people. The personal staff is divided between the member's Washington office and the offices that most members maintain in their home districts or states.

Another important group of congressional employees are committee staff members. Congress has hundreds of committees and subcommittees, and each has its own staff, which assists committee members in setting an agenda, scheduling hearings, developing legislation, and overseeing the work of the executive agencies that fall within its area of interest.

A third important group of congressional employees includes those who work for the three specialized support agencies in the legislative branch:

1. The Congressional Research Service is part of the Library of Congress; its professional staff conducts studies on a wide range of topics at the request of members and subcommittees.
2. The Congressional Budget Office, established in 1974, provides Congress with its own source of economic information and analysis.
3. The General Accounting Office determines whether government programs have been cost-effective (it is described in detail later in this chapter).

The number of people employed in congressional staff and support functions has risen sharply over the last few decades. This rapid expansion has resulted partly from a series of important changes in Congress itself and in the federal government as a whole. The federal budget increased tenfold from the mid 1970s to the mid 1990s and hundreds of new government programs have been initiated. Moreover, public dissatisfaction with the presidencies of Lyndon Johnson and Richard Nixon created a demand for greater congressional effectiveness and more vigilant oversight of executive actions. All these changes provided incentives for increases in congressional capabilities and led directly to staff expansion.

Another, equally important reason that congressional staffs have continued to grow has been the widespread perception among members of Congress that staff aides help members do things that contribute directly to reelection. The more legislation members can be involved in, the more publicity their offices can generate; and the more efficiently and successfully they can respond to constituents' requests for help, the more likely they are to succeed at election time. To the intensely political people who serve in Congress, the prospect of reelection has been a powerful motive for the steady enlargement of congressional staff and support agencies—yet another way in which politics helps to determine the shape of American government.

THE ORGANIZATION OF CONGRESS

The internal structure of Congress has changed and grown over time, as each generation of legislators has shaped Congress to fit its needs. Early in the nation's history, parties emerged to organize the business of the initial Congresses, and party caucuses hammered out important policy decisions. For a few decades after the Civil War, committees began to play a more dominant role in lawmaking. By the last decade of the nineteenth century, however, party leaders in Congress, particularly the Speaker of the House and the majority leader of the Senate, had become the principal powers.

But the party leaders of the time, notably Speaker Joseph G. Cannon (R, Ill.) and Speaker Thomas Brackett Reed (R, Maine), became so dominant that the rank and file staged a revolt at the end of the first decade of the twentieth century. The authority of the party leaders was reduced, and for most of the next seventy years committees were again the power centers in Congress. A **seniority system** ensured that the member of the majority party with the longest consecutive service on each committee would automatically chair the committee for as long as he or she remained in Congress.

Throughout these decades of change, two principles have remained at the core of congressional organization: (1) control of the legislative agenda and the legislative machinery ought to be in the hands of the majority party; and (2) for purposes of efficiency and enhanced expertise, most day-to-day details of legislative work ought to be handled by small groups of legislators meeting as committees. Indeed, since the early decades of the nineteenth century the party system and the committee system have been the dominant elements in every scheme of congressional organization.

Congressional Parties

The single most distinctive feature of political parties in Congress is their limited control over their own members, particularly over the way their members vote. In legislatures in other countries, **party discipline** is normal. Party leaders in the legislatures of Britain and France, for example, can count on the members of their party to support them on virtually every vote, and if they do not, the party can impose penalties on them. Not so in the United States. When the two parties take opposing positions on an issue, typically some—and sometimes many—members of each party will defect to the opposition.

The absence of party discipline reflects, more than anything else, the limited authority of party leaders in Congress. In both the House and the Senate, leaders have very little direct control over the members of their own party and therefore have few ways either to force them to vote for the party's position on a bill or to punish them if they do not. They cannot prevent party members from running for reelection; they have little influence on the outcome of elections; and, without the support of the majority of their party, they cannot even affect committee assignments.

Parties in the House Because the House is larger than the Senate, parties play a more important role there in organizing the legislative agenda and building legislative majorities. The majority party has the principal responsibility for both tasks. It controls the selection of the Speaker of the House, and its members compose a majority on each committee and subcommittee.

The **Speaker** is almost always the most important figure in the House. Political leadership of the majority party is the Speaker's dominant concern. Working with other party leaders—especially those designated as **whips**—the Speaker helps determine the issues that will be given top priority in the House.[3]

Although the Speaker's leadership is based more on persuasion and political skill than on any real authority over individual House members, an astute Speaker has a substantial impact on the kinds of policy issues that come before the House and the way they are decided. Strong Speakers make full use of the tools of authority available to them: parliamentary direction of floor debate and assignment of bills to committee, control over the flow of information within the House, scheduling of legislative action, appointment powers, and

Senate Minority Leader Thomas Daschle (at podium) and a group of Democratic colleagues at a news conference. After the Republican takeover of Congress in 1995, Daschle earned a reputation as a skilled leader who took maximum advantage of his party's limited power, blocking initiatives by the Republicans and maneuvering them into public-relations blunders.

personal prestige and influence with other political actors in Washington. For example, a member who consistently supports the Speaker can expect assignment to preferred committees, assistance in securing campaign funds from political action committees, and help from the leadership in gaining passage of legislation introduced by that member.[4]

The Speaker does not act alone in attempting to guide the operations of the House. The Speaker is supported by, and works through, a variety of committees and networks that enhance internal communication in the party, aid in the formation of party positions on policy issues, and help improve the chances of the party's candidates for seats in the House.

The size and complexity of the majority party leadership in the House reflect the difficulty of maintaining unity and building legislative majorities among a group with several hundred members whose leaders lack the authority to demand support. A less complex leadership structure would be sufficient if the majority party leaders had more authority.

The minority party in the House has its own elected leaders and a structure that mirrors, on a reduced scale, the organization of the majority party. There are, of course, fewer members to organize in the minority party, and the minority party has less responsibility for managing the House agenda. The leader of the minority party is the minority leader, who is assisted by the minority whip. Both are elected by the minority party caucus, made up of all the minority party members.

Parties in the Senate Because the Senate is smaller and individual senators are able to deal with each other directly on most matters, parties play a much less important role there than in the House. The majority party elects a majority

Senate Majority Leader Trent Lott meets with reporters. The majority leader is a important spokesperson for his party on policy matters, especially when the president is a member of the other party. However, both majority and minority leaders in the Senate have less control than their counterparts in the House over the votes and activities of other members of their party.

leader and a majority whip; the minority party elects a minority leader and a minority whip. Each party also has a structure of leadership committees, but these have less influence on party operations than do their counterparts in the House.[5]

The primary job of the party leaders, especially the majority leader, is to organize the business of the Senate: to nudge legislation along through the legislative process, to schedule debate, and to oversee most aspects of day-to-day administration. Party leaders also help the proponents of legislation round up the votes necessary to make a majority, meet regularly with the president to discuss policy and legislative strategy, and serve as public spokespersons for their party on important policy matters.

Despite the extent of their duties and their public visibility, party leaders in the Senate are severely constrained in their ability to influence the outcome of policy debates. Their control over the votes and activities of other members of their party is even weaker than that of their House counterparts. In the Senate, therefore, leadership is even more dependent on persuasion and political sensitivities than it is in the House.

The Committee System

Most of the work of Congress is done in committees, which serve a number of important functions. Committees prepare legislation for consideration on the floors of the House and Senate, but they also delete from the legislative agenda matters that are not important, urgent, or politically viable. In fact, only a small percentage of the bills that are referred to a committee survive its scrutiny.

Congressional Leadership

The character of congressional party leadership has evolved considerably during this century. In the first decade, Joseph G. Cannon (R, Illinois) in the House and Nelson W. Aldrich (R, Rhode Island) in the Senate dominated the legislative process. In the decades that followed, the seniority system became more rigid and the chairs of the standing committees came to share legislative power with the party leaders. Since 1960 legislative power has decentralized even further, placing new demands and constraints on party leaders. In the statements that follow, some recent party leaders describe their work.

Thomas P. O'Neill Jr. (D, Massachusetts), House Speaker (1977–1986)

[At a meeting with a handful of legislative leaders in 1942, President Franklin Roosevelt introduced Albert Einstein.] Einstein explained the theory of the atomic bomb, and told the group that Hitler also had scientists working on it, and that the first nation to get the bomb would win the war and control the world.

Einstein estimated that the project would cost two billion dollars. Not surprisingly, the president was concerned about how to allocate that kind of money without alerting the public or the press.

"Leave it to me," said Sam Rayburn [then Speaker of the House]. The next day Sam called all the committee and subcommittee chairmen and told them to put an extra hundred million dollars into their budgets.

"Yes, Mr. Rayburn," they all said. There were no questions asked and no meetings held. The Manhattan Project was one of the best-kept secrets in history. The money was allocated and nobody on the committees ever questioned why a chairman was setting aside a certain amount for reasons he didn't even know about.

But that's the way things worked in Sam's time. Today, of course, you'd have ninety-two guys wanting to know what was happening and where the money was going.[1]

Committees also hold public hearings at which experts, leaders of interest groups, and other supporters and opponents of bills are permitted to express their views. In addition, they initiate studies, conduct investigations, and publish information.

Another important function of committees is **administrative oversight**. Committees monitor the work of the executive agencies in their areas of jurisdiction, review budget requests, and pass judgment on the qualifications of presidential appointees. In fact, they are the principal contact points between the executive and legislative branches. (The oversight function is discussed in detail on pages 267–268.)

Most important, however, committees are the primary source of creativity and policy leadership in Congress. The most knowledgeable military specialists in Congress are members of the House and Senate Armed Services Committees. Those who are most familiar with farm issues are on the Agriculture Committees. Because the senior members of most congressional committees have been dealing for several decades with the policy issues that fall within their committee's area

JOHN MCCORMACK (D, MASSACHUSETTS), HOUSE SPEAKER (1962–1970)

I have never asked a member to vote against his conscience. If he mentions his conscience—that's all. I don't press him any further.[2]

CHARLES HALLECK (R, ILLINOIS), HOUSE MINORITY LEADER (1959–1964)

You get pressure from guys who have come along with you on a tough vote about the fellows who went off the reservation. Some of them want to read these guys out of the party. But, hell, there may be a vote next week when you need a fellow who has strayed real bad and you can catch him on the rebound.[3]

CARL ALBERT (D, OKLAHOMA), HOUSE SPEAKER (1971–1976)

If you can't win them by persuasion, you can't win them at all. If you whip them into line every time, by the time you reach the third vote you're through.[4]

MIKE MANSFILD (D, MONTANA), SENATE MAJORITY LEADER (1961–1976)

It's pretty hard to hold the leadership accountable, because we can't dictate to our associates how they should vote. I think that these people who are representing the various states have been sent here to exercise their own judgment, that they should not be pressured because that's a counterproductive tactic.

I watched Lyndon Johnson while I was assistant majority leader for four years, and our styles are diametrically different. He was a man who liked to keep power in his own hands. He would like to collect IOU's. . . . I don't collect any IOU's. I don't do any special favors. I try to treat all Senators alike, and I think that's the best way to operate in the long run, because that way you maintain their respect and confidence. And that's what the ball game is all about.[5]

[1]Thomas P. O'Neill Jr. and William Novak, *Man of the House* (New York: Random House, 1987), 129.

[2]Quoted in Donald G. Tacheron and Morris K. Udall, *The Job of the Congressman,* 2nd ed. (Indianapolis: Bobbs-Merrill, 1970), 18.

[3]Ibid., 19.

[4]Ibid.

[5]Quoted in Daniel Rapoport, "It's Not a Happy Time for House, Senate Leadership," *National Journal*, February 7, 1976, 173.

of jurisdiction, they are as well informed about those issues as anyone in the federal government. And they have the support of specialists on the committee staffs. It is not surprising, therefore, that committees initiate much of the legislation that makes its way to the floors of the House and Senate.[6]

Of the several kinds of committees that Congress uses, the most common and most important are **standing committees**, permanent committees that have full authority to recommend legislation. A few of them, like the Rules Committee in the House, are responsible for organizing and regulating the operations of Congress. Most standing committees have jurisdictions defined along substantive policy lines: energy, agriculture, foreign relations, and so on.

Most of the standing committees are divided into subcommittees, which hold most of the hearings and conduct the initial review of most legislation. Full committees rarely convene to consider a piece of legislation until after it has been carefully reviewed by the appropriate subcommittee. As the legislative workload has grown in size and complexity, experience and specialized knowledge have made the subcommittees increasingly important.

The committee system also includes a variety of **select**, or **special, committees**. These are temporary committees created to deal with specific issues; they disband when they have completed their work. Many select committees have clearly limited functions and authority. Most, for instance, are not authorized to recommend legislation. Among the best-known recent temporary committees were the Senate Select Committee on Presidential Campaign Activities, which uncovered much of the Watergate scandal in the 1970s, and the House Select Committee to Investigate Covert Arms Transactions with Iran, which joined its Senate counterpart in exploring the Iran-contra affair in the 1980s. The standing and select committees of the 105th Congress are listed in Table 10-1.

Joint committees comprise members of both houses of Congress. Some of them, called standing joint committees, are permanent groups with no authority

TABLE 10-1 ***Committees of the 105th Congress, 1997***

House Committees	Number of Subcommittees	Senate Committees	Number of Subcommittees
Agriculture	5	Agriculture, Nutrition, and Forestry	4
Appropriations	13	Appropriations	13
Banking and Financial Services	5	Armed Services	6
Budget	0	Banking, Housing, and Urban Affairs	5
Commerce	5	Budget	0
Education and the Workforce	5	Commerce, Science, and Transportation	7
Government Reform and Oversight	7	Energy and Natural Resources	4
House Oversight	0	Environment and Public Works	4
International Relations	5	Finance	5
Judiciary	5	Foreign Relations	7
National Security	5	Government Affairs	3
Resources	5	Indian Affairs	0
Rules	2	Judiciary	6
Science	4	Labor and Human Resources	4
Select Intelligence	2	Rules and Administration	0
Small Business	4	Select Ethics	0
Standards of Official Conduct	0	Select Intelligence	0
Transportation and Infrastructure	6	Small Business	0
Veteran's Affairs	3	Special Aging	0
Ways and Means	5	Veteran's Affairs	0
Total 20	**86**	**Total 20**	**68**

SOURCE: Michael Barone and Grant Ugifusa, *The Almanac of American Politics 1998* (Washington D.C.: National Journal, 1997), 1572–1595.

to initiate legislation; the most important of these is the Joint Committee on the Economy, which receives and reviews the president's annual Economic Report and conducts studies of the national economy. In addition to the standing joint committees, hundreds of temporary joint committees known as **joint conference committees** are formed during each Congress. Their principal function is to resolve the differences that occur when the House and Senate pass varying forms of the same bill. At the end of the 101st Congress, for example, House and Senate conferees wrangled over different versions of the Clean Air Act. The House bill had included tougher controls than the Senate bill on emissions from steel plants, and a compromise in the conference committee retained the House standards but gave steelmakers more time to comply with them. Conference committee deliberations frequently produce compromise outcomes of this sort.

THE FUNCTIONS OF CONGRESS

Because the framers of the Constitution viewed the legislative branch as the safest and most reliable arbiter of the disagreements that are likely to arise among a democratic people, they gave Congress a number of important functions. Those functions have expanded in number and complexity as the scope of the federal government's responsibilities has grown. Historically, the two most significant congressional functions were legislation and representation. In this century, the expansion of presidential power and the growth of a large federal bureaucracy have added a third major function—administrative oversight—to the legislature's responsibilities.

Legislation

People who are not very familiar with Congress tend to regard it as a kind of factory where laws are made. In reality, Congress makes very few public laws, a couple of hundred at most, even in its most productive years; and many of those laws are of very minor consequences.

Legislation, or lawmaking, is accomplished through deliberation and partisan adjustment, a process that involves information gathering, prolonged discussion, complex and often tedious negotiation, bargaining, and compromise. Most of the time the result of this process is nothing. In fact, 90 percent of the bills introduced in a typical Congress never become law, and enactment of the few that survive may require years, even decades. For example, Congress debated tax reform for more than five years before it passed the Tax Reform Act of 1986. Federally funded health care for the elderly, a proposal first introduced during the Truman administration, was not enacted (as Medicare) until 1965. The line-item veto bill passed in 1996 had been debated repeatedly over the entire history of the United States.

In recent decades, the impediments to legislation have been greatly increased by the proliferation and growing sophistication of political interest groups (see Chapter 7), which affect lawmaking at every stage. They propose and help draft legislation. They testify at hearings. They lobby members in committee and during floor debate. They try to pressure the president to veto bills that they oppose.

The pervasiveness of political maneuvering and bargaining among groups means that most legislative decisions are compromises, and compromise usually weakens the impact of legislation. Yet the openness of congressional lawmaking to politics can also be viewed as one of its strengths. Politics flourishes in Congress, that is, because the setting provides a forum for a broad spectrum of voices and opinions, and because the legislative process provides many opportunities for individuals and groups to express the content and the intensity of their concerns. Everyone has opportunities to speak out about legislation and to try to influence its ultimate shape. Few laws are totally abhorrent to any group, because all groups are able to achieve at least some protection for the interests they value most.

The lawmaking process It is no simple matter to enact a law in the United States (see Figure 10-1). The process begins when an individual member of the House or Senate introduces a bill. A **bill** is a proposal, drafted in the form of a law, that a member would like his or her colleagues to consider. A bill may be introduced in either house of Congress by any member of that house. When a bill is introduced, it is assigned a number by the clerk and referred to a committee by the presiding officer. Many bills go no farther; they die because the committee lacks the time or interest to deal with them.

For bills that do not die, the next step is examination by the committee.[7] Most congressional committees have subcommittees that conduct the initial examination of legislative proposals. Subcommittees hold hearings at which they gather written and oral testimony from witnesses who have knowledge of, or interest in, the bill. At the conclusion of the hearings, the subcommittee votes on the bill. Usually the voting occurs after a **mark-up session** in which all the members of the subcommittee participate in revising the bill to put it into a form that is acceptable to a majority of them. If the subcommittee supports the bill, it is returned to the full committee, where another mark-up may take place, followed by a vote of the full committee.

Mark-up sessions are a key battleground for all the political forces that seek to shape the text—and thus the impact—of a bill. In 1986, for example, Congress passed the most significant reform of federal tax policies in decades. The mark-up in the Senate Finance Committee occurred in a room full of tax lobbyists who communicated with senators and staff throughout the process, often haggling over the tiniest details. In a tax bill, of course, a tiny detail can be worth hundreds of thousands of dollars to individual taxpayers.

If a majority of the full committee supports the bill, it is reported to the full House or Senate. The House's procedure at this point differs from the Senate's. Bills reported out of committee in the Senate go directly to the floor, where debate is scheduled by the party leaders. The House, because of its larger size, has a Rules Committee that determines when a bill will be debated, how long the debate will last, and what kinds of amendments (if any) may be introduced during debate.

Once a bill has been reported to the floor, it is placed on a legislative calendar. In the House, debate is usually limited to a few hours or less, depending on how important or controversial a bill is. Senate floor rules are less rigid, and debate there may last for several hours or days or, in some cases, weeks. In each house, debate is usually controlled by members who are designated as floor managers for the bill. The floor manager for the proponents (typically a committee or subcommittee chair who has worked on the bill) and the floor

FIGURE 10-1 How a Bill Becomes a Law

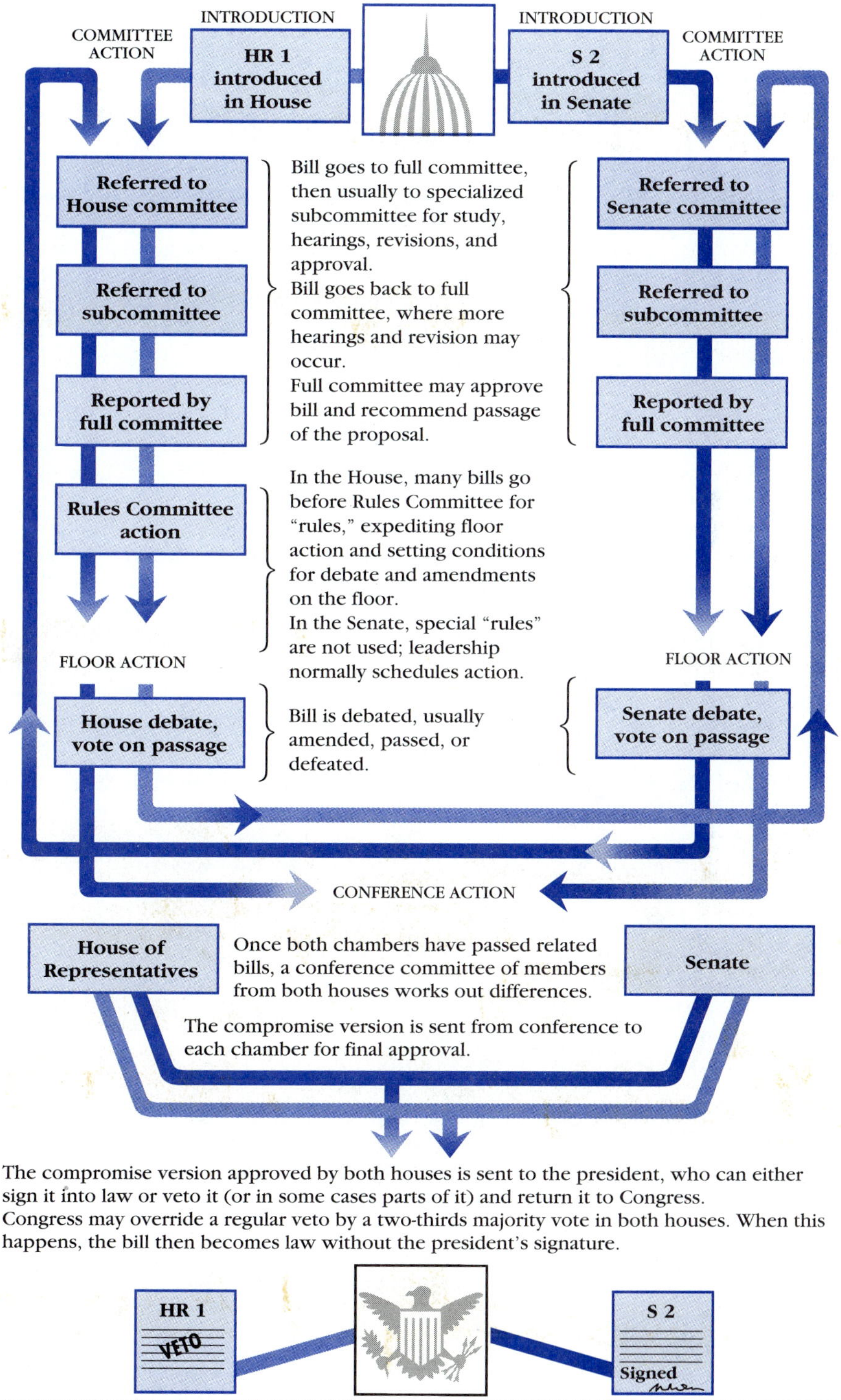

INTRODUCTION

HR 1 introduced in House

INTRODUCTION

S 2 introduced in Senate

COMMITTEE ACTION

Referred to House committee

Referred to subcommittee

Reported by full committee

Rules Committee action

COMMITTEE ACTION

Referred to Senate committee

Referred to subcommittee

Reported by full committee

Bill goes to full committee, then usually to specialized subcommittee for study, hearings, revisions, and approval. Bill goes back to full committee, where more hearings and revision may occur. Full committee may approve bill and recommend passage of the proposal.

In the House, many bills go before Rules Committee for "rules," expediting floor action and setting conditions for debate and amendments on the floor. In the Senate, special "rules" are not used; leadership normally schedules action.

FLOOR ACTION

House debate, vote on passage

FLOOR ACTION

Senate debate, vote on passage

Bill is debated, usually amended, passed, or defeated.

CONFERENCE ACTION

House of Representatives

Senate

Once both chambers have passed related bills, a conference committee of members from both houses works out differences.

The compromise version is sent from conference to each chamber for final approval.

The compromise version approved by both houses is sent to the president, who can either sign it into law or veto it (or in some cases parts of it) and return it to Congress. Congress may override a regular veto by a two-thirds majority vote in both houses. When this happens, the bill then becomes law without the president's signature.

SOURCE: *Guide to Congress* (Washington, D.C.: Congressional Quarterly, 1976), 345; updated by the authors. Reprinted by permission of Congressional Quarterly, Inc.

manager for the opposition (usually, but not always, a member of the minority party) organize the debate and allot time to other members who share their views on the bill.[8]

During the debate, individual members may introduce amendments that change the substance of the bill in some way. The House has much more rigid rules about amendments than the Senate. Unless the rule on the bill specifically permits otherwise, amendments offered in the House must be directly related, or germane, to the substance of the bill. In the Senate, there are few restrictions on amendments, and senators are more prone to attaching nongermane amendments to any bill that happens to be under consideration. A common political tactic in the Senate, for example, is to attach a controversial unrelated provision to an essential or popular piece of legislation. Such additions are called **riders** because they "ride" through the legislative process on the backs of other bills when they might not have survived on their own.

Amendments are voted on as they are introduced. Those that receive the support of a majority are integrated into the bill. When debate is completed and all amendments have been considered, a final vote on the bill occurs. Today, this is almost always a recorded vote—that is, the position of each member is noted and recorded in the *Congressional Record*, the official journal of House and Senate proceedings.

Even if a majority of the members present vote in favor of a bill, to become law it also requires approval by the other house, which must go through the same process. It often happens that when a bill passes in the second house, it differs from the version passed in the first house. To resolve the differences, a joint conference committee is created. Its sole purpose is to construct from the differing versions a single bill that can win the approval of both houses. When the conference committee has completed its work (usually by forging a compromise), it reports to each house, and another floor vote is taken in each house. If both houses agree to the conference committee's version of the bill, it is sent to the president for signature.

The president has several options. One is to sign the bill, at which point it becomes law. Another is to allow the bill to become law without a signature; this will occur ten working days after the bill is received, if Congress is still in session. The president may also veto the bill by declining to sign it and returning it within ten days to the house where it originated, accompanied by a message stating the reasons for the veto. Congress then has an opportunity to override the president's veto. An override, however, requires a two-thirds majority in each house and, as Table 10-2 indicates, rarely happens.

If the annual session of Congress ends within ten days of the passage of a bill, the president may exercise another option, the **pocket veto**, simply by declining to sign the bill. Because Congress is not in session, the president does not return the bill, nor is there any possibility of a congressional override. Because many bills are passed in the legislative rush that comes at the end of a congressional session, opportunities for pocket vetoes occur with some frequency.

In 1996, presidents were given still another option in some cases, when President Clinton signed a bill creating a **line-item veto**. This permits the president to veto portions—or line items—of certain kinds of legislation while allowing the remainder of the bill to become law. Traditionally, presidents could kill objectionable portions of a bill only by vetoing the entire bill.

The line-item veto went into effect on January 1, 1997. Under its provisions, Congress may replace a line item that a president has vetoed only by passing

TABLE 10-2 Presidential Vetoes of Congressional Bills, 1933–1996

PERIOD	PRESIDENT	REGULAR VETOES	POCKET VETOES	TOTAL VETOES	OVER-RIDDEN
1933-1945	Roosevelt	372	263	635	9
1945-1953	Truman	180	70	250	12
1953-1961	Eisenhower	73	108	181	2
1961-1963	Kennedy	12	9	21	0
1963-1969	Johnson	16	14	30	0
1969-1974	Nixon	24	18	42	6
1974-1977	Ford	53	19	72	12
1977-1981	Carter	13	18	31	2
1981-1989	Reagan	39	39	78	9
1989-1993	Bush	31*	15	46	1
1993-1996	Clinton	17	0	17	1

*President Bush contended that four of his regular vetoes were pocket vetoes. Some members of Congress disagreed, noting that the president can exercise a pocket veto only after Congress has adjourned for the year, not during a recess. The dispute over terminology was not resolved, and all of those vetoes are listed here as regular vetoes.

SOURCE: *Congressional Quarterly Weekly Report,* December 19, 1992, 3925-3926. Post-1992 data compiled from *Congressional Quarterly Weekly Reports.*

another law for that purpose. The president may veto this new law, however, and the veto can be overridden by Congress only with the traditional two-thirds majority in each house.

Rules, procedures, and precedents The lawmaking process is governed by a highly developed set of rules and precedents that control such matters as parliamentary procedures in debate, the assignment of bills to committees, the operations of committees, and legislative recordkeeping. Because the rules shape political conflicts in Congress and play a large role in determining the strategies of political adversaries, some of their general effects on the operations and decisions of Congress are worth noting.[9]

First, the rules enforce a decentralization of legislative power in both houses of Congress. They require that legislation be considered and acted on at a number of points (committee, subcommittee, floor, and joint conference) before final passage. In effect, each of these stages is a veto point, for defeat at any one of them usually kills a bill. Hence, members who control the veto points in the legislative process—an especially strong and obdurate committee chair, for instance—have significant power in determining what will or will not become law.

Second, the rules favor the status quo by, in effect, biasing the legislative process against change. The proponents of a new piece of legislation must succeed at every stage in the process: their bill must win majorities in subcommittee, in full committee, on the floor, and so on. Opponents must win at only one of these stages: they can defeat the bill in subcommittee, in full committee, or wherever they can construct a majority in opposition to the bill. The cards thus are stacked against new legislation.

Third, the rules work to slow the pace of legislative consideration. Congress has occasionally shown an ability to legislate quickly, particularly when confronted with a national security crisis. But quick action is the exception, not the norm. Most of the time the legislative process grinds away slowly because so many participants at so many stages have to study and deliberate.

Fourth, the rules provide several mechanisms by which determined minorities can thwart the will of congressional majorities. In the Senate, for instance, much is accomplished through a procedure called **unanimous consent**. Action can be taken without debate when all members consent to that procedure, but only one dissenting senator can prevent action under unanimous consent and thus slow the progress of the Senate. Senator Jesse Helms (R, N.C.) has sometimes used this tactic to force the Senate to pay attention to issues that are important to him personally. His objections to unanimous consent resolutions have earned him the title "Senator No."

Also in the Senate, which has a long tradition of unlimited debate, a small group of senators may delay or even prevent a vote on a bill by carrying out a **filibuster**. They do this by gaining recognition to speak in debate and then not relinquishing the floor. Some senators have held the floor for more than twenty-four consecutive hours, and a group of senators working together can hold the floor indefinitely. It now takes a vote by three-fifths of the entire Senate (sixty senators) to invoke **cloture** and thereby end a filibuster. This means that if 41 percent or more of the senators are intensely opposed to a bill that has majority support, final action on the bill can be slowed or prevented. Even after cloture, loopholes in the Senate rules permit a single senator to prolong debate.

Finally, a bill can die when a majority of the members of a committee or a subcommittee opposes it, even though a majority of the members of the house in which it was introduced favors it. In these and other ways, the rules permit the will of a determined minority to supersede that of a majority.

The legislative process is decentralized, slow, and tedious, and it crushes most bills. For members of Congress who have legislative goals, it is a demanding consumer of time and effort and an unrelenting source of frustration. But it does ensure that in most cases new laws are carefully considered and solidly supported before they are enacted.

Representation

In the United States, participation in the national government occurs through the process of **representation**. Every member of Congress represents two groups of citizens. In that every member has some responsibility to the national interest, he or she represents the nation as a whole. The member also represents a **constituency**, the state or congressional district that elects her or him to Congress.

The interests of these two groups may be in conflict. Sometimes what is best for the district may not be best for the nation. Higher farm prices benefit individual farmers but not the nation's consumers. Federal subsidies for the construction of a dam in a particular district will have local benefits but will cause an increase in everyone's taxes. Members also confront conflicts between their own views and the views of their constituents. Some policies that a representative believes to be best for the nation may have little support in his or her own district.

Constituent relations How do members of Congress keep in touch with their constituents? How do they know their constituents' opinions? How do they deal

PRACTICING DEMOCRACY

Contacting Your Representatives in Washington

The United States Congress is one of the most accessible legislatures in the world. Debates and votes are open to the public and are reported in full. Anyone can phone, write, or visit the office of a member of Congress.

A good source of background information about members of Congress is *The Almanac of American Politics,* published biennially. To find out exactly what a member has said on the floor of Congress and how he or she has voted on a bill, check the *Congressional Record,* the official journal of congressional proceedings. It is published every day that Congress is in session. To learn a member's position on any issue, start with the *Congressional Quarterly Weekly Report,* a magazine known as *CQ*. At the end of each week's *CQ* is a list of each member's vote on every bill on which there is a recorded vote.

When writing to a member of Congress, address the letter as follows:

Honorable John A. Cruz
United States Senate
Washington, DC 20510

Honorable Sally S. Goodman
United States House of Representatives
Washington, DC 20515

Normally, the member's office will respond by mail within two or three weeks on a policy issue. A response may take longer if you write about a personal problem involving an agency of the government.

To contact a member's local office, look for the address and phone number in the government pages (blue pages) of the local phone book. A call to the local office will often provide the quickest solution to a problem or the most efficient (and least expensive) way to register your views on a policy issue. To phone your representative's Washington office, call the Capitol switchboard: (202) 224-3121.

Most members of Congress also have e-mail addresses. These can be located in many ways, but one of the most efficient is to look them up in the "Congressional E-mail Addresses" page on the World Wide Web portion of the Internet. The Internet address is

http://lcweb.loc.gov/global/legislative/congress.html#legbranch

If you wish to visit your representative's office to get help with a problem or to express your views while you are in Washington, D.C., please call ahead. Members of Congress are always happy to see their constituents. Remember, though, that their schedules are hectic, and that they are rarely available for unscheduled visits.

Republican representative David McIntosh greets citizens in his Indiana district. Public expectations require all members of Congress to stay in close touch with the people they represent.

with disagreements within their constituency? Each member develops his or her own ways of doing these things.

Constituencies comprise people with varying attitudes, levels of information, interests, and partisan preferences. They are quite complex, with overlapping and often conflicting interests. As a consequence, members must constantly interact with the "folks back home" to discern the direction and intensity of their constituents' opinions.

The representative at work Although many people think that representation is a one-way process, that representatives are given "instructions" by their constituents and simply react to those instructions, this is a misperception. Members rarely receive anything resembling instructions from home. They do tend to hear a good deal from the people they represent, but studies of congressional mail suggest that this type of communication has a number of limitations.

First, although members may receive thousands of letters, faxes, and e-mail communications each week, most of their constituents never write or call. A flood of communications about some particular issue is likely to indicate a campaign "stimulated" by one or more interest groups. The communications that members receive on such occasions often look or sound exactly the same, and this somewhat diminishes their impact. Public opinion polls indicate that only about 15 percent of all adults have ever communicated with their representatives in Congress.[10]

Second, many of the communications that members receive have little to do with legislative issues. They are requests for help with specific problems such as expediting a passport, assisting with a grant application, or getting a disabled veteran into a veterans' hospital.

Third, many of the communications that a member receives contradict each other. Some constituents may recommend a vote for a bill, others a vote against it. On clean-air legislation, for instance, environmentalists may want the member to vote for stringent regulations, but factory owners may want weaker regulations. Members hear a lot from constituents—veterans, farmers, schools, hospitals, and others—who want increases in the benefits they receive from the government. But they also hear frequently from people who want budget cuts and lower taxes.

Fourth, members hear nothing or next to nothing from their constituents about many issues, especially issues that have little direct bearing on the district. Members from inner-city districts hear little from their constituents about agricultural subsidies, for example; representatives from New England hear little from the folks at home about coal mine safety.

To overcome deficiencies in the communications received from constituents, many members of Congress work hard to interact with the people they represent. They have developed a number of successful techniques for doing so. A generous **franking privilege** enables them to mail newsletters and questionnaires to every postal box in their states or districts, free of charge, and the congressional recording studios enable them to send video- or audiotapes to television and radio stations back home. Members also receive ample funds for travel between Washington and their districts. Most spend at least part of every month back home, aided by the typical monthly schedule of Congress: three weeks in session and one week for "district work periods." In addition to their Washington offices, all members have one or more offices in their districts with full-time staffs. Members also keep in touch by reading local newspapers, telephoning district leaders, and meeting with visitors from the district when they come to Washington.

But the relationship between members and their constituents is based on more than just the frequency and technology of communication. Most members have grown up in their districts. Their political socialization took place there; they entered politics and achieved their first political successes there. As a result, they tend to share the economic and social values of the people they represent, not simply because it is politically expedient to do so but because those are their personal values as well. In reality, much of the relationship between members and their districts is felt rather than communicated.

Chapter 8 noted the extraordinary success rate of members of Congress who run for reelection. Here is an important part of the reason. In their voting behavior, Americans seem to be expressing considerable satisfaction with the way they are represented by their own member of Congress. Far from being easy or automatic, this satisfaction reflects the substantial effort that contemporary members of Congress apply to their responsibilities as representatives and the abundant array of resources available to them in carrying out those responsibilities.

Congress

Do you need to know the status of an item in this year's federal budget? Perhaps you want to contact your representative in Congress or find out which committees will be holding hearings on a bill that concerns you. Or maybe you need to do research for a term paper on the congressional leadership. For information about Congress, the following Internet locations are good starting points.

THOMAS: CONGRESS'S GATEWAY

Named after Thomas Jefferson, this site, **http://thomas.loc.gov/** was created early in 1995 to be the central repository of information about Congress. Here one can find the full text of the *Congressional Record* and all bills introduced in Congress, information about each member's vote on every bill, and a wide variety of other information. All the databases at this site are searchable by key words, name, or bill number.

GPO ACCESS ON THE WEB

This site at **http://thorplus.lib.purdue.edu:80/gpo/** provides several valuable databases, most of which start with information from the 103rd Congress in 1993. Congressional bills, the *Congressional Record Index* and the full text of the *Congressional Record,* the *History of Bills*, the full text of public laws, the *Congressional Directory,* House and Senate calendars, and a wide range of other legislative documents are available.

CONGRESSIONAL DIRECTORIES

Check out **gopher://marve.loc.gov/11/congress/directory/** for addresses and committee assignments of members of Congress, or try **http://www.house.gov/memberwww.html** for a link to e-mail addresses and homepages of members of the House of Representatives. The main entry page for information on the Senate and individual senators is **http://www.senate.gov,** which includes e-mail addresses for senators but is not as complete or well developed as the House homepages.

CONGRESSIONAL QUARTERLY

The address **http://cq.com** is an entry page for information and resources from the *Congressional Quarterly* service. The site includes lead stories from the *Congressional Quarterly Weekly Report,* analysis of major issues, members' votes on individual issues, and congressional election results.

VOTING, CAMPAIGN FINANCE, ISSUE POSITIONS OF MEMBERS

The address **http://www.vote-smart.org/congress/index.html** will link you to a variety of information about members, voting patterns, sources of campaign funds, and issues before Congress.

CONGRESSIONAL LEADERSHIP

The site at **http://www.vote-smart.org/reference/primer/clead.html** provides special information about and by the congressional leadership.

Administrative Oversight

Administrative oversight is another essential congressional function. Because Congress is ill-equipped to make every important public policy decision, in many areas it delegates responsibility to bureaucratic agencies, charging them with making expert decisions but subjecting those decisions to legislative review. When this process works as intended, it combines bureaucratic expertise and popular control. The policy experts in the executive branch of government make the day-to-day decisions of public policy, and the people's representatives in the legislative branch review them and, when necessary, attempt to alter them.

Techniques Congress performs its oversight function in a great many ways.[11] Most of the standing committees of Congress conduct **oversight hearings** as a regular part of their responsibilities. During an oversight hearing the activities of an executive agency or the management of a specific program are reviewed in depth. The report produced by an oversight hearing may suggest changes in administrative procedures, reauthorization of the agency or program, or legislation to remedy its perceived defects.

In addition to oversight hearings, Congress conducts **special investigations**. Some of these investigations are virtually indistinguishable from oversight hearings. They are conducted by permanent committees and subcommittees with no special appropriations of funds or additions to committee staffs. More commonly, however, investigations differ from routine oversight hearings in the depth of their examinations, the vigor with which they are conducted, and the amount of funds and staff resources committed to them.

Employees of the executive branch also fall under congressional oversight through **personnel controls**. Those who serve at the top levels—cabinet secretaries, agency heads, regulatory commissioners—are presidential appointees whose appointments are subject to Senate confirmation. When the president nominates a candidate to fill one of these positions, the nomination must be reviewed and approved by majority vote in the Senate before it takes effect. The Senate can, and occasionally does, reject candidates proposed by the president, as it did in the case of Henry Foster.

In addition, Congress has control over the salaries and employment conditions of all federal employees, both career civil servants and presidential appointees. It sets pay scales; establishes "personnel ceilings" that limit the number of people who can work in a specified agency or office; creates general hiring qualifications; and approves routine personnel policies regarding annual leave, sick pay, dismissals, retirements, and pensions. This range of control gives Congress some discretion in determining who will work where in the executive branch and under what conditions. Congress sought to enlarge its political control over the activities of the inspector general of the CIA, for example, by enacting legislation making that position a presidential appointment subject to Senate confirmation.

Financial control—the power of the purse—is the most important and effective of Congress's techniques for overseeing the work of the executive branch. Before Congress appropriates funds to an agency or program, it assesses the manner in which previous appropriations have been used, and it examines the stated plans for the use of the funds being requested. This work is usually conducted by the House and Senate Appropriations Committees, which hold annual hearings for virtually every program and agency in the government. At the hearings, executive-branch officials must explain their past activities and defend their budget requests for the coming year.[12]

Another tool of congressional oversight is the General Accounting Office (GAO), the federal government's accounting arm. Located in the legislative branch, the GAO conducts audits of government programs to determine whether they have been well managed and whether their benefits justify their costs. GAO audit reports are submitted to Congress, which sometimes uses them to target inefficiency or malfeasance in the management of federal programs or in the use of federal funds. Much of the information that led to intense congressional review of mismanagement in the Department of Housing and Urban Development (HUD) during the Reagan administration came from GAO audits.

Finally, should other means of oversight prove insufficient, **impeachment** constitutes the legislature's weapon of last resort. It is the power to remove from office the president, the vice president, or any other civil officer of the United States who has been found guilty of (in the words of Article II, Section 4, of the Constitution) "treason, bribery, or other high crimes and misdemeanors."

The impeachment process begins with the introduction of a bill of impeachment in the House of Representatives. This bill is referred to the Judiciary Committee, which may do nothing or may debate the bill and report it to the full House. In the latter case, the House debates the charges and then votes. If a majority opposes the bill, the charges are dropped; if a majority supports the bill, the person is impeached. The process then moves to the Senate for trial, with the members of the Senate serving, in effect, as the jury. When the impeached officer is the president, and only then, the Chief Justice of the United States presides over the Senate trial. Conviction by the Senate requires the assent of two-thirds of the senators present and voting.

As this description suggests, the framers of the Constitution devised an impeachment procedure that is unwieldy and difficult to use.[13] They did not intend impeachment to be routinely used, and it has not been. Over the course of American history, impeachment proceedings have been initiated in the House more than sixty times, but as of the end of 1995 only fifteen federal officials had ever been impeached and only seven had been convicted. Most of them were federal judges, including three who were impeached and removed from office in the 1980s.

CONGRESSIONAL REFORM AND ITS IMPACT

After 1968, Congress changed its rules and procedures in dramatic ways. To understand those changes, put yourself in the position of a new member who is trying to establish a legislative career. To establish a career, you need to accomplish two things: (1) get yourself reelected every time your term is over, and (2) make your influence felt in legislative policy making. The former is essential to any legislative career at all; the latter is essential to achieving a measure of satisfaction and success.

During the 1950s and early 1960s, however, a new legislator could not easily accomplish either goal. The electoral process was dominated by party leaders outside Congress to whom members were often beholden. The internal operations of

Congress were dominated by the chairs of the powerful committees and by the party leaders. Junior members had small staffs, meager allowances, little access to committee and subcommittee influence, and minimal impact on the policy agenda.

Slowly over the 1960s and 1970s, a group of reformers emerged and grew in Congress. The first target of reform was the seniority system. For most of the twentieth century, committee chairs had automatically gone to the member of the majority party with the longest consecutive service on the committee. No meaningful provision existed for altering that selection process or for removing committee chairs who were unresponsive to their party leaders or colleagues.

In the 1970s House reformers succeeded in loosening the hold of the seniority system. Although most committees continue to be chaired by the senior majority party member of the committee, the majority party caucus now elects committee chairs at the beginning of each Congress. Some senior members have been removed by this procedure, and those removals have had a chastening effect on the others. In addition, committee chairs have lost much of the control they once had over subcommittees and committee resources. Though still powerful figures in Congress, committee chairs are no longer an unassailable oligarchy.

During the 1970s, junior members also started to get seats on the most prestigious committees. The number of subcommittees grew to the extent that virtually every member of the majority party could expect to chair a subcommittee after just a few years in Congress, and the enlargement of subcommittee and personal staffs and the growth in support agencies like the Congressional Research Service made individual members less reliant on congressional leaders for information. All these changes enhanced the ability of new members to develop legislation and conduct their own inquiries.

The most far-reaching reform took place in the House, but similar efforts were under way in the Senate. In both houses, individual members achieved greater and more effective involvement in the legislative process, and they acquired more autonomy than their counterparts had at any time in this century.

In the early 1980s, a reaction set in to this powerful wave of congressional reform, leading to what some scholars have referred to as the "postreform Congress."[14] It is characterized principally by a resurgence in partisanship. Party leaders, especially in the House, have regained a significant portion of the influence they lost during the previous two decades. In part, their success has resulted from internal efforts to reinvigorate and institutionalize the party caucuses. Party leadership committees like the Republican Policy Committees in the House and Senate have become important forums for the development of substantive party positions. The whip system in the House, an essential element of the party leadership structure, has grown so that now nearly a quarter of House Republicans have whip responsibilities.

Two other changes in the 1980s abetted the revitalization of congressional partisanship. One was the growing ideological homogeneity of the legislative parties. As politics in the South was changing, the southern Democrats in Congress came to resemble their northern colleagues more closely than at any time since World War II. At the same time, the liberal, or moderate, wing of the Republican party was shrinking almost to the vanishing point. Beginning in the late 1970s, therefore, party unity in floor voting began to grow. Although the congressional Democrats and Republicans can hardly be compared to the tightly disciplined parliamentary parties of western Europe, they did reach important new levels of inter-

FIGURE 10-2
Party Unity Scores in House and Senate Combined, 1965–1995

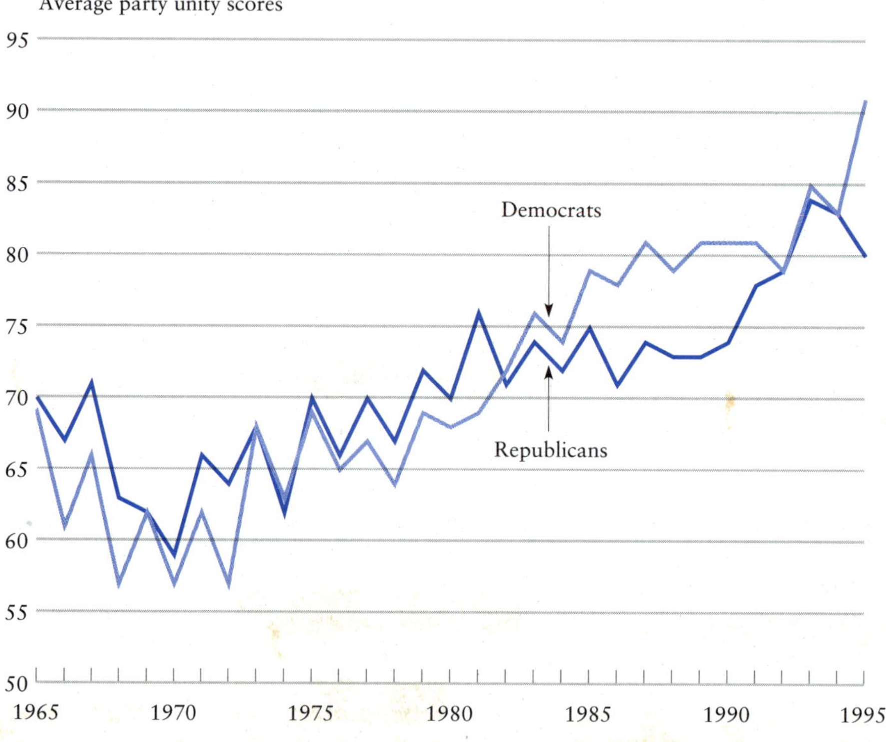

SOURCE: **Calculated by the author from data in several issues of *Congressional Quarterly Weekly Report.***

nal unity and consistency in the postreform period. This trend is shown in Figure 10-2, which charts the extent to which members vote with their own party on issues where a majority of one party opposes a majority of the other.

When the Republicans took control of both houses of Congress after the 1994 elections, they wasted no time in taking policy initiatives in a number of areas. In the House especially, the new Speaker, Newt Gingrich, asserted firmer leadership over his party than had any Speaker in decades. He was highly successful in maintaining Republican cohesion in support of a lengthy agenda of legislative proposals.

The contemporary Congress thus is a product of two recent trends. One was driven by the needs of individual members for electoral security and internal influence, the other by institutional needs for centralized leadership. Coping with policy issues that require painstaking compromises that impose sacrifices on specific segments of the population has always been difficult for Congress. Those, however, are precisely the kinds of issues that occupy the most prominent positions on the current legislative agenda. And because of recent reforms, compromise is more difficult to accomplish.

CASE STUDY

MANDATORY TERM LIMITS

Beginning in the late 1980s, the combination of public dissatisfaction with the performance of Congress and remarkably high reelection rates for its members led to calls for the imposition of limits on the number of terms a member could serve. The framers of the Constitution had debated this matter at some length, concluding that the decision was best left to the voters in individual states and districts. No term limits were included in the language of the Constitution.

In 1988 and 1992, however, the national Republican party platform called for mandatory term limits for members of Congress, which at that time was firmly under Democratic control. The party's nominees for president and vice president, George Bush and Dan Quayle, strongly endorsed the proposal. In 1990, voters in California, Colorado, and Oklahoma imposed term limits on members of their state legislatures, and citizens in the state of Washington narrowly defeated a proposal to impose limits on the terms of their representatives in Congress. In 1992 and 1994, a number of state ballots included referendum questions on legislative term limits. Public opinion polls suggested that term limits was an idea whose time had come.

Most of the proposals for congressional term limits called for a maximum of twelve consecutive years of House or Senate service. Senators would be forced to retire after two six-year terms, House members after six two-year terms. Proponents argue that this limitation is the only effective way of ensuring significant turnover in Congress and thereby of keeping control of government out of the hands of career politicians. Incumbents are so well financed and so deeply entrenched, the proponents point out, that it is very hard for challengers to raise the money and gain the name recognition necessary to dislodge them. Indeed, when incumbents run for reelection, they do nearly always win. As a result, the proponents argue, Congress has become increasingly insulated and self-serving and decreasingly responsive to the will of the American people. As Republican Ernest Jim Istook argued in a House speech:

> our country has grown large and government has grown even larger. It has created a system whereby too many people in politics know no other way to make a living. And too often they are isolated and unfamiliar with normal and everyday life. This is not healthy for America. It is especially fascinating to read studies which show the longer somebody serves in Congress, the more they tend to vote for big government, and bigger taxes, and to oppose cutting spending and cutting the size of government. The system has become a narcotic for too many people.

Opponents of term limits believe that they are too blunt an instrument for solving the problems of Congress. They would force the retirement of good legislators as well as bad ones and deny voters the right to choose whomever they wanted to represent them. They would produce, especially in the Senate, a sizable class of lame-duck legislators who would have little incentive to be responsive to the public after winning their last election before mandatory retirement. And, by removing from Congress its most experienced and powerful members, term limits would inevitably enhance the influence of nonelected congressional staff and executive-branch bureaucrats. Many opponents admit the magnitude of an incumbent's advantages in congressional elections but believe that the problem should be addressed by campaign finance reform rather than by term limits.

Term limits were a key item in the Contract with America, the list of pledges that Republicans used to help them gain a congressional majority in the 1994 elections. On several occasions thereafter, the House of Representatives voted on an amendment to the Constitution that would limit congressional terms. In each case, however, the vote fell short of the two-thirds majority a constitutional amendment requires. Representative Henry Hyde (R, Ill.), serving his eleventh two-year term, led the opposition to the amendment in 1995:

> When that dentist bends over with the drill whirring, do you not hope he has done that work for a few years? And when the neurosurgeon has shaved your head and they have made the pencil mark on your skull where they are going to have the incision and he approaches with the electric saw, ask him one question: Are you a careerist?
>
> Is running a modern complex society of 250 million people and a $6 trillion economy all that easy? To do your job . . . you have to know something about the environment, health care, banking and finance and tax policy, farm problems, weapons systems, Bosnia and Herzegovina and North Korea, not to mention Nagorno-Karabakh, foreign policy, the administration of justice, crime and punishment, education and welfare, budgeting in the trillions of dollars, and immigration. And I have not scratched the surface. We need our best people to deal with these issues. We in Congress deal with ultimate issues: life and death, war and peace, drawing the line between liberty and order. And do you ever really doubt that America will never again have a real crisis? With a revolving-door Congress, where will we get our Everett Dirksens, our Scoop Jacksons, our Arthur Vandenbergs, our Hubert Humphreys, our Barry Goldwaters, our Sam Ervins? You do not get them out of the phone book. Where did Shimon Peres and Yitzhak Rabin get the self-confidence to negotiate peace for their people with the PLO? I will tell you where: experience, bloody, bloody experience.

Despite the defeat of these proposed amendments in Congress, support for term limits remains high among the American people. The issue will return to be debated another day. And those who view politics as a complex set of activities where experience helps will do battle once again with those who believe that tenure in office leads to self-interest, isolation, and unresponsiveness.

Discussion Questions

1. What are the central political issues in the term-limits debate?
2. Who supports term limits for members of Congress, and why?
3. Where does the issue stand at this time?
4. What impact has this debate had on contemporary American politics?
5. What is your position on this issue?

SUMMARY

Congress is a *bicameral legislature* comprising two legislative bodies: the House of Representatives and the Senate. Each member of the House represents a district with a population of about 600,000 and serves for a two-year term. Senators serve six-year terms; there are two senators from each state.

In the initial Congresses, party caucuses hammered out important policy decisions. Committees began to play a more dominant role after the Civil War, but by the end of the nineteenth century party leaders in Congress had become the principal powers. Within a decade, they had become so powerful that a revolt occurred and the committees again became the power center. The *seniority system* ensured that the member of the majority party with the longest consecutive service on a committee would automatically be its chair.

Whereas tight party discipline is normal in legislatures in other countries, political parties in Congress have limited control over their own members. In the House, the majority party controls the selection of the *Speaker of the House.* Working with other party leaders, especially *whips,* the Speaker helps determine the issues that will be given top priority.

Most of the work of Congress is done in committees. Committees hold public hearings at which supporters and opponents of bills may express their views. They also engage in *administrative oversight*—monitoring the work of the executive agencies in their areas of jurisdiction, reviewing budget requests, and passing judgment on the qualifications of presidential appointees. *Standing committees* are permanent committees that have full authority to recommend legislation; most are divided into subcommittees. *Select (special) committees* are created to deal with a specific set of issues and have limited functions and authority. *Joint committees* comprise members of both houses of Congress; *joint conference committees* are formed to resolve the differences that occur when the two houses pass varying forms of the same bill.

The lawmaking process begins when a member of the House or Senate introduces a *bill,* or proposal, for consideration. The bill is assigned to a committee, which may decide not to consider it. If the bill is considered, it is initially examined by a subcommittee, which may hold hearings on the subject of the bill. At the conclusion of the hearings, the subcommittee holds a mark-up session, in which the bill is revised and then voted on. If the subcommittee supports the bill it is returned to the full committee, where another mark-up and vote take place.

If a majority of the full committee supports the bill, it is reported to the full House or Senate. It is then placed on a legislative calendar and sent to the floor for debate. During the debate, individual members may introduce amendments. If a majority of the members present vote in favor of the bill, it is sent to the other house, where the process is repeated. If the two houses pass different versions of the bill, it is sent to a conference committee. If both houses agree to the conference committee's version, the bill is sent to the president for signature.

The president may sign the bill or allow it to become law without a signature. He may also veto the bill by declining to sign it and returning it to Congress within ten days. Congress may override a veto, but an override requires a two-thirds majority in each house and hence is rare. If the annual session of Congress ends within ten days of the passage of a bill, the president may exercise a *pocket veto* by simply declining to sign the bill. Under legislation enacted in 1996, he may also use a *line-item veto* to kill portions of certain kinds of legislation.

Congressional rules and procedures require that legislation be considered and acted on at a number of points; defeat at any of those points usually kills the bill. The rules thus favor proponents of the status quo, work to slow the pace of legislation, and enable determined minorities to thwart the will of majorities.

Many members of Congress work hard to interact with people they represent. Their *franking privilege* enables them to mail newsletters and questionnaires to their constituents free of charge. They travel frequently between Washington and their home state or district, where they also maintain offices with full-time staffs.

Most of the permanent committees of Congress conduct *oversight hearings,* in which the activities of an executive agency or the management of a specific program is reviewed in depth. In addition, Congress often establishes a temporary committee to conduct special investigations. Employees and agencies of the executive branch fall under congressional oversight through *personnel controls* and *financial control.* The legislature also has the power to remove a public official by means of *impeachment.*

During the 1970s, a number of reforms were made in congressional rules and procedures. In the House, the majority party now elects committee chairs at the beginning of each Congress. Junior members may get seats on prestigious committees and may chair subcommittees. In both houses of Congress, individual members have more effective involvement in the legislative process and more autonomy than their counterparts of earlier decades had.

KEY TERMS

bicameral legislature
seniority system
party discipline
Speaker of the House
whip
administrative oversight
standing committee
select (special) committee
joint committee
joint conference committee
legislation
bill
mark-up session
rider
pocket veto
line-item veto
unanimous consent
filibuster
cloture
representation
constituency
franking privilege
oversight hearings
special investigation
personnel controls
financial control
impeachment

RESOURCES

READINGS

Davidson, Roger H. *The Postreform Congress*. New York: St. Martin's Press, 1992. A collection of readings exploring the readjustments that occurred in both houses of Congress after the dynamic reforms of the 1970s.

Fenno, Richard F., Jr. *Homestyle: House Members in Their Districts*. New York: HarperCollins, 1987. An examination of the relationship between members of Congress and their constituents. Identifies different ways in which members conceptualize the people and regions they represent.

Hibbing, John R. *Congressional Careers: Contours of Life in the U.S. House of Representatives.* Chapel Hill: University of North Carolina Press, 1991. An exploration of the career patterns and professional lifestyles of members of the House of Representatives.

Jones, Charles O. *Separate But Equal Branches: Congress and the Presidency.* Chatham, N.J.: Chatham House, 1995. A new and insightful analysis of the roles of Congress in the late twentieth century.

Light, Paul C. *Forging Legislation.* New York: Norton, 1991. A revealing case study of the legislative process; the author follows from inception to enactment a bill to create the Department of Veterans Affairs.

Rohde, David W. *Parties and Leaders in the Postreform House.* Chicago: University of Chicago Press, 1991. An empirical analysis of revitalized partisanship in the House of Representatives after 1980.

ORGANIZATIONS

Center for Democracy, 1101 15th Street, N.W., Washington, DC 20005; phone (202) 429-9141, fax (202) 293-1768. Nonpartisan organization that works to strengthen democratic institutions. Monitors elections and provides democratizing governments with technical and informational assistance.

Center for Responsive Politics, 1320 19th Street, N.W., Washington, DC 20036; phone (202) 857-0044, fax (202) 857-7809; Internet http://www.vote-smart.org/congress/finance/crp.html Conducts research on Congress and related issues with particular interest in campaign finance and congressional operations.

U.S. Capitol Historical Society, 200 Maryland Avenue, N.E., Washington, DC 20002; phone (202) 543-8919, fax (202) 544-8244. Conducts historical research and maintains information centers in the Capitol.

11

The Presidency

PREVIEW

- The authority of the presidency
- Exercising leadership: bargaining and going public
- Institutional and personnel resources: the cabinet; the executive office of the president; the president's spouse; the vice presidency
- The personal dimension: physical health, character, managerial style, and belief system
- The politics of presidential policy making: setting the agenda; influencing the legislation; building public support; implementing priorities in the executive branch; presidential leadership

Bill Clinton faced major economic and budgetary problems when he entered the presidency. But they came as no surprise. He had talked about them during his campaign. He held a public seminar to discuss them as president-elect. He spoke about them during his first address to Congress and throughout his first six months in office. But he didn't realize how difficult they would be to solve.

The basic issue was simple enough to articulate but hard to resolve. The economy was in recession in 1992, and Clinton had promised to stimulate it. The federal budget was out of balance, and Clinton had promised to reduce that imbalance substantially. How could he do both simultaneously?

Several groups vied for the president's attention. Clinton's political advisers urged him to pursue a populist policy in which economic stimulation would be the primary objective and a middle-class tax cut a principal stimulator. The president's economic advisers, on the other hand, cautioned against decreased taxes, increased spending, and any programs that would increase burdens on business.

Whatever policy Clinton chose, Congress would have to be involved. Congressional sentiment was divided, largely along partisan lines. The Republican minority in 1993 were dead set against any increase in taxes; they wanted deficit reduction to be achieved through massive government spending cuts. As the party out of power, they would not have to take the heat for such cuts from those who would be adversely affected by them. Congressional Democrats were much less united, with liberal members, particularly those from urban areas, wanting the president to stimulate the economy in order to create more jobs. Not only did they support continued government spending, but they opposed reductions to programs that benefited their traditional political constituencies. Moderate and conservative Democrats, primarily those from the South, were more sympathetic to spending cuts and opposed new taxes.

Over the first four months of his administration, Clinton vacillated among the positions of his various advisers and congressional allies. A politician who desired to please, he struggled to find a consensus, one that would meet with some approval from each of these groups. In doing so, he made decisions and then was forced to reverse some of them when new information became available. Moreover, his decision making was affected by leaks of potential policy options to the news media. These leaks embarrassed the president and limited his discretion, forcing him to back off from proposals that had produced a strongly negative public reaction. The leaks also contributed to the impression of mixed messages that emanated from the White House.

As delay and indecision continued, the media depicted a presidency in disarray with little leadership from the top. All these factors lowered public confidence in Clinton and weakened his already weak political position (he had received only 43 percent of the vote). In the end, he proposed a $16 billion economic stimulus package as his number-one priority. It was enacted by the House of Representatives but defeated in the Senate by a Republican-led filibuster. His second priority, a deficit-reduction bill, was substantially modified by Congress before it was enacted by the barest of margins in August 1993. In the process, the president was forced to make a number of highly publicized compromises. He had finally achieved a major goal, but his reputation as a decision maker, legislative leader, and communicator-in-chief all suffered in the process. His political capital had been depleted and his presidential image damaged.

Clinton's first six months in office had been rough, but his difficulties are characteristic of the modern presidency. Moreover, the manner of his defeat and victory, and the methods he used to pursue his objectives, were not unique. All presidents face a multitude of problems when taking office. Part of their challenge is to establish priorities to deal with them. Presidents also face a multitude of choices with differing payoffs. Part of their challenge is to evaluate these payoffs and select the options that are both optimal and feasible. Finally, presidents are subject to a multitude of pressures to which they must respond, and they have to do so in a manner that is consistent with the dignity of their office, the goals of their policy, and the political environment in which they find themselves. In other words, they have to be political leaders if they are to be successful.

Politics pervades the presidency. It affects how presidents get into office, what they do while there, and when and how they do it. Whereas politics inflates expectations of presidential performance, it also can make the achievement of those expectations more difficult over time. And it does this in all aspects of the policy-making process, from agenda setting to consensus building to the implementation of legislation.

But presidents have no choice. Their presidency has to function as a political institution. Only effective political leadership can overcome the constitutional constraints, generated by separate institutions sharing powers and responsibilities, to initiate national policy; only effective political leadership can unite a diverse nation and build a policy consensus behind that policy; only effective political leadership can coordinate the various officials who will oversee the implementation of that policy and are held accountable for its success or failure. Thus politics creates the dilemma of the modern presidency, but it also provides presidents with their only solution to that dilemma in normal times: strong political leadership.

Presidents often face a "damned if they do, damned if they don't" dilemma. They are expected to be sensitive to public interests and pressures even though those interests and pressures may be ambiguous, contradictory, and fluid. They are expected to respond quickly and decisively to policy problems, to initiate and propose solutions, and to build support for them even though their information may be incomplete, their advisers may be divided, and the environment within which they operate may be hostile. And they are expected to solve the problems even though they do not control all or even most of the factors that generated them. Moreover, if the problems persist, they will probably be blamed and their capacity to lead in the future may be impaired.

Presidents have a persistent leadership dilemma whose roots lie in the American system of government.[1] To achieve their goals, presidents need the cooperation of many individuals over whom they may have little or no influence. Yet the Constitution divides authority, institutions share power, and political parties often lack cohesion and have difficulty maintaining long-term policy positions. Faced with these hurdles, how can presidents successfully lead? They can do so through the skillful use of three kinds of powers:

1. *Legal powers*. Presidents can utilize the formal authority that is vested in the presidency. Here they command by virtue of constitutional and statutory powers as well as by precedent.
2. *Institutional powers*. Presidents can utilize subordinates in the executive branch. Here they delegate to others the job of collecting information and assessing options while reserving the critical decisions for themselves.
3. *Political powers*. Presidents can utilize the informal powers of the presidency. Here they persuade on the basis of their elected position, political reputation, and public approval.

This chapter focuses on these powers and the environment in which they are exercised. It begins by exploring the legal basis of presidential authority and the evolution of presidential powers through statute and precedent. Next, it looks at presidential leadership and the institutional and personal resources necessary to achieve it. The chapter concludes by examining how presidents use their political powers to try to get things done—how they attempt to make, sell, and implement public policy. In each of these areas, it explores the politics of the contemporary presidency.

THE AUTHORITY OF THE PRESIDENCY

Article Two of the Constitution gives the president a broad grant of executive power, which is checked by the requirement for joint institutional involvement in the exercise of most of these powers. Thus presidents can appoint people to many offices, subject to the advice and consent of the Senate. Some presidential appointees, such as cabinet secretaries and ambassadors, hold office at the discretion of the president. Others, however, who hold quasi-legislative or quasi-judicial positions, such as members of independent regulatory agencies, serve fixed terms and can be removed only by impeachment. As chief executive, a president can direct subordinates to perform a certain task by issuing **executive orders** and **executive memoranda**. But Congress retains the authority to structure the executive branch, authorize its programs, and appropriate money for them.

The Constitution also gives the president some legislative and judicial duties and responsibilities. A president may recommend legislation and veto bills enacted by Congress. But in each case Congress has the final word; it does not have to act on the president's recommendations, and it can override a veto by a two-thirds vote of both houses. The president can also affect the federal judiciary through nominations. But Senate approval of nominees is required, and the president cannot remove judges, who serve during "good behavior" for life. In addition, presidents can issue pardons, grant clemency, and provide amnesty for those convicted or accused of a federal crime.

These limited constitutional powers have been supplemented by statutory authority, or powers granted by ordinary legislation. The power to propose an annual budget, for example, is a congressional requirement, not a constitutional obligation. Similarly, Congress has enacted laws that give presidents power to help settle labor disputes; President Clinton used this power when he intervened in the threatened strike of pilots against American Airlines in 1997. Congress has also provided the president with money for emergency relief efforts, which presidents can designate by simply declaring parts of the country ravaged by natural disasters as eligible for these funds. The line-item veto enacted in 1996 allows the president to negate specific items in appropriations bills without having to veto the entire bill. In foreign affairs, presidents have used fast-track authority given to them by Congress to negotiate treaties such as the North American Free Trade Agreement (NAFTA) with Canada and Mexico and the General Agreement on Tariffs and Trade (GATT) both during Clinton's first term. Moreover, Congress has acquiesced in a number of other ways in the expansion of presidential powers in foreign affairs.

But Congress has also enacted legislation to constrain the exercise of statutory presidential powers. The War Powers Resolution (1973) requires that the president report to Congress and, ultimately, obtain its approval in order to commit American armed forces to hostile or potentially hostile situations for more than sixty days. The Budget and Impoundment Control Act (1974) provides Congress with an alternative budgetary capacity that includes a Congressional Budget Office, budget committees in both houses, and a process by which Congress competes with the president in preparing an annual budget. It also limits the president's ability to refuse to spend money that Congress has appropriated. More recently, Congress has also allowed other discretionary executive authority to lapse, such as the authority that had been given to Presidents Roosevelt through Nixon to reorganize their Executive Office subject to congressional objection. Thus Congress at different times has both strengthened and weakened the president's statutory power.

Finally, precedent has expanded the presidency. The president's domestic agenda-setting role, foreign policy initiatives, legislative lobbying, public appeals, even the role as crisis manager have all evolved and become expectations of the contemporary office. These precedents have created performance expectations that presidents can find difficult to meet.

EXERCISING LEADERSHIP

Presidents need to exercise political leadership to close the gap between expectations and performance. They must try to persuade others to follow their lead by bargaining behind closed doors and making a public appeal.

Bargaining

In his classic study, *Presidential Power,* Richard E. Neustadt points out that presidents must be persuasive; they must be able to convince others that it is in *their* interest to do what the president wants.[2] Being persuasive often involves bargaining behind closed doors.

In the give-and-take of bargaining, presidents enjoy certain advantages. Their office is respected. Others look to them for guidance and leadership. Moreover, they control some valued commodities such as publicity, nominations, even social invitations, and they can use their discretion to propose and implement programs that benefit particular groups and constituencies. They can also impose a variety of sanctions, usually as a last resort. Sanctions range from not doing favors, not raising money, or not offering jobs to campaigning against those who oppose presidential policies.

In addition to wielding rewards and sanctions, however, presidents need to be able to be persuasive. Neustadt identifies two strategic imperatives that contribute to a president's persuasive ability: reputation in Washington and prestige with the general public. Reputation affects what presidents can do. Presidents who say what they mean and do what they say are likely to gain more support than those whose priorities are unclear and whose positions are subject to continual change.[3] Reputation in turn helps shape the public's perceptions, which are closely linked to the president's prestige. In general, presidents who enjoy the broadest public support are likely to be most persuasive with Congress, executive officials, foreign leaders, and others.

Political scientists have found empirical evidence to support the proposition that presidents' legislative influence increases as their popularity, measured in terms of public approval, increases. Political scientist George C. Edwards III, who has analyzed the results of Gallup polls and congressional voting patterns over several decades, found that the more popular presidents were, the more congressional support they received regardless of their partisan affiliation.[4]

For public approval to be converted into congressional votes, however, there must be a relationship between the basis of the president's popularity and the issue before Congress. George Bush found this out the hard way during the budget deficit debate of 1990. His plea to the American people and to Republican members of Congress to support the compromise that his administration had negotiated with the Democratic leadership fell on deaf ears despite his high standing in the polls. In 1990, Americans approved of Bush's performance as president in foreign affairs, but many did not support his budget policy. Similarly, despite Bush's popularity after the Persian Gulf War in 1991, Congress did not rush to support his domestic legislative initiatives.

Going Public

Appealing to the public by giving major addresses, holding press conferences and town meetings, and participating in other citizen-oriented events augments presidential power in two fundamental ways.[5] First, it legitimizes the position of the president in the eyes of others. Public support enables presidents to withstand criticism better, and it decreases the amount of criticism they are likely to receive. People are less likely to oppose a popular president than an unpopular one.

Going public also enables the president to apply pressure more effectively. Elected officials are usually very responsive to the beliefs and desires of organized groups and coalitions that may support or oppose them the next time they

Turnover within the cabinet is usually heavy at the end of a president's first term. Here President Clinton announces four of his nominees for cabinet posts for his second term: Anthony Lake (left) as CIA director, Madeleine Albright (second from left) as secretary of state, William Cohen (second from right) as defense secretary, and Sandy Berger (right) as national security adviser.

seek office. Political appointees and even civil servants are also sensitive to the needs of the groups affected by their decisions and policies. On the other hand, there are dangers to relying too heavily on the public. Its opinion tends to be volatile and inconsistent. Moreover, public approval is usually tied to visible short-term results.

Presidents face another problem when they go public: they raise expectations, sometimes to unrealistic heights. Failure to meet these expectations results in disappointment and damages a president's reputation, making it difficult to generate support for other proposals down the line. The high priority that President Clinton gave to health-care reform early in his administration is a classic example. By emphasizing this issue and his plans for dealing with it, Clinton heightened public awareness of the problem and created expectations. When his plan failed to win the support of Congress, the president's prestige fell.

The electoral process also tends to inflate public hopes. In his quest for the presidency, Jimmy Carter talked in unequivocal terms about the strong, honest, purposeful leadership he would provide as president. His inability to project that type of leadership or to make good on the 125 promises he had made during the campaign and reiterated after he took office contributed to the sharp decline in his popularity during his four years in office. All presidents are judged to some extent by the promises they make, duly recorded by the news media.

TABLE 11-1 *Government Departments Whose Heads Are Part of the Cabinet*

DEPARTMENT	ESTABLISHED	HEADS DURING CLINTON ADMINISTRATION
State	1789	Warren Christopher; Madeleine Albright
Treasury	1789	Lloyd Bentsen; Robert Rubin
Interior	1849	Bruce Babbitt
Justice	1870	Janet Reno
Agriculture	1889	Mike Espy; Dan Glickman
Commerce	1913[a]	Ron Brown; Mickey Kantor; William Daley
Labor	1913[a]	Robert Reich; Alexis Herman
Defense	1947[b]	Les Aspin; William Perry; William Cohen
Housing and Urban Development	1965	Henry Cisneros; Andrew Cuomo
Transportation	1966	Federico Peña; Rodney Slater
Energy	1977	Hazel O'Leary; Federico Peña
Health and Human Services	1979[c]	Donna Shalala
Education	1979[c]	Richard Riley
Veterans Affairs	1989	Jesse Brown

[a]Split from Commerce and Labor (est. 1903).
[b]Replaced Departments of War (est. 1789) and Navy (est. 1798).
[c]Split from Health, Education, and Welfare (est. 1954).

INSTITUTIONAL AND PERSONNEL RESOURCES

Presidents need help. Their job is too big, their tasks are too diverse, and the expectations placed on them are too great for them to operate alone. The Constitution anticipated that the president would have advisers, but it did not establish an advisory structure. Beyond the role of the Senate in providing advice and consent to appointments and treaties, presidents were left to their own devices.

The Cabinet

In 1792, President Washington began to meet frequently with the heads of the three executive departments in existence at that time—State, War, and Treasury—plus the attorney general, who initially had no department. These meetings became more frequent and eventually evolved into an informal advisory system. Known as the **cabinet**, it assumed a partisan character in 1794 after Thomas Jefferson resigned as secretary of state to protest the administration's economic and foreign policies.

For more than 160 years the cabinet functioned as the president's principal advisory body. (Table 11-1 shows the departments whose heads, together with the vice president and certain other high officials such as the national security adviser, make up the cabinet.) Administration positions on controversial proposals were often thrashed out at cabinet meetings. Department secretaries also lent their prestige to the president, helping the administration maintain its political support in the party, Congress, and the country.

As the president's influence began to increase at the beginning of the twentieth century, particularly during the administrations of Theodore Roosevelt and

Woodrow Wilson, the cabinet's influence declined. Its meetings became more of a forum for discussion than a mechanism for making decisions. Franklin Roosevelt even trivialized the forum. His practice was to go around the table asking each participant what was on his or her mind. Frequently after the session, several secretaries would remain to discuss their important business with the president out of the earshot of others. Eisenhower was the last president to use his cabinet as a formal advisory body.

Although presidents have continued to consult with department heads individually or in small groups, they have turned increasingly to smaller, more cohesive bodies for policy advice and coordination. Presidents Reagan and Bush created cabinet councils, organized on the basis of broad policy areas, to debate policy, develop recommendations, and help in the implementation of key presidential priorities. President Clinton has used a variation of this approach, with three policy councils operating in the economic, domestic, and national security spheres, respectively.

The Executive Office of the President

With the cabinet declining in importance, presidents have turned increasingly to their own staffs for advice, coordination, and public relations. Before 1939, presidential staffs were very small. In fact, not until 1857 did Congress authorize the president to hire a secretary. What help presidents had before that year, they paid for themselves.

Small staffs forced chief executives to do much of the administrative work themselves. George Washington maintained custody of the public papers; Abraham Lincoln wrote his own speeches; Grover Cleveland often answered the White House phone; Woodrow Wilson typed the final drafts of his principal addresses.

The inadequacy of presidential staffing became evident during the first term of Franklin Roosevelt's administration. In 1936, responding to criticism that his presidency was not being run efficiently, Roosevelt appointed a committee to study the problem. The committee proposed the establishment of an official presidential office, and in 1939 Congress gave the president the authority to construct one.

The first **Executive Office of the President** (EOP) consisted of five separate units: three wartime agencies, the Bureau of the Budget, and a White House Office. Over the years, the EOP has grown in size, responsibility, and power. Today, it consists of twelve offices (including the president's) and two executive residences and has approximately 1,700 full-time employees and a budget of $230 million (see Figure 11-1). The largest and most powerful units are the Office of Management and Budget and the White House Office.

The Office of Management and Budget The Budget and Accounting Act of 1921 created a Bureau of the Budget to help the president prepare an annual budget to be submitted to Congress. Initially housed in the Department of the Treasury, the bureau was moved into the newly created EOP in 1939. This move converted the Budget Bureau into an important presidential agency, extending the president's reach and influence to the ongoing budgetary process.

As the substantive policy-making responsibilities of the presidency increased, the bureau was given an additional role—to coordinate legislative policy for the president. The increasing importance of the budget office led President Nixon to rename and restructure it in 1970. Now called the **Office of Management and**

FIGURE 11-1
The Executive Office of the President—at Its Inception and in 1998

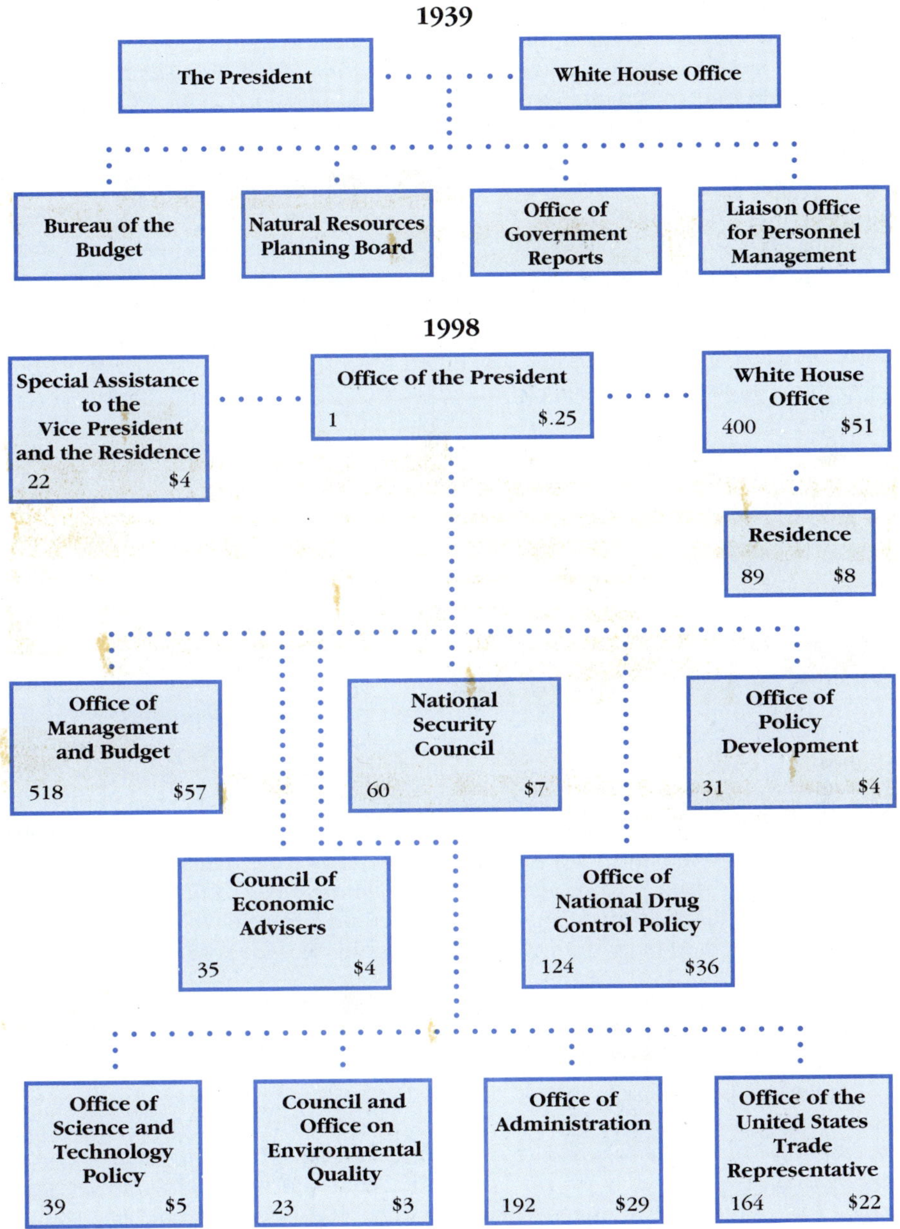

Numbers on left indicate full-time personnel. Dollar amounts in millions indicate proposed budget authority for the 1998 fiscal year.

SOURCE: Budget of the United States Government, Fiscal Year 1998. Washington, D.C.: Government Printing Office, 1997.

Budget (OMB), it assumed management advisory responsibilities in addition to its budgetary review and legislative policy functions.

To the extent that presidents require executive departments to consult with the OMB and allow it to have the last word, it has become both feared and powerful. It has gained a reputation as the institution that says no. In the process, it has generated considerable controversy, much of it stemming from the OMB's budgetary orientation and presidential perspective in contrast to the service orientation and more parochial views of the executive departments and agencies.

In its policy recommendations, the OMB traditionally tries to save money by limiting spending, thereby pitting departments and agencies against one another and against the OMB in the battle for funds. The OMB is also concerned with setting precedents, in contrast to the departments, which are more sensitive to protecting their interests and those of their clientele. Thus the OMB would be inclined to oppose a program likely to result in a large increase in expenditures, but a department whose clientele benefited from the program would probably support it. The conflict resulting from the politics of budgeting is continuous.

In addition to its budgetary and management functions, the OMB performs another critical role for the president. It acts as a central clearinghouse, monitoring what the executive departments and agencies want to do and how they want to do it. All proposals for new legislation, positions on existing legislation, and testimony before congressional committees must be cleared in advance by the OMB to make certain that they are in accord with the president's objectives. This is known as the **central clearance process**. At the end of the legislative process, the OMB also coordinates executive branch recommendations to the president to approve or disapprove legislation enacted by Congress. This is known as the **enrolled bill process**.

The OMB performs still another clearance operation for pending regulations to be issued by the departments and agencies. In exercising this **regulatory review**, the OMB must determine if a regulation is necessary, consistent with administration policy and legislative intent, and cost effective.

In short, since its inception the OMB has been a potent instrument of presidential power. Nixon and Ford turned to it to improve the management of government. Carter used it to reorganize parts of the executive branch, including his own office. Reagan, Bush, and Clinton relied on it to achieve significant budget cuts as well as to help them maintain oversight over the executive branch.

The White House Office Like the OMB, the **White House Office** has evolved into a large and potent presidential staff. From its inception in 1939 until the mid 1960s, the office was relatively small and informal. A handful of administrative aides performed assignments dictated by specific presidential needs, such as writing a speech, planning a trip, or getting sufficient information for the president to make a decision. The president's assistants did not exercise exclusive domain over a policy or functional area; they did not rival cabinet secretaries for status and influence. Rather, they acted as personal assistants, enhancing the information available to the president, extending the influence of the presidency, and coordinating presidential activities with those of the rest of the government.

Gradually, the staff began to expand. During the 1950s, an official liaison with Congress was established. During the 1960s, a policy-making capacity in national security and domestic affairs was created. During the 1970s and 1980s, regular links with the president's principal constituencies—interest groups, state and local governments, and the political parties—were set up. By the 1990s, an economic policy council was formally added.

As presidential responsibilities have grown, so has the White House Office staff. In 1950, it numbered about 300 people; by 1960, it exceeded 400; by 1970, it was close to 500. After the Watergate scandal, in which a number of presidential aides were implicated, the size of the White House payroll declined. Today, the White House Office has an official staff size of approximately 400, plus another 100 people from the executive departments and agencies who are detailed to the White House for special assignments. Its budget is $51 million.[6]

In theory, most White House Offices in recent decades have had similar structures and decision-making processes. There is a formalized structure with a chief of staff, policy assistants, a large public relations operation, and the traditional units that help the president meet his day-to-day responsibilities and link him to his principal constituencies. In practice, however, recent Republican staffs have tended to be more hierarchical in organization, more clear-cut in areas of responsibility, and more formal in decision-making processes than have their Democratic counterparts. Further, recent Republican presidents have distanced themselves more from day-to-day operations and middle-level policy-making issues than have recent Democratic presidents, who have tended to place themselves in the midst of their administrations' political, policy, and personnel decisions.

The bureaucratized White House has presented presidents with their own internal management problems: how to supervise the operation of a sizable, diverse, and increasingly specialized staff. Presidents Ford and Carter tried unsuccessfully to do this supervision themselves. Inundated with decisions that could have been settled by others, both presidents eventually turned to a chief of staff to oversee these and other administrative tasks. Since then, all presidents have depended on a chief of staff to run the White House.

The chief of staff has three important responsibilities: (1) to act as an honest broker, ensuring that the president has a wide range of information and advice; (2) to offer recommendations to the president about decisions that need to be made and actions that need to be taken; and (3) to serve as a lightning rod for criticism directed at the president. The general rule of thumb in the White House is that the president should be credited with all the good news and favorable actions and the staff should be blamed for the major foul-ups and problems.

As the White House Office has expanded in functions and responsibilities, power has shifted to it from the departments and agencies. The shift has enhanced the status, visibility, and influence of the president's principal aides and decreased those of many cabinet secretaries. Proximity to the president's Oval Office, illustrated in Figure 11-2, growing policy-making responsibilities, and large support staffs have placed White House aides in a better position than other executive branch officials to shape administration goals and coordinate strategies to achieve them.

By providing a cadre of politically loyal strategists and technicians, the larger, more powerful White House Office has increased presidential discretion and influence. But these changes have also created tensions between the officials in the White House and those in the departments and agencies. Complaints have been heard from cabinet officials that the White House is formulating more and more major policies, that presidents and their staffs are getting more directly involved in the implementation of policy, and that the access of department sec-

FIGURE 11-2
An Exploded View of the West Wing of the Clinton White House

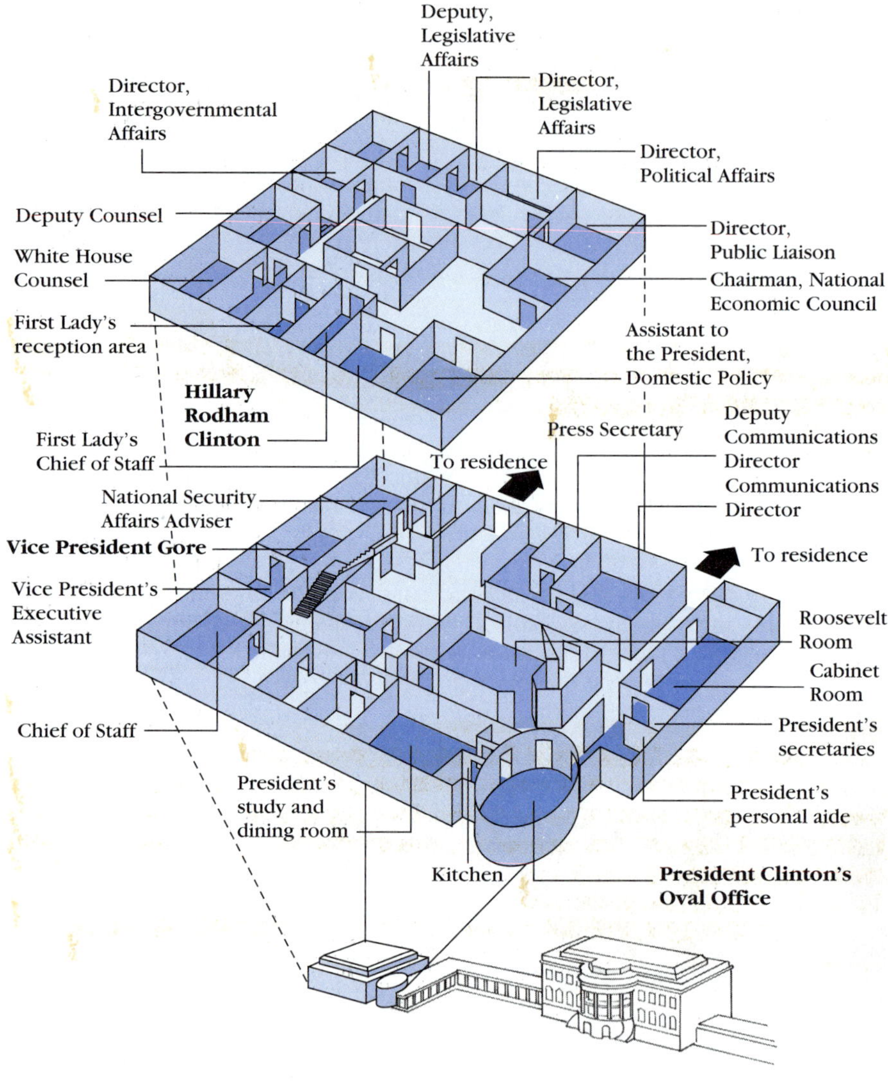

SOURCE: *Washington Post*, February 5, 1993, A23. Copyright © 1993 The Washington Post. Reprinted with permission.

retaries and their deputies to top White House policy makers is being impaired. Tension has also increased between political appointees and civil servants.

Internal staff conflicts within the White House Office have also become evident and the subject of considerable speculation in the news media. Turf battles, policy disputes, and personality clashes have now become standard fare. These conflicts, which often become public, make it harder for an administration to speak with a single voice. Leaks have become more frequent, along with "kiss-and-tell" books and articles by departing presidential aides. In short, the White House has become a battleground in which personal and institutional politics *within* the administration influence decisions almost as much as political pressures from outside it.

President Clinton had particular difficulty in finding the right people for his White House. Several embarrassing incidents during the early years of his administration forced him to shift senior aides and revise White House operations. In his first three years, Clinton had two chiefs of staff, five deputy chiefs of staff, four counsels, three legislative liaison heads, three communication directors, two press secretaries, and many other changes in White House personnel.

The President's Spouse

The role of the president's spouse has expanded to include more than simply ceremonial and social responsibilities. A president's spouse is expected to campaign, to make speeches, and to attend events in the president's absence and on the president's behalf. Communicating public reactions and perspectives to the president is another important task, one that Eleanor Roosevelt pioneered as first lady. Mrs. Roosevelt traveled across the country for her husband, monitoring public opinion and reporting the country's mood to him, and writing a newspaper column entitled "My Day."

All too often, personal aides are reluctant to tell a president bad news. A presidential spouse may be in a better position to do so. For example, Nancy Reagan was instrumental in conveying to her husband which of his top aides and department secretaries were not serving him well. Her efforts culminated in

After the health-care reform plan she had put together died in Congress, Hillary Rodham Clinton refocused her public activities on less controversial areas and ones in which she played a less visible policy-making role. Here she addresses a convention of the American Association of Retired Persons.

the resignation of two senior administrative officials in the president's second term, his chief of staff and his attorney general.

Presidential spouses have also involved themselves on issues of public policy. Betty Ford and Rosalynn Carter spoke out on health-care issues, and Mrs. Carter was the first spouse to attend cabinet meetings regularly. Nancy Reagan promoted the Reagan administration's campaign against illegal drugs.

Hillary Rodham Clinton has been the most active spouse thus far in the formulation and coordination of policy. The first to be given an office in the west wing of the White House with the rest of the president's principal policy advisers, Mrs. Clinton coordinated and tried to gain support for the administration's health-care initiatives. She also began writing a newspaper column.

Mrs. Clinton's role was not without controversy, however. Critics complained that her unique relationship to the president made her less subject to the usual constraints on presidential advisers—she could not be fired—and placed her in a position to impose her own views on the president and those around him and to prevent others from reaching him. Mrs. Clinton's support of a comprehensive health-care plan that provided universal care for all Americans is a good example of an issue in which the first lady's strongly held views carried the day with the president despite concerns that the plan was too costly, too complex, and too bureaucratic.

A reluctance to be disrespectful to the first lady may also act to inhibit critical discussion in her presence, particularly on issues in which her position is well known. This reluctance makes her less vulnerable to criticism than are others in a position to influence public policy. Moreover, the first lady's involvement in an issue heightens public awareness, focuses media attention, and indicates the importance the administration attaches to a proposal. Thus when the proposal is defeated, as was the case with health care, the loss has larger political implications for the president than it otherwise would. Since that defeat, Mrs. Clinton has played a less visible policy-making role in the Clinton administration.

Mrs. Clinton's political and policy roles can only be advisory. By law, members of the president's immediate family may not hold a paid appointed position with the federal government, although they may hold a private sector job.

The Vice Presidency

Like the roles of the OMB and the White House Office, that of the vice presidency has been enlarged, and the stature of the office enhanced. Today, the vice presidency is considered prestigious in its own right. That was not always the case.

Throughout much of American history, in fact, the position was not well regarded even by those who served in it. The nation's first vice president, John Adams, complained, "My country has in its wisdom contrived for me the most insignificant office that ever the invention of man contrived or his imagination conceived."[7] Thomas Jefferson, the second person to hold the office, was not quite as critical. Describing his job as "honorable and easy," he added, "I am unable to decide whether I would rather have it or not have it."[8]

Why was such a position created in the first place? The framers did not discuss a vice presidency until the end of the Constitutional Convention. Although they wanted to ensure an orderly succession if the presidency became vacant, there were other ways to do so. The manner in which the vice president was to be selected, however, offers a clue as to why the framers established this position. Originally, the candidate with the second-highest number of Electoral Col-

Al Gore and Bill Clinton share a close personal and professional relationship, to the point that after their reelection in 1996 Clinton began openly supporting his vice president's bid to succeed him.

lege votes was to become the vice president. This placed the second-most-qualified person (in the judgment of the electors) in a position to take over if something happened to the president.

In 1800, however, the presidential election ended in a tie in the Electoral College. Since the electors could not designate which position, president or vice president, they wished Jefferson and Burr to have, both Democratic-Republican candidates received the same number of votes and the House of Representatives had to determine the winner. To prevent this situation from happening again, Congress proposed and the states ratified the Twelfth Amendment to the Constitution, which requires separate Electoral College ballots for president and vice president. This modification in voting upset the logic of the framers' reasoning, because the political parties began to choose their vice presidential nominees for reasons of partisanship rather than merit. It is probably no coincidence that the office declined in importance following the enactment of this amendment.

Until the middle of the twentieth century, vice presidents performed very limited functions. But after Franklin Roosevelt's sudden death in 1945, Eisenhower's illnesses in the 1950s, and Kennedy's assassination in 1963, the position of vice president became a subject of public concern and congressional action, namely, the Twenty-Fifth Amendment. Ratified by the states in 1967, this amendment permits the president to appoint a vice president if that position becomes vacant, subject to the approval of a majority in both houses of Congress.

Since the end of World War II, presidents have also done more to prepare their vice presidents for the job that they might have to assume eventually. Eisenhower invited Vice President Richard Nixon to attend cabinet, National Security Council, and legislative strategy meetings and to preside over these ses-

PRACTICING DEMOCRACY

Keeping Up with the President

In addition to the Internet, there are other ways of finding out what the president is saying and doing.

Everything the president officially says is a matter of public record. All the president's public speeches, remarks, proclamations, executive orders, letters, and so on are preserved and published by the National Archives and Records Administration. These documents are found in all federal depository libraries and in many other research libraries.

The *Federal Register* publishes a daily record of the president's words and official actions. A weekly record, along with a digest of the president's activities that week, is found in the *Weekly Compilation of Presidential Documents.* A complete record of the president's speeches appears annually in the *Public Papers of the Presidents.* In fact, *Codification of Presidential Proclamations and Executive Orders* contains these documents from 1945 to 1989 in one convenient, indexed volume. More recent executive orders and memoranda can be found in the *Federal Register* and in the *Weekly Compilation of Presidential Documents.*

The *New York Times* usually runs the full text of major presidential speeches and transcripts of most presidential press conferences on the day after they occur.

A recorded message for the press listing the president's schedule for the day can be heard by calling (202) 456-2343. A similar message for the first lady can be heard at (202) 456-6269.

sions during Eisenhower's absences. Nixon also represented the president on a number of well-publicized trips abroad. Lyndon Johnson, John Kennedy's vice president, also participated in a variety of administrative activities, from coordinating efforts to eliminate racial discrimination to promoting the exploration of outer space and lobbying Congress.

Despite their own "enhanced" experiences, neither President Johnson nor President Nixon gave major new responsibilities to their own vice presidents. But Presidents Ford and Carter did. Vice Presidents Nelson Rockefeller and Walter Mondale regularly advised Ford and Carter, respectively, on policy issues, particularly in the domestic sphere, and acted as their liaison with Congress, interest groups, and the president's political party. Symbolically, Jimmy Carter gave Walter Mondale an office in the west wing of the White House, close to the Oval Office, thereby indicating to others how he regarded his vice president. Although Vice Presidents George Bush and Dan Quayle did not exert as much clout in their respective administrations as Mondale did in his, they too participated in major policy discussions, headed committees to examine interagency problems, and represented their president on trips abroad.

Vice President Al Gore has been an important Clinton adviser with regular input into major decisions about policy and strategy. He has a weekly lunch with the president and is a regular participant in political strategy meetings. Heading the administration's National Performance Review, its effort to "reinvent government," Gore has also been charged with overseeing the coordination of regulatory priorities and agendas. A key legislative lobbyist, he cast the tie-breaking vote in the Senate on the 1993 deficit reduction proposal. Additionally, he has performed the traditional vice presidential roles of public outreach and political fund-raising. The latter got him into trouble when it was revealed that he had solicited campaign and party contributions from his West Wing office in the White House. He has also been accused of raising money at a non-profit religious institution, a Buddhist temple.

Gore's involvement in questionable activities points to the critical linkage between the president and vice president. Although the vice presidency has gained in stature and is now regarded as a stepping stone to the presidency, vice presidents cannot successfully distance themselves from the problems of the administration in which they serve. Their fate is inevitably tied to the president's. To make matters worse, a vice president who hopes to have any influence in the administration, to be chosen as a running mate for a second term, or to gain the president's support for a future presidential campaign cannot disagree publicly with the "boss," take attention away from him, or appear eager to have the number one job. Thus after President Reagan was shot in 1981, Vice President Bush, who was in Texas at the time of the assassination attempt, had his helicopter land at the vice president's residence in Washington, D.C., rather than at the White House to avoid any appearance that he was eager to take over as president.

THE PERSONAL DIMENSION

Presidents need advice, but they also have discretion in making decisions and conditioning their relationships with others. How skilled and smart they are, what they believe, how quickly they absorb information and take action, how they view their roles and tasks, how they feel on a particular day, and how they feel about themselves in general all affect their perceptions, their evaluations, and ultimately their words, decisions, and behavior.

Physical Health

Despite the importance of health, public information about the diagnosis and treatment of presidential illnesses is usually vague and incomplete, particularly at the onset of a problem. In an effort to prevent precipitous reactions and maintain continuity, White House spokespersons have tended to downplay the president's medical problems and not fully inform the public about them. Thus it was not until weeks after Ronald Reagan left the hospital following the 1981 attempt on his life that the public learned how close to death he actually had come. Similarly, Grover Cleveland's two cancer operations in 1893, Woodrow Wilson's incapacity after a stroke in 1919–1920, Franklin Roosevelt's worsening health during the mid 1940s, and John F. Kennedy's affliction with Addison's disease were not publicized during their tenure in office.

In the second half of the twentieth century, presidents seem to have had more than their share of illnesses.[9] Dwight Eisenhower had three major illnesses: coronary thrombosis in 1955, acute ileitis in 1956, and a minor stroke in 1957. In addition to Addison's disease, Kennedy had a back problem that was treated with special braces, exercises, and a chair designed to alleviate pressure. Lyndon Johnson had gall bladder and hernia operations during his presidency and

WHERE ON THE WEB?

THE PRESIDENCY

The White House went on the Internet in 1993. Today, you can obtain a variety of information about the presidency, such as speeches, reports, press briefings, even letters—all updated daily from the White House homepage. You can also access from it all cabinet-level websites as well as sites sponsored by several independent agencies and commissions. Moreover, you can send e-mail to the president, vice president, and other executive officials. Here's how to do so.

Direct e-mail can be sent to the following addresses: **president@whitehouse.gov** and **vice.president@whitehouse.gov.** The White House homepage can be accessed at **http://www.whitehouse.gov.** You can then choose from the menu shown here.

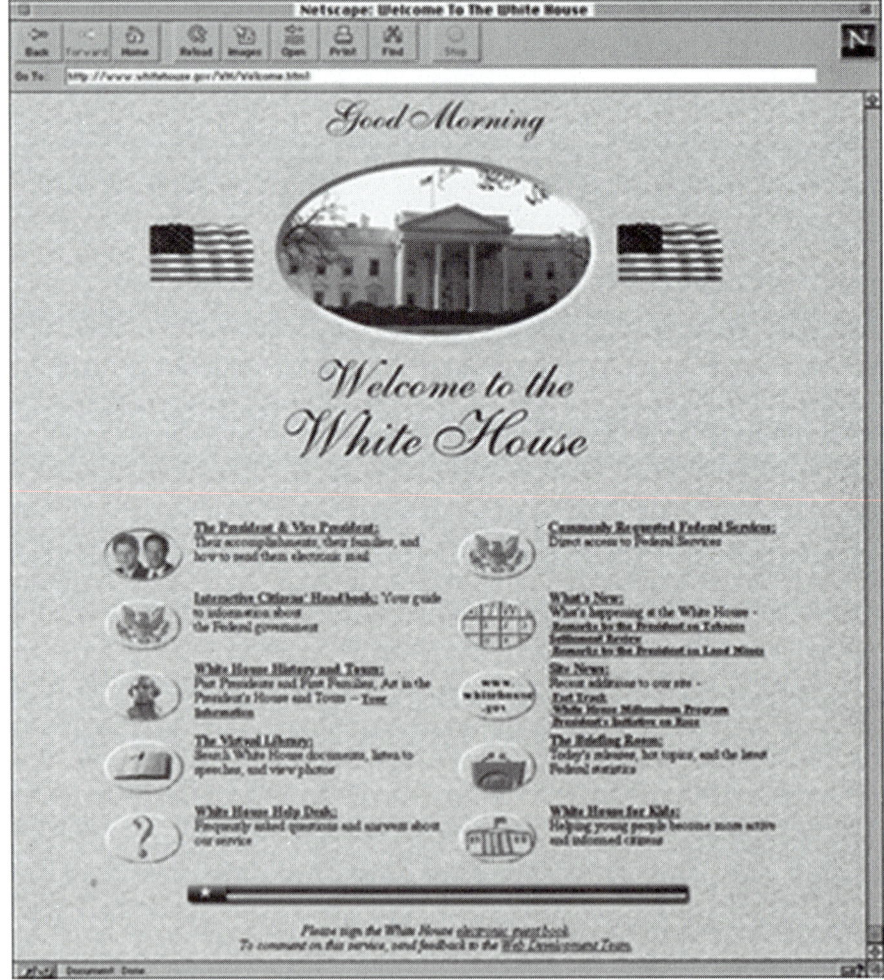

caught pneumonia on at least one occasion; moreover, the burdens of the Vietnam War put both him and his successor, Richard Nixon, under severe psychological strain. (Nixon also was stressed by the Watergate scandal.) Reagan had malignant growths removed from his colon and face and may have been subject to the onset of Alzheimer's disease during the later years of his presidency. George Bush was treated for an overactive thyroid (Graves' disease) and had precancerous skin growths removed. Bill Clinton regularly gets shots for allergies and his characteristic hoarseness. He tore a ligament in his knee, which required surgery to repair and the use of crutches during his recovery period. He has begun also begun using a hearing aid.

The effects of illness, injury, and mental stress on presidential performance vary. Some presidents are better able than others to cope with them. In general, the more serious the medical problem and the longer the recovery period, the more removed presidents have become from the day-to-day functioning of their office, with critical decisions delayed or delegated to others.

What is more difficult to discern is how decision making is affected when presidents are not feeling up to par or when their judgment is affected by medication or pain. Consider, for example, the incredible amount of activity that President Bush engaged in at the beginning of the Persian Gulf crisis. Determined not to become a prisoner of the White House as Jimmy Carter had been during the early months of the Iranian hostage crisis in 1979, Bush frantically vacationed in Maine with what a journalist described as "nonstop golf and horseshoes, iron-man jogs, marathon set of tennis, relentless trolls for bluefish aboard his speedboat, *Fidelity*."[10] Was this activity a consequence of his overactive thyroid, frustration over his inability to prevent or thwart the Iraqi invasion of Kuwait, or simply business-as-usual for George Bush?

Character

Common sense suggests that personality also affects behavior, but the impact of personality is very hard to discern even by those who are trained to do so. It must be inferred from rhetoric and behavior. How much did George Bush's reaction to press stories that he was weak and indecisive in the failed Panamanian coup attempt in 1989 influence his later decision to use overwhelming military force to invade Panama and remove dictator Manual Noriega from power? How much has Bill Clinton's penchant for compromise been a consequence of his need to play the kind of mediating, healing role that he did between his mother and alcoholic stepfather? Although these questions are difficult to answer with any degree of certainty, the assumption that underlies them still seems valid: that self-esteem, confidence, and feelings of being appreciated, attractive, approved, and in control affect how presidents organize their White House, make decisions, and interact with their aides.

Political scientist James David Barber has advanced a psychological model for explaining presidential behavior in terms of their level of activity (active or passive) and their ability to relate to others and enjoy their work (positive or negative).[11]

Of the four character types in this schema, Barber considers the *active-positive* to be best suited to the presidency. Such a person brings to the office the high level of activity needed to sustain the multiple roles a president must assume. Moreover, a positive attitude toward work generates its own psychological and physical benefits. It contributes to a heightened energy level; it eases the inevitable conflicts that result from competing perspectives, interests, goals,

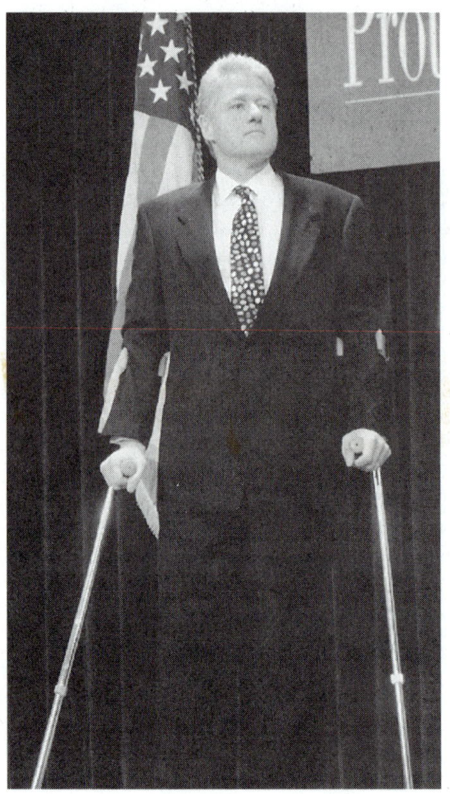

A president's health may affect his decisions and actions, although it is hard to judge exactly how. Shortly into his second term, President Clinton tore a ligament in his knee. The injury required surgery and put him on crutches for weeks, a disability that left the normally vigorous president visibly frustrated.

and ambitions; and it increases tolerance. Presidents who enjoy their work tend to be more eager and better able to take on new and difficult challenges than those who do not. *Active-negative* presidents, on the other hand, tend to be dangerous because they become rigid and unyielding when their decisions are challenged. They take those challenges personally.

Barber's model had been criticized on a number of grounds: (1) his categories are too simplistic and too broad; (2) personalities do not fit neatly or easily into them; and (3) the expectations that flow from them are too general to be useful as explanations for individual behavior, much less as predictions of future actions. Despite these criticisms, the model continues to frame much of the debate on personality and the presidency. Although he has not succeeded in providing a comprehensive theory or an airtight explanation of why presidents behave as they do, Barber has focused attention on the importance of personality and has identified certain facets of it that must be considered in discussions of presidential leadership.

Managerial Style

Presidents interact with their subordinates and make decisions in a variety of ways. Some presidents feel that they must dominate. For example, Lyndon Johnson monopolized discussions with his staff and was unable to accept criticism. Kennedy and Bush treated their assistants more as equals.

Some presidents need to operate in a protective environment. Nixon saw only a few trusted aides and wanted all recommendations and advice to be presented to him in writing. Ford, Eisenhower, and Reagan were more open, saw more people, and were willing to make decisions on the basis of oral presentations.

Some presidents need to be involved in everything. Johnson, Carter, Bush, and Clinton have taken a hands-on approach to decision making. In contrast, Eisenhower and Reagan delegated considerable authority to others, waiting for issues to be brought to them rather than reaching out for them. Obviously, a president's managerial style affects the way his White House works.

Belief System

Belief systems are shaped by the way in which individuals view themselves and others. Beliefs about how the world works provide a frame of reference for presidents, who must filter information, evaluate options, and choose a course of action that is consistent with their policy goals.[12]

The president's world view is especially likely to limit consideration of alternatives in a crisis. The North Korean invasion of South Korea in 1950, the domestic strife in Nicaragua in the mid 1980s, and the Iraqi invasion of Kuwait in 1990 were seen by presidents Truman, Reagan, and Bush, respectively, as threats to the United States and its interests, and they decided that American armed forces needed to be employed. In contrast, President Carter did not view the hostage crisis in Iran as a grave threat to American national security. Preoccupied with safeguarding the lives of those who had been taken prisoner, he spent a year trying to find an acceptable, diplomatic solution to the crisis.

In some situations, presidents do not have strongly held opinions that dictate a particular response. Under such circumstances they will follow opinion—their advisers', the public's, or both—rather than lead it.

THE POLITICS OF PRESIDENTIAL POLICY MAKING

The increasing number of presidential decisions that have major national and international consequences has inflated the importance of the president's character, managerial style, and beliefs. It has also directed attention to the president's changing policy role. The framers of the Constitution intended for presidents to have an impact on public policy, but they did not expect them to dominate the policy process. Yet that is precisely what happens much of the time.

Although presidents have considerable personnel resources at their disposal—policy experts, political strategists, and support staff in the executive branch and the Executive Office—these advisers frequently disagree about what to do and how to do it. Their disagreement, combined with the absence of a public consensus on most major issues, makes the formulation and management of public policy a time-consuming and difficult process. Presidents use diverse strategies and techniques to overcome these constraints in setting an agenda, influencing Congress, building public support, and implementing their priorities.

Setting the Agenda

Presidential agendas used to be laundry lists of proposals designed to appeal to as broad a segment of electoral supporters as possible. Beginning in the 1980s and continuing into the 1990s, however, policy agendas have been of necessity more limited, as scarce resources and continuing budget deficits have forced presidents to reduce the number and costs of their programs.

By limiting their proposals and establishing clear priorities, presidents try to set the pace and tone of public debate and hope to give the impression that they are in charge. Limiting priorities has several advantages for presidents. Not only does it enable them to concentrate their administrations' resources on the issues that are most important to them, but it also gives them leverage over the news media's agenda.

Timing is another strategic concern of presidents intent on achieving their legislative policy goals. Presidential influence tends to decrease over time. As members of Congress position themselves for the next election, as bureaucrats begin to press their claims on political appointees, and as the opposition party begins to coalesce against the incumbent, achieving domestic policy goals may become more difficult for the president. This problem may become acute following a midterm election, as it did for Clinton in 1994. Presidents tend to be least influential at the end of their term, and particularly if it is their second term. During this period, the phrase **lame duck** is often used to describe the incumbent. Like a duck that cannot fly because its wings have been clipped, presidents lose momentum and power as policy makers as their administration draws to a close.

Influencing the Legislature

Presidents have to work hard at influencing Congress. Differing interests, constituencies, and even parties affect presidential and congressional perspectives and policy decisions. Key to success is a president's ability to focus and orchestrate the administration's major efforts, a task that requires the mobilization of cabinet heads, other executive officials, party leaders, and representatives of sympathetic interest groups behind presidential priorities. During the Reagan administration, the White House Office assembled a legislative strategy group to accomplish this task. The Bush and Clinton administrations operated in a more ad hoc manner initially when dealing with Congress, although the Clinton administration improved its legislative coordination after Leon Panetta, a former member of Congress, took over as White House chief of staff, and maintained it under his successor, Erskine Bowles.

The congressional leadership must also be involved in the development of legislative proposals. The nature of that involvement depends on the policy in question as well as on the political composition of Congress. Carter and Reagan relied on their own party's congressional leaders, bringing in the opposition leaders when necessary. Facing opposition majorities in both houses of Congress, Bush in 1989 and Clinton in 1997 tried to assume a more bipartisan approach, which became increasingly difficult as partisan issues emerged and especially as the next election approached.

Regardless of their strategic approach, presidents must be personally involved in lobbying for their legislative goals. The extent of this involvement is often taken as a sign of how much importance is attached to a particular issue. There are a variety of ways for getting involved, ranging from requesting support to twisting arms to making deals. Lyndon Johnson was legendary for effective lobbying. Nixon, Ford, and Carter were not nearly as successful. Presidents cannot dictate to Congress, nor can they easily reverse overwhelming sentiment on an issue. Since 1968, divided government, with different parties controlling Congress and the White House, or geographic or ideological divisions within

FIGURE 11-3
Presidential Success in Congress

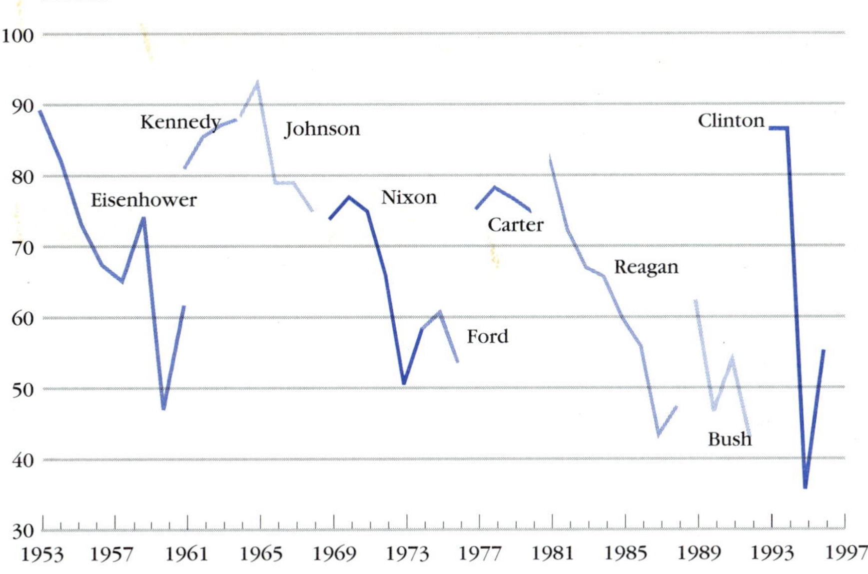

SOURCE: *Congressional Quarterly Weekly Report,* December 21, 1996, 3455.

the majority party in one or both houses, has been the norm. These partisan divisions have reduced the president's effectiveness in dealing with Congress, although they have not eliminated it entirely.

How effective can presidents be? According to political scientist George Edwards, presidents can influence Congress only at the margins.[13] In a closely divided legislature, however, affecting the votes of a few members of Congress can be crucial. One measure of how influential presidents actually are is the proportion of legislation on which members of Congress vote in accordance with the stated position of the president. Figure 11-3 graphs the support scores of presidents since 1953.

Presidential support increases when the president's party controls both houses of Congress. But partisan control is not the guarantee of legislative success that it is in parliamentary systems such as those of Great Britain and Israel, in which straight party voting is expected and prime ministers are selected because they control a partisan legislative majority. In the United States, presidents have to work to build and maintain majorities even within their own party. On the other hand, they may have more success in attracting opposition support than do executives in a parliamentary system. Clinton received more support from Republicans than Democrats in the votes on two free trade initiatives, the North American Free Trade Agreement (NAFTA) and the General Agreement on Tariffs and Trade (GATT), in 1993 and 1994, respectively.

Although presidential influence varies with the issue, presidents generally have had more success on foreign policy issues than on domestic ones. This success, which was particularly evident in the period from the end of World War II to the Vietnam War, led some political scientists to conclude that there were actually two presidencies: one in foreign affairs and one in domestic policy.[14] Today, the distinction between foreign and domestic policies is less clear-cut. Foreign policy issues have a greater impact on domestic policy than they did in earlier decades, and therefore, Congress has become more interested and involved in foreign policy matters. As a consequence, presidents can no longer be assured that their foreign policy initiatives will always prevail. They must mobilize support for them much as they do in the domestic arena.

Although in normal times presidents cannot impose legislation on Congress, by exercising a veto they usually can prevent legislation that they do not like from becoming law. The veto is not absolute, but it is a potent weapon. A very low percentage of all presidential vetoes have been overridden (see Table 10-2 on page 261). In addition, as noted earlier, Congress granted the president a line item veto for appropriations bills. This legislation, if upheld by the courts, allows the president to veto individual items in spending bills. The items could be restored by Congress but would then be subject to a regular veto and the regular override requirement of a two-thirds vote in both houses.

The threat of exercising the veto power is frequently used to try to get Congress to modify a proposal. To make a veto threat stick, however, the president must be prepared to exercise it and must have reason to believe that it will be sustained. George Bush and Bill Clinton have both used the veto effectively as a tactic for dealing with congressional majorities of the opposite party. They indicated how far they were willing to go on legislative proposals, suggested what they were prepared to veto, and sustained their threat by doing so. Both however, suffered veto overrides.

Clinton's most effective use of the veto occurred during his budget battle with the Republican Congress in 1995–1996. First he vetoed a comprehensive budget reconciliation bill in which the Republicans wished to impose greater spending and tax cuts than the president wanted. He then vetoed several appropriations bills that contained what he considered insufficient funding for particular departments and agencies. Because of the failure of Congress and the president to agree on these appropriations, much of the government was forced to shut down twice, suspending many services in the process. The public blamed the Republicans more than Clinton for the shutdowns, creating pressure on them to compromise with the president.

Building Public Support

Because public backing contributes to the president's success in Congress, presidents devote much time and effort to shaping public opinion. The White House Office works hard to promote a favorable image and public response by influencing the form, content, and timing of information that flows from the government. It provides a host of services for the media, from information packets to daily briefings to interviews and photo opportunities. These efforts to shape news coverage of the president can succeed if the media are primarily dependent on material supplied by the White House.

The pomp and ceremony of the presidency also help the president. The public aspects of the institution receive extensive coverage and enhance the stature of the person who occupies the Oval Office. Recognizing this effect, presidents go public more now than in the past.

Jimmy Carter is a good example of a president who used symbolism to boost his popularity. In the aftermath of Watergate, he played down the grandeur of

President Clinton shakes hands with Mexican president Ernesto Zedillo after the two leaders signed a joint declaration on drug trafficking in 1997. Such images of the president as international statesman often boost public support for his administration.

office: he walked down Pennsylvania Avenue following his inauguration, wore a sweater when he delivered his first address to the nation, and dispensed with the playing of "Hail to the Chief" at public ceremonies. But when his popularity declined, he began dressing more formally and reinstated "Hail to the Chief." Other examples of presidents using ceremony to enhance their public image include Bush's address to a joint session of Congress to announce the end of the Persian Gulf War in 1991 and Clinton's involvement in the Bosnian peace accord in 1995, his frequent meetings with world leaders, and his public extensions of empathy to victims of terrorism and natural disasters.

One device that some presidents have used successfully to demonstrate their mastery of the issues and to build support for their programs is the press conference. Roosevelt, Kennedy, Carter, Bush, and Clinton have done well in these forums, where their extensive knowledge about policy and personnel have stood them in good stead with the White House reporters. Reagan fared less well. Lacking detailed information, he was unable to answer questions as accurately and fully as the press demanded. The need for extensive preparation and the fear of making embarrassing mistakes discouraged him from holding many press conferences. Even though Clinton's performances at press conferences have been favorably evaluated, he also has not held many prime-time press conferences, preferring the more congenial public format of a town meeting with average citizens to the more adversarial confrontation with the Washington press corps.

The extensive efforts by the White House to secure favorable media coverage are a direct response to the situation in which presidents often find themselves. The general public is often divided, uninterested, and uninvolved; but organized groups, political parties, and public officials are not shy about taking stands and promoting their positions. Thus the president has to take his communicator-in-chief role seriously and try to build consensus both inside and outside the government.

Implementing Priorities in the Executive Branch

Implementation is the final stage in the policy process. Here the president must deal primarily with officials in the executive branch. Traditionally presidents have not gotten deeply involved in the details of implementation because of the size of the bureaucracy, time constraints, and their limited resources for affecting executive-branch decisions. However, with the increased attention given to management issues such as bureaucratic red tape, federal contracting, nonperformance of services, and allegations of mismanagement, the efficient operation of government has become a salient concern for every administration.

The easiest and most direct way for presidents to exercise control over policy implementation is to have White House aides communicate their wishes to those in the departments and agencies who are responsible for implementing them. In most cases a telephone call or White House meeting will suffice. Occasionally an executive order may be necessary.

The president can also oversee the regulations that departments and agencies issue to implement legislation. President Carter standardized procedures for issuing these regulations, and President Reagan created the division in the Office of Management and Budget that reviews them. Their successors have continued this review process.

A significant part of the president's management problem is rooted in the sharing of powers, which creates multiple allegiances for executive branch agencies; they must be sensitive both to the interests of Congress and to those of the presidency. Part of the difficulty also stems from a civil service system based on merit and not partisanship. Finally, the development of an outside clientele for the departments and agencies has also eroded the president's influence. Even political appointees must be sensitive to the interests and needs of their department's constituency. When those interests and needs are at odds with the president's, political appointees face a dilemma. If they are to maintain credibility with the clients they serve, they must be advocates for them; but over time this advocacy may strain their relationship with the president.

Presidential Leadership

The problems that presidents encounter in their efforts to make and implement public policy are the consequences of multiple pressures that affect all aspects of presidential decision making. In a pluralistic society in which political actors and institutions are responsive to their clienteles, politics is likely to occur within and among institutions of government, making it hard for any one of them to dominate the policy-making process.

This situation is precisely what the framers desired and the Constitution intended. It places the burden on the advocates of change: it is they who must form coalitions and gain the support of those who share power. This burden of consensus building often falls on the president's shoulders, and it is a heavy one. Reflecting on his first two years in office, Clinton commented: "I was a prime minister, not a president. I got caught up in the parliamentary aspect of the presidency and missed the leadership, the bully pulpit function which is so critical."[15]

The dilemma, as we explained at the beginning of this chapter, is the gap that often exists between public expectations and presidential performance. Sometimes the gap can be bridged by the exercise of strong political leadership. But even if the president does try to exercise that leadership, even if the president is sensitive to the politics of the presidency, success is not guaranteed. Presidents still must contend with factors beyond their personal and institutional control; they are still hostage to events. In the end, their reaction to events, what they say and do when conditions are not favorable, is the true test of their leadership skills. In good times, it is harder to exercise these skills; presidents tend to merely preside over the government. In bad times, power flows to them; they may prevail.

CASE STUDY

THE CLINTON HEALTH-CARE FIASCO

This is a story that illustrates the difficulty of exerting presidential leadership. It is a story of a problem, a promise, and a proposal, but no policy solution. It is also a story of shifting public moods, conflicting interest-group pressures, and partisan and ideological divisions, all of which combined to thwart a major presidential initiative. It is the story of the health-care issue that preoccupied the Clinton administration during 1993 and 1994 and ultimately brought it to its knees.

During his campaign for nomination and election in 1992, Bill Clinton talked about the need for changes in the nation's health-care system and promised to propose legislation to reform it within the first 100 days of his administration—a promise that he tried but failed to keep. Five days after he took his oath of office, Clinton met with senior White House staff, cabinet officials, and his wife, Hillary Rodham Clinton, to discuss health-care issues and what to do about them. There were two major problems: more than 37 million Americans were uninsured or underinsured, and their numbers were rising; and medical costs were increasing by more than 10 percent per year, far more than the rate of inflation. Americans were concerned. They believed the system was broken and needed fixing; it was too expensive and inefficient. But a majority of them were also satisfied with their own doctors and with the quality of the health care they personally received. The dilemma for the president, then, was how to address the coverage, cost, and efficiency issues without adversely affecting the choice of physicians and the quality of health care that Americans had come to expect.

The president decided to form a task force to explore these problems and make recommendations to him within the first 100 days of his administration. To demonstrate his resolve, he asked his wife to oversee the task force's effort. By creating a presidential task force and putting Mrs. Clinton in charge of it, the president raised the political stakes for himself and for his administration.

The initial plan was to assemble a relatively small group of policy experts, primarily from outside the government, to design an innovative health-care system that addressed the president's two primary concerns: cost and coverage.

But the number of participants mushroomed when Democratic members of Congress and department secretaries, anxious to get in on the action, volunteered their staffs. Eventually the total exceeded 600, an extraordinarily large figure considering that maintaining presidential control over the reform initiative, constraining outside pressures on it, and preventing leaks were three of the principal rationales for setting up a presidential task force in the first place.

To combat the size problem, the task force was organized into eight teams and thirty-four groups that examined different aspects of the health-care problem, drafted working papers, and designed proposals for a senior group of advisers to consider. The senior group met every night, sometimes until two or three o'clock in the morning, for several months to iron out problems, propose solutions, and figure out their cost. "It was grueling, exhausting," said one of the participants. "Every night it was always, 'God we gotta get this done tonight.' It drove some of the policy people who had different opinions berserk, but that's how decisions were made."

To combat the leaks problem, the task force teams and groups at first met behind closed doors. Republican members of Congress, whose staffs had not been invited to join the policy-making groups, objected to the secrecy. They instituted a legal challenge on the grounds that officials on government salary were participating and that therefore the public had a right to know what was happening. A federal court agreed, forcing the task force to open its doors.

Although the task force was officially disbanded on May 31, it was not until early September, almost 200 days into the new administration, that the president made his final decisions on health care, with the help, of course, of the first lady. The president's delay in arriving at a policy was caused by two factors: the complexity of the problem and comprehensiveness of the proposed solution, and the need to focus on his other priorities, especially deficit reduction, during this period.

On September 22, 1993, the president finally delivered his health-care address to a joint session of Congress. "The health care system is badly broken and we need to fix it," he said. "We must make this our most urgent priority." Despite the appeal to urgency, however, it took more than three weeks for the administration's bill, all 1,342 pages of it, to reach Congress. The bill was so large and comprehensive that it went to five separate House and Senate committees, along with other health-care proposals that had been introduced by both Republican and Democratic members.

As Congress considered the legislation, numerous interest groups, which had initially been reluctant to criticize the president's proposals and Mrs. Clinton's defense of them, sprang into action. They raised objections to almost every aspect of the administration's plan. Small business opposed the bill's requirement that employers pay the health insurance costs of their employees; private insurers criticized the health-care alliances that employers and employees had to join, particularly the limited choices of doctors, insurers, and benefits that would be available for participants; health-care providers, including pharmaceutical companies, public and private hospitals, and some medical professionals, opposed any attempt by the government or a special commission to set prices.

Many of the groups active in the health-care debate mounted extensive public relations campaigns to supplement their congressional lobbying efforts to convince the American people of the merits of their arguments. Most effective were the "Harry and Louise" ads sponsored by the Health Insurance Association of America, a well-financed trade association headed by a former member of Congress, Willis (Bill) Gradison, who had served on one of the health subcommittees while in Congress. Harry and Louise, a typical middle-class couple, feared that the administration's proposals would limit their choice of doctors and health-care providers, would bankrupt the federal treasury, and would create another huge government bureaucracy. Their objections became the principal criticisms of the Clinton plan.

In the face of these criticisms, public opinion began to turn against the administration. Within months, opponents outnumbered supporters. The shift in public sentiment naturally affected members of Congress as they performed their dual roles of lawmaking and representation. Members wrestled with the intricacies of the issue and at the same time tried to respond to the needs, interests, and demands of their constituents. Their quandary and inability to reach a consensus was captured by the news media, whose coverage highlighted the disagreements within Congress and between it and the White House.

Diverted by other issues, defensive about its own proposal, encountering increasing opposition from within its own party, the administration was unable to mount an effective counterattack. The plan was too comprehensive to explain easily to the American people. Health-care reform, which had held so much promise in 1992, gradually died of its own weight in Congress in 1994.

It was a bitter loss for the president, Congress, and its Democratic majority. The president had failed to achieve his principal legislative priority. He had also lost most of his other legislative proposals, which were delayed because of health care. In fact, health care became *the* metaphor for failed presidential leadership. The president's prestige suffered; his political capital was depleted; his party lost control of Congress in the 1994 elections; and the problems the legislation was intended to address remained unresolved.

Discussion Questions

1. Who were the principal protagonists in the health-care controversy, and what did they want?
2. What were the issues, and why weren't they resolved?
3. What was the impact of the health-care fiasco on the president, on his party, and on the country? Was this impact long or short term?

SUMMARY

The presidency is a political institution. It operates within a political environment that requires the skillful exercise of power. Politics generates the demands and pressures on the president, the issues and conflicts that need to be resolved, and the resources that can be utilized in that resolution. In this sense, the politics of the presidency creates both challenges and opportunities; how presidents handle them becomes in large measure the criterion by which their performance in office and place in history are evaluated.

In empowering the president with executive responsibilities, the framers gave the institution a broad grant of authority, to be checked by the requirement for joint institutional involvement in the exercise of most of those powers. Thus the president could nominate subject to the advice and consent of the Senate; subsequently the president was given the right to remove political appointees in the executive branch. As chief executive, the president could direct subordinates through *executive orders* and *executive memoranda,* but Congress retained the authority to structure the executive branch as well as authorize its programs and appropriate funds for them. The president was also given some legislative duties and responsibilities, including the right to recommend and the power to veto. But Congress has the last word. The president can also affect the judiciary through the nomination of judges, and the issuance of pardons, clemency, and amnesty for those convicted or accused of federal crimes.

The president's limited constitutional and statutory authority but growing roles and responsibilities have forced those who have occupied the Oval Office to utilize their political skills to compensate for their lack of formal powers. In doing so, they have had to bargain with and cajole others in the government and build support outside of it by *going public.* How they perform these tasks affects their reputation and prestige, which impact on their ability to achieve their policy goals.

The institutional resources of the presidency contribute to its exercise of power. These resources include the *cabinet* and the *Executive Office of the President,* which together function to maximize presidential information, liaison, and influence. In addition, the vice president and the president's spouse now play important and sometimes controversial roles in the administration.

How presidents interact with others, how they approach their job, and how flexible they are all depend to a large extent on their character, style, and world views. These aspects of their personality affect their performance in office.

A key to presidents' success is their ability to set and promote a policy agenda, mobilize support for it, and oversee its implementation. These are not easy tasks, because the problems are complex, the time frames for fixing them are usually short, and the resources at the president's disposal are limited. But the real difficulty for presidents is getting others with different goals, different perspectives, different time frames, and different constituencies to follow their lead. This requires great skill in defining the issue, shaping the political environment, selling a course of action to the American people, and bargaining with other public officials. In general, in normal times, presidents have more discretion and influence on foreign than domestic policy.

KEY TERMS

executive order
executive memorandum
going public
cabinet
Executive Office of the President
Office of Management and Budget
central clearance process
enrolled bill process
regulatory review
White House Office
lame duck

RESOURCES

READINGS

Barber, James David. *The Presidential Character.* 4th ed. Englewood Cliffs, N.J.: Prentice-Hall, 1992. A pioneering but controversial study of the impact of personality on performance in office. Short, psychologically oriented chapters on individual presidents make for interesting reading and speculative interpretations.

Edwards, George C., III, and Stephen J. Wayne. *Presidential Leadership.* 4th ed. New York: St. Martin's Press, 1997. A comprehensive text that synthesizes the principal political science literature on and knowledge about the presidency.

Jones, Charles O. *The Presidency in a Separated System.* Washington, D.C.: Brookings Institution, 1994. Assesses the presidency within the framework of the constitutional system of separate institutions competing for shared powers.

Kernell, Samuel. *Going Public.* 3rd ed. Washington, D.C.: Congressional Quarterly, 1997. Argues effectively that presidents need to adopt a public strategy to achieve their policy objectives.

Nelson, Michael. *The Presidency and the Political System.* 5th ed. Washington, D.C.: Congressional Quarterly, 1997. An excellent collection of readings on multiple aspects of the contemporary presidency.

Neustadt, Richard E. *Presidential Power and the Modern President.* New York: Free Press, 1990. The classic study, originally published in 1960, of the president's basic leadership dilemma: how to exert influence within a highly decentralized political system in normal times. To this work, Neustadt has added his reflections in chapters dealing with presidents Kennedy through Carter.

Skowronek, Stephen. *The Politics Presidents Make.* Cambridge, Mass.: Belknap Press, 1993. An intellectually sophisticated study of leadership patterns in the presidency from John Adams to George Bush.

ORGANIZATIONS

Center for the Study of the Presidency, 208 East 75th Street, New York, NY 10021; phone (212) 249-1200, fax (212) 628-9503. E-mail thecsp@aol.com Publishes the journal *Presidential Studies Quarterly* and occasional books; organizes annual conferences on the presidency.

White Burkett Miller Center of Public Affairs, University of Virginia, Charlottesville, VA 22901; phone (804) 924-7236, fax (804) 982-2739; Internet http://www.virginia.edu/miller Holds seminars and publishes monographs and articles on the contemporary presidency.

12

The Executive Bureaucracy

PREVIEW

- The organization of the federal bureaucracy: types of organizational structures; staffing the bureaucracy
- Functions of the executive bureaucracy; implementation; policy making; determinants of bureaucratic influence
- Problems of accountability: legal and legislative controls; popular participation; the adequacy of controls

On April 19, 1995, Americans were horrified by sights of devastation from the terrorist bombing of the Alfred P. Murrah Federal Building in Oklahoma City. But not many thought of this awful attack as having much to do with politics. In fact, it did—in many ways.

After weeks of dangerous digging, it was determined that 167 people had died in the rubble. Some of these were children in a day-care center. Many were citizens tending to their business with the Social Security Administration, the Department of Transportation, or one of the twelve other federal agencies and departments that had offices in the building. Many more were employees in these offices—bureaucrats—doing their jobs.

One of those employees was Julie Welch. Twenty-three years old and a recent graduate of Marquette University, Welch was starting her career as an interpreter for the Social Security Administration, helping Spanish-speaking citizens in their dealings with the federal government. At her funeral the following week, her friends noted her compassion for people less fortunate than she was and her pleasure at having found a job that allowed her to help them.[1]

Over the next few months, investigators began trying to put together the story behind the bombing. According to federal indictments, it was the work of several men upset with the actions of the Federal Bureau of Investigation (FBI) and the Bureau of Alcohol, Tobacco, and Firearms (ATF). The indictments alleged that the perpetrators particularly resented the bureaus' 1993 raid on the Texas compound of the Branch Davidian religious sect, which resulted in dozens of deaths, and the 1992 attack on the Idaho home of white separatist Randy Weaver, in which ATF agents shot and killed Weaver's wife.

Whether or not it was the target of the Oklahoma City bombing, the ATF has long been a controversial federal agency. Its mission is to regulate traffic in three commodities—alcohol, tobacco, and guns—that are widely possessed in America, sometimes legally, sometimes not. Often, ATF agents must track and arrest citizens who are breaking laws that many Americans dislike or routinely disobey. Moreover, these citizens are often violent and heavily armed criminals who would rather shoot than surrender.

So ATF agents are often in the spotlight and often criticized for heavy-handedness and overreaction. In fact, in the months that followed the Oklahoma City bombing, several congressional committees conducted investigations of the ATF and FBI to determine whether their actions in the Texas and Idaho incidents had violated the law or appropriate administrative procedure.

In a complex government like America's, there is a constant tension between the need to delegate authority to executive agencies to implement the law and the need to hold these agencies accountable for their exercise of that authority. Americans often disagree about whether administrative agencies perform well or badly. Some want to give agencies more latitude to do their jobs; others want tighter restraints to prevent them from exceeding their proper authority. Often the debates take place in Congress, in the legislative and oversight processes. And sometimes, as perhaps in Oklahoma City, there is no debate at all—only wanton acts of violence seeking to make a political point.

The federal bureaucracy is the part of the government that implements decisions made by the president, Congress, and the federal courts. The administrative offices and the people who staff them are important political actors. Having their own policy preferences and prejudices, they fight to protect and expand their own vision of what is best for the country. They are not merely neutral implementors of decisions made elsewhere in the political process; they are at the center of that process, involved in the struggles among individuals, interest groups, and government institutions to affect decisions. One cannot understand the administration of public policy without acknowledging its fundamental political character. Politics is as common an occurrence and as profound a force in the halls and offices of federal agencies as it is anywhere else in government.

The word *bureaucrat* is loosely used to describe career government employees. It often brings to mind a bored and rigid person interested only in collecting a paycheck and putting in the time to get a lucrative pension. But among the millions of career government employees, many have demanding, important, and interesting jobs, and most enjoy their work and do it skillfully.

This chapter looks at American public servants, the work they do, and the political environment they do it in. The discussion begins with the size and shape of the contemporary executive branch, how it is structured and staffed. Then the chapter examines the roles that bureaucratic agencies play in the policy-making process. It concludes by probing the issue of bureaucratic accountability.

THE ORGANIZATION OF THE FEDERAL BUREAUCRACY

Bureaucracy is a system for carrying on the business of an organization by means of a clear hierarchy of authority and an emphasis on fixed routines. Bureaucracies have jurisdictions established by law or administrative rules, and their employees are specialists who are trained to perform the specific tasks assigned to them and who maintain written records of their decisions and activities. The point of bureaucracies is to achieve objectivity, precision, efficiency, continuity, consistency, and fairness.

Except for the Post Office Department, the administrative agencies of the United States government were few in number and small in size until the second half of the nineteenth century. Their growth began to accelerate after the Civil War as the population and the range of federal activities expanded. Nevertheless, the federal bureaucracy remained a relatively small enterprise until the onset of the Great Depression and World War II. Today, the executive branch is the largest component of the federal government. Its civilian employees number 3 million; its military employees, 1.4 million, and there are more than a hundred separate organizational units. In size and complexity, the federal executive branch is an entity without peer in American society.

Types of Organizational Structures

The federal bureaucracy comprises many kinds of organizations. Because the labels attached to particular units do not always precisely define their functions or levels of authority, its structure is a little difficult to comprehend at first. Sometimes an "agency," a "bureau," and an "office" are indistinguishable from one another. Some agencies are subunits of cabinet departments, and others are independent from those departments. A bureau may be a small, barely visible unit like the Bureau of Quality Control in the Health Care Financing Administration, or it may be relatively large and highly visible, like the FBI.

Politics is responsible for this apparent confusion, because the creation of bureaucratic organizations is itself a political process. What a unit is called, where it is placed in the executive branch, the degree of authority it is granted, and the qualifications established for its leaders are all political decisions. They reflect the balance of political forces existing at the time the unit was created. Because the balance of political forces changes over time, units created in one period often differ from units created in another. Figure 12-1 shows the organizational structure of the entire federal government.

Departments The major operating units of the federal government are **departments**. There are fourteen of them, each an aggregate of many related functions. As noted in Chapter 11, the head of a department—the secretary or, in the case of the Justice Department, the attorney general—is a member of the president's cabinet. The number of departments is not fixed. In the late 1970s, two new ones were added: the Department of Education and the Department of Energy. In 1988, the Veterans Administration, an independent agency, was replaced with the Department of Veterans' Affairs.

Agencies In general, an **agency** is responsible for a narrower set of functions than a department. Some agencies exist within departments, and some are independent. The Social Security Administration, a very large agency, is part of the Department of Health and Human Services. The Coast Guard, another agency, is located in the Department of Transportation in peacetime and in the Department of Defense in wartime. The General Services Administration and the United States Information Agency are independent agencies; they are not components of any of the departments.

Although an agency's jurisdiction is likely to be narrower than a department's, some agencies spend more money and employ more people than some departments do. For example, the National Aeronautics and Space Administration is an independent agency that had an annual budget of more than $14 billion for fiscal year 1996. The State Department had an annual budget of $5 billion in the same year.

Bureaus, offices, administrations, services The subunits of agencies and departments have a variety of names, none denoting a set of consistent, distinguishable characteristics. In the Department of Agriculture, for instance, the Food and Nutrition Service, the Packers and Stockyards Administration, and the World Agricultural Outlook Board are all located at roughly the same level in the hierarchy. The differences in their titles do not indicate significant differences in their authority or functions. Bureaus and other subunits are the specialized operating units of the government. Their jurisdictions are defined by the programs Congress has assigned to them and tend to be quite specific.

Independent regulatory commissions Each **independent regulatory commission** is independent of any department and to some extent is independent of presidential control. Each is run by a group of commissioners and has both quasi-legislative and quasi-judicial authority—that is, it can issue rules and regulations and can adjudicate disputes and issue rulings. The principal purpose of the regulatory commissions is to regulate commerce and trade in an assigned area of jurisdiction. For example, the Securities and Exchange Commission (SEC) regulates the stock markets, and the Federal Communications Commission (FCC) regulates telephones and the use of the public airwaves for radio and television broadcasting.

Currently, there are about a dozen independent regulatory commissions. Each has at least five commissioners, who serve for fixed but staggered terms. The president is permitted to make appointments only as vacancies occur and thus does not have the same degree of control over personnel in these units as over employees in the agencies and departments.

FIGURE 12-1
The Government of the United States

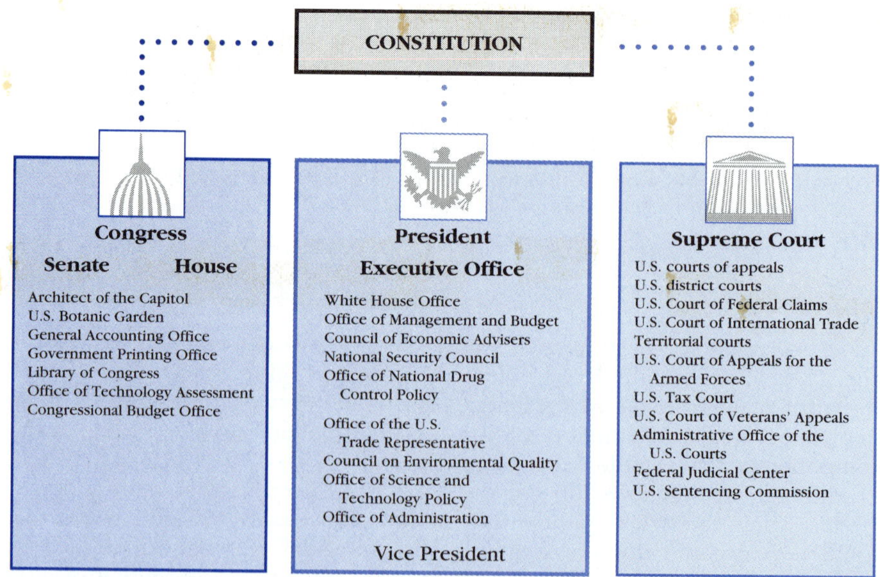

FIGURE 12-1 *(Continued)*

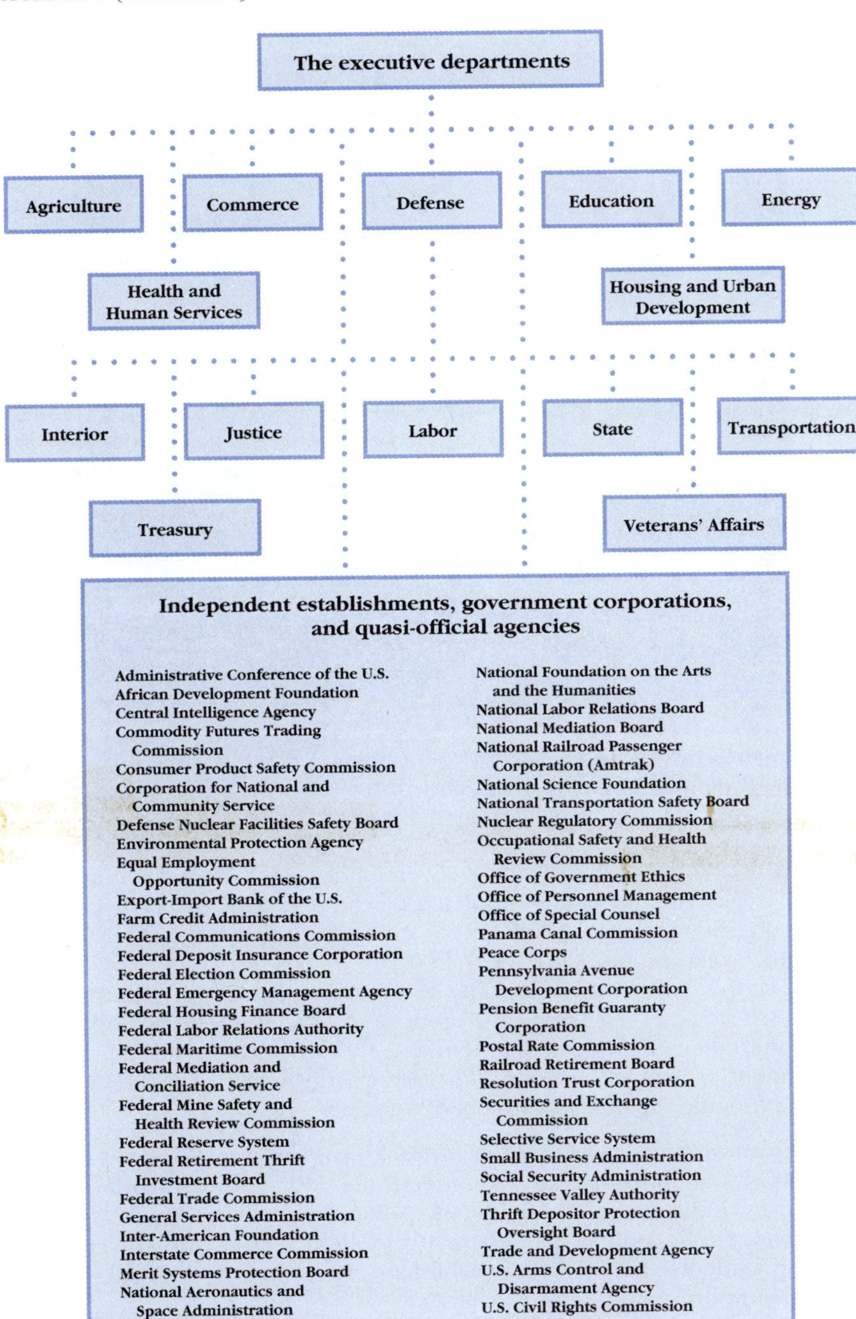

The executive departments
Agriculture
Commerce
Defense
Education
Energy
Health and Human Services
Housing and Urban Development
Interior
Justice
Labor
State
Transportation
Treasury
Veterans' Affairs
Independent establishments, government corporations, and quasi-official agencies
Administrative Conference of the U.S.
African Development Foundation
Central Intelligence Agency
Commodity Futures Trading Commission
Consumer Product Safety Commission
Corporation for National and Community Service
Defense Nuclear Facilities Safety Board
Environmental Protection Agency
Equal Employment Opportunity Commission
Export-Import Bank of the U.S.
Farm Credit Administration
Federal Communications Commission
Federal Deposit Insurance Corporation
Federal Election Commission
Federal Emergency Management Agency
Federal Housing Finance Board
Federal Labor Relations Authority
Federal Maritime Commission
Federal Mediation and Conciliation Service
Federal Mine Safety and Health Review Commission
Federal Reserve System
Federal Retirement Thrift Investment Board
Federal Trade Commission
General Services Administration
Inter-American Foundation
Interstate Commerce Commission
Merit Systems Protection Board
National Aeronautics and Space Administration
National Archives and Records Administration
National Capital Planning Commission
National Credit Union Administration
National Foundation on the Arts and the Humanities
National Labor Relations Board
National Mediation Board
National Railroad Passenger Corporation (Amtrak)
National Science Foundation
National Transportation Safety Board
Nuclear Regulatory Commission
Occupational Safety and Health Review Commission
Office of Government Ethics
Office of Personnel Management
Office of Special Counsel
Panama Canal Commission
Peace Corps
Pennsylvania Avenue Development Corporation
Pension Benefit Guaranty Corporation
Postal Rate Commission
Railroad Retirement Board
Resolution Trust Corporation
Securities and Exchange Commission
Selective Service System
Small Business Administration
Social Security Administration
Tennessee Valley Authority
Thrift Depositor Protection Oversight Board
Trade and Development Agency
U.S. Arms Control and Disarmament Agency
U.S. Civil Rights Commission
U.S. Information Agency
U.S. International Development Cooperation Agency
U.S. International Trade Commission
U.S. Postal Service

SOURCE: *United States Government Manual,* 1995/96 (Washington, D.C.: Government Printing Office, 1995), 22.

The range of jobs is extremely varied—everything from guarding presidents to maintaining trails at national parks.

Government corporations The federal government owns, in whole or in part, a variety of economic enterprises. Most of these are operated as **government corporations**,[2] a form of ownership that is supposed to protect the enterprises against political meddling and encourage them to use businesslike and efficient methods of operation. Most of the government corporations have a board of directors whose members are appointed by the president, usually for long and staggered terms that make it difficult for any single president to radically change the board's composition.

Most of the corporations can operate their own personnel systems, borrow money, sell stock, even operate at a profit. Some, like the Federal Deposit Insurance Corporation (FDIC) and the Tennessee Valley Authority (TVA), are totally independent. Others fall within a department's jurisdiction, like the Commodity Credit Corporation in the Department of Agriculture.

Boards, committees, commissions, advisory committees In addition to the major structural entities already identified, the federal government contains a great many units of lesser significance. Few of these have any significant impact on public policy. Rather, many of them serve primarily as places where presidents can make appointments to reward individuals for their political support.

Staffing the Bureaucracy

Despite the variations in the organizational units that make up the executive bureaucracy, and the efforts that have been made to limit political influence in some of them, no bureaucratic structure can be immune from or insensitive to the strong political forces at work in its environment. Administrative decisions have political consequences and hence are subject to political pressures and cross-pressures. The nature of democracy requires that government officials be responsive to the publics they serve. However, the extent to which that responsiveness is partisan in character has long been the subject of controversy, especially in the selection of personnel to serve in the executive branch.

Before 1883, nonelective positions in the federal bureaucracy were filled by means of **patronage**—the distribution of jobs by winning candidates to those who had worked for their political campaign and supported their party. "To the victor go the spoils" was the rallying cry of the day, and the spoils of election victory were usually jobs in government. This use of patronage in federal employment was known as the **spoils system**.[3]

By the latter part of the nineteenth century, the spoils system had fallen into disrepute: administration was often in the hands of political hacks, corruption was common, and fending off job seekers was a major burden for successful politicians. In 1881, a disappointed applicant for a federal job shot and killed President James A. Garfield, an event that strengthened cries for reform of the federal personnel system. In 1883, Congress responded by passing the Pendleton Act, which established the **civil service system**.

The civil service system requires that two important criteria be met in hiring people for government jobs. First, jobs must be open to any citizen regardless of his or her political preference; everyone must have an opportunity to compete. Second, civil servants must be chosen on the basis of some objective measure of their abilities—that is, on their merits. Historically, the second criterion has meant qualification based on open, competitive examinations.

The civil service system Today, the civil service system includes more than 90 percent of all federal employees. About two-thirds of the civil service employees are in what is known as the regular **civil service**, a group that includes most of the career employees of the departments and the major agencies. Regardless of where they work, their salaries and fringe benefits are determined by Congress and implemented by the Office of Personnel Management, an independent agency in the executive branch. All civil service positions are graded according to the character of the work to be done, and a pay range is assigned to each grade level.

In 1979, the **Senior Executive Service (SES)** was created to provide departments and agencies with greater flexibility in deploying, compensating, and (if necessary) removing senior managers and technical specialists. There are now about eight thousand SES members, of whom at least 90 percent must always be career federal employees. Although they are entitled, and sometimes encouraged, to move from one agency to another where their skills and experience are needed, most spend their entire careers in a single agency.

About one-third of the federal government's civilian career employees work in agencies that have their own merit systems, distinct from the regular civil service. These agencies include the TVA, the FBI, the Public Health Service, the Foreign Service, and the Postal Service. In addition, members of the uniformed armed services are part of an entirely separate career system with its own ranks and rules.

Among the 10 percent of federal employees who are not part of the career merit system are a variety of people whose jobs are incompatible with systematic personnel procedures or competitive selection techniques. These include presidential appointees to the top positions in the government, some attorneys, faculty members at the military service academies, undercover drug enforcement

Most political appointees in the executive branch serve at the pleasure of the president. In 1994, President Clinton fired Joycelyn Elders, his first surgeon general, after her candid public remarks about young people's sexuality became too politically embarrassing for him.

agents, foreign nationals who work at United States installations overseas, and employees who hold short-term or summer jobs.

Political appointees Nearly all the top-level positions in the executive branch are held by political appointees. Typically, they are individuals from the private sector who serve in the government for only a short time (about two years on average). Included in this group are cabinet secretaries and the senior officers in each of the cabinet departments, heads of the independent agencies, and members of the federal regulatory commissions, all of whom are appointed by the president and confirmed by the Senate.

The system of drawing the highest-ranking executive-branch officials from the private sector is uniquely American. No other country relies so heavily on leaders who are not career government employees. The American approach has several advantages. It ensures a constant infusion of new creative energy and fosters responsiveness to the popular will. Moreover, the dual tests of presidential nomination and Senate confirmation promote care and judiciousness in the choice of people to fill important government offices.[4]

But there are disadvantages as well. For one thing, leaders often lack experience or technical competence in the complex policy areas over which they have jurisdiction. Many members of regulatory commissions, for example, receive their appointments as rewards for previous support of the president. In addition, the short tenure of most appointees leads to inconsistency in administration and policy direction and creates a greater potential for ethical violations, since appointees tend to be less aware of and less influenced by ethical codes for government employees than are career civil servants. Many appointees are more concerned with making an impact in a brief time than with management or program initiatives that may take a while to bear fruit.

FUNCTIONS OF THE EXECUTIVE BUREAUCRACY

Many people assume that the executive bureaucracy merely executes policy decisions made by Congress and the president. In fact, the administrative agencies of the federal government are themselves important participants in policy making. Almost every public policy is shaped in some ways by the characteristics and the actions of the agencies that oversee its implementation.

Implementation

The primary task of federal agencies is to interpret and implement the public policies that emerge from the legislative process. For example, if a statute declares that the average fuel efficiency of automobiles sold in the United States must be 23 miles per gallon, an agency has to determine when and how to measure fuel efficiency, how to certify satisfaction of the standard, and how to bring companies that fail to meet the standard into compliance. Authority to perform these functions is delegated to the agency by Congress. In exercising such authority, however, the agency normally has a great deal of discretion.[5]

The principal responsibility of most public agencies is action. They are the delivery end of the policy-making process, the government's agents in dealing directly with the people (hence the name *agency*). Their task is to translate the policy objectives determined in the legislative process into goods and services that will help accomplish those objectives. They do this in a number of ways, including regulation, rule making, adjudication, and compliance enforcement.

Regulation In regulating economic and social activity, agencies are guided by two primary objectives: (1) to maintain the stability of the free-market system and its openness to competition, and (2) to protect the health, safety, and welfare of the American people. The first agency designed solely to perform regulatory activities was the Interstate Commerce Commission, established in 1887. Many others have been added since. There are now few economic functions that do not fall under the regulatory jurisdiction of one or more federal agencies in what has become a heavily regulated American economy.[6]

Since the late 1960s, however, there has been a significant movement toward **deregulation**—freeing some industries from the broad government control of earlier years.[7] The effects of deregulation on commercial air travel are generally well known. For more than four decades, the Civil Aeronautics Board (CAB) regulated domestic air travel. During that time, no major new national air carriers entered the marketplace, and CAB decisions tightly controlled airline fares and routes. In the 1970s, the president and Congress moved to deregulate the airline industry in order to stimulate competition. The CAB went out of existence, price competition intensified, new airlines sprouted up, and several mergers occurred. In the years that followed, many airlines experienced financial problems, the cost of some air travel escalated, concern about safety grew, and some people called for reregulation of the industry by the federal government.

Rule making Most agencies, operating within the jurisdiction granted them by Congress, have the authority to issue rules. Rules are best described as elaborations of the law. If the law says that you cannot fly an airplane without a pilot's license, rules will describe in detail the steps that you must take to get a license and the penalties you will incur if you fly without one. Rules have the force of law.

WHERE ON THE WEB?

THE FEDERAL BUREAUCRACY

Would you like to apply for a federal job? Have you ever wondered whether a bill you've heard about has become a law? Would you like to visit an Internet site that links you to any agency or department in the federal government? The following Internet sites can help you navigate the complicated bureaucracy that makes up the federal government.

FEDWORLD

http://www.fedworld.gov/

A gateway site to most federal agencies and sources of federal government information. FedWorld is a good starting point for any search for information about the federal government.

FEDERAL REGISTER

http://www.gpo.ucop.edu/search/fedfld.html

The *Federal Register* is the official publication for presidential documents and executive orders as well as notices, rules, and proposed rules from federal agencies and organizations. The *Federal Register* is published Monday through Friday, except federal holidays.

GOVERNMENT MANUAL

http://www.gpo.ucop.edu/catalog/govman.html

The Government Manual is prepared by the Office of the Federal Register, National Archives. It contains a description of the functions, organization, and leading officials of every federal department and agency, as well as organizational charts of most agencies.

UNITED STATES CODE

http://www.gpo.ucop.edu/search/uscode.html

The United States Code is prepared and published by the Office of the Law Revision Counsel, U.S. House of Representatives, and contains the general and permanent laws of the United States in effect as of January 1994 or January 1995, depending on the title.

APPLYING FOR A FEDERAL JOB

http://helix.nih.gov:8001/jobs/of510.html

Complete information on how to apply for federal jobs provided by the U.S. Office of Personnel Management.

In making rules, agencies must follow procedures laid down in the Administrative Procedures Act of 1946 and its amendments. A number of steps must be completed before a new rule can take effect.[8] For example, the draft of a new rule must be published in the *Federal Register* at least thirty days before the rule is to go into effect. When the draft of the rule is published, the agency must invite public comment on it. After the comments have been reviewed (a task that may take months or even years) and any changes are made, the rule is issued officially when it is published in final form in the *Federal Register* and codified in a volume called the *Code of Federal Regulations*.

Adjudication No matter how diligently executive agencies strive to remove ambiguity from the rules they issue, they are never completely successful. There are always some areas of uncertainty about the application of a specific law or rule to a particular circumstance. An agency may interpret a rule to mean one thing; a corporation may interpret it to mean another. When such differences of opinion occur, the agency is often asked to hold a hearing at which the affected party appeals what it perceives as an inappropriate or unfair interpretation.

Each year, for example, the National Highway Traffic Safety Administration (NHTSA) inspects automobiles for safety defects. If it finds a defect, the NHTSA informs the manufacturer and holds a hearing to determine whether to order the automaker to recall all the affected vehicles and repair the defect. To avoid embarrassment and potential financial loss, manufacturers usually voluntarily recall vehicles before the NHTSA requires them to.

The hearings are often run like legal proceedings. Attorneys are usually present for both sides. Sometimes a hearing is presided over by an **administrative law judge**, an independent third party whose rulings are binding on both the agency and the complainant, although either side may appeal a ruling in the federal courts. Many of the rulings are published in the *Federal Register* so that other interested parties can get a clearer picture of the application of rules and laws to specific cases.[9]

Compliance enforcement Ensuring that laws and rules are obeyed is one of the important tasks of executive agencies. For some—the FBI and the Bureau of Alcohol, Tobacco, and Firearms, for instance—it is the dominant concern, but virtually all agencies spend some of their efforts on compliance enforcement.

Some agencies conduct regular, scheduled inspections to ensure that agency guidelines are followed. For example, the Department of Agriculture routinely inspects food-processing facilities; the tag "USDA inspected" on food products indicates that they were processed under conditions that satisfied federal government standards. Other agencies prefer to make unscheduled inspections. The Coast Guard, for instance, follows the practice of stopping private boats without prior notice to inspect their life-saving equipment. In addition, many government agencies employ accountants to examine the financial records of individuals, corporations, or groups to ensure that they are complying with applicable laws and rules. The Internal Revenue Service audits individual and corporate tax returns for this purpose, and the Comptroller of the Currency audits the financial records of national banks.

The imposition of reporting requirements is another way in which compliance enforcement is carried out. Institutions and corporations are required to file periodic reports on their activities. Employers, for instance, must file regular reports on the number of workers they employ, the amounts they have withheld from paychecks for taxes, and other matters relevant to specific businesses.

One other important way in which agencies oversee compliance with laws and rules is by responding to complaints. Noncompliance often harms someone, and the harmed party may bring a complaint to the government agency that has jurisdiction.

PRACTICING DEMOCRACY

USING THE *FEDERAL REGISTER*

The *Federal Register* publishes government regulations and legal notices as they are issued by federal agencies. These include presidential proclamations and executive orders, federal agency documents having general applicability and legal effect, documents required to be published by act of Congress, and other federal agency documents of public interest.

Using the *Federal Register* can be a challenge. The documents it contains are organized by type—notices, proposed rules and regulations, final rules and regulations, and presidential documents. In the notices section are found notices of hearings and investigations, committee meetings, agency decisions and rulings, and other administrative matters. The proposed and final rules and regulations sections contain regulatory documents having general applicability and legal effect. Presidential documents include executive orders, proclamations, and other documents from the president.

Within each type, the documents are organized alphabetically by agency. Each document is filed with the *Federal Register* by the agency; it is then assigned a *Federal Register* document number. For example, the Appalachian States Low-Level Radioactive Waste Commission notice of an open meeting, filed on May 15, 1992, was assigned the number FR Doc 92-11362. The 92 in the number indicates the year the document was filed; the rest of the number indicates that it was the 11,362nd document filed with the *Federal Register* that year. The notice appears on page 21057 of volume 57, number 96, dated May 18, 1992.

A specific document is relatively easy to find if you know its *Federal Register* document number. This number immediately narrows the search to a par-

Policy Making

That agencies play an important role in making public policy is not surprising if you think about it, for agency employees are usually experts in a particular policy area. Because their day-to-day activities provide a unique vantage point for observing the strengths and weaknesses of particular programs, it is only natural for them to suggest policy changes. Soldiers who find that their rifles jam in wet weather may suggest changes in weapon design. Tax auditors who see that much revenue is being lost because of a loophole in the tax laws may recommend changes to close the loophole.

More important, agency employees have ideas of their own. Their training, their experience, and the values that prevail in their work environment shape their perceptions of the form policies should take. Agency staffs may care deeply about the policies for which they are responsible, and they play a very active role in trying to define and perfect them. Often they become vigorous advocates of their own views, negotiating with their superiors in the bureaucracy, with members and staff in Congress, and with their political constituencies to try to bring policies into line with their ideas.[10]

Bureaucratic agencies share some of the characteristics of other institutions that participate in policy making. They are concerned about their own interests; they seek to enlarge their resources and protect their turf; they develop mutually beneficial long-term relationships with other political actors; and they engage in

ticular year and quickly narrows it to a specific week. If you do not know the document number, you must search through the quarterly or cumulative indexes to find the document. The index entries are arranged first under the name of the agency that issued the document, then by the type of document (rule, notice, and so on). The number that appears at the end of each index entry identifies the page in the *Federal Register* on which the document begins.

Determining which agency might have issued a document is often the most difficult part of finding it. A helpful tool is the *United States Government Manual.* This volume, found in most libraries, lists and describes all the branches and departments of the government. Deciding into what category the document falls is a simpler step. Generally, if an issue is still in the decision-making process, documents relating to it (notices of hearings, for example) will be found in the notices section. Once a decision has been made, look in the rules and regulations section to see how it is being implemented. To find presidential documents, two other publications from the *Federal Register* are also useful: *Codification of Presidential Proclamations and Executive Orders* and *Weekly Compilation of Presidential Documents.*

Even experienced researchers sometimes have trouble finding documents in the *Federal Register*. Fortunately, helpful staff members in the Finding Aids Unit of the National Archives are readily available by telephone at (202) 523-5227. The *Federal Register* is published daily, Monday through Friday, by the Office of the Federal Register, National Archives and Records Administration. Copies are found in most large libraries and in all federal depository libraries. In addition, access to the *Federal Register* is increasingly available through the Internet. The Government Printing Office maintains a Website **(http://thorplus.lib.purdue.edu.80/gpo/)** that provides text from the *Federal Register* for 1994 to the present.

bargaining and negotiation to accomplish their objectives. The political character of the American policy-making process shapes the bureaucracy as thoroughly as it shapes Congress, the courts, the presidency, and interest-group activity. But bureaucratic agencies are also distinct from other kinds of government decision makers in some important ways: their hierarchical organization, their character and culture, their professionalization, and their organizational pathologies.

Hierarchy Most bureaucratic decision making is hierarchical. Policy proposals typically emerge first at the lowest organizational levels, in the offices and bureaus that are most directly exposed to specific policy environments. Officials there make recommendations to their superiors, who in turn make recommendations to their superiors, and so on up the levels of hierarchy.

Along the way, two important things happen. One is filtering, a process by which some proposals are eliminated as unnecessary, too costly, or untimely. Part of the responsibility of managers in the bureaucratic hierarchy is to filter out policy proposals that should not be recommended for further consideration higher up. Many proposals die this way, in the internal review process of the agencies in which they originate. Often they are rejected after political struggles that may involve people and interests from outside the agency.

The secretary of defense, for example, may receive a proposal from the Navy for a new carrier-based fighter airplane. Although the Navy may be enthusiastic about the plane, the secretary may reject the proposal after determining that the plane is not a significant enough improvement over current fighters to justify the cost of a new weapons system. This is a filtering decision.

Another important activity of bureaucratic agencies is enforcing coordination. Every agency has many subunits that propose new policies and new expenditures of funds. Because the sum of these proposed expenditures always exceeds available resources, managers must set priorities. Priority setting occurs at every level in the hierarchy, so programs that survive initial review at the lowest levels may die at higher levels when they come into conflict with other proposals. A recommendation to improve dairy price supports may appear perfectly sensible when compared with a proposal to increase cotton price supports. But it may not fare so well when it is compared with a proposal for developing new soil conservation projects. The first comparison, between price supports for various agricultural commodities, is made at a low level in the hierarchy. The second comparison, involving two different kinds of policies, is made at a much higher level.

Character and culture Bureaucratic agencies are not empty vessels into which new programs are poured for implementation. Every agency has its own character and culture, and over time it acquires certain biases. Initially, these come from the kinds of programs an agency is asked to administer, but they are reinforced by the agency's contacts with the interest groups it serves, by the ways in which it recruits new employees, and by the operating procedures it employs.

An agency often reflects the philosophy and interests of its leader. James Watt, President Reagan's secretary of the interior in the early 1980s, had little patience with environmentalists and let it be known.

One of the important ways in which agencies institutionalize their biases is by routinizing their work. They develop **standard operating procedures (SOPs)**—predetermined ways of responding to a particular problem or set of circumstances. For example, the State Department has SOPs for dealing with foreign citizens who enter American embassies seeking political asylum. The Navy has SOPs for responding to contacts with foreign vessels in international waters. The IRS has SOPs for determining whether a tax return will be audited. Although SOPs simplify bureaucratic decisions and contribute to their consistency, they also channel bureaucratic activity into rigid patterns and thus make agencies less adaptable to change, especially change that is imposed from outside—by Congress or the president.

Professionalization In recent years, decision making by the executive bureaucracy has become increasingly professionalized because of the technical complexity of modern public policy. To deal with this complexity, agencies hire experts. For example, in recent years the federal government employed 150,000 architects and engineers, 10,000 physicians, 14,000 scientists, and more than 30,000 attorneys.[11] Because of their command of specific and detailed information, such experts have steadily enlarged their role in bureaucratic policy making. What experts add to this process is a reliance on professional as well as political criteria. Striking a balance between professional advice and political realities is a constant struggle for executive-branch officials.

Bureaucratic pathologies The natural characteristics of bureaucratic agencies often produce certain pathologies, unhealthy conditions that adversely affect the way they approach policy decisions. These reduce the efficiency and effectiveness of some agencies and are a principal source of the criticism directed at the federal bureaucracy.

Persistence is a bureaucratic pathology. Agencies often endure long after their reason for existence has passed. Once created, they are hard to abolish. The National Screw Thread Commission, for instance, was established during World War I to standardize screw threads for military equipment. It had little to do after the war ended in 1918 and did not hold a meeting or issue a report for a decade. Yet it continued to occupy a suite of offices and employ a staff until 1934.

Conservatism is a bureaucratic pathology. As noted earlier, agencies become set in their ways and tend to resist new ideas or new techniques that threaten to disrupt business as usual. For example, when General Billy Mitchell pushed for the creation of a permanent air force after World War I, he was resisted by the military establishment, which viewed airplanes as little more than glamorous gimmicks. Mitchell took his case to the public, arguing that air power would be critical in future wars. Demoted, transferred, and ultimately court-martialed for his efforts, he died a frustrated man in 1936, just five years before the Japanese attack on the United States naval base at Pearl Harbor demonstrated convincingly how right he had been.[12]

Expansionism is a bureaucratic pathology. The one change that nearly all agencies seem to welcome, growth creates new opportunities for promotion, prestige, power, and policy impact—all matters of importance to bureaucrats. The desire to grow is based in large part on the perception that growth will make life in the agency more pleasant and meaningful. But agency growth is often driven by self-interest rather than public need. Even in agencies whose programs are outmoded or whose benefits are difficult to demonstrate, expansionism is a strong and common tendency. Only the vigilance of executives and legislators can keep it in check.

The *territorial imperative*, the irresistible urge of an agency to jealously guard its own territory or turf, is a bureaucratic pathology. Indeed, the most furious conflicts that agencies wage are those with other agencies that seem to be encroaching on their area of jurisdiction. Most turf battles center on control over programs. For decades, for instance, the Department of Agriculture has battled successfully to keep the Forest Service under its jurisdiction, despite the reasonable claim that the Forest Service's function (managing the national forests) more closely fits the mission of the Interior Department (which oversees the national parks). The relevant congressional committees and affected interest groups have been in the middle of this political struggle. In this case, as in all others, the interest groups look to Congress to help them with the bureaucracy, and they look to the bureaucracy to help them with Congress.

Every agency suffers, at least occasionally, from some of these pathologies. They add new dimensions to the political struggles within the executive branch and between executive agencies and other political actors. And they help account not only for the difficulties in imposing a rational pattern of organization on the federal executive branch but also for the problems that presidents encounter in their efforts to use the executive branch for their own purposes.

Determinants of Bureaucratic Influence

Agencies vary in their ability to affect public policy. Some, like the Marine Corps, are potent and respected. Others, like the Occupational Safety and Health Administration, are weak and maligned. Still others, like the Energy Department, are influential in some periods and less influential in others.

Many scholars have tried to identify factors that help certain agencies play a substantial role in shaping public policy. Francis E. Rourke has identified four such factors: expertise, political support, organizational vitality, and leadership.[13] To a significant extent, the ways in which these variables combine determine an agency's impact.

Expertise Specialized knowledge has long been regarded as bureaucracy's principal contribution to the process of government. But some kinds of expertise are more valuable than others. The more technical and specialized an agency's expertise is, the greater will be the agency's opportunity to dominate policy making in its area of concern. If an agency has technical capabilities that few people possess or understand, challenges to its judgment will be rare. For many years, the space program was in this position. Because most of the country's experts on space and rocketry worked for the government, there was little opportunity for serious technical criticism of the federal space program. Once the political decision to explore space was made, policy decisions on how to go about it were left largely to the National Aeronautics and Space Administration.

Conversely, the more widely expertise is available outside an agency, the less valuable it is likely to be as a source of agency influence on public policy. The federal agencies that specialize in economic policy, for instance, have no corner on the market of economic expertise. Their recommendations are routinely challenged by other experts, both in and out of the government.

Political support The more widespread and intense an agency's support is in Congress, in the White House, among interest groups, and in the public mind, the greater its ability to affect policy making in its area of jurisdiction. Agencies therefore work hard to cultivate external support.

During the forty-eight years that J. Edgar Hoover was FBI director, for example, the FBI was remarkably successful in cultivating external support. It assisted in the production of radio programs and films that glorified its accomplishments, and it created the "Ten Most Wanted" list to dramatize its crime-busting efforts. Hoover himself devoted considerable attention to relations with his congressional overseers. As a result, FBI budget requests were rarely cut and FBI recommendations regarding crime policies were usually heeded.

The close relationships that often develop among executive agencies, special interest groups, and congressional subcommittees are called **iron triangles** or **subgovernments**. All across the government, in almost every policy area, these mutually supportive relationships exist. Some of the most powerful participants in each triangle endure year after year: the subcommittee's ranking members and staff, the agency bureaucrats, and the leaders of the special interest groups (see Figure 12-2). They come to know each other well, and over time they develop understandings and procedures that allow all three points on the triangle to serve the interests of the affected constituents.

Organizational vitality Like people, organizations have the capacity to stir the emotions. Such organizational vitality is most likely in an agency that is new and fresh. The agency bursts onto the scene, full of enthusiasm, staffed by bright,

FIGURE 12-2

The Iron Triangle of Merchant Shipping Policy

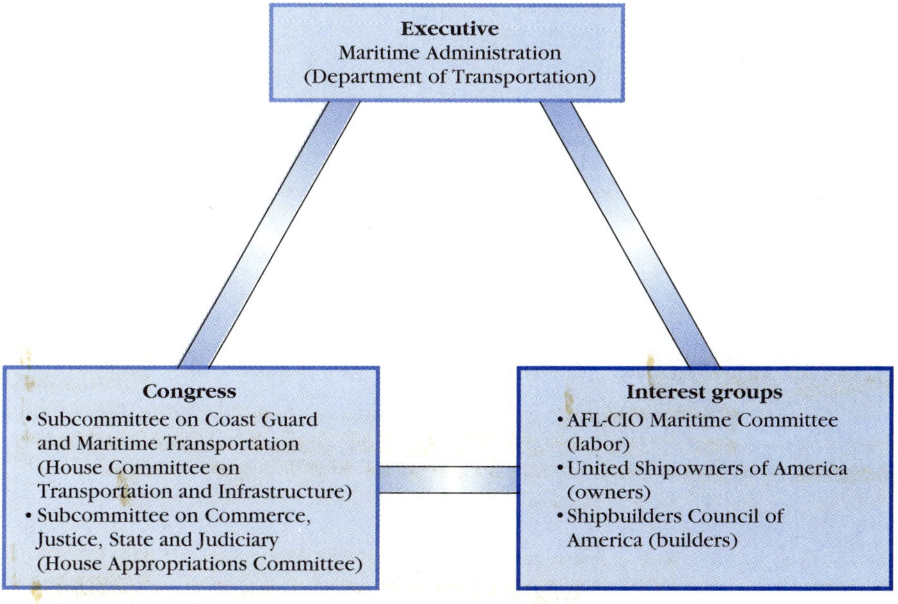

aggressive people carrying out a popular mission. Many of the New Deal agencies did this in the 1930s. The Peace Corps did it in the early 1960s, and so did the Army's Green Berets a few years later. A high level of vitality facilitates the recruitment of talented people and opens the budget floodgates. The president is happy to be associated with such a popular enterprise, and people are likely to defer to the agency's judgment.

Unfortunately, organizational vitality is difficult to sustain. As an agency ages, it makes enemies. Its routines harden, slowing the decision-making process. The enthusiasts who ran the agency in its early days go on to other pursuits, and the quality of performance declines. Before long the agency begins to drop back into the pack. As its vitality decreases, so too does its influence on policy making.

Leadership The way an agency is run can make a difference in the way the agency is perceived and in the attention given to its recommendations. To improve an agency's effectiveness, leaders can boost internal morale. By providing a sense of excitement and improving the work environment, they can enhance performance. Good leaders can also be persuasive and effective in dealing with the agency's constituencies, especially with the interest groups and the congressional committees most concerned with the agency's programs.

PROBLEMS OF ACCOUNTABILITY

Although bureaucrats are not elected, many of them spend their entire careers in government, often in the same agency. Although they make critical decisions about the economy, human welfare, protection of the environment, and war and peace, only the most important, the most misguided, or the most blatantly corrupt of those decisions attract much public attention. Bureaucrats are often isolated from direct public scrutiny and public review.

That isolation is a significant concern in a democracy, where public policy is supposed to serve the public interest. What can be done to ensure that bureaucratic choices will give due priority to the public interest and that bureaucrats will be held accountable for their actions? How can the checks and balances that are so essential to curb the excesses of authority be imposed on agencies and individuals whose work is so often out of public view? Chapter 11 discussed what efforts presidents undertake to control and direct the work of the executive branch. Several other approaches have been used to accomplish these objectives, including legal and legislative controls.

Legal Controls

Bureaucratic decisions are subject to judicial review—that is, they may be challenged in the federal courts. Most legal challenges are based on one of two grounds. The first is that the agency has acted outside its legal authority or jurisdiction. The second is that the agency's decision-making process has violated one or more of the legal rights and protections guaranteed by the Constitution. If a court finds that such a challenge is valid, it can respond in several ways. It can issue a declaratory judgment against the agency, restricting its actions in specified ways. Or it can grant an **injunction**—an order that usually prohibits the agency from taking further action against the aggrieved party until certain conditions, such as a rehearing, are satisfied. If the plaintiff has sued for damages, the court may also order an agency to pay a sum of money as compensation for those damages.

Such lawsuits take many years to wend their way through the courts, and the high cost of litigation deters the filing of suits by many people who have a genuine grievance. Even those who file suits rarely get satisfaction, because agencies win most of the cases in which they are involved. Legal controls thus provide an imperfect guarantee of bureaucratic accountability.

Legislative Controls

Because administrative oversight is conducted by Congress, the popularly elected branch of the government, it provides the most important guarantee of agency responsiveness to the public interest. The most important of these are its review of personnel policy and presidential appointments and its ultimate control over agency budgets. Congress also exercises oversight through its central role in determining the organizational structure and location of administrative agencies. Congress determines the maximum number of people an agency may employ. It also determines the qualifications that certain executive-branch officials must possess.

Congress determines which positions are subject to Senate confirmation, and it has tended to expand that requirement when it has been in conflict with the executive branch. Congress determines the location and level of new agencies and sometimes alters these aspects of existing agencies. When it approved the establishment of the Environmental Protection Agency (EPA) as an independent agency, for example, it did so to keep the EPA from falling under the control of one of the existing cabinet departments. Organizational decisions of this sort are one of the ways in which Congress imposes its political preferences on the executive branch.

The General Accounting Office (GAO), an arm of Congress, plays a very important role in legislative efforts to control the bureaucracy. The GAO was first created in 1921 to perform financial audits of agency accounts. Over the years, its functions have expanded, and now congressional committees often ask it to investigate agency management practices and the effectiveness of substantive programs.

The most important form of legislative control is the power of the purse—the control that Congress exercises over agency budgets.[14] Each year, agencies must appear before congressional appropriations subcommittees to present and defend their budgets. Those subcommittees then make recommendations that find their way into budget and appropriations bills.

Subcommittee decisions rarely follow the agency presentations precisely. Sometimes the subcommittees add funds for certain programs; more often they reduce funding. Frequently, the subcommittees or the full Congress shift funds from one program to another, replacing agency and presidential preferences with those that have gained political support in the subcommittee or in Congress.

The Adequacy of Controls

As the United States government's reliance on bureaucracies increases and as the complexity and power of bureaucracies increase, the need for effective control mechanisms grows more acute. Bureaucracies are crucial to the efficient management of the national government, because of their expertise and their ability to simplify and routinize complex tasks. To get those benefits, however, Congress and the president have to delegate considerable authority and discretion to bureaucratic agencies.

Controlling those delegations is no easy task. Effective checks and balances, ever difficult to create and sustain, are especially elusive in the web of relationships that enmesh the bureaucratic agencies of the executive branch. The executive bureaucracy is huge, many of its functions are technically complex, and some of its functions must be conducted in secret. Moreover, the routine and repetitive nature of much government work encourages bureaucrats and other political actors to develop and maintain enduring and mutually beneficial relationships. The desire to sustain these relationships and the shared rewards they produce often inhibits efforts to control bureaucratic activity.

The record shows that oversight has been uneven and incomplete, and there is no reason to expect that it will improve significantly in the years ahead. It is hard to strike the proper balance between giving bureaucracies the freedom and encouragement they need to be effective, and at the same time retaining sufficient control to redirect them when they go astray.

CASE STUDY

Government Regulates Too Much! Or Does It?

When asked whether there is too much or too little government regulation, Americans today nearly always say "too much." Many share Ronald Reagan's often expressed view that "government is the problem, not the solution." The resurgence of the Republican party in the 1980s and 1990s rested firmly on its promise to reduce the size and intrusiveness of government, and one of its prime targets has been federal regulations and the federal bureaucrats who implement them.

Most college students, like most other Americans, believe that government is too large and too intrusive in their lives. Students often join the chorus calling for less federal spending, less regulation, and smaller bureaucracies. But what would that mean in a student's life? What policies and regulations affect you most directly, and what would your life be like without them?

You're about to call it a night. As you review the events of the day, it never occurs to you that you had any contact at all with government. But you did—in more ways than you could possibly have imagined.

You did not get food poisoning when you ate your eggs for breakfast. Those eggs were inspected by the United States Department of Agriculture. Your coffee pot did not give you an electric shock when you had your midmorning coffee break. When you blew your hair dry, no cancer-causing asbestos fibers were blown out with the forced air. Both the coffee pot and the hair dryer were inspected and approved by the United States Products Safety Commission.

The building in which you attended classes did not catch fire; and, even if it had, the fire probably would not have spread quickly enough to endanger your life. The exit signs were clearly marked, and there were fire extinguishers on each floor. Local building codes require that.

The lecture in your physics course was given by a professor who spent the summer doing research on a grant from the National Aeronautics and Space

Administration. The library in which you worked during the afternoon was recently remodeled with the help of a large grant from the National Endowment for the Humanities, a federal agency. The touring exhibit you went to view at the college museum was mounted with funds provided by the National Endowment for the Arts, also a federal agency. The museum itself was recently able to stay open longer hours because of a grant from another federal agency, the Institute of Museum Services.

When you went for your late afternoon dip at the public swimming pool, you were not infected by harmful bacteria, nor did you contract polio. In 1952, 59,000 Americans died from polio. That was before Dr. Jonas Salk, with generous federal support for his research, discovered the polio vaccine.

The microwave oven in which you prepared your dinner did not endanger your health by emitting intolerable levels of radiation. The Consumer Products Safety Commission again. When you drove your car to the movies, the exhaust did not emit unhealthy levels of lead into the atmosphere, and your seatbelt enhanced your safety in case of an accident. The Environmental Protection Agency and the National Highway Safety Board made sure of that.

You attend a public university at which the cost of your education is directly subsidized by your state government. But still the costs are more than your family can afford. So you receive financial aid, principally in the form of student loans guaranteed by the federal government. But those don't cover all of your costs, so you also contribute to your own education with the money you earn from a federally subsidized work-study job on campus.

You didn't think much about government today. But government was with you in almost everything you did. Like most college students, you are the direct beneficiary of a wide range of government regulatory and subsidy policies.

To those who say there's too much government interference in the economy and in our personal lives, others respond that government provides important protections and opportunities for individuals, especially those with limited resources. Disagreement over the proper role for government is the central political debate of our time. Think about the ways government affects your life. Where do you stand in this debate?

Discussion Questions

1. Why do the American people seem to seek a smaller government?
2. Does your reading in this chapter suggest ways in which the government is shrinking?
3. Why did the federal government grow to its present size after World War II?
4. What would you cut and what would you keep if you had the power to reshape the government?

SUMMARY

The federal bureaucracy—the executive branch—is the largest component of the federal government and includes several types of organizations. The fourteen *departments* are the government's major operating units. *Agencies* have responsibility for a narrower set of functions and may exist either within a department or independently. Bureaus, offices, administrations, and services are subunits of agencies.

Independent regulatory commissions are independent of any departmental affiliation and to some extent are independent of presidential control. The federal government also owns a variety of economic enterprises, most of which are operated as *government corporations*.

Before 1883, nonelective positions in the federal bureaucracy were filled by means of *patronage*. People who had supported winning candidates received government jobs, in what was known as the *spoils system*. Calls for reform led to the establishment of the *civil service system*, in which federal employment is based on merit rather than on political considerations. The regular *civil service* now includes most of the career employees of the departments and the major agencies. The positions of senior managers and technical specialists are covered by the *Senior Executive Service*. Nearly all the top-level positions in the executive branch are held by political appointees.

The primary task of federal agencies is to interpret and implement the public policies that emerge from the legislative process. They do this in a number of ways, one of which is regulation. Most agencies have the authority to issue rules, or elaborations of laws. The draft of a new rule must be published in the *Federal Register* at least thirty days before it is to go into effect. The agency invites and reviews public comment on the rule and then publishes the rule in its final form.

Executive agencies perform quasi-judicial functions when they hold hearings to resolve conflicting interpretations of a rule. The hearings are often presided over by an *administrative law judge*, whose rulings are binding on both the agency and the complainant.

To ensure that laws and rules are obeyed, agencies make scheduled inspections, conduct audits, and impose reporting requirements. Agencies also oversee compliance by responding to complaints by parties that believe they have been harmed as a result of noncompliance.

Executive agencies also play an important role in the initiation of policy, because agency employees usually are experts in a particular policy area. Their training, experience, and values shape their perceptions of the form policies should take.

The natural characteristics of bureaucratic agencies may produce certain pathologies. Among these unhealthy characteristics are persistence, conservatism, expansionism, and the territorial imperative, the common urge of an agency to jealously guard its own territory or turf.

Several factors determine an agency's ability to affect public policy. The more technical and specialized an agency's expertise is, the greater will be the agency's opportunity to dominate policy making in its area of concern. Similarly, the more widespread and intense an agency's external political support is, the greater will be the agency's ability to affect policy making. Agencies try to develop supportive clienteles among the groups that benefit from their programs.

Organizational vitality, another source of influence, is difficult to sustain. A good leader can increase an agency's influence by boosting internal morale and dealing persuasively with the agency's constituencies.

Several approaches have been used to make bureaucratic agencies more accountable to the public. Bureaucratic decisions are subject to judicial review, and courts can issue a declaratory judgment against an agency, grant an *injunction* that prevents the agency from taking certain actions, or order an agency to compensate a plaintiff for damages. Legislative controls on the bureaucracy include congressional review of personnel policy and presidential appointments, control of the structure of administrative agencies, and control over agency budgets.

KEY TERMS

bureaucracy
department
agency
independent regulatory commission
government corporation
patronage
spoils system
civil service system
civil service
Senior Executive Service (SES)
deregulation
administrative law judge
standard operating procedures (SOPs)
iron triangle
subgovernment
injunction

RESOURCES

READINGS

Rourke, Francis E. *Bureaucracy, Politics, and Public Policy.* 3d ed. New York: HarperCollins, 1987. A clear and comprehensive exploration of the way politics shapes the organization, operation, and policy products of the federal executive branch.

Seidman, Harold, and Robert Gilmour. *Politics, Position, and Power.* 4th ed. New York: Oxford University Press, 1986. A study of the creation and management of political influence within the federal bureaucracy. Provides a good feel for how the bureaucratic universe appears from the inside.

Shafritz, Jay M., and Albert C. Hyde, eds. *Classics of Public Administration.* 3d ed. Belmont, Calif.: Wadsworth Publishing, 1992. A book of readings that includes most of the seminal articles in the scholarly study of public administration and bureaucratic operation.

ORGANIZATIONS

American Society for Public Administration, 1120 G Street, N.W., Washington, DC 20005; phone (202) 393-7878; fax (202) 638-4952; e-mail dcaspa@aol.com Sponsors workshops and conferences, disseminates information about public administration. The society's mission is to promote high ethical standards for public service.

National Academy of Public Administration, 1120 G Street, N.W., Washington, DC 20005; phone (202) 347-3190; fax (202) 393-0993; e-mail napa@tmn.com Conducts studies and offers assistance to federal, state, and local government agencies and public officials on problems of public administration and public policy implementation.

13

The Judiciary

PREVIEW

- Judicial federalism: federal and state courts
- The power of judicial review: the political question doctrine; judicial review and political influence; activism versus self-restraint
- How judges are chosen: appointment of federal and Supreme Court justices
- The Supreme Court: caseload; deciding what to decide; oral argument; discussing cases and voting in conference; writing opinions; opinion days; Supreme Court decision making as a political process
- The politics of judicial policy making

With public concern about teenage pregnancy and the spread of AIDS growing, in 1991 the Falmouth Public Schools in Falmouth, Massachusetts, joined many other school districts around the country in making condoms available free of charge to high school students. But the condom distribution program, in which students were also counseled about the proper use of condoms and about sexually transmitted diseases, was challenged in court by parents who argued that it violated their rights to familial privacy and freedom of religion. Although a New York state court had struck down a similar program in 1993, the Massachusetts state supreme court upheld the Falmouth program. In January 1996, the United States Supreme Court declined to consider an appeal of the decision.

The Court's refusal to take the case did not mean that its nine justices agreed with the Massachusetts court. Nor did letting the Massachusetts decision stand mean that the New York decision was overruled. Rather, it simply meant that no more than three of the justices, if that, considered the issue worth reviewing at the time. The Court has almost absolute power to decide what issues it wants to decide and when it wants to decide them.

The issue of access to contraceptives has long been politically controversial and subject to litigation. In 1943, a doctor brought a lawsuit challenging the constitutionality of an 1879 Connecticut law that prohibited virtually all individuals, whether married or single, from using contraceptives and barred physicians from giving advice about their use. When the state court upheld the law, the doctor appealed that decision to the United States Supreme Court. But the Court ruled that he failed to meet its tests for bringing such a lawsuit. Because he had not been arrested and had failed to show that he had suffered any personal injury as a result of the statute, the Court said, he lacked standing—the basis for bringing a lawsuit.

Over a decade later, Dr. C. Lee Buxton and a patient were likewise denied standing on the grounds that the law had not been enforced for eighty years, even though the state had begun to close birth control clinics.

In this case, *Poe v. Ullman* (1961), Justice Felix Frankfurter argued that the Court should exercise judicial self-restraint by not declaring a largely unenforced law unconstitutional.

Finally, after Dr. Buxton and Estelle Griswold, executive director of the Planned Parenthood League of Connecticut, had been found guilty of prescribing contraceptives to a married couple, the Court struck down what Justice Potter Stewart called Connecticut's "uncommonly silly law." In announcing the court's ruling in the case, *Griswold v. Connecticut* (1965), Justice William O. Douglas explained why challengers of the law were now being granted standing. Because Buxton and Griswold had given medical advice on how to prevent conception, he said, they therefore had a professional relationship with the couple. This gave them standing to challenge the constitutionality of Connecticut's law as a violation of a married couple's right to privacy.

No less important for the Court's ruling in *Griswold* was the fact that in 1962, the year after *Poe v. Ullman,* Justices Frankfurter and Charles Whittaker had resigned from the Court. They had been replaced by President John F. Kennedy's two appointees, Justices Byron White and Arthur Goldberg. With that change in the Court's composition came major changes in the Court's view of individuals' standing to sue and the kinds of rights they could claim in the courts. The Court's recognition of a constitutional right of privacy in *Griswold,* in turn, provided a basis for extending that right to include a woman's right to decide whether to have an abortion in *Roe v. Wade* (1973).

The controversy that began with challenges to the constitutionality of Connecticut's birth control law illustrates the importance of the Supreme Court's power to decide what cases it will review as well as how the Court responds to social forces. Individuals must have standing to bring cases and controversies to the courts, but whether they are granted standing may also depend on the composition of the court. In addition, the controversy illustrates the operation of the American system of judicial federalism, in which each state maintains a system of courts whose standards and rulings may differ from those of other states and of the federal court system.

The shift in the Court's position in the Connecticut birth control cases also indicates how political dynamics affect judicial decision making and how changes in the composition of the bench may significantly alter the Court's role in larger controversies. Although the judiciary can decide only cases and controversies that are properly brought to it, it is nevertheless a political institution. Judges and justices are political actors who exercise great power in the United States, far more than their counterparts in other democracies. Their decisions, based on interpretations of law, sometimes have enormous political consequences. They may affect millions of people and involve billions of dollars. They may settle conflicts between special interest groups, alter the relationship between the president and Congress or between the federal and state governments, and defend the rights of individuals and businesses against the coercive powers of government.

This chapter begins by focusing on the organization and operation of courts and the politics of judicial federalism. It looks at the power of judicial review, the politics of selecting and appointing judges, the judicial process itself, and the Supreme Court. Finally, it examines the politics of judicial decision making and explores the interaction between courts and other political institutions. In all these areas, courts and judges are integral players in the politics of American government.

JUDICIAL FEDERALISM

In most countries, there is a single, unitary system of courts, but in the United States, judicial power is decentralized and divided between two separate judicial systems. Alongside the federal judiciary, each of the fifty states has its own independent judiciary. Within both the federal and the state systems, judicial power is further divided between trial courts (and other lesser courts such as traffic courts) and one or two levels of appellate courts, which hear appeals from the lower courts. (The organization of the federal judicial system is shown in Figure 13-1.)

The importance of these dual judicial systems, termed **judicial federalism**, is that federal courts largely consider disputes over national law and state courts consider only disputes arising under state law. If there is a conflict between

FIGURE 13-1

The Organization of the Federal Judiciary System

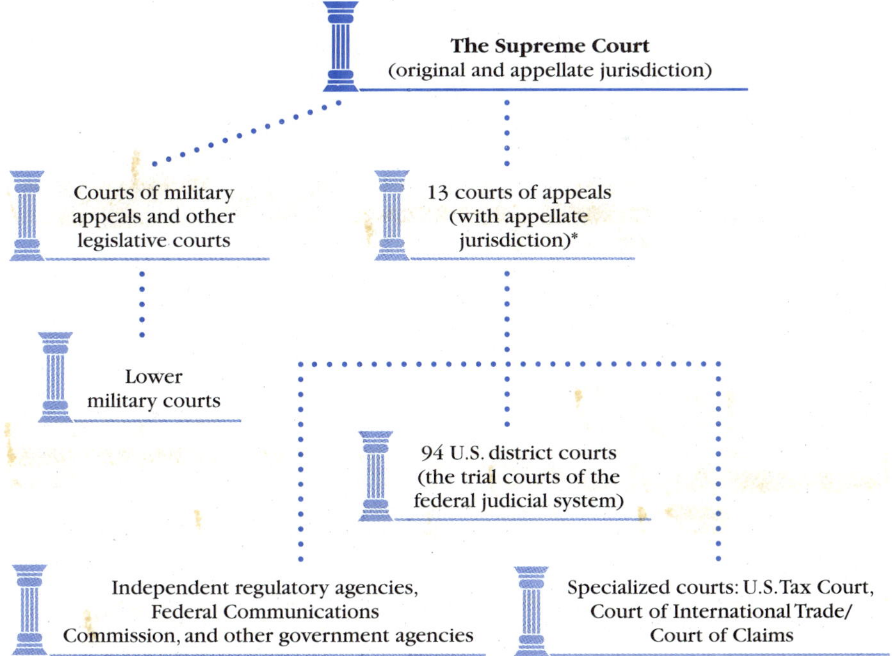

*This includes eleven regional courts of appeals, one Court of Appeals for the District of Columbia Circuit, and one Court of Appeals for the Federal Circuit.

national and state law, the matter is settled by the federal courts and ultimately by the Supreme Court. This is so because (as discussed in Chapter 2) the Constitution and federal law are supreme over state law. Judicial federalism and the decentralized structure of federal and state courts have a number of important consequences for judicial policy making, as we will see in this chapter.

Federal Courts

Article III of the Constitution vests judicial power "in one Supreme Court, and in such inferior courts as Congress may from time to time ordain and establish." Courts created under Article III are called **constitutional courts**. In addition, under Article I, Congress may create **legislative courts** to carry out its own powers. The United States Court of Military Appeals, which applies military law, is one such court; federal bankruptcy courts are another type of legislative court. These courts have more specialized jurisdiction than those created under Article III, and their judges do not hold lifetime appointments.

Congress has established a number of courts under Article III. In 1789, it divided the country into thirteen districts (one in each state) and created a federal district court for each. **District courts** are the trial courts of the federal system. In addition, the Judiciary Act of 1789 created three federal **courts of appeals** to hear appeals from decisions of the district courts or from state courts. But Congress did not provide for any appellate court judges. Instead, these courts were staffed by two Supreme Court justices who twice a year sat with a district court judge to hear cases. The federal courts of appeals were not staffed by full-time appellate judges for another hundred years.

As the country grew, so did the number of district courts, along with the number of appeals of their rulings to the Supreme Court. Eventually, the workload of the Supreme Court became too large for the justices to handle. Congress responded in 1891 by creating the circuit courts of appeals, which now hear most of the appeals coming from them or from state courts. Today, aside from legislative courts, the federal judiciary consists of ninety-four district courts, thirteen courts of appeals, and the Supreme Court.

State Courts

State courts are by no means inferior to the federal judiciary, even though their decisions may be appealed to the federal courts and to the Supreme Court if they involve the application of federal law or issues governed by the federal Constitution. State courts play a crucial role in the administration of justice. When interpreting state constitutions and bills of rights, they have great freedom to pursue their own directions in policy making rather than simply following the direction of the Supreme Court.

State courts handle by far the greatest volume of litigation. Well over 90 percent of all lawsuits filed each year are in state courts. The business of state courts also tends to diverge from that in federal courts. Apart from criminal cases, the largest portion of state supreme court litigation involves economic issues.

THE POWER OF JUDICIAL REVIEW

Article III of the Constitution, along with congressional legislation, specifies the **jurisdiction** of federal courts, the kinds of cases and controversies that courts may decide. Under Article III, the Supreme Court has **original jurisdiction** in all cases involving disputes between two or more states and in cases brought against the United States by ambassadors of foreign countries. Original jurisdiction means that the case originates in the Supreme Court rather than a lower court, but in practice the Court appoints a "special master" to hear the case and to recommend a decision. Out of the more than seven thousand cases that come to the Court each year, only two or three involve matters of original jurisdiction. The rest arrive under the Court's **appellate jurisdiction**, as established by congressional legislation. Under its appellate jurisdiction, the Court hears appeals from lower federal courts and state courts. Federal legislation also defines the jurisdiction of the lower federal courts; state constitutions and legislation define the jurisdiction of state courts.

Courts have jurisdiction only over disputes involving adverse interests and a real controversy. They will not take "friendly lawsuits" brought by two parties who simply want to have some question settled. The parties must have **standing to sue**; they must show that they are suffering or are in danger of suffering an immediate and substantial personal injury (see the box on page 338).

More individuals and interest groups may now gain access to the courts, and they may raise a wider range of disputes. They may bring test cases and controversies in which they have a stake in the outcome but which also represent a conflict over the public interest. In the 1940s and 1950s, the National Association for the Advancement of Colored People brought a series of test cases challenging the constitutionality of racially segregated public schools. These cases led to the Supreme Court's landmark ruling, in *Brown v. Board of Education of Topeka, Kansas* (1954), that struck down the doctrine of "separate but equal" facilities. More recently, environmental groups like the Natural Resources Defense Council and the Sierra Club have brought suits against polluters in order to protect the environment; and the United States Chamber of Commerce, business groups,

The Supreme Court has original jurisdiction in all cases involving disputes between states. In 1997, the Court ruled that New York State had to give New Jersey control of part of Ellis Island, the historic immigration facility in the harbor of New York City.

Requirements for Gaining Standing

1. *A personal injury must be claimed.* For example, an individual must have been denied some right under federal or state law.
2. *The dispute must not be hypothetical.* Real adverse interests must be at stake.
3. *A case must be brought before a court authorized to hear such disputes.* Cases must be within a court's jurisdiction.
4. *Other remedies must have been exhausted.* For example, litigants must have exhausted administrative appeals and appeals in other lower courts.
5. *The dispute must not be moot.* Circumstances since filing the lawsuit must not have changed so as to end the dispute or make it hypothetical.
6. *A case must be ripe for judicial resolution.* The dispute must not be hypothetical, and other opportunities for resolving it must have been exhausted.
7. *The dispute must be capable of judicial resolution.* The dispute must not involve a political question that should be decided by other branches of government.

and conservative legal foundations have used litigation to challenge the enforcement of health, safety, and environmental regulations.[1]

The Political Question Doctrine

After a lawsuit has been filed, judges may still refuse to decide a dispute. For example, they will not decide hypothetical disputes or give "advisory opinions" on possible future conflicts. Courts also avoid deciding **political questions**—issues that judges think should be resolved by other branches of government, either because of the separation of powers or because the judiciary is not in a position to provide a remedy. Thus courts generally avoid disputes involving foreign policy and international relations. But this does not make the judiciary less political. Deciding what is a "political question" is itself a political decision and an exercise of judicial review.

Judicial Review and Political Influence

In the United States, the judiciary, particularly the Supreme Court, exercises great political power because its members have the authority to interpret the Constitution and the laws of the nation. This power of *judicial review* (see Chapter 2) gives the courts the power to strike down any law enacted by Congress or by the states and to declare official government actions unconstitutional.

The political influence of the judiciary has grown dramatically since the nation's founding. No longer is the judiciary, as Alexander Hamilton claimed in *The Federalist, No. 78,* "the least dangerous branch" of the government. Instead, it has become truly a coequal branch. The Supreme Court increasingly asserts its power in striking down congressional legislation, state laws, and municipal ordinances. Likewise, lower courts no longer serve simply as tribunals for private dispute resolution but more often serve as problem solvers and policy makers.

Activism versus Self-Restraint

Do courts exercise too much power? Have they usurped the power of other branches of the government? The power of judicial review has been criticized,

George E.C. Hayes, Thurgood Marshall, and James M. Nabrit celebrate on the steps of the Supreme Court after hearing its decision in Brown v. Board of Education of Topeka, Kansas (1954). *As attorneys for the National Association for the Advancement of Colored People's legal defense fund, they had spearheaded the litigation that led to the decision, which abolished legal segregation in public schools. Thirteen years later, Marshall was himself appointed to the Court by President Lyndon Johnson.*

at different times, by both liberals and conservatives. In the 1920s and 1930s, liberals attacked the Supreme Court for its **judicial activism** in striking down progressive economic legislation such as minimum-wage laws. (Judicial activism is the use of judicial review to invalidate state and federal laws.) Criticizing the Court for substituting its conservative economic views for the more progressive views of Congress and state legislatures, the liberals urged the Court to exercise **judicial self-restraint** and defer to legislative authority. (Judicial self-restraint is the practice of deferring to the executive and legislative branches, rather than asserting the Court's own view.) By contrast, the Court's activism in defending civil liberties and civil rights in the 1960s and 1970s led conservatives to charge that the Court was usurping the power of other political institutions and thwarting the will of the majority. Presidents Nixon, Reagan, and Bush all called for the appointment of judges who would exercise judicial self-restraint.

But the political role of contemporary courts is only partially explained by judges' exercise of judicial review. Courts respond (more or less slowly) to the problems created by technological advances and political and social changes. The expansion of judicial power is also related to changes in government policies for dealing with illegal activities. For instance, the federal judiciary played a minor role in environmental protection until the 1970s, when Congress passed legislation such as the Clean Air and Clean Water Acts and the National Environmental Protection Act. Then the courts had to resolve conflicts over the implementation of that legislation by federal agencies.

Other social trends have been no less significant in increasing and changing the business of courts. Even before the 1920s and 1930s, railroads and other businesses relied on the judiciary to protect property rights and to strike down progressive economic legislation enacted under the influence of the labor and populist movements beginning in the late nineteenth century. The civil rights movement of the 1950s and 1960s brought lawsuits challenging racial discrimination in schools, in employment, and in public accommodations.

The pace of litigation is also influenced by economic cycles. This is so because increased economic activity gives rise to new issues involving property rights and disputes over government regulations affecting labor–management relations; health, safety, and environmental matters; and other economic issues.

No less important is the fact that American society is exceedingly litigious—so much so that the United States is sometimes called an adversial democracy. In the mid 1990s, for instance, more than 300,000 cases a year were filed in the federal courts, more than twice the number in the preceding decade. Moreover, as noted earlier, the federal judiciary handles but a small percentage of all litigation that occurs in the United States; state courts face over 25 million cases a year. Another measure of the increasing litigiousness of the United States is the rather dramatic increase in the number of lawyers and judges since the end of World War II. In 1995, it was estimated that there was one lawyer for every 290 American citizens.

Even more fundamental to the political role of the judiciary are cultural factors that condition the way democratic politics works in the pluralistic and litigious American society. The competition for power among diverse interest groups in other political arenas inexorably finds its way into the courts. As the astute French commentator Alexis de Tocqueville observed in the 1830s, "Scarcely any political question arises in the United States that is not resolved, sooner or later, into a judicial question."[2] This situation results from a distinguishing feature of democracy in America: the peculiar "legal habit" that accompanies Americans' devotion to civil rights and to the idea of the rule of law.

HOW JUDGES ARE CHOSEN

A hallmark of the federal judiciary is the relative isolation of judges from political pressures such as the direct personal lobbying faced by senators, representatives, and other elected officials. Under the Constitution, federal judges are given lifetime appointments, and Congress is barred from decreasing their salaries. Still, judges are appointed largely for political reasons, get involved in political controversies, and make judgments that affect the rules that govern politics.

In contrast with the system for appointing federal judges, the means of selecting state court judges varies from one state to another and among different courts within the states. In states on the Atlantic seaboard, judges have historically been appointed by either the governor or the state legislature. In other states, particularly in the South, they are elected on either a partisan or a nonpartisan basis. In the Midwest and West, as well as in a growing number of states elsewhere, some combination of those methods—a so-called **merit system**—is used. Under a merit system a nonpartisan commission usually provides a list of possible nominees from which the governor or legislature makes appointments to fill vacancies. After one or two years of service, an appointee's name is placed unopposed on a ballot, and voters decide whether he or she should be retained. Under this system, judges may or may not come up for retention elections every ten or fifteen years.

Politics ultimately determines the choice of state court judges. Regardless of the method of selection, the same kinds of individuals tend to be selected. White male lawyers from upper-middle-class Protestant backgrounds who have been politically active have historically predominated. Since the late 1970s, however, an increasing number of women and members of minority groups have been appointed or elected to state judgeships.

Appointment of Federal Judges

Politics also determines who is appointed to the federal bench. Article II of the Constitution gives the president the power to nominate and appoint, with the advice and consent of the Senate, all federal judges. Since federal judgeships provide lifetime tenure, these appointments are a prized form of political patronage. In fact, presidents try to "pack" the federal courts in the hope of influencing the direction of public law and policy long after they have left the Oval Office.

In the 1980s and early 1990s, for instance, Republican presidents Ronald Reagan and George Bush promised to appoint judges who were opposed to abortion. Political scientists studying the decisions of federal judges appointed by recent presidents found that "Reagan appointees were much more resistant to abortion rights than were the appointees of his predecessors, including the appointees of fellow Republican Richard Nixon. Likewise, President Carter's appointees were much more supportive of abortion claims than were the appointees of other presidents."[3] Compared with those of Carter, Reagan, and Bush, President Clinton's appointees have been less ideologically aligned and more racially and ethnically diverse; they have also included a much higher proportion of women (see Tables 13-1 and 13-2.)

TABLE 13-1 ***Number of Judicial Appointments from Roosevelt through Clinton***

	Roosevelt	Truman	Eisenhower	Kennedy	Johnson
Supreme Court	9	4	5	2	2
Circuit Court	52	27	45	20	40
District Court	137	102	127	102	122
Special Courts[b]	14	9	10	2	13
Total	212	142	187	126	177

	Nixon	Ford	Carter	Reagan	Bush	Clinton[a]
Supreme Court	4	1	0	4	2	2
Circuit Court	45	12	56	78	37	31
District Court	182	52	202	290	148	171
Special Courts[b]	7	1	3	10	0	0
Total	238	66	261	382	187	204

[a]Appointments made through March 1997.
[b]Includes Customs, Patent Appeals, and Court of International Trade.

TABLE 13-2 ***A Profile of Presidential Appointees to the Lower Federal Courts***

	Number of Appointments						
	Johnson	Nixon	Ford	Carter	Reagan	Bush	Clinton[a]
Gender							
Male	159	226	63	217	340	149	139
Female	3	1	1	41	28	36	63
Ethnicity or race							
White	152	218	58	202	344	165	146
Black	7	6	3	37	7	12	38
Hispanic	3	2	1	16	15	8	14
Asian		1	2	2	2		3
Native American				1			1
ABA ratings							
Exceptionally well qualified	89	117	31	145	203	109	134
Qualified	68	110	32	110	165	76	65
Not qualified	4		1	3			3
Total number of appointees	162	227	64	258	368	185	202

[a]Appointments made through March 1997.
Note: One Johnson appointee did not receive an ABA rating.

SOURCE: Sheldon Goldman, "Bush's Judicial Legacy: The Final Imprint," *Judicature* 282 (1993); Alliance for Justice, *Judicial Selection Project Annual Report,* 1993; and *Alliance for Justice* (for appointments through March 1997).

Despite their constitutional authority, however, presidents often must compete with the Senate and other political bodies in appointing judges. In addition to the president, the Senate, and judicial candidates themselves, other key actors include the Department of Justice, the Standing Committee on the Federal Judiciary of the American Bar Association, and leading political party officials. The practice of senatorial courtesy, in which the president consults with senators from the president's party and from a prospective nominee's home state prior to making a formal nomination, developed in part to achieve this accommodation.

The appointment process encourages the Senate and the president to bargain with each other to achieve their political objectives. The president may trade lower-court judgeships for legislation and good relations. That is, the president may agree to nominate a senator's preferred candidate for a district court judgeship in exchange for the senator's vote on crucial legislation and support of the administration's policy goals. Federal judgeships are opportunities for the Senate, no less than for the president, to influence national policy and confer political patronage.

Appointment of Supreme Court Justices

Unlike other federal judgeships, appointments to the Supreme Court are usually considered a prerogative of the president. Although the Senate has the power to defeat a nominee, in this century only seven have been blocked: four were defeated, two were withdrawn, and no action was taken on one.

Most presidents delegate the responsibility for selecting candidates and getting them through the Senate to their attorney general and other close advisers. The assistant attorney general in charge of the Office of Legal Policy in the Department of Justice usually compiles a list of candidates from recommendations by White House staff, members of Congress, governors, and state and local bar associations. The president and a committee of his top advisers narrow the number of candidates to two or three on the basis of a political evaluation and an informal rating by the Standing Committee on the Federal Judiciary of the American Bar Association. (The ABA committee ranks candidates as "well qualified," "qualified," or "not qualified.") At some point when the president is making the final choice, an exhaustive FBI investigation of the candidate(s) is initiated and a formal evaluation by the ABA is received. Once these reports have been reviewed by the attorney general and White House counsel, a recommendation is sent to the president. If he approves, the nomination is formally submitted to the Senate. The Senate Judiciary Committee then holds a **confirmation hearing** and recommends approval or rejection of the nominee by a vote of the entire Senate.

The rejection of President Reagan's nomination of Robert H. Bork to the Supreme Court in 1987 vividly illustrates the political nature of the appointment process (see the Case Study on pages 353-355). It indicates the range of forces that can affect judicial appointments and the difficulty the president can encounter if he does not take these forces into account. It also demonstrates the need for cooperation in a process that requires agreement between two government institutions.

All presidents try to fill vacancies on the Supreme Court with political associates and individuals who share their ideological views. They make little or no effort to balance the Court by crossing party lines. Of the 108 individuals who have served on the Supreme Court, there have been 13 Federalists, 1 Whig, 8 Democratic-Republicans, 42 Republicans, and 44 Democrats.

In earlier eras, presidents sought geographic balance on the Court as well as ideological compatibility. In the early nineteenth century, representation of different geographic regions was considered crucial to establishing the legitimacy of the Court. As the country expanded westward, presidents were inclined to give representation to new states and regions. But in this century, appointments have rarely turned on geography. President Nixon, for instance, named two justices from Minnesota, and three of President Reagan's four appointees came from the West.

Some observers believe that religion, race, and gender have become more important considerations in judicial selection in recent years. But historically they have been barriers to appointment to the Court. The overwhelming majority (93) of the 108 justices have come from mainstream Protestant backgrounds. Of the remaining 15, 8 were Catholics and 7 were Jews. Justice Thurgood Marshall, who was appointed by President Lyndon Johnson in 1967, was the first African American to serve on the Court. When he retired in 1991, President George Bush named another African American, Judge Clarence Thomas, to fill his seat. In 1981, President Reagan fulfilled a campaign pledge to appoint the first woman to the Supreme Court, nominating Sandra Day O'Connor. In 1986, Antonin Scalia, a Catholic and Reagan's second appointee, became the first Italian American to serve on the Court. Reagan also named another Catholic, Anthony Kennedy, in 1988. President Clinton appointed another female justice, Ruth Bader Ginsburg, in 1993; both she and his second appointee, Stephen G. Breyer, were Jewish.

Considerations such as religion, race, and gender are politically symbolic and largely reflect changes in the electorate. In the future, expectations for more diverse representation—particularly from among Hispanics and Asians—are likely to continue. Still, they are likely to remain less important than personal and ideological compatibility in presidents' attempts to "pack" the judiciary with judges who share their political views.

THE SUPREME COURT

The Supreme Court is perhaps the least understood government institution in the United States. Although the public may attend oral arguments and the Court's rulings are handed down in the form of published opinions, a tradition of secrecy surrounds the justices' decision making. The Court stands as a temple of law—an arbitrator of political disputes and an expression of the ideal of "a government of laws, and not of men." But it remains a fundamentally political institution. Behind the marble facade, the justices compete for influence.

The Court's annual term (or work year) begins on the first Monday in October and runs until the end of June. For most of this time, the justices are hidden from public view. They hear oral arguments only fourteen weeks a year—on Mondays, Tuesdays, and Wednesdays of every other two-week period from October through April. On Wednesday afternoons and again on most Fridays, they hold private conferences to decide which cases they will review and to make decisions on cases for which they have heard oral arguments. The rest of the time they work alone in their chambers with their law clerks, writing opinions and studying drafts of opinions circulated by other justices.

The Court's Caseload

The public learns about only a few of the Court's rulings each term. Usually only the most controversial decisions are given media coverage. The Court actually reviews and decides by written opinion only about one hundred cases each year. Still, that is only about 1 percent of the nearly eight thousand cases filed and placed on the Court's **docket** each year. The vast majority of these cases are denied review, leaving the lower-court rulings untouched.

The Court's caseload has grown (see Figure 13-2) and changed throughout its history. In the nineteenth century, almost all cases came to the Court as mandatory appeals, which the justices had to decide. But as the caseload grew, Congress eliminated most provisions granting rights of appeal and substituted **petitions for a writ of certiorari** (a petition requesting a court to order a review of the ruling of a lower court), which the Court may simply deny. Congress thus permitted the justices to determine which cases they would review. Figure 13-3 (page 346) presents the main avenues of appeal to the Supreme Court.

The Court now exercises virtually absolute control over its caseload. The power to turn away cases enables it not only to limit the number of cases it reviews but also to pick what issues it wants to decide and when. In this sense, the modern Supreme Court functions like a legislative body, setting its own agenda for adjudication and policy making.

Deciding What to Decide

When the justices meet in conference, they vote on which cases to review. Prior to each conference the chief justice circulates two lists of cases. On the first—

FIGURE 13-2

Docket of and Filings in the Supreme Court, 1800–1995

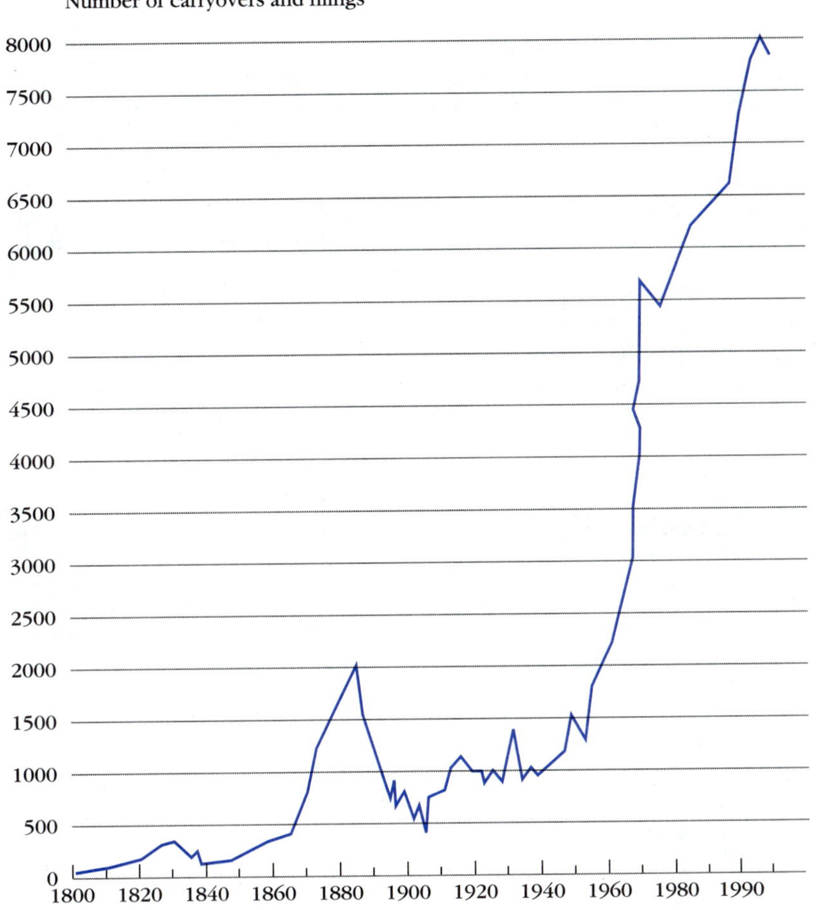

SOURCE: David M. O'Brien, *Storm Center: The Supreme Court in American Politics,* 4th ed. (New York: Norton, 1996), 180. Reprinted by permission of W. W. Norton & Company, Inc.

the Discuss List—are all the cases he thinks are worth considering, based on a review of the clerks' recommendations. Any justice may add other cases, but the list typically includes only forty to fifty cases. Attached is a second list—the Dead List—containing cases that are considered unworthy of discussion. Over 90 percent of all cases are unanimously denied without discussion, and most of those that make the Discuss List are denied as well. The conference lists are an important technique for saving time and focusing attention on the few cases deemed worthy of consideration.

The chief justice presides over conferences, as he does over oral arguments and all the Court's other public functions. At a conference, he usually begins by summarizing each case and indicating why he thinks it should be accepted or denied. Discussion then passes from one justice to another in order of their seniority on the bench.

FIGURE 13-3
Avenues of Appeal to the Supreme Court

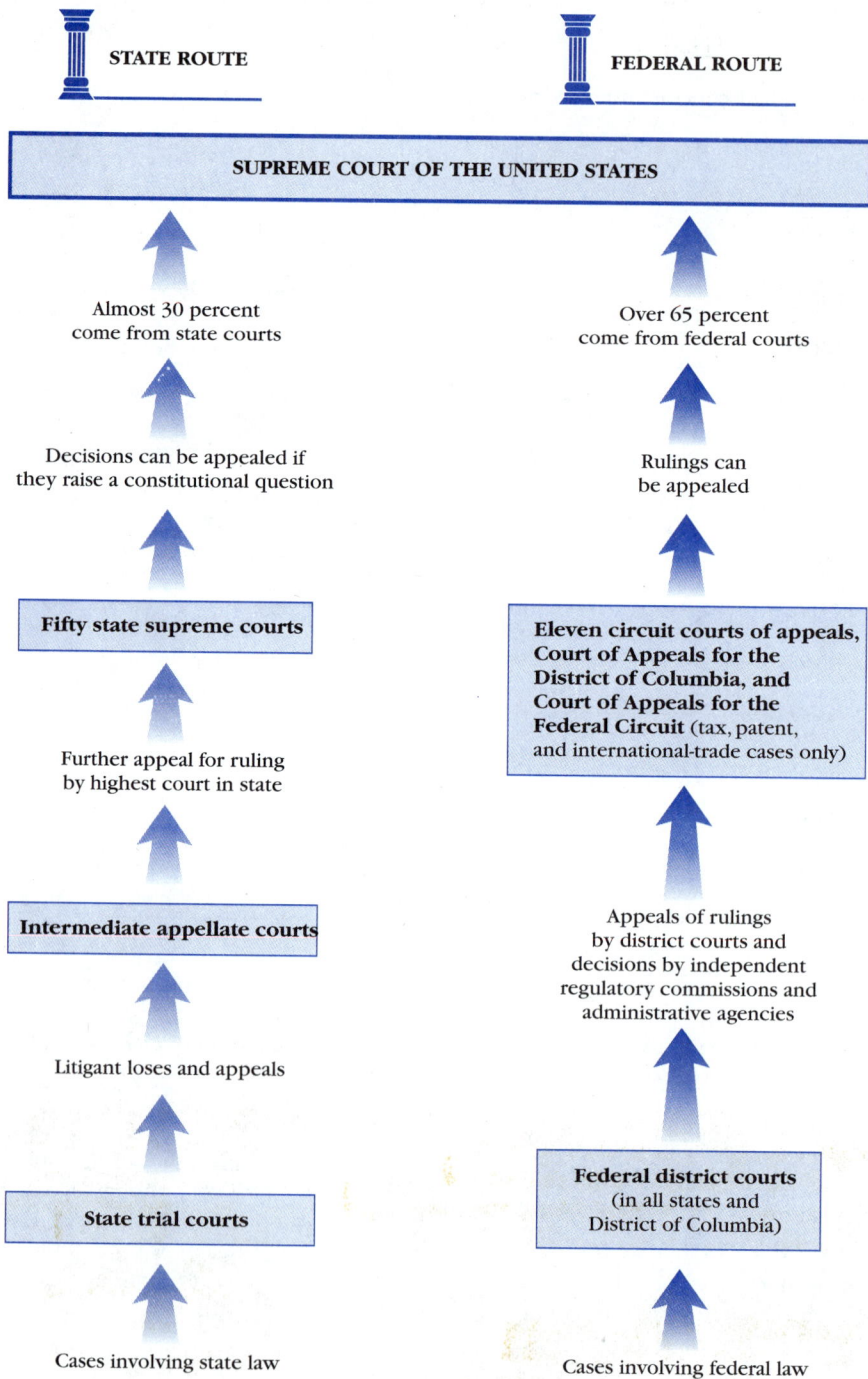

STATE ROUTE

FEDERAL ROUTE

SUPREME COURT OF THE UNITED STATES

State route

Almost 30 percent
come from state courts

Decisions can be appealed if
they raise a constitutional question

Fifty state supreme courts

Further appeal for ruling
by highest court in state

Intermediate appellate courts

Litigant loses and appeals

State trial courts

Cases involving state law

Federal route

Over 65 percent
come from federal courts

Rulings can
be appealed

Eleven circuit courts of appeals, Court of Appeals for the District of Columbia, and Court of Appeals for the Federal Circuit (tax, patent, and international-trade cases only)

Appeals of rulings
by district courts and
decisions by independent
regulatory commissions and
administrative agencies

Federal district courts
(in all states and
District of Columbia)

Cases involving federal law

SOURCE: David M. O'Brien, *Storm Center: The Supreme Court in American Politics,* 4th ed. (New York: Norton, 1996), 197. Reprinted by permission of W. W. Norton & Company, Inc.

The United States Supreme Court in 1997. The chief justice always sits in the middle, with associate justices alternating out to his right and left, in descending order of years of service. (Seated) *Antonin Scalia (appointed by Reagan in 1986); John Paul Stevens (Ford, 1975); Chief Justice William Rehnquist (associate justice, Nixon, 1972; chief justice, Reagan, 1986); Sandra Day O'Connor (Reagan, 1981); Anthony M. Kennedy (Reagan, 1988).* (Standing) *Ruth Bader Ginsburg (Clinton, 1993); David H. Souter (Bush, 1990); Clarence Thomas (Bush, 1991); and Stephen G. Breyer (Clinton, 1994).*

Although the Court decides all other matters by majority rule, review can be granted on the vote of only four justices—the informal **rule of four**. However, only a small number of the cases granted review are actually accepted on this basis. For well over 70 percent of the cases accepted for review, a majority of the justices agree on the importance of the issues presented. The rule of four was adopted by the Supreme Court when Congress expanded the Court's discretionary power to pick the cases it accepts. The purpose was to assure Congress that important cases would be granted review even if less than a majority of the justices deemed them to present substantial questions of federal law. In addition, because less than a majority of the Court may grant review, the denial of a particular case is not considered a precedent that would be binding on lower courts.

Because of the Court's heavy docket, it does not grant cases in order to decide questions of fact, such as a person's guilt or innocence, or simply to correct mistakes made in lower courts. Instead, it takes cases that involve questions of law on which lower courts have disagreed. The Court thus tends to decide only cases that have national scope and involve significant controversies over public law and policy.

After a conference, the clerk of the Court is told which cases have been accepted or denied. The justices do not explain why they deny review of a case. This policy not only saves them time but also enhances their flexibility: the Court may take up an issue in a later case without feeling bound by an earlier denial.

For the few cases that are granted review, the clerk notifies the litigants that they have thirty days to submit briefs on the **merits**—the questions to be decided. The clerk then sets a date for oral argument, usually about four months later.

Oral Argument

Counsel once had unlimited time to present oral arguments; but as the caseload increased, the justices cut back on the time. Each case now gets only one hour—thirty minutes for each side. The Court hears four cases on each oral argument day, which is virtually the only time that the public may see the justices.

Oral arguments are also the only opportunity attorneys have to communicate directly with the justices, who want crisp, concise, and conversational presentations. They do not want attorneys to read their briefs, and the time limit is strictly enforced. Although Chief Justice Charles Evans Hughes reportedly called time on a lawyer in the middle of the word *if,* the Court is more tolerant now. As former chief justice Warren Burger once explained, "We allow a lawyer to finish a sentence that is unfolding when the red light goes on, provided, of course, the sentence is not too long."[4]

Discussing Cases and Voting in Conference

Within a day or two after oral arguments, the justices meet in secret conference to discuss and vote on the cases. The chief justice opens the discussion, which moves to each of the other justices in order of their seniority. For much of the Court's history, the justices voted in reverse order of seniority, the junior ones voting first so as not to be swayed by the votes of their senior colleagues. But that practice has been abandoned. Because of the heavier caseload, each justice has only about three minutes to express his or her views and vote on each case. As a result, conferences involve less collective deliberation than was generally true in the past.

The justices' votes at conference are always tentative. Until the day the final decision comes down, justices may use their votes in strategic ways to influence the disposition of a case, offering or threatening to switch sides depending on whether or not their conditions are met. Before and during conference as well, justices bargain and negotiate the treatment of issues and the language of opinions. Justice Harlan F. Stone, for example, once candidly told Justice Frankfurter: "If you wish to write [the opinion] placing the case on the ground which I think tenable and desirable, I shall cheerfully join you. If not, I will add a few observations for myself."[5]

Writing Opinions

After every three-day oral argument session, one of the justices is assigned to write the **opinion** for the Court on each case. This is a crucial aspect of the work of the Court because how an opinion is written—the legal reasoning used to justify the decision—is just as important as the decision itself. The justice selected must be one who voted with the majority during conference, and if the chief justice did so he assigns the opinion, either to himself or to another justice. By tradition, if the chief justice did not vote with the majority, the senior associate justice who was in the majority makes the assignment.

The power of opinion assignment presents significant opportunities for the chief justice to influence the final outcome of cases. In unanimous and landmark cases, chief justices often write opinions themselves. Chief Justice Earl Warren wrote the opinion striking down segregated schools in *Brown v. Board of Education* (1954). Chief Justice Warren Burger likewise delivered the opinion in *United States v. Nixon* (1974), rejecting President Nixon's claim of executive privilege to withhold tape recordings made in the Oval Office during the Watergate crisis.[6]

Chief justices usually try to see that all the justices are assigned about the same number of opinions (thirteen to fifteen per year), so as to distribute the workload evenly and to avoid angering their colleagues. They may make assignments on the basis of a justice's background and particular expertise or in anticipation of public reactions to a ruling. In addition, they sometimes ask the justice who is closest to the dissenters to write the opinion in the hope that other justices will switch their votes and thereby bolster the authority of the Court's decision. Not surprisingly, the power of assigning opinions invites resentment and lobbying by other members of the Court.

Writing and circulating opinions is the justices' most difficult and time-consuming task. Although the justices differ in their styles and approaches to writing opinions, most delegate the preliminary drafting of opinions to their law clerks. Only after a justice is satisfied with an initial draft does it go to other justices for their reactions.

Opinions announcing the decision of the Court are not statements of the author's particular views of jurisprudence. Rather, they are negotiated documents forged from ideological divisions within the Court. The justice writing the Court's opinion must avoid pride of authorship and attempt to reach a compromise that will secure a majority and an **institutional opinion** for the Court's decision. If a justice fails to achieve this goal, the opinion is reassigned.

What makes writing an opinion for the Court so difficult is that all the other justices are free to write their own individual opinions. They may write **concurring opinions**—opinions agreeing with the result reached by a majority but disagreeing with its reasons or legal analysis. Justices differ on the propriety of such opinions, which reflect failure or unwillingness to compromise. Some think that they are a sign of "institutional disobedience"; others believe that they are a valuable record of the justices' differing views. In any event, every justice now writes several concurring opinions each term.

Justices who disagree with the majority opinion usually write **dissenting opinions**. In the words of Chief Justice Hughes, dissenting opinions appeal "to the brooding spirit of the law, to the intelligence of a future day, when a later decision may possibly correct the error into which the dissenting judge believes the Court to have been betrayed."[7] Because dissenting opinions undercut the Court's decision, justices may use them as threats when trying to persuade the majority to narrow the scope of its ruling or tone down its language. Some justices write more dissents than others, but as a group they average about ten each term.

Opinion Days

Litigants, lawyers, the media, and the public finally learn the outcome of the justices' votes on opinion days, the days when the Court hands down its final published opinions. The Court once announced opinions only on "Decision Mondays," but now it may do so on any day of the week. By tradition, there is no prior announcement as to when cases will be handed down. Instead of reading their opinions from the bench, as was once done, the justices simply announce them in two to four minutes, merely stating the result in each case. Copies of opinions may be obtained from the offices of the clerk of the Court and the public information officer at the Court. The "Where on the Web?" box on page 351 suggests ways to access opinions as well as other legal materials in electronic form.

Supreme Court Decision Making as a Political Process

Decision making by the Supreme Court is a political process. The justices often follow their own political agendas when granting and deciding cases. Because the Court decides what cases to review on the basis of the vote of only four justices, the justices may form voting blocs to determine which cases will be granted review. But the justices decide the merits of those few cases by majority vote. In deciding those cases, the process of opinion writing is crucial to the final outcome and affords the justices opportunities to bargain and compromise with each other, as well as to write concurring or dissenting opinions.

The political struggles within the Court come to an end on opinion days, though the justices continue to compete for influence and try to persuade each other to reconsider their views in other cases. Opinion days, however, may also mark the beginning of larger struggles for influence between the Court and rival political forces.

THE POLITICS OF JUDICIAL POLICY MAKING

The Court decides conflicts over public law and policy by bringing them within the language, structure, and spirit of the Constitution. In this way, the Court determines public policy. The struggles that follow are central to American politics. The key actors in that competition are the lower courts, Congress, the president, political interest groups, and ultimately the general public. Their reactions may enhance or thwart the implementation of the Court's rulings and determine the extent of compliance with judicial policy making.

Although the Court depends on lower courts to enforce its rulings, compliance is invariably uneven because the ambiguity of judicial opinions allows lower courts to pursue their own policy goals. Crucial language in an opinion may be treated like *dicta*—language that is not binding in other cases. Or differences between the facts on which the Court ruled and the circumstances of another case may be emphasized so as to reach a result opposite to that reached by the Court. For example, lower courts interpreted *Abington School District v. Schempp* (1963), which struck down a law requiring the reciting of the Lord's Prayer in public schools, to permit voluntary and nondenominational prayer in public schools.[8] Likewise, state courts in Texas refused to extend the Court's ruling in *Norris v. Alabama* (1935) forbidding racial discrimination against blacks in the selection of juries.[9] They continued to allow the exclusion of Mexican Americans from juries until the Court finally ruled, in *Hernandez v. Texas* (1954), that all kinds of racial discrimination in jury selection violate the Fourteenth Amendment's equal protection clause.[10] In sum, open defiance is infrequent but not unprecedented. When it occurs, it reflects the differing policy preferences of state and federal judges.

On major issues of public policy, Congress is likely to prevail or at least to temper the impact of the Court's rulings. Congress may pressure the Court in a

WHERE ON THE WEB?

Supreme Court Decisions and Other Legal Materials

Are you especially interested in a decision that's just been handed down by the Supreme Court? Do you need to research the history of the Court's decisions on civil rights or flag burning? Are you interested in copyrighting a story or song you've written? The following information will be invaluable to you in finding what you need in electronic form.

In 1991, the Supreme Court began a project called *Hermes* that makes Court decisions available on the Internet on the day they are announced. Further, a number of university servers, such as Cornell Law School, are part of network sites that make the Court's opinions available to the public. Here are several ways to reach the Cornell server:

Gopher: **law.cornell.edu** or **http://www.law.cornell.edu** (specify the path: *U.S. Law: Primary Documents and Commentary*)

World Wide Web: **http://www.law.cornell.edu**

Telnet: **telnet gopher.law.cornell.edu** or **telnet www.law.cornell.edu** (specify the path above)

This server is one of the most accessible and useful; it contains all Supreme Court decisions from the 1991 term to the present, as well as some earlier landmark rulings. A database on selected state and federal judges, along with federal laws on copyright, patents, and other commercial practices, is also available.

listserv@law.cornell.edu (leave the subject line blank and in the message area, type: subscribe liibulletin *your name, address, phone number*)

Syllabi and opinions of the court may be accessed through e-mail on the preceding list server. On the very day the Court hands down a decision, syllabi of the decisions will be sent to your address. The full opinions may be requested through the methods given here or through e-mail. To receive a decision, you must submit the docket number of the case—for example: 95-0000, where 95 is the year and 0000 is the number of the case. Send an e-mail message to: **liidelivery@law.cornell.edu** and leave the subject blank. In the message area, type **request 95-0000.** To stop the messages from this site, send an e-mail message to **listserv@law.cornell.edu** and type **unsubscribe liibulletin** in the message area. New cases are also available from the base address for Supreme Court materials at **http://www.law.cornell.edu/supct/**

number of ways. The Senate may try to influence future judicial appointments, and the House may even try to impeach the justices. More often, Congress uses institutional and jurisdictional changes as weapons against the Court.

Under Article III of the Constitution, Congress has the power to "make exceptions" to the appellate jurisdiction of the federal courts. That authorization has been viewed as a way of denying courts the power to review certain kinds of cases. During the Reagan administration, for instance, there were numerous unsuccessful proposals to deny courts the power to decide cases involving

Sandra Day O'Connor, the first woman justice on the Supreme Court, plays a key centrist role in the Court's decisions, often providing the critical fifth vote needed to swing the outcome in one direction or the other.

school prayer and abortion. But Congress has succeeded only once in cutting back on the Supreme Court's jurisdiction; this occurred in 1868 with the repeal of the Court's jurisdiction over writs of habeas corpus.

Congress has had slightly greater success in reversing the Court by means of a constitutional amendment, which three-fourths of the states must ratify. The process is cumbersome, and thousands of amendments designed to overrule the Court have failed. But four Court decisions (see Chapter 2) have been overturned by constitutional amendments.

More successful has been congressional enactment or rewriting of legislation in response to the Court's rulings. In *Zurcher v. The Stanford Daily* (1978), for example, the Court held that there is no constitutional prohibition against police searching newsrooms without a warrant for "mere evidence" of a crime, such as photographs.[11] Two years later, however, Congress essentially reversed that ruling by passing the Privacy Protection Act of 1980, which prohibits unannounced searches of newsrooms and requires that police obtain a subpoena ordering writers to turn over desired evidence. So, too, Congress overrode more than a dozen rulings of the conservative Rehnquist Court when it enacted the Civil Rights Act of 1991.

Although Congress cannot always overturn the Court's rulings, it can often thwart their implementation. For example, Congress delayed implementation of the school desegregation decision in *Brown v. Board of Education* (1954) by not authorizing the executive branch to enforce the ruling until the passage of the Civil Rights Act of 1964. Later, by cutting back on appropriations for the Department of Justice and the Department of Health, Education, and Welfare during the Nixon and Ford administrations, Congress registered opposition to busing and further attempts to achieve integrated public schools.

Presidents may undercut the Court's policy making as well. By issuing contradictory directives to federal agencies and assigning low priority to enforcement by the Department of Justice, they may limit the impact of the Court's decisions. Presidents may also make broad moral appeals in opposition to the Court's rulings. For example, President Reagan's opposition to abortion served to legitimate resistance to the Court's decisions in this area.

When it threatens to go too far or too fast in its policy making, the Court is ultimately curbed by public opinion. Except during transitional periods or critical elections, however, the Court has usually been in step with major political and social movements.[12] Moreover, the public tends to perceive the Court as a temple of law rather than of politics—as impartial and removed from the pressures of special or partisan interests. But the public also tends to understand little about the operation of the Court, and for this reason only about 30 percent of Americans express "great confidence" in the Court.

Some Court watchers warn of an "imperial judiciary" and a "government by the judiciary."[13] They point out that judicial review is antidemocratic because it enables the Court to overturn laws enacted by popularly elected legislatures. But the Court's duty is to interpret the Constitution, and compliance with and enforcement of the Court's rulings depend on the cooperation of other political institutions as well as on public acceptance. Major confrontations over public policy are determined as much by what is possible in a pluralistic society with a system of free government as by what the Court says about the meaning of the Constitution.[14] That is the essence of politics in a constitutional democracy.

CASE STUDY

The Battle over Bork

In 1987, a fierce political battle erupted over President Ronald Reagan's nomination of Judge Robert H. Bork to the Supreme Court. Instead of becoming the 104th justice, Bork became the 28th Supreme Court nominee to be rejected or forced to withdraw because of opposition in the Senate. This confirmation battle underscored both the Reagan administration's effort to make the Court a symbol and an instrument of the Reagan presidency, and the power of the Senate to defeat a nominee.

In nominating Bork the president chose, over more moderate Republicans and conservative jurists, one of the most outspoken critics of the Court's liberal rulings under chief justices Earl Warren and Warren Burger. The president did so even though Democrats had regained control of the Senate in 1986 and were determined to oppose any nominee who was closely aligned with the right wing of the Republican party. Reagan underestimated the extent of this opposition, which was heightened by the pivotal nature of the appointment. The justice whom Bork was to replace, Lewis Powell, had often cast the crucial fifth vote in cases upholding such liberal-backed policies as legal abortion and affirmative action programs.

The president's nomination of Bork was immediately denounced by Democratic senator Edward Kennedy of Massachusetts and by the chair of the Senate

Judiciary Committee, Democratic senator Joseph Biden of Delaware. More than eighty-three organizations followed. Calling Bork "unfit" to serve on the high court, the American Civil Liberties Union abandoned its practice of not opposing nominees. The AFL-CIO also came out in opposition to Bork.

Right-wing organizations were no less active in support of Bork, though they were initially encouraged to downplay their support by White House chief of staff Howard Baker. Over the objections of the Justice Department, the White House adopted a strategy of recasting Bork's conservative record in order to make his opponents appear shrill and partisan. A 70-page White House briefing book was prepared, followed by a 240-page report released by the Justice Department; both attempted to portray Bork as a "mainstream" jurist.

The publicity surrounding the nomination was extraordinary. Numerous reports analyzing Bork's record were distributed to editorial boards around the country by both sides in the struggle. People for the American Way, a liberal group, launched a $2 million media campaign opposing the nomination, and the National Conservative Political Action Committee committed more than $1 million to lobbying for Bork's confirmation.

What had far greater impact, however, was Bork's own role in the preconfirmation fray and the Senate confirmation proceedings. Even before the hearings began, Bork took the unusual step of granting newspaper interviews to explain, clarify, and amend his twenty-five year record as a Yale Law School professor, United States solicitor general in the Nixon administration, and federal judge. These actions broke with tradition and gave the appearance of a public relations campaign.

During his five days and thirty hours of nationally televised testimony before the Judiciary Committee, Bork continued to give the appearance of refashioning himself into a moderate, even "centrist," jurist. By the time he finished, he had contradicted much of what he had stood for in the past. A key consideration thus became, in the words of Senator Patrick Leahy (D, Vt.), one of "confirmation conversion." Noting the "considerable difference between what Judge Bork has written and what he has testified he will do if confirmed," Arlen Specter, a Republican senator from Pennsylvania, observed, "I think that what many of us are looking for is some assurance of where you are." Even Bork seemed troubled, and at the end of his testimony he told the committee, "It really would be preposterous to say things I said to you and then get on the Court and do the opposite. I would be disgraced in history."

Bork's testimony weighed far more than that of the 110 witnesses assembled for and against him in the following two weeks. To be sure, they contributed to the atmosphere of campaign politics that surrounded the hearings. For the first time a former president, Gerald Ford, introduced a nominee to the committee. And former president Jimmy Carter sent a letter expressing his opposition to the nomination. Nor had justices ever before come out as allies of a president or his nominee. Yet retired chief justice Warren Burger testified on behalf of Bork, and justices John Paul Stevens and Byron White publicly endorsed him.

In spite of the publicity and pressure group activities, the hearings were illuminating. They focused on the nature of the Constitution. Is the Constitution defined by the intent of the framers, as Bork's supporters maintained? Or is the Constitution a living document, one that has become more democratic through amendments and interpretations? In the end, this debate turned the tide against Bork in the Senate. Conservative southern Democrats and moderate Republicans joined liberal Democrats to oppose the nomination. The politics in their states, the position of their parties, and the opinion of a majority of the public would not have supported a return to an era in which civil rights and liberties were not protected as they are today.

Discussion Questions

1. What role does and should the Senate play in the appointment of federal judges?
2. Has the appointment of Supreme Court justices become too politicized?
3. What standards should apply in the selection and confirmation of nominees to the federal bench?

SUMMARY

The judiciary is a political institution and often must rule on some of the most divisive social issues of the day. Courts provide forums for individuals and interest groups to obtain hearings of their disputes and legal claims. Courts and judges are thus integral players in the politics of American government.

The United States has two separate judicial systems, federal and state; these dual systems are termed *judicial federalism*. If there is a conflict between national and state law, the matter is settled by the federal courts and ultimately by the Supreme Court. Article III of the Constitution vests judicial power in the Supreme Court and any other courts created by Congress. Courts created under Article III are *constitutional courts*. Today, the federal judiciary consists of ninety-four district courts, thirteen courts of appeals, and the Supreme Court.

Courts have jurisdiction only over disputes involving adverse interests and a real controversy. The parties must have *standing to sue;* they must show that they are suffering or are in danger of suffering an immediate and substantial personal injury. Courts avoid deciding *political questions* that the judges think should be resolved by other branches of government. Disputes that are open to judicial resolution are referred to as *justifiable disputes*.

The power of judicial review gives the courts the ability to strike down any law enacted by Congress or by the states and to declare official government actions unconstitutional. Although judicial review is controversial because it enables the Supreme Court to thwart the democratic process, the Court has nevertheless increasingly asserted this power. As a result it has been criticized for its *judicial activism* and urged to exercise *judicial self-restraint*—to defer to Congress and state legislatures.

The method of selecting state court judges varies from one state to another. Federal judges are appointed by the president with the advice and consent of the Senate. Senators exercise considerable influence on lower-court appointments; and the president often encounters considerable senatorial opposition to his nominations of Supreme Court justices, who are usually political associates and individuals who share his political views.

The Supreme Court decides less than 2 percent of the cases placed on its *docket* each year. The Court takes only cases that involve questions of law on which lower courts have disagreed. Litigants then submit briefs on the *merits*—the questions to be decided.

The Court hears oral arguments in only about one hundred cases a year. Each side in a case has thirty minutes to present its arguments. Within a day or two after oral arguments, the justices meet in secret conference to discuss and vote on the case. One of the justices in the majority is assigned to write an *opinion* for the Court on the case. The justice writing the opinion must attempt to reach a compromise that will serve as an *institutional opinion* stating the reasons for the Court's decision. The other justices are free to write *concurring opinions*, which agree with the decision but for different reasons, or *dissenting opinions*.

The Court decides conflicts by bringing them within the language, structure, and spirit of the Constitution. In this way, it determines public policy. The reactions of other institutions of government and the public may enhance or thwart the implementation of the Court's rulings. Congress can temper the impact of a ruling by means of jurisdictional changes, through a constitutional amendment, or by rewriting legislation. The president can undercut the Court by issuing contradictory directives to federal agencies, assigning low priority to enforcement, or publicly disagreeing with its rulings. Ultimately, however, the Court is curbed by public opinion.

KEY TERMS

judicial federalism
constitutional courts
legislative courts
district courts
courts of appeals
jurisdiction
original jurisdiction
appellate jurisdiction
standing to sue
political question
judicial activism
judicial self-restraint
merit system
confirmation hearing
docket
petitions for a writ of certiorari
rule of four
merits
opinion
institutional opinion
concurring opinion
dissenting opinion

RESOURCES

READINGS

Abraham, Henry. *Justices and Presidents*. 3rd ed. New York: Oxford University Press, 1992. An excellent political history of appointments to the Supreme Court.

O'Brien, David. *Storm Center: The Supreme Court in American Politics*. 4th ed. New York: Norton, 1996. A detailed institutional history of Supreme Court politics.

Rosenberg, Gerald. *The Hollow Hope: Can Courts Bring About Social Change?* Chicago: University of Chicago Press, 1991. A well-written, provocative study that argues that courts cannot bring about massive social change.

ORGANIZATIONS

Administrative Office of the United States Courts, Thurgood Marshall Federal Judiciary Building, One Columbus Circle, N.E., Washington, DC 20544; (202) 273-3000; Internet http://www.ncsc.dni.us/ Conducts some research and collects data on federal caseloads; is responsible for the administration of the federal courts.

Federal Judicial Center, Thurgood Marshall Federal Judiciary Building, One Columbus Circle, N.E., Washington, DC 20544; (202) 273-4000. Conducts research and training programs for the federal judiciary and publishes a newsletter, *The Third Branch*.

Public Information Office, Supreme Court of the United States, One 1st Street, Washington, DC 20543; (202) 223-2584. Distributes opinions of the Court and occasional speeches by the justices.

Supreme Court Historical Society, 111 2nd Street, N.E., Washington, DC 20002; (202) 543-0400. Collects materials related to the history of the Supreme Court and funds research projects. Publishes newsletters and *The Yearbook of the Supreme Court Historical Society*.

14

The Policy-Making Process

PREVIEW

- Types of policy
- Stages in the policy-making process: problem recognition; policy formulation and adoption; policy implementation, policy evaluation, and policy reconsideration or termination
- Politics and the policy process: incrementalism; major policy shifts; mixed results

Declaring "crime ravaging our neighborhoods and communities . . . [to be] a threat to [the nation's] security, economic revival, and our most basic values," President Clinton in August 1993 proposed a mammoth anticrime bill. The measure he outlined represented an unprecedented federal initiative in crime fighting, typically thought of as an issue mainly for state and local governments to handle. The president asked for enough money to help state and local officials hire 100,000 new police officers. His proposal also called for new federal death penalties, an overhaul of the appeals process for inmates on death row, a ban on assault weapons, and a waiting period and background check for handgun purchases. "It's time we put aside the divisions of party and philosophy," the president declared. "There is no conceivable excuse to delay this action one more day."

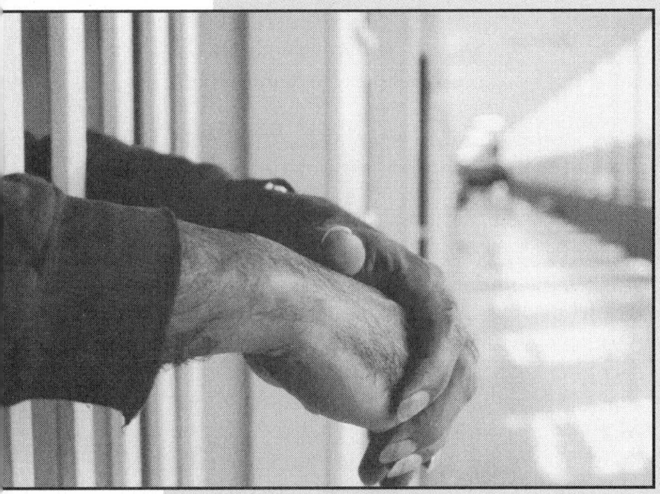

But despite President Clinton's pleas for rapid, nonpartisan action—and despite polls that consistently showed crime and security to be top public concerns—almost one full year of rancorous legislative debate passed before Congress ultimately approved an anticrime bill. Passage required marshaling the support of "friends," overcoming the opposition of "enemies," compromising on many important issues, and effectively utilizing the legislative skills of party leaders in both houses of Congress. In all these ways, the consideration and passage of the anticrime bill provide a good illustration of the politics of making public policy in America.

Sponsors of the bill crafted a measure designed to appeal to liberals and conservatives alike. For liberals, the legislation included gun control provisions, rehabilitation programs, expanded shelters and services for battered women, drug treatment centers, and youth crime prevention programs. For conservatives, the bill provided for more prisons, more harsh sentencing, and more police.

Opposition to the bill came both from some Democrats—especially members of the black and Hispanic caucuses—who believed the bill was *too punitive,* and from some Republicans who believed the bill was *too soft* on crime. Other Republicans felt the administration had not adequately consulted with them in preparing the bill. In particular, Republicans opposed a provision allocating to cities and communities funds that could be spent pretty much as they saw fit. "That's $1.6 billion that could go for law enforcement that is going right down the drain," complained Senator Orrin Hatch (R, Utah).

Lobbying efforts, both pro and con, were fierce. Formidable opposition to the bill came from the National Rifle Association (NRA) and other gun rights advocates, who waged massive telephone and radio campaigns. In March 1994, just prior to congressional action on the bill, the NRA reportedly made $150,000 in congressional campaign contributions. So concerned was the NRA about this measure that Senator Tom Harkin (D, Iowa) commented, "The real reason that many senators are opposing this bill can be summarized in three letters: NRA."

Supporters of the bill marshaled their own lobbying efforts. President Clinton personally contacted dozens of members of Congress, as did Treasury Secretary Lloyd Bentsen and Attorney General Janet Reno. The administration persuaded former presidents Ronald Reagan, Jimmy Carter, and Gerald Ford to sign a letter of support. Democratic supporters also called upon the nation's police chiefs and mayors (including such Republicans as Mayor Rudolph Giuliani of New York and Richard Riordan of Los Angeles) to lobby Congress.

In the end, skillful maneuvering by House and Senate leaders resulted in the bill's passage. Supporters agreed to cuts totaling more than $3 billion in funding for crime prevention programs—areas that critics described as "pork." Opponents also were able to win modest adjustments to the provision banning assault weapons and to force the dropping of the provision permitting defendants to use sentencing statistics to challenge a death sentence as racially discriminatory. Overall, despite some defections in their own ranks, the Democratic majorities in both the House and the Senate made enough concessions to win sufficient moderate Republican support to pass the bill.

Among the major provisions of the $30.2 billion bill were the authorization of $8.8 billion over six years to help communities hire 100,000 police officers; $7.9 billion in construction grants for state prisons and boot camps; $6.9 billion for crime prevention programs; and the banning for ten years of the manufacture, sale, or possession of 19 types of assault weapons. As such, the bill represents a major step toward redefining the traditional relationship between the federal government and state and local governments in the law enforcement area. Prior to this act, federal law enforcement activity generally meant bigger federal budgets for *federal* agents, prosecutors, and prisons. As a result of the law, the Justice Department will be funneling billions of dollars back to *states, counties, and cities* for crime prevention programs.

In signing the bill on September 13, 1994, President Clinton declared, "Today the bickering stops. The era of excuses is over, the law-abiding citizens of our country have made their voices heard. Never again should Washington put politics and party above law and order."

The struggle for passage of the anticrime bill illustrates several aspects of policy making in America. First, in spite of President Clinton's appeals to "put aside the divisions of party and philosophy" and not to "delay this action one more day," policy making is almost always conflictual, and the process is almost never rapid. Policy making is a struggle between groups advocating one side or another. This struggle is especially intense when the stakes are high, and it does not always end with the passage of legislation. Second, private lobbying groups are critical in the policy-making process. They play important roles in formulating and adopting various policy positions and in shaping public opinion. The anticrime legislation also shows that the policy-making process rarely leaves everyone completely satisfied and that, indeed, compromise is essential if the process is to succeed. Finally, this example shows the importance of politics in the policy-making process. A certain amount of bargaining, negotiating, and old-fashioned arm twisting is often critical to the adoption of new policy initiatives.[1]

How do issues like crime and crime prevention become part of the national political agenda? How do they come to be viewed as important enough to warrant attention and consideration by the political system? How is government persuaded to act on public issues? These questions are examined in this chapter.

TYPES OF POLICY

Public policy is action by government designed to address public problems. Simply stated, public policy is what government does (or does not do). In a more formal sense, public policy can be said to be "a goal-directed or purposive course of action [taken by government] in an attempt to deal with a public problem."[2] This definition focuses on the actual *accomplishments* of government.

Public policies may be classified in a number of ways. Some experts classify them in terms of who pays the cost of the programs. Some classify them in terms of who benefits. Others focus on issues or on social impacts. Classification of policies in terms of their impacts on society sheds light on the political strategies associated with different policies. An example of this approach is Theodore Lowi's classification of policies as distributive, regulatory, or redistributive.[3]

Distributive policies are those that distribute goods and services to citizens. Policies that provide recreational, public safety, transportation, and educational services are examples of distributive policies. Distributive policies also include subsidies to farmers, the Social Security program, the interstate highway system, grants for scientific research, grants-in-aid to cities and states, tax deductions for interest on home mortgage loans, and the construction of harbors, reservoirs, and dams. The important point about distributive policies is that although some group or groups may gain something from a particular policy, the costs associated with the policy are viewed as minimal because they are shared by the public as a whole.

In distributive policy making everyone seems to win; no one appears to lose, or at least no one appears to lose very much. The politics of distributive policy making is generally described as "pork-barrel politics"—there is something for everyone, and individual legislators support each other's particular programs. Although such programs may cost billions of dollars, they generate surprisingly little controversy.

Regulatory policies are those through which the government establishes rules and standards and thereby regulates or controls the behavior of individuals, groups, businesses, or other entities. Often developed in response to practices that are deemed harmful or destructive, regulatory policies include laws that regulate child labor, automobile emissions, minimum wages, harmful additives in food, and the dumping of industrial wastes in streams and rivers. Regulatory policy making generally is associated with intense lobbying, as groups attempt to secure legislation that will be advantageous to them or defeat legislation that will be disadvantageous.

Redistributive policies are those that are clearly perceived to take benefits (wealth, property, or other values) from some groups and give them to others. For example, some people view welfare programs as taking resources away from them in order to benefit poorer people. Similarly, some whites view policies designed to enhance the voting strength and participation of minorities as taking power away from them. Because policy making on such questions can be seen as a zero-sum game (one group will win, and another will lose), redistributive policies are the type least amenable to compromise. Usually there are two consistent and clearly identifiable sides. Liberals and conservatives often line up on opposite sides, and rhetoric is intense from both sides. The politics of redistributive policy making often is described as "class politics" because those with many resources are battling those with few.

STAGES IN THE POLICY-MAKING PROCESS

Policy making can best be thought of as a *process*. Although it is not possible to describe in detail the elements of the formation of every policy, it is possible to discuss five general stages by which most policies are made: problem recognition, policy formulation and adoption, policy implementation, policy evaluation, and policy reconsideration or termination.

Problem Recognition

Problem recognition is probably the most important stage in the policy-making process. Before Congress considers an issue, before an agency of the executive branch administers a program, and before the courts consider any disputes that may have arisen, the issue must first be recognized as a problem requiring government attention.

Public awareness is critical for an issue to receive serious consideration. Dramatic social and economic events often trigger that awareness. The Great Depression of the 1930s is a classic example of an event that forced the country to pay attention to the need for significant public action in welfare, employment, housing, and social policy. The Iraqi invasion of Kuwait in 1990 was an attention-getting event in international affairs and precipitated American involvement in the Persian Gulf War.

Often, the president can use his unique position of high public visibility to bring to the nation's attention issues that he particularly wishes to place on the policy agenda. For example, President Clinton has been very concerned about public education. His recommendation in 1997 of a series of measures designed to set minimum standards and evaluate performance for the nation's elementary and secondary students sparked a national dialog on the quality of public education in America, and the role of the national government in maintaining that quality.

But sometimes seemingly small, unexpected events provide the spark that leads to significant public awareness of a problem and perhaps eventually to

Public awareness of an issue can lead to public support for policies that address it. Images of clear-cut forests on the Olympic Peninsula of Washington helped to focus attention on the controversy between the logging industry and environmental groups over the preservation of the spotted owl, as well as on the broader ecological effects of clear-cutting.

new or modified policy solutions. Environmentalists, for example, succeeded in bringing to the public's attention the plight of the northern spotted owl. This 2-pound bird, whose habitat is the fir and spruce forests in Washington, Oregon, and California, is threatened by logging. In the late 1980s, environmentalists succeeded in having the bird placed on the endangered species list and forcing at least a temporary reduction of logging activities.

The resulting battle between environmentalists and the timber industry was the most intense ever generated by the Endangered Species Act. Environmentalists argued that the ecosystem including the habitat of the spotted owl was in decline and that more than one hundred other species of plants and animals were also threatened with extinction. The timber industry countered that the forest provided employment for thousands of families as well as lumber for millions of American homes. Environmentalists filed a number of lawsuits claiming that the Interior Department and the United States Forest Service, the two federal agencies managing the forests, were not protecting the owl or its habitat and were breaking the law. After more than a decade of struggle, in 1992 President Bush grudgingly approved a plan to restrict logging on 5.4 million acres of Pacific Northwest forest where the spotted owl lives.

The spotted owl controversy continued to be a catalyst for policy change into the Clinton administration. One of the early actions of Clinton's secretary of the interior, Bruce Babbitt, was the announcement of a major policy shift in the department's method of wildlife protection. Babbitt's plan, as he described it in congressional testimony in 1993, was to focus on entire ecosystems rather than on individual plants and animals. Babbitt's proposal would provide for intervention before any crises arose and individual species were endangered, thereby avoiding lengthy and contentious legal battles like those over the spotted owl. On the other side, after the Republicans took control of Congress in 1995, they passed a waiver of environmental laws, permitting the resumption of logging across vast sections of public land. Although President Clinton had vowed to veto the measure, he did ultimately sign it.

Public awareness of an issue is not enough to guarantee that the issue will be placed on the policy agenda. Skillful advocacy by interest groups is also critical. As noted in Chapter 7, political interest groups see to it that issues of concern to them are brought to the public's attention and make their way to the agenda-setting stage of the policy process. In the case of the northern spotted owl, environmental groups like the Wilderness Society and the Environmental Defense Fund were instrumental in bringing the issue to the public's attention. Other groups, such as political parties, the media, academics, and even influential public and private individuals, may also serve as important advocates of particular policy issues.

Policy Formulation and Adoption—Subgovernments and Issue Networks

Once a problem has been placed on the government's agenda, an effective and feasible solution to the problem must be found. This stage is called **policy formulation**. Usually, there are many possible courses of action for resolving a problem. For example, the perceived problem of declining test scores among college-bound high school seniors might be addressed by policies to encourage more effective teachers, smaller classes, curriculum modification, or some combination of these. From the variety of options that exist, policy makers must identify a solution or set of solutions that will be effective in addressing the problem, acceptable to the parties concerned, and affordable.

Many actors and organizations may be involved in the actual formulation of policy. Legislators and their staffs, the president and the White House staff, government bureaucrats and agencies, specially appointed commissions, and "think tanks" (such as the Brookings Institution and the American Enterprise Institute) all may be involved in the drafting of policy alternatives. Moreover, policy is rarely formulated without active involvement on the part of those *interest groups* most likely to be affected.

Policy formulation does not always result in a new law or administrative action. Frequently policy makers may decide not to act at all. The fact that an issue has made it to the agenda-setting stage does not automatically mean that action will be taken.[4]

Marshaling the support needed to win official approval of a specific course of action is called **policy adoption**. At this stage, lobbying, bargaining, negotiating, and compromising may be needed. Seldom does any policy emerge from the process in the form in which it was initially proposed. To be adopted, to gain sufficient political support, policies often must be modified significantly.

Often the activities that take place during the formulation and adoption stages occur among a cluster of actors and institutions. The special relationship that sometimes develops among executive agencies, interest groups, and congressional committees has been called an "iron triangle" (see Chapter 12). Three decades ago, Douglas Cater described this phenomenon as a **subgovernment**:

> In one important area of policy after another, substantial efforts to exercise power are waged by alliances cutting across the [executive and congres-

> sional] branches of government and including key operatives from outside. In effect, they constitute *subgovernments* of Washington comprising the expert, the interested, and the engaged. [emphasis added][5]

Figure 14-1 shows the energy subgovernment. When energy policy is formulated, the most active and influential participants will come from the executive departments and agencies, congressional committees, and interest groups listed in the figure. Subgovernments also exist in education, employment and labor, health, urban affairs, agriculture, transportation, national security, and other issue areas.

Hugh Heclo has extended the subgovernment concept by arguing that for many of today's highly technical issues it is impossible to identify clearly a few dominant actors. In the many policy areas that are highly intricate and confusing, Heclo argues, influential individuals and groups move freely in and out of the policy arena, and in many cases it appears that no group is actually "in control" of policy making. Heclo uses the term **issue network** to describe the adoption of policy in many contemporary problem areas. An issue network, he says, "is a shared-knowledge group having to do with some aspect (or as defined by the network, some problem) of public policy."[6] Issue networks supplement those actors traditionally identified as belonging to the iron triangle with a host of other policy professionals and experts.

FIGURE 14-1

The Energy Subgovernment

EXECUTIVE DEPARTMENTS AND AGENCIES

Energy Department
Interior Department
Nuclear Regulatory Commission

KEY CONGRESSIONAL COMMITTEES

Senate
Energy and Natural Resources
Environment and Public Works

House of Representatives
Commerce
Resources
Science

SELECTED INTEREST GROUPS

American Public Power Association
Environmental Action
Environmental Defense Fund
Friends of the Earth
Resources for the Future
Sierra Club
Union of Concerned Scientists
Worldwatch Institute

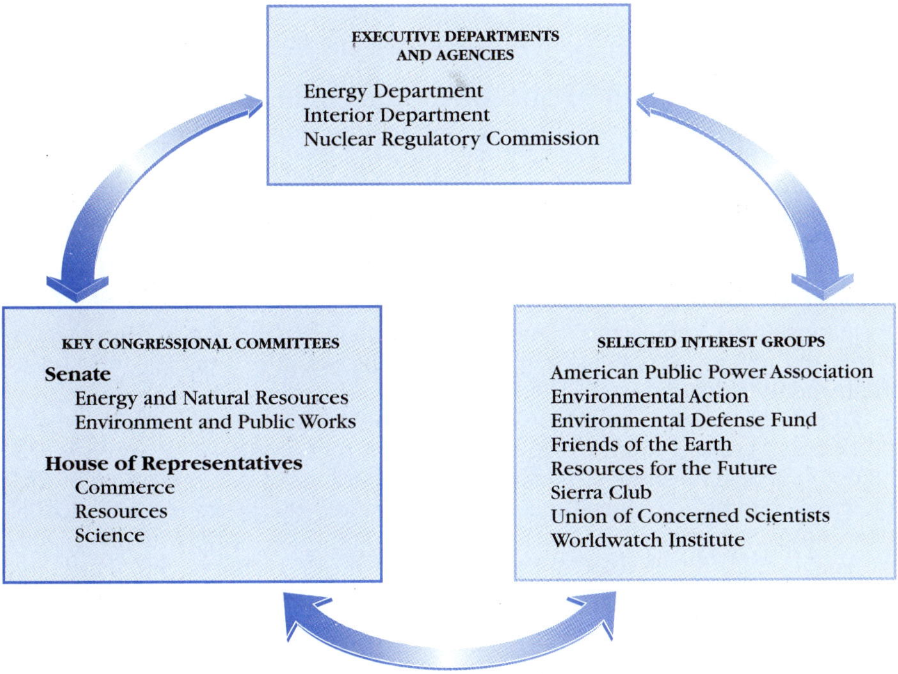

SOURCE: *Washington Information Directory, 1995–1996* (Washington, D.C.: Congressional Quarterly, Inc., 1996); and *The Capital Source* (Washington, D.C.: National Journal, Spring, 1996).

Health policy, for example, is characterized by many sets of people who are knowledgeable about various aspects of this complex issue: physicians and other health-care professionals, hospitals and clinics, mental health centers, nursing homes, pharmaceutical companies, insurance companies, patients, senior citizens, and so forth. Health policy cannot possibly be made in isolation from these, and many other, groups. In Heclo's view, issue networks have not replaced traditional subgovernments, but they have added a new and complicating dimension to policy formation and adoption. Issue networks, he says, "overlay the once stable political reference points with new forces that complicate calculations, decrease predictability, and impose considerable strains on those charged with government leadership."[7]

Policy Implementation

Policies that have been adopted must be administered. Putting policy into place is called **policy implementation**. In a few cases, policy decisions may be self-executing: for example, the decision to extend formal diplomatic recognition to a new foreign government is a policy that is essentially in place as soon as it is adopted. The vast majority of laws and policy decisions, however, are not implemented automatically. Many may require a complex implementation structure, perhaps involving hundreds of thousands of people and the expenditure of millions or billions of dollars.

Policy implementation is not a simple, routine process. The administration of policy can be highly political, sometimes involving struggles as intense as those occurring during the policy adoption process. For example, in recent years the EPA and its staff have been constantly embroiled in debates with environmentalists and certain members of Congress over the implementation of environmental legislation. Environmental groups frequently charge that the EPA is too slow in implementing legislation, and some members of Congress believe the EPA has ignored or significantly modified congressional intent in certain areas.

Administrators and bureaucrats in any agency frequently have wide latitude in the implementation and administration of policy. Such latitude is desirable when they need to modify policy to fit changing times and conditions. It can be detrimental, however, if administrators actively change the direction of policy. By choosing to apply laws rigorously or leniently, bureaucrats may actually shape the impact of policies and thus incur the wrath of Congress, the president, and outside groups.

The courts too may be important in shaping policy during the implementation phase. Judicial rulings often establish the precise direction a policy will take. In public education, for example, court decisions have required the busing of schoolchildren to achieve racial balance, limited the power of local school boards to set student dress codes, forced local authorities to provide more educational options for disabled and other disadvantaged children, and altered the methods of state school financing to achieve greater equity among local school districts.

Policy Evaluation

A policy that has been formulated, adopted, and implemented is ready to be evaluated. **Policy evaluation** involves the set of activities designed to determine whether a policy is working as intended. Does an energy policy actually reduce the wasteful use of energy? Did the Patriot missile perform effectively under combat conditions? Does an environmental policy result in a less polluted environment? Does a child nutrition policy result in healthier children? Does an educational program for disadvantaged children result in better education for those children? Does an antipoverty policy result in the reduction of poverty? And what is the cost of each of these programs?

Not only *intended* consequences but also *unanticipated* ones need to be evaluated. A highway construction program, for example, may relieve traffic congestion as hoped but may also stimulate commercial growth and development in areas that are unprepared for such growth. Moreover, it may generate unexpectedly higher levels of pollution or reduce ridership on mass transit.

Policy evaluation may be conducted in two ways. The first is informal or "seat of the pants" evaluation.[8] For example, if residents and administrators of a housing program express satisfaction with the program, there is at least an informal indication that the program is working. The problem with such impressionistic evaluations is that the evaluators may not be disinterested parties. If they have been advocates of the program, have a stake in its success, or depend for their information on those who do, this can affect their judgments.

To avoid this problem, evaluators try to measure the impact of policy in more rigorous ways. They do so by collecting information from a variety of sources, by using sophisticated statistical analyses, and by following accepted methods of social-scientific research. When this is done, others can check the results, and analysts can determine whether the policy is having the desired impact. This leads to the last stage in the policy process.

Policy Reconsideration or Termination

Programs that are not meeting their objectives or have outlived the problem for which they were created may be overhauled or may undergo **policy termination**. As one team of policy analysts has noted, "policies get old, they wear out, or they keep solving problems that have long since been resolved or replaced by more pressing social priorities. . . . Releasing dollars and other resources invested in outdated programs makes them available for deployment against new problems."[9] In 1993, for example, Congress—bowing to pressure to cut spending—terminated support for the $11 billion Superconducting Supercollider (SSC) project being built in Texas. And in 1995, citing the need to set an example for cost savings in other areas of government, Congress abolished its Office of Technology Assessment, an agency that for twenty-three years had provided members with advice on technical issues such as nuclear proliferation, medical research, and telecommunications policy.

But there are many obstacles to program termination, and halting an ongoing project can be very difficult. As California representative George Brown commented, with some exaggeration, during debates on the SSC, "Something you learn quickly around here is that nothing ever dies."[10] Obviously, employees of the agency that was created to administer a program will fight to hold on to their jobs. Agency employees typically seek ways to demonstrate their value and to publicize the severe negative consequences of terminating the program. The agency's clients—those who are served by the program—will also rally around a continuation of the program, as may legislators responding to pressure from potential voters or government contractors. Despite such difficulties, however, program terminations and modifications do occur—they are part of the policy-making process.

POLITICS AND THE POLICY PROCESS

The making of public policy is a process that moves through several identifiable stages and is never complete. What, then, are the implications of the continually changing and incomplete nature of policy?

Incrementalism

Incrementalism is a salient characteristic of policy making in the United States. Policy is made in slow, halting steps, or increments. Often policy makers seem to take two steps forward and one step back. Many factors account for the slow pace. Social problems often are complex, simple solutions are rarely possible, and funds are almost always limited. The most important factor, however, is the fragmentation of political power.

Responsibility for any policy area is shared by a host of congressional committees and subcommittees; by numerous executive departments, commissions, and agencies; and by the already overloaded and overburdened court system. Moreover, the fragmentation found at the national level is magnified many times over at the state and local levels. Fragmented power means that interested groups and individuals have numerous opportunities to block or alter suggested policy changes and that an extraordinary amount of coalition building is necessary to bring about any significant change. Not only does coalition building take time, but it also necessitates a considerable amount of bargaining and compromise. Most policies that are adopted have been modified to satisfy the concerns of numerous groups and organizations.

Major Policy Shifts

Major changes in policy sometimes do occur, however. In the mid 1990s, significant change in the nation's approach to welfare policy occurred, as a major federal antipoverty program was replaced with lump-sum payments to the states, giving them broad discretion to run their own welfare programs.

In the American system, large-scale, fundamental policy shifts are often associated with major social, economic, or international upheavals like the Great Depression or the emergence of the Soviet Union as a superpower after World War II. Such events create a sense of urgency. Suddenly everyone agrees that something must be done, and it is possible to overcome some of the usual delaying forces of American politics.

Major policy changes are also often associated with strong and persistent pressure from the White House. President Johnson's extraordinary interest in education played a major role in the passage of the 1965 education act. President Nixon's strong support of the general revenue-sharing program was largely responsible for its passage in 1972.

Finally, chances for major policy shifts are usually enhanced when the same political party controls Congress and the presidency. President Johnson was greatly assisted in his campaign for passage of education reform, as well as other parts of his Great Society program, by the presence of large majorities of Democrats in the House and Senate who were sympathetic to his proposals.

Thousands of former welfare recipients in New York City have been put to work cleaning parks, playgrounds, and other public spaces under the city's Work Experience Program. The administration of Mayor Rudolph Giuliani touted the program as the solution to years of cutbacks in park maintenance, but unionized park workers charged that their jobs were being replaced with what amounted to slave labor.

President Reagan was aided by a Republican majority in the Senate and strong Republican unity in the House during the first years of his administration.

Mixed Results

Does public policy have much impact on the problems it is designed to solve? Successful policy initiatives include the Social Security system, the Peace Corps, the Head Start program for preschool children, the school lunch program for those who cannot afford to purchase adequate meals, and the federal job training program, which has provided numerous people with the education and skills necessary for steady employment.

Some problems persist in spite of massive efforts to wipe them out. Billions of dollars have been spent to combat poverty, but there still are poor people in the United States. Billions of dollars have been spent to clean up the environment, but there still are polluted lakes, streams, and air. Billions of dollars have been spent on housing, but there still are homeless people.

Such problems persist for a variety of reasons. One is the complexity of the problems themselves. Poverty, for example, has multiple causes, and experts often disagree about which are most important. Another reason is that the costs of a proposed solution may be more than society is willing to pay. Cleaning up the environment to a degree that satisfies the most ardent environmentalists might consume funds that most people would prefer to spend on other programs.

The high cost of solving, or even significantly affecting, complex problems is a particularly important issue—one that frequently brings its own set of policy

PRACTICING DEMOCRACY

Following an Issue through Congress

Many bills are proposed in every session of Congress, but relatively few survive the legislative process to become law. For those that do, the path is usually long and tortuous. There are several ways to track a bill as it moves along.

The first step is to get a copy of the bill itself. When a senator or representative introduces a bill, it is given a number or title. If you don't know the number of a House bill, call the clerk of the House at (202) 225-7000 and ask. Once you have the number, you can request a free copy of the House bill from the House Document Room, U.S. Capitol, Washington, D.C. 20515; phone (202) 225-3456. Senate bills are available from the Senate Document Room, U.S. Capitol, Washington, D.C. 20510; phone (202) 224-7860. You can also find the bill in the *Congressional Record* for the day it was entered.

A bill is assigned to the committee of the House or Senate that is concerned with the topic the bill covers. The committee discusses the bill and holds hearings so that interested individuals can express their opinions. Most committee meetings and hearings are open to the public. The "Daily Digest" section of the *Congressional Record* lists the next day's schedule of committee meetings. Committees and subcommittees also generally issue their own calendars. Call the Capitol switchboard at (202) 224-3121 and ask for the relevant committee; a staff member will send you the calendar.

Another way to track a bill is to use the *Calendar of the House of Representatives and History of Legislation.* Published weekly when Congress is in session, this document contains (among other things) a list of bills currently in conference committee, a list of bills out of conference, histories of all the bills before the House, and the House calendar. It can be requested from the House Document Room.

questions. Proposals for solving a particular problem almost always raise the question of how to cover the costs of the proposed solution. Should funds for a new policy initiative be generated by raising taxes, or should they be taken from funds currently being spent in another area?

Some problems are not solved because of disagreement about what the problems really are. In the area of housing, for example, public policy has had a split focus. At some times, the emphasis has been on the construction of large public housing projects. At other times, the goal has been to clean up urban blight. At still other times, policies have been designed to provide subsidies for homeowners and renters.

What exactly is the problem? How are programs going to be paid for? Which groups are going to benefit, and which are going to lose? These are the sorts of political questions that policy makers must resolve. When the groups that are most directly involved in making policy decisions—Congress and its various committees, the president, agency administrators, interest groups, and the political parties—can reach agreement about the nature of the problem, and about the measures required to resolve it, solutions tend to be reached fairly quickly. At the core of policy making in the United States

For a small fee, the LEGIS computerized database system provides detailed information on bills in Congress. For more information, contact LEGIS, Ford House Office Building, Washington, D.C. 20515; phone (202) 225-1772. The full text of congressional legislation is also available at **http//thomas.loc.gov** on the Internet. The e-mail address **thomas@loc.gov** gives more information about this Internet site.

You can also speak to staff members or listen to taped telephone messages on the status of bills and other activities in Congress. For a daily digest of the Senate portion of the *Congressional Record,* call (202) 224-2658; for the House, call (202) 225-2868. For a daily update on the status of bills in the House or Senate, call (202) 225-1772.

Both parties in Congress provide staff members and taped telephone messages that monitor the progress of legislation—so-called cloakroom messages. For daily legislative activity in the House of Representatives, call the Democrats at (202) 225-7400 or the Republicans at (202) 225-7430. For the next day's House legislative schedule, call the Republicans at (202) 225-2020 or the Democrats at (202) 225-7330. For daily legislative activity in the Senate, call the Democrats at (202) 224-8541 or the Republicans at (202) 224-8601. For the Senate legislative schedule, call the Republicans at (202) 224-5456 or the Democrats at (202) 224-4691.

For up-to-the-minute developments, many congressional debates, votes, committee meetings, and hearings are regularly televised live on the noncommercial cable channels C-SPAN and C-SPAN2. You can also observe floor debates and votes in the Senate and House chambers in person from the visitors' galleries. Write to or call the Washington office of your senator or representative to arrange for a free pass.

lies politics—the struggle among people with differing goals, objectives, and resources. Politics both defines the problems to be addressed by policy makers and shapes the solutions.

CASE STUDY

Making Welfare Work

For years politicians seeking a sure-fire campaign issue have found a safe target in the nation's public welfare system. Many critics, especially Republicans and conservatives, not only charged that waste and fraud run rampant in welfare programs but blamed the policies themselves for encouraging family breakups, unwed pregnancies, and a supposed "culture of dependency" that keeps welfare recipients from summoning up the motivation to go out and look for a job.

In the 1990s the critics have succeeded to a remarkable extent in bringing about drastic change in the system. The federal government began to allow a number of states to experiment with modifications in existing welfare programs, including time limits for eligibility and requirements that recipients work or enter job-training programs. In 1992 Bill Clinton campaigned on a pledge to do away with "welfare as we know it," and after the Republicans gained control of Congress in the 1994 elections, they began to press him to keep that pledge. In 1996, Congress approved and Clinton signed into law a welfare reform bill that ends federal guarantees of cash assistance for poor children and gives states vast new authority to run their own welfare programs through federally funded block grants.

Before the 1996 reform bill, the nation's welfare system was funded mainly through categorical grants—funds provided by the federal government (often with matching state funds) and targeted for specific areas of need. Some of the largest components of the system have been the Aid to Families with Dependent Children (AFDC), Medicaid, and food stamp programs. Most of these programs were based on the notion of "entitlement"—that is, the assumption that people are automatically qualified to receive certain benefits if they meet certain conditions. Consequently, although states generally had some discretion in establishing eligibility and funding standards, the federal government set broad—and sometimes detailed—guidelines.

The 1996 bill abolished AFDC and transferred its responsibilities to the states, as well as imposing strict new requirements and limits for those receiving assistance. For example, most adult recipients will be required to find work within two years or lose their benefits. Heads of families may not receive benefits for more than five years during their lifetime, and most unmarried mothers under 18 will have to live with an adult and attend school to be eligible. Although food stamps and Medicaid remain categorical grant programs, eligibility for them was cut back as well.

Opponents of the reform bill, largely Democrats and liberals, acknowledged the flaws in the existing system but maintained that such a drastic overhaul was unnecessary and unwise. Among other arguments, they pointed out that the value of child welfare payments has been falling as the rate of unwed pregnancies has gone up, that not enough low-skill jobs exist in the American economy for welfare recipients, and that providing enough training to prepare them for jobs that do exist would cost more, not less, than is now spent on welfare. Although proponents of a block grant approach argue that governments closest to the people—state and local governments—will make better decisions about what kinds of welfare programs are most efficient and most effective, opponents fear that such a change will pit states against each other in a "race to the bottom," leading to major reductions in support for the poor and needy and consequently to higher levels of hunger, homelessness, and other social ills.

Under the law, states were required to have at least 25 percent of their welfare caseload engaged in work in fiscal year 1997, with the proportion rising to 50 percent by 2002. Single parents would be required to work at least 20 hours a week during fiscal year 1996 (rising to 30 hours in 2000), and two-parent families would have to work at least 35 hours a week. States that failed to meet these work requirements would have their block grant reduced. At the same time, significant financial incentives were offered to states that succeed in various objectives of the bill; and states were given considerable discretion on eligibility, including the option to deny benefits to children born to welfare recipients.

When the Republican lawmakers initiated the welfare reform bill, they had three objectives: (1) to reduce federal spending; (2) to turn the federal entitlement programs into block grants and shift responsibility for their implementation to the states; and (3) to put welfare recipients to work. When the legislation became law, the first two objectives were accomplished. Federal spending was cut by $54.1 billion over a six-year period, primarily through cutting food stamps as well as the benefits for legal immigrants. Moreover, the change to block grants gave states almost complete control over benefit eligibility.

The third objective was more complex. Welfare-to-work has been the centerpiece of the welfare overhaul agenda as well as the central issue of the controversy. Critics of the law argue that there are simply not enough jobs for the current welfare population. Meanwhile, governors and the Clinton Administration say that the success of welfare reform will depend on the level of job opportunities. Since the law was enacted, they have been trying to create jobs for welfare recipients.

Will welfare reform work? It's too early to tell. The challenges that emerged in the initial stages of implementing the law are summarized below:

1. **Creating sufficient jobs.** According to the White House, to make welfare reform a success, 700,000 entry-level jobs must be created by the turn of the century. The rest of the four million welfare recipients who are forced to work are supposed to enter "workfare," in which states assume responsibility to pay the recipients' welfare benefits in exchange for their public-service work. Besides urging business leaders to hire welfare recipients, the Clinton Administration announced in 1997 that the federal government plans to hire at least 10,000 people from the current welfare rolls for a diverse assortment of permanent or temporary jobs over the next four years. (Six were to become clerical workers at the White House.)

   Still, since welfare reform has become state responsibility, job creation has now become primarily a state burden. But getting people on welfare to work requires job openings, and the new jobs have to be entry-level, low-skill positions. Many of the new jobs require college or even graduate degrees, whereas the majority of the welfare recipients don't even have high school diplomas.

2. **Defusing tension between the working poor and welfare recipients.** With government subsidies available to corporations that hire welfare recipients, hiring welfare recipients at lower wages could become a cost-cutting measure. Among the 30 million low-wage American workers without high school degrees, there is widespread fear that the new law may displace their jobs. In fact, many economists predict that even if the labor force displacement is insignificant, the influx of low-paid workers will drive down the wages of those workers who currently have jobs. In 1997, Maryland became the first state to forbid employers from hiring taxpayer-subsidized welfare recipients to replace workers already on the job.

3. **Providing logistical support.** In addition to jobs, there is also intense competition between working poor families and workfare participants for subsidized child care. Without such care, welfare mothers would be forced to leave their children alone at home while they are at work, and

thus would risk losing their child to the state on the basis of child neglect. Especially in big cities, however, the demand for subsidized care is much greater than the supply. Moreover, while the majority of welfare recipients live in inner cities, most of the jobs are in suburbs. States will thus need to provide transportation to work sites.

4. **Changing welfare recipients' behavior.** On the day the welfare reform bill was debated in the Senate prior to its final vote, Senator Daniel Patrick Moynihan (D, N.Y.), one of the strongest opponents, asserted that the legislation made "a fearsome assumption": that "the behavior of certain adults can be changed by making the lives of their children as wretched as possible." Upon signing the bill into law, President Clinton stated: "Today we have a historic opportunity to make welfare what it was meant to be: a second chance, not a way of life." For better or worse, most welfare recipients will now have to change their behavior and adjust to a new way of life.

   In the states where welfare reform has been under way for several years, the results in this respect have been mixed. Some welfare recipients have shown initiative and willingness to learn—they are delighted to have the chance. Others, however, have problems that range from absenteeism and lack of discipline about work hours to poor reading and communication skills and open resentment at being given directions. Still others have more serious problems, such as alcohol and drug abuse. Many who have problems quit the program, and it's unclear what proportion will stay on the job for the long run. The current training programs in states are designed to address the behavior issue: trainees are being coached to come to work on time, put in eight hours, and avoid fights with either supervisors or co-workers.

5. **Maintaining a strong economy.** Proponents as well as opponents of the welfare reform bill agree that the economy will play a crucial role in determining its success. The 61-year-old welfare system came into place during the Great Depression; and the strength of the U.S. economy in the 1990s kept unemployment rates down and provided welfare reform a chance to succeed.

Studies in early 1997 found that the number of Americans receiving welfare had fallen nearly 20 percent nationwide since March 1994; the number had dropped in every state but Hawaii. Welfare rolls had fallen more than 40 percent in three states—Oregon, Wisconsin, and Indiana—that have been most energetic in urging recipients to work. (Indiana and Wisconsin began experimenting with a two-year eligibility limit in 1995; Oregon's experiment involved an intensive case management system that did not impose time limits.)

While most researchers were uncertain whether the caseload decline was due to good times or tough laws, a report by the White House Council of Economic Advisers in May 1997 credited the healthy economy as the dominant force, concluding that it accounted for 40 percent of the drop. Welfare reform in states was credited with 31 percent, with the rest attributed to other policies, including the Earned Income Tax Credit for low-income workers, increased child support collections, and increased spending on child care for welfare mothers. The White House findings are supported by the significant decline of caseloads in a few states that had not changed their welfare policy during this period.

References:
Congressional Quarterly Weekly Report
The New York Times
The Washington Post

Discussion Questions

1. Policy making in America is normally described as an "incremental" process. What is meant by this, and what major factors contribute to the incremental nature of policy making? Under what conditions can policy shifts occur? What explains the major shift in welfare policy in the 1990s?
2. What are the major issues in the implementation of the welfare reform bill?
3. Select a policy issue of particular interest to you, and research that issue in terms of each step in the process of policy making, paying particular attention to how "politics" has been involved at each stage.

SUMMARY

Public policy is action by government designed to address public problems; it is what government actually does or accomplishes. Policies may be classified in a number of ways. One way to classify policies is in terms of their impacts on society. *Distributive policies* are those that distribute goods and services to citizens. *Regulatory policies* are those through which the government establishes rules and standards and thereby regulates or controls behavior. *Redistributive policies* are those that are perceived to take benefits from some groups and give them to others.

Policy making can be seen as a process that unfolds in five stages. The first and most important stage is *problem recognition*. An issue must be recognized as a problem requiring government attention in order to be placed on the policy agenda. Once a problem has been recognized as requiring national attention, a feasible solution must be found. This is the stage of *policy formulation*. Usually there are many potential courses of action, and a choice must be made to pursue one of them (or not to act at all). *Policy adoption* involves marshaling the support needed to win approval of a course of action. To achieve this support, lobbying, bargaining, negotiating, and compromise may be needed. Policies that have been adopted must be administered; putting policy into place is known as *policy implementation*. *Policy evaluation* consists of activities designed to determine whether a policy is working as intended. Not only intended consequences but also unanticipated consequences need to be evaluated. The final stage of the policy-making process is *policy reconsideration* or *termination*. There are many political obstacles to program termination. Agency employees want to keep their jobs; clients served by a program want it to continue; voters place pressure on legislators to preserve the program. Nevertheless, programs frequently are terminated or overhauled.

Policy making is often extremely slow; and even when policy changes are made, the changes are likely to be very small departures from the status quo. Among the reasons for the *incrementalism* of policy making in America are the complexity of social problems and the fragmentation of political power. Nevertheless, major policy shifts sometimes occur, often associated with strong and persistent pressure from the White House.

KEY TERMS

public policy
distributive policy
regulatory policy
redistributive policy
problem recognition
policy formulation
policy adoption
subgovernment
issue network
policy implementation
policy evaluation
policy termination
incrementalism

RESOURCES

READINGS

Anderson, James E. *Public Policymaking: An Introduction.* Boston: Houghton Mifflin, 1990. An excellent brief overview that emphasizes formulation, adoption, implementation, impact, and evaluation.

Brewer, Garry D., and Peter deLeon. *The Foundations of Policy Analysis.* Homewood, Ill.: Dorsey Press, 1983. A thorough examination of all phases of the policy process, with an especially good analysis of the political aspects of the earliest phases of policy making: recognition of the problem and selection of alternatives.

Nakamura, Robert, and Frank Smallwood. *The Politics of Policy Implementation.* New York: St. Martin's Press, 1980. A look at the political aspects of implementing policy *after* legislative adoption of a particular course of action. An especially good examination of the politics of bureaucracies.

Stone, Deborah A. *Policy Paradox and Political Reason.* New York: HarperCollins, 1988. A study of public policy and policy analysis that places "politics" at the center of policy making and thoroughly examines the political struggles related to policy adoption.

ORGANIZATIONS

Brookings Institution, 1775 Massachusetts Avenue, N.W., Washington, DC 20036; (202) 797-6000; fax: (202) 797-6004; no general e-mail. Conducts research and publishes scholarly studies in many policy areas, including education, economics, government, and foreign policy.

Cato Institute, 1000 Massachusetts Avenue, N.W., Washington, DC 20001; (202) 842-0200; fax: (202) 842-3490; e-mail CATO@CATO.org A policy research organization that advocates limited government and individual liberty. Policy issues of prime concern include deregulation, privatization, limited taxation, and reduced government spending.

Heritage Foundation, 214 Massachusetts Avenue, N.W., Washington, DC 20002; (202) 546-4400; fax: (202) 546-8328; no general e-mail. Conducts research, analysis, and policy forums on a variety of policy issues; generally advocates individual freedoms, limited government, a free market, and strong national defense.

People for the American Way, 2000 M Street, N.W., Washington, DC 20036; (202) 467-4999; fax: (202) 293-2672; e-mail PFAW@PFAW.org Examines policy issues primarily in light of First Amendment rights and issues; also conducts extensive public education programs on constitutional issues through radio, television, and various print media.

Appendix A

The Declaration of Independence

When in the Course of human events, it becomes necessary for one people to dissolve the political bands which have connected them with another, and to assume among the Powers of the earth, the separate and equal station to which the Laws of Nature and of Nature's God entitle them, a decent respect to the opinions of mankind requires that they should declare the causes which impel them to the separation.

We hold these truths to be self-evident, that all men are created equal, that they are endowed by their Creator with certain unalienable Rights, that among these are Life, Liberty and the pursuit of Happiness. That to secure these rights, Governments are instituted among Men, deriving their just powers from the consent of the governed. That whenever any Form of Government becomes destructive of these ends, it is the Right of the People to alter or to abolish it, and to institute new Government, laying its foundation on such principles and organizing its powers in such form, as to them shall seem most likely to effect their Safety and Happiness. Prudence, indeed, will dictate that Governments long established should not be changed for light and transient causes; and accordingly all experience hath shown, that mankind are more disposed to suffer, while evils are sufferable, than to right themselves by abolishing the forms to which they are accustomed. But when a long train of abuses and usurpations, pursuing invariably the same Object evinces a design to reduce them under absolute Despotism, it is their right, it is their duty, to throw off such Government, and to provide new Guards for their future security. —Such has been the patient sufferance of these Colonies; and such is now the necessity which constrains them to alter their former Systems of Government. The history of the present King of Great Britain is a history of repeated injuries and usurpations, all having in direct object the establishment of an absolute Tyranny over these States. To prove this, let Facts be submitted to a candid world.

He has refused his Assent to Laws, the most wholesome and necessary for the public good.

He has forbidden his Governors to pass Laws of immediate and pressing importance, unless suspended in their operation till his Assent should be obtained; and when so suspended, he has utterly neglected to attend to them.

He has refused to pass other Laws for the accommodation of large districts of people, unless those people would relinquish the right of Representation in the Legislature, a right inestimable to them and formidable to tyrants only.

He has called together legislative bodies at places unusual, uncomfortable, and distant from the depository of their public Records, for the sole purpose of fatiguing them into compliance with his measures.

He has dissolved Representative Houses repeatedly for opposing with manly firmness his invasions on the rights of the people.

He has refused for a long time, after such dissolutions, to cause others to be elected; whereby the Legislative Powers, incapable of Annihilation, have returned to the People at large for their exercise; the

State remaining in the mean time exposed to all the dangers of invasion from without, and convulsions within.

He has endeavoured to prevent the population of these States; for that purpose obstructing the Laws of Naturalization of Foreigners; refusing to pass others to encourage their migration higher, and raising the conditions of new Appropriations of Lands.

He has obstructed the Administration of Justice, by refusing his Assent to Laws for establishing Judiciary powers.

He has made Judges dependent on his Will alone, for the tenure of their offices, and the amount and payment of their salaries.

He has erected a multitude of New Offices, and sent hither swarms of Officers to harass our People, and eat out their substance.

He has kept among us in times of peace, Standing Armies without the Consent of our legislature.

He has affected to render the Military independent of and superior to the Civil power.

He has combined with others to subject us to a jurisdiction foreign to our constitution, and unacknowledged by our laws; giving his Assent to their acts of pretended Legislation.

For quartering large bodies of armed troops among us;

For protecting them, by a mock Trial, from punishment for any Murders which they should commit on the inhabitants of these States;

For cutting off our Trade with all parts of the world;

For imposing taxes on us without our Consent;

For depriving us in many cases, of the benefits of Trial by Jury;

For transporting us beyond Seas to be tried for pretended offences;

For abolishing the free System of English Laws in a neighbouring Province, establishing therein an Arbitrary government, and enlarging its Boundaries so as to render it at once an example and fit instrument for introducing the same absolute rule into these Colonies;

For taking away our Charters, abolishing our most valuable Laws, and altering fundamentally the Forms of our Governments;

For suspending our own Legislature, and declaring themselves invested with Power to legislate for us in all cases whatsoever.

He has abdicated Government here, by declaring us out of his Protection and waging War against us.

He has plundered our seas, ravaged our Coasts, burnt our towns, and destroyed the lives of our people.

He is at this time transporting large Armies of foreign Mercenaries to compleat the works of death, desolation and tyranny, already begun with circumstances of Cruelty & perfidy scarcely paralleled in the most barbarous ages, and totally unworthy the Head of a civilized nation.

He has constrained our fellow Citizens taken Captive on the high Seas to bear Arms against their Country, to become the executioners of their friends and Brethren, or to fall themselves by their Hands.

He has excited domestic insurrections amongst us, and has endeavoured to bring on the inhabitants of our frontiers, the merciless Indian Savages, whose known rule of warfare, is an undistinguished destruction of all ages, sexes and conditions.

In every stage of these Oppressions We have Petitioned for Redress in the most humble terms: Our repeated Petitions have been answered only by repeated injury. A Prince, whose character is thus marked by every act which may define a Tyrant, is unfit to be the ruler of a free People.

Nor have We been wanting in attention to our British brethren. We have warned them from time to time of attempts by their legislature to extend an unwarrantable jurisdiction over us. We have reminded them of the circumstances of our emigration and settlement here. We have appealed to their native justice and magnanimity, and we have conjured them by the ties of our common kindred to disavow these usurpations, which, would inevitably interrupt our connections and correspondence. They too have been deaf to the voice of justice and of consanguinity. We must, therefore, acquiesce in the necessity, which denounces our Separation, and hold them, as we hold the rest of mankind, Enemies in War, in Peace Friends.

We, therefore, the Representatives of the United States of America, in General

Congress, Assembled, appealing to the Supreme Judge of the world for the rectitude of our intentions, do, in the Name, and by Authority of the good People of these Colonies, solemnly publish and declare, That these United Colonies are, and of right ought to be Free and Independent States; that they are Absolved from all Allegiance to the British Crown, and that all political connection between them and the State of Great Britain, is and ought to be totally dissolved; and that as Free and Independent States, they have full Power to levy War, conclude Peace, contract Alliances, establish Commerce, and to do all other Acts and Things which Independent States may of right do. And for the support of this Declaration, with a firm reliance on the protection of divine Providence, we mutually pledge to each other our Lives, our Fortunes and our sacred Honor.

Appendix B

The Constitution of the United States of America

We the People of the United States, in Order to form a more perfect Union, establish Justice, insure domestic Tranquility, provide for the common defence, promote the general Welfare, and secure the Blessings of Liberty to ourselves and our Posterity, do ordain and establish this Constitution for the United States of America.

[THREE BRANCHES OF GOVERNMENT]

[*The legislative branch*]

ARTICLE I

[Powers vested]

SECTION 1 All legislative Powers herein granted shall be vested in a Congress of the United States, which shall consist of a Senate and House of Representatives.

[*House of Representatives*]

SECTION 2 The House of Representatives shall be composed of Members chosen every second Year by the People of the several States, and the Electors in each State shall have the Qualifications requisite for Electors of the most numerous Branch of the State Legislature.

No Person shall be a Representative who shall not have attained to the Age of twenty-five Years, and been seven Years a Citizen of the United States, and who shall not, when elected, be an Inhabitant of that State in which he shall be chosen.

[Representatives and direct Taxes shall be apportioned among the several States which may be included within this Union, according to their respective Numbers, which shall be determined by adding to the whole Number of free Persons, including those bound to Service for a Term of Years, and excluding Indians not taxed, three fifths of all other Persons.][1] The actual Enumeration shall be made within three Years after the first Meeting of the Congress of the United States, and within every subsequent Term of ten Years, in such Manner as they shall by Law direct. The Number of Representatives shall not exceed one for every thirty Thousand, but each State shall have at Least one Representative; and until such enumeration shall be made, the State of New Hampshire shall be entitled to chuse three, Massachusetts eight, Rhode-Island and Providence Plantations one, Connecticut five, New York six, New Jersey four, Pennsylvania eight, Delaware one, Maryland six, Virginia ten, North Carolina five, South Carolina five, and Georgia three.

When vacancies happen in the Representation from any State, the Executive Authority thereof shall issue Writs of Election to fill such Vacancies.

The House of Representatives shall chuse their Speaker and other Officers; and shall have the sole Power of Impeachment.

[*The Senate*]

SECTION 3 The Senate of the United States shall be composed of two Senators from each State, [chosen by the Legislature

[1]Changed by Section 2 of Amendment XIV.

thereof],[2] for six Years; and each Senator shall have one Vote.

Immediately after they shall be assembled in Consequence of the first Election, they shall be divided as equally as may be into three Classes. The Seats of the Senators of the first Class shall be vacated at the Expiration of the Second Year, of the second Class at the Expiration of the fourth Year, and of the third Class at the Expiration of the sixth Year, so that one-third may be chosen every second Year; [and if Vacancies happen by Resignation, or otherwise, during the Recess of the Legislature of any State, the Executive thereof may make temporary Appointments until the next Meeting of the Legislature, which shall then fill such Vacancies].[3]

No person shall be a Senator who shall not have attained to the Age of thirty Years, and been nine Years a Citizen of the United States, and who shall not, when elected, be an Inhabitant of that State for which he shall be chosen.

The Vice President of the United States shall be President of the Senate, but shall have no Vote, unless they be equally divided.

The Senate shall chuse their other Officers, and also a President pro tempore, in the absence of the Vice President, or when he shall exercise the Office of President of the United States.

The Senate shall have the sole Power to try all Impeachments. When sitting for that Purpose, they shall be on Oath or Affirmation. When the President of the United States is tried, the Chief Justice shall preside: And no Person shall be convicted without the Concurrence of two-thirds of the Members present.

Judgment in Cases of Impeachment shall not extend further than to removal from Office, and disqualification to hold and enjoy any Office of honor, Trust, or Profit under the United States: but the Party convicted shall nevertheless be liable and subject to Indictment, Trial, Judgment, and Punishment, according to Law.

[*Elections*]

SECTION 4 The Times, Places and Manner of holding Elections for Senators and Representatives, shall be prescribed in each State by the Legislature thereof; but the Congress may at any time by Law make or alter such Regulations, except as to the Places of chusing Senators.

The Congress shall assemble at least once in every Year, and such Meeting shall be on the first Monday in December, [unless they shall by Law appoint a different Day].[4]

[*Powers, duties, procedures of both bodies*]

SECTION 5 Each House shall be the Judge of the Elections, Returns, and Qualifications of its own Members, and a Majority of each shall constitute a Quorum to do Business; but a smaller Number may adjourn from day to day, and may be authorized to compel the Attendance of absent Members, in such Manner, and under such Penalties as each House may provide.

Each House may determine the Rules of its Proceedings, punish its Members for disorderly Behavior, and, with the Concurrence of two thirds, expel a Member.

Each House shall keep a Journal of its Proceedings, and from time to time publish the same, excepting such Parts as may in their Judgment require Secrecy; and the Yeas and Nays of the Members of either House on any question shall, at the Desire of one fifth of those Present, be entered on the Journal.

Neither House, during the Session of Congress, shall, without the Consent of the other, adjourn for more than three days, nor to any other Place than that in which the two Houses shall be sitting.

[*Compensation, privileges, limits on other government service*]

SECTION 6 The Senators and Representatives shall receive a Compensation for their Services, to be ascertained by Law, and paid out of the Treasury of the United States. They shall in all Cases, except Treason, Felony and Breach of the Peace, be privileged from Arrest during their Attendance at the Session of their respective Houses, and in going to and returning from the same; and for any Speech or Debate in either House, they shall not be questioned in any other Place.

No Senator or Representative shall, during the Time for which he was elected, be appointed to any civil Office under the

[2]Changed by Amendment XVII.

[3]Changed by Amendment XVII.

[4]Changed by Section 2 of Amendment XX.

Authority of the United States, which shall have been created, or the Emoluments whereof shall have been encreased during such time; and no Person holding any Office under the United States, shall be a Member of either House during his Continuance in Office.

[*Origin of revenue bills; presidential approval or disapproval of legislation; overriding the veto*]

SECTION 7 All Bills for raising Revenue shall originate in the House of Representatives; but the Senate may propose or concur with Amendments as on other Bills.

Every Bill which shall have passed the House of Representatives and the Senate, shall, before it become a Law, be presented to the President of the United States; if he approve he shall sign it, but if not he shall return it, with his Objections to that House in which it shall have originated, who shall enter the Objections at large on their Journal, and proceed to reconsider it. If after such Reconsideration two thirds of that House shall agree to pass the Bill, it shall be sent, together with the Objections, to the other House, by which it shall likewise be reconsidered, and if approved by two thirds of that House, it shall become a Law. But in all such Cases the Votes of both Houses shall be determined by Yeas and Nays, and the Names of the Persons voting for and against the Bill shall be entered on the Journal of each House respectively. If any Bill shall not be returned by the President within ten Days (Sundays excepted) after it shall have been presented to him, the Same shall be a Law, in like Manner as if he had signed it, unless the Congress by their Adjournment prevent its Return, in which Case it shall not be a Law.

Every Order, Resolution, or Vote to which the Concurrence of the Senate and House of Representatives may be necessary (except on a question of Adjournment) shall be presented to the President of the United States; and before the Same shall take Effect, shall be approved by him, or being disapproved by him, shall be repassed to two thirds of the Senate and House of Representatives, according to the Rules and Limitations prescribed in the Case of a Bill.

[*Powers granted to Congress*]

SECTION 8 The Congress shall have power To lay and collect Taxes, Duties, Imposts and Excises, to pay the Debts and provide for the common Defence and general Welfare of the United States; but all Duties, Imposts and Excises shall be uniform throughout the United States;

To borrow money on the credit of the United States;

To regulate Commerce with foreign Nations, and among the several States, and with the Indian Tribes;

To establish an uniform Rule of Naturalization, and uniform Laws on the subject of Bankruptcies throughout the United States;

To coin Money, regulate the Value thereof, and of foreign Coin, and fix the Standard of Weights and Measures;

To provide for the Punishment of counterfeiting the Securities and current Coin of the United States;

To Establish Post Offices and post Roads;

To promote the Progress of Science and useful Arts, by securing for limited Times to Authors and Inventors the exclusive Right to their respective Writings and Discoveries;

To constitute Tribunals inferior to the Supreme Court;

To define and punish Piracies and Felonies committed on the high Seas, and Offences against the Law of Nations;

To declare War, grant Letters of Marque and Reprisal, and make Rules concerning Captures on Land and Water;

To raise and support Armies, but no Appropriation of Money to that Use shall be for a longer Term than two Years;

To provide and maintain a Navy;

To make Rules for the Government and Regulation of the land and naval Forces;

To provide for calling forth the Militia to execute the Laws of the Union, suppress Insurrections and repel Invasions;

To provide for organizing, arming, and disciplining the Militia, and for governing such Part of them as may be employed in the Service of the United States, reserving to the States respectively, the Appointment of the Officers, and the Authority of training the Militia according to the discipline prescribed by Congress;

To exercise exclusive Legislation in all Cases whatsoever, over such District (not exceeding ten Miles square) as may, by Cession of particular States, and the acceptance of Congress, become the Seat of the

Government of the United States, and to exercise like Authority over all Places purchased by the Consent of the Legislature of the State in which the Same shall be, for the Erection of Forts, Magazines, Arsenals, dock-Yards, and other needful Buildings; —And

[*Elastic clause*]
To make all Laws which shall be necessary and proper for carrying into Execution the foregoing Powers, and all other Powers vested by this Constitution in the Government of the United States, or in any Department or Officer thereof.

[*Powers denied to Congress*]
SECTION 9 The Migration or Importation of Such Persons as any of the States now existing shall think proper to admit, shall not be prohibited by the Congress prior to the Year one thousand eight hundred and eight, but a tax or duty may be imposed on such Importation, not exceeding ten dollars for each Person.

The privilege of the Writ of Habeas Corpus shall not be suspended, unless when in Cases of Rebellion or Invasion the public Safety may require it.

No Bill of Attainder or ex post facto Law shall be passed.

[No capitation, or other direct, Tax shall be laid, unless in Proportion to the Census or Enumeration herein before directed to be taken.][5]

No Tax or Duty shall be laid on Articles exported from any State.

No preference shall be given by any Regulation of Commerce or Revenue to the Ports of one State over those of another: nor shall Vessels bound to, or from, one State be obliged to enter, clear, or pay Duties in another.

No money shall be drawn from the Treasury, but in Consequence of Appropriations made by Law; and a regular Statement and Account of the Receipts and Expenditures of all public Money shall be published from time to time.

No Title of Nobility shall be granted by the United States: And no Person holding any Office of Profit or Trust under them, shall, without the Consent of the Congress, accept of any present, Emolument, Office, or Title, of any kind whatever, from any King, Prince, or foreign State.

[5]Changed by Amendment XVI.

[*Powers denied to states*]
SECTION 10 No State shall enter into any Treaty, Alliance, or Confederation; grant Letters of Marque and Reprisal; coin Money; emit Bills of Credit; make any Thing but gold and silver Coin a Tender in Payment of Debts; pass any Bill of Attainder, ex post facto Law, or Law impairing the Obligation of Contracts, or grant any Title of Nobility.

No State shall, without the Consent of the Congress, lay any Imposts or Duties on Imports or Exports, except what may be absolutely necessary for executing its inspection Laws: and the net Produce of all Duties and Imposts, laid by any State on Imports or Exports, shall be for the Use of the Treasury of the United States; and all such Laws shall be subject to the Revision and Control of the Congress.

No State shall, without the Consent of Congress, lay any duty of Tonnage, keep Troops, or Ships of War in time of Peace, enter into any Agreement or Compact with another State, or with a foreign Power, or engage in War, unless actually invaded, or in such imminent Danger as will not admit of delay.

[*The executive branch*]

ARTICLE II

[*Presidential term, choice by electors, qualifications, payment, succession, oath of office*]
SECTION 1 The executive Power shall be vested in a President of the United States of America. He shall hold his Office during the Term of four Years, and, together with the Vice President, chosen for the same Term, be elected, as follows:

Each State shall appoint, in such Manner as the Legislature thereof may direct, a Number of Electors, equal to the whole Number of Senators and Representatives to which the State may be entitled in the Congress: but no Senator or Representative, or Person holding an Office of Trust or Profit under the United States, shall be appointed an Elector.

[The Electors shall meet in their respective States, and vote by Ballot for two persons, of whom one at least shall not be an Inhabitant of the same State with themselves. And they shall make a List of all the Persons voted for, and of the Number of Votes for each; which List they shall sign and certify, and transmit sealed to the Seat of the Government of the United States, directed to the President of the Senate. The President of the Senate shall, in the Presence of the Senate and House of Representatives, open all the Certificates, and the Votes shall then be counted. The Person having the greatest Number of Votes shall be the President, if such Number be a Majority of the whole Number of Electors appointed; and if there be more than one who have such Majority, and have an equal Number of Votes, then the House of Representatives shall immediately chuse by Ballot one of them for President; and if no Person have a Majority, then from the five highest on the List the said House shall in like Manner chuse the President. But in chusing the President, the Votes shall be taken by States, the Representation from each State having one Vote; A quorum for this Purpose shall consist of a Member or Members from two-thirds of the States, and a Majority of all the States shall be necessary to a Choice. In every Case, after the Choice of the President, the Person having the greatest Number of Votes of the Electors shall be the Vice President. But if there should remain two or more who have equal Votes, the Senate shall chuse from them by Ballot the Vice President.][6]

The Congress may determine the Time of chusing the Electors, and the Day on which they shall give their Votes; which Day shall be the same throughout the United States.

No person except a natural born Citizen, or a Citizen of the United States, at the time of the Adoption of this Constitution, shall be eligible to the Office of President; neither shall any Person be eligible to that Office who shall not have attained to the Age of thirty-five Years, and been fourteen Years a Resident within the United States.

[In case of the removal of the President from Office, or of his Death, Resignation, or Inability to discharge the Powers and Duties of the said Office, the same shall devolve on the Vice President, and the Congress may by Law provide for the Case of Removal, Death, Resignation or Inability, both of the President and Vice President, declaring what Officer shall then act as President, and such Officer shall act accordingly, until the Disability be removed, or a President shall be elected.][7]

[6]Changed by Amendment XII.

[7]Changed by Amendment XXV.

The President shall, at stated Times, receive for his Services, a Compensation, which shall neither be encreased nor diminished during the Period for which he shall have been elected, and he shall not receive within that Period any other Emolument from the United States, or any of them.

Before he enter on the Execution of his Office, he shall take the following Oath or Affirmation:—"I do solemnly swear (or affirm) that I will faithfully execute the Office of President of the United States, and will to the best of my Ability, preserve, protect and defend the Constitution of the United States."

[*Powers to command the military and executive departments, to grant pardons, to make treaties, to appoint government officers*]

SECTION 2 The President shall be Commander in Chief of the Army and Navy of the United States, and of the Militia of the several States, when called into the actual Service of the United States; he may require the Opinion, in writing, of the principal Officer in each of the executive Departments, upon any subject relating to the Duties of their respective Offices, and he shall have Power to grant Reprieves and Pardons for Offenses against the United States, except in Cases of Impeachment.

He shall have Power, by and with the Advice and Consent of the Senate, to make Treaties, provided two-thirds of the Senators present concur; and he shall nominate, and by and with the Advice and Consent of the Senate, shall appoint Ambassadors, other public Ministers and Consuls, Judges of the Supreme Court, and all other Officers of the United States, whose Appointments are not herein otherwise provided for, and which shall be established by Law; but the Congress may by Law vest the Appointment of such inferior Officers, as they think proper, in the President alone, in the Courts of Law, or in the Heads of Departments.

The President shall have Power to fill up all Vacancies that may happen during the Recess of the Senate, by granting Commissions which shall expire at the End of their next Session.

[*Formal duties*]

SECTION 3 He shall from time to time give to the Congress Information of the State of the Union, and recommend to their Consideration such Measures as he shall judge necessary and expedient; he may, on extraordinary Occasions, convene both Houses, or either of them, and in Case of Disagreement between them, with Respect to the Time of Adjournment, he may adjourn them to such Time as he shall think proper; he shall receive Ambassadors and other public Ministers; he shall take Care that the Laws be faithfully executed, and shall Commission all the Officers of the United States.

[*Conditions for removal*]

SECTION 4 The President, Vice President and all civil Officers of the United States, shall be removed from Office on Impeachment for, and Conviction of, Treason, Bribery, or other high Crimes and Misdemeanors.

[*The judicial branch*]

ARTICLE III

[*Courts and judges*]

SECTION 1 The judicial Power of the United States, shall be vested in one supreme Court, and in such inferior Courts as the Congress may from time to time ordain and establish. The Judges, both of the supreme and inferior Courts, shall hold their Offices during good Behaviour, and shall, at stated Times, receive for their Services a Compensation which shall not be diminished during their Continuance in Office.

[*Jurisdictions and jury trials*]

SECTION 2 The judicial Power shall extend to all Cases, in Law and Equity, arising under this Constitution, the Laws of the United States, and Treaties made, or which shall be made, under their Authority;—to all Cases affecting Ambassadors, other public Ministers and Consuls;—to all Cases of admiralty and maritime Jurisdiction;—to Controversies to which the United States shall be a Party;—to Controversies between two or more States;—[between a State and Citizens of another State;—][8] between Citizens of different States;—between Citizens of the same State claiming Lands under Grants of different States, [and between a State, or the Citizens thereof, and foreign States, Citizens or Subjects].[9]

In all Cases affecting Ambassadors, other public Ministers and Consuls, and those in which a State shall be Party, the supreme Court shall have original Jurisdiction. In all the other Cases before mentioned, the supreme Court shall have appellate Jurisdiction, both as to Law and Fact, with such Exceptions, and under such Regulations as the Congress shall make.

The trial of all Crimes, except in Cases of Impeachment, shall be by Jury; and such Trial shall be held in the State where the said Crimes shall have been committed; but when not committed within any State, the Trial shall be at such Place or Places as the Congress may by Law have directed.

[*Treason and its punishment*]

SECTION 3 Treason against the United States, shall consist only in levying War against them, or, in adhering to their Enemies, giving them Aid and Comfort. No Person shall be convicted of Treason unless on the Testimony of two Witnesses to the same overt Act, or on Confession in open Court.

The Congress shall have power to declare the Punishment of Treason, but no Attainder of Treason shall work Corruption of Blood, or Forfeiture except during the Life of the Person attainted.

[THE REST OF THE FEDERAL SYSTEM]

ARTICLE IV

[*Relationships among and with states*]

SECTION 1 Full Faith and Credit shall be given in each State to the public Acts, Records, and judicial Proceedings of every other State. And the Congress may by general Laws prescribe the Manner in which such Acts, Records and Proceedings shall be proved, and the Effect thereof.

[*Privileges and immunities, extradition*]

SECTION 2 The Citizens of each State shall be entitled to all Privileges and Immunities of Citizens in the several States.

A Person charged in any State with Treason, Felony, or other Crime, who shall flee from Justice, and be found in another State, shall on demand of the executive Authority of the State from which he fled, be delivered up, to be removed to the State having Jurisdiction of the Crime.

[8]Changed by Amendment XI.

[9]Changed by Amendment XI.

[No Person held to Service or Labour in one State, under the Laws thereof, escaping into another, shall, in Consequence of any Law or Regulation therein, be discharged from such Service or Labour, but shall be delivered up on Claim of the Party to whom such Service or Labour may be due.][10]

[*New states*]

SECTION 3 New States may be admitted by the Congress into this Union; but no new State shall be formed or erected within the Jurisdiction of any other State; nor any State be formed by the Junction of two or more States, or parts of States, without the Consent of the Legislatures of the States concerned as well as of the Congress.

The Congress shall have Power to dispose of and make all needful Rules and Regulations respecting the Territory or other Property belonging to the United States; and nothing in this Constitution shall be so construed as to Prejudice any Claims of the United States, or of any particular State.

[*Obligations to states*]

SECTION 4 The United States shall guarantee to every State in this Union a Republican Form of Government, and shall protect each of them against Invasion; and on Application of the Legislature, or of the Executive (when the Legislature cannot be convened) against domestic Violence.

[MECHANISM FOR CHANGE]

ARTICLE V

[*Amending the Constitution*]

The Congress, whenever two-thirds of both Houses shall deem it necessary, shall propose Amendments to this Constitution, or, on the Application of the Legislatures of two-thirds of the several States, shall call a Convention for proposing Amendments, which, in either Case, shall be valid to all Intents and Purposes, as part of this Constitution, when ratified by the Legislatures of three-fourths of the several States, or by Conventions in three-fourths thereof, as the one or the other Mode of Ratification may be proposed by the Congress; Provided that no Amendment which may be made prior to the Year One thousand eight hundred and eight shall in any Manner affect the first and fourth Clauses in the Ninth Section of the first Article; and that no State, without its Consent, shall be deprived of its equal Suffrage in the Senate.

[10]Changed by Amendment XIII.

[FEDERAL SUPREMACY]

ARTICLE VI

All Debts contracted and Engagements entered into, before the Adoption of this Constitution shall be as valid against the United States under this Constitution, as under the Confederation.

This Constitution, and the Laws of the United States which shall be made in Pursuance thereof; and all Treaties made, or which shall be made, under the Authority of the United States, shall be the supreme Law of the Land; and the Judges in every State shall be bound thereby, any Thing in the Constitution or Laws of any State to the Contrary notwithstanding.

The Senators and Representatives before mentioned, and the Members of the several State Legislatures, and all executive and judicial Officers, both of the United States and of the several States, shall be bound by Oath or Affirmation, to support this Constitution; but no religious Test shall ever be required as a Qualification to any Office or public Trust under the United States.

[RATIFICATION]

ARTICLE VII

The Ratification of the Conventions of nine States shall be sufficient for the Establishment of this Constitution between the States so ratifying the Same.

Done in Convention by the Unanimous Consent of the States present the Seventeenth Day of September in the year of our Lord one thousand seven hundred and eighty seven and of the Independence of the United States of America the twelfth. In witness whereof We have hereunto subscribed our Names.

[BILL OF RIGHTS AND OTHER AMENDMENTS]

Articles in addition to, and amendment of, the Constitution of the United

States of America, proposed by Congress, and ratified by the several States, pursuant to the fifth Article of the original Constitution.

Amendment I [1791]

[*Freedoms of religion, speech, press, assembly*]

Congress shall make no law respecting an establishment of religion, or prohibiting the free exercise thereof; or abridging the freedom of speech, or of the press; or the right of the people peaceably to assemble and to petition the Government for a redress of grievances.

Amendment II [1791]

[*Right to bear arms*]

A well regulated Militia, being necessary to the security of a free State, the right of the people to keep and bear Arms, shall not be infringed.

Amendment III [1791]

[*Quartering of soldiers*]

No Soldier shall, in time of peace be quartered in any house, without the consent of the Owner, nor in time of war, but in a manner to be prescribed by Law.

Amendment IV [1791]

[*Protection against search and seizure*]

The right of the people to be secure in their persons, houses, papers, and effects, against unreasonable searches and seizures, shall not be violated, and no Warrants shall issue, but upon probable cause, supported by Oath or affirmation, and particularly describing the place to be searched, and the persons or things to be seized.

Amendment V [1791]

[*Protection of citizens before the law*]

No person shall be held to answer for a capital, or otherwise infamous crime, unless on a presentment or indictment of a Grand Jury, except in cases arising in the land or naval forces, or in the Militia, when in actual service in time of War or public danger; nor shall any person be subject for the same offence to be twice put in jeopardy of life or limb; nor shall be compelled in any criminal case to be a witness against himself, nor be deprived of life, liberty, or property, without due process of law; nor shall private property be taken for public use, without just compensation.

Amendment VI [1791]

[*Rights of the accused in criminal cases*]

In all criminal prosecutions, the accused shall enjoy the right to a speedy and public trial, by an impartial jury of the State and district wherein the crime shall have been committed, which district shall have been previously ascertained by law, and to be informed of the nature and cause of the accusation; to be confronted with the witnesses against him; to have compulsory process for obtaining witnesses in his favor, and to have the Assistance of Counsel for his defence.

Amendment VII [1791]

[*Rights of complainants in civil cases*]

In suits at common law, where the value in controversy shall exceed twenty dollars, the right of trial by jury shall be preserved, and no fact tried by jury, shall be otherwise reexamined in any Court of the United States, than according to the rules of the common law.

Amendment VIII [1791]

[*Constraints on punishments*]

Excessive bail shall not be required, nor excessive fines imposed, nor cruel and unusual punishments inflicted.

Amendment IX [1791]

[*Rights retained by the people*]

The enumeration in the Constitution, of certain rights, shall not be construed to deny or disparage others retained by the people.

Amendment X [1791]

[*Rights reserved to states*]

The powers not delegated to the United States by the Constitution, nor prohibited by it to the States, are reserved to the States respectively, or to the people.

Amendment XI [1798]

[*Restraints on judicial power*]

The Judicial power of the United States shall not be construed to extend to any suit in law or equity, commenced or prosecuted against one of the United States by Citizens of another State, or by Citizens or Subjects of any Foreign State.

Amendment XII [1804]

[*Mechanism for presidential elections*]

The electors shall meet in their respective states and vote by ballot for President and Vice-President, one of whom, at least, shall not be an inhabitant of the same state with themselves; they shall name in their ballots the person voted for as President, and in distinct ballots the person voted for as Vice-President, and they shall make distinct lists of all persons voted for as President, and of all persons voted for as Vice-President, and of the number of votes for each, which lists they shall sign and certify, and transmit sealed to the seat of the government of the United States, directed to the President of the Senate;—The President of the Senate shall, in presence of the Senate and House of Representatives, open all the certificates and the votes shall then be counted;—The person having the greatest number of votes for President, shall be the President, if such number be a majority of the whole number of Electors appointed; and if no person have such majority, then from the persons having the highest numbers not exceeding three on the list of those voted for as President, the House of Representatives shall choose immediately, by ballot, the President. But in choosing the President, the votes shall be taken by states, the representation from each state having one vote; a quorum for this purpose shall consist of a member or members from two-thirds of the states, and a majority of all the states shall be necessary to a choice. [And if the House of Representatives shall not choose a President whenever the right of choice shall devolve upon them, before the fourth day of March next following, then the Vice-President shall act as President, as in the case of the death or other constitutional disability of the President.—][11] The person having the greatest number of votes as Vice-President, shall be the Vice-President, if such number be a majority of the whole number of Electors appointed, and if no person have a majority, then from the two highest numbers on the list, the Senate shall choose the Vice-President; a quorum for the purpose shall consist of two-thirds of the whole number of Senators, and a majority of the whole number shall be necessary to a choice. But no person constitutionally ineligible to the office of President shall be eligible to that of Vice-President of the United States.

Amendment XIII [1865]

[*Abolishment of slavery*]

Section 1 Neither slavery nor involuntary servitude, except as a punishment for crime whereof the party shall have been duly convicted, shall exist within the United States, or any place subject to their jurisdiction.

Section 2 Congress shall have power to enforce this article by appropriate legislation.

Amendment XIV [1868]

[*Citizens' rights and immunities, due process, equal protection*]

Section 1 All persons born or naturalized in the United States, and subject to the jurisdiction thereof, are citizens of the United States and of the State wherein they reside. No State shall make or enforce any law which shall abridge the privileges or immunities of citizens of the United States; nor shall any State deprive any person of life, liberty, or property, without due process of law; nor deny to any person within its jurisdiction the equal protection of the laws.

[*Basis of representation*]

Section 2 Representatives shall be appointed among the several States according to their respective numbers, counting the whole number of persons in each State, excluding Indians not taxed. But when the right to vote at any election for the choice of electors for President and

[11]Superseded by Section 3 of Amendment XX.

Vice-President of the United States, Representatives in Congress, the Executive and Judicial officers of a State, or the members of the Legislature thereof, is denied to any of the male inhabitants of such State, being twenty-one years of age, and citizens of the United States, or in any way abridged, except for participation in rebellion, or other crime, the basis of representation therein shall be reduced in the proportion which the number of such male citizens shall bear to the whole number of male citizens twenty-one years of age in such State.

[*Disqualification of Confederates for office*]

SECTION 3 No person shall be a Senator or Representative in Congress, or elector of President and Vice-President, or hold any office, civil or military, under the United States, or under any State, who, having previously taken an oath, as a member of Congress, or as an officer of the United States, or as a member of any State legislature, or as an executive or judicial officer of any State, to support the Constitution of the United States, shall have engaged in insurrection or rebellion against the same, or given aid or comfort to the enemies thereof. But Congress may by a vote of two-thirds of each House, remove such disability.

[*Public debt arising from insurrection or rebellion*]

SECTION 4 The validity of the public debt of the United States, authorized by law, including debts incurred for payment of pensions and bounties for services in suppressing insurrection or rebellion, shall not be questioned. But neither the United States nor any State shall assume or pay any debt or obligation incurred in aid of insurrection or rebellion against the United States, or any claim for the loss or emancipation of any slave; but all such debts, obligations and claims shall be held illegal and void.

SECTION 5 The Congress shall have power to enforce, by appropriate legislation, the provisions of this article.

AMENDMENT XV [1870]

[*Explicit extension of right to vote*]

SECTION 1 The right of citizens of the United States to vote shall not be denied or abridged by the United States or by any State on account of race, color, or previous condition of servitude.

SECTION 2 The Congress shall have power to enforce this article by appropriate legislation.

AMENDMENT XVI [1913]

[*Creation of income tax*]

The Congress shall have power to lay and collect taxes on incomes, from whatever source derived, without apportionment among the several States, and without regard to any census or enumeration.

AMENDMENT XVII [1913]

[*Election of senators*]

The Senate of the United States shall be composed of two Senators from each State, elected by the people thereof, for six years; and each Senator shall have one vote. The electors in each State shall have the qualifications requisite for electors of the most numerous branch of the State legislatures.

When vacancies happen in the representation of any State in the Senate, the executive authority of such State shall issue writs of election to fill such vacancies: *Provided,* That the legislature of any State may empower the executive thereof to make temporary appointments until the people fill the vacancies by election as the legislature may direct.

This amendment shall not be so construed as to affect the election or term of any Senator chosen before it becomes valid as part of the Constitution.

AMENDMENT XVIII [1919]

[*Prohibition of alcohol*]

[SECTION 1 After one year from the ratification of this article the manufacture, sale, or transportation of intoxicating liquors within, the importation thereof into, or the exportation thereof from the United States and all territory subject to the jurisdiction thereof for beverage purposes is hereby prohibited.

SECTION 2 The Congress and the several States shall have concurrent power to enforce this article by appropriate legislation.

SECTION 3 This article shall be inoperative unless it shall have been ratified as an amendment to the Constitution by the legislatures of the several States, as provided in the Constitution, within seven years from the date of the submission hereof to the States by the Congress.][12]

AMENDMENT XIX [1920]

[*Voting rights and gender*]

The right of citizens of the United States to vote shall not be denied or abridged by the United States or by any State on account of sex.

Congress shall have the power to enforce this article by appropriate legislation.

AMENDMENT XX [1933]

[*Terms of executives, assembly of Congress, presidential succession*]

SECTION 1 The terms of the President and Vice President shall end at noon on the 20th day of January, and the terms of Senators and Representatives at noon on the 3d day of January, of the years in which such terms would have ended if this article had not been ratified; and the terms of their successors shall then begin.

SECTION 2 The Congress shall assemble at least once in every year, and such meeting shall begin at noon on the 3d day of January, unless they shall by law appoint a different day.

SECTION 3 If, at the time fixed for the beginning of the term of the President, the President elect shall have died, the Vice President elect shall become President. If a President shall not have been chosen before the time fixed for the beginning of his term, or if the President elect shall have failed to qualify, then the Vice President elect shall act as President until a President shall have qualified; and the Congress may by law provide for the case wherein neither a President elect nor a Vice President elect shall have qualified, declaring who shall then act as President, or the manner in which one who is to act shall be selected, and such person shall act accordingly until a President or Vice President shall have qualified.

SECTION 4 The Congress may by law provide for the case of the death of any of the persons from whom the House of Representatives may choose a President whenever the right of choice shall have devolved upon them, and for the case of the death of any of the persons from whom the Senate may choose a Vice President whenever the right of choice shall have devolved upon them.

SECTION 5 Sections 1 and 2 shall take effect on the 15th day of October following the ratification of this article.

SECTION 6 This article shall be inoperative unless it shall have been ratified as an amendment to the Constitution by the legislatures of three-fourths of the several States within seven years from the date of its submission.

AMENDMENT XXI [1933]

[*Repealing of prohibition*]

SECTION 1 The eighteenth article of amendment to the Constitution of the United States is hereby repealed.

SECTION 2 The transportation or importation into any State, Territory, or possession of the United States for delivery or use therein of intoxicating liquors, in violation of the laws thereof, is hereby prohibited.

SECTION 3 This article shall be inoperative unless it shall have been ratified as an amendment to the Constitution by conventions in the several States, as provided in the Constitution, within seven years from the date of the submission hereof to the States by the Congress.

AMENDMENT XXII [1951]

[*Limits on presidential term*]

SECTION 1 No person shall be elected to the office of the President more than twice, and no person who has held the office of President, or acted as President, for more than two years of a term to which some other person was elected President shall be elected to the office of the President more than once. But this Article shall not apply to any person holding the office of President when this Article was proposed by the Congress, and shall not prevent any person who may be holding the office of President, or acting as President,

[12]Repealed by Amendment XXI.

during the term within which the Article becomes operative from holding the office of President or acting as President during the remainder of such term.

SECTION 2 This article shall be inoperative unless it shall have been ratified as an amendment to the Constitution by the legislatures of three-fourths of the several States within seven years from the date of its submission to the States by the Congress.

AMENDMENT XXIII [1961]

[*Voting rights of District of Columbia*]

SECTION 1 The District constituting the seat of Government of the United States shall appoint in such manner as the Congress may direct:

A number of electors of President and Vice President equal to the whole number of Senators and Representatives in Congress to which the District would be entitled if it were a State; but in no event more than the least populous State; they shall be in addition to those appointed by the States, but they shall be considered, for the purposes of the election of President and Vice President, to be electors appointed by a State; and they shall meet in the District and perform such duties as provided by the twelfth article of amendment.

SECTION 2 The Congress shall have power to enforce this article by appropriate legislation.

AMENDMENT XXIV [1964]

[*Prohibition of poll tax*]

SECTION 1 The right of citizens of the United States to vote in any primary or other election for President or Vice President, for electors for President or Vice President, or for Senator or Representative in Congress, shall not be denied or abridged by the United States or any State by reason of failure to pay any poll tax or other tax.

SECTION 2 The Congress shall have power to enforce this article by appropriate legislation.

AMENDMENT XXV [1967]

[*Presidential disability and succession*]

SECTION 1 In case of the removal of the President from office or his death or resignation, the Vice President shall become President.

SECTION 2 Whenever there is a vacancy in the office of the Vice President, the President shall nominate a Vice President who shall take the Office upon confirmation by a majority vote of both houses of Congress.

SECTION 3 Whenever the President transmits to the President pro tempore of the Senate and the Speaker of the House of Representatives his written declaration that he is unable to discharge the powers and duties of his office, and until he transmits to them a written declaration to the contrary, such powers and duties shall be discharged by the Vice President as Acting President.

SECTION 4 Whenever the Vice President and a majority of either the principal officers of the executive departments, or of such other body as Congress may by law provide, transmit to the President pro tempore of the Senate and the Speaker of the House of Representatives their written declaration that the President is unable to discharge the powers and duties of his office, the Vice President shall immediately assume the powers and duties of the office as Acting President.

Thereafter, when the President transmits to the President pro tempore of the Senate and the Speaker of the House of Representatives his written declaration that no inability exists, he shall resume the powers and duties of his office unless the Vice President and a majority of either the principal officers of the executive department, or of such other body as Congress may by law provide, transmit within four days to the President pro tempore of the Senate and the Speaker of the House of Representatives their written declaration that the President is unable to discharge the powers and duties of his office. Thereupon Congress shall decide the issue, assembling within 48 hours for that purpose if not in session. If the Congress, within 21 days after receipt of the latter written declaration, or, if Congress is not in session, within 21 days after Congress is required to assemble, determines by two-thirds vote of both houses that the President is unable to discharge the powers and duties of his office, the Vice President shall continue to discharge the same as Acting President; otherwise, the President shall resume the powers and duties of his office.

Amendment XXVI [1971]

[*Voting rights and age*]

Section 1 The right of citizens of the United States, who are eighteen years of age, or older, to vote shall not be denied or abridged by the United States or by any state on account of age.

Section 2 The Congress shall have the power to enforce this article by appropriate legislation.

Amendment XXVII [1992]

[*Congressional pay*]

No law varying the compensation for the services of the Senators and Representatives shall take effect until an election of Representatives shall have intervened.

Appendix C

From *The Federalist*, Nos. 10 and 51

Federalist No. 10 [1787]

To the People of the State of New York:

Among the numerous advantages promised by a well-constructed union, none deserves to be more accurately developed than its tendency to break and control the violence of faction. The friend of popular governments, never finds himself so much alarmed for their character and fate, as when he contemplates their propensity to this dangerous vice. He will not fail, therefore, to set a due value on any plan which, without violating the principles to which he is attached, provides a proper cure for it. The instability, injustice, and confusion introduced into the public councils, have, in truth, been the mortal diseases under which popular governments have everywhere perished; as they continue to be the favourite and fruitful topics from which the adversaries to liberty derive their most specious declamations. The valuable improvements made by the American constitutions on the popular models, both ancient and modern, cannot certainly be too much admired; but it would be an unwarrantable partiality, to contend that they have as effectually obviated the danger on this side, as was wished and expected. Complaints are everywhere heard from our most considerate and virtuous citizens, equally the friends of public and private faith, and of public and personal liberty, that our governments are too unstable; that the public good is disregarded in the conflicts of rival parties; and that measures are too often decided, not according to the rules of justice, and the rights of the minor party, but by the superior force of an interested and overbearing majority. However anxiously we may wish that these complaints had no foundation, the evidence of known facts will not permit us to deny that they are in some degree true. It will be found, indeed, on a candid review of our situation, that some of the distresses under which we labour have been erroneously charged on the operation of our governments; but it will be found, at the same time, that other causes will not alone account for many of our heaviest misfortunes; and, particularly, for that prevailing and increasing distrust of public engagements, and alarm for private rights, which are echoed from one end of the continent to the other. These must be chiefly, if not wholly, effects of the unsteadiness and injustice, with which a factious spirit has tainted our public administrations.

By a faction, I understand a number of citizens, whether amounting to a majority or minority of the whole, who are united and actuated by some common impulse of passion, or of interest, adverse to the rights of other citizens, or to the permanent and aggregate interests of the community.

There are two methods of curing the mischiefs of faction: The one, by removing its causes; the other, by controlling its effects.

There are again two methods of removing the causes of faction: The one, by destroying the liberty which is essential to its existence; the other, by giving to every citizen the same opinions, the same passions, and the same interests.

It could never be more truly said, than of the first remedy, that it was worse than the disease. Liberty is to faction what air is to fire, an ailment without which it instantly expires. But it could not be a less folly to abolish liberty, which is essential to political life, because it nourishes faction, than it would be to wish the annihilation of air, which is essential to animal life, because it imparts to fire its destructive agency.

The second expedient is as impracticable, as the first would be unwise. As long as the reason of man continues fallible, and he is at liberty to exercise it, different opinions will be formed. As long as the connection subsists between his reason and his self-love, his opinions and his passions will have a reciprocal influence on each other; and the former will be objects to which the latter will attach themselves. The diversity in the faculties of men, from which the rights of property originate, is not less an insuperable obstacle to an uniformity of interests. The protection of these faculties is the first object of government. From the protection of different and unequal faculties of acquiring property, the possession of different degrees and kinds of property immediately results; and from the influence of these on the sentiments and views of the respective proprietors, ensues a division of the society into different interests and parties.

The latent causes of action are thus sown in the nature of man; and we see them everywhere brought into different degrees of activity, according to the different circumstances of civil society. A zeal for different opinions concerning religion, concerning government, and many other points, as well as of speculation as of practice; an attachment to different leaders ambitiously contending for preeminence and power; or to persons of other descriptions whose fortunes have been interesting to the human passions, have, in turn, divided mankind into parties, inflamed them with mutual animosity, and rendered them much more disposed to vex and oppress each other, than to cooperate for their common good. So strong is this propensity of mankind, to fall into mutual animosities, that where no substantial occasion presents itself, the most frivolous and fanciful distinctions have been sufficient to kindle their unfriendly passions and excite their most violent conflicts. But the most common and durable source of factions, has been the various and unequal distribution of property. Those who hold, and those who are without property, have ever formed distinct interests in society. Those who are creditors, and those who are debtors, fall under alike discrimination. A landed interest, a manufacturing interest, a mercantile interest, a moneyed interest, with many lesser interests, grow up of necessity in civilized nations, and divide them into different classes, actuated by different sentiments and views. The regulation of these various and interfering interests forms the principal task of modern legislation, and involves the spirit of the party and faction in the necessary and ordinary operations of the government.

No man is allowed to be a judge in his own cause; because his interest will certainly bias his judgment, and, not improbably, corrupt his integrity. With equal, nay, with greater reason, a body of men are unfit to be both judges and parties at the same time; yet what are many of the most important acts of legislation, but so many judicial determinations, not indeed concerning the right of single persons, but concerning the rights of large bodies of citizens? And what are the different classes of legislators, but advocates and parties to the causes which they determine? Is a law proposed concerning private debts? It is a question to which the creditors are parties on one side, and the debtors on the other. Justice ought to hold the balance between them. Yet the parties are, and must be, themselves the judges; and the most numerous party, or, in other words, the most powerful faction, must be expected to prevail. Shall domestic manufactures be encouraged, and in what degree, by restrictions on foreign manufactures? are questions which would be differently decided by the landed and the manufacturing classes; and probably by neither with a sole regard to justice and the public good. The apportionment of taxes, on the various descriptions of property, is an act which seems to require the most exact impartiality; yet there is, perhaps, no legislative act, in which greater opportunity and temptation are given to a predominant party to trample on the rules of justice. Every shilling, with which they overburden the inferior number, is a shilling saved to their own pockets.

It is in vain to say, that enlightened statesmen will be able to adjust these clashing interests, and render them all subservient to the public good. Enlightened statesmen will not always be at the helm: nor, in many cases, can such an adjustment be made at all, without taking into view indirect and remote considerations, which will rarely prevail over the immediate interest which one party may find in disregarding the rights of another, or the good of the whole.

The inference to which we are brought is, that the causes of faction cannot be removed; and that relief is only to be sought in the means of controlling its *effects*.

If a faction consists of less than a majority, relief is supplied by the republican principle, which enables the majority to defeat its sinister views, by regular vote. It may clog the administration, it may convulse the society; but it will be unable to execute and mask its violence under the forms of the constitution. When a majority is included in a faction, the form of popular government, on the other hand, enables it to sacrifice to its ruling passion or interest, both the public good and the rights of other citizens. To secure the public good, and private rights, against the danger of such a faction, and at the same time to preserve the spirit and the form of popular government, is then the great object to which our inquiries are directed. Let me add, that it is the great desideratum, by which alone this form of government can be rescued from the opprobrium under which it has so long laboured, and be recommended to the esteem and adoption of mankind.

By what means is this object attainable? Evidently by one of two only. Either the existence of the same passion or interest in a majority, at the same time, must be prevented; or the majority, having such coexistent passion or interest, must be rendered, by their number and local situation, unable to concert and carry into effect schemes of oppression. If the impulse and the opportunity be suffered to coincide, we well know that neither moral nor religious motives can be relied on as an adequate control. They are not found to be such on the injustice and violence of individuals, and lose their efficacy in proportion to the number combined together; that is, in proportion as their efficacy becomes needful.

From this view of the subject, it may be concluded, that a pure democracy, by which I mean a society consisting of a small number of citizens, who assemble and administer the government in person, can admit of no cure for the mischiefs of faction. A common passion or interest will, in almost every case, be felt by a majority of the whole; a communication and concert, results from the form of government itself; and there is nothing to check the inducements to sacrifice the weaker party, or an obnoxious individual. Hence, it is, that such democracies have ever been spectacles of turbulence and contention; have ever been found incompatible with personal security, or the rights of property; and have in general been as short in their lives, as they have been violent in their deaths. Theoretic politicians, who have patronized this species of government, have erroneously supposed, that by reducing mankind to a perfect equality in their political rights, they would, at the same time, be perfectly equalized and assimilated in their possessions, their opinions, and their passions.

A republic, by which I mean a government in which the scheme of representation takes place, opens a different prospect, and promises the cure for which we are seeking. Let us examine the points in which it varies from pure democracy, and we shall comprehend both the nature of the cure and the efficacy which it must derive from the union.

The two great points of difference, between a democracy and a republic, are, first, the delegation of the government, in the latter, to a small number of citizens, elected by the rest; secondly, the greatest number of citizens, and greater sphere of country, over which the latter may be extended.

The effect of the first difference is, on the one hand, to refine and enlarge the public views, by passing them through the medium of a chosen body of citizens, whose wisdom may best discern the true interest of their country, and whose patriotism and love of justice, will be least likely to sacrifice it to temporary or partial considerations. Under such a regulation, it may well happen, that the public voice, pronounced by the representatives of the people, will be more consonant to the public good, than if pronounced by the people themselves, convened for the purpose. On the other hand the effect may be inverted. Men of factious tempers, of local prejudices, or of sinister designs, may by intrigue, by corruption, or by other means, first obtain the suffrages, and then betray the interest of the people. The question resulting is, whether small or extensive republics are most favourable to the election of proper guardians of the public weal; and it is clearly decided in favour of the latter by two obvious considerations.

In the first place, it is to be remarked that, however small the republic may be, the representatives must be raised to a certain number, in order to guard against the cabals of a few; and that however large it may be, they must be limited to a certain number, in order to guard against the confusion of a multitude. Hence, the number of representatives in the two cases not being in proportion to that of the constituents, and being proportionally greatest in the small republic, it follows, that if the proportion of fit characters be not less in the large than in the small republic, the former will present a greater option, and consequently a greater probability of a fit choice.

In the next place, as each representative will be chosen by a greater number of citizens in the large than in the small republic, it will be more difficult for unworthy candidates to practise with success the vicious arts, by which elections are too often carried; and the suffrages of the people being more free, will be more likely to centre in men who possess the most attractive merit, and the most diffusive and established characters.

It must be confessed, that in this, as in most other cases, there is a mean, on both sides of which inconveniences will be found to lie. By enlarging too much the number of electors, you render the representatives too little acquainted with all their local circumstances and lesser interests; as by reducing it too much, you render him unduly attached to these, and too little fit to comprehend and pursue great and national objects. The federal constitution forms a happy combination being referred to the national, the local and particular, to the state legislatures.

The other point of difference is, the greater number of citizens, and extent of territory, which may be brought within the compass of republican, than of democratic government; and it is this circumstance principally which renders factious combinations less to be dreaded in the former, than in the latter. The smaller the society, the fewer probably will be the distinct parties and interests composing it; the fewer the distinct parties and interests, the more frequently will a majority be found of the same party; and the smaller the number of individuals composing a majority, and the smaller the compass within which they are placed, the more easily will they concert and execute their plans of oppression. Extend the sphere, and you take in a greater variety of parties and interests; you make it less probable that a majority of the whole will have a common motive to invade the rights of other citizens; or if such a common motive exists, it will be more difficult for all who feel it to discover their own strength, and to act in unison with each other. Besides other impediments, it may be remarked, that where there is a consciousness of unjust or dishonourable purposes, communication is always checked by distrust, in proportion to the number whose concurrence is necessary.

Hence, it clearly appears, that the same advantage, which a republic has over a democracy, in controlling the effects of faction, is enjoyed by a large over a small republic—is enjoyed by the union over the states composing it. Does this advantage consist in the substitution of representatives, whose enlightened views and virtuous sentiments render them superior to local prejudices, and to schemes of injustice? It will not be denied that the representation of the union will be most likely to possess these requisite endowments. Does it consist in the greater security afforded by a greater variety of parties, against the event of any one party being able to outnumber and oppress the rest? In an equal degree does the increased variety of parties, comprised within the union, increase the security? Does it, in fine, consist in the greater obstacles opposed to the concert and accomplishment of the secret wishes of an unjust and interested majority? Here, again, the extent of the union gives it the most palpable advantage.

The influence of factious leaders may kindle a flame within their particular states, but will be unable to spread a general conflagration through the other states; a religious sect may degenerate into a political faction in a part of the confederacy; but the variety of sects dispersed over the entire face of it, must secure the national councils against any danger from that source: a rage for paper money, for an abolition of debts, for an equal division of property, or for any other improper or wicked project, will be less apt to pervade the whole body of the union than a particular member of it; in the same proportion as such a malady is more likely to taint a particular county or district, than an entire state.

In the extent and proper structure of the union, therefore, we behold a republican remedy for the diseases most incident to republican government. And according to the degree of pleasure and pride we feel in being republicans, ought to be our zeal in cherishing the spirit, and supporting the character of federalists.

JAMES MADISON

FEDERALIST NO. 51 [1788]

To the People of the State of New York:

To what expedient then shall we finally resort for maintaining in practice the necessary partition of power among the several departments, as laid down in the constitution? The only answer that can be given is, that as all these exterior provisions are found to be inadequate, the defect must be supplied, by so contriving the interior structure of the government, as that its several constituent parts may, by their mutual relations, be the means of keeping each other in their proper places. Without presuming to undertake a full development of this important idea, I will hazard a few general observations, which may perhaps place it in a clearer light, and enable us to form a more correct judgment of the principles and structure of the government planned by the convention.

In order to lay a due foundation for that separate and distinct exercise of the different powers of government, which to a certain extent, is admitted on all hands to be essential to the preservation of liberty, it is evident that each department should have a will of its own; and consequently should be so constituted, that the members of each should have as little agency as possible in the appointment of the members of the others. Were this principle rigorously adhered to, it would require that all the appointments for the supreme executive, legislative, and judiciary magistracies, should be drawn from the same fountain of authority, the people, through channels, having no communication whatever with one another. Perhaps such a plan of constructing the several departments would be less difficult in practice than it may in contemplation appear. Some difficulties however, and some additional expense, would attend the execution of it. Some deviations therefore from the principle must be admitted. In the constitution of the judiciary department in particular, it might be inexpedient to insist rigorously on the principle; first, because peculiar qualifications being essential in the members, the primary consideration ought to be to select that mode of choice, which best secures these qualifications; secondly, because the permanent tenure by which the appointments are held in that department, must soon destroy all sense of dependence on the authority conferring them.

It is equally evident that the members of each department should be as little dependent as possible on those of the others, for the emoluments annexed to their offices. Were the executive magistrate, or the judges, not independent of the legislature in this particular, their independence in every other would be merely nominal.

But the great security against a gradual concentration of the several powers in the same department, consists in giving to those who administer each department, the necessary constitutional means, and personal motives, to resist encroachments of the others. The provision for defense must in this, as in all other cases, be made commensurate to the danger of attack. Ambition must be made to counteract ambition. The interest of the man must be connected with the constitutional rights of the place. It may be a reflection on human nature, that such devices should be necessary to control the abuses of government: But what is government itself but the greatest of all reflections on human nature? If men were angels, no government would be necessary. If angels were to govern men, neither external nor internal controls on government would be necessary. In framing a government which is to be administered by men over men, the great difficulty lies in this: You must first enable the government to control the governed; and in the next place, oblige it to control itself. A dependence on the people is no doubt the primary control on the government; but experience has taught mankind the necessity of auxiliary precautions.

This policy of supplying by opposite and rival interests, the defect of better motives, might be traced through the whole system of human affairs, private as well as public. We see it particularly displayed in all the subordinate distributions of power; where the constant aim is to divide and arrange the several offices in such a manner as that each may be a check on the other; that the private interest of every individual, may be a sentinel over the public rights. These inventions of prudence cannot be less requisite in the distribution of the supreme powers of the state.

But it is not possible to give to each department an equal power of self defense. In republican government the legislative authority, necessarily, predominates. The remedy for this inconveniency is, to divide the legislature into different branches; and to render them by different modes of election, and different principles of action, as little connected with each other, as the nature of their common functions, and their common dependence on the society, will admit. It may even be necessary to guard against dangerous encroachments by still further precautions. As the weight of the legislative authority requires that it should be thus divided, the weakness of the executive may require, on the other hand, that it should be fortified. An absolute negative, on the legislature, appears at first view to be the natural defense with which the executive magistrate should be armed. But perhaps it would be neither altogether safe, nor alone sufficient. On ordinary occasions, it might not be exerted with the requisite firmness; and on extraordinary occasions, it might be perfidiously abused. May not this defect of an absolute negative be supplied, by some qualified connection between this weaker department, and the weaker branch of the stronger department, by which the latter may be led to support the constitutional rights of the former, without being too much detached from the rights of its own department?

If the principles on which these observations are founded be just, as I persuade myself they are, and they be applied as a criterion, to the several state constitutions, and to the federal constitution, it will be found, that if the latter does not perfectly correspond with them, the former are infinitely less able to bear such a test.

There are moreover two considerations particularly applicable to the federal system of America, which place that system in a very interesting point of view.

First. In a single republic, all the power surrendered by the people, is submitted to the administration of a single government; and usurpations are guarded against by a division of the government into distinct and separate departments. In the compound republic of America, the power surrendered by the people, is first divided between two distinct governments, and then the portion allotted to each, subdivided among distinct and separate departments. Hence a double security arises to the rights of the people. The different governments will control each other; at the same time that each will be controlled by itself.

Second. It is of great importance in a republic, not only to guard the society against the oppression of its rulers; but to guard one part of the society against the injustice of the other part. Different interests necessarily exist in different classes of citizens. If a majority be united by a common interest, the rights of the minority will be insecure. There are but two methods of providing against this evil: The one by creating a will in the community independent of the majority, that is, of the society itself; the other by comprehending in the society so many separate descriptions of citizens, as will render an unjust combination of a majority of the whole, very improbable, if not impracticable. The first method prevails in all governments possessing an hereditary or self appointed authority. This at best is but a precarious security; because a power independent of the society may as well espouse the unjust views of the major, as the rightful interests, of the minor party, and may possibly be turned against both parties. The second method will be exemplified in the federal republic of the United States. While all authority in it will be derived from and dependent on the society, the society itself will be broken into so many parts, interests and classes of citizens, that the rights of individuals or of the minority, will be in little danger from interested combinations of the majority. In a free government, the security for civil rights must be the same as for religious rights. It consists in the one case in the multiplicity of sects. The degree of security in both cases will depend on the number of interests and sects; and this may be presumed to depend on the extent of country and number of people comprehended under the same government. This view of the subject must particularly recommend a proper federal system to all the sincere and considerate friends of republican government: Since it shows that in exact proportion as the territory of the union may be formed into more circumscribed confederacies or states, oppressive combinations of a majority will be facilitated; the best security under the republican form, for the rights of every class of citizens, will be diminished; and consequently, the stability and independence of some member of the government, the only other security, must be proportionally increased. Justice is the end of government. It is the end of civil society. It ever has been, and ever will be pursued, until it be obtained, or until liberty be lost in the pursuit. In a society under the forms of which the stronger faction can readily unite and oppress the weaker, anarchy may as truly be said to reign, as in a state of nature where the weaker individual is not secured against the violence of the stronger: And as in the latter state even the stronger individuals are prompted by the uncertainty of their condition, to submit to a government which may protect the weak as well as themselves: So in the former state, will the more powerful factions or parties be gradually induced by alike motives, to wish for a government which will protect all parties, the weaker as well as the more powerful. It can be little doubted, that if the state of Rhode Island was separated from the confederacy, and left to itself, the insecurity of rights under the popular form of government within such narrow limits, would be displayed by such reiterated oppressions of factious majorities, that some power altogether independent of the people would soon be called for by the voice of the very factions whose misrule had proved the necessity of it. In the extended republic of the United States, and among the great variety of interests, parties and sects which it embraces, a coalition of a majority of the whole society could seldom take place on any other principles than those of justice and the general good; and there being thus less danger to a minor from the will of the major party, there must be less pretext also, to provide for the security of the former, by introducing into the government a will not dependent on the latter; or in other words, a will independent of the society itself. It is no less certain than it is important, notwithstanding the contrary opinions which have been entertained, that the larger the society, provided it lie within a practicable sphere, the more duly capable it will be of self government. And happily for the *republican cause,* the practicable sphere may be carried to a very great extent, by a judicious modification and mixture of the *federal principle.*

James Madison

Appendix D

Presidential Elections

Candidates	Party	Electoral Vote
1789		
George Washington	Federalist	69
John Adams	Federalist	34
Others		35
1792		
George Washington	Federalist	132
John Adams	Federalist	77
George Clinton		50
Others		5
1796		
John Adams	Federalist	71
Thomas Jefferson	Democratic-Republican	68
Thomas Pinckney	Federalist	59
Aaron Burr	Democratic-Republican	30
Others		48
1800		
Thomas Jefferson[1]	Democratic-Republican	73
Aaron Burr	Democratic-Republican	73
John Adams	Federalist	65
Charles C. Pinckney		64
1804		
Thomas Jefferson	Democratic-Republican	162
Charles C. Pinckney	Federalist	14
1808		
James Madison	Democratic-Republican	122
Charles C. Pinckney	Federalist	47
George Clinton	Independent-Republican	6
1812		
James Madison	Democratic-Republican	122
DeWitt Clinton	Federalist	89
1816		
James Monroe	Democratic-Republican	183
Rufus King	Federalist	34
1820		
James Monroe	Democratic-Republican	231
John Quincy Adams	Independent-Republican	1
1824		
John Quincy Adams[1]	Democratic-Republican	84
Andrew Jackson	Democratic-Republican	99
Henry Clay	Democratic-Republican	37
William H. Crawford	Democratic-Republican	41
1828		
Andrew Jackson	Democratic	178
John Quincy Adams	National-Republican	83

Candidates	Party	Electoral Vote
1832		
Andrew Jackson	Democratic	219
Henry Clay	National-Republican	49
William Wirt	Anti-Masonic	7
John Floyd	National-Republican	11
1836		
Martin Van Buren	Democratic	170
William H. Harrison	Whig	73
Hugh L. White	Whig	26
Daniel Webster	Whig	14
1840		
William H. Harrison[2]	Whig	234
(John Tyler)	Whig	
Martin Van Buren	Democratic	60
1844		
James K. Polk	Democratic	170
Henry Clay	Whig	105
James G. Birney	Liberty	
1848		
Zachary Taylor[2]	Whig	163
(Millard Fillmore)	Whig	
Lewis Cass	Democratic	127
Martin Van Buren	Free Soil	
1852		
Franklin Pierce	Democratic	254
Winfield Scott	Whig	42
1856		
James Buchanan	Democratic	174
John C. Fremont	Republican	114
Millard Fillmore	American	8
1860		
Abraham Lincoln	Republican	180
Stephen A. Douglas	Democratic	12
John C. Breckinridge	Democratic	72
John Bell	Constitutional Union	39
1864		
Abraham Lincoln[2]	Republican	212
(Andrew Johnson)	Republican	
George B. McClellan	Democratic	21
1868		
Ulysses S. Grant	Republican	214
Horatio Seymour	Democratic	80
1872		
Ulysses S. Grant	Republican	286
Horace Greeley	Democratic	66

Candidates	Party	Electoral vote
1876		
Rutherford B. Hayes	Republican	185
Samuel J. Tilden	Democratic	184
1880		
James A. Garfield[2]	Republican	214
(Chester A. Arthur)	Republican	
Winfield S. Hancock	Democratic	155
James B. Weaver	Greenback-Labor	
1884		
Grover Cleveland	Democratic	219
James G. Blaine	Republican	182
Benjamin F. Butler	Greenback-Labor	
1888		
Benjamin Harrison	Republican	233
Grover Cleveland	Democratic	168
1892		
Grover Cleveland	Democratic	277
Benjamin Harrison	Republican	145
James R. Weaver	People's	22
1896		
William McKinley	Republican	271
William J. Bryan	Democratic, Populist	176
1900		
William McKinley[2]	Republican	292
(Theodore Roosevelt)	Republican	
William J. Bryan	Democratic, Populist	155
1904		
Theodore Roosevelt	Republican	336
Alton B. Parker	Democratic	140
Eugene V. Debs	Socialist	
1908		
William H. Taft	Republican	321
William J. Bryan	Democratic	162
Eugene V. Debs	Socialist	
1912		
Woodrow Wilson	Democratic	435
Theodore Roosevelt	Progressive	88
William H. Taft	Republican	8
Eugene V. Debs	Socialist	
1916		
Woodrow Wilson	Democratic	277
Charles E. Hughes	Republican	254
1920		
Warren G. Harding[2]	Republican	404
(Calvin Coolidge)	Republican	
James M. Cox	Democratic	127
Eugene V. Debs	Socialist	
1924		
Calvin Coolidge	Republican	382
John W. Davis	Democratic	136
Robert M. LaFollette	Progressive	13
1928		
Herbert C. Hoover	Republican	444
Alfred E. Smith	Democratic	87
1932		
Franklin D. Roosevelt	Democratic	472
Herbert C. Hoover	Republican	59
Norman Thomas	Socialist	
1936		
Franklin D. Roosevelt	Democratic	523
Alfred M. Landon	Republican	8
William Lemke	Union	

Candidates	Party	Electoral vote
1940		
Franklin D. Roosevelt	Democratic	449
Wendell L. Wilkie	Republican	82
1944		
Franklin D. Roosevelt[2]	Democratic	432
(Harry S Truman)	Democratic	
Thomas E. Dewey	Republican	99
1948		
Harry S Truman	Democratic	303
Thomas E. Dewey	Republican	189
J. Strom Thurmond	States' Rights	39
Henry A. Wallace	Progressive	
1952		
Dwight D. Eisenhower	Republican	442
Adlai E. Stevenson	Democratic	89
1956		
Dwight D. Eisenhower	Republican	457
Adlai E. Stevenson	Democratic	73
1960		
John F. Kennedy[2]	Democratic	303
(Lyndon B. Johnson)	Democratic	
Richard M. Nixon	Republican	219
1964		
Lyndon B. Johnson	Democratic	486
Barry M. Goldwater	Republican	52
1968		
Richard M. Nixon	Republican	301
Hubert H. Humphrey	Democratic	191
George C. Wallace	American Independent	46
1972		
Richard M. Nixon[3]	Republican	520
(Gerald R. Ford)	Republican	
George S. McGovern	Democratic	17
1976		
Jimmy Carter	Democratic	297
Gerald R. Ford	Republican	240
1980		
Ronald Reagan	Republican	489
Jimmy Carter	Democratic	49
John Anderson	Independent	
1984		
Ronald Reagan	Republican	525
Walter Mondale	Democratic	13
1988		
George Bush	Republican	426
Michael Dukakis	Democratic	111
1992		
Bill Clinton	Democratic	370
George Bush	Republican	168
Ross Perot	Independent	
1996		
Bill Clinton	Democratic	379
Bob Dole	Republican	159
Ross Perot	Reform Party	

[1]Elected by the House of Representatives.

[2]Died while in office.

[3]Resigned from office.

The 1996 Presidential Vote

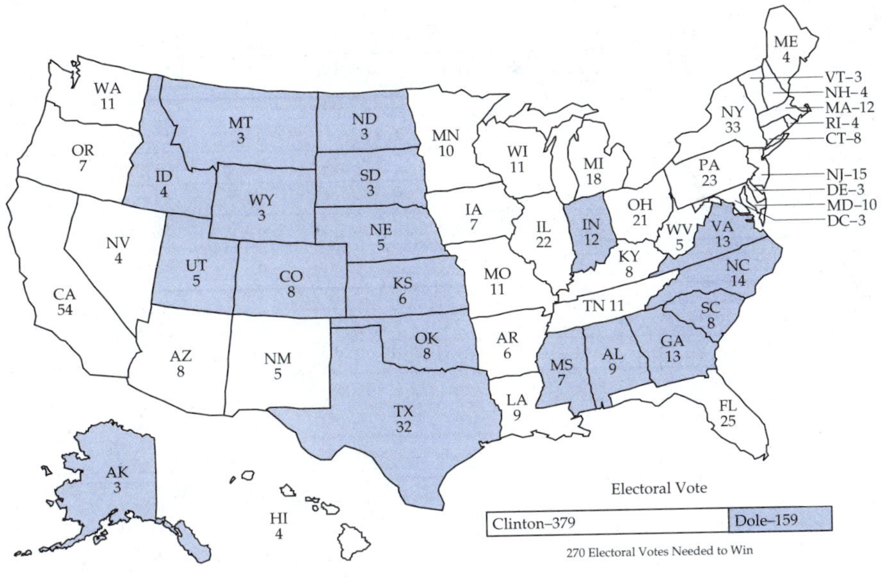

State	Total Vote[1]	Clinton	Percent	Dole	Percent	Perot	Percent
Alabama	1,534,349	662,165	43.2	769,044	50.1	92,149	6.0
Alaska	241,620	80,380	33.3	122,746	50.8	26,333	10.9
Arizona	1,404,405	653,288	46.5	622,073	44.3	112,072	8.0
Arkansas	884,262	475,171	53.7	325,416	36.8	69,884	7.9
California	10,019,484	5,119,835	51.1	3,828,380	38.2	697,847	7.0
Colorado	1,510,704	671,152	44.4	691,848	45.8	99,629	6.6
Connecticut	1,392,614	735,740	52.8	483,109	34.7	139,523	10.0
Delaware	270,810	140,355	51.8	99,062	36.6	28,719	10.6
District of Columbia	185,726	158,220	85.2	17,339	9.3	3,611	1.9
Florida	5,300,927	2,545,968	48.0	2,243,324	42.3	483,776	9.1
Georgia	2,298,899	1,053,849	45.8	1,080,843	47.0	146,337	6.4
Hawaii	360,120	205,012	56.9	113,943	31.6	27,358	7.6
Idaho	491,711	165,443	33.6	256,595	52.2	62,518	12.7
Illinois	4,311,391	2,341,744	54.3	1,587,021	36.8	346,408	8.0
Indiana	2,135,431	887,424	41.6	1,006,693	47.1	224,299	10.5
Iowa	1,234,075	620,258	50.3	492,644	39.9	105,159	8.5
Kansas	1,074,300	387,659	36.1	583,245	54.3	92,639	8.6
Kentucky	1,388,707	636,614	45.8	623,283	44.9	120,396	8.7
Louisiana	1,783,959	927,837	52.0	712,586	39.9	123,293	6.9
Maine	605,897	312,788	51.6	186,378	30.8	85,970	14.2
Maryland	1,780,870	966,207	54.3	681,530	38.3	115,812	6.5
Massachusetts	2,556,459	1,571,509	61.5	718,058	28.1	227,206	8.9

State	Total Vote[1]	Clinton	Percent	Dole	Percent	Perot	Percent
Michigan	3,848,894	1,989,653	51.7	1,481,212	38.5	336,670	8.7
Minnesota	2,192,640	1,120,438	51.1	766,476	35.0	257,704	11.8
Mississippi	893,857	394,022	44.1	439,838	49.2	52,222	5.8
Missouri	2,158,065	1,025,935	47.5	890,016	41.2	217,188	10.1
Montana	407,083	167,922	41.3	179,652	44.1	55,229	13.6
Nebraska	677,415	236,761	35.0	363,467	53.7	71,278	10.5
Nevada	464,279	203,974	43.9	199,244	42.9	43,986	9.5
New Hampshire	499,053	246,166	49.3	196,486	39.4	48,387	9.7
New Jersey	3,075,860	1,652,361	53.7	1,103,099	35.9	262,134	8.5
New Mexico	556,074	273,495	49.2	232,751	41.9	32,257	5.8
New York	6,316,129	3,756,177	59.5	1,933,492	30.6	503,458	8.0
North Carolina	2,515,807	1,107,849	44.0	1,225,938	48.7	168,059	6.7
North Dakota	266,411	106,905	40.1	125,050	46.9	32,515	12.2
Ohio	4,534,434	2,148,222	47.4	1,859,883	41.0	483,207	10.7
Oklahoma	1,206,713	488,105	40.4	582,315	48.3	130,788	10.8
Oregon	1,377,760	649,641	47.2	538,152	39.1	121,221	8.8
Pennsylvania	4,506,118	2,215,819	49.2	1,801,169	40.0	430,984	9.6
Rhode Island	390,247	233,050	59.7	104,683	26.8	43,723	11.2
South Carolina	1,151,422	506,152	44.0	573,339	49.8	64,377	5.6
South Dakota	323,826	139,333	43.0	150,543	46.5	31,250	9.7
Tennessee	1,894,105	909,146	48.0	863,530	45.6	105,918	5.6
Texas	5,611,644	2,459,683	43.8	2,736,167	48.8	378,537	6.7
Utah	665,629	221,633	33.3	361,911	54.4	66,461	10.0
Vermont	258,449	137,894	53.4	80,352	31.1	31,024	12.0
Virginia	2,416,642	1,091,060	45.1	1,138,350	47.1	159,861	6.6
Washington	2,253,837	1,123,323	49.8	840,712	37.3	201,003	8.9
West Virginia	636,459	327,812	51.5	233,946	36.8	71,639	11.3
Wisconsin	2,196,169	1,071,971	48.8	845,029	38.5	227,339	10.4
Wyoming	211,571	77,934	36.8	105,388	49.8	25,928	12.3
Totals	96,273,262	47,401,054	49.2	39,197,350	40.7	8,085,285	8.4

[1]Official results. Total includes votes for minor-party candidates.

Source: Federal Election Commission, January 16, 1997.

Glossary

administrative law judge a quasi-independent employee of a federal agency who supervises hearings at which disputes between the agency and a regulated party are resolved. The judge's rulings are binding on both the agency and the complainant, although either side may appeal a ruling in the federal courts.

administrative oversight the review and control by congressional committees of the work conducted by the executive branch of the federal government.

adversary (accusatory) system a system of criminal justice in which a neutral judge presides over the introduction of evidence by a prosecutor and a defense attorney. The defendant is presumed to be innocent until proven guilty and cannot be forced to testify.

affirmative action government and private policies or programs designed to help women and minorities advance in areas in which they have historically been discriminated against or disadvantaged.

agency a unit of the federal government with responsibility for a set of functions that are generally less broad than those of a department. Some agencies are independent; others exist within departments.

agents of political socialization groups and individuals, such as parents, peers, and churches, from whom citizens acquire political information and learn political attitudes and values.

Aid to Families with Dependent Children (AFDC) a federal social welfare program that made monthly payments to any family with children and an income below a certain level. This program was ended by Congress in 1996.

America 2000 a report issued during the presidency of George Bush that established six national educational goals to be attained by the year 2000.

American ethos what Americans believe; the attitudes, values, and traditions of American society. At its core, the American ethos consists of a commitment to a democratic political system and a capitalistic economic system.

***amicus curiae* brief** a written opinion on a judicial case submitted to the court by a party who is not directly involved in the litigation but has an interest in the outcome. Such a brief is also known as a "friend of the court" brief.

Anti-Federalists the group of people who opposed adoption of the Constitution following its drafting in 1787.

appellate jurisdiction the authority of courts to review decisions of lower courts and administrative agencies. Under Article III of the U.S. Constitution, Congress has the power to provide for the appellate jurisdiction of the Supreme Court and courts of appeals.

Articles of Confederation the first constitution of the United States, approved by the Second Continental Congress in 1777 but not ratified by all thirteen former colonies until 1781. It provided for a unicameral legislature, the Continental Congress, which had extremely limited powers.

astroturfing the practice by interest groups of mounting grassroots lobbying campaigns that evoke a highly charged but artificial public response.

authority lawful power. In a democracy, authority is derived directly or indirectly from the people. It is embodied in the rule of law—the Constitution, statutes, treaties, executive orders, and judicial opinions.

balance of trade the difference in value between a country's imports and its exports.

belief system a set of related ideas, such as a religion or a political ideology, that helps

people understand and cope with the world around them. People use belief systems as guides for thought and action.
bicameral legislature a legislature composed of two houses, such as the U.S. Congress.
bilateral relations one-to-one dealings between the United States and a foreign government. The most common such relations involve routine interactions among diplomats and officials, as in the processing of visas, passports, and customs claims.
bill a proposal, drafted in the form of a law, that a member of Congress would like the other members to consider. A bill may be introduced into either house of Congress by any member of that house.
bill of information a document specifying the charges and evidence against a criminal defendant, which in some states prosecutors may obtain from a judge instead of seeking a grand jury indictment.
Bill of Rights the first ten amendments to the U.S. Constitution, which guarantee specific civil rights and liberties. Introduced in the First Congress, the amendments were ratified by the states in 1791.
Bill of Rights, nationalization of the Supreme Court's application to the states of guarantees in the Bill of Rights, made on the basis of the guarantee of "due process of law" in the Fourteenth Amendment to the Constitution. As a result, the First Amendment, for example, limits the power of both the national government and the states.
block grants grants-in-aid that state and local governments can spend as they wish within specified broad policy areas, such as housing, transportation, or job training.
broad reading an approach to interpreting the U.S. Constitution that allows its general principles to be widely applied to different cases in light of changing circumstances.
bundling a means by which political action committees circumvent rules limiting their donations to individual candidates. A PAC solicits donations for a group of candidates but asks that the checks be made out to specific candidates. The checks received for each candidate are then bundled together and sent to that candidate.
bureaucracy an organization of activity based on hierarchies of authority and fixed routines. Bureaucracies have jurisdictions established by law or administrative rules. Their employees are specialists, and they maintain written records of their decisions and activities. Bureaucracies are created to achieve objectivity, precision, efficiency, continuity, consistency, and fairness.
cabinet a body consisting of the heads of the executive departments of the federal government, plus the vice president. Historically, presidents have used the cabinet to counsel them on policy issues, to build support for their programs and positions, and to gain legitimacy for their administrations. In recent decades, however, the cabinet has become less important as an advisory body.
candidate an aspirant for public office. Normally candidates enter primary elections to obtain their party's nomination and if successful, run as the party's nominee in the general election. Candidates who lack a party label are considered independents.
capitalism a system of private ownership and control of the means of economic production and distribution that operates within a free market. It is often contrasted with socialism and communism, systems in which government controls some or all of the means of production and distribution.
categorical grants grants-in-aid that can be used only for narrowly defined purposes, such as education for homeless children or prevention of drug abuse.
caucus a meeting of partisans. Both major political parties permit the use of caucuses at the precinct level as the first stage in a process by which delegates may be chosen for the parties' national nominating conventions. The Democratic party requires that the number of delegates awarded to each candidate be proportional to the support the candidate receives in the caucus; the Republican party does not impose this requirement.
central clearance process a procedure by which all legislative proposals, positions, and testimony of the executive departments and agencies are cleared beforehand by the Office of Management and Budget to ensure that they are in accord with the president's program.
citizen a member of a political society, with rights and obligations that structure political participation.
civil liberties freedoms that the government must respect, such as the freedom of speech, press, and assembly, that are guaranteed under the U.S. Constitution or legislation or through judicial interpretation of laws.
civil rights rights that the government may not deny or infringe on because of an individual's race, gender, national origin, age, or ethnicity.
civil service the career employees of the federal departments and major agencies whose salaries and fringe benefits are determined by Congress and implemented by the Office of Personnel Management.

civil service system the system for filling most federal government jobs that was established by the 1883 Pendleton Act, whereby jobs must be open to any citizen and merit must be the basis for choosing employees.

Clean Air Act, 1963 the first major federal law attempting to set standards of air quality and to regulate air pollution.

Clean Water Act, 1972 the law by which the federal government took over from the states the establishment of minimum water quality standards.

clear and present danger test a test created by Supreme Court Justice Oliver Wendell Holmes for determining the scope of freedom of speech under the First Amendment to the U.S. Constitution. Under this test, only speech that poses a "clear and present danger" to the country may be punished.

cloture the limitation of debate on a measure before the Senate. It takes a vote by three-fifths of the entire Senate (sixty senators) to invoke cloture and thereby end a filibuster.

cold war the period of intense and often hostile competition between the United States and the Soviet Union from 1945 through the late 1980s.

comity the principle by which federal courts respect and leave undisturbed rulings of state courts that are based solely on independent state grounds.

commercial speech advertising, which for many years was interpreted by the Supreme Court as lacking social redeeming value and thus falling outside the scope of protection for free speech under the First Amendment. But recent rulings of the Court have extended First Amendment protection to many kinds of commercial speech, so long as it is truthful and not deceptive.

community development block grant a federal grant to a local government for urban renewal projects; it gives localities the flexibility to use the funds for projects tailored to their communities.

concurring opinion a document submitted by one or more justices or judges of a court that agrees with the decision reached in a case but not with all of the reasoning or explanations offered in the institutional opinion. It explains how the same result would have been reached by different reasoning.

confirmation hearings hearings held by a legislative body before approving the appointment of a government official. Under the U.S. Constitution, the president nominates federal judges and other high officials in the executive branch, but they must be confirmed by the Senate.

confront witnesses, right to a criminal defendant's right, guaranteed by the Sixth Amendment to the U.S. Constitution, to call and question witnesses who testify as to the defendant's guilt.

conservatism a political ideology that emphasizes economic rights and liberties for individuals with a minimum of government restraint. Compared with liberals, conservatives favor a more active role for government in national defense and law enforcement and tend to be more satisfied with the status quo.

constituency the residents of the state or district that elects a particular member of Congress.

constitutional courts the U.S. Supreme Court and other federal courts created under Article III of the U.S. Constitution, which gives Congress the power to establish "inferior courts" below the Supreme Court. Federal district courts and courts of appeals are constitutional courts and have general jurisdiction over virtually all matters of federal law.

consulate an office outside a country's capital at which a foreign country is represented.

Consumer Price Index (CPI) a measure of inflation based on the costs of certain goods commonly purchased by American consumers.

containment a policy designed to prevent the spread of Soviet influence into noncommunist countries, which formed the central thrust of American foreign policy from World War II to the late 1980s.

continuing appropriations resolution stopgap legislation passed when Congress has failed to pass an agency's budget before the beginning of a new fiscal year. Such a resolution typically continues spending in the new fiscal year at the same level as in the preceding year.

cooperative federalism a view of federalism held between the mid 1930s and the 1960s that stressed a partnership and sharing of government functions between the states and the national government.

cost of living adjustment (COLA) an annual increase in government benefits, intended to keep pace with inflation.

courts of appeals the courts within the federal judicial system that hear appeals of decisions of lower courts, state courts, or administrative agencies. There are thirteen courts of appeals.

crosscutting requirements conditions imposed on almost all grants-in-aid to further various social and economic objectives, such as nondiscrimination or environmental protection.

crossover sanctions conditions imposed on grants-in-aid in one program area that are designed to influence state and local government policy in another area.

dealignment a weakening of the attachment people feel toward political parties. A dealignment of the American electorate has been occurring since the 1960s, with the result that increasing numbers of voters consider themselves independent and vote on the basis of candidates' qualifications rather than party affiliation.

debt service the amount of each year's budget that the government pays as interest on the federal debt. It has been growing steadily as a proportion of federal expenditures.

de facto segregation racial segregation due to housing patterns rather than laws or official government policies.

de jure segregation racial segregation due to laws or government policies. The Fourteenth Amendment to the U.S. Constitution has been interpreted by the Supreme Court as forbidding de jure segregation.

democracy a political system in which the people as a whole have the ultimate authority; citizens make public policy themselves or choose people to make it for them. In an ideal democracy, all citizens have the same opportunity to affect policy; this goal is accomplished by having equal representation and by having electoral and governing decisions made on the basis of majority rule.

department one of the major operating units of the federal government and of the president's cabinet.

deregulation an effort begun in the late 1960s to reform the federal regulatory process by reducing or eliminating regulations that seemed to stifle competition.

determinate sentencing a system of sentencing criminals in which mandatory sentences are specified for particular offenses, leaving judges and juries little discretion in individual cases.

devolution federalism a possible contemporary trend, beginning with the 1994 Republican congressional victories, in which many federal government responsibilities may be returned to state and local governments.

diplomacy the conduct of relations between nations, usually through negotiation and consultation between foreign ministers and ambassadors.

direction in reference to public opinion, the proportion of the population that holds a particular view.

direct orders legal measures adopted by the national government, and enforced by civil or criminal penalties, that require certain actions by state and local governments.

discount rate the interest rate that Federal Reserve Banks charge when they lend money to member banks. When the Federal Reserve Board of Governors lowers the discount rate, it is cheaper for member banks to get money from the Federal Reserve Banks, and they can pass the savings on to their own customers in the form of lower interest rates.

dissenting opinion a document submitted by one or more justices or judges of a court that disagrees with the majority's reasoning and decision in a case.

distributive policy a public policy that distributes goods and services to citizens and whose costs are perceived as widely shared by the public as a whole. Examples are policies that provide recreational, public safety, transportation, and educational programs.

district courts the trial courts of the federal judicial system. There are ninety-four federal district courts, at least one in each state.

docket the list of filings or cases that come before a court. The U.S. Supreme Court, for example, has an annual docket of over seven thousand cases.

double jeopardy trying a person in court more than once for the same crime, a practice forbidden by the Fifth Amendment to the U.S. Constitution.

dual federalism a view of federalism held between the time of the Civil War and the mid 1930s that attempted to recognize and maintain separate spheres of authority for the national and state governments.

due process fair and regular or usual procedures. Them Fifth and Fourteenth Amendments to the U.S. Constitution provide that no one shall be deprived of life, liberty, or property by the government "without due process of law."

Education Consolidation and Improvement Act, 1981 a federal education program consolidating a number of small categorical grants into one major block grant.

elector a person chosen to vote for candidates to office. In presidential elections, the voters of each state select electors to vote for president. Initially these electors were expected to exercise independent judgment in their choice; today they are expected to ratify the choice of the majority or plurality of the state's voters.

Electoral College the body that selects the president and vice president, consisting of the 538 electors chosen in the fifty states and the District of Columbia. A majority of the college's votes is required for election.

Elementary and Secondary Education Act, 1965 one of the most significant federal education programs, which distributes aid to school districts on the basis of the proportion of low-income-family children in those districts.

embassy the headquarters of a country's diplomatic corps in a foreign country.

enrolled bill process a procedure by which the Office of Management and Budget coordinates executive branch recommendations on legislation that has been passed by Congress and is awaiting presidential action.

Environmental Protection Agency the federal agency, created in 1970, that is charged with enforcing the nation's environmental laws.

equality of opportunity a situation in which members of historically disadvantaged or discriminated-against groups, such as women or ethnic minorities, have a chance to obtain an education or employment that is equal to that of other individuals in a society.

equality of result a situation in which groups unequal in terms of such factors as educational background and historical socioeconomic advantages enjoy the same benefits or status in income or employment.

espionage the deployment of operatives who spy on foreign governments or pay foreign nationals to reveal secrets about their own governments.

establishment clause the part of the First Amendment to the U.S. Constitution that forbids Congress from establishing a national religion or favoring particular religions. As a result of the Supreme Court's interpretation of the amendment, state governments are subject to the same prohibitions.

exacting scrutiny test (strict rationality test) the test generally used by federal courts when reviewing whether laws and regulations involving nonracial discrimination violate the equal protection clause of the Fourteenth Amendment to the U.S. Constitution. Under this test, discrimination on the basis of gender, age, or wealth is unconstitutional unless it furthers some legitimate government interest in a reasonable way. This test is more rigorous than the minimal scrutiny test but less rigorous than the strict scrutiny test.

executive memorandum a formal statement of official policy or procedure, issued by the president to inform his subordinates of what he wishes them to do.

Executive Office of the President a bureaucracy created in 1939 to provide institutional staff support for the president.

executive order a presidential order to subordinates to perform a particular task in a particular way.

executive privilege the power claimed by the president to keep certain communications within the White House confidential from Congress and the courts.

express powers powers that are enumerated in a constitution. Article I, Section 8, of the U.S. Constitution, for example, enumerates seventeen specific powers of Congress, including the power to tax, coin money, regulate commerce, and provide for the national defense.

Federal Reserve Board of Governors (the Fed) an independent agency of the federal government outside the executive and legislative branches that makes general credit, monetary, and operating policy for the Federal Reserve System as a whole.

Federal Reserve System the system that serves as the central bank for the United States, setting standards and rules that constrain the actions of other banks. It is composed of twelve Federal Reserve Banks, their twenty-five branches throughout the country, and many of the nation's commercial financial institutions. The system is managed by the Federal Reserve Board of Governors.

federalism a system of government in which powers are shared between a central or national government and state or regional governments. The U.S. Constitution establishes a federal system.

fighting words words that may incite violence or a breach of the peace and public order. Historically, they have not been considered protected speech under the First Amendment to the U.S. Constitution, but in recent years the Supreme Court has overturned all convictions on these grounds.

filibuster a technique for preventing a vote in the Senate, in which senators gain recognition to speak in debate and then do not relinquish the floor. A filibuster can be ended only by a vote of cloture, and even then, loopholes in the Senate rules permit a single senator to prolong debate.

financial controls the most important and effective of Congress's techniques for overseeing the work of the executive branch. Before it appropriates funds to an agency or a program, Congress assesses the manner in which previous appropriations have been used and examines the stated plans for use of the funds currently being requested.

fiscal policy government economic policy dealing with the amounts of annual government expenditures and revenues, the purposes for which money is spent and the sources from which it comes, and the relationship of expenditures to revenues. The primary instrument of fiscal policy is the annual federal budget.

food stamps government-issued coupons that can be used to purchase food.

formula grants grants-in-aid distributed on the basis of a formula applied to all eligible recipients.

franking privilege the right of members of Congress to mail newsletters and questionnaires free of charge to every mailbox in their states or districts.

free exercise clause the part of the First Amendment to the U.S. Constitution that guarantees individuals the freedom of religious belief. As a result of the Supreme Court's interpretations of the amendment, state governments are barred from coercing individuals' religious beliefs.

freedom of association a right that the First Amendment to the U.S. Constitution has been interpreted as guaranteeing to individuals, including the right to organize and to belong to political parties and religious, economic, and other kinds of social organizations.

free-enterprise system a competitive economic system in which people are encouraged to pursue their own financial interests and the market determines their success or failure. Such a system rewards individual initiative and discourages government involvement.

general ticket system a winner-take-all method of selecting presidential and vice presidential electors that is used in all states but two, Maine and Nebraska. Under this system, the entire slate of electors pledged to the candidate who receives the most votes in the state is elected.

gerrymandering the practice of drawing legislative districts in such a way as to give one party an advantage.

going public making an appeal to the people for support for presidential policies. Presidents go public to obtain the backing they need from other public officials, particularly members of Congress.

government the formal institutions within which processes and procedures of decision making about public policy are formulated, implemented, and adjudicated.

government corporation an economic enterprise owned in whole or in part by the federal government; examples are the Tennessee Valley Authority and the Federal Deposit Insurance Corporation.

grand jury a group of twelve to twenty-three persons who meet in private to determine, on the basis of evidence presented by prosecutors, whether to approve an indictment against an individual.

grants-in-aid federal payments to state and local governments.

grantsmanship efforts by state and local governments to maximize the federal aid they receive.

Great Compromise the compromise reached at the Constitutional Convention in 1787 between the Virginia and New Jersey plans. It provided that each state would be equally represented in the Senate and that representation in the House of Representatives would be based on population.

gross domestic product (GDP) a statistical indicator of economic growth that measures the value of goods and services produced by factors of production—land, labor, and capital—located in the United States.

Housing and Community Development Act, 1974 the legislation that established the Community Development Block Grant program, which provided cities with money for a wide variety of housing and development needs such as public housing, street paving, lighting, and attracting commercial development.

ideological party a political party whose members share a belief system distinct from those of other parties. Ideological parties in the United States, such as the Socialists and the Libertarians, have been minor parties with a limited membership base.

impeachment the power of Congress to remove any civil officer of the United States who has been found guilty of "treason, bribery, or other high crimes and misdemeanors." The impeachment process begins with the introduction of a bill of impeachment in the House of Representatives. If the House approves the bill by majority vote, the impeached person is then tried in the Senate. Conviction requires the votes of two-thirds of the senators present and voting.

implied powers government powers that are inferred from the powers expressly enumerated in a written constitution. The "necessary and proper" clause of Article I, Section 8, of the U.S. Constitution has been interpreted to give Congress broad implied powers.

incrementalism the tendency for public policy to be made in slow, halting steps; a characteristic of policy making in the United States.

independent regulatory commission a unit of the federal government whose principal purpose is to regulate commerce and trade in an assigned area of jurisdiction. Commissions are independent of any department and, to some extent, of presidential control. All are run by a group of commissioners rather than a single executive.

indictment the formal statement of charges against a criminal defendant, based on evidence presented by a prosecutor to a grand jury.

inflation an increase in the general price level in an economy.

in forma pauperis "in the manner of a pauper." When appealing a decision to the U.S. Supreme Court, indigents may file an *in forma pauperis* petition, stating that they are too poor to pay the Court's $300 fee for filing an appeal and asking that it be waived.

inherent powers powers possessed by a national government that are not enumerated in a constitution. In the conduct of foreign affairs, presidents have often claimed that they possess inherent powers.

injunction a prohibitory court order, such as one that prevents a federal agency from taking further action against an aggrieved party until certain conditions—a rehearing, for example—have been met.

inquisitorial system a system of criminal justice used in some countries, such as France, in which the accused person is presumed guilty, interrogated by magistrates, and denied other rights afforded in adversary systems.

institutional opinion an official explanation or justification of a decision by a court with multiple judges or justices.

intensity in reference to public opinion, the depth of feeling on an issue.

intergovernmental lobby the group of state and local government organizations, such as the National League of Cities and the National Governors' Association, that lobby the national government for legislation and decisions favorable to state and local governments.

iron triangle the close, mutually supportive relationship that often develops among executive agencies, special interest groups, and congressional subcommittees.

isolationism disengagement from the affairs of foreign countries except when they intersect directly with those of the United States. This approach characterized American foreign policy almost continuously until World War II.

issue network an interconnected group of specialists in a particular subject area working in bureaucratic agencies at all levels of government, along with experts employed by legislative committee staffs, interest groups, think tanks, and universities. Issue networks play an important role in developing the national policy agenda, shaping consensus about preferred policies, and directing political leaders to develop and implement new policy proposals.

issue party a party created out of dissatisfaction with one or both of the major parties when they ignore an important issue, take an unpopular stand, or nominate an unattractive candidate. An issue party exercises power by threatening the major parties with loss of electoral support until they change their ways. In recent decades issue parties have tended to become vehicles for individuals to promote their presidential candidacy.

Jim Crow laws laws passed in the late nineteenth century that required racial separation in public transportation, restaurants, and other places of accommodation and discriminated against African Americans in various other ways.

Joint Chiefs of Staff (JCS) a body that advises the president on military matters, made up of the highest-ranking uniformed officer in each of the military services. It is chaired by an officer from one of the services who is appointed by the president to a two-year term.

joint committees committees composed of members of both houses of Congress. They are permanent study committees with no authority to initiate legislation.

joint conference committees temporary joint committees whose principal function is to resolve the differences between forms of the same bill passed by the House and the Senate, respectively.

judicial activism the use of judicial review to invalidate a law or other official action.

judicial double standard the Supreme Court's tendency since 1937 to uphold virtually all economic regulations under the Fifth and Fourteenth Amendments' guarantees of due process but to give heightened scrutiny to laws and regulations that affect individuals' noneconomic civil rights and liberties.

judicial federalism the dual judicial system in the United States, consisting of a system of federal courts and separate judicial systems in each of the fifty states.

judicial review, power of the power and authority of a court to determine whether acts of a legislature or an executive violate a constitution. The U.S. Supreme Court, for instance, has the power to strike down any congressional or state legislation, as well as any other official government action, that it deems to violate the U.S. Constitution.

judicial self-restraint deference by courts to the decisions of other branches of government.

jurisdiction the authority of a court to

decide particular cases. The jurisdiction of federal courts is provided for in Article III of the U.S. Constitution and by Congress in statutes.

lame duck a label often applied to a president in the last two years of a second term because the president is ineligible to run for reelection and may thus have difficulty building and maintaining political support.

legislation the making of laws, one of the major functions of Congress.

legislative courts courts created by Congress under Article I of the U.S. Constitution and having jurisdiction or authority over particular areas of law. The U.S. Court of Military Appeals, which applies military law, is one such court.

libel false statement of fact about a person or defamation of his or her character in print or by visual portrayal on television. Libel falls outside the scope of protection for free speech under the First Amendment to the U.S. Constitution.

liberalism a political ideology that emphasizes political rights and liberties for individuals and equal opportunity for all. Liberals oppose government restraints on the exercise of political freedoms but favor government programs that help the less fortunate.

limited government the idea that government powers are limited and specified or are traceable to enumerated powers in a written constitution.

line-item veto the presidential power, created in 1996, to veto portions of certain kinds of legislation while allowing the rest of the bill to become law.

loan guarantee a government guarantee that if a company or an individual is unable to pay back a loan, the government will do so.

lobbying the art of persuading public officials to support a particular policy position. The term alludes to legislators' being accosted by interest group representatives in the lobby outside the legislative chamber.

macroeconomics the study of the behavior of the economy as a whole.

mandatory entitlement program a federal program that confers benefits, usually in the form of payments or loan guarantees, to any citizen who meets certain stipulated qualifications. Examples include Social Security, veterans' benefits, and student loan guarantees.

mark-up session a meeting at which all of the members of a congressional subcommittee or committee participate in revising a bill to put it into a form that is acceptable to a majority of them.

meaningful choice the opportunity for voters to select among at least two candidates whose views are dissimilar and who have sufficient resources to present their views to the public.

Medicaid a federal program established in 1965 to help people with low incomes pay for hospital, doctor, and other medical bills.

Medicare the federal health insurance program for people over 65, added to the Social Security system in 1965.

merit system a system of appointing judges or other government officials on the basis of ability, competitive examinations, or comparisons with other qualified candidates. Some states have so-called merit systems for the selection of state judges, in which a nonpartisan commission recommends a list of possible nominees from which the governor or legislature makes appointments.

military-industrial complex a term, first used in the 1950s, referring to the close and mutually beneficial relationship between the Defense Department and the companies that manufacture weapons for it.

minimal scrutiny test the test used by federal courts when reviewing whether laws and regulations dealing with economic matters violate the equal protection clause of the Fourteenth Amendment to the U.S. Constitution. On this test, laws and regulations will be upheld if they have a rational basis.

***Miranda* warnings** a set of reminders about constitutional rights that police must give before interrogating criminal suspects. Suspects must be told that they have the right to remain silent and to consult an attorney and that an attorney can be provided if they cannot afford to hire one. This requirement was the result of the Supreme Court's ruling in *Miranda v. Arizona* (1966).

monetarists economists who believe that monetary policy is the most important instrument of government economic policy, especially for maintaining price stability.

monetary policy government control of the availability and flow of money in the economy. Its central concern is the terms on which money can be borrowed—that is, interest rates and repayment requirements.

mutual assured destruction an element of containment policy holding that for nuclear deterrence to be effective, the United States had to convince the Soviet Union and other potential adversaries that it possessed the capability to inflict significant damage in a nuclear attack, even if that attack came as a retaliatory response to a nuclear attack on the United States. This capability implied that nuclear attack on the United States would be suicidal for the country that launched it.

National Defense Education Act, 1958 a federal program designed to upgrade the science, math, and foreign-language skills of schoolchildren.

National Security Council (NSC) a component of the Executive Office of the President that is intended to facilitate the coordination of foreign and defense policy. It consists of the president, the vice president, the secretary of state, and the secretary of defense, advised by the director of central intelligence and the chairman of the Joint Chiefs of Staff. The head of the NSC staff, the assistant to the president for national security affairs, is often the principal presidential adviser on national security issues.

National Service Act, 1993 a federal program providing college loans that can be paid off by working at community service jobs.

nation-centered federalism a view of federalism held in the pre–Civil War era that advocated an active and expanded role for the national government.

negative advertising commercials that seek to discredit a political candidate. First used in 1964, such advertising has come to characterize modern media campaigns.

new federalism the view of federalism associated with presidents Nixon and Reagan, which stressed greater flexibility in the use of grants-in-aid by the recipients and, in the Reagan years, reductions in the total amount of grants.

New Jersey Plan one of the main proposals for the overall structure of government that was presented at the Constitutional Convention in 1787. It was proposed by William Paterson and called for a unicameral legislature in which all states would be represented equally, a multimember executive with no power to veto legislation, and a supreme court. This plan was favored by smaller states.

newsworthiness the characteristic of stories and events that merit attention by the news media because they capture public interest. Frequently they involve conflict, drama, and surprise in addition to timeliness and importance.

nullification, doctrine of the claim, associated most closely with South Carolina senator John C. Calhoun, that states could declare acts of Congress null and void within their borders.

obscenity material that because of its sexual content is not considered protected speech under the First Amendment to the Constitution. The Supreme Court determines obscenity by three measures: (1) whether local community standards would find a work prurient; (2) whether the work depicts sexual conduct defined as obscene under the law; and (3) whether the work lacks serious literary, artistic, political, or scientific value.

Office of Management and Budget (OMB) the president's principal office for preparing a budget, coordinating legislative and regulatory activities, and improving management in the executive branch.

one person, one vote the principle that all legislative districts within the same state must be approximately equal in population in order to ensure that all citizens have equal representation in government. This principle was enunciated by the Supreme Court in *Westberry v. Sanders* (1964).

opinion (1) a judgment made about current issues, including feelings people have, positions they take, and conclusions they reach. (2) the written explanation or justification of a court's or an individual judge's decision.

original jurisdiction the authority of a court to have a case originate in it. Article III of the U.S. Constitution specifies the "cases or controversies" over which the Supreme Court has original jurisdiction.

oversight hearings regular in-depth reviews by congressional committees of the activities of executive agencies or the management of specific programs. Such a hearing is usually preceded by an investigation by the committee staff. At the hearing itself, executive branch officials are called to explain their activities and to answer the committee's questions. The product of an oversight hearing may be a report suggesting changes in administrative procedures, remedial legislation, or reauthorization of the agency or program.

partial preemption the national government's establishment of minimum standards in a policy area and its requiring state and local governments to meet those standards or lose their authority in that area.

partisan a person who identifies with a political party.

party caucus a meeting of all members of a party in a legislative body to set legislative strategy or seek to determine a party position on important policy decisions.

party discipline the ability of party leaders in a legislature to count on the members of their party to support them on votes and to impose sanctions on members who do not. It is normal in legislatures in other countries but rare in the U.S. Congress.

party platform a formal statement of a party's beliefs, opinions, and policy stands, tied together by a set of underlying principles based on the party's ideological orientation.

patronage the distribution of government jobs as a reward for working on a winning candidate's campaign or providing other service to a party or political machine.
personnel control congressional control over presidential appointments and over the number, qualifications, salaries, and employment conditions of all federal employees.
petition for a writ of *certiorari* a legal request that the U.S. Supreme Court hear an appeal of a particular case.
plea bargaining an arrangement whereby a criminal defendant pleads guilty to lesser charges than those originally brought in exchange for a reduced sentence. As a result, both the prosecution and the defense are saved the time and expense of a trial.
pocket veto a presidential veto of a bill that occurs when a congressional session concludes within ten days of the bill's passage and without the president having signed it. Because Congress is not in session, the president does not return the bill, nor is there any possibility of a congressional override.
policy adoption marshaling the support needed to win official approval of a specific public policy. This stage of the policy-making process is typically characterized by bargaining, negotiating, and compromise.
policy evaluation determination of whether a particular public policy is working as intended.
policy formulation the stage in the process of making public policy during which an effective and feasible solution to a problem is developed.
policy implementation the stage in the process of making public policy during which the policy is actually put into action.
policy termination the process of halting public policies that are not meeting their objectives or have outlived the problem for which they were created.
political action committee (PAC) a nonparty group that solicits contributions from its members and uses the money to influence the outcome of elections.
political correctness the avoidance or prohibition of language and behavior that are offensive to certain segments of the population, such as women or minority groups. Opponents claim that such a prohibition violates individuals' rights protected by the First Amendment to the U.S. Constitution.
political culture the dominant values, beliefs, and attitudes of members of a society about their governance, their history, and their rights and responsibilities as citizens. A political culture conditions the structure of the society's political system, the rules by which it operates, and the bounds of acceptable behavior within it.
political efficacy an individual's sense of his or her own ability to influence political outcomes and to participate in politics in ways that make a difference.
political equality the principle that the vote of each citizen in a democracy counts equally. Two conditions apply: the majority rules, and the candidate with the most votes wins.
political ideology a set of interrelated attitudes that shape judgments about and reactions to political issues. Political ideologies, such as liberalism and conservatism, provide people with a general orientation toward government that helps them form opinions and react to events.
political interest group an organization that attempts to influence the staffing and policies of government.
political party a group organized to win elections in order to influence the policies of government. American political parties are broad-based, decentralized, pragmatic political organizations.
political questions issues presented to courts that judges decide would more appropriately be resolved by other branches of government.
political socialization the ongoing process whereby individuals acquire the information, beliefs, attitudes, and values that help them comprehend the workings of a political system and orient themselves within it.
politics the process by which people pursue their own needs and preferences within a society. Politics frequently involves a struggle to achieve power in order to attain individual and group goals.
popular sovereignty the idea that government is based on the consent of the people and is accountable to the people for its actions.
power the influence that some individuals, groups, or institutions have over others; the ability to get people to do something they might not otherwise do. It may be exercised through the use of persuasive skills, legal authority, force or the threat of force, or the promise of rewards.
preemption the national government's removal of an area of authority from state and local governments.
prime rate the interest rate that banks charge their best customers to borrow money. A lower prime rate encourages economic activity by reducing the cost of borrowing.
privacy, right of a constitutional right not

enumerated in the Bill of Rights but construed by the U.S. Supreme Court to be in the "penumbras," or shadows, of the First, Third, Fourth, and Fifth Amendments and enforceable against the states under the Fourteenth Amendment.

probable cause reasonable justification; specifically, sufficient evidence for an arrest or a police search, a requirement of the Fourth Amendment to the U.S. Constitution.

problem recognition the stage in the process of making public policy during which decision makers and the public become aware of the existence of a problem possibly requiring public attention.

procedural due process the application of laws and regulations according to fair and regular procedures. It imposes limits on how government may carry out its activities.

project grants grants-in-aid for which potential recipients must apply to a federal agency; such grants are usually awarded on a competitive basis.

proportional voting the principle by which delegates chosen in the Democratic party's presidential nominating primaries and caucuses are awarded to candidates in proportion to the number of popular votes that they receive.

prospective voting judgments about how to vote that anticipate candidates' future decisions and actions. According to this model of voting behavior, voters compare their own values and positions on issues with those of the candidates and parties in an effort to determine which party and which candidates are likely to benefit them the most.

public assistance social welfare programs providing money and other forms of support, such as food, medical care, or housing subsidies, to needy people. These programs may be administered by the federal government or by the states.

public opinion the opinions, attitudes, and values of the public as they relate to the issues of the day.

public opinion poll a survey of the beliefs, attitudes, and/or opinions of the general population. Public opinion polls have been conducted regularly since the 1940s to gauge opinion on a wide range of contemporary issues.

public policy government decisions designed to address public problems. Public policy is established by Constitution, law, and precedent; it constitutes the rules by which a society lives.

realignment a shifting of partisan attitudes among the electorate. Realignment occurs over a period of years when the dominant party loses the allegiance of some of its supporters and the other party gains the allegiance of some of these voters as well as a majority of newer ones coming into the electorate. The last realignment in American politics occurred during the 1930s, when the Democrats became the dominant party.

reapportionment the redistribution of seats in the U.S. House of Representatives among the states every ten years on the basis of population changes since the previous census.

rebuttal, right of the requirement that broadcasters give people who are criticized on the air or political candidates whose opponents are endorsed by a station the opportunity to reply free of charge. This right, upheld by the U.S. Supreme Court in 1969, has discouraged broadcasters from airing controversial issues or endorsing candidates.

redistributive policy a public policy, such as a welfare program, that is perceived to take benefits from one group and give them to others.

redistricting redrawing the boundaries of legislative districts to reflect geographic shifts in population.

regulatory policy a public policy that establishes rules and standards and thereby controls behavior. Examples include laws that regulate child labor, minimum wages, and industrial pollution.

regulatory review a procedure by which the Office of Management and Budget oversees regulations that executive agencies wish to issue to implement legislation. In assessing regulations, the OMB examines their necessity, cost-effectiveness, and consistency with administration policy and congressional intent.

representation the processes through which members of Congress seek to determine, articulate, and act on the interests of residents of their state or district.

republic a government whose powers are exercised by elected representatives, who are directly or indirectly accountable to the people governed.

required reserve ratio the percentage of deposits that member banks of the Federal Reserve System must keep as reserves, as determined by the Fed. As the reserve ratio goes up, the amount of money available for banks to lend goes down; this makes credit harder to obtain, causes interest rates to rise, and cools economic activity.

responsible party government the idea that a party that controls the government must try to implement its platform and the promises made by its candidates.

restrictive covenants contracts in which it is stipulated that property may not be sold or leased to members of certain racial or religious groups. In *Shelley v. Kraemer* (1948), the Supreme Court held that such covenants were unconstitutional under the Fourteenth Amendment.
retrospective voting judgments about how to vote that are based on the past performance of the parties and their elected officials in light of the promises they made and the conditions that resulted from their actions. According to this theory of voting behavior, voters look back and decide whether they (and society) are better or worse off as a result of the performance of the people in power.
reverse discrimination discrimination against whites and/or men, the basis on which affirmative action programs have been challenged under the equal protection clause of the Fourteenth Amendment to the U.S. Constitution.
revolving door politics the practice by which former government officials represent organized interests in the private sector.
rider one or more controversial provisions attached to a piece of legislation. Proposals that might have difficulty surviving on their own are thereby permitted to "ride through" the legislative process on the backs of other bills.
rule of four the informal rule that for a case to be accepted for review by the U.S. Supreme Court, at least four of the justices must vote to take it.
salience importance. The most salient public policy issues are those that arouse the most attention and interest.
secondary group a group, such as a labor union, church congregation, or bridge club, that individuals choose to join and that may help shape or reinforce their political views and values.
Section 8 a provision of the 1974 Housing and Community Development Act that established a rental subsidy program for needy families and encouraged the construction of subsidized rental housing units.
secular regulation rule a rule used by the U.S. Supreme Court in applying the First Amendment's guarantee of the free exercise of religion. It requires that national and state laws have a secular (nonreligious) purpose and not discriminate on the basis of religion.
seditious libel libel or slander that defames or criticizes the government or its officials. The First Amendment to the U.S. Constitution has been interpreted as forbidding governments from punishing seditious libel.
select committees (special committees) temporary congressional committees created to deal with a specific set of issues. They usually disappear once they have completed their work. Many such committees have explicitly limited functions and authority, and most are not authorized to recommend legislation.
selective perception the tendency of most people to use their reading and television watching to acquire information and opinions that support their existing political views and party preferences.
self-incrimination confessing to a crime or testifying in a court in a way that implicates oneself in a crime. The Fifth Amendment to the U.S. Constitution provides a guarantee against forced self-incrimination.
Senior Executive Service (SES) the highest-ranking group of federal civil service employees, created in 1979 to provide agencies with greater flexibility in deploying, compensating, and, if necessary, removing their senior managers and technical specialists. There are now about eight thousand SES members, of whom at least 90 percent must always be career federal employees.
seniority system the former system under which the member of the majority party with the longest consecutive service on each congressional committee was automatically its chair for as long as he or she remained in Congress.
separate but equal doctrine the principle that laws requiring separate facilities for white and black citizens were permissible under the U.S. Constitution's Fourteenth Amendment guarantee of equal protection. The doctrine was upheld by the Supreme Court in *Plessy v. Ferguson* (1896) but abandoned in the mid twentieth century.
separation of powers the division of power and authority within a government among three branches, typically the legislature, the executive, and the judiciary.
Servicemen's Readjustment Act, 1944 a federal program, also known as the G.I. Bill, that provided financial assistance to military veterans for completing their education.
single-member district an electoral district in which only one of the candidates for a particular office can be elected. Districts for members of Congress are of this type.
slander a false statement of fact about a person or defamation of his or her character by speech, for which individuals may be subject to prosecution.
social insurance a "pay as you go" social

welfare program in which employees and employers contribute to a national insurance fund. Examples in the United States are Social Security, Medicare, and unemployment insurance.

social redeeming value the criterion used by the Supreme Court in determining whether speech is protected under the First Amendment. Only the categories of libel and slander, obscenity, fighting words, and commercial speech have been deemed to lack social redeeming value and to receive less protection under the First Amendment.

Social Security the federal social insurance program that provides monthly payments to retired and disabled workers, and to survivors of workers who are eligible for the benefits.

socioeconomic status (SES) an analytic measure of relative social and economic standing.

soft money campaign contributions and expenditures not subject to federal limits which can only be used in "bipartisan" efforts to educate and inform the voters about the candidates and the issues. Subject of considerable controversy during and after the 1996 elections.

sound bite short excerpt taken from a speech or statement made by a candidate or public official that is highlighted in a television news show.

Speaker of the House the elected leader of the majority party in the House of Representatives, who serves as the presiding officer of the House.

special committees select committees.

special investigations special examinations by Congress of executive branch or presidential activities. Some are conducted by permanent committees and subcommittees with no special appropriations of funds or additions to committee staffs. More commonly, however, investigations differ from routine oversight hearings in the depth of their examinations, the vigor with which they are conducted, and the amount of funds and staff resources committed to them.

speech-plus-conduct the communication of ideas through marching, picketing, and sit-in demonstrations. Under the Supreme Court's interpretation of the First Amendment, such forms of expression are protected speech so long as they are not disruptive or destructive of public or private property.

speedy and public trial a right guaranteed to criminal defendants by the Sixth Amendment to the U.S. Constitution. As a result, secret trials are forbidden, and an arrested person must be tried within a period specified by Congress.

split-ticket voting the practice of voting for candidates of different parties on the same ballot. Split-ticket voting has increased in recent decades with the weakening of partisan allegiances.

spoils system the distribution of federal jobs to supporters of the victorious presidential candidate. It was the primary way of staffing the federal bureaucracy prior to the creation of the civil service system.

stability permanence; persistence. When public opinion is stable, it persists with little or no change.

standard operating procedures (SOPs) predetermined ways of responding to a particular problem or set of circumstances. SOPs simplify bureaucratic decisions and contribute to their consistency, but they also channel bureaucratic activity into rigid patterns and make agencies less adaptable to change.

standing committees permanent congressional committees that have full authority to recommend legislation. A few, like the Rules Committee in the House, are responsible for organizing and regulating the operations of Congress; most have jurisdictions defined along substantive policy lines.

standing to sue the right or legal status to initiate a lawsuit or judicial proceedings. To have standing to sue, parties must show that they are suffering or in danger of suffering an immediate and substantial personal injury.

state-centered federalism a view of federalism held in the pre–Civil War era that opposed increasing national power at the expense of the states.

strict construction the idea that the U.S. Constitution can and should be interpreted in a narrowly literal sense, as it was written and understood by its framers.

strict rationality test the exacting scrutiny test.

strict scrutiny test the test used by federal courts when reviewing whether the equal protection clause of the Fourteenth Amendment to the U.S. Constitution is violated by laws or regulations that limit or deny individuals' "fundamental rights" or that discriminate on the basis of race, national origin, or religion. Under this test, government must have a "compelling interest" that justifies the law or regulation.

structural unemployment the "natural" or lowest possible rate of unemployment, reflecting the number of people who at any given time are just entering the work force, leaving one job to look for another, or having difficulty finding a job because they lack valuable skills.

subgovernment an alliance that develops among executive agencies, interest groups, and congressional committees in a particular policy area. (Also called an *iron triangle*.)
subsidy direct government intervention in the economy in the form of cash grants, loan guarantees, and tax advantages extended to particular industries or economic areas.
substantive due process conformity of the subject matter of laws and regulations to a standard of reasonableness. It imposes limits on what government may do.
suffrage the right to vote.
summit meeting a meeting between the American president and an important foreign leader.
superdelegates delegates to the Democratic party's national nominating convention who are chosen from among the party's elected and appointed leaders. Unpledged to any candidate, they constituted approximately 18 percent of the convention's delegates in 1996.
symbolic speech nonverbal communication through the use of symbols that the U.S. Supreme Court has ruled to be protected speech under the First Amendment, such as the wearing of black armbands as a sign of protest.
Synthetic Fuels Corporation a program passed during the Carter presidency that provided subsidies for the production of fuel from sources other than oil, such as wind, garbage, and plants. It was abolished during the Reagan presidency.
territorial imperative the tendency of federal agencies to guard their own area of jurisdiction against other agencies that seem to be trespassing on it.
terrorism the use of violence to disrupt the routines of international activity and to demoralize and frighten a country's population or regime.
three-fifths compromise the decision made at the Constitutional Convention in 1787 to count three-fifths of slaves as persons for the purposes of determining taxation and representation in the U.S. House of Representatives.
Three Mile Island a nuclear power plant in Pennsylvania that in 1979 experienced the worst nuclear accident in United States history. That event dramatically focused the public's attention on energy issues in general and nuclear dangers in particular.
travel, right to a right not enumerated in the Bill of Rights but construed by the U.S. Supreme Court to be a basic guarantee of the Fourteenth Amendment. As a result, states are forbidden from infringing on individuals' right to travel from one state to another.
treaty an official, written set of accords between nations in which the parties agree to certain specific actions. When the United States enters into a treaty with a foreign government, it is negotiated by American diplomatic officials, sometimes including the president. It must then be approved by two-thirds of the members of the Senate.
unalienable rights in the social theory of John Locke, certain natural rights of individuals that are believed to precede the creation of government and that government may not deny. The Declaration of Independence proclaimed that individuals have the unalienable right to "Life, Liberty, and the Pursuit of Happiness."
unanimous consent a common device used for procedural efficiency in the Senate, in which action is taken without debate when all members consent to it.
unconventional participation efforts to influence public policy, such as street demonstrations, boycotts, and sit-ins, that fall outside the normal channels of political participation.
unemployment insurance a federal program, created as part of the 1935 Social Security Act, that pays benefits to people who lose their jobs.
universal suffrage the right of all citizens who have reached maturity to vote. It reflects the democratic principle that if government is to be based on the consent of the governed, all citizens should be able to participate in the selection of their public officials.
urban renewal an approach to federal housing policy, established in 1949 and terminated in 1974, that was designed to clear blighted and deteriorating areas of inner cities and replace them with new commercial and residential establishments.
Virginia Plan one of the main proposals for the overall structure of government that was presented at the Constitutional Convention in 1787. It was drafted by James Madison and called for a strong central government, including a bicameral legislature with representation of states based on their wealth and population, a chief executive chosen by the legislature, and a powerful judiciary. This plan was favored by larger states.
void for vagueness a judicial standard used to strike down laws that are overly broad or so vague that it is uncertain what they apply to or whether they infringe on freedoms such as those protected under the First Amendment to the U.S. Constitution.
Water Quality Act, 1965 the first major federal law attempting to establish standards for water quality.

whip the member of each party's leadership structure in the House and the Senate who works closely with rank-and-file members to determine party positions and to seek to form legislative coalitions.

White House Office the president's principal political aides, who provide staff support for formulating presidential policy, communicating it to the public, and helping the president meet the day-to-day responsibilities of the office.

winner-take-all voting the principle by which the candidate who receives the most votes in an electoral district or state wins all of the delegates or electors at stake. The Republicans permit this method of voting in their presidential nominating primaries and caucuses; the Democrats do not.

writ of *certiorari* a formal order issued by the U.S. Supreme Court to a lower federal court or state court requesting the record of the decision in a case that the Supreme Court has accepted for review. Four of the Court's nine justices must agree to grant a writ of certiorari in order for a case to be reviewed.

writ of mandamus an order issued by a superior court that directs a lower court or other government authority to perform a particular act.

References

Chapter 1 The American Political Environment

1. Herbert McClosky and John Zaller, *The American Ethos: Public Attitudes Toward Capitalism and Democracy* (Cambridge, Mass.: Harvard University Press, 1984).

Chapter 2 The Constitutional Basis of American Politics

1. See Max Farrand, *The Framing of the Constitution* (1913); and John P. Roche, "The Founding Fathers: A Reform Caucus in Action," *American Political Science Review* (December 1961): 799.
2. For further discussion, see Gordon S. Wood, *The Creation of the American Republic, 1776–1787* (Chapel Hill: University of North Carolina Press, 1969).
3. "Resolution of Federal Convention (May 30, 1787)," in *The Records of the Federal Convention of 1787,* ed. Max Farrand (New Haven, Conn.: Yale University Press, 1913), vol. 1, 30.
4. James Madison, in *The Federalist Papers,* ed. Clinton Rossiter (New York: New American Library, 1961), no. 39, 240–246.
5. See Forrest McDonald, *Novus Ordo Seclorum: The Intellectual Origins of the Constitution* (Lawrence: University of Kansas Press, 1985).
6. James Madison, in Farrand, *The Records of the Federal Convention of 1787,* vol. 1, 122–123.
7. Patrick Henry, in *The Complete Anti-Federalist,* ed. Herbert J. Storing (Chicago: University of Chicago Press, 1981), vol. 5, 211.
8. For studies of the debates in the various state ratification conventions, see *Ratifying the Constitution,* ed. Michael Gillespie and Michael Lienesch (Lawrence: University of Kansas Press, 1989).
9. See Peter Onuf, "State Sovereignty and the Making of the Constitution," in *Conceptual Change and the Constitution,* ed. Terence Ball and J. G. A. Pocock (Lawrence: University of Kansas Press, 1988).
10. See John Reid, *The Concept of Liberty in the Age of the American Revolution* (Chicago: University of Chicago Press, 1988).
11. See Ellis Sandoz, *A Government of Laws: Political Theory, Religion, and the American Founding* (Baton Rouge: Louisiana State University Press, 1990).
12. *Meyers v. United States,* 272 U.S. 52 (1926).
13. This discussion draws on David O'Brien, "Federalism as a Metaphor in the Constitutional Politics of Public Administration," *Public Administration Review* 49 (1989): 411.
14. For two studies of judicial review and the founding, see Robert Clinton, *Marbury v. Madison and Judicial Review* (Lawrence: University of Kansas Press, 1989); and Sylvia Snowiss, *Judicial Review and the Law of the Constitution* (New Haven, Conn.: Yale University Press, 1990).
15. Felix Frankfurter, "The Zeitgeist and the Judiciary," in *Law and Politics,* ed. A. MacLeish and E. Prichard (New York: Capricorn, 1939), 6.
16. Edward White, "The Supreme Court of the United States," *American Bar Association Journal* 7 (1921), 341.

Chapter 3 Federalism in Theory and Practice

1. *McCulloch v. Maryland,* 17 U.S. 316 (1819).
2. It should be noted that the Virginia and Kentucky Resolutions were drawn to address specific political issues of the

time and that neither Madison nor Jefferson governed as president in a way that was congruent with the resolutions. Further, neither accepted Calhoun's extended nullification theories. For further discussion, see Andrew C. McLaughlin, *A Constitutional History of the United States* (New York: Appleton-Century, 1935).

3. See Edward S. Corwin, *The Twilight of the Supreme Court* (New Haven, Conn.: Yale University Press, 1934), ch. 1.
4. *United States v. E. C. Knight Company,* 156 U.S. 1 (1895).
5. For elaboration, see David B. Walker, *The Rebirth of Federalism* (Chatham, N.J.: Chatham House Publishers, Inc., 1995), 76–91.
6. See *Hodel v. Virginia Surface Mining & Reclamation, Inc.,* 452 U.S. 264 (1981); and *EEOC v. Wyoming,* 460 U.S. 226 (1983).
7. *Intergovernmental Perspective* 11, No. 2/3 (Spring–Summer 1985): 23. In response to this "Garcia update," it should be noted that Congress in 1986 amended the Fair Labor Standards Act to allow states and localities to use compensatory time in lieu of overtime pay for their workers. See John J. Harrigan, *Politics and Policy in States and Communities* (New York: HarperCollins, 1991), 58.
8. *Garcia v. San Antonio Metropolitan Transit Authority,* 469 U.S. 528 (1985).
9. Timothy J. Conlan, James D. Riggle, and Donna E. Schwartz, "Deregulating Federalism? The Politics of Mandate Reform in the 104 Congress" *Publius: The Journal of Federalism* 25 (Summer 1995): 23–40. U.S. Advisory Commission on Intergovernmental Relations, Intergovernmental Perspective (Fall, 1993).
10. For an interesting look at these regional debates, see Dick Kirschten, "Formula Friction," *National Journal,* February 2, 1991, 272–273.

Chapter 4 Civil Rights and Liberties

1. On the debate over whether the Fourteenth Amendment was intended to apply to the states, see Horace E. Flack, *The Adoption of the Fourteenth Amendment* (Baltimore, Md.: Johns Hopkins University Press, 1908); Charles Fairman, *Reconstruction and Reunion,* 1864–88 (New York: Macmillan, 1971); and Raoul Berger, *Government by Judiciary* (Cambridge, Mass.: Harvard University Press, 1977).
2. *Gitlow v. New York,* 268 U.S. 652 (1925).
3. For an excellent history of the nationalization of the Bill of Rights, see Richard C. Cortner, *The Supreme Court and the Second Bill of Rights: The Fourteenth Amendment and the Nationalization of Civil Liberties* (Madison: University of Wisconsin Press, 1981).
4. *Joint Anti-Fascist Refugee Committee v. McGrath,* 341 U.S. 123 (1951).
5. *Rochin v. California,* 341 U.S. 165 (1952).
6. *Griswold v. Connecticut,* 391 U.S. 145 (1965).
7. *California v. Hodari D.,* 499 U.S. 621 (1991).
8. *Olmstead v. United States,* 277 U.S. 438 (1928).
9. *Katz v. United States,* 389 U.S. 347 (1967).
10. *Escobedo v. Illinois,* 378 U.S. 478 (1964).
11. *Gideon v. Wainwright,* 372 U.S. 335 (1963).
12. *Miranda v. Arizona,* 384 U.S. 436 (1966).
13. *Furman v. Georgia,* 408 U.S. 238 (1972).
14. See *Gregg v. Georgia,* 428 U.S. 153 (1976).
15. See *National Association for the Advancement of Colored People v. Alabama,* 357 U.S. 449 (1958).
16. *Bowers v. Hardwick,* 478 U.S. 186 (1986).
17. Edward White, "The Supreme Court of the United States," 7 *American Bar Association Journal* (1921), 341.

Chapter 5 Issues of Freedom and Equality

1. *Texas v. Johnson,* 491 U.S. 397 (1989).
2. Quoted in David M. O'Brien, *Storm Center: The Supreme Court in American Politics,* 4th ed. (New York: Norton, 1996), 124.
3. *United States v. Eichman,* 110 S.Ct. 2404 (1990).
4. See Walter Berns, *The First Amendment and the Future of American Democracy* (New York: Basic Books, 1976), ch. 1.
5. *Engel v. Vitale,* 370 U.S. 421 (1962); and *Abington School District v. Schempp,* 374 U.S. 203 (1963).
6. *Witters v. Washington Department of Services for the Blind,* 474 U.S. 481 (1986); and *Rosenberger v. The Rector and Visitors of the University of Virginia,* 115 S.Ct. 2510 (1995).
7. *Reynolds v. United States,* 98 U.S. 145 (1879).
8. *New York Times Co. v. Sullivan,* 376 U.S. 254 (1964).
9. *Schenck v. United States,* 249 U.S. 47 (1919).
10. *New York Times Co. v. United States,* 403 U.S. 670 (1971).
11. *R.A.V. v. City of St. Paul, Minnesota,* 505 U.S. 377 (1992).

12. *Wisconsin v. Mitchell,* 113 S.Ct. 2194 (1993).
13. *Roth v. United States,* 354 U.S. 476 (1957).
14. *Miller v. California,* 413 U.S. 15 (1973).
15. See *Cohen v. California,* 403 U.S. 15 (1971).
16. *Bethel School District No. 403 v. Fraser,* 478 U.S. 675 (1986).
17. *New York v. Ferber,* 458 U.S. 747 (1982).
18. *California v. LaRue,* 409 U.S. 109 (1972); and Barnes v. Glen Theatre, Inc., 501 U.S. 560 (1991).
19. See *Pacific Gas & Electric v. Public Utilities Commission of California,* 475 U.S. 1 (1986).
20. *Tinker v. Des Moines Independent Community School District,* 393 U.S. 503 (1969).
21. *Stromberg v. California,* 283 U.S. 359 (1931).
22. *Spence v. Washington,* 418 U.S. 405 (1974).
23. *Brown v. Socialist Worker '74 Campaign Committee,* 459 U.S. 87 (1982).
24. *Gibson v. Florida Legislative Investigating Committee,* 371 U.S. 539 (1963).
25. *Elfrandt v. Russell,* 384 U.S. 11 (1966).
26. *Application of Stolar,* 401 U.S. 23 (1971).
27. *United States v. Harris,* 347 U.S. 612 (1954).
28. *Minor v. Happersett,* 88 U.S. 162 (1875).
29. *Baker v. Carr,* 369 U.S. 186 (1962).
30. *Miller v. Johnson,* 115 S.Ct. 2475 (1995).
31. *Plessy v. Ferguson,* 163 U.S. 537 (1896).
32. *Brown v. Board of Education of Topeka,* 347 U.S. 483 (1954).
33. *Brown v. Board of Education of Topeka,* 349 U.S. 294 (1955).
34. *Alexander v. Holmes County Board of Education,* 396 U.S. 19 (1969).
35. *Rostker v. Goldberg,* 453 U.S. 57 (1981).
36. *Michael M. v. Superior Court,* 450 U.S. 464 (1981).
37. *Craig v. Boren,* 429 U.S. 190 (1976).
38. *Dothard v. Rawlinson,* 433 U.S. 321 (1977).
39. *Geduldig v. Aiello,* 417 U.S. 484 (1974).
40. *Frontiero v. Richardson,* 411 U.S. 677 (1973).
41. *Nashville Gas Co. v. Satty,* 434 U.S. 136 (1977).
42. *Meritor Savings Bank, FBD v. Vinson,* 477 U.S. 57 (1986).
43. *Regents of the University of California v. Bakke,* 438 U.S. 265 (1978).
44. *City of Richmond v. J. A. Croson,* 488 U.S. 469 (1989).

Chapter 6 Political Socialization, Participation, and Public Opinion

1. David Maraniss, *First in His Class* (New York: Simon and Schuster, 1995), 55–56.
2. William J. Clinton, as quoted in David Maraniss, "Clinton's Life Shaped by Early Turmoil," *Washington Post,* January 26, 1992, A1, 17.
3. M. Kent Jennings and Richard G. Niemi, "Patterns of Political Learning," in *Political Opinion and Behavior,* ed. Edward C: Dreyer and Walter A. Rosenbaum (North Scituate, Mass.: Duxbury, 1976), 80–97; and Martin P. Wattenberg, *The Decline of American Political Parties* (Cambridge, Mass.: Harvard University Press, 1984).
4. Fred I. Greenstein, *Children and Politics* (New Haven, Conn.: Yale University Press, 1965).
5. Jennings and Niemi, "Patterns of Political Learning."
6. For a discussion of different explanations of the socialization process, see David O. Sears, "Whither Political Socialization Research? The Question of Persistence," in *Political Socialization, Citizenship Education, and Democracy,* 69–97.
7. Harold W. Stanley and Richard G. Niemi, *Vital Statistics on American Politics* (Washington, D.C.: CQ Press, 1995), 47, 49.
8. Steven H. Chaffee, Clifford I. Nass, and Seung-Mock Yang, "The Bridging Role of Television in Immigrant Political Socialization," *Human Communication Research* 17, No. 2 (Winter 1990): 266–288.
9. See, for example, Douglas Kellner, *Television and the Crisis of Democracy* (Boulder, Colo.: Westview, 1990).
10. See Henry E. Brady, Sidney Verba, and Kay Lehman Schlozman, "Beyond SES: A Resource Model of Political Participation," *American Political Science Review* 89, No. 2 (1995): 271–294.
11. See, for example, Stephen Earl Bennett, *Apathy in America, 1960–1984: Causes and Consequences of Citizen Political Indifference* (Dobbs Ferry, N.Y.: Transnational, 1986), 63–70.
12. See Samuel L. Popkin, *The Reasoning Voter: Communication and Persuasion in Presidential Campaigns* (Chicago: University of Chicago Press, 1991).
13. "Low-Income Voters' Turnout Fell in 1994, Census Reports," *New York Times,* June 11, 1995.
14. See, for example, Stephen J Rosenstone and John Mark Hansen, *Mobilization, Participation, and Democracy in America* (New York: Macmillan, 1993), 36, 244–248; Verba and Nie, *Participation in America,* 284–285; Brady, Verba, and Schlozman, "Beyond SES," 285.

15. "Politics Quiz," *Washington Post,* January 29, 1996, A6.
16. Joan Biskupic, "Has the Court Lost Its Appeal?" *Washington Post,* October 12, 1995, A23.
17. The Center reported that only 20 percent of those under age 30 followed the news very closely, compared with 23 percent of those between age 30 and 40 and 29 percent of people over age 50. "The Times Mirror News Interest Index: 1989-1995," *The Pew Research Center for The People & The Press,* 7.
18. "How Americans View the Contract with America," *New York Times/CBS News Poll,* February 28, 1995, A21.
19. In 1988, approximately 80 percent of people who identified themselves as conservative supported Bush, and a similar percentage of self-identified liberals supported Dukakis. In 1992, although the candidacy of independent H. Ross Perot reduced these percentages, 68 percent of the liberals voted for Clinton and 64 percent of the conservatives cast their ballots for Bush, according to the large exit poll conducted for the major news networks on election day.
20. One question that pollsters have asked with some frequency in recent years is "Which do you say you favor—a larger government with many services or a smaller government with fewer services?" Here are some of the responses, given in percentages:

	Larger	*Smaller*
1984	43	49
1988	45	49
1992	38	55
1993	29	60
1994	24	66

"Disillusionment with Washington," *American Enterprise,* January/February 1994, 101; "The Mood on Washington," *American Enterprise,* November/December 1995, 106.
21. Richard Morin and Dan Balz, "Americans Losing Trust in Each Other and Institutions," *Washington Post,* January 28, 1996, A6.
22. Martin B. Abravnel and Ronald J. Busch, "Political Competence, Political Trust, and the Action Orientation of University Students," *Journal of Politics* 37 (February 1975): 57–82; and Joel Aberbach and Jack L. Walker, "Political Trust and Racial Ideology," *American Political Science Review* 64 (December 1970): 1199–1219.
23. James W. Prothro and Charles M. Gregg, "Fundamental Principles of Democracy: Bases of Agreement and Disagreement," *Journal of Politics* 22 (May 1960): 276–294. Also see McClosky, "Consensus and Ideology"; and McClosky and Brill, *Dimensions of Tolerance.*
24. Benjamin I. Page and Robert Y. Shapiro, "Effects of Public Opinion on Policy," *American Political Science Review* 77 (March 1983): 175–190; and Gerald C. Wright Jr., Robert S. Erikson, and John P. McIver, "Public Opinion and Policy Liberalism in the American States," *American Journal of Political Science* 31 (November 1987): 980–1001.
25. Robert Erikson, Norman Luttberg, and Ken and L. Tedin, *American Public Opinion: Its Origins, Content, and Impact,* 4th ed. (New York: Macmillan, 1991), 332.

Chapter 7 Interest Groups and Political Parties

1. Disagreements within the group, however, may exist over specifics. During the national health-care debate in 1993, the national organization of the AARP supported the managed-care, private-insurer approach of the Clinton administration, whereas its California affiliate backed the single-payer option. David S. Hilzenrath, "AARP's Nonprofit Status Comes Under Scrutiny," *Washington Post,* May 22, 1995, A8.
2. Today, with a larger membership of approximately 2.5 million, the NRA is not as powerful because of the rise of opposition groups and general public concern with crime.
3. In 1993 Democrats received $24.8 million in PAC contributions compared with $10.8 million for the Republicans; in 1995, they received $18 million compared with $25.3 million for the Republicans. John E. Yang, "House GOP on a Roll," *Washington Post,* February 12, 1996, A9.
4. A new business has even been created to help lobbyists perform this task. Since congressional committee rooms have a limited seating capacity and are filled on a first-come, first-served basis, a service now exists to save places in line for busy, highly paid lobbyists. Students are paid by the hour to wait until the committee room opens. Sometimes the lineup for an extremely popular hearing will begin on the previous day and involve camping outside the House and Senate office buildings throughout the night.
5. For an excellent discussion of how and

why presidents try to mobilize groups' support, see Mark A. Petterson, "The Presidency and Organized Interests: White House Patterns of Interest Group Liaison," *American Political Science Review* 86 (September 1992): 612–625.

6. One of the changes in rules that the House of Representatives adopted after the Republicans took over in 1995 was to open all committee meetings to the public "except in extraordinary circumstances" and to permit public broadcasting as a matter of right.
7. Consider the case of James H. Lake, a well-known Washington lobbyist who was asked by a senior executive of one of the agricultural companies he represented to help retire the debt of a defeated congressional candidate whose brother just happened to be secretary of agriculture at the time. Lake requested that the five top executives of his firm, including himself, contribute $1,000 each to the defunct but still in debt congressional campaign. Four did; one refused to do so. After checks totaling $4,000 were sent to the campaign, the executive of the agricultural company that had requested the contributions had his company issue a check for $5,000 to Lake's firm for expenses they had incurred on behalf of the company. Lake returned $1,000 to each of the contributors and kept the balance. It is illegal for companies to make campaign contributions and Lake subsequently pleaded guilty to charges that he violated the law. "Prominent GOP Consultant Admits Fraud," *Washington Post,* October 24, 1995, A1 and A6.
8. E. E. Schattschneider, *The Semi-Sovereign People: A Realist's View of Democracy* (Hillsdale, Ill.: Dryden, 1960), 34–35.
9. The early Republicans were not the forerunners of the modern Republican party, which was organized in 1854 and nominated its first presidential candidate in 1856. Democrats, however, claim Thomas Jefferson as their first president and trace their party's origins to the Democratic-Republican party at the end of the eighteenth century.
10. See John F. Bibby, Cornelius P. Cotter, James L. Gibson, and Robert J. Huckshorn, "Parties in State Politics," in *Politics in the American States: A Comparative Analysis,* ed. Virginia Gray, Herbert Jacob, and Robert B. Albritton (Glenview, Ill.: Scott, Foresman/Little, Brown, 1990) 108–111.
11. James L. Gibson, Cornelius Cotter, John F. Bibby, and Robert J. Huckshorn, "Assessing Party Organizational Strength," *American Journal of Political Science* 17 (May 1983): 193–222.
12. John F. Bibby, *Politics, Parties, and Elections in America,* 2d ed. (Chicago: Nelson-Hall, 1992), 104.
13. Gerald M. Pomper with Susan S. Lederman, *Elections in America* (White Plains, N.Y. : Longman, 1980), 161.
14. Jeff Fishel, *Presidents and Promises* (Washington, D.C.: Congressional Quarterly, 1985), 38.
15. For a discussion of the concept of responsible party government, see Committee on Political Parties of the American Political Science Association, *Toward a More Responsible Two-Party System* (New York: Holt, Rinehart and Winston, 1950); and Austin Ranney, *The Doctrine of Responsible Party Government* (Urbana: University of Illinois Press, 1962).
16. David W. Rohde, "The Reports of My Death Are Greatly Exaggerated: Parties and Party Voting in the House of Representatives," in *Changing Perspectives on Congress,* ed. Glenn R. Parker (Knoxville: University of Tennessee Press, 1990); and Malcolm E. Jewell and David M. Olson, *Political Parties and Elections in American States* (Chicago: Dorsey, 1988), 246–249.
17. "1994 Party Unity Votes," *Congressional Quarterly,* December 31, 1994, 3658.
18. Randall L. Calvert and John A. Ferejohn, "Coattail Voting in Recent Presidential Elections," *American Political Science Review* 77 (June 1983): 407–419; and John A. Ferejohn and Randall L. Calvert, "Presidential Coattails in Historical Perspective," *American Journal of Political Science* 28 (February 1984): 164–183.
19. Paul Allen Beck and Frank J. Sorauf, *Party Politics in America,* 7th ed. (New York: HarperCollins, 1992), 423.
20. This subject is discussed in Robert A. Carp and Ronald Stidham, *The Federal Courts* (Washington, D.C.: Congressional Quarterly, 1985), 142–148; also see Craig Ducat and Robert L. Dudley, "Federal District Judges and Presidential Power During the Postwar Era," *Journal of Politics* 51 (February 1989): 98–118. An examination of the influence of party on state judges can be found in Stuart Nagel, "Political Party Affiliation and Judges' Decisions," *American Political Science Review* 55 (December

1961): 843-850; and David W. Adamany, "The Party Variable in Judges' Voting: Conceptual Notes and a Case Study," *American Political Science Review* 63 (March 1969): 57-83.

Chapter 8 Campaigns and Elections

1. For all practical purposes, people are deemed to be responsible for their own actions if they are 18 years of age or older and are mentally competent. In some states, individuals who have been convicted of a felony or dishonorably discharged from the military may not vote.
2. Angus Campbell, Philip E. Converse, Warren E. Miller, and Donald E. Stokes, *The American Voter* (New York: Wiley, 1960), 101-107.
3. Raymond E. Wolfinger and Steven J. Rosenstone, *Who Votes?* (New Haven, Conn.: Yale University Press, 1980), 13-26.
4. James A. Barnes, "Tainted Triumph?" *National Journal,* November 7, 1992, 2539.
5. Ruy A. Teixeira, "What If We Had an Election and Everybody Came?" *American Enterprise* 3 (July-August 1992): 55.
6. William H. Flanagan and Nancy H. Zingale, *Political Behavior of the American Electorate,* 7th ed. (Washington, D.C.: Congressional Quarterly, 1991), 49-54.
7. Mitofsky International, *New York Times,* November 13, 1994.
8. Flanagan and Zingale, *Political Behavior of the American Electorate,* 124.
9. For an excellent discussion of the retrospective model of voting behavior see Morris Fiorina, *Retrospective Voting in American National Elections* (New Haven, Conn.: Yale University Press, 1981), 65-83.
10. John S. Jackson, Barbara Brown, and David Bositis, "Herbert McClosky and Friends Revisited: 1980 Democratic and Republican Party Elites Compared to the Mass Public," *American Politics Quarterly* 10 (1982): 158-180; and Martin Plissner and Warren J. Mitofsky, "The Making of the Delegates, 1968-1988," *Public Opinion* 3 (September-October 1988): 46.
11. The Equal Rights Amendment, which would have prohibited all discrimination on the basis of gender, failed to achieve ratification. In the 1980s, Republican platforms opposed the amendment and Democratic platforms supported it.
12. Thomas E. Patterson, *The Mass Media Election* (New York: Praeger, 1980), 72-74.
13. Ibid., 103.
14. In Maine and Nebraska, one elector is chosen in each state congressional district, and two electors are selected at large; thus in these states a divided electoral vote is possible.
15. To gain an advantage, parties attempt to draw legislative districts so that their partisans constitute a stable but not overwhelming majority in as many districts as possible and their opponents constitute a majority in as few of them as possible.
16. For a discussion of redistricting in the 1990s, see Beth Donovan, "Political Dance Played Out Through Legal Wrangling," *Congressional Quarterly,* December 21, 1991, 3690-3695.
17. But they must be careful in using staff that are on the congressional payroll. It is against federal law for United States government employees, such as congressional staffs, to engage in campaign activities in the course of their official duties. To circumvent this rule, candidates may have their staff members take a leave of absence during the campaign.

Chapter 9 Politics and the News Media

1. Austin Ranney, "Broadcasting, Narrowcasting, and Politics," in *The New American Political System,* 2d version, ed. Anthony King (Washington, D.C.: American Enterprise Institute, 1990), 195.
2. "NBC's Believability Burned," *Times Mirror Center for the People and the Press,* March 3, 1993, 1-2.
3. U.S. Bureau of the Census, *Statistical Abstract of the United States 1995* (Washington, D.C., 1995), 571.
4. Ranney, "Broadcasting, Narrowcasting, and Politics," 190-191.
5. Ibid., 192.
6. Rajiv, Chandrasekaran, "Internet Use Has More Than Doubled in Last 18 Months, Survey Finds," *Washington Post,* March 13, 1997, E3.
7. Clinton's the One," *Media Monitor* (November 1992): 2.
8. "The Bad News Campaign," *Media Monitor* (March-April 1996): 2.
9. "Clinton's the One," 3-4.
10. "The Bad News Campaign," 2.
11. "Dole's Summer Doldrums: TV News Coverage of the 1996 Presidential Election," *Media Monitor* (July/August 1996): 3.
12. "Take This Campaign—Please!" *Media Monitor* (September/October 1996): 2.
13. Almost 70 percent of Clinton's ads were negative in 1992, compared with 56

percent for Bush. L. Patrick Devlin, "Contrasts in Presidential Campaign Commercials of 1992," *American Behavioral Scientist* 37 (November 1993): 288; Lynda Lee Kaid and Anne Johnston, "Negative Versus Positive Television Advertising in U.S. Presidential Campaigns, 1960–1988," *Journal of Communications* 41 (Summer 1991): 54.
14. Edwin Diamond and Adrian Marin, "Spots," *American Behavioral Scientist* 32 (March–April 1989): 386.
15. "The Invisible Man," *Media Monitor* (May–June, 1995): 2.
16. Timothy E. Cook, *Making News and Making Laws* (Washington, D.C.: Brookings Institution, 1989), 7.
17. O. J. Simpson was acquitted of the murders of his ex-wife, Nicole Brown Simpson, and a friend of hers, Ronald Goldman. Rodney King was a motorist who was stopped and beaten by Los Angeles police. A private citizen who witnessed the beating recorded it on videotape.
18. "Public Interest and Awareness of the News," *Pew Research Center New Interest Index* (January 1996): 6.
19. Media coverage of the budget battle between Congress and the president, which resulted in two brief partial shutdowns of the government, had an impact on the Republican Congress similar to that which the hostage crisis had had on President Carter. By showing how the shutdowns affected people, the coverage helped turn opinion against Congress.

Chapter 10 Congress

1. Information on the assault weapons ban repeal was drawn from Alan Greenblatt, "Repeal of Assault Weapons Ban Unlikely to Go Beyond House," *Congressional Quarterly Weekly Report,* March 23, 1996, 803; "Victory in the House!" *NRA Grassfire* (newsletter), April 1996; "Clinton Firm on Assault Ban," Associated Press, January 28, 1996; "Assault Weapons Ban, Statement of Senate Majority Leader Bob Dole," March 21, 1996, released by the National Rifle Association Institute for Legislative Action.
2. The members of each Congress and their districts are described in detail in Congressional Quarterly's *Politics in America* series, which is updated after each congressional election.
3. The term *whip* derives from a participant in English fox hunts, the "whipper-in," whose task was to keep the hounds from leaving the pack.
4. For a former Speaker's view, see Thomas P. O'Neill Jr. and William Novak, *Man of the House* (New York: Random House, 1987).
5. See Frank H. Mackaman, ed., *Understanding Congressional Leadership* (Washington, D.C.: Congressional Quarterly, 1981).
6. See Richard L. Hall, "Participation and Purpose in Committee Decision Making," *American Political Science Review* 81 (1987): 105–127.
7. See Steven S. Smith and Christopher J. Deering, *Committees in Congress* (Washington, D.C.: Congressional Quarterly, 1984).
8. See Steven S. Smith, *Call to Order: Floor Politics in the House and Senate* (Washington, D.C.: Brookings Institution, 1989).
9. See Walter J. Oleszek, *Congressional Procedures and Policy Process,* 3rd ed. (Washington, D.C.: Congressional Quarterly, 1989).
10. House of Representatives, Commission on Administrative Review, *Final Report,* 95th Cong., 1st sess. (1977), 830.
11. See, for example, Morris S. Ogul, *Congress Oversees the Bureaucracy* (Pittsburgh, Penn.: University of Pittsburgh Press, 1976).
12. A dated but rich analysis is Richard F. Fenno Jr., *The Power of the Purse* (Boston: Little, Brown, 1966). A more recent study is D. Roderick Kiewiet and Mathew D. McCubbins, *The Spending Power* (Chicago: University of Chicago Press, 1990).
13. See Raoul Berger, *Impeachment* (Cambridge, Mass.: Harvard University Press, 1973).
14. See, for example, David W. Rohde, *Parties and Leaders in the Postreform House* (Chicago: University of Chicago Press, 1991).

Chapter 11 The Presidency

1. For an excellent discussion of the leadership dilemma that contemporary presidents face, see Bert A. Rockman, *The Leadership Question* (New York: Praeger, 1984).
2. Richard E. Neustadt, *Presidential Power and the Modern Presidents* (New York: Free Press, 1990).
3. In his first year of office, George Bush reiterated his pledge not to raise taxes; in his second year, he abandoned that pledge. Almost as soon as he took office, Bill Clinton backed away from his campaign promises to cut taxes on the middle class, allow homosexuals to openly serve

in the armed forces, and admit Haitian refugees seeking political asylum into the United States. Ronald Reagan, in contrast, stuck to his promises to cut taxes, increase defense spending, and reduce the role of government in the domestic sphere. Bush's and Clinton's vacillation and Reagan's steadfastness helped shape their initial reputations as presidents.

4. George C. Edwards III, *At the Margins* (New Haven, Conn.: Yale University Press, 1989), 124.
5. Samuel Kernell, *Going Public,* 2d ed. (Washington, D.C.: Congressional Quarterly, 1993).
6. Although President Clinton proposed that the White House Office be reduced by 25 percent, he actually increased its size and cost. The 25 percent reduction was obtained by reducing not the White House Office but the Office of Drug Abuse and several other councils in the Executive Office of the President. Moreover, the budget of the White House Office was increased by more than $3.5 million in 1993 to update its communications technology.

   In addition, the White House Office budget is supplemented by other executive departments that provide services for the president and his staff. These include units of the Defense Department, such as White House Communications (secure communications), the Air Force (air transportation for the president and vice president), the Army (explosives detection and ground transportation), and the Navy (helicopter transportation, Marine guards, food and medical facilities). They also include the General Services Administration (buildings and grounds), National Park Service (visitors and the fine arts collection), National Archives (custody of official documents), Secret Service (protection of the president, the vice president, and their families), and State Department (state visits and receptions).
7. John Adams, *The Works of John Adams,* vol. 1, ed. C. F. Adams (Boston: Little, Brown, 1850), 289.
8. Thomas Jefferson, *The Writings of Thomas Jefferson,* vol. 1, ed. P. L. Ford (New York: Putnam, 1896), 98–99.
9. For discussions of presidential illnesses, see Michael P. Riccards, "The Presidency: In Sickness and Health," *Presidential Studies Quarterly* 7 (Fall 1977): 215–231; Robert E. Gilbert, *The Mortal Presidency: Illness and Anguish in the White House* (New York: Basic Books, 1994); "Special Symposium on Presidential Health," *Political Psychology* 16 (December 1995): 757–860.
10. Tom Mathews, "The Road to War," *Newsweek,* January 28, 1991, 60.
11. James David Barber, *The Presidential Character,* 4th ed. (Englewood Cliffs, N.J.: Prentice-Hall, 1992).
12. John P. Burke and Fred I. Greenstein, *How Presidents Test Reality* (New York: Russell Sage, 1989).
13. Edwards, *At the Margins,* 213–234.
14. This theory of the two presidencies was first postulated by Aaron Wildavsky in "The Two Presidencies," *Trans-Action* 4 (December 1966): 7–11. It has subsequently engendered considerable debate. Much of that debate appears in Steven A. Shull, ed., *The Two Presidencies: A Quarter Century Assessment* (Chicago: Nelson-Hall, 1991).
15. Quoted in Bob Woodward, *The Choice* (New York: Simon & Schuster, 1996), 22.

Chapter 12 The Executive Bureaucracy

1. CNN report, "Julie Welch Will Never See Her Future," by correspondent Judy Woodruff, April 27, 1995.
2. See Francis J. Leazes, *Accountability and the Business State: The Structure of Federal Corporations* (New York: Praeger, 1987).
3. See Martin Tolchin and Susan Tolchin, *To the Victor: Political Patronage from the Clubhouse to the White House* (New York: Random House, 1971).
4. See G. Calvin Mackenzie, ed., *The In and Outers* (Baltimore, Md.: Johns Hopkins University Press, 1987).
5. Randall B. Ripley and Grace A. Franklin, *Policy Implementation and Bureaucracy* (Chicago: Dorsey, 1986).
6. Faith Hawkins and John M. Thomas, *Making Regulatory Policy* (Pittsburgh, Penn.: University of Pittsburgh Press, 1989).
7. See Susan J. Tolchin and Martin Tolchin, *Dismantling America: The Rush to Deregulate* (New York: Oxford University Press, 1985).
8. See Jerry L. Mashaw, *Due Process in the Administrative State* (New Haven, Conn.: Yale University Press, 1985).
9. See,Philip J. Cooper, *Public Law and Public Administration* (Englewood Cliffs, N.J.: Prentice-Hall, 1988).
10. A classic study of such bureaucratic cultures is Herbert Kaufman, *The Forest Ranger: A Study in Administrative Behavior* (Baltimore, Md.: Johns Hopkins University Press, 1967).

11. Kenneth J. Meier, *Politics and the Bureaucracy: Policymaking in the Fourth Branch of Government,* 2d ed. (Monterey, Calif.: Brooks/Cole, 1987), 65.
12. See Alfred F. Hurley, *Billy Mitchell: Crusader for Air Power* (New York: Franklin Watts, 1964).
13. Francis E. Rourke, *Bureaucracy, Politics, and Public Policy,* 3d ed. (Boston: Little, Brown, 1984), 91–122.
14. The classic and still-valuable study is Fenno, *The Power of the Purse.* Also see Aaron Wildavsky, *The New Politics of the BudgetaryProcess* (New York: HarperCollins, 1992).

Chapter 13 The Judiciary

1. See, for example, Lee Epstein, *Conservatives in Court* (Knoxville: University of Tennessee Press, 1985); Nan Aron, *Liberty and Justice for All: Public Interest Law in the 1980s and Beyond* (Boulder, Colo.: Westview, 1989); and Clement Vose, *Caucasians Only* (Berkeley: University of California Press, 1959).
2. Alexis de Tocqueville, *Democracy in America,* ed. Philip Bradley (New York: Doubleday, 1945), 151.
3. Steve Alumbaugh and C. K. Rowland, "The Links Between Platform-Based Appointment Criteria and Trial Judges' Abortion Judgments," *Judicature* 74 (1990): 153.
4. Quoted in O'Brien, *Storm Center,* 290.
5. Quoted by Alpheus T. Mason, *Harlan Fiske Stone: Pillar of the Law* (New York: Viking, 1956), 222.
6. *United States v. Nixon,* 418 U.S. 683 (1974).
7. Charles E. Hughes, *The Supreme Court of the United States* (New York: Columbia University Press, 1928), 68.
8. *Abington School District v. Schempp,* 374 U.S. 203 (1963).
9. *Norris v. Alabama,* 294 U.S. 587 (1935).
10. *Hernandez v. Texas,* 347 U.S. 475 (1954).
11. *Zurcher v. The Stanford Daily,* 436 U.S. 547 (1978).
12. See Robert Dahl, "Decision-Making in a Democracy: The Supreme Court as a National Policy-Maker," *Journal of Public Law* 6 (1957): 279; and Richard Funston, "The Supreme Court and Critical Elections," *American Political Science Review* 69 (1975): 795.
13. See Donald Horowitz, *The Courts and Social Policy* (Washington, D.C.: Brookings Institution, 1977); and Raoul Berger, *Government by the Judiciary* (Cambridge, Mass.: Harvard University Press, 1977).
14. For further discussion of the Court's role as a policy maker, see Gerald Rosenberg, *The Hollow Hope: Can Courts Bring About Social Change?* (Chicago: University of Chicago Press, 1991).

Chapter 14 The Policy-Making Process

1. "Lawmakers Enact $30.2 Billion Anti-Crime Bill," 1994 *CQ Almanac,* 273–294; "$30 Billion Anti-Crime Bill Heads to Clinton's Desk," *CQ Weekly Report,* August 27, 1994, 2488–2493; David Johnson and Steven A. Holmes, "Experts Doubt Effectiveness of Crime Bill," *New York Times,* September 14, 1994.
2. James E. Anderson, David W. Brady, and Charles Bullock, *Public Policy and Politics in America* (North Scituate, Mass.: Duxbury, 1978), 5.
3. Theodore J. Lowi, "American Business, Public Policy Case Studies, and Political Theory," *World Politics* 16 (July 1964): 677–715. In later works, Lowi added a fourth policy type, "constituent policies," which are administrative and of little concern to the general public. For a critique of the Lowi scheme, see Hugh H. Heclo, "Review Article: Policy Analysis," *British Journal of Political Science* 2 (1972): 83–108.
4. See James E. Anderson, *Public Policy-Making* (New York: Praeger, 1975), 66–75, for a discussion of this point.
5. Douglas Cater, *Power in Washington* (New York: Random House, 1964), 17 (emphasis added).
6. Hugh Heclo, "Issue Networks and the Executive Establishment," in Anthony King (ed.), *The New American Political System* (Washington, D.C.: American Enterprise Institute, 1978), 103.
7. Ibid., 105.
8. "Seat of the pants" is a term used by Anderson, Brady, and Bullock in *Public Policy and Politics in America,* 11.
9. Gary D. Brewer and Peter deLeon, *The Foundations of Policy Analysis* (Homewood, Ill.: Dorsey, 1983), 387.
10. Quoted in *New York Times,* October 20, 1993.

Photo Credits

Chapter 1: Page 1: Porter Gifford/Gamma Liaison; **4:** David Butow/Black Star; **8:** Matthew Neal/Stock, Boston; **16:** Chris Maynard/NYT Pictures

Chapter 2: Page 25: Michael Anderson/Folio Inc.; **29:** National Geographic Society/White House Historical Association; **30:** © Louis Glanzman/Courtesy, Independence National Historical Park Collection

Chapter 3: Page 47: Michael Newman/PhotoEdit; **52:** Bettmann; **56 (top):** Bill Anderson/Monkmeyer; **56 (bottom):** Bob Daemmrich/Stock, Boston

Chapter 4: Page 71: Rick Kopstein/Monkmeyer; **81:** Sam Mircovich/Archive Photos; **85:** Wide World Photos

Chapter 5: Page 91: Catherine Smith/Impact Visuals; **94:** Wide World Photos; **101:** Bettmann; **106:** Wide World Photos

Chapter 6: Page 115: Wide World Photos; **118:** Donna Binder/Impact Visuals; **120:** Lawrence Migdale/Stock, Boston; **123:** Bettmann; **127:** Lee Corkran/Sygma; **138:** Bettmann

Chapter 7: Page 149: Stephen Agricola/Folio, Inc.; **153:** Wide World Photos; **158:** Jose R. Lopez/NYT Pictures; **162:** Wide World Photos/National Geographic Society; **168:** Wide World Photos; **173 (left):** Jeff Mitchell/Archive Photos; **173 (right):** Mike Theiler/Archive Photos

Chapter 8: Page 187: Wide World Photos; **190:** Library of Congress; **192:** Wide World Photos; **199:** © Rick Winsor/Woodfin Camp; **202:** Wide World Photos; **212:** Wide World Photos

Chapter 9: Page 221: Wide World Photos; **225:** Franklin D. Roosevelt Library; **228:** Wide World Photos; **230:** C-Span; **233:** Wide World Photos; **238:** Wide World Photos

Chapter 10: Page 247: Wide World Photos; **249:** Wide World Photos; **252:** Wide World Photos; **253:** Wide World Photos; **264:** Mary Ann Carter/NYT Pictures

Chapter 11: Page 277: Reuters/Ira Swarz/Archive Photos; **282:** Wide World Photos; **289:** Wide World Photos; **291:** Reuters/Corbis–Bettmann; **296:** Wide World Photos; **301:** Wide World Photos

Chapter 12: Page 309: Paul Moseley/Fort North Star Telegram/SIPA Press; **314 (left):** Courtesy, Secret Service; **314 (right):** Jeff Henry; **316:** Wide World Photos; **322:** Bettmann

Chapter 13: Page 333: Dan Habib/Impact Visuals; **337:** Wide World Photos; **339:** Wide World Photos; **347:** Brad Markel/Gamma Liaison; **352:** Wide World Photos

Chapter 14: Page 359: Jack Kurtz/Impact Visuals; **363:** Paul Conklin; **369:** George Cohen/Impact Visuals

Index

Throughout this index, the lower case letters *c, t,* and *f* indicate *captions, tables,* and *figures* respectively.

Abington School District v. Schempp, 95, 350
Abortion
amicus curiae briefs related to, 163
and federal judge appointments, 341
history in U.S., 84–86
information sources on, 86
political battle over, 84–86
right of privacy and, 83
Roe v. Wade, 78, 84, 163, 334
Activism, judicial, 338–340
Acton, James, 71
Adams, John, 38, 290
Adarand Constructors, Inc. v. Pena, 110
Administrative law judge, 319
Administrative oversight, 267–268
Congressional committees, 254
financial controls, 267–268
impeachment, 268
personnel controls, 267
special investigations, 267
Administrative Procedures Act, 318
Adversary justice system, nature of, 79
Advertising, political, 234
Advisory committees, 314
Affirmative action, 12–13, 106
criticisms of, 12, 108, 109–111
reverse discrimination, 109–111
Supreme Court decisions related to, 108–109
AFL-CIO, 151, 354
African Americans
civil rights movement, 104–105
Partisanship, 169
political participation of, 125
racial discrimination, 104–105
slavery, 30–31
voting rights, 102, 104
Age
conservatism in, 131
and party affiliation, 170–171
and political knowledge/information, 128
and political participation, 125*t*
and public opinion, 128
voting age, 195
and voting behavior, 194–195, 195*t*
Agencies
federal bureaucracy, 311–312
organization of, 312–313*f*
Agenda setting, by president, 297–298
Agents of political socialization, 119–121
AIDS
condom distribution issue, 333–334
Ryan White Act, 57
Aid to Families with Dependent Children (AFDC), 10
and welfare reform, 2, 54, 372
Airlines, deregulation, 317
Albert, Carl, 255
Alcohol, Drug Abuse, and Mental Health grant, 59
Aldrich, Nelson W., 254
Alexander, Lamar, 232
Allen, George F., 26
Almanac of American Politics, The, 263
Amendments
amendment process, 40
Bill of Rights, 32, 40
ratification of, 32, 40
Supreme Court decisions overturned by amendments, 40, 352
American Airlines, 280
American Association of Retired Persons (AARP), 2, 151
American Automobile Association, 151
American Bar Association (ABA), 341
in judicial appointment process, 343
American Civil Liberties Union (ACLU), 153, 241, 354
American ethos, meaning of, 11–14
American Federation of Teachers (AFT), 163
American Indian Bar Association, 163
American Jewish Congress, 14, 163
American Manufacturers Association, 149

American Medical Association (AMA), 2, 9
American Revolution, 11, 32–33
Americans with Disabilities Act of 1990, 55, 56*c*
American Tort Reform Association, 160
Amicus curiae brief, 163
Amish, 13
Animal sacrifice, and freedom of religion, 96
Anthony, Susan B., 102
Anticrime bill, 359–360
Anti-Federalists
  on state rights, 31, 73
  view of federalism, 49
Appeals, Supreme Court, 346*f*
Appellate courts, 336
Appellate jurisdiction, 337
Appropriations Committees, 267–268
Arab American Institute, 14
Archer, Bill, 180
Argersinger v. Hamlin, 75*t*
Aristotle, 4
Arizona, immigration backlash in, 18
Armed forces. *See* Department of Defense
Arms, right to bear, 6
Articles of Confederation, 28–29
Assault weapons ban, Republican/National Rifle Association relationship, 247–248
Association of National Advertisers, 241
Astroturfing, 160
Authority, governmental, 9–10

Babbitt, Bruce, 363–364
Baker, Howard, 354
Baker v. Carr, 103
Bakke, Alan, 108
Barber, James David, 295–296
Barr, Bob, 63
Belief system
  of presidents, 297
  and public opinion, 130
Benton v. Maryland, 75*t*
Bentsen, Lloyd, 360
Bicameral legislature, meaning of, 29–30, 248
Biden, Joseph, 354
Bill of information, 81
Bill of Rights
  amendments of, 32
  application to states, 41
  and civil rights/liberties, 73–89
  historical roots, 73–74
  nationalization of, 74–75
  ratification of, 32, 40
Blackmun, Harry, 85
Block grants, 53, 58
  under devolution federalism, 54
Bork, Robert H., 162, 343, 353–355
Bowers v. Hardwick, 83
Branch Davidians, 309
Brandeis, Louis D., 35–36
Brennan, William J., Jr., 82, 92, 96, 98
Breyer, Stephen G., 86, 344, 347*c*
Bristol-Myers Squibb, 180
Broad reading, of Constitution, 41
Brown, George, 367
Brown, Jerry, 233
Brown v. Board of Education of Topeka, Kansas, 36, 104, 163, 337, 339*c*, 349, 352
Buchanan, Patrick, 232
Buckley v. Valeo, 192, 214
Budget and Accounting Act of 1921, 284
Bureaucracy. *See also* Federal bureaucracy
  nature of, 310
  overview of, 312–313*f*
Bureau of Alcohol, Tobacco, and Firearms (ATF), 309–310, 319
Bureau of Quality Control, 311
Bureau of the Budget, 284
Bureaus, federal bureaucracy, 312
Burger, Warren E., 43, 95, 348, 349, 353, 354
Burr, Aaron, 291
Burton, Dan, 213
Bush, George, 92, 110, 127, 142, 171, 177, 187, 188, 232, 233, 281, 293, 295, 298, 363
  on abortion, 85
  cabinet of, 284
  and Congress, 299
  election of, 197, 201, 208*f*, 209
  environmental policy, 150
  and executive office, 286
  federal judge appointments, 341
  managerial style of, 296, 297
  new Federalism under, 53
  personal style of, 301
  and Supreme Court, 339, 343
  on term limits, 271
  as vice president, 292
  on voting rights, 26, 103
Bus Regulatory Reform Act, 56
Buxton, Dr. C. Lee, 333–334

Cabinet, 283–284
  listing of, 283*t*
Cable News Network (CNN), 299
Cable Satellite Public Affairs Network (C-SPAN), 229, 230*c*, 299
Cable television, 228–229
  narrowcasting, 299
  news stations, 299
Cajuns, 12
Calendar of the House of Representatives and History of Legislation, 370
Calhoun, John C., 49
California
  immigrant backlash in, 18
  lobbyists for, 61

California v. Hodari D., 78
Campaign finance, 192
  increasing costs for, 202
  legal restrictions, 192
  loopholes to law, 214
  nonpresidential nominations, 205
  and political action committees (PACs), 214
  preconvention fundraising, 202
  problems, 213–216
  and soft-money expenditures, 192, 214
Campaigns. *See* Election campaign
Campbell, Tom, 115
Canada, federalism of, 50
Cannon, Joseph G., 251, 254
Capitalism
  definition of, 12
  and democracy, 12
  free-enterprise system, 12
Capital punishment. *See* Death penalty
Caplan, Thomas, 115
Carpetbaggers, 119
Carter, Jimmy, 110, 169, 187, 197, 282, 286, 292, 295, 298, 302, 354
  belief system, effects of, 297
  and Congress, 299*f*
  election of, 201
  federal judge appointments, 341
  Iran hostage crisis, 240, 297
  managerial style of, 297
  staff organization, 287
  symbolism, use of, 300–301
Carter, Rosalynn, 290
Categorical grants, 57–58
Cater, Douglas, 364–365
Central clearance process, 286
Central Intelligence Agency (CIA), 267
Chicago, Burlington & Quincy Railroad v. Chicago, 75*t*
Chief of staff, role of, 287
Christian Coalition, 161
Christians, born-again
  and voter behavior, 197
Citadel, 106*c*, 163
City of Richmond v. J.A. Croson, 108–109, 110
Civil Aeronautics Board (CAB), 317
Civil liberties, 73
Civil rights
  and Bill of Rights, 73–89
  and Constitution, 72–73
  and criminal justice. *See* Criminal justice and civil rights
  versus economic interests, 83–84
  interest groups and, 163
Civil Rights Act of 1875, 104
Civil Rights Act of 1964, 57, 109, 352
Civil Rights Act of 1991, 352
Civil rights movement, 104–105
  media coverage of, 227
  protests, 101*c*, 123
Civil service system, 315–316
Civil War, 119, 169
  causes of, 39, 49
  and political parties, 169
  and state-federal relations, 51
Civil War Amendments, 40
Clean Air Act, 257, 339
Clean Air Act Amendments, 150
Clean Water Act, 150, 339
Clear and present danger test, 97
Cleveland, Grover, 284, 293
Clinton, Bill, 115–116, 119, 127, 137, 142, 161, 162*c*, 163, 165, 169, 177, 178, 181, 197*c*, 232, 233*c*, 291*c*, 295, 296*c*, 298, 303
  on affirmative action, 110
  anticrime bill, 359–360
  and block grants, 58
  cabinet of, 284
  campaign finance problems, 213
  and Congress, 299*f*
  economic policy, 277–278
  education policies of, 362
  election of, 209*f*
  environmental policy, 150, 364
  and executive office, 286
  federal judge appointments, 341
  fund-raising problems of, 162*c*, 164
  and grants-in-aid, 62
  gun control, 247
  health care reform, 282, 303–305
  managerial style of, 297
  and news media, 234, 235, 237*f*, 238*c*
  and power, 5–6
  and 1992 presidential election, 209
  and 1996 presidential election, 4, 209
  and Republican Congress, 1–3, 187–188
  and same-sex marriage, 63-64
  and Supreme Court, 86, 343
  symbolism, use of, 301, 301*c*
  on voting rights, 26, 104
  and welfare reform, 372
  White House staff, 288*f*, 289
Clinton, Hillary Rodham, 289*c*
  activities as first lady, 290
  health care reform, 303–305
Cloture, 262
Coalition to Save Student Aid, 159
Coast Guard, 311, 319
Coca-Cola, 180
Code of Federal Regulations, 319
Codification of Presidential Proclamations and Executive Orders, 292, 321
Commercial speech, 99–100
Commissions, 314
Committee of Eleven, 30
Committees, federal bureaucracy, 314
Committee staff members, Congress, 250
Commodity Credit Corporation, 314
Communications Decency Act, 240–242
Communist party, 167

Comptroller of the Currency, 319
Concentrated power, 7
Concord Coalition, 2
Concurrent powers, meaning of, 36
Concurring opinions, Supreme Court, 349
Condoms, school distribution issue, 333–334
Confirmation hearing, 343
Congress. *See also* House of Representatives; Senate
  administrative oversight, 267–268
  as bicameral legislature, 30, 248
  committees of. *See* Congressional committees
  compared to parliaments in other countries, 251, 299
  constituency, 262
  contacting members of, 263
  election to. *See* Congressional elections
  and federal bureaucracy, 327
  and foreign policy, 280
  information sources on, 370–371
  lawmaking function, 257–262
  lobbying of, 160–161
  members, profile of, 248–249
  news media coverage of, 237–239
  organization of, 250–257
  party influence on, 177
  personal staff aids, 249–250
  and political action committees (PACs), 157
  political parties in, 269–270
  powers of, 34*f*, 34–35
  and president, 298–300
  presidential success in, 299*f*
  reform, impact of, 268–270
  representation process, 262–266
  seniority system, 251, 269
  separation of powers, 34–36
  specialized agencies/workers, 250
  and Supreme Court, 350–353
  term limits, 271–272
  whips, 251
  work environment of, 248–249
  on World Wide Web, 266
Congressional Budget and Impoundment Control Act, 280
Congressional Budget Office, 250, 280
Congressional committees, 253–257
  administrative oversight, 254
  committee staff members, 250
  of 1995 Congress, 256*t*
  joint committees, 256–257
  joint conference committees, 257, 261
  select committees, 256
  standing committees, 255
Congressional districts
  gerrymandering, 205–206, 206*f*
  reapportionment, 205–206
  single-member districts, 167
Congressional elections, 205–206
  campaign activities, 249
  campaign strategy, 211
  incumbency, advantages of, 206–208
  midterm elections, 210
  and political action committees (PACs), 157
  and reapportionment/redistricting, 205–206
Congressional Quarterly Weekly Report, 263
Congressional Record, 260, 264, 370
Congressional representation, 262–266
Congressional Research Service, 250, 269
Congress of Racial Equality (CORE), 15
Consensus, in democracy, 17
Conservatism, 130-131, 136*t*
Constituency, 262
  communication with representative, 263
  definition of, 262
  reelection constituency, 265
  relationship with representatives, 262-263
Constitution
  amendment process, 40
  Articles of Confederation, weakness of, 28–29
  Bill of Rights, 32
  and civil rights/liberties, 72–73
  Constitutional Convention, 28–31
  flexibility of, 39
  and governing process, 39–40
  and judicial review, 37–39, 41
  ratification of, 31–32
  and Revolutionary War, 27–28
  signing of, 30*c*
  strict *versus* broad interpretation, 41
Constitutional concepts
  federalism, 36–37
  judicial review, 37–39
  limited government, 33
  popular sovereignty, 32–33
  separation of powers, 34–36
  unalienable rights, 33–34
Constitutional Convention, 28–31
  formation of, 28–29
  Great Compromise, 29–30
  New Jersey Plan, 30
  on republic, 29
  three-fifths compromise, 30–31
Constitutional courts, 336
Continental Congress, 28–29
Contract with America (Republican), 1–3, 188, 212, 240, 272
Convention, national. *See* Presidential election convention
Cooperative activity, as political participation, 122
Cooperative federalism, 51–52
Cousins v. Wigoda, 190
Cox, Archibald, 42–43
Criminal justice and civil rights, 76–83
  cruel and unusual punishment, prohibition against, 82–83
  double jeopardy, 82

due process, 76–78
fair trial, right to, 81–82
Miranda warnings, 80–81
plea bargaining, 79
search and seizure, 78–79
self-incrimination, right against, 79–81
Criminal justice process, 76*f*
death penalty issue, 82–83
double jeopardy, 82
grand jury, 81
jury trial, 81–82
sentencing, 82–83
Crosscutting requirements, for grants-in-aid, 57, 58*f*
Crossover sanctions, for grants-in-aid, 56*c*, 57, 58*f*
Cruel and unusual punishment, 32, 75*t*
death penalty, 82–83
prohibition against, 82–83
Cubanos, 13

Daley, William, 161
Daschle, Thomas, 252*c*
Dealignment, political parties, 171
Death penalty, 82–83
Declaration of Independence, 32, 101
drafting of, 28
intent of framers, 8–9
De facto segregation, 105
Defense of Marriage Act, 63–65
DeJonge v. Oregon, 75*t*
De jure segregation, 105
Democracy, 11–12
consensus and conflict in, 17
definition of, 8
and elections, 189–198
and equality, 11–13
and majority rule, 8–9
and news media, 222–223
and political participation, 121
and representation, 262
representative *versus* direct, 9
Democratic beliefs
about political efficacy, 138–139
about support for democratic processes, 139
about tolerance of others, 139
about trust in public officials, 136–138
on role of government, 135–136
Democratic National Committee, 172, 173*c*
Democratic party
delegate selection process, 172
Democratic electorate, portrait of, 210–211*t*
demography of, 170*t*
history of, 169–171
party platform of, 175
phone numbers for party, 174
and reapportionment, 205
supporters of, 169–170
and voter turnout, 196
Democratic Party of the U.S. v. La Follette, 190
Democratic-Republicans, 169
Department of Agriculture, 314, 324, 328
inspections, 319
organization of, 312
Department of Defense, 311
Department of Education, 311
Department of Energy, 311
Department of Health and Human Services, 311
Department of Justice, 341
Department of Transportation, 311
Departments, federal bureaucracy, 311
Deregulation, 317
Determinate sentencing, 82
Devolution federalism, 54–55
Direct democracy, 9
Direct orders, 55, 58*f*
Discrimination
and affirmative action, 12–13, 109–111
age discrimination, 105
civil rights movement, 104–105
gender-based, 105–106
legal tests of, 105–106
nonracial discrimination, 105–106
reverse discrimination, 109–111
Dissenting opinions, Supreme Court, 349
Distributed power, 7
Distributive policies, characteristics of, 361
District courts, 336
Diversity, 12–15
and ethnic identity, 14–15
and public opinion, 129–130
and subcultures, 12–15
Diversity of public opinion, 132–133*t*
Docket, Supreme Court, 344, 345*f*
Doctrine of nullification, 49
Dole, Bob, 109
gun control, 247
Dole, Elizabeth, 202*c*
Dole, Robert, 188, 202, 232
campaign by, 212*c*
and 1996 election, 4, 209
support for, 197
vote for, 209*f*
Dominos, 180
Double jeopardy, 32, 75*t*, 82
Douglas, William O., 334
Dred Scott v. Sanford, 39
Drug problem
public opinion about, 140
Drug testing, 71–72
Dual federalism, 51
Due process, 32, 49, 51, 74, 76–78
historical roots, 76–77
procedural due process, 77
substantive due process, 77–78
Dukakis, Michael, 127, 234
Duke, David, 127*c*
Duncan v. Louisiana, 75*t*

Earned Income Tax Credit, 374
Economic interests versus civil rights, 83–84
Educational level
and political knowledge/information, 128
and voting behavior, 194, 210–211*t*
Edwards, George C. III, 281, 299
Eighth Amendment, 32, 82
Einstein, Albert, 254
Eisenhower, Dwight D., 284, 291, 293
and Congress, 299*f*
managerial style of, 297
Elastic clause, 33
Elders, Jocelyn, 316*c*
Election campaign, 198–208
financing of. *See* Campaign finance
as vehicle for political participation, 121
Elections. *See also* Congressional elections; Presidential election
analysis of results, 208–211
campaigns. *See* Election campaign
congressional, 157, 205–206
and democracy, 189–198
effects on governance, 212–213
and meaningful choice, 189, 190
and news media, 234–235
nonpresidential, 205–208
and political interest groups, 154–158
and political parties, 173–175
presidential election convention, 199–203
primary elections, 175
and suffrage, 189–190
Electoral College, 168
and candidates' campaign strategy, 204
historical view, 203
popular votes versus electoral college votes, 203, 209*f*
and vice president, 204
Electors, 203
Electronic media, 224–228
Elementary and Secondary Education Act, 368
Eleventh Amendment, 40
Ellis Island, ownership of, 337*c*
Emily's List, 154
Eminent domain, 74, 75*t*
Endangered Species Act, 363
Energy Department, 324
Engel v. Vitale, 95
English, as "official" language, 13
English Bill of Rights, 73
English language, as official American language, 18
Enrolled bill process, 286
Entitlements, 372
Environmental Defense Fund, 149, 364
Environmental policy
under Bush, 150
under Clinton, 150
EPA on policy implementation, 366
under Reagan, 149–150
spotted owl issue, 363*c*, 363–364
from 1970s to 1990s, 149–150
Environmental Protection Agency (EPA), 55, 149–150, 327, 329, 366
Equality, 11–13
of opportunity, 11–13
political equality, 11
and voting rights, 101–103, 103
Equal protection clause, tests of, 105–106
Equal Rights Amendment, 40
Equal time doctrine, 223
Ervin, Sam, 42
Escobedo v. Illinois, 79–80
Espionage Act of 1917, 97
Establishment clause, 75*t*, 94–95
Ethnic identity, 14–15
Everson v. Board of Education of Ewing Township, 75*t*, 94
Exacting scrutiny test, 106, 109
Exclusionary rule, 75*t*
debate related to, 78–79
Executive agreements, 280
Executive branch. *See also* Presidency; President
lobbying of, 161–162
news media coverage of, 235–237
party influence on, 177–178
Executive federalism, 50
Executive memoranda, 279
Executive Office of President
in 1998, 285*f*
evolution of, 284
historical view, 284
Office of Management and Budget (OMB), 284, 286
White House Office, 286–289
Executive order, 279
Executive privilege, 41
Express powers, of government, 33

Fairness doctrine, 223
Family Research Council, 161
Farrakhan, Louis, 15
Farrand, Max, 27
Federal bureaucracy
adjudication by, 319
agencies, 311–312
boards/committees/commissions/advisory committees, 314
bureaus/offices/administrations/services, 312
character and culture of, 322–323
civil service system, 315–316
compliance enforcement by, 319
coverage of, 328–329
departments, 311
government corporations, 314
hierarchical decision making by, 321–322
historical view, 310–311, 314–315
independent regulatory agencies and commissions, 312

iron triangles, 325, 325*f*
legal controls on, 326–327
legislative controls on, 327
pathologies of, 323–324
and policy making, 320–326
political appointments, 316
professionalization of, 323
regulatory activities, 317
rule making, 318–319
Senior Executive Service (SES), 315
and spoils system, 315
standard operating procedures (SOPs), 323
on the World Wide Web, 318
Federal Bureau of Investigation (FBI), 309, 311, 315, 319, 325
Federal Communications Commission (FCC), 312
fairness doctrine, 223
and obscene language, 99
Federal courts, 335–336
appellate courts, 336
appointment of judges, 341
constitutional courts, 336
district courts, 336
Federal Deposit Insurance Corporation (FDIC), 314
Federal Election Campaign Act, 192, 213–214
Federal Elections Commission (FEC), 192, 194, 201
information sources on, 201
Federal Flag Protection Act of 1989, 92
Federal government
American beliefs about, 137*f*
authority of, 9–10
limited government concept, 33
public attitudes toward, 12*f*, 14*t*
and states. *See* State-federal relationship
Federal government, shut down of, 2
Federalism, 36–37
Anti-Federalists' view of, 49
of Canada, 50
cooperative federalism, 51–52
devolution federalism, 54–55
dual federalism, 51
Federalists' view of, 38, 49
and founding fathers' intent, 48
of Mexico, 50
nation-centered view, 49
new federalism, 53
as political issue, 48
and same-sex marriage, 63–65
state-centered view, 49, 51
United States system of, 36–37
Federalist, The
No. 51, 34
No. 78, 338
No. 84, 34
Federalists
history of, 169
view of federalism, 49
Federal Register, 292, 318, 319
guidelines for use of, 320–321
Fifteenth Amendment, 40, 101–102, 103
Fifth Amendment, 32, 51, 74, 76, 79
Fighting words, 99
Filibuster, 262
Finance, campaign, 168
Financial controls, and administrative oversight, 267–268
Fireside chats, 224, 225*c*
First Amendment, 32, 74–75, 94, 96, 139, 223
First Continental Congress, 27
First lady, role of, 289–290
Flag burning, 91–92
Food stamps, 372
Forbes, Steve, 168, 214, 232
Ford, Betty, 290
Ford, Gerald, 110, 286, 292, 298, 354
and Congress, 299*f*
managerial style of, 297
nomination of, 201
staff organization, 287
Foreign policy. *See also* Defense policy
and Congress, 280
and president, 280
Foreign Service, 315
Forest Service, 324, 363
Formula grants, 59
Foster, Dr. Henry, 161, 237, 267
Fourteenth Amendment, 40, 74, 76, 78, 101, 102, 104–105
Fourth Amendment, 32, 78–79
France, Parliament compared to Congress, 251
Frank, Barney, 63
Frankfurter, Felix, 41, 77, 98, 334, 348
Franking privilege, 265
Freedom of assembly and petition, 32, 75*t*
Freedom of association, 100–101
Freedom of Information Act, 224, 225
obtaining information under, 224
Freedom of press, 75
Freedom of religion, 32, 75*t*, 92–96
accommodationist approach to, 95
establishment clause, 75*t*, 94–95
free exercise clause, 75*t*, 96
high wall of separation approach, 94
and public opinion, 130
secular regulation rule, 95
separation of church/state, 94–95
Freedom of speech, 32, 74, 75*t*, 96–101
clear and present danger test, 97
commercial speech, 99–100
fighting words, 99
libel and slander, 99
obscenity, 98–99
protected speech, 97–98
social redeeming value speech, 97–98
speech-plus-conduct, 100–101
symbolic speech, 100
unprotected speech, 98–100

Freedom of the press, 223–242
Free-enterprise system, 13
Free exercise clause, 75*t*, 94
Free speech, 6
Frostbelt, federal aid to, 59
Furman v. Georgia, 82–83

Gallup poll, 134
Garcia v. San Antonio Metropolitan Transit Authority, 53
Garfield, James A., 315
Gender discrimination, 106*c*
  path to equality, 15–17
  types of discriminatory practices, 106
General Accounting Office (GAO), 250, 268, 327
General Agreements on Tariffs and Trade (GATT), 280, 299
General Electric, 180
General Services Administration, 311
General warrants, 78
Generation X, political participation of, 141–143
George III, King of England, 27, 28, 33
Gerry, Elbridge, 205
Gerrymandering, 205–206, 206*f*
Gideon v. Wainwright, 75*t*, 80
Gingrich, Newt, 7, 137, 180, 214–215, 249*c*
  campaign finance problems, 213
  and Contract with America, 176
  gun control, 248
Ginsburg, Ruth Bader, 86, 343, 347*c*
Gitlow v. New York, 74, 75*t*
Giuliani, Rudolph, 360
Going public, by president, 281–282
Goldberg, Arthur, 334
Goldwater, Barry, 167
GOPAC, 214–215
Gore, Albert, Jr., 197*c*
  campaign finance problems, 213
  role in redesigning government, 291*c*, 292–293
Government. *See* Federal government
Government corporations, 314
Gradison, Willis (Bill), 305
Gramm, Phil, 176
Grandfather's Pizza, 180
Grand jury, 81
Grant, Ulysses S., 101
Grants-in-aid, 51–52
  block grants, 58
  categorical grants, 57–58
  and Clinton administration, 58, 62
  conditions of aid, 56*c*, 57, 58*f*
  formula grants, 59
  grantsmanship, 61
  and intergovernmental lobby, 61–62
  project grants, 59
  and Reagan administration, 61
  regionalism and distribution, 59–60, 60*t*
  slowdown of, 53
  types of, 52, 57
Grantsmanship, 61
Great Britain, Parliament compared to Congress, 251, 299
Great Compromise, 29–30
Great Depression, 10, 169, 362
  and dual federalism, 51
  and New Deal recovery program, 51–52
  and party loyalty, 119
Great Society programs, 52*c*, 368
Greece, ancient, city-state, 4
Green Berets, 326
Griswold, Estelle, 334
Griswold v. Connecticut, 75*t*, 78, 334
Group Health Association of America, 2
Gun control
  assault weapons ban, 247–248
  NRA support of Republicans, 247–248
  as state versus national issue, 47–48
Gun-Free School Zones Act, 47

Hall, Arsenio, 233*c*
Halleck, Charles, 255
Hamilton, Alexander, 34, 73, 338
Hamilton v. Regents of the University of California, 75*t*
Hammer, Marion P., 153*c*
Hanks, Jack, Jr., 115
Harkin, Tom, 360
Hart, Gary, 127–128
Hasidic Jews, 13, 16*c*
Hatch, Orrin, 360
Hatch Act, 100, 294
Hatfield, Mark, 176
Hawaii, same-sex marriage in, 63–64
Hayes, George E.C., 339*c*
Head Start program, 52*c*, 369
Health care, Clinton proposal for, 160, 282
Health Care Financing Administration, 311
Health care proposal, 161–162
Health Insurance Association of America, 2, 305
Heclo, Hugh, 365–366
Helms, Jesse, 262
Henry, Patrick, 31
Hermes, 351
Hernandez v. Texas, 350
Hewlett-Packard, 180
Hicklin rule, 98
Hispanics, voting rights of, 103
  partisanship, 169
Holmes, Oliver Wendell, 97
Homosexuals, same-sex marriage, 63–65
Hoover, Herbert, 119
Hoover, J. Edgar, 325
Horton, Willie, 234
House and Senate Armed Services Committees, 254
House Ethics Committee, 215
House of Representatives

and lawmaking, 257–262
majority party, 251–252
reapportionment, 205–206
Rules Committee, 258
size of membership, 248
House Select Committee to Investigate Covert Arms Transactions with Iran, 256
House Ways and Means Committee, 158*c*, 180
Housing and Urban Development, Department of (HUD), 268
Hughes, Charles Evans, 348, 349
Hunt, E. Howard, 42
Hyde, Henry J., 63, 272

Ideology. *See* Political ideology
Image, of president, 300–302
Immigration, backlash against, 17–20
Immigration and Naturalization Service, 19
Impeachment, process of, 268
Implementation phase, policy-making, 366
Implied powers, of government, 33
Income level, public opinion and, 128
Incrementalism, 368
Incumbency
and congressional elections, 206–208
and presidential elections, 204
Independent regulatory commissions, 312
Indictment, 81
Inequality. *See also* Discrimination; Equality
politics of, 15
Infomercials, presidential campaign, 234
Information USA, 225
Inherent powers, of government, 33
Injunctions, 326–327
Inquisitorial justice system, nature of, 79
In re Oliver, 75*t*
Institute of Museum Services, 329
Institutional opinion, Supreme Court, 349
Integration, school, 366
Intensity, and public opinion, 126
Interest groups. *See* Political interest groups
Intergovernmental lobby, 61–62
Interior Department, 363
Intermodal Surface Transportation Act of 1991, 57
Internal Revenue Service (IRS), 319, 323
Internet, 229–230. *See also* World Wide Web
censorship of, 240–242
lobbying on, 159
White House on, 229, 292
Interstate commerce, Court interpretation of, 51
Interstate Commerce Commission, 51, 317
Intrastate commerce, 51
Iran-contra affair, 237, 256
Iran/Contra arms sales, 222
Iran hostage crisis, 240, 297
Iron triangles, 325
merchant shipping policy example, 325*f*
Israel, parliamentary voting in, 299
Issue networks
example of, 366
and policy-making, 365
Issue parties, 167–168
Istook, Ernest Jim, 271

Jackson, Andrew, 169, 204
Jackson, Jesse, 15, 249*c*
Jackson, Jesse, Jr., 249*c*
Japanese American Foundation, 14-15
Jaworski, Leon, 43
Jefferson, Thomas, 28, 38, 49, 94, 283, 291
Jeffersonian Republicans, position of, 38
Jim Crow laws, 104
Johnson, Gregory "Joey," 91
Johnson, Lyndon B., 107, 109, 165, 169, 250, 292, 293, 298
Great Society programs, 368
managerial style of, 296, 297
relations with Congress, 255
Johnson, Richard, 204
Johnson & Johnson, 180
Joint Committee on the Economy, 257
Joint committees, 256–257
Joint conference committees, 257, 261
Judges, appointment of, 340–344
federal judges, 341
merit system, 340–341
number of appointments (Roosevelt through Clinton), 342*t*
profile of presidential appointees, 342*t*
Supreme Court judges, 341–344
Judicial activism, 338–340
Judicial double standard, meaning of, 83
Judicial federalism, 335–336
Judicial review, 37–39, 41, 336–340
and activism *versus* self-restraint, 338–340
and Constitution, 37–39, 41
definition of, 41
Marbury v. Madison, 38
and political influence, 338
and political question doctrine, 338
and strict *versus* broad interpretation, 41
Judicial self-restraint, 339
Judiciary. *See also* Supreme Court
federal courts, 335–336
judges, appointment of, 340–344
and judicial federalism, 335–336
judicial review, 336–340
lobbying of, 162–163
news media coverage of, 239
organization of, 335*f*
party influence on, 178
state courts, 336
Supreme Court, 344–350
Judiciary Act of 1789, 38
Judiciary Committee, 268
Jurisdiction
appellate jurisdiction, 337
original jurisdiction, 337

Jury trial, 32, 75*t*, 81–82
Justice
  adversary system of, 79
  inquisitorial system of, 79

Kaczynski, David, 221–222
Kaczynski, Theodore, 221-222
Katz v. United States, 79
Kennedy, Anthony M., 85, 95, 343, 347*c*
Kennedy, Edward, 353
Kennedy, John F., 115, 165, 169, 227, 291, 292, 293
  and Congress, 299*f*
  managerial style of, 296
  personal style of, 301
Kent State tragedy, 123*c*
King, Rev. Martin Luther, Jr., 102, 227
King, Rodney, 239
Klopfer v. North Carolina, 75*t*
Korean War, 297
Ku Klux Klan, 94*c*, 127*c*

Labor, organized, 180
Labor disputes, 280
Labor unions, 151, 354
Lame duck, 298
Lamm, Richard, 168*c*
Law, sources of, 9–10
Lawmaking process, 257–262
  bill, introduction of, 258
  cloture, 262
  and congressional committees, 258
  filibuster, 262
  and lobbying, 160–161
  mark-up session, 258
  monitoring legislation by public, information sources on, 370–371
  and president, 261–262
  process, flowchart of, 259*f*
  rules/procedures/precedents, 262
  unanimous consent, 262
  veto, 261–262
Lawsuits
  requirements for gaining standing, 337, 338
  rise in, 340
Leahy, Patrick, 354
LEGIS, 371
Legislation. *See* Lawmaking process
Legislative branch. *See* Congress; House of Representatives; Senate
Legislative courts, 336
LEXIS, 93
Libel
  and free speech, 99
Liberalism, 130
  ideals of, 136*t*
Libertarian Party, 167
Liberty, social welfare and, 6
Library of Congress, 229
Lichter, S. Robert, 232, 237
Liddy, G. Gordon, 224
Limbaugh, Rush, 224
Limited government, 33
Lincoln, Abraham, 169, 284
Lincoln bedroom, 162*c*
Line-item veto, 257, 261–262, 280, 300
Lobbying, 158*c*, 158–166
  astroturfing, 160
  changes in, 163–164
  of Congress, 160–161
  consequences of, 164–166
  direct and indirect lobbying, 159–160
  the executive branch, 161–162
  on health care reform, 304–305
  intergovernmental lobby, 61–62
  the judiciary, 162–163
  regulation of, 163–164
Local areas, political party structure, 173
Local governments
  direct orders, 55, 58*f*
  preemption, 55–56
Locke, John, 33–34
Logging, spotted owl issue, 363*c*, 363–364
Lopez, Alfonso, Jr., 47–48
Lott, Trent, 253*c*
Lowi, Theodore, 361

Madison, James, 8, 29, 29*c*, 34, 38, 49, 84, 92, 97
  and creation of Constitution, 73–74, 94
  and ratification of Constitution, 31
Magna Carta, 73, 77
Majority rule
  and democracy, 8–9
  versus minority rights, 7–9
Malloy v. Hogan, 75*t*
Managerial style, of president, 296–297
Manhattan Project, 254
Mansfield, Mike, 255
Mapplethorpe, Robert, 241
Mapp v. Ohio, 75*t*
Maraniss, David, 115
Marbury, William, 38
Marbury v. Madison, 38, 41
Marine Corps, 324
Marketplace concept, news media, 223
Mark-up session, 258
Marshall, John, 38, 41, 49
Marshall, Thurgood, 95, 339*c*, 343
Mass media. *See also* News media
  cost factors, 202
  and image of candidates, 227
  impact of, 234–235
  local *versus* national news, candidate use of, 203, 239
  and political parties, 175
  and political socialization, 120–121
  presidential press conferences, 301–302
  reports on private lives/personalities of candidates, 231

and slant of news coverage, 230–232
talk-shows, candidates on, 233–234
use by consumers, 227*t*
McCarthy, Joseph, 226–227
McCormack, John, 255
McCulloch v. Maryland, 49, 93
McGovern, George, 167
McIntosh, David, 264*c*
Meaningful choice, and elections, 189, 190
Media. *See* Mass media; News media
Medicaid
funds for abortion, 85
threatened cuts to, 2
and welfare reform, 372
Medicare, 2, 257
Merits, potential Supreme Court cases, 348
Merit system, appointment of judges, 340–341
Messer, Kim, 106*c*
Mexican American Legal Defense and Education Fund, 15
Mexicans, 13
Mexico, federalism of, 50
Midterm elections, 210
Military. *See* Department of Defense
Militia groups, 138
Milk and Ice Cream Association, 153
Miller v. California, 98–99
Miller v. Johnson, 104
Million Man March, 15
Minimal scrutiny test, 105
Minimum wage legislation, 179–181
Minorities. *See* under names of specific groups
Miranda, Ernesto, 80
Miranda v. Arizona, 80
Miranda warnings, 80–81
Missouri Compromise, 39
Mitchell, Billy, 323
Molinari, Susan, 202*c*
Mondale, Walter, 292
Motorcycle helmet law, 57
Motor-voter laws, 25–26, 194
Movies, regulation of, 241
Moynihan, Daniel Patrick, 374

Nabrit, James M., 339*c*
National Aeronautics and Space Administration, 311–312, 324, 328-329
National Association for the Advancement of Colored People (NAACP), 104, 163, 337
National Association of Convenience Stores, 180
National Association of Counties, 62*t*
National Association of Home Builders, 153
National Association of Towns and Townships, 62*t*
National Bankers Association, 153
National committees, organization of, 171–172, 173*c*
National Conference of State Legislatures, 62*t*
National Council of La Raza, 14, 15, 16
National Election Center, 208
National Endowment for the Humanities, 329
National Environmental Protection Act, 339–340
National Federation of Independent Businesses, 180
National Governors' Association, 62*t*
National Highway Safety Board, 329
National Highway Traffic Safety Administration, 319
National League of Cities, 62*t*
National League of Cities v. Usery, 53
National Lumber Association, 149
National Organization for Women (NOW), 17, 151
National Performance Review, 292–293
National Rifle Association (NRA), 153*c*, 153
opposition to anticrime bill, 360
support of Republicans, 247–248
National Right to Life Committee, 84
National Screw Thread Commission, 323
National Taxpayers Union, 2
National Treasury Employees Union v. Von Raab, 72
National Voter Registration Act of 1993, 25–26
National Wildlife Federation, 149
Nation of Islam, 15
Native Americans, 15
Natural Resources Defense Council, 149, 337
Navy, 323
Near v. Minnesota, 75*t*
Necessary and proper clause, 33
Negative advertising, 234
Neustadt, Richard E., 281
New Deal, 119
First and Second, 52
grants-in-aid during, 51–52
New Federalism, 53
meaning of, 53
under Nixon, 53
under Reagan, 53
New Jersey Plan, 30
News media
Congress, coverage of, 237–239
and democracy, 222–223
and elections, 234–235
freedom of the press, 223–242
history of, 223–228
Internet, 229–230
judiciary, coverage of, 239
national government, coverage of, 235–239
news slant, 230–232
newsworthiness, meaning of, 230
political advertising, 234
and public policy, 239–240
radio, 224–226

New York, 61
New York Times, 292
New York Times Co. v. Sullivan, 99
Nicaragua, 297
Nicholson, Jim, 173*c*
Nickles, Don, 63
Nineteenth Amendment, 40, 102
Ninth Amendment, 32, 75
Nixon, Richard, 227, 250, 284, 286, 291, 292, 295, 298
and affirmative action, 110
and Congress, 299*f*
federal judge appointments, 341
and Kennedy, debates, 227
managerial style of, 297
New Federalism of, 53
and Supreme Court, 339
Supreme Court appointees, 343
and Watergate, 42–43, 222
Nomination campaigns, nonpresidential, 205
Noriega, Manuel, 295
Norris v. Alabama, 350
North, Oliver, 226
North American Free Trade Agreement (NAFTA), 280, 299
Northwestern University, 221
Nullification theory, 51

Obscenity, 98–99
and Federal Communications Commission (FCC), 99
Supreme Court decisions, 98–99
tests for, 98–99
Occupational Safety and Health Administration, 324
O'Connor, Sandra Day, 53, 72, 85, 108–109, 343, 347*c*, 352*c*
Office of Legal Policy, 343
Office of Management and Budget (OMB), 284, 302
central clearance process, 286
enrolled bill process, 286
regulatory review, 286
Office of Personnel Management, 315
Office of Technology Assessment, 367
Oklahoma City bombing, 7, 137, 138*c*, 139
investigation of, 309–310
Olmstead v. United States, 79
O'Neill, Thomas P., Jr., 254
One person, one vote principle, 40
Operation Rescue, 85
Opinion of Supreme Court
opinion days, 349–350
Opinions. *See* Public opinion
Opinions of Supreme Court, 348–349
concurring opinions, 349
institutional opinion, 349
Opportunity, equality of, 11–13
Original jurisdiction, 337
Oversight hearings, 267

Panetta, Leon, 298
Parker v. Gladden, 75*t*
Partido Revolutionario Institucional (PRI), 50
Party affiliation
and political socialization, 118–119
and voting behavior, 196–197
Party discipline, 269
Party platform, 175–176
Paterson, William, 30
Patronage, 315
Patterson, Thomas E., 232
Peace Corps, 326, 369
Pendleton Act, 315
Pentagon Papers, 97
Pepsi, 180
Perot, H. Ross, 168*c*, 214, 232
and presidential elections, 168, 208
and talk shows, 233
vote for, 209*f*
Persian Gulf War, 137, 187, 281, 297, 362
Personality, character-type model of presidents, 295–296
Personal staff aids, Congress, 249–250
Personnel controls, and administrative oversight, 267
Petition of Right, 73, 76–77
Petitions for writ of certiorari, 344
Philadelphia plan, 110
Pizza Hut, 180
Planned Parenthood of Southeastern Pennsylvania v. Casey, 85–86, 163
Plato, 4
Plea bargaining, meaning of, 79
Plessy v. Ferguson, 104
Pocket veto, 260
Poe v. Ullman, 334
Pointer v. Texas, 75*t*
Policy-making. *See also* Foreign policy; Public policy
evaluation phase, 366–367
implementation phase, 366
incrementalism, 368
and issue networks, 365
policy formation stage, 364–366
policy shifts, 368–369
policy termination, 367–368
problem recognition stage, 362–364
public policy, 361
results of policy, 368–371
and subgovernment, 364–365
Political action committees (PACs), 154–158
big spenders, 156*t*
and buying influence, 179–181
growth of, 155*f*
health care reform, 304–305
legal challenges by, 162–163
pros and cons of, 157–158
Political advertising, 234
Political appointments, 316

Political correctness, and First Amendment rights, 139
Political culture
and capitalism, 12
definition of, 10–11
and diversity, 12-15
and women, 15–17
Political efficacy
levels among American public, 138–139
and trust, 138–139
and voting behavior, 192–193
Political equality, 11
public attitudes towards, 12*f*, 13*t*
Political ideology
conservatism, 130-131
gender differences, 131
of Generation X, 141–143
liberalism, 130
meaning of, 130–131
percentages in American population, 136*t*
and public opinion, 130–134
Political information levels, and public opinion, 128–129
Political interest groups. *See also* Lobbying
characteristics of, 151–154
and lawmaking, 257–258
lobbying, 158–166
political action committees (PACs), 154–158
and public policy, 363, 365
and Supreme Court appointments, 354
Political participation, 121–126
activities of Americans, 122*t*
and age, 125, 125*t*
campaign activity, 121
cooperative activity, 122
of Generation X, 141–143
nonparticipation, 124
and public policy, 125–126
and race, 125
and socio-economic status, 124
unconventional participation, 122–123
voting, 121–122
and women, 125
Political parties
and Congress, 177, 251–253
and electoral process, 173–175
and executive branch, 177–178
in House of Representatives, 251–252, 269
ideological parties, 167
issue parties, 167–168
and judiciary, 178
at local level, 173
major parties, 166–167
minor parties, 167–168
at national level, 171–172
organization of, 171–173
party platform, 175–176
and public policy, 176–177
in Senate, 269
at state level, 172–173
working with, contact phone numbers, 174
Political parties, history of, 169–171
Democratic-Republicans, 169
Democrats, 169–171
Federalists, 169
realignment, 171
Republicans, 169–171
and Roosevelt administration, 169
Whigs, 169
Political question doctrine, and judicial review, 338
Political socialization, 114–146
alienation from, 119
in childhood, 118*c*
of Generation X, 141–143
as life-cycle process, 117–119
and major political events, 119
mass media and, 120–121
meaning of, 117
party affiliation, 118–119
and school, 120*c*
Political Victory Fund, 247–248
Politics
elements of, 3–5
and power, 5–10
Polls. *See* Public opinion polls
Popular sovereignty, meaning of, 33
Populist Party, 167
Pork-barrel politics, 361
Postal Service, 315
Post Office, 311
Powell, Lewis F., 353
Powell v. Alabama, 75*t*
Power
concentrated power, 7
of Congress, 34*t*, 35*f*, 34–35
Constitutional powers, 33
distributed power, 7
meaning of, 5
of president, 34*t*, 35*f*, 279
of states, 36, 37*f*
Preemption, 55–56
Presidency
and appointments/removals from office, 279–280
and Cabinet, 283–284
creation by framers, 279–280
difficulties related to, 277–278, 302–303
evolution of authority of, 279–280
and Vice President, 290–291
White House Office, 286–289
President
agenda-setting by, 297–298
bargaining position of, 281
belief systems of, 297
character-type model for, 295–296
and Congress, 298–300
executive agreements, 280
and foreign policy, 280

President *(continued)*
going public by, 281–282
image of, 300–302
implementation of policy, 302
and lawmaking process, 261–262
leadership of, 279, 280–282
managerial style of, 296–297
new media focus on, 235–237
physical health, effects of, 294–295
power-checking by, 35*f*
powers of, 34*t*, 35*f*, 279
public support building, 300–302
spouse, role of, 289–290
Presidential election, 203–204
analysis of results, 208–211
and Electoral College, 203–204
financing. *See* Campaign finance
and incumbency, 204
media influences. *See* Mass media
national party activities in, 173–175
and nonpresidential nominations, 205
winner-take-all voting, 203
Presidential election convention
assessment of public opinion, 203
delegate selection, 200–201
national nominating conventions, 202–203
preconvention activities, 201–202
proportional voting, 200
Presidential Power, 281
Press, freedom of. *See* Freedom of press
Press conferences, presidential, 301–302
Preview of the United States Supreme Court Cases, 93
Primary elections
historical development, 175
news coverage of, 231*f*
Printz v. United States, 54
Privacy Act of 1974, 224
Privacy Protection Act of 1980, 352
Privacy rights, 75, 75*t*, 83
and abortion, 83
associational privacy, 83
and Fourth and Fifth Amendments, 83
Problem recognition, and policy-making, 362–364
Procedural due process, 77
Project grants, 59
Pro-life abortion position, 163
Prospective voting, 198
Protests, 122–123
civil rights, 101*c*
Vietnam War, 123, 123*c*, 199*c*
Public knowledge, characteristics of, 128–129, 129*f*
Public officials, Americans' trust in, 136–138, 137*f*
Public opinion
characteristics of, 129–130
and democratic beliefs, 135–139
discovering, 126–128
diversity of, 132–133*t*
and information/knowledge, 128–129
and political ideology, 130–134
and public policy, 140
and religion, 130
Public opinion polls, 127–128
construction of questions, 127
data on World Wide Web, 134–135
Gallup poll, 134
guidelines for interpretation of, 127–128
purpose of, 127–128
Public Papers of the Presidents, 293
Public policy, 5, 361. *See also* Policy-making
definition of, 5, 361
distributive policies, 361
and federal bureaucracy, 320–324, 324–326
and interest groups, 363, 365
and news media, 239–240
and political participation, 125–126
and political parties, 176–177
and public opinion, 140
redistributive policies, 362
regulatory policies, 361–362
relationship to law, 5
and Supreme Court, 350–353
Puerto Rico, investment in, 180–181

Quayle, Dan, 271, 292
Quota systems, 108

Racial discrimination
de facto segregation, 105
de jure segregation, 105
Jim Crow laws, 104
restrictive covenants, 104
school segregation, 104–105
separate but equal doctrine, 104
voting rights, 101–102
Radio
historical view, 224–226
regulation of, 224–226
talk radio, 224
Rainbow coalition, 16
Randolph, Edmund, 29
Ranney, Austin, 229
R.A.V. v. City of St. Paul, Minnesota, 98
Rayburn, Sam, 254
Reagan, Michael, 224
Reagan, Nancy, 289, 290
Reagan, Ronald, 110, 119, 127, 165, 170, 178, 233, 293, 295, 298, 302, 360
on abortion, 85
belief system, effects of, 297
and Bork nomination, 353–355
cabinet of, 284
and Congress, 10, 299*f*
environmental policy under, 149–150
and executive office, 286
federal judge appointments, 341

and federal regulation, 56
and grants-in-aid, 61
managerial style of, 297
New Federalism of, 53
personal style of, 301
and Supreme Court, 339
Supreme Court appointments, 343
voter behavior for, 197
Realignment, political parties, 171
Reapportionment, 205–206
and gerrymandering, 205–206
meaning of, 205
Record, 201
Redistributive policies, characteristics of, 362
Redistricting, 103, 205–206
Reed, Thomas Brackett, 251
Reform Party, 168
Regents of the University of California v. Bakke, 108, 163
Regulation, 317
compliance enforcement, 319
coverage of, 328–329
deregulation, 317
regulatory policies, characteristics of, 361–362
Regulatory review, 286
Rehnquist, William H., 47, 78, 82, 85, 95, 347*c*
Religion. *See* Freedom of religion
Remote control television devices, 229
Reno, Janet, 360
Reno v. American Civil Liberties Union, 242
Representation, meaning of, 262
Representation process, 262–266
and franking privilege, 265
representative/constituency communication, 265
Representative democracy, 9
Republic
and Constitution, 29
nature of, 29
Republican National Committee, 172, 173*c*
Republican Party
on abortion issue, 85
on affirmative action, 109
and born-again Christians, 197
and Clinton health care package, 304
and 1995 Congress, 1–3, 7, 54, 187–188, 239, 270
Contract with America, 1–3, 54, 212
demography of, 170*t*
history of, 169–171
party platform of, 175–176
phone numbers for party, 174
and reapportionment, 207
Republican electorate, profile of, 210–211*t*
supporters of, 169–170
and voter turnout, 196
Reserved powers, of states, 37*f*
Restrictive covenants, 104
Retrospective voting, 198
Revenue-sharing program, 368
Reverse discrimination, 109–111
Revolutionary War, 27–28
Reynolds v. United States, 96
Riders to bill, 260
Right of rebuttal, 223
Rights of accused. *See* Criminal justice
Right to counsel, 32, 75*t*
Riordan, Richard, 360
Riots. *See* Protests
Robinson v. California, 75*t*
Rochin v. California, 77
Rockefeller, Nelson, 292
Roe v. Wade, 78, 84, 163, 334
Romer, Roy, 173*c*
Roosevelt, Eleanor, 289
Roosevelt, Franklin D., 119, 211, 284, 291, 293, 301
fireside chats, 225*c*
and Great Depression, 10, 77–78
New Deal, 51–52
and party realignment, 169
and radio, 224
reelection of, 204
relations with Congress, 254
Roosevelt, Theodore, 283
Rosenberger v. Rector and Visitors of the University of Virginia, 95
Roth v. United States, 98
Rourke, Francis E., 324
Rule making, federal bureaucracy, 318–319
Rule of four, 347
Rules Committee, 255, 258
Ryan White Act, 57

Salient issues, 126
Salk, Dr. Jonas, 329
Same-sex marriage, 63–65
Sanctions, 281
Scalia, Antonin, 72, 85, 98, 343, 347*c*
Schattschneider, E.E., 164–165
Schenck, Charles T., 97
Schenck v. United States, 97
School, and political socialization, 120*c*
School prayer issue, 95
School segregation, 104–105
Brown decision, 104
and busing, 105
de jure and de facto segregation, 105
Schumer, Charles, 248
Search and seizure, 32, 75*t*, 78–79
exclusionary rule, 78–79
and wiretapping, 79
Seat belt law, 57
Second Amendment, 32, 75
Second Continental Congress, 27
Secular regulation rule, 95
Securities and Exchange Commission (SEC), 312
Select committees, 256

Self-incrimination, 32, 75*t*
historical roots, 79
Miranda warnings, 80–81
and plea bargaining, 79
right against, 79–81
right to counsel, 32, 75*t*
Senate
confirmation of Supreme Court justices, 353–355
and lawmaking, 258–259
majority leader, 250
political parties in, 252–253
size of membership, 248
Senate Judiciary Committee, 343
Senate Select Committee on Presidential Campaign Activities, 256
Senior Executive Service (SES), 315
Seniority system, Congress, 251, 269
Sentencing, criminals, 82
Separate but equal doctrine, 104
Separation of church/state, 94–95
Separation of powers, 34–36
as Constitutional principle, 34–36
executive branch powers, 279
legislative powers, 34*f*, 34–35
power-sharing structures, 35–36
Seventh Amendment, 32, 75, 82
Shays, Daniel, 28
Shays's Rebellion, 28
Sherman Anti-Trust Act of 1890, 51
Sierra Club, 149, 337
Simpson, O.J., 81*c*, 239, 240
Single-member districts, 167
Sirica, John, 42
Sixteenth Amendment, 40
Sixth Amendment, 32, 79, 82
Skinner v. Railway Labor Executives' Association, 72
Slander, 99
Slavery
and state *versus* federal government issue, 49, 51
three-fifths compromise, 30–31
Smith, Susan, 239
Smoking laws, 8*c*
Socialist Party, 167
Social redeeming value speech, 97–98
Social Security Administration, 311
Social Security program, 369
Socioeconomic status
measures of, 102*f*
and political participation, 124
Souter, David H., 72, 85, 347*c*
Southern Christian Leadership Conference (SCLC), 15
Speaker of the House, 250
Gingrich as, 270
impact of, 251–252
Special investigations, administrative oversight, 267
Specter, Arlen, 354
Speech, free. *See* Freedom of speech
Speech-plus-conduct, 100–101
Speed limit, revision of, 54
Spoils system, 315
St. Clair, James, 43
Stability, and public opinion, 126
Standard operating procedures (SOPs), 323
Standing Committee on the Federal Judiciary, 343
Standing committees, 255
Standing to sue, 337, 338
Stanford, Edward T., 74
State courts, 336
State Department, 312, 323
State-federal relationship
concurrent powers, 36, 37*f*
direct orders, 55, 58*f*
and federalism, 49, 51
grants-in-aid, 57–59
interstate commerce, 51
power distribution, 37*f*
preemption, 55–56
States
government web sites, 63
political party structures, 172–173
and welfare reform, 372–373
States' rights, 31, 73, 85
Stevens, John Paul, 47–48, 72, 85, 347*c*, 354
Stewart, Potter, 98, 334
Stone, Harlan F., 348
Strict construction, of Constitution, 41
Strict rationality test, 106
Strict scrutiny test, 105
Student loans, lobby related to, 159
Subcultures, types of, 12–15
Subgovernment, 364–365
energy, 365*f*
Substantive due process, 77–78
Suffrage, 102, 189–190. *See also* Voting rights
Sunbelt, federal aid to, 60
Superconducting Supercollider (SSC), 367
Superfund, 149
Supreme Court, 15, 344–350
appeals to, 346*f*
caseload of, 344
and civil rights/liberties, 71–74
and Congress, 350–353
decision making as political process, 350
decisions overturned by amendments, 352
docket, 344, 345*f*
information sources about decisions, 93
judicial activism *versus* self-restraint, 338–340
and judicial double standard, 83
judicial review, 37–39, 41, 336–340
limiting jurisdiction of, 352
opinion days, 349–350
opinions, 348–349
oral arguments to, 348
petitions for writ of certiorari, 344

and policy making, 350–353
power-checking by, 35*f*
powers of, 34*f*, 35*f*
and president, 353
rule of four, 347
on term limits, 9
voting of justices, 348
on the World Wide Web, 351
Supreme Court justices
appointment of, 341–344
confirmation hearing, 343
justices in 1997, 347*c*
nomination of judges opposed by Senate, 353–355
political aspects of appointment, 341–344
religion/race/gender issues, 343–344
Supreme Court Reporter, 93
Sustein, Cass, 64
Symbolic speech, 100

Talk-shows, presidential candidates on, 233–234
Tax Reform Act of 1986, 257
Television
cable TV, 228–229
and political parties, 175
political socialization and, 120–121, 142
regulation of, 226–228
and satellite technology, 299
Television broadcasting, regulation of, 241
Tennessee Valley Authority (TVA), 314, 315
Tenth Amendment, 26, 32, 51, 53
Term limits, Congressional, 271–272
Territorial imperative, by federal bureaucracy, 324
Texas v. Johnson, 91–92
Third Amendment, 32, 75
Thirteenth Amendment, 40
Thomas, Clarence, 85, 128, 162, 237, 239, 343, 347*c*
Three-fifths compromise, 30–31
Tocqueville, Alexis de, 340
Tolerance of Americans, 139
Trial, right to fair trial, 81–82
Truman, Harry, 127, 211, 297
Trust
and political efficacy, 138–139
in public officials, 136–138, 137*f*
Twelfth Amendment, 291
Twenty-Fifth Amendment, 291
Twenty-Fourth Amendment, 40, 102
Twenty-Sixth Amendment, 40, 192
Twenty-Third Amendment, 40

Unabomber, 221–222
Unalienable rights, 33–34
Unanimous consent, 262
Unconventional political participation, 122–123
Unfunded Mandates Reform Act, 62
Unicameral legislature, meaning of, 30
United Farm Workers, 163
United Mine Workers, 163
United States Conference of Mayors, 62*t*
United States Consumer Products Safety Commission, 328, 329
United States Court of Military Appeals, 336
United States Government Manual, 225, 321
United States Information Agency, 311
United States Law Week, 93
United States Supreme Court Reports, Lawyer's Edition, 93
United States v. Eichman, 92
United States v. Lopez, 47–48, 54
United States v. Nixon, 43, 349
Unreasonable search and seizure. *See* Search and seizure
Urban League, 15
U.S. Chamber of Commerce, 149, 151, 241, 337
U.S. Civil Service Commission, 102
U.S. Term Limits v. Thornton, 9

Van Buren, Martin, 204
Vernonia School District 47J v. Acton, 72
Veterans Administration, 311
Veto, 261–262
leverage power of, 300
line-item veto, 257, 261–262, 280, 300
pocket veto, 260
as presidential power, 35
presidential vetoes (1933-1996), 261*t*
Vice President, 290–291
and Electoral College, 204
role/responsibilities of, 290–291
Vicktora, Robert A., 97–98
Vietnam War, 136
media coverage of, 227, 228*c*
protests, 123, 123*c*, 199*c*
Virginia Military Institute, 106*c*, 163
Virginia Plan, 29–30
"Void for vagueness," 77
Volunteerism, 143
Voter registration, motor-voter law, 25–26
Voting
one person, one vote principle, 40
percentage, 141
prospective voting, 198
redistricting, 103
retrospective voting, 198
voter registration form, 194
for 18-year-olds, 191
Voting behavior, 192–198
and group associations, 197
and issues, 198
mass media effects, 235
nonparticipation, 121–122
and partisan identification, 196–197
and party affiliation, 196
and perception of candidates, 198
of Republicans/Democrats, 196
turnout, reasons for, 192–196

Voting rights, 102
  African Americans, 102
  and poll taxes, 102
  and qualifications for voting, 102
  suffrage and voting turnout, 193*t*
  voting age, 191
  women, 15–17, 102, 190*c*
Voting Rights Act of 1965, 102

War Powers Resolution, 280
Warren, Earl, 75, 80, 349, 353
Washington, George, 169, 283, 284
Washington Post, 228
Watergate, 136, 222, 237, 256, 287
  events of, 42–43
  media coverage of, 228
Water Quality Act of 1965, 55
Watt, James, 322*c*
Weaver, Randy, 309
Webster v. Reproductive Health Services, 163
Weekly Compilation of Presidential Documents, 293, 321
Welch, Julie, 309
Welfare system, 18-19, 369*c*
  reform of, 371–375
  in regions, 59
Whigs, 169
Whips, 251
White, Byron, 85, 334, 354
White, Edward, 41, 84
White House Council of Economic Advisers, 374
White House Office, 286–289
  conflict within, 288–289
  physical layout of, 288*f*
White House web site, 294
Whitewater, 235
Whittaker, Charles, 334
Wilderness Society, 364
Wilson, Pete, 26, 110
Wilson, Woodrow, 102, 284, 293
Wiretaps, 79
Wisconsin v. Mitchell, 98
Witnesses, right to confront, 75*t*, 82
Witters, Larry, 95
Witters v. Washington Department of Services for the Blind, 95
Wolf v. Colorado, 75*t*
Women
  interest groups of, 17
  path to equality, 16–17
  and political participation, 125
  Supreme Court judges, 343
  voting rights for, 15–17, 102, 190*c*
Women's Political Caucus, 17
World Wide Web
  Congress on, 266
  federal bureaucracy on, 318
  Federal Elections Commission (FEC), 201
  interest groups and political parties on, 152–153
  judiciary website, 229
  public opinion data, 134–135
  state governments on, 63
  Supreme Court decisions, 351
  White House web site, 294
Writ of certiorari, 344
Writ of habeas corpus, 352
Writ of mandamus, 38
Writs of assistance, 78

Yeldell, Carolyn, 115
Yellow journalism, 223

Zedillo, Ernesto, 301*c*
Zurcher v. The Stanford Daily, 352